Studies in Eighteenth-Century Culture

VOLUME 19

Studies in Eighteenth-Century Culture

VOLUME 19

Edited by

Leslie Ellen Brown
West Chester University
and

Patricia Craddock
University of Florida

Published for the

American Society for Eighteenth-Century Studies

by COLLEAGUES PRESS

Published 1989

Colleagues Press Inc.
Post Office Box 4007
East Lansing, Michigan 48826

Distribution outside North America
Boydell and Brewer Ltd.
Post Office Box 9
Woodbridge, Suffolk IP12 3DF
England

First printing

Printed in the United States of America

LC 75-648277

ISBN 0-937191-14-0
ISSN 0360-2370

Editorial Policy

> The editors of *Studies in Eighteenth-Century Culture* select papers of the highest quality and broadest intellectual interest in eighteenth-century studies. Papers presented at regional and national meetings of the American Society for Eighteenth-Century Studies between July 1 and June 30 must be submitted by August 1 each year to be considered for publication. Papers written for oral presentation require revisions and the addition of scholarly apparatus. Contributions will be judged according to the highest standards of scholarship. Papers should be written in English, but quotations in foreign languages are permissible. Papers have usually averaged about 20 to 25 pages, but the editors encourage articles of greater length.

Current editorial practice follows the *Chicago Manual of Style*, 13th edition. The entire paper, including block quotations and footnotes, should be double–spaced. Footnotes should be numbered consecutively and typed on separate sheets following the text. Submit FOUR copies of the paper. Photocopies of illustrations should also be submitted in quadruplicate. Please accompany the typescript with a self-addressed envelope and enough loose stamps to cover the cost of returning one copy of the paper.

19

Editorial Readers for Volume Nineteen

135871

Contents

Preface

In this day when the humanities are assailed from many directions with accusations of diffusion, vagueness, over-specialization, and irrelevancy, it is extremely gratifying to play a part in editing the work of the American Society for Eighteenth-Century Studies and its equally important regional organizations. From the dozens of papers submitted and reviewed by the Editorial Board and its distinguished body of readers and from those select few which make up volume 19 of *Studies in Eighteenth-Century Culture*, we arrive at a happy conclusion on the state of at least one major branch of humanistic study. Indeed, these essays are full of vibrant detail, the accuracy of which attests to the care and patience of the Society's members. Likewise, the essays are attuned to leading issues which punctuate critical thought today, giving credence to the notion that it is not only important what we study but how we study it. And finally, the essays collected here uniformly illustrate "the chief thing" of the Society—that is, the limitless, imaginative, often serendipitous, and profoundly significant interconnections of true cross-disciplinary scholarship. Thus, in acknowledging Mozart, may the readers of this volume discover the music within.

—Leslie Ellen Brown

Studies in Eighteenth-Century Culture

VOLUME 19

Figure 1. Jean-Baptiste-Siméon Chardin, *The Return from Market*. Courtesy of the National Gallery of Canada, Ottawa.

Chardin and the Domestic Sublime

JACK UNDANK

In spite of some critical haggling over the iconography of Chardin's paintings, people seem to agree that "meaning," in a discursive sense, is not finally or most importantly what he produced. But the question of meaning still haunts us and has led to a great deal of confusion largely because art historians, philosophers, and literary critics want to understand the nature of the extraordinary innovation that took place in the eighteenth century when historical and pointedly moral painting was challenged by what Francastel too vaguely called "l'observation directe du monde extérieur"[1] – the discovery of a world that was, presumably, without myth, story, and legend, a world anyone could spot through the window, in the parlor, or down in the kitchen. The ungrounded presumption of an eye so innocent that it ceased to "read" or "understand," its gaze falling with perfect neutrality, indolence, and fascination upon the freshness, the "primal plentitude" (as Norman Bryson puts it[2]), of the images before it, has led to a series of exceedingly innocent and misleading questions: how could those who easily moved in the eloquent and programmed space of classicism have borne the shock of a mute, uninflected world? how did objects speak, what meanings did they compose, when they had lost their tongues? Only our obsession with language in general and linguistic models or analogies in particular can account for the rigid distinction these questions draw between meaning as pure discursivity and a hypothetical void of meaninglessness, between what is cognitively construed and the puzzling static of things unenlisted in the drama of an institutionalized intelligibility.

The far more awkward truth of the matter seems to be that the slow, historic movement from classical traditions of allegory, symbol, and transcendence to the new semiotics of immanence did not create a vacuum; it did not end by severing signifiers from signifieds so that, as Bryson views it, "the signified [was] effectively in exile" (114), unless the narrowest rational or linguistic construction is placed on meaning or signification. In this movement toward immanence, which, in fact, existed side by side and in contiguous relationship with history painting, painters or other practitioners of the "ordinary" did not imprison themselves in merely reflexive gestures, gestures without meaning, "painterly traces" that have, as Bryson says, "no implications other than beauty" (121).

It goes without saying that philosophically unsettled terms like meaning, signification, beauty, and intelligibility have their own history. They live within the changing circumstance of perception itself—not merely within those historically fluctuating assumptions concerning certain physical and physiological laws of vision that Michael Baxandall has carefully studied,[3] but within the temporal codes, principles, and values that saturate all acts of attention. They did not arise, in the anthropic, Lockean world of Chardin's century, from things in and of themselves but from our interanimating encounter with things as we aligned them with our already acculturated and idiosyncratic habits of mind, and as, in the process, these things immediately solicited from us their intelligibility. We, or people then, contented ourselves with what was humanly, and in human terms, perceivable—a "beau perçu" (to use the terms of Diderot's article "Beau" for the *Encyclopédie*) if not a "beau réel." And, above all, we perceived, knew, or understood something that was sufficiently if not absolutely "real," since Nature, according to Condillac and others, did in fact "offer" us this beauty and everything else; we were not simply fashioning them out of whole cloth. We, or they, apprehended especially the "rapports" or relationships objects entertained with one another, most interestingly in our context, the way some of them, to use Condillac's example once again, unmistakably dominated others, while those others "*seem[ed]* to arrange themselves *about* them" and created a space of "intervals."[4] Vision was a dance in which subjects and objects so happily accepted each other's delicate embrace that there was no telling who led from who followed.

There was in our instantaneous reception and recognition of phenomena or in the "idées accessoires" they generated—the associations that accompany them or the expressivity with which, in the act of representation, they are invested—an implied but active intelligibility, a sensuous or conscious "idea" or understanding that we labored to organize in the admittedly delinquent or inadequate medium of metaphorical abstraction and analysis. Or, more spontaneously and incautiously, we allowed ourselves to experience the "real" as a form of ontological and moral assent or repugnance, as—to use a then current analogy—a sympathetic or dissonant vibration caused by the noise of the world. All "ideas" and therefore meaning and significance—whether they arose, in full complexity, from abstraction, memory, and imagination or from the simpler impact of sensations—were the products of an effect, experienced as an effect within us, as the not always articulatable result of every reciprocal engagement of spectacle and historic witness. It was not therefore accidental that words like "effect" and "sentiment" spread like wildfire; from Du Bos and the Abbé Batteux, to Cochin, Saint-Mard, and Marmontel (who was scandalized, later in the century, by the way "effect" had, among modern authors, usurped all other criteria), they came to be used as catchwords for the very purpose and end of art.[5] The mute but eloquent intelligibility of the world as it was being freshly valued and apprehended had been reproduced in artworks that seemed to defy a traditional aesthetic formulation. Under these circumstances, so unlike the ones operating in the works of Beckett, Derrida, and a recent book by Clément Rosset called *Le Réel: traité de l'idiotie*, the object in art or life, reality itself, was an idiot only if we were idiots. This then is my first and shortest proposition: the ordinary world speaks; we, in our own admittedly human and circumstantial fashion, understand it.

My second, very unspectacular, proposition concerns the artistic, social, axiological, and economic codes and so the predictable effects Chardin was able to deploy. Well, they were not always entirely predictable. Diderot, for example, thought that the proportions of the servant returning from the market (Figure 1) were "a little colossal" and that she was "mannered in her attitude."[6] He was absolutely right in what he saw, but he refused to be gulled into believing that a kitchen was the place for a figure whose proportions and pose come straight out of Watteau, De Troy, and Boucher. On the positive side, Diderot thought that Chardin had an abundance of "taste," but he could not stomach the inappropriate use of it, the outrageous clash of form and content—the use of these proportions and that attitude on "une nature basse, commune et domestique" (1:125). Surely Chardin knew what he was doing, though it could not have been easy to make his subject matter palatable to what was then called "la véritablement bonne compagnie"—the aristocrats and members of the upper bourgeoisie who purchased his paintings and who enjoyed not nature but nature refined by art. He drew on all the resources available to him — an appropriately subdued baroque lighting, atmosphere, and theatricality, rococo colors and delicacy — in order to bestow upon this "base, common, and domestic" subject matter (rather like Fielding seeking to borrow the epic's glory for his novels) some of the prestige, stylishness, or numinousness that had incorporated themselves into the exalted or seductive images he found about him in art or life. His servant, however "domestic," must not be thought "common" or "base" — any more than his brioche, which, like a bride, wears a sprig of orange blossom on its head. Just as Diderot, in his domestic dramas and their theories, consciously spliced together inherited codes or genres, Chardin was uneasily but at times triumphantly fusing a "high" style and a "low" subject matter, producing not what we mistake for a reflection of perceptual reality, but the wistful, historically grounded, dream of one. His children are clean, pink, rosy-cheeked, well-mannered, and starched beyond belief — rather like his scrubbed and glistening pots, glasses, and porcelains, the perfect fuzz of his peaches, or the swollen freshness of his carnations. Set Chardin alongside of Hogarth and Jan Steen on the one hand and Oudry or Desportes on the other, and there before you, in Chardin, is not Francastel's "observation directe du monde extérieur," not the raucous or grotesque bustle of "ordinary life" nor the heaving symbols of wealth and nobility displayed, but a hybrid, rose-tinted vision of domesticity, comparable only to the Dutch *banketjestukken* of Pieter Claesz and Willem Heda a full century earlier.

But Chardin's images carry, of course, a very different ideological weight: we see in them the effluence and projection of a class eminently discreet and "tasteful" in its aesthetic, familial, and financial attitudes. More accurately, these are the attitudes of certain male members of a class that, in France, encompassed those aristocrats who secretly envied what they took to be bourgeois self-reliance, security, and calm, the easy and productive reconciliation of work, virtue, and passion. With a classical decorum that spurns any mention of the labor, the precise economic activity that went into the production of the modest wealth, the leisure, and even the smooth domestic fealty we see portrayed, Chardin never allows us to catch sight of the tradesman, the merchant, the man on the job. His toils are invisible, properly off in the wings. But the absent father, lord, and proprietor of Chardin's splendid but unpretentious objects can, like the absent artist himself, stand unseen before these images for which he is ultimately responsible and burst with pride or longing. Never was a child so wholesome and obedient, nor wife so tender, nor servant so industrious. Never were tables or boards so amply but unostentatiously provided, nor their very *négligence* more fully a sign of a truly well-bred sufficiency, independence, and nonchalance. And notice (Figure 2) how Chardin favors those succulently rounded shapes or rounded receptacles that, for Rudolf Arnheim, speak of receiving, giving, and containing, attributes of the submissive woman,[7] shapes that support themselves upon or take their relief from the firmest and most virile of horizontal lines or from the more tacit and gentler signature of less pronounced verticals.

My third proposition, ideologically related to the second, has to do with those qualities in Chardin's work that we associate with sculpture. Diderot was neither the first nor the last to exclaim that Chardin's paintings were a triumph of trompe-l'oeil illusionism nor to go from there to wondering how he achieved it. It would seem that Chardin's mastery of what we might call the materiality of figural space induces an immediate reflection about his workmanship, so that his images, in Diderot's words, "speak eloquently to the artist" (2:111) above all—and of course to the critic: "a lot of technique and truth; and that's about all" (2:111). There is only one step to take from our astonishment at Chardin's "magic" to the locked door of "that's about all" and to think that his work must therefore be about the processes, mental or physical, involved in the representation of visual phenomena. If we project our fascination with this aspect of his painting upon Chardin himself, we are easily led—and no doubt with some, but (it has to be stressed) very partial justification—to speak of his slow, laborious production, of a concentration on technique, of a self-consciousness that betrays itself not only in the theme of "work" (as Bryson sees it) or in the merely formal and reflexive "absorption" that Michael Fried finds in his models, but even more overtly in the witty gesture of a painting like *The Girl with a Shuttlecock*, where the feathers of the shuttlecock delicately introduce the harmonic range of the artist's palette as he paints this very picture, the tools of his own childish "game." In this severely blinkered view—which can and has been used, deconstructively, reductively, and by now tediously, in interpreting works of literature—Chardin has less to say about the things or events before him than about the circumstances of their production, less to say about his times than about our own very modern theoretical enthrallments. It is certainly valuable to notice a repeated motif or formal design in Chardin's paintings—the use of "absorbed" figures and reflexive gestures that he and his contemporaries did not so much introduce as perpetuate from a tradition extending well into the seventeenth century—if one also explains the changing cultural contexts that generate the vast semiological differences within that tradition. And what, furthermore, may be a part of Chardin's paintings cannot in his case (or perhaps in any case) be pressured into serving as an emblem of the whole without enlisting the

Figure 2. Chardin. *Pitcher and Cover, Copper Pot, Napkin, Three Eggs, Wicker Basket, Slice of Salmon on a Pot Cover, Leek, and Crock on a Stone Shelf.* Courtesy of the National Gallery of Scotland, Edinburgh.

blinding violence all synecdoches perform. It seems hardly necessary to add, though nobody has suggested it, that Chardin's sitters, who stood or sat for endless hours, may necessarily have taken on the stiff, dazed, and vacant pose of slightly anesthetized beings, so that the slow, scrupulous artist may indeed have painted what he beheld. Or did he even more intrusively pose them in attitudes that he thought they could hold, without too much strain, over long periods of time? The effect would have been the same, and his paintings would still bear the imprint of a predominantly technical and material circumstance — a circumstance about which we could weave Heisenbergian theories of artists disturbing their field of vision in the very act of preparing to capture it or of objects so shaped under the pressures of a long, merciless gaze that they themselves quite literally assume it.[8]

Chardin's work, however, reveals a materiality of another sort — one that takes his mastery and effort for granted and concentrates instead and yet once more on the way his objects themselves are made to appear. "It is a shame," Diderot wrote, again apropos of *The Return from Market* (Figure 1), "that Chardin infuses everything with his manner and that in moving from one object to another it sometimes becomes ponderous and heavy; it works marvelously well with the opaqueness, flatness, and solidity of inanimate objects; it clashes with the liveliness and delicacy of living things. Notice it here in an alcohol stove, in loaves of bread, and other accessories, and judge whether it performs as well on the face and arms of that servant" (4:83). It is not only Chardin's notorious impasto and scumbles that cause objects and beings to resemble one another. He seems, in all his paintings, to create qualities we associate with sculpture: movement arrested, a marmoreal tranquility, a sense of the heft, weight, and bearing of a hand reaching for a teapot, of a favorite copper urn pressing down upon the three legs that angle out to support it (Figure 3), of the volume of objects as they position themselves in space, a simple drawer repeatedly left open, a carnation or knife breaking across a horizontal plane. All of these provide markers for our awareness of that space, its relationship to us, and its many grave velocities or directions. Whether as a result or as an intention, his people become reified, their clothes heavy or stiff with the palpable densities of cloth, while his ordinary objects become strangely "humanized," as though they were settled and painted not only, as Diderot noticed, with the same brush but with the same phenomenological intentionality.

It may be in the context of this fascination with plasticity, volume, and stasis that we can perhaps best understand Chardin's early and late paintings of bas-reliefs, paintings in which people, animals, and greenery, severely reduced to a grisaille image registering the finest variations of

Figure 3. Chardin, *Woman, Drawing Water from a Copper Water Urn*. Courtesy of the Nationalmuseum, Stockholm.

value and depth, stretch across the canvas in a display of interlocking and differentiated bulk. It is as though Chardin, the son of a *maître menuisier* (a master carpenter), working to recreate those fundamental masses over which color eventually comes to pour its secondary harmonies, had in fact produced not a painting but an object, a painting wittily masquerading as creamy stone or bronze, a thing to be decoratively hung above a door, not merely as a tribute to illusion and to his own craftsmanship, but as part of the furnishings of a room. These are, moreover, paintings in which every figure, acceptably reduced at last to its formal, substantive essence, protrudes from a slab of the same inanimate matter from which it was fashioned. This rear girding of stability becomes, in his still lifes, a favored support from below: a stone ledge or, in his genre scenes, the hard surface of a table, a rough cobblestone ground (Figure 3), or an insistent expanse of flooring. Immobilized, his people announce their weight and materiality by leaning on sills, on buffets, on the back of a chair, or by standing or sitting beside voluminous objects, a washtub, a ballooning wooden vat, a butcher block whose solidity is tested by a cleaver (Figure 4). And in the light of this, his more delicate constructions, the house of cards, the spinning top, the bubbles, provide not the usual iconographic commentary about the fragility of things but a foil for the more positive assertion of an ideal of things anchored and stabilized. Everything, in Chardin's paintings, submits to an impulse that wants to represent the world as the site of numinous and palpable things and these transvalued things as the only hope for rest and stability.

But this fully ideological reification, which speaks of a form of contentment and stirs the hearts of critics to speak of the "timelessness" and "peace" of Chardin's images, exists once again in a historical context whose outlines my fourth proposition can hope only to suggest. Chardin's timelessness and peace, his moments and moods "without interval" (as Rousseau might have said), are built out of a desire firmly planted in what we take to be the shiftless modernity of the rococo. We pass, I believe, too gingerly over the genre scenes of Boucher or De Troy, and, puffed up with the complacency of old and settled discriminations, we hardly notice the complementary, anironic hope concealed beneath the surface ironies of rococo paintings in general — just as we fail to insist sufficiently on the grounding but muted sensibility of contemporary authors like Montesquieu and Crébillon. The desire we find here for order and repair, for a social and personal harmony that naturally, immanently dwells in every tender, aristocratic heart — a slow, unemphatic desire to be found even in Watteau's or Boucher's half-imagined scenic parks and sylvan haunts — will intensify and produce, toward mid-century, plays, novels, and paintings portraying households tragically sundered but reunited, scenes of chaos settling down into wordless joy and domestic solidarity. I am aware that laying out the history of painting in this manner, representing it as a ramble through sanctified images, celebrities, and best-sellers, has its obvious limitations, but it may also yield a certain measure of truth if what appears to be a diachronic, progressive series of changes in taste discloses a surprising sameness and continuity. Why is it that the same aristocratic collectors who hung their wall with engravings of Dutch genre scenes, Flemish Watteaus, and "historical" Bouchers simultaneously or eventually acquired the works of Chardin and Greuze? Studying painting from Watteau to Greuze from the point of view of the spectator's response rather than from our own puzzled concern with the shift from a "worldly" and figurative space to the earthier, more literal realm of the lower social orders (academic questions of subject matter and genre that interested theorists then and

Figure 4. Chardin, *The Kitchen Maid*. Courtesy of the National Gallery of Art, Washington; Samuel H. Kress Collection.

continue to interest them now), one comes to suspect that beneath all demonstrable difference it may be possible to detect a persistent hope, a constantly modified search for the rapturous objectification of a new social or personal harmony, for an intimacy that carried no hint of transcendence or tragedy or the impingements of external political authority.[9] Here were paintings sufficiently comfortable and agreeable to live with. They brought the gentility and taste of classical *bienséance* and the widest range of *vraisemblance* (as it was then generously defined) to bear upon pleasurable concerns or, more accurately, upon the concern with independent pleasure and happiness in the here and now.

My point is that Chardin, who strikes the unknowing as either a misfit or a timeless heavenly angel, speaks to us from a completely recognizable and historic middle ground: he draws upon the spiritual and technical resources of the early century; he offers, in its mildest form, a promise of order that will become more strident, desperate, and violent as the century wears on. Like Rousseau, whom he actually anticipates, he creates the mildest of domestic scenes — a scene that, in terms of its solicited response, lies somewhere between the unthreatened, enviable easefulness of the rococo (Watteau's theatrical rituals, Boucher's decorative scenarios, Jean-François De Troy's powdered perfection) and the no less wistful and theatrical fantasy of a stable domestic order as we see it in the images of Greuze. His secluded islands of contentment are no longer islands of Cythera, though some Cytherian grace and slow time still cling. There are no progressive departures from his middle-class households, no topological stages and developments. They are not only beyond courtship, but beyond chance and public history, beyond the sway of courts and salons, yet several safe notches above the hovels of the "people" — an altogether palatable *mediocritas*. (Their bourgeois proprietors, by their very rank — if they held to it — could seem, to a writer like Marivaux, the modern embodiments of an ancient wisdom that praised the "golden mean."[10]) Chardin transfers ravishing fantasies or allegories of "worldly" peace and stability to kitchens, cellars, servants, children, and things — the least sociable of subjects and so, figuratively speaking, the most basic, manageable, and private. Contemplating these unself-conscious objects and beings, viewers discover within themselves not only the proprietary satisfactions previously mentioned, but the secret precincts of an authentic and unself-conscious self, a self so receptive and benign that it is content with the hushed securities, the tiny, unpretentious movements of sequestered beings and objects as they shape themselves into agreeable and polite arrangements. Already in the 1730s, Chardin points toward that single, swelling wave within the current of sensibility that will turn from every shore, every social support — a current that will bear along with it all beings longing simply to exist among the unmenacing grace and therapeutic presence, the sight and sounds, of natural, inanimate things.

It may indeed be helpful, as some of my metaphors suggest, to think of Chardin, in the composition of his still lifes, as a very special kind of dramatist, a painter who adumbrates the effects and moods soon to be more rousingly theatricalized by Diderot's and Sedaine's *drames domestiques*. These canvases do in fact create mini-dramas or, rather, a series of *dénouements* that bind together and unify the disjunctive effects of chance or accident even as they seem to recapitulate, in the appearance of objects as in what passes between them, those agitations that brought them to this point of rest. Diderot, who appears to have intuited as much, asks us to notice the way "objects separate from one another, advance, draw back, as though they were real" (2:112), the way they produce, in spite of their separate spaces—the spaces, let us say, of "individual grapes, a macaroon, and isolated lady-apples" (2:114)—a "general harmony" (3:128). He emphasizes repeatedly "the disparities of objects" (2:111), their "number" (2:112), the "diversity of forms and colors" (2:113) and the "small space" they occupy (2:112), as though, miraculously, they had been made peaceably to settle together in close proximity. He does not overlook the ennobling schemata I've referred to, the "noblesse et . . . élégance" (2:113) of a garland of grape leaves, the "tasteful" composition of "disorder" (3:128), a certain "relish in the assortment and the ordering" (3:128) of masses. But he focuses repeatedly and even here on the establishment of order out of disorder, on the submission of particularities to the general good—on the constitution of a new, mysterious unity that does not smack of classical symmetries and yet produces "calm and peace" (3:129): "It is a harmony beyond which one does not dream of desiring; it weaves its way imperceptibly through the composition, in every part of the expanse of the canvas; it is, as theologians say of spirit, perceptible in the whole and yet hidden at any part" (4:83). Indeed both the chaos and its resolution are reflected—one might say reenacted—in the viewer's pleasure as he or she moves from the turbulent physical surface of Chardin's paintings to a comfortable distance from it. This too was a paradox that fascinated Diderot, as it has many since.[11]

Chardin's appeal, then, was in part the appeal of quiescence—easily confused with senescence. Diderot called him a painter for the old (2:111), and he was, at least metaphorically, right. His paintings, comparable in mood and tone only to the pietistic naturalism one finds in Fénelon or many years later in Rousseau, exude the death of desire or rather its transfigured culmination—not the paroxysmal instant but what lingers with diminished and calmer appetency in its wake. Like the eloquent *tableau* of a brief aftermath in the last act of a domestic drama— something Théophile Gautier had already noticed in 1864[12]—everything in his paintings finds its ultimate place with respect to everything else and becomes incorporated in a softly palpitating, perdurable harmony. It is not only the case that, as Diderot said, we stop before his paintings, "like exhausted travellers" dropping down in some verdant glade beside silence, running water, and cool shade (2:129); we rest before scenes that induce that feeling because they so often actually represent it. His weary servant has returned from the market; a little boy has played his games and done that mischief about which he is, perhaps, being quietly instructed by his governess; the top has been spun, the bubble blown, the strawberries mounded up to perfection beside a glass filled with water; the child has been carefully dressed for a visit; the preparations for a meal are over or we see what is left of it; a clay pipe has been smoked and rests atop a thick, unbroken slab, among other worn, angular, and masculine things; a tired copper pot, cherished for its nicks and irregularities, the look of labor and wear, has again been scoured; jars, biscuits, fruit, a meat pie, and wine have casually, mindlessly accumulated—or so Chardin, who plans this artful negligence, wants us to believe. Though the olives and, in another painting, the preserved apricots are corked or covered, their store is partially depleted. Like the wine glasses in *The Jar of Olives* or the crumbs in the *Jar of Apricots* (Figure 5), they intimate a satisfaction with things consumed, but these epicurean paintings deliberately pause, like Grafigny's Zilia in the 1740s or Rousseau's Julie in the early 1760s, to suggest moderation and economy rather than surfeit, to advertise in a steaming cup, an as yet uneaten pie or loaf of bread, the possibility of further, leisurely satisfactions and postponements without risk. We see the results or the remainders of activity, the traces, the aftermath, of effort or act—often, in his atmosphere, a kind of dust settling, a milky haze that gives his subjects and the paintings themselves a faint hallowing glow, the patina of old, commemorated things. Though energy and time have passed like a wind through Chardin's canvases, we find ourselves in a temporary lull, the future, if we care to contemplate it, unthreatened or unthreatening, predictably regular and steady in its routine successivity.

Where there is still effort or the lingering residue of it, the figure pauses to catch her breath or, as in *The Morning Toilet*, to make a small, final adjustment. Often this momentary respite lifts the figure away from care, duty, and circumstance altogether. A washerwoman distractedly turns her head as she bends to scrub things already used; a scullery maid and a tavern-keeper boy star blankly into space. A woman stops peeling

Figure 5. Chardin, *Jar of Apricots*. Courtesy of the Art Gallery of Ontario, Toronto.

vegetables and, resting both hands on her lap, mindlessly lets a turnip dangle by her side (Figure 4). But how remarkable this turnip is! Lightly grasped by its tenuous root, turned upside down, suspended and released from function, a metonymic image of the woman's inner being, it hangs from the end of a serpentine line that curves from head to upper arm before collapsing drowsily into a zigzag. It sinks down like the woman's elbow and the cleaver, angled off course like the unused knife, the skillet idling against a wooden block, or the woman herself—directed away from service and intention. The people in these paintings (and their sympathetic accessories) reenact, rather unsurprisingly for members of a "primitive" class, what had been, throughout the early century, the enviable privilege of youth and innocence but also a dream of the sophisticated upper classes: the pursuit of a loss of consciousness or self-consciousness, a surrender to the gifts of imagination or to the grace of a distraction that might liberate the mind from the tyrannies of worldly necessities, appearances, words, and obligations. From Dufresny, Marivaux, and Crébillon to Rousseau—who elaborates this dream into a positive ethic, a philosophy of existence, even the basis of a political economy—we find characters and narrators for whom a principle of digression, the turning away from social or esthetic expectations, represents the most naturally independent but also the most stylishly aristocratic behavior. Indeed it often becomes impossible to separate what is coquettishly imitated from its authentic and clearly desirable counterpart, so thoroughly does a "natural" art of behavior hide the motives and processes of its production. Characters speaking or acting inattentively, narrators composing "negligent" letters, memoirs, and essays, writing (well before Richardson) "to the moment," wandering loosely and alone through the perpetual present of their thoughts, want us so believe that they are genuinely "lost" to themselves and others, *étourdis*, *indifférents*, *distraits*, *extravagants*, spontaneously veering from public and polite awareness, incapable of smooth transitions or formal closure.[13] And in the light of these deflections from a wakeful, merely conventional center toward the eccentric, associative movements of a private spirit, Chardin's more intensely absorbed figures—the boys with their tops, cards, and bubbles, the young artist sitting on the floor to sketch yet another copy of an old academic drawing, his shabby clothes the very image of wear—appear to sever themselves from the social world and from all self-awareness, to take refuge in wonder and transfixed attention. From eye to object, a line of intensity as firm as any of Chardin's palpable supports, fixes them in place—and, as usual, with respect to something else. They act the way everything conspires to act, or rather, to be suspended, in Chardin's work, within the space of a framed intimacy and within an untroubled and repetitive time, a time without violence or interruption—the time, as Rousseau might say, of wordless melody and pure being; that time of childhood before spring has waned, before Emile's preceptor can say "the clock strikes."

It hardly matters whether we are speaking of genre scenes or still lifes, of people or things. They are not only made out of the same painterly stuff, as Diderot suggests; they also speak that same spatial, atmospheric language through which colors and values come, like shapes and figures, to refer to one another. Which is why Proust could speak so beautifully and truthfully of the "special friendships" between "a tablecloth and the sunlight," between "beings and things, between past and present, between light and shade."[14] All of Chardin's objects and beings are caught in the bliss of that privileged moment of benevolent fusion or of self-forgetful enthrallment and *rêverie* portrayed in domestic drama, in novels like Graffigny's *Lettres d'une péruvienne* (1747), and especially in the *Nouvelle Héloïse*, a moment that only painting can arrest and suspend indefinitely—exactly as Rousseau himself would have wished it. This moment holds forth as a promise, but also provisionally grants, a state of being and of desire toward which so much of eighteenth-century literature strived in spite of itself, an escape from the questionable strategies of rational persuasion and manipulation, a mood in which the agitations, curiosity, and provocations of the art and literature of the early century could find their post-climactic rest. If we are looking for an implied narrative or occult meaning in Chardin, this is where we had best find it: not in easily communicable messages, which even history paintings invariably complicate or disturb, but in a message about states of being that come to life as the mute, indefinitely suspended closure of a special kind of narrative or drama—narratives and dramas that configure themselves only as we reconstitute the world and the longing that sponsored them.

NOTES

1 Pierre Francastel, "Esthétique des lumières" in *Utopie et institutions au XVIIIe siècle*, ed. Pierre Francastel (Paris and The Hague: Mouton, 1963), 345. After an initial citation, page references will appear parenthetically in the text. All translations are my own.

2 *Word and Image: French Painting of the Ancien Régime* (Cambridge: Cambridge University Press, 1981), xvi.

3 See his *Patterns of Intention: On the Historical Explanation of Pictures* (New Haven and London: Yale University Press, 1985), 74–104.

4 Etienne Bonnot de Condillac, *La Logique; ou, les premiers développemens de l'art de penser* (Geneva: n.p., 1785), 16–17.

5 The *Encyclopédie* article called "Effet" (1755), written by Watelet, describes the word as a "terme de peinture" used by artists and spectators alike: "For the artist, *effect* is the combination of different parts of his art, a combination that stirs in his viewers the feelings that filled the painter composing it."

6 Denis Diderot, *Salons*, ed. Jean Seznec and Jean Adhémar, 4 vols. (Oxford: Clarendon Press, 1957–67), 4:83.

7 Rudolf Arnheim, *Toward a Psychology of Art: Collected Essays* (Berkeley and Los Angeles: University of California Press, 1966), 192.

8 For a longer assessment of Fried's contribution to the field of eighteenth-century painting, see my "Between the Eye and the Word: Eighteenth-Century Readers and Viewers," *Boundary 2* 10 (1982): 319–41.

9 In spite of what has come to be called the "anti-rococo" reaction at mid-century, which may have drawn some, though not all, its strength from the political and academic disenfranchisement of a certain class (see Thomas E. Crow, *Painters and Public Life in Eighteenth-Century Paris* [New Haven and London: Yale University Press, 1985], 104–33), there was no radical discontinuity in the audience that continued to appreciate and purchase works of art, and, as I am suggesting, no discontinuity in the profoundest nature of what that audience sought. The theoretical debate that heated up many decades after Chardin began his career focused on the subject matter of paintings, more specifically on the need for a refurbished and, in some cases, a rousingly civic-minded variety of history painting. But what was at stake from the earliest years of the century to this point and no doubt beyond were those stabilizing, captivating emotional effects that once seemed the artist's stock and trade. Behind their century, painters as well as writers had discovered the degradations of an old, sometimes admittedly mythical and feudal order that was itself flawed but that had, at least as they imagined it, generated awe and approbation. They had the sense that they were not part of it or that they had arrived too late on the scene, after the curtain had fallen on a moment of greatness and grandeur. But they wanted, in some lesser or minor way—the way of uncompetitive sons and daughters—to recover those awesome, dignifying, socially unifying effects that appeared to have been lost and to ground them *elsewhere*, in some overlooked, sequestered place and in less public themes.

10 "A bourgeois who keeps to his rank, who understands its limits and extent, who preserves his character from the pettiness of the people, who does not try to rival the man of quality, whose conduct, in short, observes the golden mean—that man would be my sage" ("Lettre sur les habitants de Paris" (1717–18) in *Journaux et oeuvres diverses*, ed. Frédéric Deloffre and Michel Gilot [Paris: Garnier Frères, 1969], 15).

In his still canonical but, I suspect, barely explored masterpiece, *L'Idée du bonheur au XVIIIe siècle* (Paris: Armand Colin, 1960), Robert Mauzi, speaking of "Bonheur et condition sociale," devotes several pages to what he calls "Apologie de la médiocrité." They begin with this remarkable sentence: "Searching for the average notion of a happy life in the eighteenth-century, one invariably encounters the idea of a *bourgeois happiness*. But it would not be wise to give too much weight or precision to a particular social class, since bourgeois happiness overflows the limits of the bourgeoisie" (175).

11 I want to make plain that my phrase, "the submission of particularities to the general good," is intended to draw an analogy between, on the one hand, what Diderot described as the achievement, within a seemingly discordant multi-

plicity, of "l'accord le plus parfait" (2:114) or "harmonie générale" (3:128) and, on the other, the eighteenth-century commonplace of individual interests inclining before "the general good." The analogy deliberately fuses an aesthetic, a domestic, and a civic ideal in order to suggest how or in what sense Chardin may, with the hindsight of history, be thought to adumbrate not only a far more tormented strain of sentimental virtue, but a political ideal of neoclassical virtue as well. What men like Diderot, Caylus, La Font de Saint-Yenne, and Winckelmann were, in the 1750s and 1760s, proposing, buttressing their arguments with ancient, neoclassical, or (in literature) contemporary English examples, was the possibility of unequivocal definition and resolution — in the realm of esthetic forms, a refurbished simplicity or "sedateness and solidity" (Johann Joachim Winckelmann, "On the Imitation of the Painting and Sculpture of the Greeks" in *Winckelmann: Writings on Art*, ed. David Irwin [London and New York: Phaidon Press, 1972], 73) and in private though increasingly in public matters, a controlled, self-sacrificing decisiveness, a domestic or civic sublimity that would be fiercely hierarchical, manly, immutable — wordless and thrilling in its effects. When Diderot, writing of the new theater of "daily life," spoke of his predilection for wordless pantomime or lingering *tableaux* and conjectured that "movement almost always destroys dignity" (*Oeuvres complètes*, ed. Herbert Dieckmann, Jacques Proust, and Jean Varloot [Paris: Hermann, 1975–], 10:133), he was expressing a nostalgia, a hope for what Winckelmann called an "active tranquility" (74), an order and dignity that had already been very covertly inscribed in Chardin. This hope, magnified, was of course to shift to public settings and to exit with militant gestures, outstretched arms, and fingers so splayed that they conjure up as much despair as fervor.

The isolating, escapist arenas of private parks and parlors or the fantasy landscapes of Venus and Armida — everything, in short, that seemed to represent the vacuous, dissociated self-indulgence of modernity, the "lean tensions and hollow wrinkles" (66) Winckelmann scorned, was to make way for the electrifying strangeness, difference, and grandeur of primitive and communal energies, for a solidarity and clarity valiantly wrested from weakness, confusion, and discord. Greuze, as we know, was eventually, in the 1760s, after his return from Italy, after *A Father Reading the Bible to His Children* and *The Village Bride*, to introduce into his domestic scenes the baroque swagger and struggle of a brand of history painting theoretically reconceptualized to host a variety of supposedly ancient and authentically terrible emotions. The reformers who, for want of something better, voiced their enthusiasm for Greuze, would have to wait for David to return those effects they cherished to their proper historic and public space.

But already in Chardin, who clings to a far less grandiloquent order, we find not only a suggestion of those stabilities that will, decades later, be more tensely and programmatically dramatized, but the intimation of later domestic as well as neoclassical households. Symptomatically and symbolically, women, no longer the flighty and flirtatious embodiments of an unsettled, ambiguous, socially fragmented culture, will, in Desmahis's article "Femme," written for the *Encyclopédie*, in Diderot's first example of a "drame domestique," *Le Fils naturel*, and in Rousseau's *Nouvelle Héloïse*, incorporate and exaggerate some of the attributes Chardin had given them only to become what indeed they seem to be in David's *Oath of the Horatti* or Peyron's *Death of Alcestis*: creatures finally silenced and confined, long-suffering mothers or sisters, grave and static guarantors (or victims) of narrowly defined republican virtues. Where women do, in the later century, become active or play crucial or dramatic roles, it is always as stabilizing intercessors, as motherly or wifely influences. One of the disguised ideological motives shared by some of those who took up the cause of the new history painting and a much wider group who, like Voltaire, Rousseau, and Diderot, reached back to ancient Greek forms to recapture sublimity and grandeur, was the desire to purge the arts of what they regarded as the vapid, feminizing pursuit of intimacy and of those paltry, low relief passions involved in *galanterie*. (See Voltaire's "Discours sur la tragédie" [1731] and his Epistle preceding *Oreste* [1750] to understand how the need for something "horrible" and "terrible" works against a "goût effeminé" and finally displaces love altogether—even "furious, barbaric, and fatal love.") There was, in all their minds, a connection, most clearly announced by Burke in 1757 and by Lessing in 1766 (see W. J. T. Mitchell, *Iconology: Image, Text, Ideology* [Chicago and London: University of Chicago Press, 1986], 94–149), between the sublime and the masculine—in some, a patently homosocial and in others (e.g., Winckelmann) a homoerotic or, its usual accompaniment, a homophobic ideal (e.g., Voltaire and Rousseau) that tolerated maternal or paternal domesticity but feared other forms of intimacy. Chardin was appreciated for his skill but thought to be pointless; his imaged intimacies, whatever their effect upon the paternal instincts of the male viewer, are clearly maternal. Greuze, however, repeatedly pays tribute to tribal and paternal power; he cleverly exploits female nudity; and his notorious "intimacy," which is both stagy and hyperbolic, appears, in contrast to Chardin's, not intimate at all—which no doubt discloses one of the unacknowledged secrets of his success.

12 Cited in Pierre Rosenberg, *Chardin*, trans. Emilie P. Kadish and Ursula Korneitchouk (Cleveland: Cleveland Museum of Art and Indiana University Press, 1979), 200.

13 It might be said that these characters and narrators perform, often abusively or exaggeratedly, what had already in the sixteenth and seventeenth centuries been set down as the ethical as well as the esthetic principles of "natural" manners and conversation in aristocratic society: "easiness," "careful negligence," avoidance of "ceremony"—variations of the courtly ideal of *sprezzatura*. (For what was thought to be "natural" and naturally "negligent," see Barnard Tocanne, *L'Idée de nature en France dans la seconde moitié du xviie siècle* [Paris: Klincksieck, 1978], 395–409 and Roger Duchêne, "Madame de Sévigné et le style négligé," *Oeuvres et critiques* 1 [1976], 113–27.) The unbroken tradition continued through the eighteenth century where, from the start,

in a religious rhetorician like Fénelon, a fashionable journal such as the *Mercure de France*, and among writers as diverse as Fontenelle, Marivaux, and Montesquieu, the adaptable model it offered was justified or theorized in different ways but became the basis of a new writerly practice. Not unlike those flirtatious marquises or *petits-maîtres* for whom the dizzying, side-stepping maneuvers of "indifference," "négligence," and "extravagance" represented so many seductively attractive and distancing gestures, writers in this refurbished tradition increasingly found their freedom and individuality not in the semblance of conscious effort or in the rational, logical, or linear concatenations of thought, but in what passed for blessed moments of informal, dissociative, or merely associative release. Because of its connections with a permissible social and conversational practice, the new rhetoric or cultivated abandon of *étourderie*, was able not only to camouflage the subversive ideas it often conveyed but to discover and expose a plentitude of accident, sensation, and being repressed beneath the conventional, conscious designs of ordinary discourse.

It is not surprising that women, considered the embodiments and guardians of social decorum, were blamed by those same moralists (Montesquieu, Diderot, and Rousseau among them) who eagerly imitated the "natural," disjunctive variety, the sudden, witty eruptions and interruptions, that women's salons and a female readership were credited with having inspired. Thought to be childlike, uncontrollably natural, incapable of sustained attention, superficial, easily "distracted" (according to the very representative opinion of Malebranche in his *De la recherche de la vérité*), women were conveniently vilified for having "feminized" written as well as oral discourse. By the time of Rousseau — it was indeed his great originality — the moral propriety and civility involved in maintaining an artfully "natural" style yielded to an impulse perhaps already implied (but kept at bay) in this concept of the "natural": an impulse to turn away from civility and culture entirely, to indulge in private reveries, interior dialogues, soliloquies, rhapsodies — a wholly subjective and sequestered freedom that Shaftesbury had warned against in his *Advice to an Author*. For a more detailed account of how, given the public, conventional nature of language, this was or was not possible, see my "Rousseau's 'Useless' Sensations," *French Review* 62 (February 1989). There is a fine description of the ideologies of civility, if not of its very complex practice in art and literature, in Roger Chartier's *Lectures et lecteurs dans la France d'Ancien Régime* (Paris: Seuil, 1982), 45–86.

14 Marcel Proust, *On Art and Literature 1896-1919*, trans. Sylvia Townsend Warner (New York: Meridian Books, 1958), 333.

Dryden's Nobly Ignoble Heroine: Sigismonda from Fables

CEDRIC D. REVERAND II*

It might come as a surprise to learn that "Sigismonda and Guiscardo," a Boccaccio tale Dryden included in his last major work, *Fables Ancient and Modern* (1700), was Wordworth's favorite Dryden poem. It might come as a surprise to learn that Wordsworth actually *had* a favorite Dryden poem: "I think [Dryden's] . . . translations from Boccace are the best at least the most poetical of his Poems. . . . I think Dryden has much injured the story by the marriage, and degraded Sigismonda's character by it. He has also to the best of my remembrance degraded her character still more by making her love absolute sensuality and appetite, (Dryden had no other notion of the passion). With all these defects, and some other very gross ones it is a noble Poem."[1] However casual this response, and whatever it may be lacking in the thoughtful analytic technique of later commentators, it compensates by having a certain freshness, immediacy, and confusion about it — what Wordsworth sees is an injured, degraded, grossly defective, noble poem. He seems to be struggling; he wants to admire Sigismonda, a proper heroine for what he considers a noble poem, and yet he finds that Dryden has degraded her character. Wordsworth has discovered something important: Sigismonda as a character both succeeds and fails. Furthermore, as I hope to demonstrate, this is no accident; it is part of Dryden's strategy.

The problem begins when Sigismonda starts acting nobly; she actually

23

achieves heroic stature suddenly and unexpectedly, and one can pin down the exact moment of her transformation. In the first part of the tale, Sigismonda seems ordinary enough; she falls in love with Guiscardo, arranges for the two of them to meet secretly. Her cruel father, Prince Tancred, discovers the liaison and in a rage confronts his daughter and threatens to have the young man killed. Other star-tossed women characters in *Fables*, like Althaea and Alcyone, lose control in such situations and find themselves pushed to desperate acts by their violent passion and intense grief. Like them, Sigismonda feels "all the Pangs of Sorrow in her Breast" (371), and one might reasonably expect her to crumble, cry, and scream. But something happens. When pushed to despair, Sigismonda pushes back. She refuses to indulge in hysterical "Cries, and Tears" (373), and she discovers within herself a strength of character and self-control that were not there moments before:

> But in-born Worth, that Fortune can controul,
> New strung, and stiffer bent her softer Soul;
> The *Heroine* assum'd the Womans Place,
> Confirm'd her Mind, and fortifi'd her Face.
> (374–77)[2]

Far from being impulsive, Sigismonda is deliberate; far from being driven beyond control, she is fiercely, even coolly controlled; and far from being speechless in her grief, which is true of other sobbing and screaming heroines in *Fables*, she talks, and talks, and talks, defending herself forcefully and rationally. She begins by standing up to her demanding father:

> *Tancred*, I neither am dispos'd to make
> Request for Life, nor offer'd Life to take:
> Much less deny the Deed; but least of all
> Beneath pretended Justice weakly fall.
> My Words to sacred Truth shall be confin'd,
> My Deeds shall shew the Greatness of my Mind.
> (390–95)

She continues in this vein for nearly two hundred lines, during which she defends her act as lawful, defends Guiscardo as worthy, and argues for intrinsic merit being more important than rank. She also gives her cruel father, who does not manage to get a word in edgewise during her oration, a lesson in justice as well as kingly behavior: "Nor did her Father fail to find, / In all she spoke, the Greatness of her Mind" (582–83).

Impressed as Tancred may be by his daughter's greatness of mind, he has Guiscardo killed anyway. He then cuts out the young man's heart, puts it in a goblet, and sends it to Sigismonda, along with this witty message: "Thy Father sends thee this, to cheer thy Breast, / And glad thy Sight with what thou lov'st the best" (615–16). Greatness of mind apparently does not run in the family. Sigismonda takes the heart to heart, as it were, and decides to commit suicide. Even then she remains calm and controlled:

> Then smil'd severe; nor with a troubl'd Look,
> Or trembling Hand, the Fun'ral Present took;
> Ev'n kept her Count'nance, when the Lid remov'd,
> Disclos'd the Heart, unfortunately lov'd.
>
> (627–30)

She sternly fixes her eyes on the goblet bearer and then sends a final message to Tancred, explaining "this last Act of Love" (646) she is about to commit. After a soliloquy, she does indeed weep, but it is weeping "free from Female Noise, / Such as the Majesty of Grief destroys" (685–86). She had told Tancred that she would be "Fix'd, like a Man to die" (579), and she remains true to her word, ending her life with the same composure, quite literally composing her body on the "Genial Bed" (711) after taking the poison she has prepared. Rather than being rendered helpless and hysterical by grief, which would suggest frailty and elicit pity, Sigismonda is made articulate and heroic by the occasion.

Boccaccio's Ghismonda is noble enough, but Dryden actually fortifies his version of the heroine.[3] In the original, Ghismonda and Guiscardo are lovers only, and it is their illicit love that Tancredi wishes to punish. But Dryden, as Wordsworth complains, marries the lovers. This is a significant change. It removes one of Tancred's principal objections; his insistence that "My Justice, and thy Crime, requires thy Fate" (359) rings hollow when there is no crime. True, Sigismonda has married without her father's consent, so he has some reason to object. Dryden, however, removes even that reason or, rather, has Sigismonda argue it away. She married her first husband in compliance with her father's wishes; now that she is a widow, the obligation to await her father's selection of a husband disappears: "That Bond dissolv'd," she asserts, "the next is freely mine" (411), for parents do not have "pow'r ev'n second Vows to tie" (413). Even if they had, Tancred's "little Care to mend my Widow'd Nights" (414) by providing Sigismonda with another husband has forced her, she claims, "to recourse of Marriage-Rites, / To fill an empty Side" (415–16). Where the original Tancredi can with some justice claim his daughter has debased herself by taking an illicit lover, the new Tancred is accused of not providing for his daughter, and there he stands, objecting to a lawful match, sanctioned by a holy priest.

Dryden has even more powerful ways of weakening Tancred's position, and one can easily anticipate what Dryden might make of a cruel father who also happens to be a prince. As with many kingly figures in *Fables*, such as Theseus in "Palamon and Arcite" and Agamemnon in the first book of the *Iliad*, Tancred affords Dryden the opportunity of commenting on the use of royal power. Invariably, these comments are directed toward William III, the Protestant monarch whose ascent to power in 1688 forced Catholic Dryden to relinquish the laureate. In this case, Dryden makes prince Tancred a tyrant exerting despotic power over an unwilling people. We discover this early in Dryden's translation, when we learn of Sigismonda's first marriage, arranged by her father with some reluctance. He is reluctant because he loves his daughter, and the key phrase in Italian is "teneramente amata" (*Decameron*, 238), with "amata" (beloved) not quite the right word to use for a daughter.[4] Dryden takes Boccaccio's innuendo and drives it home; he also adds another reason for Tancred's arranging the first marriage:

> At length, as Publick Decency requir'd,
> And all his Vassals eagerly desir'd,
> With Mind averse, he rather underwent
> His Peoples Will, than gave his own Consent:
> So was she torn, as from a Lover's Side,
> And made almost in his despite a Bride.
> (19–24)

Dryden's Tancred, like the original Tancredi, is not merely dilatory about marrying off his daughter, but averse to parting with her. But Dryden adds the idea of public pressure; his Tancred agrees to the match only because his unruly vassals pressure him into it. We get a clear idea of Tancred's attitude toward "His Peoples Will," and a clear sense that his affection for his daughter is not entirely paternal. Perhaps that is why "Publick Decency" eagerly desires a marriage; it would come as a welcome relief to those who have noticed Tancred's overly keen affection for his daughter. At any event, what in Boccaccio remains a possible motive behind arranging the marriage, implied by the circumstances more than by the description, in Dryden emerges more explicitly, so much so that even vassals recognize it and protest. No wonder Tancred gets upset about Guiscardo later on. Not only is the young man a rival for the affections of Sigismonda, but he is also one of those damned vassals; later, in a line added by Dryden, Tancred in anger refers to Guiscardo as "A Man so smelling of the Peoples Lee" (317).

Throughout, Dryden colors his Tancred political, not just at those many points where he offhandedly adds the word "tyrant," but also in unexpected places.[5] When discussing the murder of Guiscardo, obviously an ideal opportunity to display Tancred's cruelty most dramatically, Dryden makes Tancred's vicious behavior seem a natural consequence of his being a Williamite king. The "Slaves to Pay" (596) who are instructed to strangle Guiscardo and cut out his heart, and who sound suspiciously like William's Dutch Guards, are

> Fit only to maintain Despotick Pow'r:
> Dang'rous to Freedom, and desir'd alone
> By Kings, who seek an Arbitrary Throne:
> Such were these Guards.
> (599–602, not in Boccaccio)[6]

Tancred would use these guards against his daughter as readily as he would use them against any of his freedom-loving subjects. No longer is Tancred's unjust behavior confined to a few innocents in his all-too-immediate family; rather, it is the evil of "Despotick Pow'r" that threatens all freedom and undermines the state itself.

This addition not only enlarges the evil that is Tancred, but also adds a new dimension to Sigismonda's argument; one cannot help noticing that her longer speeches to father are laced with added political commentary. When, for instance, she argues that her lover's worth exists despite his lowly rank, Sigismonda points out that

> His Poverty augments thy Crime the more;
> Upbraids thy Justice with the scant Regard
> Of Worth: Whom Princes praise, they shou'd reward.
> Are these the Kings intrusted by the Crowd
> With Wealth, to be dispens'd for Common Good?
> The People sweat not for their King's Delight,
> T' enrich a Pimp, or raise a Parasite;
> Theirs is the Toil; and he who well has serv'd
> His Country, has his Countrys Wealth deserv'd.
> (548–56)

The first three lines are from Boccaccio, but the rest is pure Dryden. This goes beyond defending Guiscardo, and turns into an attack on Tancred's injustice together with helpful instructions on how kings are supposed to handle public trust. These are strong words, and mostly Dryden's; they shift the argument, for they make Guiscardo not merely a poor but worthy man, but also a man who has served his country better than certain monarchs Sigismonda could mention. And, by making Tancred's cruelty an extension of his behavior as a selfish, suspicious, vindictive, arbitrary prince, Dryden gives the contrast between father and lovers a new look. Sigismonda and Guiscardo are more than tragic paramours showing their mettle in response to cruelty and injustice. They are also patriots resisting a despotic monarch; as such, they take their place alongside other model patriots in *Fables*, such as the good parson and Kinsman John Driden of Chesterton, both of whom achieve nobility by daring to withstand power-hungry kings (and both of whom also serve as Dryden *alter egos*).

Dryden is making black blacker, and white whiter, weakening Tancred's case and strengthening Sigismonda's. There is no denying the force of Dryden's additions and shifts, which cumulatively assert familiar Dryden ideals, a combination of heroine in the Cleopatra or Almeyda mode,[7] and patriot in the good parson-Kinsman Driden tradition. But that is only part of the story. If we continue the examination, focusing still on Dryden's amplifications, we discover that not only does Dryden make white whiter, but he also simultaneously makes it gray. If he makes his Sigismonda even more the heroine than Ghismonda, Dryden also makes her less a heroine; he fortifies her case, and he undermines it, sometimes in the very act of adding lines that strengthen his heroine, so that our growing acceptance of Sigismonda as heroine is constantly subverted.

Let us return to one of Dryden's most obvious changes, when he adds a priest who marries Sigismonda to Guiscardo, thereby transforming a sinful liaison into a lawful union. As I have argued, this change of plot obviously adds ammunition to Sigismonda's argument by removing her "crime" and replacing it with a holy marriage. However, the wedding itself, which we witness, raises serious questions about the holy matrimony Sigismonda is soon to defend. With the priest standing in wait, an anxious Guiscardo appears. He has made his way from a cave through the connecting passage into Sigismonda's room. He knocks:

> The longing Lady heard, and turn'd the Key;
> At once invaded him with all her Charms,
> And the first Step he made, was in her Arms:
> The Leathern Out-side, boistrous as it was,
> Gave way, and bent beneath her strict Embrace.
> On either Side the Kisses flew so thick,
> That neither he nor she had Breath to speak.
> The holy Man amaz'd at what he saw,
> Made haste to sanctifie the Bliss by Law;
> And mutter'd fast the Matrimony o're,
> For fear committed Sin should get before.
>
> (156–66)

This is marriage in the nick of time. One might add that in Boccaccio, Guiscardo is wearing this leather coat to protect himself against the brambles at the entrance of the cave. Boccaccio mentions the leather jacket only once, but Dryden, evidently taken with the idea, keeps mentioning the leather jacket well after it has finished serving its original purpose, making this a rather unusual wedding scene. As we can see from the above passage, the lovers do not, on the whole, seem to be thinking primarily in terms of honorable marriage; as a matter of fact, they do not appear to be *thinking* at all. The difference between bliss "sancifie[d] . . . by Law" and "committed Sin" is a matter of seconds, and it is only thanks to a speedy priest that the lovers make it to the legal side of the line, after which

> they took their full Delight;
> 'Twas restless Rage, and Tempest all the Night:
> For greedy Love each Moment would employ,
> And grudg'd the shortest Pauses of their Joy.
> (173–76)[8]

With the actual circumstances of the marriage in mind, how do we regard Sigismonda's subsequent defense of her action?

> For, too well I knew
> What Honor was, and Honour had his Due:
> Before the Holy Priest my Vows were ty'd,
> So came I not a Strumpet, but a Bride.
> (404–7)

Her argument is technically correct, but her own interpretation of her intentions does not match the intentions we have seen in action, which would more accurately be called desires, pure and lustful. It is worth weighing the above passages side by side, one wherein Sigismonda indulges greedily, the other in which she claims that she always had honor on her mind. What she actually has in mind is enough to upset the poor harried priest who has been summoned to unite the two lovers:

> His Work perform'd, he left the Pair alone,
> Because he knew he could not go too soon;
> His Presence odious, when his Task was done.
> What Thoughts he had, beseems not me to say;
> Though some surmise he went to fast and pray,
> And needed both, to drive the tempting Thoughts away.
> (167–72)

The priest is shocked and, although it beseems not Dryden to say it, aroused by the scene of passion. Instead of two lovers being sanctified by a priest, we have a priest nearly corrupted by two overtly erotic lovers who begrudge his presence, such is their haste to get on with the serious business of "full Delight."

The greedy and restless Sigismonda appears different to us than she does to Sigismonda. Constantly, there is a pull between what we see and what she sees, to such an extent that we find ourselves smiling at her self-deception, offered in the ringing, persuasive tones of a victimized woman, a wronged daughter, a stubborn patriot, an articulate heroine. When she describes the process of her growing affections for Guiscardo, she elicits sympathy; few would side with the sullen, tyrannical Tancred who will soon mete out a punishment ill befitting the non-crime:

> Nor took I *Guiscard* by blind Fancy led,
> Or hasty Choice, as many Women wed;
> But with delib'rate Care, and ripen'd Thought,
> At leisure first design'd, before I wrought:
> On him I rested, after long Debate,
> And not without consid'ring, fix'd my Fate.
>
> (465–70)

Yet one is tempted to laugh, especially if one has in mind an image of the deliberate care with which the two loudly collapsed upon the bed:

> Attending *Guiscard*, in his Leathern Frock,
> Stood ready, with his thrice-repeated Knock:
> . . . .
> The Door unlock'd, to known Delight they haste,
> And panting in each others Arms, embrac'd;
> Rush to the conscious Bed, a mutual Freight,
> And heedless press it with their wonted Weight.
> The sudden Bound awak'd the sleeping Sire.
>
> (225–26, 229–33)

Tancred has been napping in an adjoining room (not exactly the ideal domestic arrangement), and this is the point where he discovers the lovers. The entire scene, their second encounter alone, is more graphic than in Boccaccio: "They then went to bed in the usual way; but whilst they were playing and cavorting together, Tancredi chanced to wake up, and heard and saw what Guiscardo and his daughter were doing" (McWilliam, 335).[9] Deliberation, leisurely design, long debate, careful consideration have not been conspicuous parts of Sigismonda's behavior. To be precise, one should say she is as deliberate as she has to be to get the lover she sexually craves, and while she may again be technically correct — she did not sleep with just anybody — she is making herself sound a great deal more controlled than her actions prove her to be.

As far as Sigismonda is concerned, her deliberate choice was based on Guiscardo's obvious merits, which persuaded her judgment to bestow her love on this man "whose Mind / Is Vertuous" (519–20). She challenges her father to

measure all thy Court,
By inward Vertue, not external Port,
And find whom justly to prefer above
The Man on whom my Judgment plac'd my Love.

(523–26)

Again, we should place her explanation alongside the available facts. Who is this paragon whose intrinsic worth appealed to Sigismonda's discriminating judgment when she "measured" all the court? Guiscardo, in Boccaccio and Dryden, remains a blank, a null. He responds to Sigismonda's lust, receives a note from her (hidden in a hollow cane) telling him "The Time, the Place, the Manner how to meet" (92), follows her directions, and gets caught. He has but one short, disheartening speech (after which he is completely disheartened). As far as we know, he is one of "the Train of Courtiers" who is "With all the Gifts of bounteous Nature crown'd" (47–48), but what sort of gifts were these that persuaded Sigismonda's discriminating judgment?

When we consider Sigismonda's actual "decision" to wed Giuscardo, who, by the way, has little to say in the matter one way or the other, we discover that, since her first husband died,

Youth, Health, and Ease, and most an amorous Mind,
To second Nuptials had her Thoughts inclin'd:
And former Joys had left a secret Sting behind.
. . . .
Resolv'd at last to lose no longer Time,
And yet to please her self without a Crime,
She cast her Eyes around the Court, to find
A worthy Subject suiting to her mind.

(34–36, 41–44)

When she finds him, "ev'ry Day increas'd / The raging Fire that burn'd within her Breast" (57–58). The line about the absence of former joys, as well as the line about raging fire, are both Dryden additions.[10] Guiscardo may well be a "worthy Subject suiting to her mind," but this is an ambiguous piece of praise; one wonders what kind of worth it is that suits an amorous mind. Does the quiet and passive Guiscardo shine with "inward Vertue" (524), as Sigismonda declares, or is he merely a subject worthy of her pressing desires, whose crowning natural gifts are his attractiveness, his virility, his "blooming Age" (51), and his readiness to do good service, in leather, upon request? And whatever Guiscardo may be, what do we make of the noble Sigismonda? It is difficult to believe that the woman we see casting her eyes about for a second husband to fulfill secret longings is acting with the reasonable, controlled, deliberate "Judgment" she assigns to herself. Throughout, what Sigismonda says is a version of the truth rather than an outright falsehood, but it is a version that becomes difficult to accept, given our awareness of Sigismonda's actual behavior.

Separating the two Sigismondas allows us to examine the ways in which Dryden has added material to both sides of her character; if Dryden has made Tancred blacker while making Sigismonda whiter, pushing the extremes further apart, he has also pushed Sigismonda further apart, reducing her motivation to the sexual (not that Drysden disdains this) while elevating her claims for nobility. Trying to comprehend Sigismonda entails constant struggling. How does one reconcile the roving eye with greatness of mind, the impatient, impassioned seductress with the courageous public-spirited heroine who claims to have honor on her mind?

Furthermore, it is this struggle that appears in much of the critical commentary on this poem, beginning with Wordsworth who thinks this a noble poem but criticizes Dryden for degrading the character of Sigismonda.[11] Dryden's tale pulls Wordsworth in two directions, and we find Wordsworth praising the "improved" and "most poetical" while lamenting the "fallen" and "degraded." It is not merely the erotic behavior of Sigismonda that offends Wordsworth; had this been merely an obscene tale bristling with prurience, he most likely would have dismissed it outright as Restoration immorality, beneath contempt. Rather, Wordsworth seems offended at Dryden's taking away from Sigismonda what Wordsworth thinks she should have: what bothers him is not just the sensuality, but the fact that love is *made* "absolute sensuality and appetite," not the basely motivated character of Sigismonda, but the fact that her character has been "degraded." Caught between the two Sigismondas, Wordsworth finds himself endorsing the exalted one, the woman who defended her honorable love, whose passion was elevated and convincing, who made this the "noble Poem" Wordsworth would admire. Unfortunately, she is a far cry from the Sigismonda who jumps eagerly and noisily into bed with her lover, and Wordsworth rejects that side of Sigismonda to preserve the other.

Modern commentators on the tale fall basically into two schools of thought, one for each Sigismonda. For some, the sensual Sigismonda wins, and the apparent heroism is nothing more than a sham, wherein the would-be heroine reveals her narrowness in the very act of attempting to achieve nobility. In this view, the character of Sigismonda, unable to understand how little claim she has to what she claims she has, becomes not a study in passion but an object of satire.[12] For others, it is the heroine who wins, the noble soul of part two who replaces the limited woman of part one. If that is the case, the disparity between actions and claims can be explained away by arguing for a progress, a transition that occurs when Sigismonda "changes at once from a woman of uninhibited sensuality to one of Heroic Mind" (Emrys Jones, 284-85).[13] The progress is there, quite specifically, when Sigismonda assumes the heroine's mantle, but it is so swift, and so much at odds with the rest of Sigismonda's behavior, that we have every reason to wonder how the heroine could possibly assume the woman's place.

We have, then, a Sigismonda who transcends her limitations, or whose limitations subvert her claims to spirituality. And we have a Dryden who celebrates a noble woman, or whose gross errors prevent him from endorsing that nobility, unless he is a satirist criticizing a pretense to nobility, perhaps because, according to one critic, he wishes to endorse a Christian ethic.[14] Each critic not only endures the struggle with the two Sigismondas, but sees it through to some kind of civilizing ideal, in what Sigismonda is, or what she should have been if Dryden were less prurient, or what she could have been had she been a beneficiary of Christian revelation.[15] The resolutions differ; what remains the same is the process of trying to reconcile the irreconcilable. It is the nature of Sigismonda to be both persuasive heroine and limited human being incapable of the heroism with which she convinces us. It is the nature of the tale to establish ideals and also measure them, to weave a noble portrait and unravel it as well.

Furthermore, this is a strategy I think Dryden employs throughout *Fables*, where values are established and subverted, ideals offered and withdrawn. Dryden invokes a host of value systems, Christian, heroic, domestic, sentimental, consistently making appealing and convincing cases for an array of possibilities for civilizable mankind. The possibilities include passionate love, conjugal love, love of principle, love of country, love of God, all of which vie against limitations, failures that Dryden presents persuasively as equal parts of the human scene. All the ideals have their appeal and their temporary successes, but all are constantly under a subversive pressure, so that the ideals are unattainable or inapplicable to life, even as they are precious and necessary. The divided Sigismonda is not merely an unresolved character, but a further instance of Dryden measuring ideals, inducing us to seek resolution in a universe whose basic active principle is irresolution and constant change.

NOTES

* A more extensive version of this paper, which includes an exploration of the relationships between "Sigismonda and Guiscardo" and the other tales in Dryden's anthology, will appear in *Dryden's Final Poetic Mode: The Fables*, forthcoming from University of Pennsylvania Press.

1 Letter to Sir Walter Scott, 7 November 1805, quoted in *Dryden: The Critical Heritage*, ed. James Kinsley and Helen Kinsley (London: Routledge & Kegan Paul, 1971), 323–25.

2 The text used for Dryden quotations is *The Poems of John Dryden*, ed. James Kinsley, 4 vols. (Oxford: Clarendon Press, 1958); *Fables* appears in volume 4; references are to line.

3 According to Kinsley, Dryden's Boccaccio texts were "an Italian text" as well as "the anonymous English version (1620) made partly from the Italian and partly from Antoine le Maçon's French translation of the *Decameron* (1545)" (Kinsley, *Poems*, 4:2072). I have followed Dryden with similar sources in hand, using the 1620 translation, now thought to be by John Florio, from *The Decameron, Preserved to Posterity by Giovanni Boccaccio and Translated into·English Anno 1620*, intro. by Edward Hutton, 4 vols. (1909; repr., New York: AMS Press, 1967). For the Italian text, references are to *Giovanni Boccaccio: Decameron, Filocolo, Ameto, Fiammetta*, ed. Enricho Bianchi, Carlo Salinari, and Natalino Sapegno (Milan: Riccardo Ricciardi Editore, [1952]); in presenting a modern translation, I rely on *The Decameron*, trans. G. H. McWilliam (1972; repr., Harmondsworth, England: Penguin Books, 1980).

4 McWilliam renders this as "passionately fond of his daughter" (McWilliam, 332); Florio, who tiptoes politely past Boccaccio's sexual innuendos, uses the guarded phrase "over-curious respect" (Florio, 2:142).

5 In Boccaccio, Tancredi is a benevolent ruler, "se egli nello amoroso sangue nella sua vecchiezza non s'avesse le mani bruttate" (*Decameron*, 283) — "except for the fact that in his old age he sullied his hands with the blood of passion" (McWilliam, 332), which Dryden renders as "dipp'd his Hands in Lovers Blood" (6). Boccaccio's Tancredi, however, is not called a tyrant.

6 From 1688 on, Dryden seemed to take every occasion he could find, or invent, to criticize William III and his "stupid Military State," to borrow a phrase from Dryden's 1694 poem "To Sir *Godfrey Kneller*" (51). William had just dragged England through the unpopular Nine Years War, still called by historians "King William's War"; although that war had come to an end with the Treaty of Rijswijk in 1697, England, weary with war and saddled with a war debt of £5,500,000, was resisting the apparently militaristic plans of its monarch. The two related issues that came up time and again were William's desire to keep a Standing Army at the ready in the time of peace, and his wish to retain his personal Dutch Guards. William's third and fourth Parliaments (1697–1698) fought over this issue, with the fourth Parliament in December of 1698 voting to reduce William's land forces substantially. Parliament also

voted to exclude from those forces all but natural-born subjects, which meant disbanding the Dutch Guards, whose presence served as an irritating reminder of William's foreignness. Aside from this allusion in "Sigismonda and Guiscardo," one can find Dryden attacking either the Standing Army or the Dutch Guards—sometimes the two blur together as evidence of William's warlike wishes—in many tales from *Fables*, including "To Her Grace the Dutchess of Ormond," "Palamon and Arcite," "To my Honour'd Kinsman, John Driden, of Chesterton," and "Cymon and Iphigenia."

7 For a good discussion of this familiar Dryden figure, the woman of passion, see Jean H. Hagstrum in chap. 3, "John Dryden: Sensual, Heroic, and 'Pathetic' Love," from *Sex and Sensibility: Ideal and Erotic Love from Milton to Mozart* (Chicago: University of Chicago Press, 1980), 50–71; Hagstrum includes Sigismonda in his discussion. See also Judith Sloman's *Dryden: The Poetics of Translation* (Toronto: University of Toronto Press, 1985), 141–44, for a suggestive comparison of Sigismonda with Dryden's version of Dido from his translation of the *Aeneid*.

8 Comparison to the original at this point is instructive; everything pertaining to the priest and marriage is, as I have said, a Dryden addition. Dryden's starting point is the encounter of the two lovers, which in the original version is described briefly: "insieme maravigliosa festa si fecero; e nella sua camera insieme venutine, con grandissimo piacere gran parte di quel giorno si dimorarono" (*Decameron*, 284–85). McWilliam translates this as: "After giving each other a rapturous greeting, they made their way into her chamber, where they spent a goodly portion of the day in transports of bliss" (McWilliam, 334). Boccaccio does not spell out the exact details, but there is little doubt what constitutes a transport of bliss, and one can easily recognize in the passage the source of Dryden's "full Delight" ("con grandissimo piacere"). As this example suggests, and as Wordsworth notices, Dryden consistently amplifies Boccaccio's sexual innuendo. Hagstrum in *Sex and Sensibility* finds this true of Dryden's general treatment of Ovid and of Virgil as well: "If Dryden's sexualization of the decorous Virgil . . . does not surprise, perhaps his intensification of Ovid's already assertive sexuality will. Just as the pagan love poet was more specifically erotic than his Latin predecessors, so Dryden surpassed in sexual meaning earlier English translators, reversing the tendency to tone down the ancient to please modern Christian taste" (52).

9 "E andatisene in su 'l letto, come usati erano, e insieme scherzando e sollazzandosi, avvene che Tancredi si svegliò, e sentí e vide ciò che Guiscardo e la figliuola facevano" (*Decameron*, 285).

10 Boccaccio's Ghismonda falls madly in love, but without the fire imagery, which Florio adds to his translation of the passage: "her affections being but a glowing sparke at the first, grew like a Bavin to take flame" (Florio, 2:143). This may be the source for Dryden's "raging Fire that burn'd within her Breast" (58), but Dryden adds more, thereby considerably fanning the flames: "as the Fire will force its outward way, / Or, in the Prison pent, consume the Prey; / So long her earnest Eyes on his were set" (61–63).

11 Tempting as it may be to dismiss Wordsworth's unsympathetic, casual remarks, I think they have to be weighed seriously because of their influence. They impressed Walter Scott, whose commentary on "Sigismonda and Guiscardo" closely echoes Wordsworth. See Scott, *The Life of John Dryden*, ed. Bernard Kreissman (1808; repr., Lincoln: University of Nebraska Press, 1963), 422. Much later, even Mark Van Doren, whose enthusiasm for Dryden helped rescue the poet from oblivion, quoted Wordsworth's remarks and commented that the poet's "criticism can hardly be improved upon." See Van Doren, *The Poetry of John Dryden* (1920); rev. and retitled *John Dryden: A Study of His Poetry* (1946; repr. Bloomington: Indiana University Press, 1963), 229. Emrys Jones, in "Dryden's Sigismonda," from *English Renaissance Studies: Essays Presented to Dame Helen Gardner in Honour of Her Seventieth Birthday*, ed. John Carey (Oxford: Clarendon Press, 1980), 279–90, remarks that the marriage scene has been made into a "leering intrusion" by a "whole tradition of criticism" (286–87); Jones quotes Wordsworth and Van Doren, and adds C. S. Lewis into the bargain.

12 In "Dryden's Originality in *Sigismonda and Guiscardo*," *Studies in English Literature* 12 (1972): 445–57, Judith Sloman, whose argument I am here summarizing, rejects Sigismonda's nobility because, "in spite of her claims to spiritual grandeur, she has acted all along to satisfy her passions" (448). Sloman reconciles the disjunction between claims and actions by resorting to "the irony in the poem," which "lies not just in the fact that these characters are moved by lust, but in the way their efforts at nobility are undercut by their limited knowledge" (451). However, earlier in the same article, Sloman pays tribute to Sigismonda, remarking on her defense of freedom in the face of tyrannical authority, and even justifying her taking the initiative with Guiscardo as an act appropriate to "a person conscious of his or her greatness of soul" (447). By responding positively to Sigismonda's claims, Sloman seems to be demonstrating that the irony she here ascribes to Dryden does not work.

13 This is essentially Emrys Jones's argument in "Dryden's Sigismonda." Instead of seeing a clash between fraudulent claims on the one hand and solid reality on the other, Jones regards the character as being divided between two contradictory but equally persuasive motivations, "an aspiration to the noble and magnanimous on the one hand, and on the other a frank, and to many readers disconcerting, delight in coarseness and indecency" (279). Jones reconciles the two in favor of the nobler character, calling this tale an "undoubted success" (279) in the heroic vein.

14 For Judith Sloman, Sigismonda's limitations occur because she is not a Christian. Speaking more generally in "An Interpretation of Dryden's *Fables*," *Eighteenth-Century Studies* 4 (1970/1971): 199–211, Sloman maintains that "most of the characters in *Fables*" act "without benefit of divine truth as revealed in Christ's lifetime," but instead act "within the framework of limited truth and passionate response" (200). However, in *Dryden: The Poetics of Translation* (Toronto: University of Toronto Press, 1985), Sloman seems to have shifted toward my own argument, for here she treats this "ambiguous

character" (141) more in terms of unresolved opposites, describing the heroine as "a genuine attack on tyranny," who is also "flawed by the dubious impulses that afflict everyone" (143).

15 Other critics who comment on the two sides of Sigismonda include Hagstrum in *Sex and Sensibility* and Rachel Trickett in *The Honest Muse: A Study in Augustan Verse* (Oxford: Clarendon Press, 1967). Hagstrum accepts the coexistence of "unabashed sexuality" and "love heroism" (54) as simply a part of Dryden's sensibility, as does Trickett, although Trickett's commentary is little more than diluted Wordsworth; she mentions "Dryden's insensitivity to all but the sensual aspect of love" (70), and, although she does not use the term "gross errors," she blames Dryden for not having a mind sensitive and subtle enough "to reconcile these views of human nature" (71).

Emma*grammatology*

GRANT I. HOLLY

"Do I like parlor games? My dear I am a parlor game."
Tallulah Bankhead

I

What do we say when we talk about literature? Disconcertingly, what we already know, as if the work were a bell that announced our turn to speak. As if it were a prefiguration and vindication of our own beliefs. As if the experience of reading, of finding a coherence, at once hidden and apparent, in the text, recapitulated the orphan phantasy of childhood — the phantasy of finding the real parent, the true noble ancestor and likeness, whose identity, which would authorize our identity, emerges in our "recognition" of the mirror-like similarity, the uncanny kinship, of (both) our views. Literature is a glass, we might say paraphrasing Swift, in which the reader sees everybody's face as his or her own, precisely because our relationship to literature, or, for that matter, representations in general, recapitulates the conditions that opened the very possibility of identity.

This briefly-sketched problematic of our relationship to literature is also meant to serve as a description of the scenes of both Lacanian psychoanalysis and Jane Austen's *Emma*; when I say the scene of Jane Austen's *Emma*, I am referring not only to the scene within the novel,

39

that is, Emma's interpretive relationship to her world, but also to the critics' relation to the novel, and by implication to Jane Austen.[1]

The intention is not, here and now, to develop a reading of Lacan – an undertaking that becomes both less and less necessary and more and more difficult as Lacan's writings gain popularity. Rather, what will be attempted is an emphasis of certain of Lacan's ideas that seem to me to be important in relationship to the way in which we read *Emma*.

Jane Austen as Moral Realist

One of the most striking features of Lacan's work is that he makes what in large measure constitutes literary analysis, or, for that matter, the analysis of representations in general, that is, the discovery of coherences and correspondences, of closure – within the work, between the work and historical events or modes of thought, among works, etc. – symptomatic and the subject of psychoanalysis. To put it even more strongly, these features of what would traditionally be called rational, careful, thorough, "realistic" analysis, Lacan would make the features of what is traditionally called hallucinatory behavior – part of an imaginary construct that allows the subject to maintain the illusion of self-coherence by basking in the reflection of a discovered (invented) coherence. What is at stake here is the reinterpretation of the realistic and the moral, figured in the novel in terms of closure, that is, whether or not things hold together, as part of the ideology of patriarchal culture. The search for closure in Jane Austen's work is doubly important, since, as Gilbert and Gubar have shown, Austen's work is thought of as "woman's work," and, for that reason, especially subject to policing by patriarchal culture.[2] This situation is tantalizingly thematized in *Emma* in particular, because of the way both author and character are frequently judged to fall short of the demands of the moral and the realistic: Austen through the limitations of her subject, Emma through the errors of interpretation that develop out of her persistent playfulness.

Emma as Artist Manqué

This tendency to hallucinate closure, to discover design, coherence, meaning – to write literary criticism, for example – Lacan labels "the Imaginary," and he attributes it to what he calls the mirror stage – the moment in infancy when the infant, spastic and fragmented, develops the idea of a coherent self from seeing "its" reflection in a mirror (actual or metaphorical). Among the points Lacan is making here are 1) that the idea of coherence and closure produced in this situation is exaggerated, an illusion perpetrated by the technology of the mirror's surface; 2) that the exaggeration of coherence per se is built into the ego from the very beginning, continually leading it in a pursuit of a closure it can never reach; and 3) that this desire for closure and identity is fundamentally frustrated by the fact that the self is the product of the other (the technology of the mirror, for example) and therefore is "itself" an alterity, a perpetual lack. What has been held against Emma is her lack of mastery, but it is also possible to read the novel as the disconcerting assertion of lack in opposition to mastery.

The Importance of Charades in Emma

The lack built into the Imaginary is underscored by what Lacan calls the Symbolic, the arbitrary representational systems by means of which the Imaginary attempts to construe closure, but which, precisely because of their arbitrariness, make closure unreachable. In the drama of the mirror stage, the mirror itself plays the part of the Symbolic, that is what makes the self appear, what apparently establishes identity, is in fact discontinuous with the ideas of self and identity. The mirror is merely a rigorous technology which will signify whatever crosses its path. The self produced by such a technology is a kind of prosthesis, something added in the place —of what, we cannot say. Indeed the symbolic order is a prosthetic order. Its paradigm, for Lacan, is language. The symbolic order is dominated by the signifier and the letter, which it tries to control by means of the law, or what Lacan calls the Name-of-the-father. The charades in *Emma* contribute to a generalized and uncontrollable spread of the arbitrary potential of signification.

Educating Emma and Jane

This situation, as Lacan describes, it is anxiety-laden. The dynamic relation of the Imaginary and the Symbolic consists of doomed attempts to create the motivated out of the arbitrary, the coherent out of the fragmented. Lacan characterizes this situation in the context of the sexual politics of a patriarchal society. The anxiety implicit in the Imaginary's trying to fashion identity out of difference, the self out of that which is cut off from the self—the Other—Lacan identifies as castration anxiety. The symbolic order, then, becomes the order of the phallus—not the penis, but the prosthesis, that which is added in place of, and thereby signifies incompleteness while it makes closure its signified. The way in which these anxieties are allayed in the patriarchal world is through the control of the phallus, of the symbolic order, and of discursive practices (such as literary criticism). Those in control of these practices and of the symbolic order have the phallus and make meaning. Those who are not in control, are castrated, become the phallus, and are made meaningful. As Laura Mulvey puts it: men are the makers of meaning; women are the bearers of meaning.[3] Mulvey is, of course, writing about visual pleasure in the cinema, but her thesis does apply to the way critics commonly treat Emma Woodhouse, and Jane Austen. One alternative way of treating them is grammatology, a way of making meaning without attempting to create closure — similar to the techniques of Lacanian analysis.

II

Let us return now to the question of moral realism. In the range of opinion about Jane Austen's novels, there has been general agreement that they should be discussed in terms of moral realism. Some readers have found her work neither moral nor realistic, it is true, but it is still morality and realism that provide the standards for the decision.

The "two inches" of ivory and the fine brush certainly contribute to this view. It is paradoxical but true that the miniature implies realism. We can say with some certainty that there are no abstract expressionist miniatures. What would be the point? The miniature is about closure; it mirrors the world to the last detail. We look at it as we look at the newborn, nervously counting the toes, amazed that all the parts are there. The miniature is, as Bachelard pointed out, related to immensity. In it we expect to find everything, completion (in the object and in ourselves; for finding the object complete somehow valorizes the completeness of the self). Behind the little fence and beyond the little trees, we see the little house; and through the little window, we see the little family — mother, father, child — nestled among their tiny furniture. A dog sleeps by the fire; a doll lies next to the dog. On the wall hangs a painting — recognizable, a Dutch painting of a much more numerous family, in a much more cluttered house; and in the background, the darkened hallway down which, no doubt, the family pace out Zeno's paradox, when night falls or the book is closed.

Similarly, the miniature stands for concentrated empiricism: an exhaustive, painstaking, faithful reproduction of detail. In the empiricism and the detail — a gaze that never deserts the object, but (here again is our paradox) turns to represent it — we imagine reality; in the pain, exhaustion, and faithfulness, the morality. Whether it is inscribing endless angels on the head of a pin, or *The Raft of the Medusa* on the back of a postage stamp, or the manners and passions of human beings within the narrow bounds of the social regulations of a small circle of acquaintances in a rural English community, the work seems selfless, an act of penance that shows devotion to the world, or to the masters, in its exactitude. We like it that way. We are consoled by the presence of the humble, which is to say the castrated. Consoled that is, until it dawns on us, and this is the heart of the paradox, that the miniaturist has hitched reality to a trick, has subordinated the world to the skillful manipulation of the tools, no matter how small. The miniature is also, as Burke pointed out, a version of the self-annihilation imagined by the sublime.[4] On the one hand the miniature is patronized because its form seems to flatter the self-sufficiency of the beholder. On the other, it turns out to be a profound undercutting of the possibility of self. To allay such disturbing ideas, the miniaturist is usually disciplined with charges of triviality.

All of this describes a persistent reading of Jane Austen. In his recent biography, John Halperin has found her petty, cold, and materialistic.[5] Alistair Duckworth finds in her "an unlikable fondness for obstetrical humor," with a personal cattiness which he takes to be the source of the cattiness of some of her characters and which is in fact in keeping "with the banal monotony" of her life.[6] What characterizes her life and, to a degree, weakens her work, according to these readings, is a certain lack which is evidenced in "female behavior" and manifests itself in her inability to grasp what is great and grand, so to speak. The same view is common in discussions of the novels. The absence of Napoleon has been noted more than once, which is also a way of noting the absence of what is great and grand, what is imperialistic (closure) and patriarchal. In raising technique over theme, the miniaturist disrupts the smooth functioning of the symbolic order, intercepts the phallus in its circulation, exposes it as the apparatus, awakens the fear of castration by pointing to a lack at the very heart of being that makes closure impossible, and for this she must be punished. Punishment, of course, involves calling the miniaturist trivial, which is to say, castrated, but it does so in a way that frequently shows that the miniaturist is feared because the miniature thematizes the threat of castration. Gilbert and Gubar's account records the way the history of the response to Jane Austen repeatedly demonstrates this point. D. H. Lawrence's reaction is exemplary. He attacks her by calling her an "old maid," and describes her characterization as "the sharp knowing in apartness, instead of knowing in togetherness."[7] Joel Weinsheimer puts it pretty straightforwardly when he says: "Perhaps what we lack in reading Jane Austen," by which, of course he also means what she lacks, "is a chapter on whales, . . ." or a confrontation "with an existential doorknob."[8]

It is important to note here that this critique of Jane Austen as person and novelist is exactly congruent with one of the most popular ways of understanding her novels: that is, as revelations of the way the heroines are shown to be incompetent and ill-suited for dealing with the symbolic order. Emma, who cannot finish a book or really develop her talent for painting, is an artist manqué in this view. Within the novel, she nevertheless plots several novels, all of which she gets wrong, and she would have continued to go wrong had she not submitted to Knightley, re-entered the narrative and moved towards closure as his character. The motif here, as Joseph Wiesenfarth has shown, is the story of Pygmalion and Galatea.[9] Emma tries to play Pygmalion to Harriet's Galatea, fails miserably, and finally assumes her proper role, Galatea to Knightley's Pygmalion. "The *hard truth* (italics mine) in these novels," as Wiesenfarth puts it, "is that Pygmalion is inevitably male."[10]

It is interesting that readers have stopped at this point. Pygmalion is certainly a male pig story. It conforms exactly to the paradigm that Mulvey sets up in her work on visual pleasure, construing woman as the bearer of meaning rather than the maker of meaning — that meaning being the lack that demands the direction of the patriarchal order. Emma, according to Wiesenfarth, has a "vulgarity of mind," while "true elegance . . . is inherent in Mr. Knightley's keen judgment of character, genuine English amiability, and straightforward humane action."[11] Why can't a woman be more like that!

It is not a question here of identifying critics who do not like Jane Austen or Emma Woodhouse. By and large, the views characterized here are produced by critics in the process of demonstrating their admiration for Austen, for *Emma* and its heroine. Indeed, it is also true that elements of the kind of reading I myself am suggesting have their place in established readings of *Emma*, as well. Mark Shorer, for example, talks about the way "the irresolution of the book gives it its richness . . .," and Wayne Booth discusses the way the novel's being constructed so that we "travel" with Emma, engages our sympathy on Emma's behalf. Marvin Mudrick, who admittedly likes the novel better than he likes Emma or Jane Austen, talks about the novel's "multiple" and "unresisting irony," and its relentless "deceptiveness of surface" that leads to there being "no happy ending." Of course Mudrick worries over these features, even as he praises them. They constitute a castrating threat. Emma "prefers women," "loves Harriet," has no "tenderness," and therefore "exhibits the strong need to dominate, the offhand cruelty, the protective playfulness, the malice of Jane Austen. . . ."[12]

What recurs in all this criticism is the language of lack and phallocentrism. Shorer, for example, has no sooner praised the richness of the book's irresolution than he turns to a discussion of Knightley in order to see "Jane Austen's values as they positively underlie her drama." That drama has to do with the underscoring of Emma's lack. In a process that

Shorer describes as both humiliating and "beautiful," she is "reduced" and "diminished" in her social position and "enlarged" by her submission to Knightley's moral/phallic influence. Shorer represents Knightley as "a cone," stretching from Harriet to the end of the book.[13] Booth defines Knightley as "the man who throughout the book has stood in the reader's mind for what [Emma] lacks." It is that lack which is figured in Booth's defining of the novel's "sustained inside view." As he puts it, "seen from the outside, Emma would be an unpleasant person. . . ."[14]

What makes this view seem persuasive is that Emma, herself, seems to hold it. Having blundered at Box Hill, and with Harriet, and having perhaps lost Knightley, she is covered in shame and humiliation—the admission of her lack—and swears off trying to manipulate the symbolic order, or, as it is put, "mystery" and "finesse." Where the novel differs from the criticism, however, is in its relentless engendering of the play and difference that undermine closure. From this point of view, we can reread Emma's lack of mastery to mean, not the absence of control, but "mastery's lack"—a calling forth of the lack that mastery veils.

Recently, a series of works has suggested a way of reading the novels, alternative to their being humiliating educational experiences for their heroines. I have already mentioned Gilbert and Gubar's important study, *The Madwoman in the Attic.* Another of these works is the section on Jane Austen in D. A. Miller's 1981 book *Narrative and Its Discontents.* The fundamental point of Miller's wonderfully rich and complex essay is that there is a struggle in Jane Austen's work between the ideology of closure and the production of narrative. The novel owes its existence to the very features it would seem to condemn: mistakes, blunders, vulgarity, mystery, finesse, etc. If Emma had submitted to Knightly's elegance earlier, there would have been no novel. Whatever moral lesson we try to extract from the novel exists by virtue of its opposite. A third is Joseph Litvak's 1985 *PMLA* essay, "Reading Characters: Self, Society, and Text in *Emma.*" Litvak acknowledges his indebtedness to Miller, and then takes Miller's idea of narratability and extends it to include the letter, demonstrating the way the novel can be seen as a continuing series of plays on words. It is a brilliant essay and a major contribution to ways of thinking about Jane Austen's work. A fourth work is Tony Tanner's 1986 book on Jane Austen, which makes similar points to those made by Miller and Litvak but seems unaware of their work.[15]

III

What these works point to is the grammatological reading of *Emma.* Alistair Duckworth sees the riddles, games, and charades in the novel as a kind of false wit which Jane Austen "transforms" in order make "*Emma* a far more generally palatable affirmation of culture."[16] I would ask how we could see *Emma* as anything but continually underwritten, a kind of palimpsest, by the anagrammatic possibilities of misreading and rereading—possibilities that undermine closure and even cultural affirmation. Part of our assessment of *Emma*'s realism, for example, is based on its careful depiction of character. The novel, however, relentlessly makes character a mere function of language. After Mr. Weston quits the militia, we are told, "the next eighteen or twenty years of his life passed cheerfully away"(16). It is true, of course, that this formulation reflects in complex and ironic ways on Mr. Weston's character—says that he lacks a certain intelligence and sensitivity, for example—but its form foregrounds signifying as a power that produces rather than reproduces worlds. The "or," which throws away two years as if they meant nothing, is a *tour de force*. The picture of "cheerfully" caught in the cold embrace of "passed away," suggests the way the sentence always sentences its subject and is frequently a death sentence. What we see here is the dazzling superficiality of the juvenalia remaining uncannily fundamental to the serious works of Austen's maturity. The consequence of the fundamental importance of the superficial is that the serious is undermined in the very mode of its production.

What ought to be pointed out, then, is the inexactitude, the vagueness, the substitutability that regulates the deployment of character and characteristics in *Emma*. Throughout the novel, for example, the characters and their opinions are defined against a background of what we might call characters in general, or even pure or essential characters. I refer here to the recurrence of "somebody," "nobody," "everybody," "anybody," examples of sheer prosopopoeia, personifications of personification itself. "Harriet Smith," we are told, "was the natural daughter of somebody. Somebody had placed her, several years back, at Mrs. Goddard's school, and somebody had lately raised her from the condition of scholar to that of parlour-boarder" (22-23). In volume 1, chapter 28, Emma and Knightley debate the propriety of Frank Churchill's behavior by juxtaposing it against the imagined behavior of somebody, anybody, everybody, and nobody. After Elton's proposal, Emma consoles herself in the recognition that "if Miss Woodhouse of Hartfield, the heiress of thirty thousand pounds, were not quite so easily obtained as he had fancied, he would soon try for Miss Somebody else with twenty, or with ten"(135).

A faceless multitude beings to emerge here, but this facelessness characterizes precisely that which opens the possibility of the appearance of face, of the depiction of character. Every body in literature, we might say, is no body, produced in such a way that there seems to be some body. Late in the novel, as if to make this point, the narrative, in order to make the next move in the Frank and Jane plot, introduces Old John Abdy and his son (383). Abdy: in terms of the name *qua* name, or in terms of the character's role in the novel, we are invited to say—this could be any-body, anybody and the son of anybody. Abdy is *a body*: a body without vowels, and therefore, somehow more rawly a literal body, since it presents itself in the aspect of an articulation, a physicality of the letter that has not allowed itself to be softened and rationalized into pronunci-ation. This is a body in pieces, the body as signifiers. Abdy and Abdy's son suggest that character in the novel could be anybody, that character, in other words, is character in the literal sense, a play of letters, and it is this sense that is figured in the novel's being underwritten by word play and charade.

The underwriting of the novel as a directed, authoritative narrative, is also an underwriting of the Name-of-the-father, and in the double and contradictory sense suggested by the idea of underwriting. On the one hand, the devices of riddle, charade, and word play, access and support the symbolic order and seem to demand participation in it—even as Emma attempts to use these devices as an entrance to the world of story-telling, the world of authoritative narrative. On the other, these devices undermine that order by suggesting that it is an arbitrary system of mere writing. In the first place, Emma is punished for trying to be the maker of meaning. She registers the appropriate response to her lack: "ashamed of every sensation but the one revealed to her—her affection for Mr. Knightley. —Every other part of her mind was disgusting"(412). She becomes the handmaiden of manliness, rebuking Frank Churchill for trading the symbolic order and its phallic accouterments for the poor stuff that she has grown ashamed of: "So unlike what a man should be! —None of that upright integrity, that strict adherence to truth and principle, that disdain of trick and littleness, which a man should display in every transaction of his life"(397). In the second place, however, Emma is vindicated, not as a "realistic" character, for the symbolic order produces realism as a talisman to ward off, with its wholeness, its "upright integrity," the fear of castration, but as character in the literal sense—part of the transgressive flow of signification through the text. In this sense "trick and littleness" are vindicated: without them we realize there would be no story, because in them we see the technology of signifi-cation that comprises the warp and woof of the text. Emma, the "realis-tic" character, may say she has given up "mystery," and we doubt it. In terms of the play of the letter, however, there can be no question of its disappearance. It remains on the surface, the phonic level, the level of pun and play. Here, appropriately, since I am arguing that the mystery of the novel is joined to the mystery of the letter, "mystery" becomes "Mr. E.," that is, Mrs. Elton's appellation for her husband.

As we watch the novel move towards anagram and the subversion of the symbolic order, it is appropriate that Mr. Woodhouse should play a role in the undermining of the Name-of-the-father. His contribution to the charades, "Kitty, a fair but frozen maid," already copied down by the group, seems to cause, as he struggles to remember it, some little embarrassment. The solution to Garrick's puzzle is "the chimney-sweeper," apparently harmless enough. What makes it interesting, though, is the way it plays off against the sexual innuendo. The frozen Kitty of the first stanza, who kindles a flame that calls for the attention of the phallic "hood-wink'd boy," succeeds, in the third stanza, to Fanny, bleeding victims, and strange desires. The father, here, would seem to be bringing forward the material of a primal scene, the scene in which the threat of the phallus enforces itself as the law, but in his forgetfulness and insensitivity to the innuendo, the phallus loses it potency.

What he does promote, by his very inability to control the symbolic order, is the continual slippage that undermines it. "If I had but her memory!"(78), he says of his wife, oblivious of the fact memory is all he has of her, or that it is her memory that he has forgotten. It is at this point, and with this disarming arbitrariness, that we learn the name of Emma's grandmother: "The name [Kitty]," says Mr. Woodhouse, "makes me think of poor Isabella; for she was very christened Catherine after her grandmama"(79). The circulation of signifiers, here, is very rapid indeed, and we have the sense that such a train of associations could connect anybody with anybody—which is precisely the point, especially if we join it with the way this circulation that threatens the seriousness of the patriarchal order seems to be promoted by the memory/threat of the other/grandmother. In the space, the gap, between Mr. Woodhouse's remarkable forgetting of the memory of his wife, and the disjunctive recollection of the grandmother, we see figured the name, which because it is unuttered denies closure, that constitutes a counter to the patriarchal tradition, the *horror vacui* that it dreads—the absent name of absence, what we might call the Name-of-the-mother. There is a hint of both mother and Emma in "grandmama." Mr. Woodhouse's first name, Henry, which, we learn through a similar pattern of displacement, is the name of one of John and Isabella's boys, itself figures in the subversion of the Name-of-the-father. Emma's trifling with authority and storytelling are centered around Harriet, and "Harriet" is both the diminutive and the feminization of Henry.

The pattern of slippage and displacement, which energizes the narrative on the level of the signifier, asserts itself in generalized themes of disconnectedness throughout the novel. From the outset, we enter a world of virtual orphans — almost every character in the novel is lacking one or both parents. It is worth making at least something of a list. This condition does not apply only to Emma, and Harriet, and Jane, and Miss Bates, but also to Elton, and to Robert Martin, and to young Captain Weston, and to his bride, Miss Churchill, and to her brother, Mr. Churchill, among others. The lack of parents frees characters from the tether of certain cultural significations and confuses their relationships with others. The orphaned character is an orphaned or floating signifier that construes the text as a network of partial likenesses. Emma's family situation is the mirror reversal of Miss Bates's. The possible sexual relationships are worked out in a calculus of the marriageable. In this world of likenesses, Emma and Knightley develop their relationship through the simulacra of other relationships: Harriet/Elton, Harriet/Robert Martin, Elton/Emma, Jane/Knightley. Finally, it is by imagining Harriet's relation to Knightley that Emma is able to recognize her own feelings.

The incomplete likenesses that Emma is charged with producing are actually crucial (likeness, after all, depends on difference) to the play of signification that constitutes the narrative. What is Miss Taylor to Emma: mother, sister, friend? — according to the rhetorical description of that relationship, something of all of these, but not perfectly any one of them. And besides, Miss Taylor is really Mrs. Weston, as Frank Churchill is really Frank Weston. We enter a world, in short where the riddle is fundamental, what everything has been and is about to become. Consider the names. Highbury, Hartfield, Taylor, Smith, Fairfax, Woodhouse, etc., all awaiting or suggesting their riddle, their figuration in the form of a parlor game, such as the games which are in fact played within the novel — My first, — My second, My third — thus supplementing by a factor of innuendo the fictions and errors upon which the narrative in fact depends. For Frank Churchill, for example, we might say (very schematically): My first is honesty and openness; my second what man has built for God; my third what God has built for man. Together they identify one who is neither honest nor godly, who is in fact Weston, the coming darkness, the setting sun, the son disappearing behind the church hill, another riddle. Emma. Am a. The mirrored anagram for am me. Emma Woodhouse, as in I am a wood house (both wood and house, says Freud, are symbols of female sexuality). The novel opens by placing its protagonist in the symbolic order as the bearer of meaning: I am a wood house. Knightley, the chivalric knight, and the nightly visitor Emma would house—When "N takes M for better, for worse," as Emma puts it (463). Enscombe, home of Frank Churchill, the "coxcomb," turns out not to be where "ends come" from for Emma. For her there is another ending: Enscombe, literally, "N's come," as an anagram for "Becomes N," acting out the transformation of her infatuation for Churchill into her love for Knightley. Emma's reducing her and Knightley's names to letters points to the importance of the literal in the novel. Central characters seem to grow out of a cluster of letters: K, L, M, N: Knightley, Elton, Emma, and Knightley again. Letters which seem (along with the silent E) to rotate into one another. I am suggesting here, not an alternative to the patriarchal, but a reading in resistance—especially to the tradition of judging by the standard of closure: of asking, for example, whether by the end of the novel Emma knows her place, or whether she will spin again. The play of the letter is fundamental, or elemental, to the novel, but anathema to the patriarchal order which sees the floating letter as the sign of castration. One thinks here of Kristeva's semiotic chora—a kind of articulation before order, the pleasure of merely signifying, and of that character whose absence and namelessness haunts the novel, and empowers the play of the letter, Emma's mother. In this regard perhaps the most suggestive reading is Emma as mama, the book's first word and perhaps ours, as in the puzzle, M. A., "Em" "Ma" or "Ma," "two letters of the alphabet that express perfection"(371)—a play of the lips that we call the mother tongue.

NOTES

1 References to *Emma* are from the edition of R. W. Chapman, 3rd ed. (London: Oxford University Press, 1933) and will be made in the text, parenthetically, by page number. My discussion of Lacan is derived from a general reading of his work. Especially important here is "The Mirror Stage as Formative of the Function of the I as Revealed in Psychoanalytic Experience," in *Ecrits: A Selection*, trans. Alan Sheridan (New York: W. W. Norton, 1977), 1–7; "The Signification of the Phallus," ibid., 281–91; Lacan's essays and the editors' introductions in *Feminine Sexuality: Jacques Lacan and The Ecole Freudiènne*, ed. Juliet Mitchell and Jacqueline Rose, trans. Jacqueline Rose (New York: W. W. Norton, 1985).

2 Sandra M. Gilbert and Susan Gubar, *The Madwoman in the Attic: The Woman Writer and the Nineteenth-Century Literary Imagination* (New Haven: Yale University Press, 1979), 107ff.

3 Laura Mulvey, "Visual Pleasure in Narrative Cinema," in *Art After Modern-*

ism: Rethinking Representation, ed. Brian Willis (New York: Godine, 1984), 361–73; repr. from *Screen* 16, no. 3 (1975):6–18.

4 Edmund Burke, *A Philosophical Enquiry into the Origin of Our Ideas of the Sublime and Beautiful*, ed. J. T. Boulton (London: Routledge and Kegan Paul, 1958), 72–73.

5 John Halperin, *The Life of Jane Austen* (Brighton, England: Harvester Press, 1984).

6 Alistair M. Duckworth, " 'Spillikins, paper ships, riddles, conundrums and cards': Games in Jane Austen's Life and Fiction," in *Jane Austen: Bicentenary Essays*, ed. John Halperin (Cambridge: Cambridge University Press, 1975), 281.

7 Gilbert and Gubar, *Mad Woman*, 109–10.

8 Joel Weinsheimer, "Jane Austen's Anthropocentrism," in *Jane Austen Today*, ed. Joel Weinsheimer (Athens: University of Georgia Press, 1975), 134.

9 Joseph Wiesenfarth, "*Emma*: Point Counterpoint," in Halperin, ed., *Austen: Bicentenary Essays*, 213.

10 Ibid., 216.

11 Ibid., 210,214.

12 Mark Shorer, "The Humiliation of Emma Woodhouse," in *Jane Austen: Emma*, Casebook Series, ed. David Lodge (London: Macmillan, 1972), 185, reprinted from *Literary Review* (Summer 1959); Wayne C. Booth, *The Rhetoric of Fiction* (Chicago: The University of Chicago Press, 1961), 243–66; Marvin Mudrick, *Jane Austen: Irony as Defense and Discovery* (Princeton: Princeton University Press, 1952), 192,194,206.

13 Shorer, "Humiliation," 174–75.

14 Booth, *Rhetoric*, 244,246.

15 D. A. Miller, *Narrative and Its Discontents: Problems of Closure in the Traditional Novel* (Princeton: Princeton University Press, 1981), 3–106; Joseph Litvak, "Reading Characters: Self, Society, and Text in *Emma*," *PMLA* 100 (1985): 763–73; Tony Tanner, *Jane Austen* (Cambridge, MA: Harvard University Press, 1986), 176–207.

16 Duckworth, " 'Spillikins,' " 292.

Bookselling and Canon-Making:
The Trade Rivalry over
the English Poets, 1776–1783

THOMAS F. BONNELL

Some months before his improbable encounter with Victor Frankenstein on the arctic seas, Robert Walton wrote to his sister in England, Mrs. Saville. Friendless and impatient at delays in the port of Archangel, he reminisced: "for the first fourteen years of my life I ran wild on a common, and read nothing but our Uncle Thomas's books of voyages. At that age I became acquainted with the celebrated poets of our own country." When did this poetic discovery take place? Details in the epistolary framework to *Frankenstein* hint at the period to which Mary Shelley alludes. Dated 28 March 17—, Walton's letter invokes Coleridge's "Rime of the Ancient Mariner," making the year 1798 or 1799, and the author identifies himself as twenty-eight years old.[1] His fourteenth year, therefore, when he turned from voyages to poetry, must have been 1784 or 1785. The "celebrated poets" he came to know were likely the ones just then enshrined as "English classics."

Walton's formative years coincided with a critical phase for the English book trade. Early in the 1770s sundry Scottish booksellers began to publish multi-volume collections of British poetry, a trend which eventually spread to London, resulting in rival editions of unprecedented scope: *The Poets of Great Britain* (109 vols., 1776–82), John Bell's series which was completed the year before Walton turned to the poets,[2] and *The Works of the English Poets* (68 vols., 1779–81), the set for which

Samuel Johnson wrote biographical and critical prefaces. Publishing enterprises of this kind and magnitude had never before been undertaken in Britain. Now there were several; they put before the public a cultural heritage apparently vital to be known. Defined for the first time in uniform print were *the* poets, *the* works—in effect, canons of English poetry, worthy of honor, study, and preservation.

The dual nature of that definition is evident in Walton's formulation: *celebrated poets / of our own country*. The phrase seems to beg the question historically. On the one hand, how can one know who the celebrated English poets are without a notion of English literature first having gained currency? On the other, how can one develop a sense of national literary identity until standard works in that literature have been designated? What appears to be a chicken/egg dilemma, however, does not in this case reduce to a matter of which comes first. The two terms presuppose one another—the selected poets (a canon) and the field from which they are drawn (English poetry)—in a way that discourages hunting for chronological precedence. A developing notion of canon fosters the awareness of a literary culture; similarly, the growing consciousness of a literary heritage sharpens the perception of canon. This is not to say, however, that an advance on one side of the equation is never at times more conspicuous than the corresponding advance on the other side.

Consider Keith Walker's claim in a recent issue of *TLS*. He traces the idea of a specifically English literature to the late seventeenth century. Of Dryden's mature years he writes: "This was the period of the long and fruitful collaboration with Jacob Tonson, the inventor of English literature. This is a large claim, but consider: Tonson published editions of Spenser, Shakespeare, and Milton, and such contemporaries as Dryden, Rochester, Addison, and Steele. With Dryden, he planned and published an almost complete translation of Ovid, a complete Virgil, and a Juvenal and Persius. Dryden and Tonson showed future writers the way to live by their pens, and they also established a pattern of author/publisher relations that has continued much the same to the present day."[3] England could boast of a literature long before Tonson's day, to be sure, some of it strongly colored by English themes and patriotic sentiment. Yet the idea of "English literature" may be traced to Tonson, Walker suggests, because he was instrumental in fostering the consciousness of a literary culture endemic to England. His importance lay not in publishing any particular author, but in publishing so many fine authors, old and new, that their writings together under his imprint gave the impression of coherence, of being part of an extended literary project. Even the translations mattered, perhaps especially so. Tonson's was a wholesale plan, a systematic appropriation of several *oeuvres* from Latin into English. The center of gravity was shifted from the individual Romans, where the emphasis lay in earlier ad hoc translations, to an orderly body of "Latin" authors now situated in English. What accrued to the translating tongue, and hence to English letters, was a new integrity.

Where Walker fixes the invention of English literature is where I locate the inventor of a broadly disseminated poetical canon: in the bookseller. Through their large-scale undertakings and actual rivalry, booksellers of the 1770s and early 1780s celebrated the poets as a group by putting their complete works, via the marketplace, into a wider cultural arena than had previously been possible. These collections were the first self-conscious declarations of an English poetic canon in published form.[4]

Of course the notion of canon was not new. By the sixteenth century English writers were beginning to discuss who among them and their literary forebears deserved to be canonized. But if men of letters jotted lists of candidates worthy of lasting fame, their preferences were known to few. Essentially private conceptions, such canons existed in a covert realm, unrealized in so far as any broader audience was concerned, or were brought into physical being in idiosyncratic form: a library of miscellaneous imprints; or an assemblage of paintings, such as the portraits of twenty-two poets which hung in Lord Chesterfield's library;[5] or the busts in the Temple of British Worthies at Stowe, honoring the greatest of English royalty, science, philosophy, and poetry, and where Pope was tucked around the corner to await the verdict of time. More accessible, it might be argued, were the scores of poetic miscellanies whose titles fill up column after column in the *New Cambridge Bibliography of English Literature*. Not until late in the eighteenth century, however, was English poetry addressed in a form and manner systematic enough to call for public scrutiny: Thomas Warton and Samuel Johnson helped to order the art of poetry,[6] but the booksellers were necessary to put actual canons into readers' hands. Printing and publishing were key—not of lists, but poetic works, huge collections that represented the complete works of dozens of poets. Anyone believing that canons should be left to priests in the inner sanctum would have worried over this development. So too, for other reasons, did many London booksellers; the canon now posed an economic threat to their preferred way of business.

Tremors began upon Scottish soil early in the 1770s. The Edinburgh booksellers William Creech and John Balfour charted plans for a multi-volume collection of poets. Creech was on good terms with William Strahan, Samuel Johnson's printer, and hoped through him to draw the London poetry market into their design. Strahan recoiled at the plan, however, writing to Creech in January 1773 to report "a good deal of Altercation with Mr. Balfour on the Subject of the proposed Edition of the English Poets." Not from any consideration of his "own private Interest" did Strahan refuse, he insisted, but from worry "for the Trade in general; which must soon be destroyed if every body is permitted to print every Thing. . . . I find there are about ten Printers with you, that print every Thing, and who are now beginning to print upon one another. Do you not see the obvious and unavoidable Tendency of this?" The picture of printers in Edinburgh printing "every Thing" is an exaggeration projected by Strahan's fear. By the phrase "printing upon one another" he implied outright *piracy*: yet he attached nearly the same degree of horror to another practice consistent with the phrase, outright *competition* — say, two or three booksellers publishing the same works of Milton. If this was in store for the trade, Strahan advised looking "for another Occupation"; bookselling, as far as he was concerned, would "become quickly the most pitiful, beggarly, precarious, unprofitable and disreputable Trades [sic] in Britain."[7]

Strahan hoped that Alexander Kincaid, a third Edinburgh bookseller, would see the danger as he did and refuse to enter into the nefarious project. It was too late, however, for the idea of an "Edition of the English Poets" to be scuttled. Kincaid joined Creech and Balfour to publish *The British Poets*, whose forty-four volumes took shape from 1773 to 1776. Through its failure to be distributed in London, this collection — albeit an early canon — made less of a mark than it otherwise might have. How well it fared in the provinces, if, like other works unwelcome in the capital, it saw distribution there, is a matter worth further research.[8] For the moment London was spared.

Not, however, for long. In 1774, after years of skirmishing between the booksellers of Scotland and London over copyright, the case of *Becket v. Donaldson* decided the matter. At issue were the terms of the 1710 copyright act, or 8 Anne, c. 19, which stipulated protection of twenty-one years, or until 1731, for books already published, and fourteen years for new works, renewable once — if the author was still alive — for another fourteen years. Pretty straightforward, it would appear, but many London booksellers argued that an author enjoyed a non-statutory, common-law right to his work, which he could assign at sale to a bookseller, who then held the right in perpetuity. Reasoning against the idea of "Perpetual Property," the House of Lords held that the Statute of Anne effectively took away the common-law right, leaving an author — or his assign, the bookseller — only the prescriptive right spelled out by statute.[9] Glumly resigned, Strahan observed: "We have now nothing else for it, unless when they [offending booksellers] meddle with Books still protected by Q. Anne's Statute. In that Case we must prosecute. . . ."[10] The legal murkiness cleared up, the works of many poets previously in dispute were now without doubt in the public domain, freeing the way for a monumental edition of English poetry. With the works of Shakespeare behind him (9 vols., 1773–74) and *Bell's British Theatre* (21 vols., 1776–80) underway, John Bell was soon to move on to *The Poets of Great Britain.*

Bookselling and the classics were, to Bell's mind, complementary halves of one great endeavor. From the start he conceived of his series as mirroring the publication of the ancient classics. "While the Greek and Roman classics were the only authors studied or generally known," his prospectus recounted, "the polished nations of Europe vied with each other in embellishing these inestimable models of antiquity with every ornament." If the implicit definition of a "classic" here entails an author's being studied, or subject to the peculiar attentions of teachers, critics, and scholars, it equally embraces being generally known, a condition best served by energetic and knowledgeable booksellers. The "numerous sets of the classics" produced by the book trade in many countries — printed opulently for the shelves of magnificent libraries or sturdily for "general use" — taken together were an "honour to modern ingenuity." Booksellers had now to turn their solicitude upon the authors of their own countries. Italy and France, it was claimed, had already "rewarded the memories of their illustrious countrymen." By the 1770s thus it was "high time" for Great Britain to follow suit, to "assume the consequence due to her merit, and pay her worthies that tribute to which their distinguished genius ha[d] so justly entitled them." Due consequence for the nation and just tribute to her authors lay near at hand in Bell's collection, to be executed in such a manner, it was declared, as would make the "English classics" second to none.[11]

As if to emphasize the continuity between Bell's edition and the heritage of printing the ancient classics, the prospectus announced that *The Poets of Great Britain* would be printed "in a most delicate size, resembling the Elsevier editions of the Latin classics." More than an advertising ploy, this allusion to the famed Dutch printers underscored the aim of Bell's enterprise, for he planned to give reliable and attractive texts of the classics to readers in small format at modest cost.[12] Bell vowed "to furnish the public with the most beautiful, the correctest, the cheapest, and the only complete uniform edition of the British Poets." No longer would it be a "business of time, difficulty, and vast expense" to collect the English poets, nor impossible to collect them "uniformly printed, so as to appear in a library as one and the same book." Inevitably that had been the case, for booksellers had had "no great or general object in view" when publishing English poetry. Bell's object was both great and general. His collection, said to represent "all the British Poets from the time of

Chaucer to Churchill," was vigorously promoted as "a complete and uniform set of our native classics."[13] If one takes into account Bell's self-conscious aim and persistent advertising, the tremendous scale of his undertaking, his imitation of other publishers of classics, and his appeal to nationalistic pride, then the importance of *The Poets of Great Britain* becomes clear: it was the first serious attempt to publish a comprehensive English poetical canon.

No longer could Strahan and other London printers and booksellers balk at publishing a poetical canon. Time was short to defend their poetry market with a competing collection of their own. Thirty-six book-sellers joined interests to become the proprietors of *The Works of the English Poets*. As Edward Dilly confided to James Boswell, the proprietors viewed Bell's edition as "an invasion of what we call our Literary Property." (The wilful nostalgia of the phrase "what *we call* our Literary Property" shows them reluctant to accept the 1774 copyright ruling.) To strengthen their defenses they engaged Johnson to write prefaces and forged ahead with what was to be "an elegant and accurate edition of all the English Poets of reputation, from Chaucer to the present time." The tone of this remark, in addition to Dilly's characterizing the proprietors as "a select number of the most respectable booksellers" and boasting that their edition would "do honour to the English press," catches the accent of *noblesse oblige*, as though their collection was meant as a curatorial service to the nation.[14] Nevertheless, their motives in part were undisguisedly financial. While this fact muffles the clapper on Dilly's high-sounding phrases, it is no reason to be reductive. A highly complex enterprise, the canon was shaped by literary values, patriotic impulse, and an urge for self-definition as well as by materialist causes.

Conspicuously, Bell and the proprietors both used the term "all": the upstart invited the public to expect "all the British Poets from the time of Chaucer to Churchill"; the established trade, eager to mimic Bell's sweep, intended to publish "all the English Poets of reputation, from Chaucer to the present time." Grandiose claims both, Bell's was especially so — staggering in fact. What such a collection might have looked like we can glean from Boswell, who recounts a conversation at Ashbourne in September 1777, the first time he had met with Johnson since learning of the proprietors' projected *Works*: "At night Dr. Johnson and I talked of a collection being made of all the English poets who had published their volumes. He said that a Mr. Coxeter, whom he knew, had gone the greatest length towards this, having collected about five hundred volumes, I think, of unknown poets; but that upon his death Tom Osborne bought them, and they were dispersed, which [Johnson] thought a pity, as it was curious to see any series complete; and in every volume of poems something good might be found."[15] The impulse "to see any series complete" is foreign to current notions of the canon as something rear-guard and exclusionary. Yet to fix the limits of English poetry and sanc-tion a collection as "complete" does serve a canonic end. Here was the phantom of an all-inclusive collection, its motto being that "something good might be found" in every volume. But five hundred volumes? And still only the "unknown poets"? Imagine the complete works.

Coxeter's library demonstrated the need for a published canon. First, although it was deeply interesting to the intellectually curious, like any private collection it was hidden from all but few. Second, the rarity of the library proved that it had been a "business of time, difficulty and vast expense" for Coxeter to assemble it; the success of any such attempt was measured explicitly in terms of the "great lengths" to which the collector had gone. Lastly, it was a pity for the poetry to have been dispersed, for once the volumes had been sold, Coxeter's peculiarly whole vision of English literature had vanished. Its potential for Johnsonian usefulness had, in the final analysis, wasted into the shadow of an aristocratic conceit. If canons were to emerge from the private realms of professional scholars or individual collectors, if they were going to be accessible to the public and become common national property, booksellers were needed to sink money into multi-volume collections of poetry on an unprece-dented scale.

Neither Bell nor the proprietors lived up to their rhetoric of all-inclusiveness. Instead of all, Bell published fifty poets, the proprietors fifty-two. (See Table 1.) Common to both collections were forty-two poets, their works spanning close to 140 years, from the early poems of Milton, Waller, and Cowley in the 1630s to the final works of Gray and Akenside in the late 1760s. The eight writers exclusive to Bell's *Poets of Great Britain* extend this period significantly, to roughly four hundred years. Though the coverage is sparse, Chaucer, Spenser, and Donne rep-resent earlier periods of English poetry untouched by Bell's rivals; at the other end Bell reached for the more up-to-date in the works of Cun-ningham and Churchill. In contrast to this extension, concentration was the proprietors' guiding principle. Notwithstanding a somewhat more realistically-worded goal of including all poets *of reputation* from Chaucer to the present, nothing prior to the middle of the seventeenth century appeared in *The Works of the English Poets*. To judge from the ten poets exclusive to the *Works*, all of them belonging to Restoration and early eighteenth-century verse, the proprietors opted for a more thorough picture of a literary age. Conceivably they abandoned Chaucer and other early poets so as neither to publish a collection that was spotty

TABLE 1
The Canons of Bell and the Proprietors

The Poets	Volume numbers in	
	Poets	*Works*

Bell's Exclusively

Geoffrey Chaucer (c. 1343–1400)	1–14	
Edmund Spenser (c. 1552–99)	15–22	
John Donne (1572–1631)	23–25	
Richard West (1716–42)	103	
Edward Moore (1712–57)	98	
Charles Churchill (1732–64)	107–109	
John Cunningham (1729–73)	106	
John Armstrong (1709–79)	102	

The Proprietors' Exclusively

John Wilmot, 2nd Earl of Rochester (1647–80)		10
Thomas Otway (1652–85)		11
Charles Sackville, 6th Earl of Dorset (1638–1706)		11
George Stepney (1663–1707)		12
William Walsh (1663–1708)		12
Richard Duke (1658–1711)		11
Thomas Sprat (1635–1713)		9
Charles Montague, 1st Earl of Halifax (1661–1715)		12
Sir Richard Blackmore (1654–1729)		24
Thomas Yalden (1670–1736)		10

Common to Both Collections

Abraham Cowley (1618–67)	36–39	1–2
Sir John Denham (1615–69)	35	9
John Milton (1608–74)	28–31	3–5
Samuel Butler (1613–80)	32–34	6–7
Wentworth Dillon, 4th Earl of Roscommon (?1633–85)	43	10
Edmund Waller (1606–87)	26–27	8
John Dryden (1631-1700)	40–42	13–19
John Pomfret (1667–1702)	51	21
John Philips (1676–1709)	66	21
Edmund Smith (1672–1710)	102	21
William King (1663–1712)	45–46	20
Thomas Parnell (1679–1718)	67–68	44
Nicholas Rowe (1674–1718)	58	26–28
Sir Samuel Garth (1661–1719)	69	20
Joseph Addison (1672–1719)	57	23
John Hughes (1677–1720)	70–71	22
Matthew Prior (1664–1721)	47–49	30–31
John Sheffield, 1st Duke of Buckingham (1648–1721)	44	25
William Congreve (1670–1729)	56	29
Elijah Fenton (1683–1730)	72	29

TABLE 1, Continued

The Poets	Volume numbers in	
	Poets	*Works*
John Gay (1685–1732)	80–82	41–42
George Granville, Baron Lansdowne (1667–1735)	50	25
Thomas Tickell (1685–1740)	73	26
James Hammond (1710–42)	97	49
William Somervile (1675–1742)	74–75	47
Richard Savage (c. 1697–1743)	88–89	45
Alexander Pope (1688–1744)	76–79	32–38
Jonathan Swift (1667–1745)	52–55	39–40
William Broome (1689–1745)	83	43
Christopher Pitt (1699–1748)	90	43
James Thomson (1700–48)	91–92	48–49
Isaac Watts (1674–1748)	59–65	46
Ambrose Philips (1674–1749)	93	44
Gilbert West (1703–56)	95	56
John Dyer (1699–1757)	94	53
William Collins (1721–59)	97	49
William Shenstone (1714–63)	99–100	54
Edward Young (1683–1765)	84–87	50–52
David Mallet (?1705–65)	101	53
Mark Akenside (1721–70)	104–5	55
Thomas Gray (1716–71)	103	56
George Lyttelton, 1st Baron Lyttelton (1709–73)	96	65

Note: Poets are listed in chronological order by date of death.

in the earlier periods, like Bell's, nor to bind themselves to a grander scheme than was practicable for their present purposes.

Any further insight into their principles of selection must be left to inference and guesswork. A headnote to either collection might have been illuminating, if even as brief as the classification and rationale sketched out by Joseph Warton in the "Dedication" to his *Essay on the Writings and Genius of Pope*. Warton grouped English poets into four "classes and degrees," the first class comprised of "sublime and pathetic poets" (Spenser, Shakespeare, Milton, Otway, Lee); the second of poets "such as possessed the true poetical genius, in a more moderate degree, but had noble talents for moral and ethical poesy" (Dryden, Donne, Denham, Cowley, Congreve); the third of "men of wit, of elegant taste, and some fancy in describing familiar life" (Prior, Waller, Parnell, Swift, Fenton); and a fourth class of "mere versifiers" (Pitt, Sandys, Fairfax, Broome, Buckingham, Landsdowne).[16] Warton's listing dramatizes what the rival collections lacked: a ranked interpretation of merit based on a more or less consistent scheme of literary value.

Nothing so detailed as Warton's outline is found in Johnson's "Advertisement" to the 1779 *Prefaces, Biographical and Critical, to the Works of the English Poets*. Less than 200 words, it reveals that Johnson had been asked for "a few dates and a general character" of each poet but that he had been led beyond this purpose by a "desire of giving useful pleasure."[17] That Johnson had done much more, even lent his shaping intelligence to the whole project, was implied by the epithet which the proprietors, to Johnson's vexation, printed on the spines of their volumes: "Johnson's Poets." Actually the only poets included on his recommendation were Pomfret, Yalden, Blackmore, and Watts. Upon first learning of the collection, Boswell had expected Johnson to enjoy supervisory control. When it turned out that the proprietors were in full charge, he was dismayed. If Johnson was "to furnish a preface and life to any poet the booksellers pleased," Boswell sarcastically asked whether "he would do this to any dunce's works if they pleased. 'Yes,' said [Johnson], 'and *say* he was a dunce.' "[18] This offhand exchange betrays an opinion at odds with Boswell's deference to booksellers in other contexts: distrust of their judgment. No doubt the fillip is principally a measure of Boswell's trust in the choices Johnson would have made — had it been his prerogative — and not a conviction that the proprietors had little taste. Still, what if the dunces were let in?

In his *Prefaces* Johnson criticized poets with meager talent, but called no one a dunce. A more candid estimate of a few of the minor poets may be found in *Rambler* 106, where Johnson gloomily assesses the vanity of human hopes embodied in a public library: "Of the innumerable authors whose performances are thus treasured up in magnificent obscurity, most are forgotten, because they never deserved to be remembered." What about works that had perished? "The learned often bewail the loss of ancient writers," Johnson reflected, "but, perhaps, if we could now retrieve them, we should find them only the Granvilles, Montagues, Stepneys, and Sheffields of their time, and wonder by what infatuation or caprice they could be raised to notice."[19] Why anyone would bother with these poets was hard to imagine, yet there they were, Granville and Sheffield in both collections, Montague and Stepney among the ten exclusive to the *Works*. Publication in the canon indeed raised such poets to notice. Were the rival collections then the work of "infatuation or caprice"?

Too much effort and money had been invested in them for that to have been the case. The canon was serious business for booksellers battling over new terrain opened up by a clarification of copyright. Alexander

Chalmers, editor of an expanded edition of *The Works of the English Poets* (1810), defended the proprietors for their expertise in trade: "It has often been objected to Dr. Johnson's Collection, that it includes authors who have few admirers, . . . but it ought always to be remembered, that the collection was not formed by that illustrious scholar, but by his employers, who thought themselves, what they unquestionably were, the best judges of vendible poetry, and who included very few, if any, works in their series for which there was not, at the time it was formed, a considerable degree of demand."[20] Even if we admit those hedging phrases—"very few, if any," "at the time it was formed," and "considerable"—the observation rings false. How can we account for the inclusion of poets like Walsh, Duke, Sprat, Smith, Hughes, Fenton, and several others, let alone Granville, Montague, Stepney, and Sheffield? The work of some had not been reprinted on its own for decades: for Stepney, not since 1701; for Sprat, not since 1709; for Fenton, 1717; Blackmore, 1727. How could any of this poetry be characterized as vendible?

However unconvincing on the face of it, Chalmers's notion of "vendible poetry" cannot easily be dismissed. First, how "vendible" a poet is cannot be measured prior to a specific market situation: vendible poetry presupposes a vendor as well as a buyer, and the skill of the vendor—the bookseller—helps to determine which poetry sells and which does not. Second, the competitive context needs to be analyzed. A trade rivalry, in which booksellers try to out-do one another, might provide an opportunity for stretching the limits of what is vendible. To test these hypotheses, we can look at the 1779 *Works* in context as a response to and defense against the challenge of Bell's *Poets*.

Bell's intention to publish the English classics was met with hostility. He was denied the reciprocal amenities enjoyed by other London booksellers: credit, help with distribution, shelf space in bookshops other than his own, and the chance to advertise in most London newspapers. Lacking much capital, he published his collection serially, poet by poet, hoping to recover his investment along the way. Given this necessity, Bell began with poets sure to sell briskly, his inaugural line-up serving as an index of best-selling poets: Milton, Pope, Dryden, Butler, Prior, Thomson, Gay, Waller, Young, and so on.[21] Bell could ill afford to publish poets whose works did not appeal individually to the buying public. This constraint is most evident if one sets the eight poets chosen uniquely by Bell against the ten chosen by the proprietors. With the exception of Donne—a fascinating inclusion—more of Bell's choices were apt to be purchased on their own merits. Yet with fifty poets all told, many were bound to be less popular. On this score serial publication worked to Bell's advantage: to some eyes, a poet who is fifteenth or thirty-first in a series will appeal more than the same poet whose works lie singly on a shelf filled with other titles.

"Non-literary" means of appeal were important. The portable size of the books became a selling point; Bell's collection fit into two boxes the shape of thick folios and made a convenient poetic library for travel. Evidence too suggests that Bell might have included Aaron Hill, William Hamilton, and John Gilbert Cooper if only he had unearthed portraits of them to copy for frontispiece engravings. Using portraits to sell volumes was deplorable, thought Thomas Tyrwhitt, who was incensed with Bell for having used his name and text of *The Canterbury Tales* in the Chaucer volumes. Such a tack could work only with the "very young persons" who were, he suggested, Bell's principal customers. "Having given them a picture at the beginning of each volume," Tyrwhitt sneered, Bell "seem[ed] to have thought (and perhaps with reason) that they would be perfectly unconcerned about every thing else."[22] Fair or not, Tyrwhitt's point is well taken: commercial strategy was central to the bookseller's way of thinking.

The proprietors of the *Works* were also keenly alert to vendibility, as we see from Edward Dilly's outline of their initial plans. Making their product different from Bell's had been on Dilly's mind when he wrote to Boswell in 1777: "My brother will give you a list of the Poets we mean to give, many of which are within the time of the Act of Queen Anne, which Martin and Bell cannot give, as they have no property in them."[23] Copyright law would ensure that the *Works* included poets whom Bell could not put in his series, and Dilly's enthusiasm suggests he believed the difference would make their set more attractive to buyers. Their edge would be increased, they also calculated, if Johnson's name were connected with their endeavor. Johnson drew customers so effectively in fact that some wished to purchase the *Prefaces* without the accompanying poetry. Had that been allowed, the proprietors would have defeated their own purpose.

On better footing than Bell with their pooled resources, the proprietors were in a position to publish their whole collection at once. They decided that the set had to be purchased complete, a policy with a risk. Fewer could afford the edition, but by the same token fewer purchases were necessary for the booksellers to profit. Besides, the proprietors still had separate financial interests in various poets, and if no volumes were sold individually, the collection would interfere less with their own bookselling. More fundamentally, the sales policy hints that, in the proprietors' assessment, some of the poetry had no independent commercial value. Strahan had once confided that "Poetry, unless excellent, is good for nothing, and seldom sells to pay Paper and Print." Charles Dilly agreed: "Poetry of all things is the most doubtful in the sale, unless the Author is well known."[24] One wonders then what their attitude was towards poets who had not seen print for fifty, sixty, or seventy years. Surely the complete works of such poets would not have repaid the investment of "Paper and Print," were it not for the circumstances of their publication. If the set had to be purchased complete, it did not matter that Stepney's works had little appeal—but then, why canonize him?

The answer, in part, is that both collections aspired to be definitive. Bell piled up fifty poets in an effort to be comprehensive, while the proprietors needed fifty-two to shore up the bulwark to their Literary Property. Both undertakings, if they were plausibly to present *the* poets and *the* works, had to guard against incompleteness, that is, giving the impression of a fragmentary set. Each canon stretched the limits of what must have seemed a feasible number of poets and volumes for any collection to include.[25]

Capital outlay, the market for individual poets, order of publication, format, illustration, sales policy, copyright restrictions, product differentiation, the impression of completeness—all were factors crucial to the booksellers in shaping marketable editions. While neither collection reduces to a materialist equation, this angle is indispensable for understanding the formation of canons. Because of the peculiar chronology involved (*Poets*, 1776-82; *Works*, 1779-81) the collections took shape partly in response to each other. Bell outlined a panorama from Chaucer to Churchill; his competitors projected the same, but later reduced their scope. The proprietors sought biographical and critical prefaces because Bell had them; then, after Johnson's prefaces were published in 1779 and 1781, passages from them were incorporated into Bell's prefaces. And as both parties had a chance to copy at least some of the choices of poets from the other collection, one may assume there was cross-fertilization of this type also. The trade rivalry was an intricate affair, perhaps just as complicated for the participants as for us in retrospective analysis. Bookselling had entered a new phase; some must have thought it had become what Strahan dreaded, "the most pitiful, beggarly, precarious, unprofitable and disreputable Trade[] in Britain."

"[B]ecause every canon requires the existence of some authoritative group of *canonizers*," writes Douglas Lane Patey, "radical changes in canons are usually accompanied by rearrangements in the social structure of such authority." To the changes in legal and economic structure that I have sketched Patey adds a key conceptual ingredient: a shift in aesthetic theory. In the latter half of the eighteenth century "disinterestedness" came to characterize a new way of viewing art. An "aesthetic attitude" was born, one that disentangled the moral and the intellectual from the purely artistic, that prepared readers to approach "literature" through a special frame of mind — disinterested, desiring neither practical knowledge nor possession.[26] If this was the case, one wonders how conscious of it the booksellers were in judging the market to be ready for a large-scale canonization of poetry. Yet we must be wary of an ideal as slippery as disinterestedness. Just as the arbiters of canons may be influenced by financial motives, readers too may buy poetry for a variety of reasons. More needs to be known about the purchasers of these sets — their whereabouts, their economic strata, their education — but the fact that the collections sold, and sold well, is itself a phenomenon which may be interpreted, in the broadest sense of the term, politically.[27]

The period of the trade rivalry was coterminous with the American revolution; while Britain was losing her colonies, the literary canon was taking shape. To what extent the impending loss of prestige conditioned the urge to regulate the literary integrity of the country may be difficult to gauge, but the conjunction is provocative, especially in the light of Gerald Newman's recent study. Newman argues that English nationalism grew out of the period between the mid-1740s and mid-1780s, and central to its identity were various cultural institutions, particularly a literary heritage. Times of war, heightened patriotism, and perceived impotence abroad only accelerated the process.[28] Also helpful to place the canon formation of the 1770s and 1780s into political context is the work of Benedict Anderson. In his analysis, a printed language lays the bases for national consciousness in three ways, two of which are pertinent here: 1) when fellow readers are connected through print, the embryo of a nationally-imagined community is formed; 2) print-capitalism gives a fixity to language that in the long run helps "to build that image of antiquity so central to the subjective idea of the nation."[29] If print technology sowed the seeds of these tendencies, then uniform collections of 68 or 109 volumes represented their flowering. In buying the "English classics," readers could feel connected to their fellow citizens as never before, and the fact that sets of their classics had been published fueled pride in their literary heritage and its antiquity. It is well worth noting the difference in title between the two series printed in Edinburgh, *The British Poets* and *The Poets of Great Britain*, and the set printed in London, *The Works of the English Poets*. The booksellers were sensitive to the nationalistic nuances of their canons.

What the booksellers did not see was that their collections, pushed to expansive limits by competition, would be regarded one day as narrow, a hindrance to personal growth and broader cultural awareness. In Robert Walton we find a distrust of canon that may well reflect the experience of

Mary Shelley herself. To return to his reminiscence: "At that age [fourteen] I became acquainted with the celebrated poets of our country; but it was only when it had ceased to be in my power to derive its most important benefits from such a conviction, that I perceived the necessity of becoming acquainted with more languages than that of my native country. Now I am twenty-eight, and am in reality more illiterate than many school-boys of fifteen."[30] Much more than the bookselling world had changed by the time these lines were written. Explosive polemics had surrounded the issues of both gender and nation, and the canons of forty years earlier could be read to embody a constricting spirit that promoted illiteracy, not enlightenment or growth. For those virtues, Walton came to see, one had to travel beyond one's own national and psychological borders to explore the languages and fruits of other peoples.

NOTES

1 Mary Wollstonecraft Shelley, *Frankenstein: Or, The Modern Prometheus*, ed. James Rieger (Chicago: University of Chicago Press, 1982), 13–15.

2 Although the years 1776–82 appear on Bell's title-page imprints, the volumes were actually published from 1777 through mid-1783.

3 Keith Walker, review of James Anderson Winn, *John Dryden and His World, Times Literary Supplement*, 19–25 February 1988, 193.

4 To apply the term *canon* to these constructs of the booksellers is to deviate from current usage. This does not trouble me. Rigidity in defining the term, when "the canon" itself as monolith has been shattered, serves no useful end. Some leeway is needed if we are to characterize modes of canonical activity in times prior to our own. A history of English canons which ignored the phenomenon I am describing would neglect a distinctive type of canon formation, and fail of an opportunity to put the social, economic, and political dimensions of our own canon debate into perspective.

5 See David Piper, "The Chesterfield House Library Portraits," in Rene Wellek and Alvaro Ribeiro, eds., *Evidence in Literary Scholarship: Essays in Memory of James Marshall Osborn* (Oxford: Clarendon Press, 1979), 179–95.

6 See Lawrence Lipking, *The Ordering of the Arts in Eighteenth-Century England* (Princeton: Princeton University Press, 1970).

7 William Strahan to William Creech, 1 January 1773, The Creech Papers, Scottish Record Office, West Register House, Edinburgh. These papers are quoted with the kind permission of Mr. L. P. K. Blair Oliphant.

8 For guidance one would begin with John Feather, who maps out this terrain, though he makes no mention of *The British Poets*. See *The Provincial Book Trade in Eighteenth-Century England* (Cambridge: Cambridge University Press, 1985), esp. chap. 4, "The Distribution System."

9 For the legal details, see Lyman Ray Patterson, *Copyright in Historical Perspective* (Nashville: Vanderbilt University Press, 1968), 143-79; for the social and economic background, see Gwyn Walters, "The Booksellers in 1759 and 1774: The Battle for Literary Property," *The Library*, 5th Series, 29 (1974): 287-311.

10 Strahan to Creech, 25 August 1774, The Creech Papers.

11 Advertisement in the form of a three-page prospectus at the back of John Dryden, *The Spanish Fryar* (London, 1777), sig. H5^{r-v}.

12 See David W. Davies, *The World of the Elseviers 1580-1712* (The Hague: Nijhoff, 1954), 53-75, and passim.

13 *The Spanish Fryar*, sig. H5^r-H6^r.

14 Edward Dilly to James Boswell, 26 September 1777, in Boswell, *Life of Johnson*, ed. George Birkbeck Hill, rev. L. F. Powell, 6 vols. (Oxford: Clarendon Press, 1934-50), 3:110.

15 James Boswell, *Boswell in Extremes, 1776-1778*, ed. Charles McC. Weis (New York: McGraw-Hill, 1970), 159-60.

16 Joseph Warton, *An Essay on the Writings and Genius of Pope* (London, 1756), xi-xii.

17 Samuel Johnson, *Lives of the English Poets*, ed. George Birkbeck Hill, 3 vols. (Oxford: Clarendon Press, 1905), 1:xxvi.

18 Boswell, *Boswell in Extremes*, 150.

19 Samuel Johnson, *The Rambler*, ed. W. J. Bate and Albrecht B. Strauss, *The Yale Edition of the Works of Samuel Johnson*, vols. 3-5 (New Haven: Yale University Press, 1969), 4:201.

20 Alexander Chalmers, "Preface," *The Works of the English Poets*, 21 vols. (London, 1810), 1:vi.

21 As the series progressed the ordering principle became less evident. For the full record of publication, see Thomas F. Bonnell, "John Bell's *Poets of Great Britain*: The 'Little Trifling Edition' Revisited," *Modern Philology* 85 (1987): 128-52.

22 Thomas Tyrwhitt, letter dated 12 June 1783, *Gentleman's Magazine* 53 (1783): 461. There were no portraits of Richard West, Edward Moore, and eleven other poets in Bell's edition, a fact which shows that the portrait — the lack of one or access to one — was not a sufficient criterion for inclusion or exclusion.

23 *Life of Johnson*, 3:111. Gilbert Martin printed the volumes to Bell's edition at the Apollo Press in Edinburgh.

24 Strahan to Creech, 9 September 1774; Charles Dilly to Creech, 6 May 1773; The Creech Papers.

25 The issue of inclusion is complex. If it be argued that the booksellers copied choices made previously, as in the several mid-century editions of Dodsley's *Collection of Poems*, one then has to explain why dozens of poets in such miscellanies were not chosen. Even more puzzling: what became of the proprietors' intention to include works that Bell legally could not publish? To have been protected in 1779 by the Act of Queen Anne, a poet's works would have

had to be published for the first time, or in a significantly new form, after 1751. But look (in Table 1) at the poets exclusive to the *Works*: they had been dead for decades. Did the proprietors change their mind? Why did Bell not include Rochester and Otway? These and other questions remain.

26 Douglas Lane Patey, "The Eighteenth Century Invents the Canon," *Modern Language Studies* 18 (1988): 23–25.

27 For evidence of the popular reception of the *Poets* and the *Works*, see Bonnell, "John Bell's *Poets*," 147–52. Perhaps the proprietors and Bell were, after all, "the best judges of vendible poetry."

28 Gerald Newman, *The Rise of English Nationalism: A Cultural History 1740–1830* (New York: St. Martin's Press, 1987), 67, 125–26, 163, 193.

29 Benedict Anderson, *Imagined Communities: Reflections on the Origin and Spread of Nationalism* (London: Verso Editions, 1983), 47.

30 Shelley, *Frankenstein*, 13–14.

I wish to thank the NEH for a summer stipend enabling me to conduct research in London and Edinburgh.

Durazzo, Duni, and the Frontispiece *to* Orfeo ed Euridice

BRUCE ALAN BROWN

The preeminent position of Gluck's *Orfeo ed Euridice* (1762) in the mid-eighteenth-century reform of serious opera is undisputed. While other works — notably by Mattia Verazi and Niccolò Jommelli in Stuttgart, Carlo Frugoni and Tommaso Traetta in Parma (and Traetta in Vienna itself) — may have anticipated it to some degree, *Orfeo* was the first truly uncompromising answer to the challenge laid down by Francesco Algarotti in his *Saggio sopra l'opera in musica* of 1755, and even more concretely in the anonymous *Lettre sur le méchanisme de l'opéra italien*, published the following year: to create "un Opéra, qui ne sera ni François ni Italien, mais un composé de l'un & de l'autre, purgé des défauts de tous le deux. . . "[1] The artistic success of the opera was due in large measure to the efforts of Count Giacomo Durazzo, theatrical intendant in Vienna, who was able to coordinate the contributions of poet, composer, and choreographer; dancers, chorus, and vocal soloists (drawn from the two companies under his control) without engendering the personal jealousies and imbalances of components that chronically afflicted public opera in Italy.[2] The Genoan Count was also responsible for *Orfeo*'s almost immediate recognition, across Europe, as the masterpiece it was. Having already cultivated extensive connections in Paris — chiefly through his theatrical and literary correspondent, the playwright Charles Simon Favart — Durazzo ensured that Gluck's opera would receive ample

71

treatment in the press, including Abbé Arnaud's widely-read *Journal étranger*. These same resources he used also to put *Orfeo* before the world in a sumptuously engraved score.

The first edition of *Orfeo* has received much attention since its appearance, principally on account of a notorious case of plagiarism that resulted from it. Asked by Favart to proofread the score sent by Durazzo from Vienna, the composer François André Danican Philidor used the opportunity to pilfer Orpheus's first solo air, inserting it (retexted) as a *romance* in his opéra-comique *Le Sorcier*, which was given its premiere in January of 1764. Although this and other Philidor's larcenies were already known during his lifetime,[3] indignant critics dredged up the *Sorcier* scandal in the next century too. The lexicographer François-Joseph Fétis, misled by the erroneous indication "Rappresentata in Vienna, nell 'anno 1764" in the *Orfeo* edition, tried to turn the charge against Gluck.[4] Hector Berlioz, armed with the published correspondence of Favart, set matters straight as to priority, but confused them otherwise by, on the one hand, accusing Philidor of intentionally altering the date in the score, and on the other defending his "borrowing."[5] Adolphe Jullien's definitive words on the matter in 1878 have not prevented the issue of Philidor's plagiarism from distracting attention from his very real contributions to music, and from the *Orfeo* score's significance as cultural propaganda.[6]

In broaching the subject of *Orfeo*'s first edition again, my aim is neither to cast blame on, nor to exonerate the opéra-comique composer Philidor, but rather to explore the connections—both musical and visual—between this burgeoning Parisian genre and Gluck's *azione teatrale*, as well as the motivations behind Durazzo's publication of the score in Paris. The most telling evidence on these matters is to be found in the music itself, and in a collection (at the Bibliothèque de l'Opéra in Paris) of some seventy letters from Durazzo to Favart, which were either omitted from the poet's *Mémoires et correspondance* (edited by his grandson),[7] or printed with substantial deletions. Though mentioned in print in 1894,[8] and used occasionally since then,[9] these materials—in many ways more illuminating than the published correspondence—have yet to be taken fully into account by students of Viennese and Parisan theatrical life.[10]

* * *

A core of essential facts concerning the process by which the *Orfeo* edition came about was already to be gleaned from the Favart *Mémoires*. The poet was considerably alarmed when, after two months, the manuscript score Durazzo had alerted him to expect had still not materialized. Favart was able to reconstruct part of its peregrinations: "J'ai envoyé M. Duni à la découverte, il m'a rapporté que M. Blaudel [Blondel] étoit chargé de la partition d'Orphée pour me la remettre, mais qu'il l'avoit communiquée d'abord au baron d'Olbac [d'Holbach], ensuite au baron Vomssuieten [van Swieten] qui, après en avoir fait copier quelques airs, l'a remise à M. Blaudel [Blondel]."[11]

As we shall see, the Italian Egidio Duni, since 1757 a composer of opéra-comique in Paris, was to play a central — if largely passive — role in the publication of *Orfeo*. The *philosophe* d'Holbach and the Viennese diplomat and patron of music Gottfried van Swieten (then stationed in the French capital) were only the first of many illustrious admirers of the opera.[12] Once the score had finally been delivered to him, Favart continued to show it widely, reporting to Durazzo that "Mondonville, in leafing through *Orfeo*, was ecstatic over the talent of M. Gluck,"[13] and later, that Philidor "was enchanted by the beauty of the work; in several places, he shed tears of pleasure."[14] Whereas Duni had refused to correct the score — purportedly teeming with copyist's errors — even for a fee of 500 *livres*, Philidor gladly offered his services, asking only for a copy of the finished edition.[15] Progress on its engraving was repeatedly held up as Favart awaited the arrival of Gluck — in vain, in May of 1763, and again the following spring, when the composer did appear and inspected the proofs — as well as a drawing from Vienna which a French artist would engrave as a frontispiece. In the end the drawing was supplied by Charles Monnet (and engraved by Noël Le Mire), and by 6 April 1764 Favart could announce that the entire run of the edition would be completed during the following week. Public response was disappointing, to say the least; besides the copies taken by Durazzo, and the numerous *exemplaires de droit* for the Bibliothèque Royale, the censor, Favart, and so forth, only nine copies of the score had been sold in the French capital by April of 1766.[16]

It is tempting to infer a plan for Gluck to bring *Orfeo* to the stage in Paris already in 1763 or 1764, a decade before it was actually realized. Durazzo, personally acquainted with Favart from visits in 1748 and 1759, had every reason to expect that his literary agent would show the score of the opera to "[the] most skilled connoisseurs in music" — who were unanimous in thinking it "an epoch-making work, which will pass into posterity."[17] And on the basis of the published memoirs, we are justified in thinking that the poet's hope (expressed a few days later) that "the admirers of this opera, who have manuscript copies, will be even more anxious to possess the print"[18] was in reference to these Parisian musicians, and interested local parties such as d'Holbach and van

Swieten. Confirmation of Durazzo's intentions in sending his composer to Paris in 1763 is provided in a letter from L. H. Dancourt, an Arlequin and author who had recently found employment at the Viennese court's French theater. Writing on 5 July to his intimate friend Favart, he announced "Vous ne verrez point le chevalier Gluck; il est de retour ici. Il mettoit le pied dans sa chaise de poste à Bologne [where he was directing his opera *Il Trionfo de Clelia*], et partoit pour Paris, lorsqu'il a reçu une lettre du Comte qui le rappeloit à Vienne, parce qu'ayant appris [in a letter from Favart] que l'opéra étoit brûlé, le voyage du chevalier devenoit inutile selon lui. . . ."[19] Furthermore, Gluck was clearly beginning to extricate himself from the day-to-day operations of Vienna's French theater, having turned over the composition of ballet music to Giuseppe Scarlatti (in the 1762–63 season), and most conducting chores to Florian Gaßmann.[20]

Much about the structure, the poetry, and the music of *Orfeo* seems calculated to impress a Parisian as well as a Viennese audience. The large role accorded the chorus and ballet was characteristic of productions of the Opéra more than of Italian spectacles, the opening scene in particular recalling the funeral tableau at the start of the first act of Rameau's *Castor et Pollux* (in its original version). Favart, in allaying Durazzo's fears about the consequences of delays in the production of the edition, made explicit reference to French *tragédie-lyrique*: "Les opéras de Lulli, de Rameau, et de tous nos meilleurs compositeurs, en paroissant deux ans après les représentations, n'en ont pas moins ici de débit; et la musique de M. Gluck . . . n'aura pas un moindre avantage."[21] More pertinently, the opera was bound to appeal to the progressive among the capital's cultural elite, who in recent years had been comparing opera seria favorably to their own spectacle (in the press and other forums), without remaining blind to the weaker features of Italian opera.[22] The reviewer of the published score of *Orfeo* for the *Affiches, annonces et avis divers* praised the simplicity of the action, saying that it would be "an excellent model for our young lyric authors to follow."[23] Of librettist Calzabigi's verses for the scene wherein Orpheus leads his spouse out of the underworld, he commented "Ce ne sont ni des Madrigaux, ni des Pensées alambiquées, ni d'ingénieuses pointes, ou de petits traits d'Epigramme, comme dans la plupart de nos Opéras: c'est le langage de la nature, c'est l'action simple & l'expression d'une femme sensible. . ."[24]

And yet there are strong indications, in the materials at the Bibliothèque de l'Opéra, that it was precisely the Viennese spectators and court that Durazzo had uppermost in mind in arranging for a Parisian edition of *Orfeo*. After twice alerting Favart, in the briefest of terms, of this project that would end up claiming so much of his time,[25] Durazzo wrote on 19 February 1763 laying out his request in full:

> Nous avons eû à la fin du carnaval une reprise d'Orphèe, qui a eû autant de succès que la premiere fois, et je prevois que je serois contraint de le reprendre après Pâques. Vous m'obligerez en ordonnant qu'on travaille d'abord à en graver la Musique. il y aura probablement dans la partition que je vous ai envojée des fautes grossieres du Copiste, soit pour les notes, soit pour les paroles. il faut que je me rapporte à vôtre amitié, et j'espere que vous trouverez des personnes capables dans les deux genres pour la correction. je vous enverrai la semaine prochaine le titre, et une lettre qui doit être à la tête. je voudrois le Format ordinaire des Opera que Vous m'avez envoié. je prefere sur tout l'Isle des Foux. j'aimerois une Vignette dans le même genre. On pourroit y representer Orphee qui attendrit les Ombres, et les Furies à l'entrée de l'Enfer. Vous voïez que je voudrois indiquer l'endroit principal de l'action, ou Orphee chante *Deh placatevi con me Ombre* &c. et le Choeur repond: *Nò*.[26]

The wording of the letter suggests that for Durazzo, the wish to engrave *Orfeo*'s score was a direct consequence of the opera's resounding success in the theatre.[27] Indeed, its success was even greater than has been thought: two performances during February and, with the substitution of a new Euridice, eleven more from July through September. The possibility of a Viennese-produced edition would scarcely have occurred to Durazzo, for music publishing was all but non-existent in the Austrian capital at this time.[28] The vignette for the title page (to be treated more fully below) was inspired by a work—Duni's *L'Isle des foux*—which, like *Orfeo*, had found great favor with Viennese spectators. Durazzo's choice of scene here also comes as a surprise, for it is not the one depicted in the finished engraving. As for the letter to be placed at the front of the volume—such did not appear; ultimately, from subsequent references it emerges that this was to be a "lettre pour la dedicace à S. M." [i.e. Sa Majesté], whom we must take to mean Empress Maria Theresia, in the absence of further information.[29] Several months later Durazzo announced another change of plan, making explicit who the original market for the edition had been, and implicitly explaining why the dedication was dropped: "Je vous dirai méme, que, puisque Nous avons deja attendu si longtems, je ne voudrois pas me charger de Ledition Entiere par ce quen attendant, p[r]esque tous Les amateurs ont eû le tems de sen faire des copies. Jen prendrai cinquante ou Cent Exemplaires, que je payrai au prix dont Vous Conviendrés, laissant le reste a Paris pour etre débité, soit pour mon Compte, ou Celui des gens qui y ont travaillé, Comme Vous Jugerés apropos."[30]

One sees that the amateurs of whom Favart had written were in fact Viennese. In this same letter Durazzo informed his correspondent that he would not be sending the drawing for the frontispiece from Vienna, as originally planned — perhaps for practical reasons, but also conceivably because it would no longer be as critical that the engraving correspond clearly to the original stage picture, now that a substantial number of buyers would not have had actual experience of the opera.

The extent of Philidor's involvement with the publication of the *Orfeo* score is another matter clarified by the unpublished correspondence between Durazzo and Favart, and surprisingly it turns out to be quite negligible. In one of the notebooks into which the poet had drafts of his letters copied, there is a passage excluded from the printed version of his letter of 1 December 1763:

> il ya longtems que cet ouvrage auroit du etre achevé. Philidor setoit chargé de le conduire mais après nous avoir trainé 4 mois, il s'est trouvé qu'il n'a rien fait &c. il n'exigeoit rien de son travail, je n'ai pas eté dans le cas de lui faire des reproches réels[.] j'ai eté obligé de m'adresser ailleurs[.] jai employe [sic] sodi qui en moins de *15 jours* un mois a mis l'ouvrage en etat d'être gravé[.] il va tous les jours ~~chez le graveur~~ donner ses soins; ~~pour~~ [illeg.] ~~n'est pas gratis~~ mais il n'est pas en etat de les donner gratis et je me suis engagé a les payer[.] la copie que V E m'a envoyée fourmille de fautes: il falloit qu'un homme de l'art les corrigeât et Sodi joint à l'avantage d'etre musicien [et] compositeur celui de posseder la langue italienne[.][31]

Again, Favart was being less than candid; the manuscript score that had been sent from Vienna survives (likewise at the Bibliothèque de l'Opéra) and proves to be no less and no more accurate than others produced by its scribe, Theresia Ziβ — the "Wittib Ziβin," principal copyist for Italian opera at the Viennese Burgtheater during the 1750s and 1760s .[32] The first of the two layers of annotations in the score — almost certainly by the same Carlo Sodi spoken of by Favart — consists of ink corrections of unclear or faulty orthography (for example, reinforced accents, "Schalamaux" changed to "Chalumeaux"), and a mere two musical errors, both involving accidentals. In addition, a number of pencil marks indicated to the engraver such things as ends of pieces, entrances of characters, and changes of clef. In sum: an effort requiring not more than a few afternoons, for someone working with a printed libretto in hand.

* * *

Returning to Durazzo's initial words on the frontispiece (quoted above), we are at first puzzled as to what association he might have seen between the scene in which Orpheus sways the furies, and the vignette of

Example 1

an opéra-comique by Duni, depicting the miser Sordide as he whiningly sings "Je suis un pauvre misérable, / Rongé de peine et de souci." Dancourt provides a strong hint, in an observation made to Favart soon after his arrival in the Austrian capital: "on m'a fourni, sans le vouloir, un argument contre le chant brodé, c'est qu'on m'a parlé ici avec enthousiasme de l'air de M. Duny: *Je suis un pauvre misérable.*"[33] (See Musical Example 1.)

While not actually sounding like Duni's air, the music of *Orfeo* did similarly startle and impress by its simplicity. In opéra-comique this feature could be explained by the humbleness of the genre's origins and the relative lack of skill of its singers; in opera seria such directness was possible only by consciously departing from tradition. That the comic genres might have something of use to serious opera is suggested—but only in passing—in both of the above-named manifestos. Algarotti, in lamenting the affectations most modern music had fallen into, points out that "some image of truth" is still occasionally to be found in Italian music, principally in "Intermezzi, and Opere buffe."[34] The author of the *Lettre sur le méchanisme de l'opéra italien*, mocking Rousseau's assertion that no one would ever succeed in writing good music to French words, responds that "Quelques Airs de Titon & l'Aurore [by Jean-Joseph Cassanéa de Mondonville], du Devin de Village, des Trocqueurs [by Antoine Dauvergne] doivent exciter le courage au lieu de l'abattre. . . "[35] But the independence of action required to give substance to such hints could only be found—as Algarotti had predicted—at a court theatre (such as that in Vienna), headed by "an able director, in whom good intentions are united with power,"[36] and not at an institution as weighted with habit and bureaucracy as the Académie Royale de Musique. That opéra-comique and opera seria regularly alternated already on one and the stage made a Viennese alliance of these genres all the more likely.

Missing from the score of *Orfeo* was all coloratura display, and even the usual places (in the repeats of da capo arias) where singers could improvise it. While the tune sung by Sordide in *L'Isle des foux* was not so much a dramatic highlight as a musical one (the opera being essentially episodic), Durazzo's choice for the frontispiece to *Orfeo* was both. The moment he singled out, Orpheus's song "Deh placatevi con me," was the centerpiece of an extended scene complex built of alternating or recurring blocks of dance (by the furies and shades), menacing choral outbursts, and lyrical pleadings from Orpheus. Gluck rendered dynamic the classicizing symmetry set up by Calzabigi's text, making each successive utterance of the protagonist more urgent, and the chorus less adamant. Whereas for the infernal horde Gluck and his librettist drew on longstanding traditions of Italian opera (the obsessive sdrucciolo rhythms for the chorus, and the imitations of Cerberus's barking, for example),[37] for Orpheus's music the style was closer to that of opéra-comique. If one disregards the interventions of the chorus — with their unresolving C flats (spelled B natural), so admired by Rousseau[38] — what remains is essentially an ariette in the latest Parisian manner, with regular phrases, a wealth of appoggiaturas and relatively little text repetition. (See Musical Example 2.)

Rare was the opera seria singer who would be content with such restrained material; Gaetano Guadagni's training under David Garrick put him in sympathy with Durazzo's desire to maintain dramatic illusion,[39] and thus an ideal candidate (besides vocally) for the role of Orpheus. The soprano who took the part of Amore was even more suited to music in the style of opéra-comique, for this genre was her usual repertory. And in fact the aria Gluck composed for Lucile Clavereau, who along with several members of her family performed regularly in the Viennese French troupe, shares a number of features with pieces he had written for his own comic operas. The alternation of fast and slow sections in "Gli sguardi trattieni" he had employed to good effect in *L'Ivrogne corrigé* of the previous year ("Tu n'auras que la bastonnade," sung by "Pluto" as he imposes his sentence on the drunkards Mathurin and Lucas); the plan derives ultimately from "A Serpina penserete" in Pergolesi's *La Serva padrona*, a piece given in Vienna both in its original form and in French translation. For an air in *Le Diable à quatre* of 1759 ("Quel plaisir me transporte") Gluck had employed the same combination of turns and trills for the violins to suggest the giddy pleasure described in such *galant* terms here by Calzabigi. (See Musical Examples 3a and 3b.) The debt owed to opéra-comique by *Orfeo*'s most famous number, "Che farò senza Euridice," has been long acknowledged. Criticized from the start as too cheerful for its context,[40] the piece derives from what was the most poignant number in *L'Ivrogne corrigé*: "Avec nous il prit naissance," in which Cléon sings of his love for Colette.

More direct still, of course, was Philidor's use of "Chiamo il mio ben così" in his opéra-comique *Le Sorcier*. It is worth pointing out that in calling his cosmetically retouched version a "Romance" he was in effect designating the true genre of Gluck's original.[41] The *romance*, which would receive its most cogent definition in Rousseau's *Dictionnaire de musique* of 1768, had become a fixture in opéra-comique largely on the basis of the *citoyen de Genève*'s example of it in *Le Devin du village* of 1752. Naïve, often slightly antique in expression, and strophic in form, the *romance* was allied more with song than with aria. Even though as musical director of the Burgtheater Gluck had seen ample evidence of the genre's favor in Vienna, he remained aloof from it in his own comic operas, and Orpheus's first-act air is in fact the only *romance* to come from the composer's pen. Though ostensibly a foreign element in this Italian opera, Orpheus's *romance* works perfectly in its context. Its three strophes reflect the bereaved husband's three-fold cries of "Euridice" in the opening chorus, and indeed Orpheus begins the first strophe by saying "Thus I call my beloved." The requisite archaizing touch is provided by the echo-orchestra with chalumeau (a primitive form of clarinet), and the instrumentation also lends naïvely poignant word-painting in each of the subsequent strophes: hunting horns joining in as Orpheus sings "Cerco il mio ben così," and throaty English horns as he weeps for her. The three stanzas are separated by accompanied recitative—which may have prevented the audience from immediately identifying the form of the piece with opéra-comique. In Philidor's version the strophes follow one another without pause.

Curiously, it is not the music but the text in which the reviewer of *Le Sorcier* for the *Mercure de France* saw a prior model: "*Bastien*, seul alors sur la scène, chante cette jolie Romance que nous avons reconnu être imitée d'un sonnet italien du Chevalier ZAPPI."[43]

After reproducing the text ("Nous étions dans cet âge encore . . ."), the writer argues that "L'imitation du Poëte Italien ne déprime point l'honneur du talent de l'Auteur françois, elle prouve au contraire le bon usage qu'il fait de la connoissance d'une langue étrangere."[44] What is condoned here is, in reverse, precisely the sort of borrowing practiced by Gluck throughout *Orfeo ed Euridice*. These examples illustrate—as does Durazzo's recourse to the frontispiece of Duni's opera—the increasing common ground at this time between serious and comic opera.

* * *

Of all the many scores sent to Durazzo from Paris, that of *L'Isle des fous* was unique in having a title page vignette—and one by artists of the calibre of Cochin and Flipart at that. (See Figure 1.) Frontispieces were fairly common in opéra-comique libretti, but the folio page of a typical

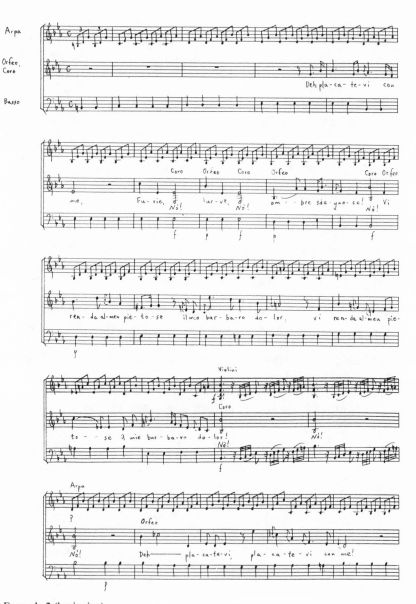

Example 2 (beginning)

Example 2 (concluded)

French engraved score offered a larger field for the artist, and for this reason too *L'Isle des foux* would have recommended itself as a model. Durazzo continued to refer to this engraving even after having had second thoughts about the scene from *Orfeo* he would like depicted in the edition being supervised by Favart. On 17 December 1763 he wrote giving the poet a new list of options:

Venons a present au frontispice. Je ne Lenverrai plus de Vienne. faites faire une Vignette a peu pres de la Grandeur et de la forme de Celle de

Example 3a

Example 3b

Figure 1. J. J. Flipart, after C. Cochin: "Je suis un pauvre misérable," title-page vignette from Egidio Duni, *L'Isle des foux* (Paris, n.d.). Photo Bibl. Nat. Paris.

Lisle des foux. on a choisi dans Cette piece la Scituation, et Lair de *Je suis* un pauvre *miserable*. je voudrois que lon pris de Lorphée la scituation ou Celui ci, voit sa femme tomber morte sur un bout de Rocher, qui se trouve sur le devant de la scene, au Moment quil la regarde, et quil chant lair, dont Les Parolles sont *ché faro senza Euridice*. ou bien La scituation, ou, Orpheé, au Milieu des monstres qui veulent lempecher d'entrer aux enfers, joüe de la lire et chante *Deh per pieta placatevi*. ou bien Encore la scituation ou orpheé au milieu des chants [sic] Eliseés tient par la main son Epouse sans la regarder et que le Coeur [sic] Lui chante *Euridice Amor ti rende*. Je donne la preference a cette derniere scituation. Cependant je Vous laisse la Liberté de choisir Celle que Vous Voudrés.[45]

(Note the information provided here—and not in the libretto—on the stage picture during "Che farò.") Indeed, it was this last scene that was engraved by Noël Le Mire, after a design by Charles Monnet. (See Figure 2.)

The moment in the drama Durazzo finally settled upon was less forceful musically than his original choice, coming in the middle of a mainly decorative chorus, but visually it was more satisfying. Both Orpheus and Euridice were included, and the stage picture was now that most amply described in the libretto—an important factor for an artist 600 miles from the site of the premiere.[46] One finds copious stage directions guiding Monnet's hand, as regards both setting and action:

[Mutazione] Terza. Deliziosa per i boschetti che vi verdeggiano, i fiori che rivestono i prati, ritiri ombrosi che vi si scuoprono, i fiumi ed i ruscelli, che la bagnano.

Da un Coro di Eroine vien condotta Euridice vicino ad Orfeo, il quale senza guardarla, e con atto di somma premura la prende per mano, e la conduce subito via. . . .

(Third [Scene], delightful on account of its green woods, the flowers which cover the fields, the shady retreats found there, the rivers and brooks that bathe it.

A Chorus of Heroines leads Euridice close to Orpheus, who without looking at her, and with a gesture of utmost urgency takes her by the hand, and leads her quickly away. . . .)

Orpheus himself describes what he finds upon arriving in the Elysian Fields, in an arioso preceding the chorus:

Che puro ciel, che chiaro sol,
Che nuova serena luce è questa mai!
Che dolce lusinghiera armonia
Formano insieme il cantar degli augelli,

Figure 2. "Euridice Amor ti rende," frontispiece from Christophe Gluck, *Orfeo ed Euridice* (Paris, 1764). Photo from the Music Library of Yale University.

Il correr de' ruscelli,
Dell'aure il susurar.
Questo è il soggiorno de' fortunati Eroi!
Quì tutto spira un tranquillo contento,
Ma non per me. . . .

(How pure the sky, how bright the sun,
What unwonted, serene light is this!
What sweet, enticing harmony
Is formed by the singing of birds,
The rushing of streams,
The murmuring of the breezes?
This is the soujourn of the fortunate Heroes!
Here everything breathes a tranquil
happiness,
But not for me. . . .)

Monnet and Le Mire faithfully reproduced the essentials of the libretto's descriptions, omitting only the "puro ceil" and "chiaro sol," probably
on account of the medium. They also clearly took the frontispiece of the
Duni opera into consideration; in both pictures the two central figures
occupy a protrusion of the foreground, and are sheltered by a canopy of
trees—completed in L'Isle des foux by what seems to be an incarnation
of la Folie. The upright format of the Orfeo frontispiece is due to
Favart's desire to give "more grandeur, nobility and expression to the
figures, and more room for les accessories," as well as to enable the
picture to be detached and framed separately.[47] Though much indebted
to a vignette from an opéra-comique, by Favart's action this work was
elevated to the status of a "precious piece of engraving."

Whatever dishonesty Favart may have shown on the financial side of
their dealings (and at this very time he and Dancourt were conspiring to
poison the mind of the empress with regard to her theatrical director,
claiming inadequate compensation for his efforts, among other things),[48]
he served the count well in choosing the artist he did for the Orfeo
frontispiece. A student of Vanloo as was Le Mire, the draughtsman
Charles Monnet is known primarily for his contributions to the illustrated edition of the Métamorphoses d'Ovide (1767–71), described by
Lady Dilke as "one of the most harmoniously beautiful books of the
[eighteenth] century."[49] (The composition of one of the plates Monnet
supplied for this book, "La Nymphe Salmacis veut embrasser le jeune
Hermaphrodite, qu'elle voit dans le Bain," is quite similar to that in his
Orfeo drawing [see Figure 3].) As an engraver, Noël Le Mire would
likewise be involved in the Métamorphoses project, but his work was
already well known to Durazzo from other editions he had acquired
through his literary agent: the five-volume Decamerone of Boccaccio

Figure 3. Massard, after C. Monnet: "La Nymphe Salmacis veut embrasser le jeune Hermaphrodite, qu'elle voit dans la Bain," from *Les Métamorphoses d'Ovide* (Paris, 1768), vol. 2.

(drawings by Gravelot), the 1762 edition of La Fontaine's *Contes et nouvelles*, and the frontispiece to Favart's *Soliman II* of the same year.[50] Le Mire's engraving for the *Orfeo* score was very likely what prompted his election in 1768 to the Imperial and Royal Academy of Vienna; four years later he engraved the portrait of Emperor Joseph, working "d'après une bague donnée par sa Majesté Impériale."[51]

Durazzo's indirect patronage of these two artists is only one episode in a thriving commerce in visual art between Paris and Vienna, one which flowed in both directions. The expatriate Austrian engraver Jean-Georges Wille, established in Paris as a "more or less official mandatory for the German courts,"[52] had since 1759 been sending engravings and paintings — in many cases for third parties — to his "old friend" M. Wächter, secretary to Chancellor Kaunitz.[53] For his part, Wächter put Wille in touch with the Austrian landscapist Johann Christian Brand, sent engravings, literary pamphlets, and a student: the portraitist Jakob Schmutzer, who spent several years in Wille's studio under the sponsorship of Kaunitz.[54]

In the realm of theatrical décors, as well, Paris was a major supplier to the imperial capital. For the festivities honoring the 1760 marriage of Archduke Joseph and Isabella of Bourbon Parma, Durazzo imported (through Favart) three prominent scenic artists: the machinist Gabriel Duclos of the Théâtre Italien; Charles-André Tremblin (or Tramblin), formerly a painter for the Opéra; and Jean-Nicolas Servandoni, who had worked at the Opéra in earlier decades but who was best known for his elaborate pantomime spectacles in the Tuileries palace's Salle des Machines, and elsewhere. (Already in 1752 Tremblin had been associated with the diplomat Mæcenas Kaunitz, decorating coaches for his "grande entrée à Paris" on completing his term as ambassador.)[55] The success of Durazzo's venture was at best limited. Tremblin and Duclos — the latter unable to communicate with the German-speaking workers under his direction[56] — both ended up fleeing to St. Petersburg, where Tremblin took his own life. The lateness of Servandoni's arrival prevented him, too, from being as useful as the count would have liked. But the specialized skills of Servandoni and Duclos — not available locally — did make possible some spectacular stage effects: Tetide's crystalline "monparnasce," with a working torrent, in Gluck's opera of that name, and the destruction of Armida's palace in Traetta's opera of 1761 (for which Durazzo had supplied the prose sketch).[57]

Just prior to being forced from his position as superintendent of Vienna's theatres in the spring of 1764, Durazzo entrusted one last grand project to his theatrical agent, asking him to commission a complete set of costumes, "au plus galand," from Louis René Boquet of the Opéra, for an Italian serenade to be performed at the Frankfurt coronation of Archduke Joseph as king of the Romans. At the same time, in language reminiscent of that in earlier letters, the count asked to be brought up to date on the whole range of theatrical costuming in the French capital:

> Jaurois Envie Aussi Mon cher favard, si Je vais a Paris, de Connoitre, et de voir tous les *Costhumes* et Habits de Caracters dont on sest servis dans tous les theatres de Paris depuis quelques années et Comme je ne serai pas assés de tems dans Cette Ville pour voir representer les Pieces ou ces habits auront eté employés, je voudrois, qu'a mon ariveé Vous puissiés men faire voir un de chaque Genre; ou si Je ne vais pas a Paris, Je vous prirai, peut etre, de men Envoyer un dessein Coloré de quelques unes, au vray, et tels quils ont eté Executtés; afain que lon puisse si Conformer, lorsque lon Voudra les faire faire. . . .
>
> Pour ce qui concerne, Lopera et la danse, mandé moi Jusques quel point on y suit le Costhume, si lon paroit Vouloir quitter les Paniers dans la danse Noble; Jusqu'a quel point on employe le Panier dans le demi Caractere.[58]

In ordering costumes and maquettes from Boquet — and earlier, a painter from the school of Boucher[59] — Durazzo was dealing with the most established, conservative of Parisian artists. The two followers of Vanloo whose work graced the first edition of *Orfeo ed Euridice* belonged firmly in this same camp. Yet the count shows himself to be in the forefront of theatrical developments with his eager questions on historical and national costuming (implicit in the phrase "suit le Costhume"), and on the "panier," or whale-bone corset. Vienna's French theater had already made some progress in this area: in 1761 Zinzendorf noted that "La Tragédie d'hier [by Crébillon] a été executée dans le nouveau gout qu'on doit a Melle Clairon a Paris, qui a aboli toute exclamation et demarche affectée su Théatre, point de paniers."[60] There is no contradiction in Durazzo's exploitation of opposing styles or currents of thought from the Parisian theatrical scene; his choices were consistently apposite and imaginative. Boquet's magnificent plumes and draperies were exactly what was needed for a static and allegorical piece such as the one given in Frankfurt, while a frontispiece based on an opéra-comique model, ennobled in tone through its execution, was a perfect reflection of what Gluck had accomplished in his music for *Orfeo*. The sureness with which the composer drew upon the different genres that went into the work was a direct result of Durazzo's foresight: in assigning him such a wide range of tasks (as the count himself implied in noting "la deference, qu'il a montrè à se prêter à tous les genres de musique, que je luy ai demandès, soit pour les Ballets, soit pour les opera-comiques, ou les grands opera"),[61] and in choosing as his theatrical agent a man with access to talent from the full spectrum of Parisian theatres. Demonstrating remarkable determination, the Genoan director of Vienna's theatres sought to break down barriers between music both high and low — as well as French and Italian. *Orfeo ed Euridice* of 1762 was the fullest embodiment of his vision.

NOTES

* Research for this paper was supported in part by a grant from the Faculty Research and Innovation Fund, University of Southern California.

1 *Lettre sur le méchanisme de l'opéra italien* (Naples and Paris, 1756), ix: "an opera which will be neither French nor Italian, but a composite of the one and the other, purged of the faults of both." It has recently been suggested that Durazzo was the author of the 1756 *Lettre*; while the evidence for this in the text of the pamphlet is at best suggestive, it is fairly clear that he paid for its publication, and certain that he endorsed its arguments. See Gabriella Gentili-Verona, "Le Collezioni Foà e Giordano della Biblioteca Nazionale di Torino," *Vivaldiana* 1 (1969):31–55. Durazzo's authorship is likewise assumed by Françoise Karro in "Da la Querelle des Bouffons à la réforme de Gluck: Les Lettres du Comte Giacomo Durazzo à Charles-Simon Favart conservées à la Bibliothèque de l'Opéra," *Mitteilungen des österreichischen Staatsarchivs* 38 (1985):163–96.

2 For a discussion of the larger cultural significance of *Orfeo*, see Daniel Heartz, "From Garrick to Gluck: The Reform of Theatre and Opera in the Mid-Eighteenth Century," *Proceedings of the Royal Musical Association* 94 (1967/68):111–27.

3 See, for example, the "EPÍTRE, au sujet de l'opera d'*Ernelinde*" by an anonymous *abonné* of the *Mercure de France* which appeared in the January issue (first part) of that periodical in 1768:

> D'autres [nous assurent], que dans les beaux endroits,
> Les déguisemens, quoiqu'adroits,
> Masquent en vain les ressemblances
> Des traits originaux de *Glouc*, de *Galouppi*,
> De *Pergoleze*, & de *Geomelli*; . . .

> (Others [assure us], that in the beautiful passages
> The disguises, though clever,
> Mask in vain the resemblances
> To the original features of *Glouc*, or *Galoupi*
> Of *Pergoleze*, and of *Geomelli*; . . .)

In the first volume of Framery and Ginguené's *Encyclopédie méthodique. Musique* (Paris, 1791), the latter wrote of Philidor that "on lui reproche . . . beaucoup d'emprunts ou plus que des emprunts; & il est certain que dans le

Sorcier, dans Tom Jones, dans Ernelinde & d'autres ouvrages, des motifs entiers, alors ignorés des François à qui la musique italienne étoit entièrement étrangère, mais très-connus aujourd'hui, viennent à l'appui de ce reproche" ("One reproaches him many borrowings, or more than borrowings; and it is certain that in *Le Sorcier*, in *Tom Jones*, in *Ernelinde* and in other works entire motives, unknown then to the French, to whom Italian music was entirely foreign, but very well known today, come to the support of this reproach") (621).

4 *Biographie universelle des musiciens*, 8 vols. (Paris: Firmin Didot, 2/ 1877–78), 8:31 (s.v. "Philidor").

5 In an article originally written for the *Journal des débats*, and reprinted in *A travers chants* (Paris: Lévy, 1862), 125–27.

6 Jullien, *La Cour et l'opéra sous Louis XVI* (Paris, 1878; repr., New York: AMS Press, 1978), "Favart et Gluck: La Première édition d'Orphée (1764)," 322 ff.

7 *Mémoires et correspondance*, ed. A. P. C. Favart, 3 vols. (Paris: Léopold Collin, 1808).

8 Auguste Font, *Favart: L'Opéra-Comique et la comédie-vaudeville aux XVIIe et XVIIIe siècles* (Paris, 1894; repr., Geneva: Slatkine, 1970), 152. The letters (Fonds Favart, Carton I, A, I) are mainly in the hand of two secretaries, but also include passages, and a few complete letters, penned by Durazzo himself.

9 Jacques-Gabriel Prod'homme reproduced a selection of passages dealing with the publication of the *Orfeo* score, generally without comment, in *Christoph-Willibald [sic] Gluck* (Paris, 1948; repr., Paris: Fayard, 1985).

10 The recent study by Françoise Karro (see n. 1), which treats the political dimensions of the correspondence especially well, should do much to change this situation.

11 *Mémoires*, 2:58; letter of 28 January 1763: "I have sent M. Duni to investigate; he reported to me that M. Blondel had been charged with delivering the score of *Orphée* to me, but that he had first given it to Baron d'Holbach, and then to Baron van Swieten who, after having had several airs copied out of it, returned it to M. Blondel."

12 On van Swieten's early musical activities in Brussels and Paris, see Ernst Fritz Schmid, "Gottfried van Swieten als Komponist," *Mozart Jahrbuch* 1953, 15–31, and Edward Olleson, "Gottfried van Swieten: Patron of Haydn and Mozart," *Proceedings of the Royal Musical Association* 89 (1962/63):63.

13 *Mémoires*, 2:67; letter of 6 February 1763.

14 *Mémoires*, 2:102; letter of 19 April 1763.

15 Ibid.

16 *Mémoires*, 2:225; letter of 13 April 1766.

17 *Mémoires*, 2:180; letter of 29 December 1763.

18 *Mémoires*, 2:184; letter of 2 January 1764.

19 *Mémoires*, 2:279: "You shall not see the chevalier Gluck at all; he has returned here. He was stepping into his carriage in Bologna, and leaving for Paris,

when he received a letter from the Count calling him back to Vienna, since having learned that the Opéra had burned, he judged the chevalier's trip to be useless. . . ." Dancourt added: "et par conséquent voilà mes pièces sans leur tailleur qui leur auroit fait un habit à la mode de Paris et de tous les amateurs de bonne musique" ("and consequently, there you have my pieces without their tailor, who would have made a suit in the style of Paris, and of all the lovers of good music.") While this might be construed as indicating that Gluck's business with the Opéra was to have concerned not *Orfeo*, but a work or works by Dancourt, a previous letter shows that this reference was to three pieces destined for the Comédie Italienne (2:271; letter of 13 March 1763).

20 See the manuscript *Répertoire* of the Burgtheater for 1763, compiled for Durazzo by Philipp Gumpenhuber (Vienna, Österreichische Nationalbibliothek, Musiksammlung, MS 34580 c). Durazzo also negotiated on Gluck's behalf around this time for a pension, which likewise served to free the composer for outside projects (memorandum dated 21 January 1763; Vienna, Hofkammerarchiv, Camerale 2186, Fasz. 67 1762–1789, fol. 8–9ʳ).

21 *Mémoires*, 2:184: "The operas of Lulli and Rameau, and of all our best composers, in appearing two years after their performances, do not sell any less well; and the music of M. Gluck . . . will not have any less of an advantage."

22 Besides Rousseau's *Lettre sur la musique françoise* of 1753, and Calzabigi's famous "Dissertazione" prefacing the Paris edition of the works of the Viennese court poet Metastasio, there were several explications of Italian serious opera—in addition to opera buffa, topical on account of the sojourn of Bambini's troupe of "Bouffons" in Paris—that appeared in France. See, for example, the "Mémoires d'un Musicien qui s'est instruit dans toutes les Ecoles de l'Europe, où l'on trouvera des Observations historiques & critiques sur la Musique Italienne & Françoise, sur l'Opéra des deux Nations, & sur *Zoroastre*," *Journal encyclopédique* (1 May 1756), 31–73; the review and extract of Marcello's *Il Teatro alla moda* (originally published in Venice ca. 1720) in the *Journal étranger* (October 1760), 73–91; the reviews in the above *Journaux* of productions of Italian opera abroad also furnished ample opportunity for remarks on the genre as a whole.

23 *Affiches, annonces et avis divers*, no. 23, Wednesday, 6 June 1764.

24 "They are neither madrigals, nor over-refined thoughts, nor ingenious witticisms, or little flashes of epigram; they are the language of nature, a simple action and the expression of a sensitive woman. . . ."

25 In a note at the end of a letter of 20 November 1762 (published in fragmentary form in the *Mémoires*, 2:34 ff.), Durazzo told Favart: "Vous recevrez par Mʳ: Français Beau Frere de Mʳ: Blondel [French *chargé d'affaires* in Vienna—not the architect, as surmised by Prod'homme, *Gluck*, 118] un paquet de musique dont je vous marqueraj L'usage que vous en devez faire." ("You will receive from Mr: Français, brother-in-law of Mr: Blondel, a packet of music, the use of which you are to make I will indicate to you.") In conveying New Year's

greetings on 30 December, Durazzo added a postscript in his own hand, saying

Vous aurez receù La	You will have received the
Partition de l'opera	score of the opera
d'Orpheè[.] je voudrois	*Orfeo*. I would like
sçavoir combien il	to know how much it
m'en couteroit de	would cost me to
La faire imprimer[.]	have it printed.

26 "At the end of Carnival we had a revival of *Orfeo*, which had as much success as the first time, and I predict that I will be obliged to take it up again after Easter. You will oblige me by ordering that one start right away to engrave its music. There are probably some gross copyist's errors in the score I sent you, as regards both music and words. I will have to rely on your friendship, and I hope you will find persons capable in both areas for the correction. Next week I will send you the title [page], and a letter to go at the front. I would like the ordinary format of the operas you have sent me. I prefer above all *L'Isle des foux*. I would like a vignette in the same style. In it one could show Orpheus moving the Shades to pity, and the Furies at the entry to Hell. You see that I wish to indicate the main part of the action, where Orpheus sings 'Deh placa-tevi con me Ombre' &c. and the chorus answers 'Nò.' " According to Gum-penhuber's chronicle for 1763, the two performances of *Orfeo* on Sunday, 13 February and on Monday the 14th were both part of a special program consisting of a Hannswurst play, a French comedy, and Gluck's opera (plus the usual ballets).

27 For an English translation of the reviews of the first performance that appeared in the *Wienerisches Diarium*, see Patricia Howard, *C. W. von Gluck, Orfeo* (Cambridge: Cambridge University Press, 1981), 53–56.

28 When the score to Gluck's *Alceste* was published in 1769 (two years after the premiere, as with *Orfeo*), it was by the Viennese printer Trattner, in the less elegant technique of movable type. Following the death of Maria Theresia's consort Francis of Lorraine in 1765, and the ascent of Joseph II as co-regent, increased encouragement was given to local manufacture of goods that had commonly been imported before. Although the score was dedicated to Arch-duke Leopold of Tuscany, it is perhaps significant that Trattner was the publisher to whom the young Archduke Joseph had been sent in 1756 to learn the printing trade.

29 Letter of 13 July 1763.

30 Letter of 17 December 1763: "I will even tell you that since we have waited so long already, I do not want to take the entire edition, because while we have been waiting, nearly all the amateurs have had the time to have copies made. I will take fifty or a hundred copies, which I will pay at whatever price you like, leaving the rest in Paris to be sold, either to pay your expenses, or those of the persons who have worked on it, as you see fit." Favart offered Durazzo 100 copies at 15 *livres* apiece—"une remise . . . de trois livres, car chaque exem-

plaire sera délivré au public sur le pied de dix-huit livres" (*Mémoires*, 2:187; letter of 4 January 1764) ("a discount . . . of three *livres*, for each copy will be delivered to the public at the price of eighteen *livres*"). In fact the score was advertised at 12 *livres* (in the *Affiches, annonces et avis divers*); the poet, who had taken personal responsibility for placing notices in local and international journals, had short-changed—not saved—Durazzo 300 *livres*. The price did not appear on the title page of the score, in contrast to usual Parisian practice.

31 "This work should have been finished long ago. Philidor had been charged with directing it, but after he had led us on for 4 months, it was found that he had done nothing &c. He asked nothing for his work, [and] I was not in the position of making him any real reproaches. I was obliged to address myself elsewhere. I used Sodi, who in less than 15 days a month put the piece in a state to be engraved. He goes every day to the engravers to give it his attentions; for [illeg.] isn't free but he isn't in a position to be giving them free of charge, and I have been forced to pay for them. The copy Y[our] E[xcellency] sent my is swarming with errors: It was necessary [to find] a man of the art to correct them, and Sodi combines the advantages of being a musician and of knowing Italian."

32 Mus. Ms. 3971: Orfeo / Opera Seria / Del: Sig^re Gluk. The editors of the opera for the composer's *Sämtliche Werke* recognized that the score originated in the copy workshops of Vienna's court theatre, but failed to see the significance of the annotations in it, and of its presence at the Bibliothèque de l'Opéra along with the other Favart materials. This is especially regrettable, as the Paris edition was the source on which they based their own.

33 *Mémoires*, 2:264; letter of 25 April 1762: "I was furnished, without asking for it, with an argument against embroidered singing, in that people here have talked to me with enthusiasm about M. Duny's air 'Je suis un pauvre misérable.' " One of the Viennese enthusiasts was Count Carl von Zinzendorf, who noted in his diary (now in the Staatsarchiv, Vienna) on 4 July 1761

> On donna Nanine de Voltaire, et l'Isle des Foux, Opéra Comique nouveau. . . . Sordide dont du Londel fit, on ne peut pas mieux, le rôle, chanta un tres joli air. Je suis un pauvre miserable, rongé de peines et de soucis, j'ai travailé comme un Diable, pour amasser l'or que voici.

> ("They gave *Nanine* by Voltaire, and *L'Isle des foux*, a new comic opera. . . . Sordide, whose role was played incomparably by du Londel, sang a very pretty air, "Je suis un pauvre miserable, rongé de peines et de soucis, j'ai travailé comme un Diable, pour amasser l'or que voici.")

During a soirée at the end of the next month, according to this same source, "Mlle de Kaunitz chanta sur le balcon cet air Je suis un pauvre miserable//" ("Mlle Kaunitz sang from the balcony the air "Je suis un pauvre miserable//") (30 August 1761). On the reception of Duni's air in Paris, see Daniel Heartz, "Diderot et le théâtre lyrique: 'le nouveau stile' proposé par *le Neveu de Rameau*," *Revue de musicologie* 64 (1978): 229–52.

34 Algarotti, *Saggio sopra l'opera in musica*, 2d ed. (Livorno, 1763), 38.

35 *Lettre sur le méchanisme*, 79: "Certain airs in *Titon & l'Aurore* and *Le Devin de village*, and *Les Trocqueurs* should excite one's courage, rather than discouraging one."

36 *Saggio*, 12.

37 As in the aria for Lucifer in Handel's oratorio *La Resurrezione* of 1708, and the opening scene of act 2 from the same composer's *Admeto* (1727), respectively.

38 Jean-Jacques Rousseau, "Extrait d'une Résponse du Petit Faiseur à son Prête-nom, sur un Morceau de l'*Orphée* de M. le Chevalier Gluck," *Lettre à M. Burney sur la musique avec fragmens* (Paris, 1781); repr., in *Oeuvres complètes* (Paris: L. Hachette, 1857), 4:463 ff.

39 Zinzendorf noted in his diary that the repetition of two arias in Giuseppe Scarlatti's *Il Mercato di Malmantile*, demanded by the audience, was "fort ressenti par M. de Durazzo" (16 July 1763).

40 Zinzendorf, 6 October 1762, reporting a comment by the wife of the Venetian ambassador.

41 Berlioz, in his discussion of the case in *A travers chants*, referred to this piece as "la romance de Gluck."

42 See Daniel Heartz, "The Beginnings of the Operatic Romance: Rousseau, Sedaine, and Monsigny," *Eighteenth-Century Studies* 15(1981–82):149–78.

43 *Mercure de France*, January 1764 (first part), 184: "Bastien, alone on stage at that moment, sings this pretty Romance, which we have recognized as being imitated after an Italian sonnet by the Chevalier ZAPPI."

44 Ibid., 185: "The imitation of the Italian poet in no way takes away from the French author's talent; it proves, on the contrary, the good use he makes of the knowledge of a foreign language." The supposed model used by *Le Sorcier*'s librettist (Antoine Poinsinet "le mystifié") is not immediately apparent in the *Rime dell'Avvocato Gio: Batt. Felice Zappi*, 15th ed. (Venice, 1818).

45 "Let's come to the frontispiece. I will no longer send it from Vienna. Have a vignette made of approximately the size and shape of that in *L'Isle des foux.* In that opera one chose the scene, and the piece of 'Je suis un pauvre misérable.' I would like for one to choose the scene in *Orfeo* where he sees his wife fall dead on an outcropping of rock at the front of the stage, at the moment in which he looks at her, and sings the air, of which the words are 'Che farò senza Euridice.' Or, the scene where Orpheus, in the middle of the monsters who want to prevent him from entering Hell, plays the lyre and sings 'Deh per pietà placatevi.' Or, the scene where Orpheus, in the middle of the Elysian Fields, takes his spouse by the hand without looking at her, and the chorus sings to him 'Euridice Amor ti rende.' I give the preference to this last scene. However I leave you free to choose whichever you like."

46 Another factor in dissuading Durazzo from his first choice (at least at the stage when the frontispiece was still to have been supplied from Vienna) was possibly the criticism that had been raised against the *bocca d'inferno* in the sets for the opera. The reviewer in the semi-official *Wienerisches Diarium*

wrote tactfully that "we can not convince ourselves that the brush of the painter has carried out the true intentions of the designer [Giovanni Maria Quaglio]" (Howard, *C. W. von Gluck, Orfeo*, 56).

47 *Mémoires*, 2:192-93; letter of 31 January 1764.

48 See Robert Haas, *Gluck und Durazzo im Burgtheater* (Vienna: Amalthea, 1925), 93 ff.

49 Lady Emilia Dilke, *French Engravers and Draughtsman of the XVIIIe Century* (London: G. Bell, 1902), 33.

50 Yves Sjöberg, *Bibliothèque Nationale. Département des Estampes. Inventaire du fonds français: Graveurs du XVIIIe siècle* 14 (1977):92.

51 *Mercure de France*, December 1772, 172 (quoted in Sjöberg, *Inventaire*, 184-85).

52 François Courbouin, *La Gravure en France des origines à 1900* (Paris, 1923), 106.

53 See the *Mémoires et journal de J.-G. Wille*, ed. Georges Duplessis, with an introduction by Edmond and Jules de Goncourt, 2 vols. (Paris, 1857), passim.

54 In Wille's comical description of the arrival of his new apprentice in 1762 one can see something of the general Viennese — as well as a personal admiration of French taste in the arts:

> Il me fit en entrant bien des révérences gothiques, me voulant baiser le bas de ma robe de chambre, me nommant tantôt Votre Excellence, tantôt Ihre Gnaden. . . . Il a été envoyé à Paris . . . par le grand chancelier, comte de Kaunitz; même l'argent qu'il a annuellement à dépenser sera délivré par ordre du grand chancelier. . . . Il m'a conté que la Dévideuse, Tricoteuse, etc. [engraved by Wille], qui se vendent trois livres chez moi, sont ordinairement vendues quinze liv. à Vienne.

> (On entering he made several Gothic bows, wanting to kiss the hem of my dressing-gown, calling me now Your Excellence, now Your Grace. . . . He was sent to Paris . . . by the Grand Chancellor, Count Kaunitz; even the money he has annually to spend will be delivered by order of the Grand Chancellor. . . . He told me that 'la Dévideuse,' 'la Tricoteuse,' etc., which are sold at my shop for three *livres*, are ordinarily sold for fifteen *liv.* in Vienna.)

(*Mémoires et journal*, 1:211-12; entry for 19 November 1762).

55 See Durazzo's letter of 19 March 1760 to Favart (Fonds Favart). An important dossier on these artists which had become separated from the materials in the Fonds Favart was described and reproduced by J. J. Guiffrey in "Les Peintres décorateurs du XVIIIe siècle: Servandoni, Brunetti, Tramblin, etc., etc.," *Nouvelles archives d'art francais*, 3d ser., 3 (1887):119-28.

56 See Durazzo's letter of 21 January 1764 to Favart (Fonds Favart).

57 See Duclos's letters to Favart of 15 August 1760 and 7 January 1761 (Bibliothèque de l'Opéra, Fonds Favart, Carton, I, A, IV).

58 Letter of 21 January 1764 (Fonds Favart): "I would also like, my dear Favart, if I come to Paris, to get to know, and to see all the costumes and characteristic clothing that have been used in the Parisian theatres for the last few years.

And as I won't have enough time in that city to see performed the plays in which these costumes have been used, I would like for you to have made, by my arrival, an example in each genre; or if I don't come to Paris, I would ask you, perhaps, to send me a colored drawing of some of them, true-to-life, and as they have been executed, so that we can conform to them, should we wish to have them made. . . ."

59 "Quelque Détail / au suiet du Peintre, Machiniste, ou Decorateur et du Tailleur pour le service de la Diréction Théatrale de Vienne" (March 1760) (Fonds Favart).

60 Zinzendorf, entry for Sunday, 19 April 1761: "Yesterday's tragedy was performed in the new style we owe to Mlle Clairon in Paris, who has abolished all affected exclamation and posturing on the stage—no *paniers.*"

61 Manuscript note requesting a pension for Gluck (see n. 20 above): "the deference he has shown in lending himself to all the types of music I have asked of him, be it in ballet, comic opera, or serious opera."

The Libertine Sublime: Love and Death in Restoration England

JAMES GRANTHAM TURNER

> Tho' round my Bed the Furies plant their Charms,
> I'll break 'em, with *Jocasta* in my Arms:
> Claspt in the Folds of Love, I'll wait my Doom;
> And act my Joys, tho' Thunder shakes the Room.

When Nathaniel Lee wrote these lines, in the *Oedipus* he co-authored with Dryden, he may not have suspected that within a few years they would be uttered again, in a dubious piece of fiction, by a villainous seducer. In Richardson's *Clarissa*, of course, the libertine fraternity apply *Oedipus* to the dying Belton as if it were smelling salts, and Clarissa herself quotes it in her delirium after the rape.[1] But I am thinking of an earlier and seamier fiction, Alexander Smith's *School of Venus* (London, 1716), where the earl of Rochester recites these very couplets to restore his strength as he attempts to rape a young girl (1:149). In a parallel episode of the same work, Beau Fielding recites a comparable declaration of sexual bravado from "the Earl of *Rochester's* prophane Play of *Sodom*" (1:245); Smith appears to consider the obscene burlesque and the heroic drama equivalent ornaments for the libertine character, since both provide magnificent assertions of erotic energy in the face of doom. My essay will try to establish a context and reception-history for this *topos*, following its shifts and recombinations at different levels of literature, and opening up larger questions about the status of libertinism and its rise in Restoration England. In particular it will ask how, at a specific literary-historical juncture, the cult of flamboyant sexuality encountered the discourse of sublimity.

Various thinkers, from Coleridge and Kierkegaard to Georges Bataille and Julia Kristeva, have tried to understand the exhilarating power of libertinism in its most extreme manifestation, the figure of Don Juan; the episodes studied here, from English heroic drama and libertine poetry, may be seen as variants on Don Juan's final defiance. Kristeva, for example, analyzes Don Juanism in both psychological and historical terms: she relates it to a special form of semiotic exuberance (an "ivresse des signes") that she identifies with the Baroque, but she also finds parallels in case-histories from her own practice as a psychoanalyst, cases of casual Priapism and father-fixation, attempts to transcend the impasses of sexuality by trying "the solution called perverse, to pass from the abject to the sublime, to taste the whole gamut of troubles and delights, supreme guarantee against boredom. . . ."[2] Another perceptive interpreter of "baroque" sexuality in literature, Peter Hughes, describes it as a form of heroism that replaces martial prowess, as a "constant pushing of the sexual and amorous beyond itself into the language of power," and as an anticipation of Bataille's principle that "Eroticism is the assertion of life even to the point of death."[3] My own approach will draw upon these important ideas, but it will modify them according to the specific mentality of the age.

Sexual Heroism and the Erotic Sublime

Hughes is quite right to discover a heroization of sexuality in the later seventeenth century. "No Age abounded more with Heroical Poetry," as Samuel Butler remarked, "and yet there was never any wherein fewer Heroicall Actions were performed."[4] The English Restoration was preoccupied with the search for new modes of heroism, and since militant Titanism had been so fully embodied in Cromwell, it turned to the "wars within doors" of love and sex. But how could something so morally dubious be aggrandized? In a significant and potentially unstable synthesis, a wholly unromantic cult of frank physicality and sexual freedom was grafted onto its apparent opposite—the heroic love-code of Romance, infinitely elaborated in the salon culture of mid-century France.

Contemporary French theories of *les passions de l'amour*, associated with a *préciosité* quite different from sexual libertinism, nevertheless develop a concept of erotic greatness that prepares the way for this fusion. For Descartes, for example, erotic love—the desire to fuse with the person or object that seems to be the other half of one's being—enjoyed a special status; other fundamental passions are only beneficial in moderation, but love, provided that its goal is genuinely good and not illusory or harmful, can never reach the limits of its greatness, and is all the better the more "excessive" it grows. This valorization of excess, even when the love is "déréglé," departs dramatically from the Aristotelian model of ethics that condemns excess and deficiency equally; it makes an important step towards the sublime conception of passion, as an infinite force beyond good and evil. Desire in Descartes's theory, when combined with "generosity" and directed towards a future good, may be permitted the same excess; in moral terms it "cannot be bad," and in its physical effects, though it can induce deep "langueur" in the hopeless lover, no passion does more to stimulate the heart, sharpen the senses, and activate the body. Indeed, constitutional prowess is directly linked to amorous capacity, and so "Herculeses and Rolands love more ardently than other men."[5]

The next generation of love-theorists amplified this heroic conception, and introduced the vocabulary of the sublime. Love is assumed to be a privilege of *grands esprits*. The lover's life is too stormy and tumultuous for the "mediocre," those who are mere machines and not fully human; hence it is that the Court loves and the City does not. (The court entertainments of Louis XIV make it quite clear that "love" refers to illicit sexual conquests, justified by the God-like status of the royal seducer.) Greatness is defined in contradictory and sometimes tautological terms: it is a product of social elevation, but it is also an internal capacity of mind and emotion, in theory independent of class—the greater the *esprit*, the more "pure, noble et sublime" the mind, the greater the heart and the "passions of fire." Love-passion grows in one whose heart is "too vast," and who seeks his ideal resemblance to "fill the void that he has made in going beyond himself." Yet love is also an extrinsic force which generates wit, raises and "aggrandizes" the soul, makes the common man "magnifique," and fills the entire being with its own grandeur. It propels the lover above circumstances, beyond the self, towards a solipsistic encounter with a mirror-image of the self, and towards a state of "excess" in which all concerns are dissolved into the aesthetic: indeed, "la passion ne peut pas être belle sans cet excès."[6] Similarly, in Dryden's frequently-quoted *Conquest of Granada*, the "Heroique Passion" of Love finds "No room in any base degenerate mind," and "kindles all the Soul with Honours Fire, / To make the Lover worthy his desire" (part two, 2.1. 145–48). Love is both a form of social nobility and a fiery principle which absorbs the entire soul, a transpersonal force and a variety of solipsism: the lover strives to be worthy, not of his beloved Other, but of "his desire."

This heroic ideology permeated the libertine ethos, and its repertoire of gestures spread even to the outer fringes of the English Restoration "World." The stage, particularly the tragedy, was evidently the means of transmission. The seducer-hero John of Austria in Thomas Otway's *Don Carlos*, for example, declares that "Those that are noblest born should highest prize / Loves sweets," setting his own "unconfin'd" and "Godlike mind" against the "dull Law" and "dull Moralists" who would place limits on sexuality; before the consummation of his affair he defines love in terms of infinite height — privileged lovers "should fly, / And mounted by their wishes soar on high" — and afterwards, conveniently, he redefines it as "unbounded liberty."[7] (As in Dryden, the hypostasis of desire generates an unintended ambiguity; in what ways are lovers mounted by their wishes?) Another and more villainous Don John, in Thomas Shadwell's *The Libertine*, frames his exaggerated debaucheries in similar statements: he will reject all "bounds" and "live the noble life of Sense," following "Love and mighty Lust" and disdaining those "dull insipid Fools that live by measure."[8] A version of this supra-ethical ideology was even thought appropriate for the Restoration stage-heroine, who encourages her lover with the idea that "Sublime Deserts may justify Desires."[9]

Such ideas, which should be seen as idea-gestures or performative *topoi* rather than as intellectual concepts, translated easily from the fictive stage to the theater of the world. Whereas in France the sexual sublime served to rationalize and defend the libertinism of the aristocracy, in England it could be assumed even by the minor gentry and apprentice wits who crowded into the pit, for whom it conveyed a kind of surrogate class-privilege. Thus one moralist complains that the flamboyant young hedonists of the 1670s talk of "the height of Spirit," of "a greatness of Soul that scorns to be imposed on"; "the pursuing variety of amours," they think, "is the peculiar gusto of a great wit, [and] their extravagancies are . . . inseparable proofs of extraordinary capacities." Another complains in the 1690s that poets are so devoted to libertinism that the "Thoughts sublime" of art are equated with "wanton Love and Flames unchaste."[10] Dryden cannot conceal his admiration for the "greater Gust" with which the king conceived Monmouth and scattered his seed throughout the land.[11] Other satirists convey a similar awe and relish even in their denunciations of upper-class lechery: thus Mary of Modena enjoys "sublimer Amours" with the Papal Nuncio, and the duchess of Cleveland is praised for having outshone the "glory" and the "Transcendent deeds" of Messalina.[12] Aphra Behn reverses this gender-bias in her thinly-disguised fictionalization of Lord Grey's affair with his sister-in-law: when he attacks "the dull Methods of ordinary loving" and raves about the "Excess of Joy, far above dull Sense, or formal thinking," it is evidence of his villainy and absurdity, but when his victim uses the same heroic-libertine vocabulary she is genuinely sympathetic: "I cannot fall more gloriously . . . I will be brave in Love, and lavish all. . . . If there be no boldness like that of love, nor courage like that of the lover, sure there never was so great a heroine as *Sylvia*. Undaunted, I resolve to stand the shock of all; . . . it is below the dignity of my mighty passion to justify it farther."[13]

This fetishization of greatness had two effects: energy tended to be valued over ethics, and satire and panegyric were forced closer together. When Matthew Prior proudly shows "Great Nassau" in bed with Queen Mary, and praises the "soft Excess" of Her Majesty's love-making, we are only a hair's-breadth away from burlesque.[14] The emperor Sardanapalus, in John Oldham's thinly-veiled mockery of Charles himself, shows a "Gallant height of Soul" and an "Imperial" phallic resolution that override the ostensible goal of the poem; Oldham's extreme combination of lofty Pindaric form and obscene diction — what we might call the "offensive sublime" — has the effect of emulating rather than censuring the priapic monarch. We can judge the poet's aspiration from his attack on *Sodom*, a sordid failure in the same genre: to have been "great in wickedness," to have outgone great pornographers like Petronius, Pietro Aretino, and Nicolas Chorier, would indeed have been "Heroick."[15]

Fire, excess, height, greatness, "sublimity," transcendence, the intensity of pleasure and refinement of taste that combine in the word "gust" — all these are transferred from courtly Romance to bravura sexual performance in word and deed, to what Rochester called "Love rais'd to an extream." Thenceforth libertinism would always exist in a high and a low version, corresponding to the poles of the "abject" and the "sublime," each mirroring and supporting the other, even though each threatened the other — by their very similarity — with absurdity. This intimate double relationship is clearly manifested in Rochester, both in his own writings and in those fictional and memorial reconstructions that sprang up around him. In many ways he was a champion of the anti-sublime, of course: his obscenity deflates the panoply of Romance, his intellectual satire destroys the soaring pretensions of reason, and he singles out the "sublime" literary and sexual aspirations of Mulgrave for special personal abuse.[16] And yet he does contribute to the cult of erotic sublimity. It is not simply that his satirical offensives were carried so far that, as Hazlitt later put it, they "almost amounted to sublimity," but he also positively supports the heroic ideology of sex. His obsessive repetition of the word "dull" reveals his preoccupation with those extremes of sensation that raise the spirit to a new intensity, a sublimation in the alchemical sense. To "Raise pleasure to the topp," sexual love combines with wine and poetry in a mutually-reinforcing system of "heat" and exaltation:

> For wine (whose power alone can raise
> Our thoughts so farre above)
> Affords Idea's fitt to praise
> What wee think fitt to Love.[17]

Sexuality is expansive even at its most coarse; Rochester's viciously ironic attacks on female promiscuity, like Oldham's self-undermining mock-heroics, positively assert something boundless and unconfined, "something Generous in meer lust." Love is not merely a "Cordial dropp" that sweetens an otherwise nauseous existence, but a power that can engender—momentarily at least—a state of both elevation and belief: "For none did e're soe dull and stupid prove, / But felt a God, and blest his pow'r in Love."[18]

Rochester's harnessing of self-presentation and heightened erotic energy, and his revaluation of the extreme, were faithfully echoed by his contemporaries. He was "fam'd for high Extreams, / The Hero's Talent," for a "noble and elevated mind, like Fire and Air." Behn remembered his irresistible combination of Greatness and Softness, manifested both as a lover and as a poet. His chaplain found him "one of the *greatest of Sinners*," utterly "singular," "above the reach and thought of other men"; but in "the heightening and amazing circumstances of his sins" he detected a special amorous sensibility that might have served to celebrate the love of God. Gilbert Burnet noticed in him a "sublimity" of wit that was "scarce imitable" and a "violent love" of sexual pleasure that, when "heighten'd" by the "heat" of alcoholism, "carried him to great excesses"; his diagnosis, though hostile and dissuasive, echoes at several points the portrait of the ideal lover in contemporary love-theory. Burnet also recognized, unlike other dazzled contemporaries, the inner psychological and epistemological dimension of Rochester's attempt to find sublimity in the sensual, the frustration and nihilism that follows when heat does not generate ideas, when pleasure does not reach the top, or when nothing can be found "fit to love." Burnet's Christian counter-arguments were thus aimed not at reason alone, but at the "capacity of apprehending high and sublime things": he lured the jaded earl by suggesting that the resurrected senses will enjoy "a more quick and sublime way of Operation," which will in turn "exalt the Joys . . . of the Good."[19]

Throughout the literature of the Restoration, then, we may trace the attempt to heroize sexuality by associating it with the quasi-religious exaltation of pleasure and the antinomian glories of excess, with amoral individualism and imperial absolutism, and—above all—with the sublimating "heat" of creative genius. It is a precarious attempt, since both components of the synthesis—heroism and sexuality—were deeply problematic, and led just as easily to ignominy as to exaltation. Nevertheless, these tensions could be obscured in the clouds of height and extremity, and dissolved in a common association with creativity. Rochester's obscene verses, for example, were attacked and defended for their "Fire" and "spirit," their "*Liber Spiritus*" and "unbounded Fancy" (*RCH*, 122–23, 155). Indeed, literature and sexual behavior converge in the cult of sublime passion, mutually defining and reinforcing each other; literature is drawn into the glamorous culture of upper-class erotic adventure, and sexuality can move away from moral restriction into the realm of the aesthetic.

Literary theory thus replays and refines the new heroized version of libertinism: both Hobbes and Dryden insisted that heroic literature must "raise admiration, principally, for three Vertues, Valour, Beauty, and Love"; conversely, the heroic must be found in the representation of those forms of Beauty and Love that engender "admiration" in the seventeenth-century sense—astonishment or wonder rather than strict ethical judgement.[20] Restoration tragedy acted out this percussive conception of the "Heroique Passion": as eye-witnesses vividly recall, Dryden's sexual despots and devourers would send ripples of "trembling Admiration" through the audience.[21] Dryden is in fact a central figure in this libertine refurbishment of the traditional equivalence of Eros and creativity. He declared that "Poets like lovers should be bold and dare," and that he abandoned rhyme because "Passion's too fierce to be in fetters bound"; contemporary readers defined their response, and his genius, in terms of "masculine beauty," "violence," "rapture," melting, burning, Promethean fire, orgasmic death. The future Lord Bolingbroke carried the libertine/poetic conceit even further: Dryden avoids the "stale thing" of a "Poetick Wife," which might have diminished the Fancy and put out his "Fire"; instead, like a Sultan in his harem, he enjoys all the "wishing Muses," and they in turn "no decay, no want of vigour find, / Sublime your Fancy, boundless is your Mind."[22]

Thunder in the Bedroom

What light, then, do twentieth-century theories of sexual transgression shed on this historical conjunction of erotics, poetics, and heroic ideology? Peter Hughes's stress on "the constant pushing of the sexual and amorous beyond itself" captures the restlessness and extremity of the period, but we have seen that seventeenth-century love-ideology conceived the transcendent, not as something beyond the erotic, but as an intrinsic property of sexuality itself. Nor does it pass from love to power, as Hughes asserts, but rather subsumes the language of politics into the fiction of absolute sexuality; this was an age that eroticized politics and transformed sex into "nobility," "height" and "conquest." Hughes speaks of "self-consciousness that turns into the sacrifice and even the destruction of the self," but the extreme manifestation of sexual energy could be apprehended, not as the destruction of the self, but as the ground of absolute selfhood, the "singular," the "inimitable," and "original"; the reception-history of Rochester provides many examples, to which we might add the refusal of Don John in Shadwell's *Libertine* when the Statue calls on him to repent—"Could'st thou bestow another heart on me I might, but with this heart I have, I can not"—where Coleridge would find a profound expression of identity and "a portion of sublimity."[23] Hughes's interpretation draws heavily on Bataille's concept of eroticism as "assertion of life"; but though Bataille throws a brilliant light on the process whereby "intensity is increased by intimations of destruction," his polarized psychology is an insufficient basis for the interpretation of this crucial development in mentality.

The heroization of sexuality is better understood in terms of two seventeenth-century theories of the "sublime" that evolved in response to the decline of religion: the amorous psychology of love-ideology, and the Longinian analysis of the aesthetic response. Both are concerned with a boundlessness and a "vastness" ambiguously located within the mind and exterior to it, and both discover sublimity in the attempt to accommodate this immense expansive power, to find its interior equivalent in an experience of beautiful excess, and thus to transcend the commonplace limitations of human capacity. Erotic heroism does not express anything as homogenous as Bataille's "assertion of life," but rather a rage against its inadequacies, an incessant (and obsessive) attack upon Dullness. It aims not to celebrate but to control and transcend the parameters of life. Without recourse to traditional religion, it tries to assuage the "monstruosity in love" painfully articulated by Shakespeare's Troilus—"that the will is infinite and the execution confin'd, that the desire is boundlesse and the act a slave to limit"—and reiterated in Rochester's private complaint of "soe great a disproportion twixt our desires and what [Fate] has ordained to content them."[24] This problematic engenders various forms of solution: suppression (Troilus's lines are cut from Dryden's revision), obscene reversal (the "Transcendent" whore whose flesh can actually "outdoe" her own imagination), or sudden religious conversion (in the case of Rochester). Assimilation into the heroic code, as we have seen, proved to be the most compelling of these solutions.

Bataille does define the arena of attempted transcendence, however: the point of confrontation between eroticism and death. Hubristic defiance of the forces that limit human expansion towards the infinite — death being the paradigm — thus became the most important of those "heightening and amazing circumstances" that transformed sexuality into heroism and made Love a spectacle for Admiration.

This dramatic confrontation may be traced in many genres. The effect is milder in the lyric and more strenuous in the tragedy, but the posture is common to both, and makes an appearance even in the margins of comedy. Thus Nemours in Lee's *The Princess of Cleve*, a strange hybrid of low comedy and sentimental tragedy, exercises his "Wit" by articulating a philosophy of extremity and erotic Titanism: "Thus wou'd I have Time rowl still all in these lovely Extreams. . . . The two nearest ways to enter the Closet of the Gods, and lye even with the Fates themselves, are Fury and Sleep — Therefore the Fury of Wine and the Fury of Women possess me waking and sleeping, . . . and Death I defie thee."[25] Nemours claims to be paraphrasing the recently-departed Rochester here — "Thus sung Rosidore in the Urn" — but no poem called "The Urn" has survived, and Lee probably expresses a generic response to the phenomenon of Rochester, fusing the coffee-house diabolism of "To the Post Boy," the recklessly simplified hedonism of "Upon his Drinking a Bowl," and the blithe sexual confidence of "Against Constancy" ("I'll change a Mistress till I'm dead, / And fate change me for worms"). Though Rochester does not actually "lie with the Fates" in any extant poem, the gesture is rooted in the European libertine tradition. Aretino's *Sonetti lussuriosi* begin with the urge to control death and time in the act of love, to die (literally) in a sexual spasm, and then to take Adam and Eve by storm; the French "satyrique" poet imagines himself descending to the underworld with undiminished bravado, masturbating in the face of the dead.[26] The supreme act of libertine sublimity involves not merely plunging into the pleasures of the flesh, but transcending the limits of the body in a convulsive moment of thought, achieving the illusion of God-like control — the aspiration of another of Lee's overreachers, Nero: "Swift, as quick thought, through every art I range: / Who but a GOD, like me, could Sexes change?" Like a Gnostic adept, Nero harnesses the power of sexual perversion to usurp divine creativity, "Beings [to] annihilate, and make a new" (*Works*, 1:32).

The gesture of defiance is of course absurd, ephemeral, and splendidly futile, like the attempt in Marvell's "Coy Mistress" to "roll all our strength and all / Our sweetness up into one ball." Time is not controlled but foreshortened, compressed into the brief thrill of the audience as the ranting villain outtops his own rhetoric, or the explosive brevity of the obscene parody, where the climactic violence of language coincides with the ultimate act of libertine heroism. At the end of Oldham's *Sardanapalus*, for example, the Priapic monarch collects "all [his] Strength . . . in one Thrust," and "mid'st a glorious heap of burning C—ts expire[s]." And in "The Wish," persistently ascribed to Rochester even though it appeared in print when he was fourteen, all the *topoi* of the new sexual heroics—the impatient desire to dissolve bodily limitations in total sexuality, the idea of alchemic sublimation by erotic heat, the cult of the extreme in language and experience, and the strange fantasy of control over birth as well as death—fuse into a single obscene gesture: "one thrust" will convert him all to sperm, and once growing in the womb he will "boldly f— — — [his] Passage out again."[27] The same spasmodic moment links the lowest and the highest stratum, just as aristocratic freedom and street hooliganism joined forces in the frolics of Rochester and Sedley.

This "low-heroic" posture—defying death by a sudden display that combines eroticism and contempt—shows us how the abject and the offensive may converge upon the sublime. Again, continental libertinism provides an example. Thus Claude le Petit heroizes the execution of the sodomite Chausson, an event that he witnessed a year before he was himself burnt at the stake for obscenity and atheism; the condemned man "regarda la mort sans crainte et sans frisson," refusing the ministry of the priest, until finally, as the flames rose around him, "L'infâme vers le Ciel tourna sa croupe immonde: / Et, pour mourir enfin comme il avoit vécu, / Il montra, le vilain, son cul à tout le monde." Le Petit's sonnet matches Chausson's stately and impeturbable scurrility, forcing us to resist the comic-dismissive response and to realize, by a double irony, the truth of what at first seemed merely mock-heroic: "jamais on n'expira de plus noble façon."[28] I would argue, in fact, that the elemental simplicity of Chausson's gesture—thrusting one's arse in the face of death—underlies many splendid moments in the heroic drama, gleaming through the superstructure of decorous language.

The gallant assertion of sexual bravado in the teeth of mortal threat, as we have seen in the first example of this essay, was a popular expression of heroism in Restoration tragedy (and one easily assimilated into the literary underworld). The Oedipus of Dryden and Lee defies the Furies in Jocasta's arms, and promises to "act my Joys, tho' Thunder shakes the Room." Shadwell's Don Juan outfaces not only the statue of the Commander, but the ghost of his own father, murdered by himself, whose monument he selects for the scene of nightly rapes.[29] Dryden's Morat likewise braves his imperial father, his rival for the charms of Indamora, and thereby elevates him into a malignant deity: in a splendid rant that hides a rather muddled use of myth, he promises to "snatch my *Semele*, like *Jove*," despite the "rouling Thunder" of his father's wrath, "And midst the dreadful Rack enjoy my Love" (*Aureng-Zebe* 4.1). (Indamora seems to be destroyed in either case.) In a similar mood Anthony, in *All for Love*, defies his enemies both mortal and divine, and drives off with sex all thoughts of ignominy and defeat:

> Let *Caesar* spread his subtile Nets, like *Vulcan*,
> In thy embraces I would be beheld
> By Heav'n and Earth at once:
> And make their envy what they meant their sport.
> Let those who look us blush; I would love on
> With awful State, regardless of their frowns,
> As their superior god.
>
> (3.1.17–23)

"I would love on" is a transparent euphemism, a coded evocation of the parallel of high and low, tragedy and obscene burlesque; it requires only a downward twist of the linguistic register, without changing the content or the meter, to transform Anthony into Buggeranthos or Sardanapalus.

The common source of these defiant declarations is Anchises' magnificent response in the Homeric Hymn to Aphrodite, here given in Congreve's version:

> This Instant will I seize upon thy Charms,
> Mix with thy Soul, and melt within thy Arms:
> Tho' *Phoebus*, arm'd with his unerring Dart,
> Stood ready to transfix my panting Heart;
> Tho' Death, tho' Hell, in Consequence attend,
> Thou shalt with me the Genial Bed ascend.[30]

But there are important differences between Dryden's (and Congreve's) lines and their ancient original, quite apart from the ludicrously polite diction that erodes their heroic intensity. Anchises really is in the presence of the goddess, half-recognizing her but suppressing his terror to achieve erotic immediacy, whereas Dryden's protagonists act out the confrontation of Eros and Thanatos at several removes; imperious desire is transposed into the conditional tense, distanced by simile, stiffened into a ceremonial tableau. And the primary emotional drive is no longer absolute passion overcoming awe, but regressive sentimentality in Oedipus, savage hatred of the father in Morat, and hubristic exhibitionism in Anthony—the solemn confidence that, like the Gods in the frescoes of Giulio Romano, he would appear majestic even in the act of copulation.

Dryden is a victim as well as an exponent of this heroic cult of erotic immediacy. As Harold Brooks says of *Aureng-Zebe*, "the new lucidity demanded by Restoration taste was in conflict with the endeavour at the sublime, limiting the poet's powers to suggest a dimension beyond the finite and the comprehensible."[31] Dryden was sincerely committed to the heroic-erotic code—as Jean Hagstrum has eloquently shown—and he found in sexuality not only a "Heroique Passion" but a model of the poet's creative fire. But he also saw it as what Bakhtin would call an eruption of the low material stratum: the satirist's instinct for absurdity often clashes with the dramatist's striving for "admiration," blurring the distinction between heroes and grotesques. Nor can he escape the uncertainty that runs throughout the erotic literature of the period: what is the relation between discourse and sexuality? Can language convey the immediacy of erotic experience or is it a mere compensation, as in Mulgrave's ironically-titled "Perfect Enjoyment": "But now, alas! for want of further force, / From action we are fallen into discourse"?[32] Like his fellow-dramatists, Dryden assumed the potential immediacy of language when he pursued the "admiration-effect," the mimetic enactment of extreme moments of erotic excitement or erotic hubris. But his commitment to discursiveness, his supreme control of formalized description and argumentation, often undermines his attempt to show characters *in articulo amoris*. By a strange extension of neo-classical dramatic theory, his protagonists become as it were the messengers of their own psychic events, describing their heats in a language of observation, precisely bounded, detached and cool—violating his own aesthetic of fire and freedom, clamping fetters on passion.

We find sexuality and death more perversely bonded, and the sublimity of abjection more thoroughly converted into pure theatrical effect, in writers of less verbal skill—in Otway's *Venice Preserved* or Lee's *Lucius Junius Brutus*. The whole action of *Venice Preserved* can be understood as Jaffeir's attempts to prove that—in his opening words—"I'm not that abject wretch / You think me," to run what Kristeva would call the gamut from the abject to the sublime, by tasting all the pleasures of erotic pain. He shuttles between different forms of sado-masochistic intensity, first sacrificing Belvidera to the cause, then sacrificing himself to her, and finally transferring this whole complex to the charms of Pierre: only by total abjection to his hero can he reach the sublime end, "dying well" on the scaffold in a high-tragic version of Chausson's confidence and contempt.

A similar upward spiral of eroticism and cruelty propels Lee's tragedy of political and sexual extremism. Brutus throws off the guise of a sexually-obsessed lunatic to become the scarcely less demented "Father of his Country," forcing his son Titus, on a "stain'd and reeking" dagger pulled from the breast of Lucrece, to renounce the consummation of his marriage to Tarquin's daughter. The drama of Titus — oscillating between conflicting duties and factions, impotent on his wedding night, tortured and executed at Brutus's command — is punctuated by the Father's embraces, which are both passionate and manipulative; he loves and "moulds" the boy in a way that both denies and reproduces the role of mother: "thus on my brest, / The hard and rugged Pillow of thy Honor, / I wean thee from thy Love." The final farewell of father and son resembles that of Anthony and Cleopatra — Brutus "Print[s] this last kiss upon thy trembling lips," and Titus expires blissfully in his arms. Titus's fate resembles Don Juan's as Kristeva interprets it, clasped in the arms of the destroying father. But the boundaries of gender have been shifted: duty, desire, and paternal authority are consummated on a hard and rugged breast, a petrified mother.[33]

These tensions are internalized and compressed into the outbursts of love for his bride Teraminta that provide the climactic tableaux of acts 2 and 3 — livid confections of masochism, gender-inversion, and death. Embracing Teraminta at the end of act 2, Titus is the distracted mother of a dead baby, fondling the corpse and shrieking when it is taken from his or her breast; one act later he again attempts to let amorous bravado triumph over prohibition and death, but the death-principle is already an intrinsic property of his desire:

> Come to my brests, thou Tempest-beaten Flower . . .
> Yes, by the Gods, I'll smell thee till I languish, . . .
> Fall like the Night upon thy folding beauties,
> And clasp thee dead: Then, like the Morning Sun,
> With a new heat kiss thee to life again,
> And make the pleasure equal to the pain.

This fantasy seems to combine Bataille's "assertion of life" with its exact opposite. Teraminta returns these images of deadly masculine nurture when they meet, broken and bleeding, in act 5; she offers to lean her head on his breast and "like a Cradle Babe / To suck thy wounds and bubble out my Soul."[34] Lee thus constructs, in the cruel theater of political and social conflict, the psychological situation that Kristeva discovers at the heart of libertine sexuality: the attempt to fashion a compromise between the abject sadomasochistic impulse and the sublime identification, "idealizing and terrifying," with a superego "who commands impotence" — the Father, the Commander, the embrace of stone.[35]

Kristeva's redeployment of the psychoanalytic vocabulary is rich and ingenious, and she evokes the "intoxication with appearances" and the "extravagant superiority of baroque man" with a panache that would have been appreciated in the period. But a truly historical explanation of baroque sexuality would have to acknowledge the specific social and intellectual forces that intersected with a specific moment in the evolution of the concept of sublimity. Lee's drama lays bare the psychological tensions that push sexual heroism towards perversity, but it is above all a study in crisis, a thinly-disguised indictment of an England lurching out of control, where political authority has become entangled with sexual extremism. A history of the period must give full weight to the various issues broached in this essay: the conjunction of salon love-ideology and sexual freedom in the courts of Louis XIV and Charles II, the anxieties of serving a libertine monarch, the ambiguous class-position of the sexual hero, the crisis of confidence in language, the aesthetics of passion and immediacy, and the displacement of religious sensibility in the hastily assembled secular-hedonist culture of Restoration England. And it must ask whether the cult of erotic sublimity expanded or contracted the self-realization of women, as writers and as subjects of sexuality.

Once such a history is constructed — a task far beyond my scope here — a new genealogy of the modern may emerge. According to one historian, it was Kant's theory of the sublime that cleared the way for a new and distinctly modern sensibility, one that "searches out extreme experiences in order to explore the boundaries of human life," and made possible a new art based on "a heightened sensitivity, an extreme of expressive affect which is communicated in an explosive act."[36] But these are precisely the effects valued by the ideology of heroic love, pursued by the poets and dramatists of the Restoration, exaggerated into an offensive or spasmodic sublime, grafted into a new form of high libertinism, and thence disseminated throughout the eighteenth century.

NOTES

1 Everyman's Library edn. (London: Dent, 1951), 3:209, 4:152.
2 "Eros maniaque, Eros sublime" and "Don Juan, ou aimer pouvoir," in *Histoires d'amour* (Paris: Denoël, 1983), 105, 251–63.
3 "Wars within Doors: Erotic Heroism and the Implosion of Texts," *English Studies* 60 (1979): 402 (epigraph), 403.
4 *Prose Observations*, ed. Hugh de Quehen (Oxford: Clarendon, 1979), 175.
5 *Les Passions de l'âme* (1648), ed. Geneviève Rodis-Lewis (Paris: Vrin, 1966), arts. 79, 101, 111, 119, 139 ("Je dis que cette Amour est extremement bonne, pource que joignant à nous de vrays biens, elle nous perfectionne d'autant. Je dis aussi qu'elle ne sçauroit estre trop grande; car tout ce que la plus excessive

peut faire, c'est de nous joindre . . . parfaitement à ces biens"), 141, 145; *Oeuvres*, ed. Charles Adam and Paul Tannery (Paris: Cerf, 1901), 4: 613–17 (letter to Chanut).

6 This account is based on the *Discours sur les passions de l'amour*, a synthesis of the ideas of Pascal, Rochefoucauld, Méré, and Malebranche that reflects discussions in court and salon circles; sometimes attributed to Pascal himself, it is cited from his *Oeuvres complètes*, ed. Henri Gouhier and Louis Lafuma (Paris: Du Seuil, 1963), 285–89. Louis's cult of heroic love is discussed in Philippe Beaussant, *Versailles, Opéra* (Paris: Gallimard, 1981), passim, esp. 57–61, 112–13 (I am grateful to Martha Pollak for this reference); for the cult of "le sublime dans les moeurs," see Theodore A. Litman, *Le Sublime en France (1660–1714)* (Paris: Nizet, 1971), 120–29. Even Saint-Evremond, who attacked the new valuation of excess and vastness, praises the greatness of love in modern tragedies and includes "l'excès de la joie" in a depiction of ideal love (*Oeuvres choisies*, ed. A. C. Gidel [Paris: Garnier, 1867], 102; Litman, *Sublime*, 145–57).

7 *Works*, ed. J. C. Ghosh (Oxford: Clarendon, 1932), 1:184–86, 195.

8 *Complete Works*, ed. Montague Summers (London: Nonesuch, 1927), 3:25, 28.

9 Francis Fane, *Love in the Dark* (London, 1675), 7; the high-born heroine, who speaks verse in a prose drama, is in carnival disguise when she delivers this line.

10 *Remarques on the Humours and Conversations of the Town* (London, 1673), 13, 79, and cf. 7 ("these Gentlemen thirst after the fame of Heroes, and extraordinary men"); John Phillips, *A Reflection on our Modern Poesy* (London, 1695), 1. The word "sublime" seems to have been drinking-club slang, used somewhat like "high" in the 1960s; see Hugh Crompton, *Pierides* (1658), quoted in Theodore E. B. Wood, *The Word "Sublime" and its Context 1650–1760* (The Hague: Mouton, 1972), 49. This usage is reflected in Milton, *Samson Agonistes*, ll. 1669–70.

11 *Absalom and Achitophel*, l. 20. This common way of explaining the vigor of bastards (familiar from Shakespeare) is also translated into heroic terms by Otway's Don John: "My Glorious Father got me in his heat, / When all he did was eminently great" (*Works*, 1:185).

12 Gregorio Leti, *The Amours of Messalina, late Queen of Albion* (London, 1689), 1:56; *The Penguin Book of Restoration Verse*, ed. Harold Love (Harmondsworth, England: Penguin, 1979), 224–25.

13 *Love-Letters Between a Noble-Man and his Sister* (1684), ed. Maureen Duffy (London: Virago, 1986), 3, 4, 65, 66, 81–82 (I am grateful to Judith Kegan Gardiner for this reference).

14 *Literary Works*, ed. H. Bunker Wright and Monroe K. Spears, 2d ed. (Oxford: Clarendon, 1971), 92, 133.

15 Bodleian MSS Firth c. 15, p. 163, and Rawl. poet. 123, p. 84. In Princeton MS AM 14401 Oldham's obscene satires against obscenity are included alongside *Sodom* and the first translation of Chorier and evidently did not pose a

classification-problem for the compiler. For Oldham's tendency to inflame the passions he pretended to denounce, see also Tom Brown in David Farley-Hills, ed., *Rochester: The Critical Heritage* (London: Routledge, 1972), 175. Henceforth cited as *RCH*.

16 Cf. *Poems*, ed. Keith Walker (Oxford: Blackwell, 1984), 108 ("something soe Sublime"), 112–14. Further references to Rochester's poetry will be by title and line, using this edition.

17 Song ("How happy Cloris"), alternative version, ll. 6, 29–32 (*Poems*, 40–41); line 6 is unchanged in all three versions of this poem. The concept of "heat" (and its opposite "dullness") was essential to Rochester's conception of creativity, as revealed in his conversations with Burnet (e.g., *RCH*, 54, 59, 65, and cf. 57).

18 "A Ramble in St James's Parke," line 98, "A Letter from Artemiza," lines 44–49; Artemiza also declares that Love is "the most gen'rous passion of the mynde" and could create belief even "in lands of Atheists" (ll. 40, 46–47). Cf. "Upon his leaving his Mistriss," lines 19–21: "And shall my *Celia* be confin'd? / No, live up to thy mighty *Mind*, / And be the Mistress of *Mankind*."

19 *RCH*, 113 (anon.), 37 (Fane), 102–5 (Behn), 45–46 (Parsons), 49, 51, 68, 62 (Burnet); cf. also 100 (Oldham), 138, 142, 148 (Wolseley), and 163 (D'Urfey). For Burnet sublimity could be a quality of mind or an effect of style, but in both cases he seems to have assumed an emotional or even sexual core: cf. his description of a preacher whose "Sermons have a sublimity in them that strikes the hearer as well as it edifies him," and whose "Eloquence is Masculine . . . tempered with all the softness of persuasion" (quoted in Wood, *The Word "Sublime,"* 165).

20 Cf. Jean H. Hagstrum, *Sex and Sensibility: Ideal and Erotic Love from Milton to Mozart* (Chicago and London: Chicago University Press, 1980), 65; and Hobbes, Preface to the *Odyssey* (1675), in *Critical Essays of the Seventeenth Century*, ed. Joel E. Spingarn (Oxford: Clarendon, 1908), 2:68; note the inference Hobbes makes from his statement, that as readers of heroic poetry women are just as qualified as men.

21 E.g., Colley Cibber, quoted in James and Helen Kinsley, eds., *Dryden: The Critical Heritage* (London: Routledge, 1971), 193. Hereafter cited as *DCH*.

22 *Conquest of Granada*, part two, 1.1.145; Prologues to *Tyrannick Love* and *All For Love* (in other prologues he explores the parallel of sex and writing in more comic terms); *DCH*, 38, 47 (a comic version), 97–100, 208, 222; and Theophilus Parsons, commendatory poem to *Cleomenes*. Dryden's aesthetic principles also included the valorization of excess, e.g., in his praise of Dorset in the "Discourse of Satire."

23 *Biographia Literaria*, ed. James Engel and W. Jackson Bate (Princeton: Princeton University Press, 1983), 2:212–22, esp. 219; note the cross-reference to another stage-libertine on p. 227 ("this tragic Macheath"). In view of this awareness of libertinism, it seems unwise for the editors to say that there is no sexual meaning in "orgasms of sickly imagination" (cf. "the lowest provocation of torpid feeling [in] the reader"; p. 211 and n.).

24 *Troilus and Cressida*, 3.2; Rochester, *Letters*, ed. Jeremy Treglown (Oxford: Blackwell, 1980), 241-42 (fragment of a letter to his wife).

25 *Works*, ed. Thomas B. Stroup and Arthur L. Cooke (New Brunswick, NJ: Scarecrow, 1955), 2:188.

26 "Se post mortem fotter fosse honesto / Direi: Tanto fottiam, che ci moiamo: / E di là fotterem Eva ed Adamo / Che trovano il morto si disonesto" (sonnet 1); Frédéric Lachèvre, *Le Procès du poète Théophile de Viau* (Paris: Champion, 1909), 2:417 ("J'arresserai devant les morts, / Et tu me branleras la pique").

27 Bodleian MS Firth c.15, p. 163; for "The Wish," cf. David M. Vieth, *Attribution in Restoration Poetry* (New Haven: Yale University Press, 1963), 33, 490.

28 *Oeuvres libertins*, ed. Frédéric Lachèvre, Le Libertinage au XVIIe siècle, (Paris: Capiomont, 1918), 5:xli.

29 Lee, *Works*, 1:403; Shadwell, *Complete Works,* 3:38 (and *The Libertine*, passim). Shadwell's source, Rosimond, also makes the Don a parricide, but the ghost-scene is unique to the English version; cf. August Steiger, *Thomas Shadwell's "Libertine": A Complementary Study to the Don Juan-Literature* (Berne: Francke, 1904), 50-51.

30 *Works*, ed. Montague Summers (London: Nonesuch, 1923), 4:171 (translating Hymn 5, ll. 145-53).

31 "Dryden's *Aureng-Zebe*: Debts to Corneille and Racine," *Revue de littérature comparée* 46 (1972): 34.

32 Quoted from *The Gyldenstolpe Manuscript Miscellany*, ed. Bror Danielsson and David M. Vieth (Stockholm: Almqvist and Wiksell, 1967), 234.

33 Lee, *Works*, 2:330-35, 342-44, 383; Kristeva, *Histoires d'amour*, 253.

34 Lee, *Works*, 2:347, 360, 377.

35 Kristeva, *Histoires d'amour*, 253, 262; the connection with the abject/sublime dichotomy is not explicit at this point, but is implied in Kristeva's argument.

36 Richard Kuhns, "The Beautiful and the Sublime," *New Literary History* 13 (1982): 288-89.

The Secrets of Genteel Identity in The Man of Mode: Comedy of Manners vs. the Courtesy Book

I take my text from the gospel according to George Bernard Shaw: "Acquired notions of propriety are stronger than natural instincts. It is easier to recruit for monasteries and convents than to induce an Arab woman to uncover her mouth in public, or a British officer to walk through Bond street in a golfing cap on an afternoon in May."[1] Shaw here wittily expresses a fundamental insight of good comedy of manners. So-called "natural appetites" like the drives for food and sex are commonly understood as extremely deep transhistorical and powerful determinants of human behavior. Yet Shaw sees that supposedly superficial and fleeting codes of manners may be still more powerful determinants of human action. While good comedy of manners often mocks the absurdities and unnaturalness of fashionable manners, it also often has a less judgmental side. It may non-judgmentally revel in the sheer plenitude of behavioral styles and fashionable artifacts, in the exuberantly baroque creativity with which human beings make nonutilitarian signs and ascribe meaning to them. Good comedy of manners also often expresses a more basic wonder at the power of social codes, not only to determine human behavior but also to constitute human identity itself.

Shaw's observation usefully sidesteps the oppressive question of whether manners are revelatory of morals or whether they are mere "surface" forms, perhaps of aesthetic interest, but not fundamentally

117

expressive of "deeper" morals. Some common usage, much courtesy literature, and most literary criticism have inclined to the former sober view, insisting that manners have a sacramental character, that good manners are outward and visible signs of inward and spiritual grace and moral health. That such a view no longer predominates in our own American culture may be one reason why literary critics have been inclined to worry that comedy of manners, however amusing, is lamentably trivial. In a recent study of English courtesy literature from the Renaissance through the nineteenth century, Michael Curtin has argued that early modern courtesy books and nineteenth-century etiquette books are fundamentally different from each other. The earlier Christian humanist courtesy literature "joined the more minute and ceremonious aspects of 'manners' with those broader and more substantial parts of conduct that verge onto what we call 'morals,' " Curtin argues, whereas the later etiquette books "concentrated on precise descriptions of the exact rules of interpersonal behavior with a relative disregard for moral thought." Significantly, he notes, the later etiquette books "were organized around particular social situations—dinners, balls, receptions, presentations at court, calls, promenades, introductions, salutations—rather than according to the moral virtues of an ideal individual—grace, fortitude, self-control."[2]

Sir George Etherege's *The Man of Mode* (1676), as a comedy of manners of the 1670s, is one text in a complex set of discourses on manners in the 1670s. This essay will consider Etherege's play along with a few of the contemporary courtesy books, both because we can gain some further insight into the play and because this is a nice cameo-exercise in considering what I have elsewhere written about as competing "spheres of discourse."[3] Here we have the sober discourse of courtesy books published between 1670 and 1678 to set beside the comic discourse of the stage. Some assistance in this project is available from earlier criticism. D. R. M. Wilkinson in an odd but not worthless book entitled *The Comedy of Habit: An Essay on the Use of Courtesy Literature in a Study of Restoration Comic Drama* (1964) earlier undertook a project resembling what I propose here. Wilkinson apparently began prompted by a desire to rebut L. C. Knight's animadversions that Restoration comedy was dull by providing the comedy with a more appropriate historical context, but he ended by convincing himself that the comedy was indeed not only dull but quite without moral or "artistic coherence." Moreover, Wilkinson decided that even the allegedly witty prose of Restoration comedy was not as well written as the prose of courtesy books. Focusing rather too intensely on the moral bottom line, he also concluded that "what emerges . . . from a juxtaposing of the comedy and the main body of contemporary courtesy literature is their almost complete lack of connection. . . . The conduct advocated in the plays, no less than the manners, differs radically from the ideals of conduct in the courtesy books."[4]

A different approach, one more sensitive to the different representational decorums of courtesy books and comedy, can discover more illuminating connections. Part of the conceptual muddle of Wilkinson's book was his expectation that the courtesy books, as non-fictional texts, would provide "a wealth of incidental evidence on the behaviour of the historical gallants" which would shed light on the more mysteriously fictional plays. He did, at least, have sense enough to notice how many of the Restoration books were "retreads" of earlier continental and English books, and to see that the behaviors they described were different from the behaviors at Charles II's court.[5]

Indeed, advice literature of this sort can usefully be considered not as non-fiction, but as a species of romance. Like romance, it is concerned to define ideals and to show how obstacles to the achievement of ideals may be overcome; the class ideals of the nobility and gentry are, naturally, of special concern. Like romance, too, the courtesy literature normatively represents its ideals as attainable by the virtuous, and insists that personal interest and larger social interests are congruent. Thus, Richard Graham Preston, later Viscount Preston, declares:

> He who is advanc'd to Title and Fortunes and is become an head of the people, either by his own merits or the Atchievements of his Ancestors, ought to be exemplary in virtue. Being set by Heaven on such a conspicuous place on purpose to guide the people into the paths of love, and obedience to their God, and King; and to shew them the ill effect of contrary performance: like Candles put at night in *Pharos* Towers, which at once give the Mariners a view of their fruitful *Egypt*, and lead them off those many and dangerous shelves of the *Nile*.[6]

Furthermore, this literature tends to describe generalized programs of behavior rather than particular actions in sharply delineated historical contexts.[7] Consequently, new editions and new translations of earlier Renaissance books continued to be published in the later seventeenth century, sometimes without much effort by the new publishers, translators, or adapters to alter the advice or examples given.[8] The connection between courtesy literature and romance is made exceptionally vivid in Edward Panton's *Speculum Juventutis: or, A True Mirror; Where Errors in Breeding Noble and Generous Youth, with the Miseries and Mischiefs that usually attend it, are clearly made manifest* (1671). Despite an initial warning to the reader that only plain truth and not the pleasures of Tasso will be found within his book, Panton proceeds throughout to mingle a story of Sifaris, a youth "undone by too much Idleness and libertie, in short, by ill education" with his more general advice about correct behavior in the court and in the camp.[9] Compared with the romance of the Christian humanist courtesy literature, Restoration comedy of manners, especially Etherege's, is a more realistic mode.[10]

Despite such differences between the courtesy literature and the comedy, there are revealing congruencies. An intense fascination with manners and modes in the 1670s of itself links the two. To cite only a few texts from a longer bibliography, we have Richard Lingard's *A Letter of Advice to a Young Gentleman Leaving the University* (1670); *The Rules of Civility; or Certain ways of deportment observed in France, amongst all persons of quality, upon several occasions* (1671), an English version of Antoine de Courtin's French book of the same year;[11] William Ramesey's *The Gentleman's Companion: or a character of true nobility and gentility* (1672); and *The Courtier's Calling* (1675), an English version of Jacques de Calliéres's 1661 French book. Among the better-known comedies of the 1670s clearly focusing on manners and modes besides *The Man of Mode*, we can note Wycherley's *The Gentleman Dancing Master* (1672) and Behn's *The Town Fop* (1676).

Contemporaries felt that modes and manners were changing with unusual rapidity. One impetus was the change in the locus of social power from the court to the town. Curtin notes the gradual eclipse of courtly courtesy books by those focusing on the town and argues that "only in the eighteenth century did court criticism, along with the courts themselves, decline. Increasingly, London-based 'fashionable society' assumed the role the court had previously played as the cynosure of elegant . . . manners."[12] While the elegant manners of the town could, in part, be merely imitations of the elegant manners of the court, certain real differences between the court and the town necessitated fresh invention. The shift in focus from court to town was not completed in this decade, but one does notice that the more astute Dorimant is entirely a creature of the town while Sir Fopling still seems to think it worth his while to appear at court, and futilely attempts to impress Dorimant at Lady Townley's in act 4 by regaling him with an account of a conversation he has just had earlier that evening in the state drawing room (4. 1. 228–29).[13] In the 1670s advice to courtiers continued to be published, advice both French and English in origin, but a number of the new English courtesy books show little or no interest in the court. Even the adaptation of Du Refuge's *Traicté de la court* published in 1672, as W. Lee Ustick has pointed out, implies an audience of both courtiers and non-courtiers and "extracts from the French manual only such passages as are adaptable to the more general scope of a work on conduct which is not specifically for the courtier."[14] At the same time, another set of texts explicitly addressed the character of the "town gallant."[15]

The courtesy books of this period seem unusually concerned with the rudeness of interruption. According to them, the contemporary world is littered with men who narcissisticly talk on and on about themselves and, what is worse, intrude themselves and their interminable self-regarding speeches into company where they are not wanted. For example, Panton complains:

> He is worthily blam'd of impertinency that interrupts a good discourse, and brings in by head and shoulders his loves, suits, quarrels, or such like things, which is of as little concern as the affairs of *China*: there is nothing so troublesome as these sort of people, whether in publique or private, their story is never done, but still to begin, they would have you find as much passion and pleasure to hear, as they have to speak . . . they would always speak, and never hear.[16]

Similarly, Richard Lingard in another original English courtesy book insists:

> No man . . . should be his own *Historian*, that is, talk of his own feats, his travels, his conferences with great men, &. Nor boast of his Descent and Alliance, or recount his Treasures, or the manage of his Estate, all which wears out the greatest patience, and *without a provocation* expresses an intollerable Vanity, and implyes a belief that others are *affected* and *concerned* in these things as much as himself. . . .[17]

The town, of course, was more populous and more filled with strangers than earlier courts, so it is not surprising that contemporary gentlemen should have succumbed to the temptation to become their own historians, and, in the absence of friends, thrust themselves forward clamoring for the attention of strangers. A number of the alternative topics for conversation approved by the courtesy book writers seem notably unlikely to gain a gentleman much popularity in the real world. Panton, for example, advises, "choose rather to talk of things than of persons, of historical matter rather than the *present age*."[18]

The courtesy book writers accompany their strict injunctions against self-advertising speech with advocacy of what they call "complaisance." Complaisance is usefully defined by the anonymous author of *The Art of Complaisance or the Means to Oblige in Conversation* (1673) as "an Art to regulate our works and behaviours in such a manner as may engage the love and respect of those with whom we Converse, by distributing our praises and differences, where the quality of merit of the person require it, by a seeming diligence to give our assistance, and by mildly suffering the errours and miscarriages of others."[19] The social functions of complaisance are clear: by making gentlemen slower to take affront, it avoids violence. Its benefits to the individual are also apparent: in a world where many gentlemen must survive by seeking places from patrons, complaisance attracts patrons; and in a world increasingly filled with importuning but apparently genteel strangers, complaisance is a way to avoid unwanted intimate contact with them.

If we look at the scenes between Dorimant and Sir Fopling, we can see how, in these courtesy terms, Dorimant's conduct is eminently modest, reticent, and complaisant, Sir Fopling's wildly intrusive. Dorimant and Sir Fopling are virtual strangers before the play begins. In the second speech he utters, Sir Fopling importunes Dorimant when they meet in Lady Townley's drawing room, "let thee and I be intimate; there is no living without making some good man the *confident* of our pleasures" (3. 2. 140-42). Sir Fopling, for his part, is happy to confide the details of his travels to Paris, his reception in great families in France, his shopping trips, singing lessons with Lambert, his study with the dancing master St. André, his flirtations, his troubles with his servants, and on and on. About Dorimant's history, in contrast, we know surprisingly little, and he himself is inclined to tell his public even less.

Advisors on the topic of complaisance conjure up the image of a threatening world in which considerable skill is needed to avoid giving offense. Lingard counsels, "neither would I have a man *lye open* to the scrutinies and pumpings of every *Pragmatical Inquisitor*; such assaults must be managed by *art*, you must put by the thrusts, by *slight* rather than *strength*, for no force must be discerned, in such cases he that *drolls* best evades best."[20] Dorimant's self-deprecating response to Sir Fopling's offer of intimacy and declaration that all need confidants is a model of strategic complaisance and evasion: " 'Tis true!," Dorimant obligingly agrees to the proposition that all need confidants, then modestly adds, "but there is no man so improper for such a business as I am" (3. 2. 143-44).

Throughout the play, Sir Fopling again and again noisily intrudes. In 3.3 he clatters up the Mall with his equipage, shouting at his servants, frightening off Lady Woodvill and Harriet; in act 4 he bursts into Lady Townley's private party with a crowd of strangers in masquerade; then climactically, in 4.2 he surprises Dorimant and Bellinda by erupting into Dorimant's lodgings with fiddles at six o'clock in the morning.

What is wonderful about Sir Fopling is that he violates each rule of civility with such utter aplomb. In a world where everyone else is tensely alert to decorum, even anxiously paranoid, Sir Fopling trips blithely across every taboo and feels sublimely unthreatened. He is a kind of comic villain of courtesy. For him, surfaces are entirely pleasing; inwardness nonexistent. Others whisper, talk in asides and double meanings, but Sir Fopling always speaks up audibly and plainly. We feel superior to his unconsciousness. Yet we wonder, with some suspense, will the moment ever come when he notices that he is unwanted and ridiculed? When he says in the Mall, "There never was so sweet an evening," and Bellinda replies, " 'T has drawn all the rabble of the town hither," will he not consider—as we must—that she means to include him in the class of rabble? (3. 3. 196-97). Comedy is about release and the hope of invulnerability. In a society massively anxious about civility, our hero, Sir Fopling, breaks all the rules and yet does not die; indeed, he never even has his feelings hurt.

Yet, in another way, Sir Fopling's presence in town society raises disturbing questions about what it means to be a man of mode. Sir Fopling appears to have been produced by education; notions of propriety, to return to Shaw's language, are notions he has acquired through a program of lessons made explicit in the play. In the first act, Dorimant describes Sir Fopling as a person "of great acquired follies." Medley adds, "He is like many others, beholding to his education for making him so eminent a coxcomb. Many a fool had been lost to the world had their indulgent parents wisely bestowed neither learning nor good breeding on 'em" (1. 333-37). Disdain for education pervades *The Man of Mode*. In act 2, Medley mocks a book "*The Art of Affectation*, written by a late beauty of quality" to teach fashionable manners to young ladies, a book that has been identified as Hannah Woolley's *The Gentlewoman's Companion* (2. 1. 128-29, and note at 128). Dorimant, in contrast, is admired by Young Bellair because "all he does and says is so easy and so natural" (3. 3. 22).

Etherege represents courtesy literature itself as a threat for two reasons. First, much contemporary courtesy literature paradoxically idealized gentility as a natural phenomenon that could not be achieved by effort, yet at the same time that courtesy literature appeared to present universally accessible step-by-step directions as to how to construct a genteel identity.[21] And the more the courtesy literature abandoned the generalities of the older Christian humanist books for the more particularistic, etiquette-like guides to conversation and table manners of some of the newer French and English books, the more practically threatening it was. One common rhetorical strategy in the courtesy literature was to explain publication as an almost accidental incursion into the public sphere of advice intended to be private. The preface to *The Rules of Civility; or, Certain Ways of deportment observed in France* insists, "This Treatise was never intended for the Press," and claims that it was written at the request of a friend of the writer, a gentleman of Provence whose son was about to go from an academy to the court.[22] Another common rhetorical strategy was to insist that the implied reader hardly needed the detailed advice about to be imparted. Thus, Lingard published what he represented as private advice to a nobleman he tutored, and concluded, "he that reflects upon himself and considers his passions, and accommodates himself to the world cannot need many directions."[23] The very existence of published instructions for constituting a genteel self nevertheless challenged the conservative ideology that gentility is created by nature, not by mere training; not surprisingly, Etherege resented such challenges.

A second reason why courtesy literature itself should appear in *The Man of Mode* as a threat is that Etherege wanted to represent Dorimant as natural and English, not as a servile imitator of French manners. Etherege was not comfortable aligning himself simply either with old-fashioned Christian humanist traditions in manners or with contemporary French courtesy literature. Modern fashionable and libertine manners of the town are to be defined in opposition both to Christian humanism and to the court manners of France. In the 1670s even courtesy book writers in the Christian humanist tradition were having difficulty maintaining such elements of their position as the older advocacy of male chastity. Panton soberly tried to advocate at least post-nuptial male chastity, but his syntax seems to fall apart and his position to crumble as his sentence advances: "Do not wrong your Wife, or rather God, by unlawful Loves, especially in your House, so soon as you can be rid of them, they have been the cause of great desolations, and tragick accidents."[24] The idea, advanced by some literary critics, that Etherege wanted to satirize or even criticize Dorimant's loose sexual practices seems to me unsupported by any persuasive evidence. Laura Brown's assertion, for instance, that in *The Man of Mode* "Dorimant's whole represented relationship to his cast mistresses is weighted toward a sympathy for them" strikes me as a peculiar lapse into sentimental humanism for someone who presents herself as a neo-Marxist feminist.[25]

As Etherege sets himself against the pieties of the Christian humanist tradition, so also he wishes to resist appearing a servile imitator of the French court. The English town ideal is to be acquainted with French manners, to incorporate them into English practices, then to efface the incorporation and to proclaim the Englishness and superiority of the result. *The Man of Mode* overtly and repeatedly criticizes, even stigmatizes, the rage for French culture. Sir Car Scrope's prologue immediately declares French fashion unnecessary and asks:

> Of foreign wares, why should we fetch the scum,
> When we can be so richly served at home?

As John Barnard has pointed out in a good recent article, the play's concern with the impact of French language and culture upon English society "can only be read as a reflection of tension present in the audience itself."[26] Even the Shoemaker is an English patriot, doubting that French shoemakers can make better shoes than he can and cursing his rivals: "Damn 'em, caterpillars, let 'em feed upon cabbage" (1. 259–60). The original English courtesy literature of the 1670s also sometimes lamented the power of French fashion and declared its real unimportance. Thus, Lingard observed:

> The mere *Englishman* is supposed to be *defective* in [civilities], as being rough in address, not easily acquainted, and blunt even when he obliges though I think it not worth the charge the *Gentleman* is at that *Travells* for it: Nay I am sorry for the poor return many make, that import hither the *aire* and *courage*, and *assurance* of the *French*, therewith quitting their own staple native commodities of much greater value, the *sincerity* and *generosity* of the *English disposition*.[27]

Certainly Charles II brought back elements of French manners to his court and certainly Etherege at that court and in his own travels in France picked up and valued elements of French sophistication and manners, yet in its original and most authentic form the code of French court manners so carefully developed to promote the rise of the absolutist state was alien to England, mismatched to the needs of London town society, and even remote from the much less formal and distant practices of Charles II himself. As Orest Ranum has pointed out in his study of French court manners, from the late seventeenth century both the English and the Dutch "have been suspicious of courtesy legislated from above for purposes of emptying society of its political rights."[28] English national identity was defined in opposition to French identity on this as on so many other points.

Etherege sees courtesy literature as a threat to his ideology of gentility, not so much because libertine behaviors are condemned by the Christian humanist literature as because the courtesy literature, especially the more recent and particularistic French and English literature, unwittingly exposes the secret that genteel identities can be — and are — produced by training, not by nature. And, we may say, the courtesy literature returned the compliment by its own awareness of being engaged in a contest of discourses with the comedy. Comedy threatened to expose the idealist and romance character of the courtesy literature with its parodic representations of paragons of courtesy and with its own powerful theatrical illusions of glamor and realism. Thus, Panton struggled to distinguish his ideal gentleman from a theatrical simulacrum:

> A Civil man is easily known . . . if you see him come into the company of many, you'll find his hat in his hand with a good grace, his visage free and open, his fashion modest, the carriage of his body comely, without affecting extravagant postures, such as are exposed on the theaters to be derided at. . . .[29]

Feeling the problem closer to the bone, the author of *The Art of Complaisance* observed that the two great subjects of conversation at court and in the theater were love and honor and that "according to these, do some vitious and Mercenary Poets fashion the Character of their compleat Gentlemen." The writer then confessed:

> For half an hour after I had seen a late new Play, whilst the Impression continued, I wished nothing.so much as to be like the two tearing fellows, which the Poet had designed for the Characters of Gentlemen, nor in that mood, would I have exchanged their abilities in drinking and whoring, for all the old fashioned vertues in the world, and I dare say that three parts of the men there present, would have preferd the honor of committing a thousand rapes and adulteries, to the practice of all those sullen virtues which under that name they are taught to abhor. How deplorable a thing is it![30]

What better evidence could there be that both the sober and the comic discourses of manners had real power to constitute human identity?

NOTES

1 Bernard Shaw, *Man and Superman: A Comedy and a Philosophy*, in *Collected Plays with their Prefaces*, 7 vols. (New York: Dodd, Mead & Co., 1970-74), 2:796.
2 Michael Curtin, "A Question of Manners: Status and Gender in Etiquette and Courtesy," *The Journal of Modern History* 57 (1985): 409.
3 Susan Staves, "Where is History but in Texts?: Reading the History of Marriage," in *The Golden and the Brazen World: Papers in Literature and History, 1650-1800*, ed. John Wallace (Berkeley: University of California Press, 1985), 125-44.
4 D. M. R. Wilkinson, *The Comedy of Habit: An Essay on the Use of Courtesy Literature in a Study of Restoration Comic Drama* (Leiden: Universitaire Pers, 1964), 6. A later article also directly relevant here is John C. Hayman, "Dorimant and the Comedy of *The Man of Mode*," *Modern Language Quarterly* 30 (1969):183-97. Hayman argues that Wilkinson fails to recognize the special relevance of French courtesy books to Etherege's play, maintaining,

for instance, that while English moralists condemned dissimulation, the French tended to accept its necessity. Other aids in locating the courtesy books I discuss here were: Gertrude E. Noyes, *Bibliography of Courtesy and Conduct Books in Seventeenth-Century England* (New Haven: Tuttle, Morehouse, and Taylor, 1937) and John E. Mason, *Gentlefolk in the Making: Studies in the History of English Courtesy Literature and Related Topics from 1531 to 1774* (1935; repr., New York: Octagon Books, 1971).

5 Wilkinson, *Comedy of Habit,* 6.

6 Richard Graham Preston, *Anglia Speculum morale; with the several Aspects it beareth to Virtue and Vice* . . . (London, 1670), 8. He combines statements of traditional high humanist ideals with lamentations and details about how some (not all) contemporaries have fallen away from those ideals. Preston, although a Protestant, served James II with such loyalty that he was promoted to the Scots peerage, and, in the reign of William, convicted of Jacobite treason.

7 Curtin, "Question of Manners," 398.

8 For the many incarnations of one of the most popular Italian Renaissance writers, see Antonio Santosuosso, *The Bibliography of Giovanni Della Casa: Books, Readers, Critics, 1537-1975* (Florence: Ulschki, 1979); for a good discussion of later English versions of Eustache Du Refuge's *Traicté de la court* (1616, 1618), see W. Lee Ustick, "The Courtier and the Bookseller: Some Vagaries of Seventeenth-Century Publishing," *Review of English Studies* 5 (1929):143-54.

9 Edward Panton, *Speculum Juventutis: or, A True Mirror; Where Errors in Breeding Noble and Generous Youth, with the Miseries and Mischiefs that usually attend it, are clearly made manifest* (London, 1671), 9. Somewhat similarly, Preston's volume concludes with a "Life of Theodatus" designed to present "The Idea of an exactly accomplished Gentleman" (99), and with three short "novels."

10 Preston, Panton, Walker, and Lingard (mentioned and cited in this article) write within the Christian humanist tradition. Wilkinson, *Comedy of Habit*, and also Mason, *Gentlefolk in the Making*, cited n. 4, provide adequate general descriptions of the Christian humanist courtesy book tradition in England in the seventeenth century.

11 Virgil B. Heltzel, "The Rules of Civility (1671) and its French Source," *Modern Language Notes* 43 (1928): 17-22; W. Lee Ustick, "Seventeenth-Century Books of Conduct: Further Light on Antoine de Courtin and the Rules of Civility," *Modern Language Notes* 44 (1929):148-58.

12 Curtin, "Question of Manners," 399.

13 Sir George Etherege, *The Man of Mode*, ed. John Barnard (New York: W. W. Norton, 1979). References are to act, scene, and line.

14 Ustick, "The Courtier and the Bookseller," 150.

15 Several of these texts are discussed by Max Novak in his important article, "Margery Pinchwife's 'London Disease': Restoration Comedy and the Liber-

tine Offensive of the 1670s," *Studies in the Literary Imagination* 10 (1977):1–24.

16 Panton, *Speculum Juventutis*, 152.

17 Richard Lingard, *A Letter of Advice to a Young Gentleman Leaving the University, Concerning his Behavior and Conversation in the World* (London, 1673), 14; 1st ed. Dublin, 1670. Lingard had been a professor in the University of Dublin and vice-provost of Trinity College, Dublin.

18 Panton, *Speculum Juventutis*, 19.

19 *The Art of Complaisance, or the Means to Oblige in Conversation* (London, 1673), 2; Ustick, "The Courtier and the Bookseller," has pointed out that this book derives from Du Refuge's *Traicté de la court.*

20 Lingard, *Letter of Advice*, 44.

21 Cf. a similar argument made about Renaissance courtesy literature in Frank Whigham, "Interpretation at Court: Courtesy and the Performer-Audience Dialectic," *New Literary History* 14 (1983): 625–39.

22 *The Rules of Civility; or, Certain Ways of deportment observed in France amongst all persons of quality, upon several occasions* (London, 1671), "Advertisement." This book is detailed enough to warn the reader to cut his fingernails and not to "toss or tumble" the ladies (84, 40). To illustrate the point that "customs are not invariant," the writer observes: "Heretofore for example, one might without incivility have hawkt and spit upon the ground before a person of quality; provided he put his foot upon it when he had done; now it is perfect clownishness and intolerable" (153).

23 Lingard, *Letter of Advice*, 5.

24 Panton, *Speculum Juventutis*, 279. Obadiah Walker, a more overtly religious writer, one whose *Of Education, especially of young gentlemen* (Oxford, 1673), is exceptionally sober, seems to me to convey a certain desperation in his advice to tutors on keeping their young men from "debauchery": "But if neither sense of *honour*, which this sin wounds more than any other . . . nor sense of the grievousness of the sin, nor the *expensiveness*, nor *spoiling* his parts, nor danger to his person, nor the *fear of diseases*, nor shortness of life, nor conscience of his duty and virtue, nor emploiment, nor any other remedy will serve; 'tis best to *marry* him" (58). As a noted Oxford tutor, eventually master of University College, Walker no doubt had practical experience of the inefficacy of his prudential and moral advice.

25 Laura Brown, *English Dramatic Form, 1660–1760* (New Haven: Yale University Press, 1981), 45.

26 John Barnard, "Point of View in *The Man of Mode*," *Essays in Criticism* (1984):302.

27 Lingard, *Letter of Advice*, 30.

28 Orest Ranum, "Courtesy, Absolutism, and the Rise of the French State, 1630–1660," *Journal of Modern History* 52 (1980): 426–51.

29 Panton, *Speculum Juventutis*, 150.

30 *The Art of Complaisance*, 64–65.

Derrida, Rousseau, and the Difference

ARAM VARTANIAN

The major part of *De la grammatologie* is a textual analysis in the course of which Derrida "deconstructs" Rousseau's philosophy while constructing his own. To analyze, in our turn, his reading of Rousseau, it will be useful to focus on the pivotal chapter entitled "Ce dangereux supplément," where the hermeneutic assumptions and consequences of "grammatology" are most clearly manifest. We hope that such a study, despite its limited sphere, will prove germane to the broader topics of Derrida's relationship to Rousseau, the validity of his critique of metaphysical reason, and the type of literary criticism that has resulted from his philosophical position.

Derrida realized that Rousseau would be an ideal candidate for interpretation from the standpoint of a theory of language that controverted the age-old "logocentric" primacy, indeed the repressive rule, of speech over writing.[1] Not only did Rousseauism offer an exemplary and culminating instance of the whole culture of logocentrism and the accompanying metaphysics of presence, but the privileging of phonic signs seemed to have found support in its author's *Essai sur l'origine des langues*. The only drawback was that Rousseau had neglected to make his views on language basic, or even particularly important, to his philosophy. To be sure, there was in the *Discours sur l'origine de l'inégalité* a probing account of the development of language and of its long-range impact, along with other factors, on the downward spiral of human history. But that account, besides evaluating the role of speech in moral and sociological terms foreign to Derridean concerns, also omitted the crucial distinction between oral and written modes of expression. Although, in the *Essai sur l'origine des langues*, Rousseau did eventually treat that question, he did so only incidentally; moreover, he did not regard the work central enough to his thought to have it published in his lifetime. Derrida's initial problem, therefore, was somehow to upgrade a marginal, or at least accessory, aspect of Rousseauism into one of its main preoccupations. This appeared feasible by the expedient of forging a bond between its linguistic theory, its actual use of language (or the *écriture* peculiar to it), and the concept of nature recognized unanimously as comprising its core. Derrida thus reread Jean-Jacques's *oeuvre* through the appropriate spectacles, seeking in it a pattern of features that might indicate an overarching nexus between scriptural practice, opinions on language, and metaphysical naturalism.

Derrida found what he was looking for principally in a frequent and symptomatic recurrence of the verb *suppléer* and its substantive *supplément*. What appeared significant in this "système d'écriture" was not just its repetitive character and thematic pertinence but also, he believed, the instability of meaning it betrayed. *Suppléer* could mean "to add to" or "to supplement" as well as "to replace" or "to substitute," while *supplément* meant, in the eighteenth century, both an "addition" and a "substitution" (though in modern French it has come to be used unequivocally, more or less like its English cognate).[2] Derrida's interest in this lexical anomaly was not altogether innocent. He brought to its understanding a presupposition of his own for which Rousseau had given no cause. This was the conviction that language, as now constituted, could be counted on to subvert and negate the entire tradition of philosophy, from Plato to Hegel, which it had been made to embody—an expectation that led Derrida to undertake the dismantling of Western metaphysics by a still untried critical method.

To this end, he discovered in the *supplément*, as a corollary of its semantic vacillation, a logical paradox for which he coined the neologism *supplémentarité*. As a conceptual tool, this corresponded remarkably well to Rousseau's description of nature, whose incoherencies it served at the same time to lay bare. A primordially perfect and self-sufficient nature had, incomprehensibly, been added to and substituted for. Strangely, every addition became, according to the Rousseauist version of history, a diminishment; and every substitution left a new absence. The patent self-contradiction—the "unthinkability," for Derrida—of such a thought-process confirms the fact that "le supplément est ce que ni la nature ni la raison ne peuvent tolérer" (213).[3] Rousseau's philosophy, built on the onto-theological axiom of an original, self-identical, and absolute nature, thus contained the seeds of its own destruction, both logically and linguistically. Catastrophe and decadence, not progress and happiness, were the unfortunate outcome, as nature inexplicably deviated from the total presence it was presumed to be, to a nearly total non-presence, cancelling itself out as both an ideal and a reality. In Derrida's hands, the perverse logic of the *supplément* brings into focus the underlying dilemma of Rousseau's at once natural and unnatural anthropology. Although the difficulties of his metaphysical naturalism have been analyzed along other lines, Derrida exposes them in a manner that had not occurred to anyone else, and that has, besides, the merit of being inscribed (to employ that term literally no less than figuratively) in certain stylistic traits of Rousseau's *écriture*.[4]

However, when Derrida reads that *écriture* by the wavering light of supplementarity in order to decipher its deep philosophical message, the result is less impressive. It becomes necessary, in fact, to distort or ignore the sense of a number of Rousseau's texts so as to make them cooperate with the aim of deconstruction. This, as we shall see, is notably the case with a paradigmatic passage taken from the *Confessions*, in which Jean-Jacques alludes to "ce dangereux supplément"—that is, the vice of masturbation—in a phrase that becomes Derrida's chapter-heading. Onanism thereupon acquires metaphysical significance when Rousseau's sexual "supplement" is said to be qualified, in a neighboring remark, as an "état presque inconcevable à la raison"—a formula meant to characterize also the fate of logocentrism. Similarly, Derrida claims that Rousseau's definition of writing as "un supplément à la parole," cited from another of his works, is evidence that he viewed *écriture*, in opposition to speech, as unnatural, dangerous, and self-destructive, that is, as analogous to masturbation. Thus, writing, metaphysics, and onanism, in the Derridean strategy of reading, become linked deconstructively as manifestations, or referents, of the treacherous *supplément* and are judged accordingly. The verdict is determined in advance by a general statute: "la négativité du mal aura toujours selon Rousseau la forme de la supplémentarité. Le mal est extérieur à une nature, à ce qui est par nature innocent et bon" (208-9).[5]

Because much of this explanatory scheme would have come as news—probably as unwelcome news—to Jean-Jacques, it is imperative that a means be found to affirm that he did not always know what he was saying. For that purpose, too, the *supplément* proves convenient. With its potential for ambiguity in mind, Derrida contends that "le concept de supplément est une sorte de tache aveugle dans le texte de Rousseau, le non-vu qui ouvre et limite la visibilité" (234).[6] He is taxed with hesitancy and carelessness in his handling of that elusive but persistent locution, employing it indistinctly to mean an addition or a substitution, or both: "tout cela ne traduit ni une passivité ni une activité, ni une inconscience ni une lucidité de l'auteur" (234);[7] "il ne s'en sert qu'en se laissant d'une certaine manière et jusqu'à un certain point gouverner par le système" (227).[8] The semantic booby-trap of *suppléer* and *supplément*, a "déjà-là de la langue" planted in his path, causes Rousseau, when he depends on those words, to say something which is "plus, moins ou autre chose que ce qu'il *voudrait dire*" (226).[9]

Before deciding, as a test of Derrida's competency in the matter, the extent to which all this may or may not be true, it should be realized that the ambiguity of *suppléer* and *supplément* is more a fact of lexicology than of communication. Whatever the actual situation might be involving their use, a possible uncertainty of meaning can always be averted by an attentive writer of French. If the object of *suppléer*, or the referent of *supplément* (in its dual eighteenth-century sense), exists in an incomplete or deficient state, then those terms ordinarily signify "to add to" and "addition." If the object or referent is something either absent or in need of replacement, then they mean "to substitute" and "substitution." Thus the impreciseness of the word can be obviated if its context is prepared in such a way that the nature of the subject being discussed or the description of the object to which it applies tells us which reading is appropriate. On the whole, Rousseau was a skillful enough writer to escape the pitfall of that semantic ambivalence, and, whenever it was worth his while to do so, he did.

This can be illustrated immediately with an example proposed by Derrida, who quotes the following fragment from *Emile*: "la sollicitude maternelle ne se supplée point" (209). He finds it to be equivocal: "cela veut dire qu'elle n'a pas à être suppléée: elle suffit et se suffit; mais cela veut dire aussi qu'elle est irremplaçable."[10] The alleged ambiguity makes it possible to catch the idea of nature, and consequently the author of *Emile*, off balance in a moment of "blindness" and inconsistency; for even though nature has presumably made mother-love ("la sollicitude maternelle") a self-sufficient instinct, sometimes it is necessary, as Rousseau himself admits, to replace the natural mother by a wet-nurse to assure the infant's survival. However, if we restore the phrase to its context, which has to do with a key issue of Rousseauist pediatrics—namely, breast-feeding—the confusion disappears.[11] "Ne se supplée point" does not have the alternative meaning of "cannot be added to," because such a statement would, on the face of it, be false. Indeed, "maternal care" is commonly supplemented by other kinds: that of a father, a sibling, a grand-parent, etc. Rousseau's maxim can thus only express a cliché that there is no substitute for a mother. But this does not exclude the possibility, as the passage makes clear, of a surrogate mother replacing the natural one, although Rousseau strongly believes that, for the well-being of society, the woman who satisfies the unreplaceable need in question ought to be the biological mother. As for mother's milk, that too is substitutable, because cow's milk will also serve the purpose, and often even better. What, in the phrase, is non-substitutable is the child's experience of being loved and nurtured by someone it takes to be its mother. Far from remaining unsure of his discourse, Rousseau, who had never enjoyed that advantage, knew only too well what he was talking about. He spent his life in a vain search for substitutes — including, out of desperation, "nature" herself ("O nature! ô ma mère! me voici sous ta seule garde") — and learned, to his chagrin, that "la sollicitude maternelle ne se supplée point."

As other cases of Rousseau's use of *suppléer* and *supplément* are encountered, we shall comment in passing on whether or not they betray a mental servitude or blind-spot on his part to that lexical element. Meanwhile, it should be pointed out that the ambiguity of *supplément*, even if it did typify his *écriture*, would be irrelevant to the ruination of his idea of nature. For whether an originally unmediated, flawless, and self-contained nature is "added to" or "substituted for," the result can only be a calamity. To modify an absolute in any way is to play havoc with it.

Derrida makes a connection, as already noted, between masturbation and writing in Rousseau's *oeuvre* by juxtaposing the reference to "ce dangereux supplément" in the *Confessions* with another passage where the same telltale word turns up. The passage runs: "Les langues sont faites pour être parlées, l'écriture ne sert que de supplément à la parole. . . . La parole représente la pensée par des signes conventionnels, et l'écriture représente de même la parole. Ainsi l'art d'écrire n'est qu'une représentation médiate de la pensée" (207).[12] This is one of a group of detached dicta under the rubric "Prononciation," which the author neither elaborated into a finished work, nor incorporated into the *Origine des langues* (if that had been at first his intention). In quoting Rousseau's words, Derrida wishes to persuade the reader not only that they advert to writing as a "dangereux supplément" like masturbation, but that they disparage written language as a "représentation médiate" twice removed from the truth of nature. But even if this were so, there is no suggestion of danger, nor of anything at all sinister or degenerate, in Rousseau's bland remark. Derrida feels obliged to furnish such a characterization — *en supplément*, so to speak — with his own comment on the text: "L'écriture est dangereuse dés lors que la représentation veut s'y donner pour la présence et le signe pour la chose même. Et il y a une nécessité fatale, inscrite dans le fonctionnement même du signe. . . ."[13]

Incidentally, Rousseau would seem here to view writing as a supplement to speech — something extra — rather than as a substitute for it. No doubt, writing could also replace speech, as it ordinarily does. But the context indicates that Rousseau is not concerned with that aspect of the problem. He is comparing two linguistic media, and the point of his comparison is that, whereas speech is more natural and universal ("Les langues sont faites pour être parlées"), language may, in addition, be written. There is no lack of discursive control in the passage. But especially revealing about Derrida's method of reading is the fact that, in the quoted portion of "Prononciation," the words "l'écriture ne sert que de supplément à la parole" are followed, after several suspension dots, by a section that ends with a definition of writing as "une représentation médiate de la pensée." This intimates that Rousseau's definition makes explicit his antecedent use of *supplément*, and that the two statements constitute a single meaning. Now, if we look at the text itself of "Prononciation," we notice that the two parts of the quoted passage occur in separate fragments; that these, being interrupted by others, do not form a thought-sequence; and that the notion of writing as a "représentation médiate" precedes, and therefore does not amplify, the reference to writing as a *supplément* (2:1249). In short, Derrida takes as much liberty with the physical state as with the sense of Rousseau's text.

He does, nonetheless, trace an ingenious parallel, on phenomenological grounds, between masturbation and writing: "Le supplément qui 'trompe la nature' maternelle opère comme l'écriture, et comme elle il est dangereux pour la vie. . . . De même que l'écriture ouvre la crise de la parole vive à partir de son 'image' . . . l'onanisme annonce la ruine de la vitalité à partir de la séduction imaginative" (216).[14] Masturbation is thus an act which the imagination substitutes for sexual intercourse, just as writing is a substitutive imagery for the verbal intercourse of speech. In both cases, the individual, whether writer or masturbator, is alone, and the imagined partner or "receiver" is absent. The analogy invites further development, from which Derrida discreetly refrained. In writing as in masturbation (seen from the male perspective), there is a solitary agent taking pleasure in the manipulation of a stylus/phallus which emits fluid . . . and so forth. Onanism may thus be considered an allegory of writing and, conversely, writing an allegory of onanism. "Dans la chaîne des suppléments," declares Derrida, "il n'était pas facile de séparer l'écriture de l'onanisme" (235).[15] Thanks to this rapprochement, it is inferred that "Rousseau considère l'écriture comme un moyen dangereux, un secours menaçant" (207), and as "une violence faite à la destinée naturelle de la langue;" that he "condamne l'écriture comme destruction de la présence et comme maladie de la parole" (204), framing "un réquisitoire contre la négativité de la lettre, en laquelle il faut lire la dégénérescence de la culture et la disruption de la communauté" (207); and finally that "ce type de supplément dangereux qu'on appelle masturbation . . . on ne peut pas [le] dissocier de son activité d'écrivain [i.e., Rousseau's]" (224).[16]

How much of all this is textually verifiable? In fact, Rousseau said none of these things. He denounced language, it is true, as an instrument of sociability, competitiveness, civilization, and therefore of moral depravity; but when he did so in the *Discours sur l'inégalité*, he had in mind only speech and did not even mention writing, much less regard it as a "disease of speech." And when he discussed the invention of writing in the *Origine des langues*, he was no longer interested in language as a cause of humanity's fall from natural grace, but in its material evolution and its affinities with other forms of communication, especially music.[17] The degree of mediation proper to the use of signs in written as compared to spoken language was not an issue that preoccupied Rousseau, and so he never made a philosophically significant distinction between *écriture* and *parole*. He did recognize certain differences, and the relative advantages or disadvantages, of speech viewed separately from writing. But these differences, which have nothing to do with ontology or ethics, remain essentially at the level of rhetoric. He saw writing as better suited to precision, objectiveness, and clarity of expression, while speech lent itself to greater eloquence, feeling, vivacity, and energy — a judgment which, now as then, amounts to a truism. Rousseau certainly preferred the latter qualities to the former, finding them also more "natural." But his comparison did not denigrate *écriture* as dangerous, sick, destructive, decadent, or masturbatory. Insofar as these terms pertain to language, they are Derrida's, not Rousseau's, categories.

The only evidence we are left with, then, to justify the equation that speech is to writing as sexual intercourse is to masturbation in Rousseau's works is his choice of the word *supplément* to designate both onanism and *écriture*. This, at first glance, is not overwhelming proof. But, on second thought, it is even less convincing. For we recognize that the lexical concordance in question was an isolated case in a vast literary output. It occurs, moreover, in two texts that have thematically nothing in common and were composed years apart. The function of *supplément* is dissimilar in the two occurrences: in the *Confessions*, it serves as a euphemism to avoid the offensive mention of "masturbation;" in "Prononciation," it is to be understood literally. We also know, thanks to Derrida, that Jean-Jacques had a weakness for the terms *suppléer* and *supplément*. But it should be obvious that the more a writer reverts to a particular expression, the less important its appearance in unrelated contexts becomes, and the harder it is to attach a special motive to its random combinations. Everything leads one to believe, in the absence of a more specific linkage, that Rousseau's reference to *supplément* to describe both writing and masturbation was coincidental. It strains credibility to suppose that, when he invoked the concept of substitution to characterize onanism in the *Confessions*, some associative process — whether conscious, unconscious, literal, metaphorical, causative, analogical, or other — drew his mind back to the concept of addition with which he had once characterized writing in "Prononciation." On the other hand, it is eminently plausible to assume that because Derrida had already decided that writing, like masturbation, is a pathological deviation from the plenitude of natural presence, he managed somehow to read such an associative process into Rousseau's texts.

Derrida takes for granted that the "non-logic" of supplementarity deconstructs, in Rousseau's "système d'écriture," his "système de métaphysique." He argues the point by a close analysis of the indispensable passage in the *Confessions* where "ce dangereux supplément" figures *as text*. Since, in the act of quoting, Derrida fractures it into three pieces and then rearranges these, we shall begin by giving the full passage as Rousseau wrote it:

> Je ne finirais pas si j'entrais dans le détail de toutes les folies que le souvenir de cette chère Maman me faisait faire, quand je n'étais plus sous ses yeux. Combien de fois j'ai baisé mon lit en songeant qu'elle y avait couché, mes rideaux, tous les meubles de ma chambre en songeant
> 5 qu'ils étaient à elle, que sa belle main les avait touchés, le plancher même sur lequel je me prosternais en songeant qu'elle y avait marché. Quelquefois même en sa présence il m'échappait des extravagances que le plus violent amour seul semblait pouvoir inspirer. Un jour à table, au moment qu'elle avait mis un morceau dans sa bouche, je m'écrie que j'y
> 10 vois un cheveu: elle rejette le morceau sur son assiette, je m'en saisis avidement et l'avale. En un mot, de moi à l'amant le plus passionné, il n'y avait qu'une différence unique, mais essentielle, et qui rend mon état presque inconcevable à la raison.
> J'étais revenu d'Italie, not tout à fait comme j'y étais allé; mais
> 15 comme peut-être jamais à mon âge on n'en est revenu. J'en avais rapporté non ma virginité, mais mon pucelage. J'avais senti le progrès des ans; mon tempérament inquiet s'était enfin déclaré, et sa première éruption, très involontaire, m'avait donné sur ma santé des alarmes qui peignent mieux que toute autre chose l'innocence dans laquelle j'avais
> 20 vécu jusqu'alors. Bientôt rassuré j'appris ce dangereux supplément qui trompe la nature et sauve aux jeunes gens de mon humeur beaucoup de désordres aux dépens de leur santé, de leur vigueur et quelquefois de leur vie. Ce vice que la honte et la timidité trouvent si commode, a de

plus un grand attrait pour les imaginations vives; c'est de disposer pour
25 ainsi dire à leur gré de tout le sexe, et de faire servir à leurs plaisirs la
beauté qui les tente sans avoir besoin d'obtenir son aveu. Séduit par ce
funeste avantage je travaillais à détruire la bonne constitution qu'avait
rétablie en moi la nature, et à qui j'avais donné le temps de se bien
former. Qu'on ajoute à cette disposition le local de ma situation
30 présente, logé chez une jolie femme, caressant son image au fond de
mon coeur, la voyant sans cesse dans la journée; le soir entouré d'objets
qui me la rappellent, couché dans un lit où je sais qu'elle a couché. Que
de stimulants! tel lecteur qui se les représente me regarde déjà comme à
demi mort. Tout au contraire; ce qui devait me perdre fut précisément
35 ce qui me sauva, du moins pour un temps. Enivré du charme de vivre
auprès d'elle, du désir ardent d'y passer mes jours, absente ou présente
je voyais toujours en elle une tendre mère, une soeur chérie, une
délicieuse amie, et rien de plus. Je la voyais toujours ainsi, toujours la
même, et ne voyais jamais qu'elle. Son image toujours présente à mon
40 coeur n'y laissait place à nulle autre; elle était pour moi la seule femme
qui fût au monde, et l'extrême douceur des sentiments qu'elle
m'inspirait ne laissant pas à mes sens le temps de s'éveiller pour d'autres,
me garantissait d'elle et de tout son sexe. En un mot, j'étais sage parce
que je l'aimais. Sur ces effets que je rends mal, dise qui pourra de quelle
45 espèce était mon attachement pour elle. Pour moi tout ce que j'en puis
dire est que s'il paraît déjà fort extraordinaire, dans la suite il le paraîtra
beucoup plus.[18] (1:108–9)

Derrida's misreading of this passage so central to his argument has
been the subject of a recent study.[19] In what follows I will assimilate the
author's critical remarks to my own perspective while enlarging on them.
The tactic by which Derrida tries to get the text to yield what he suspects
to be its secret is to single out and blow up the connection he finds
between Rousseau's mention of "mon état presque inconcevable à la
raison" (lines 12–13) and that of "ce dangereux supplément" (line 20).
This conflating is meant to show that the *supplément* as masturbation, a
substitute/addition which paradoxically subverts and impoverishes the
sexual act it is expected to compensate for and supplement, is as intolerable to reason as it is contrary to nature; supplementarity is not only
destructive of nature but "dangereux pour la raison." Derrida asserts, on
the force of this symmetry, that Rousseau's reference to "ce dangereux
supplément" is intended to "expliquer, précisément, 'un état presque
inconcevable à la raison' " (214), that is, it confirms the dereliction of
metaphysical reasoning based on the principle of "identité à soi."[20] It is
said, in regard to Jean-Jacques's bizarre behavior depicted in the first
paragraph, that "la découverte du dangereux supplément sera ensuite
citée parmi ces 'folies' " (219), as a privileged and crowning example of
what reason is powerless to conceive. Now such a reading is plainly in
error, because the young Rousseau's discovery of masturbation, as the

story has it, took place earlier in Italy, not during the period of the "folies" induced by the proximity of Mme de Warens after his return to her home in Chambéry. The author even makes a rueful joke about this to the effect that, unlike every other youth who went to Italy, his only sexual experience while there consisted in learning to masturbate. Because he came back from Italy still technically a "virgin" ("j'en avais rapporté . . . mon pucelage," lines 15-16), it is also evident that his use of "dangereux supplément" is not at all ambiguous: in context, *supplément* can only mean "substitute," inasmuch as Jean-Jacques at this stage was not yet involved in any sexual activity other than masturbation. Furthermore, the "folies" that he enacted out of love for "Maman" are all fetishistic rather than onanistic. In brief, Derrida misses (or distorts) the apparent sense of the passage when he states that, among the various "folies" described, Rousseau evokes his recourse to masturbation as "une sorte d'explication de l'état inconcevable à la raison" (219).

Actually, the locution "mon état presque inconcevable à la raison"—which Derrida keeps repeating as if it were an axiom negating the validity of ontological knowledge—merely recapitulates what precedes it in the paragraph. Far from anything so grand as the bankruptcy of the metaphysics of presence, it sums up Rousseau's incestuously colored feelings for Mme de Warens, which were long an obstacle to their sexual liaison, and evokes the kind of non-sexual but passionate union, complete with a whole gamut of fetishistic antics, that meanwhile he dreamed of realizing with her. The "unique" (in both senses of the French word) difference between him and "l'amant le plus passionné" (line 11) was that Jean-Jacques, living in the intimacy of a woman he adored, neither desired nor attempted to sleep with her. This strange reluctance is what made his state "presque inconcevable à la raison," that is, "incomprehensible." Indeed, many will agree that, even after two hundred years, it probably would still not be comprehended if not for the help of psychoanalysis.

But even graver, the locution is not connected in the manner imagined by Derrida to the confession of "ce dangereux supplément" in the next paragraph, although, to suggest the relationship he wants between them, he inverts the order of the passage. In first quoting lines 14-23, followed a couple of pages later by the quotation of lines 1-13, Derrida makes it appear that Rousseau referred initially to the "dangereux supplément" and then unfolded—or rather, unconsciously betrayed—its deep philosophical meaning by admitting that it constituted, as part of a series of "folies," "un état inconcevable à la raison." But just the opposite is true. After the account of his sexless idyll with Mme de Warens, Rousseau introduces the theme of masturbation as a contrasting train of events and thoughts. He does this so as to make the point that, given the stimulus of his love for that lady and his residing under the same roof with her, one might have expected him, for lack of any other sexual release, to yield uncontrollably to the onanistic habits he had already acquired. Yet we are told that, paradoxically, his exalted emotions purged him, at least for a time, of all active erotic desire for "Maman" or for any other woman, and consequently of the need for self-abuse ("Tout au contraire, ce qui devait me perdre . . . etc.," lines 34–35). Thus, the meaning of "inconcevable à la raison" and that of "ce dangereux supplément," instead of being mutually corroborative, exclude each other. There is opposition, not agreement, in Rousseau's mind between masturbation as a damaging substitute for sexual intercourse and the fetishistic effects of his desexualized ideal passion. The "état presque inconcevable à la raison" at the end of the first paragraph has its rhetorical echo, not in the "dangereux supplément," but in his description of what he felt for Mme de Warens as "déjà fort extraordinaire" (line 46) at the end of the second paragraph.[21] With Freudian hindsight, it can now be supposed that, as a result of the incest taboo, Jean-Jacques's sexual yearnings for "Maman" had been sublimated ("je voyais toujours en elle une tendre mére, une soeur chérie, une délicieuse amie, et rien de plus," lines 37–38) into a temporary fit of fetishism rather than being expressed through either real or imaginary (onanistic) intercourse with her. If this text from the *Confessions* exposes a blind-spot, it is the author's unawareness of the sexual nature of his "folies." The "folies" were actually a harmless *supplément* of the "dangereux supplément"; what the passage exemplifies, if correctly understood, is the *supplément* of a *supplément*, which turns out to be, all in all, a good — even a "life-saving" — expedient. It is this more complex structure of the *supplément* — which may be called supplementarity raised to the second degree — that defines, as we shall learn, the general economy of that conceptual as well as scriptural feature of Rousseauistic philosophy.

Derrida misconstrues "ce dangereux supplément" in yet another sense that has to do more with "dangereux" than with "supplément." In that formula, "dangereux" describes neither an inherent property nor an empirical correlate of "supplément." If masturbation is dangerous in Rousseau's judgment, this is so not because it is a "substitute" for something better, richer in "natural presence"; the danger is not in the act of mediation, as it is for Derrida. For Rousseau not only is there no necessary relation between *supplément* and its modifier, but the expression he uses is a periphrasis — a "rhetorical *supplément*" — for the blunt but crude word that it leaves unspoken. "Dangereux supplément" was one of the possible ways of alluding politely — imprecisely — to masturbation; as such, it could hardly be expected to disclose the essential nature of that vice. If Rousseau preferred the circumlocution, his choice is sufficiently explained by his lexical preference.[22] In reality, the full passage indicates that he regarded onanism as dangerous for quite mundane reasons, which were based on the medical opinion of the age. The debilitating and life-threatening effects ascribed to self-abuse had been widely and often luridly popularized — an example being Diderot's *Encyclopédie* article on the subject — and Rousseau, a notorious hypochondriac, took the warnings more seriously than most of his contemporaries. But one need hardly insist that if eighteenth-century doctors viewed masturbation as a particularly morbid practice, their motive for doing so was not that it took the place of normal intercourse with a partner; their clinical perception had led them, instead, to conclude that onanism, because of the unrestraint it encouraged, had driven some of its victims to such excess that health and even survival had been sacrificed. Rousseau's text leaves little doubt ("Que de stimulants! tel lecteur qui se les représente me regarde déjà comme à demi mort," lines 32–34) that he considered the *supplément* to be "dangereux," not because metaphysically it was "inconcevable à la raison," but because physically it could squander beyond all reason sexual energy and vital forces.

Derrida's own interest in the "dangereux supplément" also deflects his attention from the real ambiguity of that theme as it is exposed by Rousseau in the text before us, which sets forth two incompatible attitudes. On the one hand, masturbation is contrary to nature and perilous to well-being; but on the other, it is a preservative of sexual virtue ("[qui] sauve aux jeunes gens de mon humeur beaucoup de désordres," lines 21–22); and, especially for those of Jean-Jacques's timid but ardent temperament, it offers a sure, convenient, and even imperious access to erotic enjoyment ("ce vice . . . a de plus un grand attrait pour les imaginations vives; c'est de disposer . . . à leur gré de tout le sexe, et de faire servir à leurs plaisirs la beauté qui les tente sans avoir besoin d'obtenir son aveu," lines 23–26). The ambivalence between a "chaste" sexlife *à la Louis XV* and one that menaces life itself is crystallized in the oxymoron "ce funeste avantage" (line 27), which is more relevant than "ce dangereux supplément" to the elucidation of this passage, because it reveals a deeper level of Rousseau's "confession" about his onanism. The perversity and harmfulness of that vice (summed up by the adjective "funeste") reflect, of course, the public view; its supposed benefits both moral and affective (summed up by the noun "avantage") express Rousseau's own original sentiment. The place of onanism in his life, thought, and writing is not a simple matter of negativity, as Derrida would have it. If Rousseau was never able, as he admitted, to break that bad habit, the reason for his inability was not merely psychological or "practical." There is a sense in which the concept of masturbation was in profound harmony with his philosophical outlook. For, in Rousseauism, the idealization of an asocial, self-sufficient nature and human nature rhymed, logically, with the solitary vice of the *promeneur solitaire* for whom the optimum happiness was to "jouir de soi-même."

Because Derrida believes that the role of supplementarity coincides with a negative, deficient, or otherwise unnatural state of affairs implied in Rousseau's writings, he misinterprets, through his own "substitutive" readings, various texts in which "suppléer" and "supplément" signify a positive and natural outcome. We shall consider three such cases. Derrida sees nothing less than a "scandal" in a statement from *Emile* which, to him, indicates that nature inversely (therefore perversely) "devient le supplément de l'art et de la société. C'est le moment où le mal paraît incurable" (211-12).[23] The remark by Rousseau that earns this dire appreciation is: "Faute de savoir se guérir, que l'enfant sache être malade; cet art supplée à l'autre, et souvent réussit beaucoup mieux; c'est l'art de la nature."[24] The context in *Emile* (4:271) clarifies the meaning of this somewhat enigmatic sentence, which is that, when one is sick, it is often better, instead of relying on the man-made art of medicine, to adopt the right disposition toward illness, as animals do instinctively; in other words, that one "know how to be sick"—a "natural art" which can restore the body to health. In this typically Rousseauist prescription for disease, nature is considered *a more effective substitute* for medical science, and there is absolutely nothing scandalous, explicitly or implicitly, in such a switching of therapeutic roles. On the contrary, it is urged as a wise and salutary step.

Derrida also selects, from the *Dialogues*, a passage in which Rousseau confides that his enthusiasm for botanizing was actually a substitute for the normal human ties that were denied him: "La contemplation de la nature eut toujours un très grand attrait pour son coeur; il y trouvait un supplément aux attachements dont il avait besoin [a "replacement," not an addition]; mais il eût laissé le supplément pour la chose, s'il en avait eu le choix, et il ne se réduisit à converser avec les plantes qu'après de vains efforts pour converser avec des humains" (1:794).[25] Derrida exclaims triumphantly: "Que la botanique devienne le supplément de la société, c'est là plus qu'une catastrophe. C'est la catastrophe de la catastrophe" (212).[26] Thus a constraint which for Rousseau was a *pis aller*, a less desirable alternative, has become, for Derrida, the worst of all possible disasters. Yet the text says only that the company of plants was to the friendless and persecuted author a "substitute" preferable to complete solitude. Derrida does bring forward next a quotation from the *Rêveries* which depicts the mining industry of the late eighteenth century in language that prefigures Zola's *Germinal*, and here "supplément" is indeed linked to catastrophic consequences. But this second text, in which Rousseau condemns the inhuman price of economic progress, is a perfect *non sequitur* with respect to the preceding one about the substitutive pleasures of botany. An interpretive comment that is applicable to one text would seem here, by a logic of mere adjacency, to be applied to another juxtaposed, but otherwise unrelated, text.

Finally, Derrida appeals to a page from the *Confessions* where Thérèse is described as a replacement for "Maman" (who, as we know, was herself a replacement for the real mother Jean-Jacques never had). The latter states: "Quand j'étais absolument seul mon coeur était vide, mais il n'en fallait qu'un pour le remplir. Le sort m'avait ôté, m'avait aliéné du moins en partie, celui pour lequel la nature m'avait fait. Dès lors j'étais seul, car il n'y eut jamais pour moi d'intermédiaire entre tout et rien. Je trouvais dans Thérèse le supplément [patently, the substitute] dont j'avais besoin" (1:332).[27] In Derrida's version of this, Thérèse as a *supplément* "tient ici le milieu entre l'absence et la présence totales. . . . Mais Rousseau enchaîne comme si le recours au supplément — ici à Thérèse — allait apaiser son impatience devant l'intermédiaire. . . . La virulence de ce concept [i.e. intermediacy] est ainsi apaisée, comme si on avait pu l'*arraisonner*, le domestiquer, l'apprivoiser" (226).[28] But in the text of the *Confessions*, there is not a hint of any indecisive and self-deluding "as if," no mention at all of being in an anguished state between total presence and total absence, and no "virulence" to appease. All these alleged ingredients of the passage amount to a "supplementary" meaning that Derrida wants it to convey. Rousseau tells us unequivocally, with a firm hold on his discourse, that for him there never was, in matters of the heart, a "compromise between all and nothing," and that Thérèse turned out happily to be just the *supplément* for Mme de Warens that he craved. The substitute is here envisaged as a satisfactory solution to an "all or nothing" predicament, and, like nature itself, as the fulfillment of a vital human longing. It is hard to see how, in such a passage, the negative economy of the "chaîne des suppléments" could be said to determine Rousseau's writing.

What conclusion can be drawn, then, about the "système d'écriture" which Derrida maintains is patterned on the underlying illogic of "ce dangereux supplément?" The texts adduced and analyzed by him fail to prove that Rousseau's writing, and therefore his unconscious thinking, took shape under the influence of a blind-spot detectable in his incapacity to master the intricacies of *suppléer* and *supplément*.[29] Judging from Derrida's own examples — to which many more could be added that are even less compatible with his method of reading—there is no reason to assume that Rousseau fell into an ambush laid for him by the French language. He was alert to the possible confusion, semantic and conceptual, lurking in *suppléer* and *supplément*, and, on every occasion thus far studied, he managed to discriminate between an addition and a substitution. He also employed those terms, in accordance with what his purpose might be, to designate either a negative or a positive result. There is nothing intrinsically illogical, or "inconcevable à la raison," in the ordinary belief that a substitute or an additive, depending on the circumstances, could be either a good or a bad thing. Even if the caveat "accept no substitutes" were justified in its usual sense, the replacement of a replacement, like the negation of a negation, can mean reversion to an original authenticity or "presence." This is in general how Rousseau understood and why he favored the notion of *supplément*. On the one hand, additions to, or substitutions for, nature had perilous and destructive effects, alienating the individual from the immediacy of his origins and from the true source of his well-being. But, on the other hand, when this "dangereux supplément" was itself replaced by something that Rousseau saw as answering a need or rectifying a fault, then there took place a "return to nature"—not in any absolute degree, of course, but quite beneficial nevertheless—which repaired an existing breach in the unity of being and reinstated consciousness in a zone closer to its primordial plenitude.[30]

If the incidence of "suppléer" and "supplément" in Rousseau's *oeuvre* is surveyed more thoroughly than Derrida has done, a quite divergent picture emerges from the one he has sketched. The works in which the "danger" and "negativity" of the *supplément* could be expected to show up most are, doubtless, the *Discours sur les sciences et les arts* and the *Discours sur l'origine de l'inégalité*, for it is there that Rousseau articulated the substance of his credo that the purity and perfection of nature had been corrupted by additions and substitutions. Yet the crucial word (as either verb or noun) does not occur germanely in the *First Discourse*. It occurs three times in the *Second Discourse*. But of these three, one is axiologically neutral, and the other two imply just the opposite of the disastrous consequences that Derrida would have us anticipate. One passage affirms: "L'homme sauvage, livré par la nature au seul instinct, ou plutôt dédommagé de celui qui lui manque peut-être par des facultés capables d'y suppléer d'abord et de l'élever ensuite fort au-dessus de celle-là, commencera donc par les fonctions purement animales" (3:142–43).[31] Here the "dédommagement"—a substitute for instinct rather than a supplementation of it—proved at first adequate and later raised the human species "far above nature," by converting a mere animal into a moral and rational being. The other illustration says: "Le droit civil étant ainsi devenu la règle commune des citoyens, la loi de nature n'eut plus lieu qu'entre les diverses sociétés, où, sous le nom de droit des gens, elle fut tempérée par quelques conventions tacites pour rendre le commerce possible et suppléer à la commisération naturelle, qui, perdant de société à société presque toute la force qu'elle avait d'homme à homme. . . ." (3:178).[32] Again, the meaning of "suppléer" is not uncertain: international law replaced "natural pity" in dealings among peoples, and the substitute would appear to have achieved its goal well enough. It would be easy to multiply instances where the *supplément* signifies for Rousseau an improvement or advantage, a good rather than an evil.[33]

Derrida's chapter on "Ce dangereux supplément" brings to the support of his interpretation of Rousseau's "système d'écriture" no more than a dozen uses of "suppléer" and "supplément." As a statistical sample, this is inadequate for a rigorously empirical study, which would have many more occurrences to consider. The works that Derrida has consulted from the standpoint of the concept of supplementarity would appear to include: *Discours sur les sciences et les arts*; *Discours sur l'origine de l'inégalité*; *La Nouvelle Héloïse*; *Du Contrat social*; *Emile*; *Essai sur l'origine des langues*; *Les Confessions*; *Les Dialogues*; *Rêveries du promeneur solitaire*. Limiting ourselves to this minimal canon, we count at least ninety-three instances of "suppléer" and "supplément." In the vast majority of them, there is no ambiguity of meaning; and if, occasionally, there is, nothing important is at stake. The same data reveal that Rousseau habitually employed "suppléer" and "supplément" to describe situations of both a positive and a negative character (where those criteria are applicable), and actually more often the former than the latter. In any event, he seems to have been under no compulsion to obey Derrida's problematic of supplementarity.

It is surely correct to view Rousseau as a writer preoccupied by substitutive thinking; and Derrida is right to claim for his own "interprétation du supplément": "Nous sommes sûrs que quelque chose d'irréductiblement rousseauiste y est capturé" (231).[34] But the corresponding "système d'écriture" is much more flexible, and even more dialectical, than he gives it credit for being. To perceive in the "chaîne des suppléments" a hermeneutic passkey to Rousseau's thought and writing is but another way of acknowledging that, compared even to the other philosophes, he felt unusually dissatisfied with the world as it was in eighteenth-century France. He rationalized that feeling, and the strong desire for change it aroused, into a historical and anthropological thesis. A long series of substitutions and additions had degraded a primitive and providential order into an unacceptable, though still reversible, disorder. The logic behind this scheme of explanation was that it legitimated, indeed required, new substitutions, additions, and compensations that would salvage what was still salvageable from the global wreck of nature. An extraordinary resolve to transform reality in keeping with the dictates of his heart was the *raison d'être* of Jean-Jacques's nostalgia for a hypothetical "state of nature," whose *présence à soi* and absolute authority, like those of God, became for him an inexhaustible source of protests, denunciations, and regenerative plans. His openness to a certain discourse of supplementarity was the product, not so much of a "système d'écriture," as of a "système de pensée," for a philosophy is determined by linguistic factors mainly to the extent that it is difficult to think, and impossible to do so abstractly, without language. Recourse to the *supplément* had the advantage of expressing both nostalgia for what was felt to be absent and a wish for what might be made present. It is consistent with Rousseauism to take *suppléer* and *supplément* as signifying, alongside their concept of danger, loss, and decadence, the complementary concept of hope, recuperation, and reform. Was there, in fact, a philosophe of the Enlightenment more eager than Rousseau to *substitute* for the existing morality and sociopolitical arrangements a whole new set of actualities that would promote his own—and therefore everyone's—pursuit of happiness?

Self-contradiction in thinking as in expression proceeds less from disparate meanings ensconced in words, metaphors, rhetorical conventions, and syntactic structures; or even from the ultimate incommensurability between signs and either things or thoughts—although, admittedly, it results frequently enough from all those causes. The more fundamental cause of self-contradiction is the difference between what we want objects and acts—including, of course, their manifestations in texts, writing, and reading—to mean and what, left to themselves, they continue obstinately to say in defiance of our designs upon them. Like perhaps all creative philosophers, Derrida is not above playing tricks on the dead. This is quite proper, in a sense, for philosophy would be immobilized without it. Every original thinker is, by definition, more interested in fabricating his own conceptual universe than in elucidating someone else's; so that for him the history of ideas is a storehouse of building materials to be used as he sees fit. Derrida's reading of Rousseau derives less from any "déjà là de la langue" than from a philosophical "déjà là" that seeks to elicit from a corpus of texts a special configuration of nature, logocentrism, supplementarity, masturbation, and written in contrast to oral language. The configuration he finds—or, in his own more accurate term, "produces"—is thus conditioned necessarily by misreading. In the end, his explication of Rousseau affirms more about itself than about its "subject" — a self-referential outcome that was perhaps to be foreseen if, as he himself postulates: "il n'y a pas de hors-texte" (227). Even so, as an interpretive strategy the notion of *supplémentarité* allows Derrida to dissect neatly and in depth the entire negative aspect of Rousseauist doctrine, or its answer to the question: what has gone wrong with society and the individual? But the *supplément*, if confined within these boundaries, fails to engage the positive aspect of Rousseau's thought, or his answer to the more fateful question: what can and should be done to put matters right? Moreover, the *supplément* works well hermeneutically as long as it espouses, in philosophical terms, the vision it analyzes. Yet a much larger demand is placed on it by Derrida, for it is expected, both as a semantic given and as a personal peculiarity of writing, also to generate and, at the same time, to undercut a logocentric system of ideas called Rousseauism. In attempting to satisfy such a demand by a novel method of reading, Derrida has deconstructed, not Rousseau's, but his own construction.

NOTES

1 "Il s'agit de reconnaître une articulation décisive de l'époque logocentrique. Pour cette reconnaissance, Rousseau nous a paru être un très bon révélateur"; Jacques Derrida, *De la grammatologie* (Paris: Editions de Minuit, 1967), 231. References to this work will be given in the body of the article.

2 In the seventeenth century, *supplément* still denoted a "replacement" and "substitute" as well as a "supplement." During the following century, that usage became obsolete, and standard dictionaries — such as Diderot's *Encyclopédie* and the *Dictionnaire de l'Académie française* (editions of 1762 and 1799) — list the word as having only the sense of an addition or supplement. Its utilization by Rousseau to mean a substitution thus had a slightly archaic flavor. The verb-form "suppléer" has kept, however, its ambiguity to the present day.

3 "The *supplément* is something that neither nature nor reason can tolerate." I will keep "supplément" in the original wherever its special ambivalence, as emphasized by Derrida, makes it untranslatable into English.

4 His success may be compared, methodologically, to that of Jean Starobinski. While the latter interprets Rousseau in reference to a criterion of *visibility* (transparence and opaqueness), Derrida does so in reference to one of *compensability* (addition and substitution).

5 "The negativity of evil will always take, according to Rousseau, the form of supplementarity. Evil is exterior to the nature of a thing, to what is by nature innocent and good."

6 "The concept of *supplément* is a sort of blind spot in Rousseau's text, the unseen that makes possible and restricts visibility."

7 "All this expresses neither passivity nor activity, neither unawareness nor lucidity on the author's part."

8 "He only makes use of it while allowing himself to be, in a certain manner and to a certain point, governed by the system." We are told also that the chameleon-like *supplément* is "à l'oeuvre dans les textes de Rousseau . . . Mais l'inflexion varie d'un moment à l'autre. Chacune des deux significations s'efface à son tour ou s'estompe discrètement devant l'autre" (208).

9 "More, less, or other than what he *would like to say*." His troubles are attributed to the general discrepancy, in all language, between *signifié* and *signifiant*: "l'écrivain écrit *dans* une langue et *dans* une logique dont, par définition, son discours ne peut dominer absolument le système, les lois et la vie propres" (227).

10 "This means that there is no need to add to it, because it suffices and is self-sufficient; but this also means that it is unreplaceable."

11 Rousseau, *Oeuvres complètes* (Paris: Bibliothèque de la Pléiade), 3: 257. Reference will henceforth be made to this edition.

12 "Languages are made to be spoken; writing serves only as a supplement to speech. . . . Speech represents thought by means of conventional signs, and writing represents speech in the same way. Thus the art of writing is nothing but a mediated representation of thought." This statement, be it said in passing, is garbled beyond intelligibility in the translation of *De la grammatologie* by Gayatri Chakravorty Spivak (Baltimore: The Johns Hopkins Press, 1976), 144.

13 "Writing is dangerous from the moment that representation claims to be presence and the sign the thing itself. And there is a fatal necessity, inscribed in the very functioning of the sign. . . ."

14 "The *supplément* which 'cheats mother nature' operates like writing, and like writing it is dangerous to life. . . . Just as writing initiates the crisis of living speech through its 'image' . . . onanism threatens the ruin of vitality through imaginative seduction."

15 "In the chain of *suppléments*, it was not easy to separate writing from masturbation."

16 "Rousseau considers writing a dangerous means, a menacing aid, and as an act of violence done to the natural destiny of language; he condemns writing as a destruction of presence and as a malady of speech, [framing] an accusation against the negativity of the letter, in which is to be read the degeneration of culture and the disruption of community; [finally] one cannot dissociate from his activity as a writer this kind of dangerous *supplément* called masturbation."

Rousseau himself did not make the association; but Derrida pretends that he did (224) by citing a passage from the *Confessions* which explains why the author abstained from sexual relations with Thérèse, his common-law wife, and took up masturbation instead. This avowal (1:594–95) sheds light on

Jean-Jacques's attitude toward both Thérèse and onanism, and also on the practical reasons for his decision (he did not want more children whom he would have had to abandon). But what it might imply about a possible tie between his penchant for the solitary vice and his activity as a writer is hard to guess.

17 The axis along which language evolved, according to Rousseau, was a geographical division between two types of speech: the "southern" and the "northern." The former, in contrast to the latter, was originally unarticulated, poetic, and musical. But the growth of society and civilization regrettably promoted the northern model; so that, as part of the general erosion of natural values, prose replaced poetry, the articulation of consonants replaced the musicality of vowels, literalness replaced metaphor, and reason replaced feeling. As Rousseau tells it, all this happened independently of the scriptural stage. In modern times, the decadence of language is said to have entailed that of musical taste by favoring harmonics over melody. The *Essai sur l'origine des langues* thus culminates as an episode of the "Querelle des Bouffons," in which Rousseau was deeply involved. Derrida likens this history of language to that of society in the *Discours sur l'inégalité* by infiltrating it, rather melodramatically, with such concepts as danger, catastrophe, evil, perversity, and death.

18 "My story would be endless if I recounted in detail all the crazy deeds to which the thought of my dear Mama prompted me when I was not in her sight. How often did I kiss my bed because I knew she had once slept in it, my curtains and all the furniture in my room because they belonged to her and her beautiful hand had touched them, the very floor on which I knelt because she had walked over it. Sometimes, in her presence, I was even driven to such extravagant acts as only the most violent love seemed capable of inciting. One day at mealtime, when she had put some food in her mouth, I exclaimed that I saw a hair; she spat out the food on her plate, I seized upon it avidly, and swallowed it. In brief, between me and the most passionate lover, there was only a single but essential difference, which makes my state of mind almost impossible to understand.

I had come back from Italy not altogether as I had gone there, but as perhaps no one of my age had ever returned from that country. I had brought back not my chastity, but my virginity. I had felt the progress of the years; my uneasy sexual temperament had finally expressed itself, and its first eruption, which was quite involuntary, had caused me to be alarmed about my health, a fact that shows better than anything my innocence until then. Soon reassured, I learned that dangerous substitute which deceives nature and keeps young persons of my emotional character from debauchery, but at the expense of their health, their vigor, and sometimes of their life. That vice, which shame and timidity find so convenient, has moreover a great attraction for lively imaginations; it disposes of the entire female sex, so to speak, according to one's wishes, and makes any tempting beauty serve one's pleasure without the need to obtain her consent. Seduced by this harmful advantage, I worked at destroying the good constitution that nature had given me, and that time had developed well. Let the reader add to this inclination of mine the physical setting of my present situation, living in the house of a pretty woman, caressing her image in the depths of my heart, seeing her continually during the day; at night surrounded by objects which remind me of her, lying in a bed where I know she has slept. What stimulants! The reader who pictures them all considers me already half-dead. On the contrary, what should have ruined me was precisely what saved me, at least for a while. Intoxicated by the charm of living in her home, by the ardent desire to pass there the rest of my days, I always saw her, absent or present, as a tender mother, a cherished sister, a delightful friend, and nothing more. I saw her always thus, always the same, and I never saw but her. Her image, always present in my heart, left no room for any other; she was for me the only woman in the world, and the extreme sweetness of the feelings she inspired in me, allowing my senses no occasion to be aroused by other women, protected me from her and from her sex. In a word, I restrained myself because I loved her. From these facts that I render poorly, let him who knows say what was the nature of my attachment to her. As for me, all I can say is that if it already appears quite out of the ordinary, it will later appear much more so."

19 Madeleine Velguth, "Le Texte comme prétexte: Jacques Derrida lit *Les Confessions* de Rousseau," *French Review* 58 (1985): 811–19. She concludes that "les phrases de Rousseau ne sont pour [Derrida] que des prétextes. Loin d'ouvrir au lecteur le texte, sa critique le transforme en tremplin pour lancer son 'exorbitante' cosmologie de non-présence."

20 Derrida theorizes that onanism as *supplément* denies the principle of self-identity, and therefore defies intelligibility, because it is a "présence absent": "Le supplément rend fou parce qu'il n'est ni la présence ni l'absence. . . . Telle est la contrainte du supplément, telle est, excédant tout le langage de la métaphysique, cette structure 'presque inconcevable à la raison' " (222).

21 Derrida omits the last three sentences of the passage, which round out the meaning of both paragraphs taken as a unit.

22 He had previously used "dangereux supplément" in *Emile* (4: 663). Thus its repetition in the later work was not occasioned by his account there of the "folies . . . inconcevables à la raison." The phrase was simply Rousseau's favorite synonym for masturbation.

23 "Becomes the *supplément* of art and society. This is the moment when the evil seems incurable."

24 "Not knowing how to cure himself, the child should know how to be sick; this art substitutes for the other, and often succeeds much better; it is nature's art."

25 "The contemplation of nature always had a very strong attraction for him [Rousseau]; he found in it a substitute for the human attachments he needed; but he would gladly have exchanged the substitute for the thing itself, if he had had a choice; and he submitted to conversing with plants only after his vain efforts to converse with human beings."

26 "That botany should become the *supplément* of society is more than a catastrophe. It is the catastrophe of catastrophies."

27 "Whenever I was completely alone, my heart was empty; but I required only another's to fill it. Fate had taken from me, had at least partly alienated, the heart for which nature had destined me. From that time on I was alone, because there was never any middle-ground for me between all and nothing. I found in Thérèse the substitute I needed."

28 "Occupies here the middle point between total absence and total presence. . . . But Rousseau goes on as if recourse to the *supplément* — in this case, Thérèse — would appease his impatience with half-way measures. . . . The virulence of this concept [i.e. intermediacy] is thus neutralized, as if it had been possible to subject it to control, to domesticate and tame it."

29 Rousseau's "blindness" has been denied also by Paul de Man in "Rhétorique de la cécité: Derrida lecteur de Rousseau," *Poétique* 1 (1970): 455-75. Concentrating on the analysis of the *Origine des langues* which fills about half the *Grammatologie*, De Man keeps his commentary at the level of theoretical principles, eschewing any examination of Derrida's actual readings of Rousseau. From his own position that the Rousseauist *oeuvre* should be read as an allegorical narrative sustained by its "rhetoricity," he rejects Derrida's deconstruction of it: "Le texte de Rousseau n'a point de points aveugles: il rend compte à tout moment de son propre mode rhétorique. Derrida interprète comme cécité ce qui est au contraire une transposition du niveau litéral au niveau figuré du discours" (473). That is, Derrida misapprehended Rousseau's philosophy of nature, history, and language because he took it literally instead of literarily, failing in the process to come to grips with the straw-man he constructed: "Rousseau sert de partenaire dans un simulacre de combat," and "Rousseau est un masque ou une ombre d'adversaire pour Derrida" (474). But De Man, who is prepared to read *De la grammatologie* as another piece of philosophical allegory, reassures us about the whole mistake: "il semble peu important que Derrida se trompe ou non à propos de Rousseau, puisque son propre texte ressemble de très près à celui de l'*Essai* [*sur l'origine des langues*] dans sa rhétorique comme dans sa formulation" (472). Since Derrida himself views neither Rousseau's philosophy nor his own critique of it as an exercise in allegory, and since De Man offers no proof that philosophical texts are primarily figurative and rhetorical statements, his taking Derrida to task on those grounds seems gratuitous and unfair.

Derrida's exegesis of Rousseauism has been discussed also in Christie V. McDonald, "Jacques Derrida's Reading of Rousseau," *The Eighteenth Century: Theory and Interpretation* 20 (1979): 82-95. She observes: "There comes the moment . . . when Derrida's text ceases to . . . protect the integrity or plenitude of the text which precedes it and seems to operate in itself as supplement . . . the truth or falsity of a reading for Derrida becomes irrelevant in the movement of the supplement" (93-94). That is, when the text does not support the interpretation, it is the text, not the interpretation, that is made to yield.

McDonald adds, without apparent irony: "one cannot deny that Derrida has permitted us to read in a way never before possible" (95).

30 In commenting on the *Essai sur l'origine des langues*, Derrida recognizes that sometimes the notion of *supplément* has a positive thrust. But these "exceptions" are passed over as incidental and prompt no reassessment or nuancing of the deconstructionist approach to his subject. Insofar as Derrida ignores rather than suppresses contrary evidence, his relationship to Rousseau is one, not merely of difference, but also of indifference.

31 "The savage, abandoned by nature to instinct alone, or rather compensated for the instinct he perhaps lacks by faculties capable of substituting for it at first and later of raising him far above nature, will therefore start out with purely animal functions."

32 "Civil law having thus become the common rule among citizens, the law of nature no longer subsisted except among different societies, where, under the name of international law, it was tempered by several tacit agreements in order to render commerce possible and to substitute for natural pity, which, losing in the relations of one society with another almost all the force it had in the relations of one individual with another. . . ."

33 Some of these require no explanation. In the *Nouvelle Héloïse*, there is: "La grâce et la facilité n'y sont pas, ni la raison, ni l'esprit, ni l'éloquence; le sentiment y est; il se communique au coeur par degrés, et lui seul supplée à tout" (2:18); and "Je ne parle point du rang et de la fortune, l'honneur et l'amour doivent en cela suppléer à tout" (2:73). In *Emile*, we find: "Il sera mieux élevé par un père judicieux et borné, que par le plus habile mâitre du monde; car le zèle suppléera mieux au talent que le talent au zèle" (4: 267); and "Comme le toucher exercé supplée à la vue, pourquoi ne pourrait-il pas aussi suppléer à l'ouïe jusqu'à certain point?" (4:389). Lastly, from the *Confessions*: "La sensualité ne présidait pas à nos petites orgies, mais la joie y suppléait, et nous nous trouvions si bien ensemble que nous ne pouvions plus nous quitter" (1:354).

34 "We are certain that something irreducibly rousseaustic is captured in it."

The "Heart" of Midlothian:
Jeanie Deans as Narrator

MARY ANNE SCHOFIELD

Sir Walter Scott historically has been thought of as a man's novelist. Twentieth-century critics from Lukács and Daiches to Brown, Fleishman, and Hart have discussed and celebrated his contribution to the novel in terms culturally defined as "masculine": that is, the nature of the hero, the meaning and/or futility of history, the evolution of society, and theories of law and justice.[1] Further, Scott has been examined in terms of his rhetorical strategies involving historical fiction, both public and private history—another structure that is conceived of as male territory. Needless to say, little criticism has been directed to the feminine/feminist aspect of a Scott novel.[2] Susan Morgan, as one exception, examines Jeanie Deans, finding her to be "the first peasant heroine in British fiction."[3] Others, however, view her only as a secondary, critical issue when discussing the novel because, at the simplest level, the Waverly novels are about heroes. Is it possible, one must ask, for a hero to be feminine? Why did Scott present heroic action dramatized through the adventures of a heroine?

Myra Jehlen provides a framework from which to examine these feminine issues in claiming that the "interior" tensions of the novel "whether lived by man or woman [are] female."[4] In other words, an examination of Jeanie Deans provides a study of the "other," non-masculine, non-assertive, imaginative side of Scott. Rather than merely labeling *The*

Heart of Midlothian "unique" (a critical stance frequently taken) because Jeanie Deans is Scott's only female protagonist, criticism should seriously examine Scott's use of her in this novel. Why did he make Jeanie Deans his spokesperson? Is Scott rejecting the masculine notions of the heroic associated with the Waverly heroes in favor of a different set of values associated with the feminine view? Is he truly concerned with the "heart" and the emotional issues that the female story raises? Clearly one cannot discount the masculine reading of the novel provided by noted Scott critics; yet a revisionist reading is necessary, if only to try and make sense of the uniqueness of Jeanie Deans's position in the Scott canon.

One of the most frequently noted critical issues in Scott criticism is his narrative method. His "layering" technique has been duly examined, with Stein, perhaps, considering the issue most seriously, noting Scott's "elaborate prefatorial apparatus"[5] and concluding that "it can be argued that the heavy editorial bracings of the Waverly novels constitute a defensive structure, which does not simply 'guide' but limits and excludes potential readings in the process of shaping our response."[6] I would argue that the narrative layers are so ordered in *The Heart of Midlothian* as to underscore and direct our attention to the unique, almost iconoclastic position Jeanie Deans holds in the story-telling of the novel, thus allowing Scott to explore the internal, non-masculine side of his creative self through her efforts.

What we are presented with in *The Heart of Midlothian* is a feminine view of history. Though Scott tries his hand at such a feminization, he is unable to sustain it. He thus encloses the "female story" of Effie and Madge—a tale of seduction and betrayal, which is at the "heart" of the novel—within several layers of male narratives and controlling forms, and particularly within that of "the law," an openly acknowledged male institution. These layers of the fable ultimately raise cogent issues about the very nature of fiction itself—who becomes the more truthful storyteller: the male or the female, in the course of the fiction.

Thus to investigate Scott's historical, narrative feminism is to examine the very liminality of fiction and the process by which this fiction is created. Is it possible, Scott questions, to address the non-masculine, non-heroic virtues in fiction? To explore and present intuitive, non-rational sides of the self? To present these views as the fiction?

In an attempt to answer these and similar questions, Scott validates an even more revolutionary strategy than his already noted one in his editorializing prefaces. Critics such as John Farrell have examined Scott's iconoclastic treatment of "history" in his historical fiction:

What finally matters about Scott's fiction is not its supreme evocation of the past but its exploration of the present. The device of historical narrative was, in Scott's hands, as in the hands of later historical novelists, a means of probing the present indirectly by filtering out the circumstantial and evanescent, and so turning the reader's mind to the deep core of historical meaning in his cultural experience. The mediating term, at least in the most powerful of the Scottish novels, is revolution.[7]

I would go further and argue that Scott consciously structures *The Heart of Midlothian* around technical revolutions of the genre. He is aware of his individual treatment of history, but he emphasizes his new rhetorical strategy with his selection of Jeanie Deans as spokesperson. Rebellion is the key here. Farrell notes that Jeanie is a revolutionary character: "Jeanie is, first of all, acting in revolt. In effect, she over-throws the authority nearest her, her father, who has committed her to his own legal system. At the same time she is symbolically acting on behalf of the murmuring Edinburgh citizens, who feel the immense remoteness of the London government. Her journey itself documents its remoteness. From the beginning, then, Jeanie's movements entail a sub-merged rebelliousness."[8] This rebellion, ostensibly on Jeanie's part, actu-ally is Scott's own. By focusing on a character whose natural attributes are ones of non-rational, emotional, intuitive behavior, who advocates rebellion against improper authority, Scott is able to explore his own creative, imaginative self to a degree unprecedented in his fiction. Despite the critical fascination with Scott's narrative technique, no one, to date, has explored this most interesting fact. Scott's process of using a female narrator as spokesperson/creator for major portions of the story enacts his exploration of the nature of the progressive act of making fiction.

What Scott investigates, then, is the very process of fiction-making and it is this investigation which makes *The Heart of Midlothian* so special. Waswo points out the extreme importance of "process" in Scott's view of history: "If formal history can be constituted by literature, so literature can constitute an historiography. How it does so is most clearly seen in the case of literary works that take history—presumed actual events and/or people—as their material: by shaping its presentation into an artistic form, they supply an historiography—not only a particular vision of historical process and change, but also a reflection of how that vision is constructed."[9] Again, Scott is testing the liminality of fiction by actively investigating, through an actual process, exactly what historical fiction is. His entire emphasis on process in *The Heart of Midlothian* is a feminine one, for the female perspective is process-oriented rather than teleological, which is the male view. The feminine point of view is concerned with how something is created — with process — rather than with the final product. Scott's position in the century after the collapse of art-as-process (romanticism) illuminates his concern with Jeanie Deans. *The Heart of Midlothian* becomes a hybrid production, a document of romantic emphasis on emotion and feeling surrounded by the rational frame of male narrators.

Through Jeanie as his spokesperson, Scott explores his own narrative skills. Both Scott as novelist and Jeanie as story-teller are charged with the same action: with discovering and presenting, by deciphering and reconstructing, a viable and credible story both for the reader and for themselves. Both manipulate the facts in order to find the passionate, imaginative tale that needs to be told. They automatically create a two-level text: of male-female, reason-feeling.

Jeanie must examine the facts and historical truths, and from them construct a plausible, emotionally true story. What Jeanie discovers at the heart of her text is the female story: one of passion and devotion without reference to rational order.

But because she is also the protagonist of a plot that concerns her ability to make a moral decision about her sister Effie's plight (Effie's affair with Staunton/Robertson, her subsequent pregnancy, and ultimate loss of the child), Jeanie's decisions about the story have human, emotional significance as well as intellectual force. Jeanie is placed "in the cruel position of either sacrificing her sister by telling the truth, or committing perjury in order to save her life."[10] The doctrines and beliefs of her father based on the 1680 persecution of the Covenanters are no longer viable for Jeanie as she faces the modern dilemma of her sister's immoral behavior and what is to be her own role in its solution.[11] Jeanie must sort out past facts and beliefs; she must separate fictitious rumors from present observations in order, first, to make her moral decision and determine her behavior at the trial, and second, to make the story which becomes The *"Heart"* of Midlothian.

The "story," which Jeanie discovers and Scott makes, is the "female story" that is at the center of the novel. It is the tale of seduction and betrayal, of misplaced power and archetypal violation, of aggression triumphing over innocence. It can be read as a gender war that pits male against female, but more importantly, it is the story that examines the validity of the non-rational, the intuitive, the feminine, versus the male-ordered and rational.[12]

At the very heart of the novel is Effie's story together with its parodic inversion in Madge's tale, which is pure imaginative passion gone mad. This account is a non-aggressive fiction of passion, powerlessness, and unhappiness. Around this Jeanie must construct an "ordered," reasonable tale so that the emotion can be contained and understood. She frequently refers to herself as the truth-seeking character, but always with the disclaimer that she is "nae great pen-woman" (347). Scott, as if he is going to take her at his/her word, does not allow her reconstruction of the feminine tale to go unchallenged, for Jeanie's own recital is blanketed by the numerous male, narrative layers introduced in the opening sections. Is it possible to have an historical novel that does not deal with male, historical events and virtues? That is one of the questions Scott poses in *The Heart of Midlothian*.

The initial sections of the novel establish the temporal primacy of the female story-storyteller. The actual kernel for the novel's story came from a woman, "the late amiable and ingenious lady . . . Miss Helen Lawson, of Girthead . . . wife of Thomas Goldie, Esq., of Craigmuie" (11). It is Helen Lawson-Goldie who met Helen Walker (the Jeanie Deans of the story) and listened to her tale. Though forced to leave Scotland the next day, she determines to pursue the story when she returns in the spring. But when Lawson-Goldie returns, she learns that Walker has died.

> My regret was extreme, and I endeavoured to obtain some account of Helen from an old woman who inhabited the other end of the cottage. I enquired if Helen ever spoke of her past history, her journey to London, etc. "Na," the old woman said, "Helen was a wily body, and whene'er ony o' the neebors asked anything about it, she aye turned the conversation." In short, every answer I received only tended to increase my opinion of Helen Walker, who could unite so much prudence with so much heroic virtue. (13)

This narrative account was sent anonymously to the male narrator, who goes on to write: "the reader is now able to judge how far the *author has improved upon*, or *fallen short* of the pleasing and interesting sketch of high principle and steady affection displayed by Helen Walker, the prototype of Jeanie Deans" (13; emphasis added). The male narrator assumes that it is his role to "fill" in the gaps and to explain away the interstices of the female text. He will correct what he thinks is the often non-direct text which the female presents. At this point, Scott is still very much the male narrator, unable to relinquish his authorial control, yet, as artist, he is capable of being faithful to this text. And so, once more in these introductory remarks, he turns back to the female text, and to Miss Goldie, the daughter, to establish the woman's story that is being told. The male narrative voice intrudes yet again in the closing paragraphs of the introduction, offering a sort of "apologia" for the ensuing tale: "If the picture has suffered in the execution, it is from the failure of the author's powers to present in detail the same simple and striking portrait exhibited in Mrs. Goldie's letter" (14). Interestingly enough, it is the woman who is considered to be the better story-teller. Further masking of the differnt narrative voices — voices that act as so many masks covering the female story that is at the heart of the novel — takes place as Scott adds an introductory "Postscript." This time Scott speaks in the voice of the male "editor" who quotes from John MacDiarmid's *Sketches from Nature* with a few more facts about Helen and Tibby Walker. It is as if Scott were still uncomfortable with the female voice, and thus he continues to explore male alternatives in the early sections.

The next layer is found in "Being Introductory," a first chapter narrated by Peter Pattieson who begins by noting the efficacy of both the printed word and the postal system (a male institution). Try as he might, however, the male voice (be it Pattieson or Scott) cannot prevent the female voice, or at least feminine imagery, from intruding, in this instance very slyly and subtly. Pattieson begins his account by describing "the summerset in good earnest" of the Somerset coach, but is forced to talk about the birth by a "Caesarean process of delivery" (19) of two women from this coach. Like the hidden female's story, they spring forth from the womblike leathern structure. Both story and females are summarily ejected. The image is an important one, however, for not only are the two women dispatched, but as an additional cover to them, two lawyers, Halkit and Hardie, are ejected as well; again the law (male) must enclose the female rhetoric.

Further enclosing of the heart/feminine story occurs as the lawyers discuss fiction and novel reading with Pattieson. The two move the narrative line totally away from the feminine by first talking about the prison and the story it could tell. Though the majority of the prisoners are male, and hence, we would be dealing with male stories, "the *real* records of human vagaries" (25; emphasis added), the feminine impulse toward human values cannot be totally ignored, for even here "every now and then you [can] read new pages of the human heart, and turns of fortune far beyond what the boldest novelist ever attempted to produce from the coinage of his brain" (25). *The Book of Adjournals* acts as a further layer, for there the tales of the heart would be presented in a rational mode. Similarly, Hardie says he will publish the *Causes Célèbres of Caledonia*, which will become the history of the mind (26) and could surpass the circulating romance fiction (26). He then tells his listeners the "tale of poor Dunover's distresses," a tale that mirrors the seduction, betrayal, and doom of the female story. Scott consciously provides a feminine counter text to his masculine one.

In the second chapter, Scott continues with the male narrative mask as he presents the "true facts" of the Porteus riots. Chapter 2 functions like the "Author's Introduction": the historical material is examined so that the statements of the fiction can be made clearer. As the narrator remarks in the beginning: "The tale is well known; yet it is necessary to recapitulate its leading circumstances, for the better understanding of what is to follow" (31).

More importantly, these first pages demonstrate the technique to be used throughout the novel; after recounting the riots that involved Staunton/Robertson and John Porteus, the male narrator goes on to give the verdict of the Porteus story, and from these facts he weaves his fiction. That is, the reader watches as the narrator encounters facts, applies his passionate imagination to these data, creates an emotive, feminine text, then finally allows his reason to rework the imaginative creation, thus circumscribing the human values of the imaginative text within the confines of reason.

All of these introductory sections continue to function as a male frame: the feminine text of passion is bound by the rational line, thus presenting the reader with the male version of the female text, long before he or she encounters the center of the novel. For example, we first read of the statute violated by Effie before we are even introduced to Effie. (Also note that it is the male narrator who introduces the women.) Further, it is another male, Sharpitlaw, who interviews Effie while she is in prison. The narrator continues to frame Effie's story up to the point of confrontation between the sisters; he is then discarded, and the scene is presented dramatically. Yet even this "heart" scene must be blanketed by the male frame: "Jeanie Deans remained with her sister for two hours, during which she endeavoured, if possible, to extract something from her that might be serviceable in her exculpation. But she had nothing to say beyond what she declared on her first examination, with the purport of which the reader will be made acquainted in proper time and place" (193).

Midway through the novel, the male narrative ceases. Once Jeanie undertakes her journey, she becomes the prime storyteller. Until this point, Jeanie has been listening to the various "versions" of Effie's story and has tried to find the truth and piece together her own notion of the tale. Once she is certain of the veracity of Effie's account, she is ready to act upon this truth: hence, the journey to London and the queen.

Jeanie becomes the surrogate novelist. She is given much data by the male structure—that is, the official statute, Saddletree's account, Robertson's first version—and she receives considerable pressure to present a tale conforming to male standards. We watch the first attempt at female control as Jeanie meets Robertson at Muschat's Cairn. He exerts male power and tries to force his version on her: "you *must* remember that she told you all this, whether she ever said a syllable of it or not. You must repeat this tale" (245). But Jeanie as truth-sayer and storyteller will not be perjured: "I shall be mansworn in the very thing in which my testimony is wanted . . . you would make me tell a falshood anent it" (146). Adhering to the truth of her feelings, Jeanie encounters the story told by the crown counsel (201), then Mr. Fairbrother's version (215–16) as counsel for the prisoner—based on a letter from Robertson which shows how he "contrived to exercise authority over the mind, and to direct the motions of this unhappy girl" (205)—and finally the testimony of two or three female witnesses by whose account it is established, "that Effie's situation had been remarked by them, that they had taxed her with the fact, and that her answers had amounted to an angry and petulant denial of what they charged her with" (206). The judge sums up the legal presentations by concluding: "For himself . . . a shadow of doubt remained not upon his mind concerning the verdict which the inquest has to bring in" (216). This section concludes with Effie's own story decoded and presented as a male text given in the judicial *Books of Adjournal*:

> Interrogated, where she was from the period she left her master, Mr. Saddletree's family, until her appearance at her father's, at St. Leonard's, the day before she was apprehended? Declares she does not remember. . . . On the question being again repeated, she declares, she will tell the truth, if it should be the undoing of her, so long as she is not asked to tell on other folk; and admits, that she passed that interval of time in the lodging of a woman, an acquaintance of that person who had wished her to the place to be delivered, and that she was there delivered accordingly of a male child. Interrogated, what was the name of that person? Declares and refuses to answer this question. (208)

Jeanie is overwhelmed by the cold formality of Effie's story presented in its convoluted and legal jargon, by Saddletree's emotional appeal, and by Robertson's imaginative, pleading account. Jeanie's own account, summed up in one word, "Nothing" (214), underscores her inability at this point to assimilate the material and produce an accurate text from it. She has had insufficient time to formulate the true history from these versions, and the first part ends on an incomplete note, though there is a hint of positive resolution, as Scott writes: "It was in that moment that a vague idea first darted across her mind, that something might yet be achieved for her sister's safety, conscious as she now was of her innocence of the unnatural murder with which she stood charged. It came as she described it, on her mind, like a sun-blink on a stormy sea; and although it instantly vanished, yet she felt a degree of composure which she had not experienced for many days" (167). On this note Jeanie prepares for her London pilgrimage. Her accounts of her journey are recorded in letters sent to her father and to Reuben. Though she claims: "I have ane ill pen" (253), she has already learned how to "organize" her presentation; for truly, "in the tenor of these epistles, Jeanie expressed, perhaps, more hopes, a firmer courage, and better spirits, than she actually felt" (253).

Her journey becomes hazardous, and her powers of story-telling are tested even more severely when she is apprehended by the highwayman and then taken in by Meg Murdockson and her daughter. Jeanie learns to decode a completely new language, that of the underworld, but more importantly she becomes the interpreter of Madge's history, for it is quite clear that Madge is the obverse, a grotesque parody of Effie, another victim of the male text. She has been so overpowered by male authority, that she has lost her reason: "Then comes the devil, and brushes my lips with his black wing, and lays his broad black loof on my mouth . . . and sweeps away a' my gude thoughts, and dits up my gude words" (274). Because her words are confused, Jeanie must decode her story, for "She was painfully interested in getting to the truth of Madge's history (275). Jeanie concludes, having listened to Madge's wild version:

> She had been courted by a wealthy suitor, whose addresses her mother had favoured, not withstanding the objection of old age and deformity. She has been seduced by some profligate, and, to conceal her shame and promote the advantageous match she had planned, her mother had not hestitated to destroy the off-spring of their intrigue. That the consequence should be the total derangement of a mind which was constitutionally unsettled by giddiness and vanity, was extremely natural. (276)

Madge's story is Effie's tale: it is the female story of victimization and exploitation by men. As decoder and interpreter, not as actor/participator, Jeanie does not change facts but only presents a coherent version of them. Scott seems incapable of totally giving himself to the powerless, female text. Though he wants to explore the imaginative, passionate, non-reasoned forces at the center of one's being, he ultimately chooses not to do so, and Jeanie Deans becomes a non-emotional "male" voice that "orders" the female story (that is, removes it from its emotional contact) so that it can be rationally understood. Jeanie becomes yet another spokesperson for Scott, and he fails to fulfill the lively expectations of the female narrator. Still, *The Heart of Midlothian* comes closer than any other Scott novel to expressing his central, imaginative, passionate core.

In the second part of the novel—after the trial to her meeting with Queen Caroline and its aftermath—Jeanie hears George Staunton's version of the story. Correcting his earlier rendition—"a tissue of folly, guilt, and misery" (197)—Staunton now tells Jeanie, because she is "a *sensible*, as well as a good woman" (197; emphasis added), the entire story of his acquaintance with low-life characters, especially Meg Murdockson, and the cruel outcome of this association:

> To make my tale short—this wretched hag—this Margaret Murdockson was the wife of a favourite servant of my father;—she had been my nurse;—her husband was dead;—she resided in a cottage near this place;—she had a daughter who grew up, and then was a beautiful but very giddy girl; her mother endeavoured to promote her marriage with an old and wealthy churl in the neighborhood;—the girl saw me frequently—she was familiar with me, as our connection seemed to permit—and I—in a word, I wronged her cruelly. (197)

His story corroborates the version Jeanie was able to piece together from Madge's account. Yet here again Scott compromises himself and his fictional investigations, for it is the male version that is giving the final approval of Jeanie's version.

The second part continues with the omniscient narrator's account of the George Staunton story (313–14), followed by the history and story of John, Duke of Argyle (315–16). Both male accounts are of a reasoned, ordered approach to life, with "measures which were at once just and lenient" (315). Here again it is the male voice that offers the "true" version. The duke tells Jeanie to "speak out a plain tale, and show you have a Scotch tongue in your head" (318). The male most forcefully here becomes the auditor and judge of the ensuing tale; the power of life and death resides in his word. Fortunately, the duke agrees to arrange a meeting with Queen Caroline and to act "as the master of ceremonies" (336). His male control nearly results in his writing her script as well (see 331, 335, 336).

This section concludes with Jeanie's interview with and "storytelling" to Queen Caroline; the tale here is a recital of facts but "with a pathos which was at once simple and solemn" (338). She is still woman enough to use her best asset: humane feelings. To mark the increase in Jeanie's knowledge and self-confidence together with her ability to interpret the facts and versions she has heard, in chapter 39, Jeanie composes letters to Staunton, her father, and Reuben Butler reviewing Effie's history and the truth of her situation as Jeanie has found it to be thus far. The second section closes with Jeanie's "fanciful" vision of "Effie restored, not to gaiety, but to Cheerfulness at least;—their father, with his gray hairs smoothed down, and spectacles on his nose;—herself, with her maiden snood exchanged for a matron's curch" (352). Part of this vision is affirmed when she reads and interprets Effie's letter to Butler. She is pleased that Effie is to marry and decides that her elopement bodes well after all.

Effie has escaped the inexorable fate usually associated with the victims of the female story—exile, madness, and/or death and, instead, undergoes the living death of becoming the fiction, that of victimized female, that was created for her. It is not a happy ending to the female text: Madge is both mad and dead; Effie lives a death-in-life. Only Jeanie survives to live happily ever-after with her Reuben. She is allowed to do so because she has not been a part of the female text: she has been the interpreter, the editor, but not a participant. She has been governed by reason and order—the male attributues—not the passionate, female ones.

In the final analysis, Scott has only partially been successful in his investigation of the feeling, feminine, imaginative side of his creative person. Jeanie's claim that she "is nae great penwoman" is accurate, for Scott controls her efforts to get at the passionate level of being, and her pen is ultimately a rational, ordered, writing implement. The true "heart" story of feeling and imagination is blanketed by many male layers, and Jeanie becomes a rational voice, not one truly and finally female.

NOTES

1 George Lukács, *The Historical Novel* (London: Merton, 1962); David Daiches, "Scott's Achievement as a Novelist," *Nineteenth-Century Fiction* 6 (1951): 81-95, 153-73; Francis Hart, *Scott's Novels: The Plotting of Historical Survival* (Charlottesville: University of Virginia Press, 1966); Avrom Fleishman, *The English Historical Novel: Walter Scott to Virginia Woolf* (Baltimore: The Johns Hopkins University Press, 1971); David Brown, *Walter Scott and the Historical Imagination* (London: Routledge and Kegan Paul, 1979).

2 George Lukács calls Jeanie Deans Scott's "greatest female character" (52); David Daiches says that the novel intimates that there is the possibility of an heroic life in the everyday world; Fleishman says that even the peasantry has nobility. None deal specifically with Jeanie as female.

3 Susan Morgan, "Old Heroes and a New Heroine in the Waverly Novels," *English Literary History* 50 (1983): 563.

4 Myra Jehlen, "Archimedes and the Paradox of Feminist Criticism," *Signs* 6 (1981): 696

5 Richard L. Stein, "Historical Fiction and the Implied Reader: Scott and Iser," *Novel* 14 (1981): 220.

6 Ibid., 119.

7 John P. Farrell, *Revolution as Tragedy. The Dilemma of the Moderate from Scott to Arnold* (Ithaca: Cornell University Press, 1980), 70.

8 Ibid., 112.

9 Richard Waswo, "Story as Historiography in the Waverly Novels," *English Literary History* 47 (1980): 9.

10 Sir Walter Scott, *The Heart of Midlothian* (1818; repr., London: Collins, 1952), 184. All subsequent references are made parenthetically.

11 Fleishman, *English Historical Novel*, 92. Fleishman argues that the novel is Jeanie's "Bildungsroman."

12 Morgan argues for the validity of humane feeling in *The Heart of Midlothian*; she does not make this the central thesis of her article nor of the book, as I do here.

Gibbon among the Aeolists:
Islamic Credulity and Pagan Fanaticism
in The Decline and Fall

THOMAS JEMIELITY

James Boswell is only one of the earliest to allege that insidious and dishonest motives prompt Edward Gibbon's analysis of Christianity in *The Decline and Fall of the Roman Empire*. Although the *Life of Johnson*, admittedly, does not appear until 1791, that 20 March 1776 conversation which impugns Gibbon's integrity is in the biography but a reshaping for public view of doubts Boswell had expressed at Oxford about Gibbon's recently published history that winter. In the *Life* Boswell refers to the *Decline and Fall* as a work "which, under the pretext of another subject, contained much artful infidelity."[1] Were we to believe Boswell, Gibbon, in a seventy-one-chapter history spanning almost two millenia, constructs only a facade behind which lurks his real objective: an infidel's attack on Christianity. Characteristically Boswellian, it is no small fantasy. Such an exclusive focussing, however, on what Gibbon says about Christianity obscures — as it does in Boswell's case — the consistency with which Gibbon treats all religion, and all abuses of religion, be it Christianity or Judaism, Islam or various forms of paganism. Principles announced and implied in the *General Observations on the Fall of the Roman Empire in the West* and introduced as well in discussing, in chapter 2, the Antonine emperors' policy on religion guide Gibbon's treatment in the history of all faiths and their excesses.[2] The main criteria which emerge from these two sections of the *Decline and Fall* are the following: first, Gibbon's uneasiness with an other-worldly concern in religions that frequently and sometimes recklessly disregards the this-worldly consequences of belief; second, his dislike for any form of religious intolerance and his preference for the tolerant policy of the Antonines; third, his suspicion about the ease with which credulity and zeal, superstition and fanaticism, can undermine any form of religious faith and, indeed, be exploited for reasons that have little to do with religion. The enlightened of his time, Gibbon hopes and implies, will, like the Antonine intelligentsia, effectively resist the divisive social and political consequences caused by excessive attachment to any single faith.

I

Completed sometime before the accession of Louis XVI in 1774,[3] the *General Observations* embody the philosophic historian's attempt to determine how "this awful revolution may be usefully applied to the instruction of this present age."[4] Echoes of Antonine religious policy in the second century, however, frequently form a counterpoint to these comments. A single, lengthy, and packed paragraph analyzes the predominantly, but not wholly, adverse effect that "the introduction, or at least *the abuse* [my emphasis] of Christianity" had on the fall of Rome. By emphatically noting at the outset that "the happiness of a *future* life [Gibbon's emphasis] is the great object of religion" (*DF*, 4:162), Gibbon encapsulates a major cause of his displeasure with the sometimes reckless this-worldly consequences of celestially oriented religious practice and belief, a major thrust of his indictment of Christianity in chapter 15. The Antonines, by contrast, locate their ethical concerns and responsibilities in the world of human beings, and follow the Greek philosophers who "deduced their morals from the nature of man rather than from that of God" (*DF*, 1:30). By contrast, chapter 15 asserts, "it was not in *this* world [Gibbon's emphasis again] that the primitive Christians were desirous of making themselves either agreeable or useful" (*DF*, 2:35). Gibbon's emphatic contrasts between "*this* world" and "a *future* life" highlight his conviction that whoever can make two ears of corn or two blades of grass to grow upon a spot where only one grew before will deserve better of mankind than the whole race of priests and theologians put together. The *General Observations* censure the adverse social and political consequences of Christianity; they praise, but not enthusiastically, some beneficent public effects of its practice; and they note the theological discord that allowed "the more earthly passions of malice and ambition" to vitiate the supposed promptings of "faith, zeal, [and] curiosity" (*DF*, 4:163). The later discussion of the state of Rome from the twelfth century on occasions a reference to ambition as "a weed of quick and early vegetation in the vineyard of Christ" (*DF*, 7:238). The context speaks of "the votes, the venality, [and] the violence" of the popular election of the Popes over a nine-century period, an abuse particularly troublesome in the absence of a civil magistrate who could lessen the effects of controversy. Yet the *Observations* are not pleased with the frequency that theological discord diverted the attention of the emperors "from camps to synods" (*DF*, 4:163). For "the church, and even the state," Gibbon continues, "were distracted by religious factions, whose conflicts were sometimes bloody, and always implacable" (*DF*, 4:163). The separation of civil and ecclesiastical authority, with each one claiming real power and the church insisting on its greater power (see *DF*, 2:318), helped prepare the way for "a new species of tyranny" that is, the ecclesiastical. Both forms of despotism, however, as Gibbon comments in chapter 53, are "more permanent evils" than "the calamities of war" (*DF*, 6:68).

The religious picture in the *General Observations* strikingly contrasts with that of Antonine Rome. The prevailing modes of worship there "were all considered by the people as equally true, by the philosopher as equally false, and by the magistrate as equally useful," a toleration effecting "mutual indulgence [and] even religious concord" (*DF*, 1:29). Likewise, Roman religion was neither embittered by theological dispute nor monolithically confined to any obligatory system, very unlike the later and extensively developed divisive intra- and inter-fraternal conflicts among the Christians and among the exclusive Jews.[5] Rome's "devout polytheist," fondly attached to his national rites, nevertheless admitted "the different religions of the earth" (*DF*, 1:29). Gibbon twice insists on this national quality in a more tolerant paganism, for the Antonine magistrates, he later observes, "were convinced that the various modes of worship contributed alike to the same salutary purposes; and that, in every country, the form of superstition which had received the sanction of time and experience was the best adapted to the climate and to its inhabitants" (*DF*, 1:31). This principle anticipates Gibbon's later use, especially in the second half of the history, of the common Protestant refusal to recognize any religious authority transcending national boundaries and to accept, rather, in the language of article 34, "the diversities of countries, times, and men's manners." Gibbon's analysis of the Paulician heresy in chapter 54 asserts this diversity at least as historical fact: "In the profession of Christianity," he writes, "the variety of national characters may be clearly distinguished" (*DF*, 6:110). "Such was the mild spirit of antiquity," the Antonine resumé claims, "that the nations were less attentive to the difference than to the resemblance of their religious worship" (*DF*, 1:29).

A comment very germane, however, to his later explicit concern in the *Observations* with the instructive value of the story of Rome's decline and fall concerns the attitude of the intelligentsia towards the religious rites in which they participate, in Antonine Rome, an "external reverence" that masks "an inward contempt": "Viewing with a smile of pity and indulgence the various errors of the vulgar, [the philosophers] diligently practised the ceremonies of their fathers, devoutly frequented the temples of the gods; and, sometimes condescending to act a part on the theater of superstition, they concealed the sentiments of an Atheist under the sacerdotal robes" (*DF*, 1:31). Although "Atheist" not at all accurately epitomizes Gibbon's religious views, is Gibbon implying here that an educated person in his time, unwilling to offend the credulity of the ignorant, will regard the mythology of eighteenth-century Europe with the same contempt and ideological indifference that characterized the pagan intelligentsia in Antonine Rome? The likelihood of such an ethical hint is strengthened by the way in which Gibbon discusses the instructive value of the history in the *General Observations*.

Eighteenth-century Europe, these *Observations* strongly imply, is a much improved reappearance of the power, stability, and humane administration of Antonine Rome, coupled with the exemplary public ideals and virtues of the Roman Republic.[6] Significantly, Gibbon sees his Europe precisely as a republic—one of his most complimentary political terms—"one great republic, whose various inhabitants have attained almost the same level of politeness and cultivation" (*DF*, 4:163). As a republic of independent states Europe operates within a continental system of checks and balances, the system that had been substantively eroded in the Empire as early as Augustus. Strikingly, the *General Observations* omit one possible contemporary threat to this "one great republic," the religion that helped to undermine and level the Roman Empire. But Gibbon has made his contemporary point implicitly in both chapter 2 and in the *Observations*: namely, that eighteenth-century Europe, most likely free of the threats of barbarism and despotism, can also be relatively free of a superstitious and enthusiastic abuse of Christianity. The enlightened of his time, Gibbon hopes and implies, will effectively resist the divisive political and social consequences of zealous and excessive attachment to any single form of faith. Europe will live as comfortably with its Christianities as Rome lived with her paganisms.

II

The application to Christianity of the evaluative norms and principles of the *General Observations* and of chapter 2 is a familiar story. Less familiar, perhaps, is the consistency and degree to which Gibbon thinks comparably about religions other than Christianity and Judaism in the *Decline and Fall*. Any religion introduced into the history, first of all, appears always for the same reason: because its fortunes somehow influenced the fortunes of the Roman Empire. The religions that enter the history also permit Gibbon to provide a comparative study of the civil and ecclesiastical orders, which so often intersect in the course of his narrative. If, for example, chapters 15 and 16 appear to explain how the "pure and humble religion" of Christianity, which "grew up in silence and obscurity," finally erected "the triumphant banner of the cross on the ruins of the Capitol" (*DF*, 2:7), Zoroastrianism enters the narrative in chapter 8 "to illustrate many of [Persia's] most important transactions . . . with the Roman Empire" (*DF*, 1:198). Islam deserves attention because "the genius of the Arabian prophet [that is, Mohammed], the manners of his nation, and the spirit of his religion involve the cause of the decline and fall of the Eastern empire . . ." (*DF*, 5:311). Julian's paganism is not irrelevant to the historian because "the phantoms which existed only in the mind of the emperor had a real and pernicious effect on the government of the empire" (*DF*, 2:432). When Gibbon, therefore, comments that several centuries of "spiritual wars" in the East did "so deeply . . . affect the decline and fall of the empire that the historian has too often been compelled to attend the synods, to explore the creeds, and to enumerate the sects, of this busy period of ecclesiatical annals" (*DF*, 6:110), he is merely applying specifically a principle of inclusion apparent throughout the *Decline and Fall*. Gibbon recognizes religion as a cultural and historical force and often directs a historian's curiosity at the way it conducts itself as an institution. Christianity receives the most attention in the history because it had the greatest effect on the Empire.

1. The Religion of Zoroaster

The first specific creed Gibbon analyzes in the *Decline and Fall* is Zoroastrianism, the religion of Persia. The brief commentary in chapter 8 revealingly anticipates the longer discussion of Christianity in chapters 15 and 16. The Magian religion, as Gibbon calls it, arose out of the mutual adopting and corrupting of the superstitions of Europe and Asia. However revered the memory of Zoroaster, "the obsolete and mysterious language" of his ZendAvesta provided a mischievously fertile opportunity for the Magian interpreters, who deconstructed, we might say, the ZendAvesta into seventy sects, "all equally derided by a crowd of infidels" (*DF*, 1:197–98). Artaxerxes' desire to secure religious unity by a general council of the wisest of the Magi unexpectedly led to the almost insurmountable and unmanageable presence of about eighty thousand Magi "from all parts of his dominions," a number Gibbon quietly acknowledges to be not very amenable either to "the authority of reason" or "the art of policy" (*DF*, 1:198). But having "so long sighed in contempt and obscurity," the Magi "obeyed the welcome summons" into the limelight. Like a competition, an elimination process reduced the participating Magi in stages from eighty thousand, to forty thousand, to four thousand, to four hundred, to forty, and at last to seven. As the result of a most convenient vision,[7] one of these Magi, Erdaviraph, fixed "the articles of the faith of Zoroaster . . . with equal authority and precision." "Supernatural evidence," encouraged by "three cups of soporiferous wine," had silenced every doubt (*DF*, 1:198). For Erdaviraph's vision had transported him to heaven to discuss the issues directly with the deity.[8]

The analysis of the Zoroastrian body of belief notes that the Persian religion condemns all unbelievers to the "infernal enemy," Ahriman, who, along with his followers, will sink at the last into "native darkness" while "virtue will maintain the eternal peace and harmony of the universe" (*DF*, 1:199). Zoroaster's was a theology "darkly comprehended by foreigners, and even by the far greater number of his disciples" — no inside advantages here. But the "philosophic simplicitly" of the faith struck even "the most careless observers" and drew specific comment from Herodotus, which Gibbon quotes (*DF*, 1:200). In this context, Gibbon explicitly announces two constituent principles of all religion, worship and ethics: "Every mode of religion, to make a deep and lasting impression on the human mind, must exercise our obedience by enjoining practices of devotion, for which we can assign no reason; and must acquire our esteem, by inculcating moral duties analogous to the dictates of our own hearts" (*DF*, 1: 200).

Significantly, Gibbon does not here mention creed, the body of belief that forms part of the customary religious trio of creed, code, and cult. The cult of Zoroastrianism Gibbon treats ironically: the "mysterious girdle" provided to the faithful Persian at puberty; the "peculiar prayers, ejaculations, or genuflexions" that accompanied "the most indifferent or the most necessary" actions of human life. A footnote mentions the fifteen genuflections, prayers, and the like required before cutting one's nails or urinating. However much Gibbon undercuts these cultic practices — for which, remember, he admits no rational explanation possible — he speaks very approvingly of the this-worldly concern of Zoroaster, as he "lays aside the prophet, assumes the legislator, and discovers a liberal concern for private and public happiness, seldom to be found among the grovelling or visionary schemes of superstition" (*DF*, 1:201). Zoroastrianism abhors fasting and celibacy. The Magian saint,

Gibbon notes, "is obliged to beget children, to plant useful trees, to destroy noxious animals, to convey water to the dry lands of Persia, and to work out his salvation by pursuing all the labours of agriculture." This injunction Gibbon reinforces with the text of the ZendAvesta itself: "He who sows the ground with care and diligence acquires a greater stock of religious merit than he could gain by the repetition of ten thousand prayers" (*DF*, 1:201). Obviously, the Zoroastrians were very desirous of making themselves agreeable and useful in this world. What went wrong, Gibbon asks? Why did Zoroastrianism fail to achieve a place with the most exemplary religious and ethical systems? Apart from the "motley composition" of "reason and passion, . . . enthusiasm and . . . selfish motives," the "useful and sublime truths" of Zoroaster were corrupted by "the most abject and dangerous superstition" (*DF*, 1:201-2). The priesthood of the Persian Magi bear a major responsibility for this prostitution. An "extremely numerous" order, the Magi enjoyed "very considerable" property. "Besides the less invidious possession of a large tract of the most fertile lands of Media, they levied a general tax on the fortunes and the industry of the Persians." Zoroaster himself, "the interested prophet," as Gibbon calls him, indispensably required tithes to make salvifically profitable the good works of believers. Magi who demanded hefty fees guarded the doors of salvation. Because the Magi "were the masters of education in Persia" (*DF*, 1:202, they exercised enormous influence. Indeed, "the administration of Artaxerxes was in a great measure directed by the counsels of the sacerdotal order" (*DF*, 1:203). Artaxerxes prohibited as well the exercise of any other form of religion, "a spirit of persecution which reflects dishonour on the religion of Zoroaster." If Gibbon is less censorious of this intolerance than usual, it is only because "it was not productive of any civil commotion." In fact, it strengthened the monarchy "by uniting all the various inhabitants of Persia in the bands of religious zeal" (*DF*, 1:203). This picture of Zoroastrianism in chapter 8 anticipates in many respects what Gibbon will shortly say about the introduction and triumph of Christianity in the Empire. That story will introduce characters and situations familiar from the tale of Zoroastrianism: deluded or ambiguously motivated civil administrators; clergy banefully influenced by authority and notoriety; specious but seasonal supernatural claim and evidence; and the ubiquitous and finally corrupting force of power and wealth.

The credulousness Gibbon wittily exposes in Zoroastrianism, like its counterpart in other faiths, constitutes a steadfast focus in the *Decline and Fall*: that "easiness of belief," as Samuel Johnson defines it, which effectively and cumulatively—for believers—asserts the frequency of supposedly tangible divine favor and intervention in human affairs. Such "prodigies" and "miracles" David Hume numbers in *The Natural History of Religion* as among those which "impress mankind with the strongest sentiments of religion. Madness, fury, rage, and an inflamed imagination," he ironically asserts, are "often supposed to be the only dispositions, in which we can have any immediate communication with the Deity."[9] Gibbon very approvingly refers to this most important source of his own principles of religious analysis, for the first time, in fact, when he takes up the distinctive features of paganism in chapter 2, where he calls *The Natural History of Religion* "the best commentary" on "the true genius of Polytheism" (*DF*, 1:29 n. 3). Like Hume, Gibbon exposes the self-gratifying attraction of a theology that defies common sense and reason to offer more exciting alternatives instead: "Amazement must of necessity be raised [Hume writes]: Mystery affected: Darkness and obscurity sought after: And a foundation of merit afforded to the devout votaries, who desire an opportunity of subduing their rebellious reason, by the belief of the most unintelligible sophisms."[10]

Gibbon's attack on credulity, it might be noted here, reflects a generic or formal requirement on his part: he is writing the history of Rome, not its romance. When the history of religion intersects the history of the Empire, Gibbon likewise seeks to penetrate the mists and shadows, the specters and the apparitions, that so easily enter and obfuscate the annals of belief. Credulity multiplies wonder. It transforms the record of religion into romance, that strange, wild tale of adventure, that chronicle of the mysterious and the preternatural peopled with lesser deities of every sort. As Gibbon challenges the romances of religion, the eery preternatural claims and qualities of their minor deities — saints, magi, priests, dervishes, and the like — come into the less easily deceived light of history to punctuate the awareness that romance also denotes the lie and the merely imaginary, the wished for rather than what was or is. What appears sometimes as an almost casually thrown off distinction — Gibbon refers in a note, for instance, to "the history or romance" of Gregory Thaumaturgus (*DF*, 6:116 n. 17) — actually highlights his ongoing effort to separate fact from fiction even in the annals of belief and his never-failing sense of how conveniently but perhaps necessarily religions can and must set their most extraordinary claims in the past. If in chapter 15, for example, he ironically exposes the credulity of the Jews of the Second Temple who believed in the Mosaic miracles which Moses' own contemporaries rejected, he later draws attention to the romantic allure of the witness-free past to locate the marvelous: "such is the progress of credulity," Gibbon remarks, in chapter 58, while speaking of the First Crusade, "that miracles, most doubtful on the spot and at the moment, will be received with implicit faith at a convenient distance of time and space"

(*DF*, 6:306). Religion, or its abuse, has an almost inescapable penchant for romance, which, in the *Decline and Fall*, receives a historian's sceptical and frequently witty analysis. To the believers who listen with credulity to the whispers of religious fancy, who pursue with eagerness the phantoms of faith, who create a marvel-filled past to reassure the present, Gibbon asks them to attend to the history of religions in the *Decline and Fall of the Roman Empire*.

2. The Religion of Mohammed

Islam's view of the afterlife draws considerable emphasis in the lengthy discussion of Mohammedanism in chapter 50. Gibbon's concern here focusses on the credulousness of next-worldly expectations. The *Decline and Fall* at least twice asserts the futility of such speculations about a next life, briefly, for instance, when it asserts that the theologians arguing about the nature of purgatory at the Council of Ferrara were seeking to resolve "a doubtful point, which in a few years might be conveniently settled on the spot by the disputants" (*DF*, 7:109). The lengthier analysis of immortality occurs in chapter 15 where Gibbon argues the moral irrelevance of the belief for the ethics and ethical sanctions of paganism and the absence of the belief among the Jews (*DF*, 2:19-28). Here, too, Gibbon asserts that only "a divine revelation" can confirm the existence or describe the qualities of an afterlife (*DF*, 2:19-20).[11] Irony, however, makes the detailed picture of Islamic immortality, like that of Christianity, appear more the product of wish-fulfillment than that of revelation.

Like the Christianity which has learned over "the revolution of seventeen centuries . . . not to press too closely the mysterious language of prophecy and revelation" about the end of time (*DF*, 2:23), so too the prudent Mohammed "has not presumed to determine the moment of that awful catastrophe, though he darkly announces the signs, both in heaven and earth, which will precede the universal dissolution . . ." (*DF*, 5:348-49). Here Gibbon again affirms the difficulty of determining "the intermediate state of the soul" as it awaits reunion with the flesh. Mohammed's picture of the final judgment uses the metaphors of "an earthly tribunal." Non-believers are universally damned: "the greater part of mankind," Gibbon states in revealing contrast, are "condemned for their *opinions* [my emphasis]," while only true believers "will be judged by their *actions* [my emphasis]" (*DF*, 5:350). However long sinful believers must suffer, eventually all of them will be saved. Like Christianity, Islam has its ideological requirements, its ideological purities, and its ideological guarantees.

The religiously familiar natural imagery[12] in Islam's description of the heavenly paradise disdains "a liberal taste for harmony and science, conversation and friendship." Instead, the prophet, says Gibbon,

> idly celebrates the pearls and diamonds, the robes of silk, palaces of marble, dishes of gold, rich wines, artificial dainties, numerous attendants, and the whole train of sensual and costly luxury, which becomes insipid to the owner, even in the short period of this mortal life. Seventy-two *Houris*, or blackeyed girls of resplendent beauty, blooming youth, virgin purity, and exquisite sensibility, will be created for the use of the meanest believer; a moment of pleasure will be prolonged to a thousand years, and his faculties will be increased an hundred-fold, to render him worthy of his felicity. (*DF*, 5:35)

Gibbon's brief interjection into this picture posits psychological impossibility along with theological unlikelihood. Although this paradise welcomes men and women, Mohammed "has not specified the male companions of the female elect, lest he should either alarm the jealousy of their former husbands or disturb their felicity by the suspicion of an everlasting marriage."[13] However much embarrassed Mohammedanism allegorizes this picture to escape its blunt sensuality, Gibbon assumes a literal intention and a literal reading. He does add, though, that "the prophet has expressly declared that all meaner happiness will be forgotten and despised by the saints and martyrs, who shall be admitted to the beatitude of the divine vision" (*DF*, 5:351).

That Gibbon should so ironically deprecate the sensuality of the Mohammedan afterlife testifies to the judicious discrimination of his religious analyses because he speaks very favorably of many features of Islam. He admires, for example, its greater toleration.[14] The summary judgment of the Moslem creed is highly complimentary: "more pure than the system of Zoroaster, more liberal than the law of Moses, . . . [and] less inconsistent with reason than the creed of mystery and superstition which, in the seventh century, disgraced the simplicity of the gospel"(*DF*, 5:487).

The concern in chapter 51 with Islamic practice towards non-believers concludes a long account of the fortunes of Arabia after the death of Mohammed in A.D. 632. The preceding chapter's more personally focussed look at Mohammed himself—with the founder rather than the faith—saves for the last the "beneficial or pernicious influence on the public happiness" of "the character of Mahomet" (*DF*, 5:395). Whatever limitations Gibbon acknowledges in Mohammed's proselytizing, he also observes that the prophet "breathed among the faithful a spirit of charity and friendship, recommended the practice of the social virtues, and checked, by his laws and precepts, the thirst of revenge and the oppression of widows and orphans" (*DF*, 5:396).

Such complimentary judgments do not preclude the incisive, ambiguous analysis of the character of Mohammed, an analysis that raises as many doubts as the supposedly neutral consideration of the five causes of Christianity. Gibbon finds it difficult "at the distance of twelve centuries . . . [to] darkly contemplate [Mohammed's] shade through a cloud of religious incense" (*DF*, 5:397), a major cause of obfuscation in religious and ecclesiastical annals. "Could I truly delineate the portrait of an hour, the fleeting resemblance," he suspects, "would not equally apply to the solitary of mount Hera, to the preacher of Mecca, and to the conqueror of Arabia" (*DF*, 5:375). The character analysis that follows refuses to resolve antitheses and moral ambiguities, and along its way even takes a glancing shot at the credulity of no less a figure than Socrates. Speaking of Mohammed, Gibbon writes:

> It was duty of a man and a citizen to impart the doctrine of salvation, to rescue his country from the dominion of sin and error. The energy of a mind incessantly bent on the same object would convert a general obligation into a particular call; the warm suggestings of the understanding or the fancy would be felt as the inspirations of heaven; the labour of thought would expire in rapture and vision; and the inward sensation, the invisible monitor, would be described with the form and attributes of an angel of God. From enthusiasm to imposture the step is perilous and slippery; the daemon of Socrates affords a memorable instance, how a wise man may deceive himself, how a good man may deceive others, how the conscience may slumber in a mixed and middle state between self-illusion and voluntary fraud. (*DF*, 5:376)

This antithetical march continues through the career of Mohammed. "Of his last years," Gibbon then notes, "ambition was the ruling passion; and a politician will suspect that he secretly smiled (the victorious imposter!) at the enthusiasm of his youth and the credulity of his proselytes" (*DF*, 5:377). The Mohammed appearing here as "the victorious impostor" is elsewhere "an eloquent fanatic" (*DF*, 5:394), founder of a religion whose fanatics, "like our fanatics of the last century, . . . spoke the language of *their* [Gibbon's emphasis] scriptures" (*DF*, 5:420 n. 66).

A historian as conscious as Gibbon of the questionable, legendary accretions to what he believes the basically simple life of Jesus,[15] not surprisingly recognizes the credulity that adds wonder to the life of Mohammed. Once again, the romance of religion is at work:

> The votaries of Mahomet are more assured than himself of his miraculous gifts,[16] and their confidence and credulity increase as they

are farther removed from the time and place of his spiritual exploits.
They believe or affirm that trees went forth to meet him; that he was
saluted by stones; that water gushed from his fingers; that he fed the
hungry, cured the sick, and raised the dead; that a beam groaned to
him; that a camel complained to him; that a shoulder of mutton
informed him of its being poisoned; and that both animate and
inanimate nature were equally subject to the apostle of God. (*DF*,
5:344)

At least in the eyes of believers, "the sword of Mahomet was not less
potent than the rod of Moses" (*DF*, 5:346). Competition has its role to
play in credulity.

Credulity, thirdly, commonly assumes unusual physical attractiveness
in its religious founders. Mohammed, so the believer was pleased to
affirm, "was distinguished by the beauty of his person, an outward gift
which is seldom despised," says Gibbon, momentarily betraying the
reader, "except by those to whom it has been refused" (*DF*, 5:335). His
father, Abdallah, had been "the most beautiful and modest of Arabian
youth; and, in the first night, when he consummated his marriage with
Amina [Mohammed's mother], . . . two hundred virgins are said to have
expired of jealousy and despair" (*DF*, 5:334).

The footnotes in which Gibbon wages so many of his battles with
Christianity's romances are an important theater of encounter with the
ease and expanse of Moslem romance. Like the footnotes on Christian
excess, these too are often of a sexual nature. Philip Guedella, we recall,
once joked that Gibbon lived out his sex life in his footnotes.[17] Certainly
a number of those notes on Mohammedanism create the impression of a
brief, in camera indulgence from which Gibbon returns to the public,
composed chamber of the text. Notice, for instance, how Gibbon han-
dles the alleged incontinence of the prophet. Perhaps, the historian spec-
ulates, this imputation "may be palliated by the tradition of his natural
or preternatural gifts: he united the manly virtue of thirty of the children
of Adam; and the apostle might rival the thirteenth labour of the Grecian
Hercules" (*DF*, 5:380). What sexual frenzy impels Gibbon not to one,
but three footnotes on this brief text that make clear the sexual nature of
these "natural or preternatural gifts," the very physical manifestation of
this "manly virtue"? The documentary Dionysian, intriguingly, adopts in
the first note the modest disguise of Latin and, in the second note, the
equally chaste cover of Greek. But in the third and final note, Gibbon's
wild abandon casts off all restraint and appears in the transparent and
nakedly revealing veils of his native English.

The first note (*DF*, 5:380 n. 175) passes on the claim that the prophet
could satisfy as many as eleven women in one hour, repeats, secondly, the

testimony of Al Jannabi that Mohammed "surpassed all men in conjugal vigour," and concludes with the astonishment of the Ali who washed the prophet's body after his death: "Beyond doubt, O prophet," the wondering Ali exclaims, "your penis is elevated towards the heavens." Modestly, of course, Gibbon hints here at one of the hitherto unconsidered attractions of a career in the mortuary arts. The second note (*DF*, 5:380 n. 176) borrows "the style" of Church Father Gregory Nazianzen in alluding to Hercules' thirteenth challenge, which the final footnote in the trio identifies as "the common and most glorious legend [that] includes, in a single night, the fifty victories of Hercules over the virgin daughters of Thestius." In something of a kill-joy moment, editor J. B. Bury denies that Gibbon's source says, " 'in a single night.' " Gibbon, however, mentions a scholarly controversy about the duration of Hercules' performance: "Atheneaeus allows seven nights," he mock-solemnly observes, "and Apollodorus fifty, for this arduous achievement of Hercules, who was then no more than eighteen years of age."[18] However much scholarship will controvert the duration of this triumph, it can unanimously agree that here at least is the one section of the *Decline and Fall* that James Boswell read with admiration, envy, and, dare I say it, credulity.

3. The Religion of Julian

The most prominent enthusiast in the *Decline and Fall* is the pagan emperor Julian, nephew of Constantine. If history provides Gibbon enough material to fashion his own *Tale of a Tub* on superstition, his Julian strikingly resembles the enthusiast Jack in Swift's *Tale*.[19] In *The Literary Art of Edward Gibbon* Harold Bond points out that the twenty-month reign of Julian occupies "three of Gibbon's most stirring chapters" because he embodied "part of the great spirit of Rome" interred with him at his death.[20] True, but one of these three chapters is wholly given over to Julian's religion in an analysis that makes clear how little the emperor's fanaticism and intolerance revealed anything of the lightly worn paganism of the Antonine emperors. Julian's was a most uncharacteristic zeal for the pagan gods.

Like Swift's Jack, Julian's imagination "was susceptible of the most lively impressions" (*DF*, 2:433). Julian, however, was a Jack with power, and so "the phantoms which existed only in the mind of the emperor had a real and pernicious effect on the government of the empire" (*DF*, 2:432). Julian's "voluntary offering of his reason on the altars of Jupiter and Apollo" (*DF*, 2:436) took the specific form of a fascination with the occult which allowed him to come under the baneful influence of fanatic pagan philosophers, one of whom, Maximus, initiates the twenty-year-old Julian at Ephesus into the mysteries of Eleusis:

> As these ceremonies were performed in the depth of caverns, and in the silence of the night, and as the inviolable secret of the mysteries was preserved by the discretion of the initiated, I shall not presume to describe the horrid sounds and fiery apparitions, which were presented to the senses, or the imagination, of the credulous aspirant, till the visions of comfort and knowledge broke upon him in a blaze of celestial light. In the caverns of Ephesus and Eleusis, the mind of Julian was penetrated with a sincere, deep, and unalterable enthusiasm; though he might sometimes exhibit the vicissitudes of pious fraud and hypocrisy, which may be observed, or at least suspected, in the character of the most conscientious fanatics. From that moment he consecrated his life to the service of the gods. (*DF*, 2:440–41)

Julian fasted to prepare himself "for the frequent and familiar visits with which he was honoured by the celestial powers." A conveniently credulous disciple, in Gibbon a ubiquitous religious phenomenon, records that Julian

> lived in a perpetual intercourse with the gods and goddesses; that they descended upon earth, to enjoy the conversation of their favourite hero; that they gently interrupted his slumbers, by touching his hand or his hair; that they warned him of every impending danger, and conducted him, by their infallible wisdom, in every action of his life; and that he had such an intimate knowledge of his heavenly guests, as readily to distinguish the voice of Jupiter from that of Minerva, and the form of Apollo from the figure of Hercules. (*DF*, 2:441)

Publicly Christian, at least initially, Julian returned privately to his pagan devotions "with the impatience of a lover" (*DF*, 2:443). In no meaningless gesture, he marked his accession by assuming "the character of the supreme pontiff" (*DF*, 2:445–46) and performed in pagan liturgies "the meanest offices which contributed to the worship of the gods": "It was the business of the emperor to bring the wood, to blow the fire, to handle the knife, to slaughter the victim, and, thrusting his hand into the bowels of the expiring animal, to draw forth the heart or liver, and to read, with the consummate skill of an haruspex, the imaginary signs of future events" (*DF*, 2: 446).

The public consequences of such an attachment were ominous. Sycophantic civil administrators who knew how to read between the lines of an apparent policy of toleration and equal treatment knew that they risked no real danger by ignoring the dictates and observing the wishes of their sovereign:

> In the exercise of arbitrary power [Gibbon writes], [the provincial ministers of his authority] consulted the wishes, rather than the commands, of their sovereign; and ventured to exercise a secret and vexations tyranny against the sectaries, on whom they were not permitted to confer the honours of martyrdom. The emperor, who dissembled as long as possible his knowledge of the injustice that was exercised in his name, expressed his real sense of the conduct of his officers by gentle reproofs and substantial rewards. (*DF*, 2:463)

A passage as darkly modern as any in the entire *Decline and Fall*. Julian, in fine, constructed and encouraged an "artful system by which [he] proposed to obtain the effects, without incurring the guilt, or reproach, of persecution" (*DF*, 2:476). The chapter-long analysis of the emperor's religion concludes with the ominous speculation that if Julian had lived longer and continued his real policy against Christianity, "he must have involved his country in the horrors of a civil war" (*DF*, 2:478).

One incident from the history of Julian nicely captures Gibbon's amusement at the fanatical excesses of Julian's faith. The historian relates how Julian hastened "to adore the Apollo of Daphne" with a devotion "raised to the highest pitch of eagerness and impatience." As he allowed his fancy to run wild with thoughts of a splendid liturgy at Antioch, Gibbon writes that Julian's "lively imagination anticipated the grateful pomp of victims, of libations, and of incense; a long procession of youths and virgins, clothed in white robes, the symbol of their innocence; and the tumultuous concourse of an innumerable people" (*DF*, 2:467). Julian's frenzy overlooked the fact that with the establishment of Christianity the temple of Apollo at Antioch had fallen into some desuetude:

> Instead of hecatombs of fat oxen sacrificed by the tribes of a wealthy city to their tutelar deity, the emperor complains that he found only a single goose, provided at the expense of a priest, the pale and solitary inhabitant of this decayed temple [who? the goose or the priest?]. The altar was deserted, the oracle had been reduced to silence, and the holy ground was profaned by the introduction of Christian and funereal rites. (*DF*, 2:467)

The temple proved not to be the best of all possible fanes. To adapt a phrase from Jaroslav Pelikan's very recently published *The Excellent Empire*, credulity and zeal, any of the excesses of superstition and enthusiasm, are in Edward Gibbon "a thoroughly ecumenical phenomenon."[21]

NOTES

1 See *Boswell's Life of Johnson, Together with Boswell's Journal of a Tour to the Hebrides and Johnson's Diary of a Journey into North Wales*, ed. George Birkbeck Hill, rev. L. F. Powell (Oxford: Clarendon, 1934), 2:447–48. See also *Boswell: The Ominous Years, 1774–1776*, eds. Charles Ryskamp and Frederick A. Pottle (Melbourne: Heinemann, 1963), 282.

One of the definitions Johnson provides for *artful* is *cunning*, and his definitions of the second term could constitute a verbal arsenal of charges levelled against Gibbon: "Artifice; deceit; sliness; sleight; craft; subtilty; dissimulation; fraudulent dexterity." The citation from Bacon underscores the ethical imputation of the term: "We take *cunning* for a sinister or crooked wisdom; and certainly there is a great difference between a *cunning* man and a wise man, not only in point of honesty, but in point of ability."

2 A third, very important source of Gibbon's religious assumptions appears in chapter 54, the study of the Paulician heresy from which Gibbon traces the Protestant Reformation in the European Renaissance. I will be directly concerned with those assumptions, however, in a separate but related study on the Protestantism of many of the principles Gibbon employs in the *Decline and Fall*.

3 Louis XVI believed that references to Arcadius or Honorius in the *General Observations* (*DF*, 4:165) unflatteringly alluded to him. In his *Memoirs*, however, Gibbon states: "I am ready to declare that the concluding observations of my third Volume were written before his accession to the throne." See Edward Gibbon, *Memoirs of My Life*, ed. Georges Bonnard (London: Nelson, 1966), 175.

4 Edward Gibbon, *The History of the Decline and Fall of the Roman Empire*, ed., intro., nn., app., and ind. J. B. Bury (London: Methuen, 1896–1900), 4:163. Hereafter incorporated into the text as *DF*.

5 Gibbon's footnote states that "the Christians as well as the Jews . . . formed a very important exception" to this Antonine policy of toleration, "so important, indeed," Gibbon alerts the reader, "that the discussion will require a distinct chapter of this work." See *DF*, 1:29 n. 3. Gibbon's later analysis of the zeal of the Jews and the early Christians repeatedly emphasizes the intolerance of both religious groups. See *DF*, 2:2–19.

6 The role of the ideals of the Roman Republic of Gibbon's history is a major theme in Harold L. Bond, *The Literary Art of Edward Gibbon* (Oxford: Clarendon, 1960). See also Lewis P. Curtis, "Gibbon's *Paradise Lost*," in *The Age of Johnson: Essays Presented to Chauncey Brewster Tinker*, ed. Frederick W. Hilles, intro. Wilmarth S. Lewis (New Haven and London: Yale University Press, 1949), 73–90. Patricia Craddock has cautioned me about the reservations Gibbon expresses for the expansionist policies of the Republic and about its treatment of women and slaves.

7 Gibbon speaks in chapter 52 of "seasonable vision" and adds: "for such are the manufacture of every religion." See *DF*, 6:4.

8 Richard N. Parkinson provides a delightful analysis of what he calls in this passage some of Gibbon's "finest comic irony" in the first of the historian's attacks "upon unreason in religion." See *Edward Gibbon* (New York: Twayne, 1973), 50–52.

9 David Hume, *The Natural History of Religion*, ed. and intro. H. E. Root (Stanford: Stanford University Press, 1957), 42. Hereafter referred to as *NHR*, 54.

10 *NHR*, 54.

11 Gibbon's analysis of the belief in an afterlife shrewdly uncovers the vanity that prompts the human refusal to accept annihilation as the ultimate human destiny. In a stimulating contemporary study, Ernest Becker advances the thesis that "the idea of death, the fear of it, haunts the human animal like nothing else; it is a mainspring of human activity — activity designed largely to avoid the fatality of death, to overcome it by denying in some way that it is the final destiny for man." See *The Denial of Death* (New York: Macmillan [The Free Press]), 1973, ix.

12 In chapter 15, Gibbon describes a Christian counterpart to such paradisiacal expectation, this one, the earth-located blissful kingdom where Christ would reign upon the earth "till the time appointed for the last and general resurrection":

> So pleasing was this hope to the mind of believers [Gibbon writes] that the *New Jerusalem*, the seat of this blissful kingdom, was quickly adorned with all the gayest colours of the imagination. A felicity consisting only of pure and spiritual pleasure would have appeared too refined for its inhabitants, who were still supposed to possess their human nature and senses. A garden of Eden, with the amusements of the pastoral life, was no longer suited to the advanced state of society which prevailed under the Roman empire. A city was therefore erected of gold and precious stones, and a supernatural plenty of corn and wine was bestowed on the adjacent territory; in the free enjoyment of whose spontaneous production the happy and benevolent people was never to be restrained by any jealous laws of exclusive property. (*DF*, 2:24)

13 Is Gibbon also joking here at the expense of Jesus? Many a Christian reader must remember how Jesus answered the trap-question about the woman who successively married seven men, after the preceding husband died, and died last herself. When asked whose wife she would be in heaven, Jesus replied — diplomatically — that "in the resurrection they neither marry, nor are given in marriage" (Matt. 22:30, King James Version).

14 Jews and Christians, he notes, "were solemnly invited to accept the more *perfect* [Gibbon's emphasis] revelation of Mahomet; but, if they preferred the payment of a moderate tribute, they were entitled to the freedom of conscience and religious worship" (*DF*, 5:486). The captive's road to Islamic faith was also simple and easy: "By the repetition of a sentence and the loss of a foreskin, the subject or the slave, the captive or the criminal, arose in a moment the free and equal companion of the victorious Moslems" (*DF*, 5:486–87).

Gibbon always displays a transcendent serenity in contemplating the sexual sacrifices of others. After recounting, for example, how Henry II's father, when master of Normandy, castrated all the bishops and the bishop-elect chosen by them because they had acted without his consent, Gibbon comments: "Of the pain and danger they might justly complain; yet, since they had vowed chastity, he deprived them of a superfluous treasure." The superfluities, by the way, were presented to Henry's father on a platter. See *DF*, 7:216 n. 16.

15 Gibbon twice speaks of the simplicity of the life of Jesus. In chapter 15 he points out that the "mild constancy [of Jesus of Nazareth] in the midst of cruel and voluntary sufferings, his universal benevolence, and the sublime simplicity of his actions and character" were insufficient, among the pagans, to compensate for "fame, . . . empire, and . . . success" (*DF*, 2:77). In a more important context, however, chapter 47, where Gibbon takes up the theological history of the doctrine of the Incarnation, the asserted simplicity of the life of Jesus marks an important introductory contrast to the record of theologically elaborate and intricate speculation which follows. Gibbon says there:

> The familiar companions of Jesus of Nazareth conversed with their friend and countryman, who, in all the actions of rational and animal life, appeared of the same species with themselves. His progress from infancy to youth and manhood was marked by a regular increase in stature and wisdom; and, after a painful agony of mind and body, he expired on the cross. He lived and died for the service of mankind; but the life and death of Socrates had likewise been devoted to the cause of religion and justice; and, although the stoic or the hero may disdain the humble virtues of Jesus, the tears which he shed over his friend and country may be esteemed the purest evidence of his humanity (*DF*, 5:97–98).

16 A comparable sceptical thrust is directed at the claim by Christian disciples that an ecclesiastical hero of theirs had exhibited miraculous power: "In the long series of ecclesiastical history," Gibbon asks in his analysis of the early church's claim of preternatural power, "does there exist a single instance of a saint asserting that he himself possessed the gift of miracles?" See *DF*, 2:30 n. 82.

17 The remark appears indirectly in Dero Saunders's introduction to *The Portable Gibbon: The Decline and Fall of the Roman Empire*, ed. and intro. Dero A. Saunders, pref. Charles Alexander Robinson, Jr. (New York: Penguin, 1977), 15.

18 The reference to Gregory Nazianzen alludes to the third to last paragraph of his first invective against the Emperor Julian. Gregory is denouncing in particular the sexually scandalous and immoral behavior to be gleaned from pagan legend and literature. He calls Hercules "the child of three nights" and expresses his puzzlement that Hercules' "labouring amongst the fifty daughters of Thestias in a single night" is "not counted, I know not wherefore, in the list." See "Gregory Nazianzen's First Invective Against Julian the Emperor," in *Julian the Emperor: Containing Gregory Nazianzen's Two Invectives and*

Libanius' Monody with Julian's Extant Theosophical Works, trans. C[harles]. W[illiam]. King (London: George Bell, 1888), 83.

19 Gibbon draws the important distinction between superstition and enthusiasm from David Hume's *The Natural History of Religion*. Hume also pursues the distinction in his essay "Of Superstition and Enthusiasm." In "Superstition and Enthusiasm in Gibbon's History of Religion," J. G. A. Pocock discusses extensively how this distinction works in the *Decline and Fall* and points out, in particular, that fanaticism can be a quality of either. See *Eighteenth-Century Life* 8, n.s. 1 (1983):83–94. Julian actually appears as enthusiast and superstitious votary, the latter as he seeks to reinvigorate the pagan priesthood and expand the presence of pagan ritual.

20 Bond, *Literary Art of Gibbon*, 66.

21 See his *The Excellent Empire: The Fall of Rome and the Triumph of the Church* (San Francisco: Harper and Row, 1987), 57.

"Soft Figures" and
"a Paste of Composition Rare":
Pope, Swift, and Memory

MELINDA ALLIKER RABB

In a letter of 1728, Swift urged Pope to make the topical allusions in the *Dunciad* less difficult, "for I have long observ'd that twenty miles from London no body understands hints, initial letters, or town-facts and passages; and in a few years not even those who live in London" (16 July 1728).[1] One can surmise how Pope felt at being told that only a few people would understand him, and that none would remember. Swift's remark is premised on a belief in the writer's complex dependence on memory; it determines what may be lost or preserved—poetic meaning, relationships with people, history, and more fundamentally, a continuous sense of self. Pope's *Dunciad* investigates the function of memory in the creation and perpetuation of art; it attacks the memory-less dunces, and foretells the dire consequences of the failure of memory. Nevertheless Swift fears that Pope's allusive techniques may cause the *Dunciad* itself to be forgotten. Thus Swift refers first to the geographical exigencies of the present moment, that those twenty miles from London may not understand satiric hints and town-passages. But, in case Pope does not care about provincial readers, Swift saves the sting until the end: "and in a few years, not even those who live in London."

Memory traditionally is set in antithesis with imagination, often benefitting imagination according to those assumptions about creativity that led to and followed romanticism. If readers have agreed to celebrate the artist for a "visionary" ability to re-make the world, opinions differ as to how the process occurs. The most common explanation is that imagination creates, transforms, bodies forth unknown shapes, articulates what has not yet been. The womb of imagination seems to have all the advantages over the grave of memory. These are the terms in which the forgetful Moderns of *A Tale of a Tub* embrace imagination, suggesting some inadequacy in this point of view:

> [T]he Question is only this: Whether Things that have Place in the Imagination, may not as properly be said to exist, as those that are seated in the Memory: which may be justly held in the affirmative, and very much to the advantage of the former, since it is acknowledged to be the Womb of Things, and the other allowed to be no more than the Grave.[2]

To the contrary, Swift and Pope imply that memory acts vitally in artistic creativity. John Sitter has argued that Mnemosyne is the mother of the Augustan muse because she represents an allegiance to history.[3] The artist's inspiration and cultural legacy would then come from the past, often from ancient precedents and models. But the wish to preserve ideals from the past does not fully account for the role of memory. At times, it supplants imagination in explanations of the transformative powers of the mind.

To a number of eighteenth-century writers, as Addison reminds us in *The Spectator*, imagination is not the only restless and fertile source of images and ideas: "The memory likewise may turn itself to an infinite multitude of objects" (*Spectator*, 600).[4] Nor is imagination the only way to turn bushes into bears: "[W]rite immediately while the impression is fresh," Johnson counsels Boswell, "for it will not be the same a week after" (*Boswell for the Defense*). That is, memory is strongly associated with processes of change. The past is not absolutely fixed, and its retrieval entails constant reshaping. Memory inevitably changes its absent original, and two people rarely remember the same thing in the same way. Hobbes believes that "imagination and memory are but one thing which for diverse considerations hath divers names." "Fancy and memory differ only in this," he explains, "that memory supposeth the time past, which fancy doth not."[5] Or, to pursue the implications of Locke's emphasis on the human ability to "revive" the past, memory enables our sense of time, and time makes everything mutable.[6] Swift and Pope agree that memory is not a fixed record book of the past but a process, suggested by the puns in the words remembering, recollecting, and reminding. Fragments from the past are reshaped, rearranged, and rethought. This essay focuses on why Swift and Pope associate different images and metaphors with memory—images and metaphors of transformation through melting, pliancy, and dissolving in Pope, and of transformation through reassembling, distorting, and congealing in Swift. In either case, the process has its liabilities as well as its rewards.

Swiftian characters are famous for their pathological disorders of memory. Some have too little, like the absent-minded Hack who digresses his way through the *Tale* and "dissects the carcass of human nature," in hope of finding a Modern "design of an everlasting remembrance." Yet Modern memory, as represented in the *Tale*, consists of images of constant flux. Like shifting clouds resembling bears, asses, and dragons, "if . . . [Prince Posterity] should in a few minutes think fit to examine the truth, tis certain they would all be changed . . . ," and the "memorial" of Modern authors, lost among men. Equally disturbing are the Struldbruggs whose immortality is made terrifying by their inability to remember anything after the age of forty.[7] While their bodies continue aging forever, memory dies. One hardly knows which is worse, to be tormented with recollections of youth or to be denied the escape of nostalgia.

Other characters suffer from excesses of memory. For Gulliver, it is memory and not imagination that gets astride on reason. His retention is severe enough to drive him mad. In order to cope with the effects of his memories of Houyhnhnmland, he must walk around with his nose stopped with rue. A similar recommendation is made for another unbalanced rememberer, Strephon. "If he would but stop his nose," the poet suggests, he might better cope with the memory of what he found in the lady's dressing-room.[8] Here the power of memory arguably displaces that of imagination. Strephon's "foul Imagination" first "links each dame he sees with all her stinks," but his inability to forget sustains his absurd obsession.

Some of the uses of memory in Swift suggest ironic reworking of classical and Renaissance precedents, such as the art of memory and the Rabelaisian grotesque. The Greek poet Simonides recommends aiding the memory with striking images that are often ugly, shocking, or comic.[9] The mnemonics built out of these images transform their originals in eccentric ways. Sometimes, the mnemonic is more interesting than the information it is supposed to call to mind. Renaissance elaborations of the art of memory, which Swift knew, are motivated by a yearning for control, probably in response to the actual quirkiness with which the mind fills itself with indelible trivia yet can seem empty when a crucial fact is needed.[10] Even worse, tenacious memories can be painful. Cicero tells the story of Simonides and his art, but he also tells the story of Themistocles. When offered the chance to remember anything he wants,

Themistocles says that he would rather learn the art of forgetting and consign to oblivion whatever he chooses.

"For fine Ideas vanish fast/ While all the gross and filthy last." Swift's reductive couplet ("Strephon and Chloe," ll. 49–50) sums up the most relevant aspects of the art of memory. Rabelais had rejected classical and Renaissance memory "claptrap," yet he exemplifies the longevity of the "gross and filthy," a quality that Swift emulates.[11] The final confluence of garbage that ends "A Description of a City Shower," Corinna's glass eye, Celia's stinking chest, an Irish child stewed and piping hot on an English mayor's table, a dissected beau and a flayed woman, the breasts of the ladies in waiting in Brobdingnag, or countless other images from *Gulliver's Travels*, *A Tale of a Tub*, or the scatological poems, demonstrate Swift's mastery of the unforgettable detail. Such details concretize intangible abstractions (like love, justice, pride, or beauty) and feelings (line anger, indignation, or fear).[12] But they not only concretize — they petrify into lasting memorials for the reader's contemplation. This process informs "The Lady's Dressing Room." The poem is constructed like the basic mnemonic of the art of memory: a man walks through a room and looks at the things (the striking image) in it.[13] Swift's images not only transform a whole woman, the absent Celia, into fragments that remind Strephon of her (such as nail parings, plucked hairs, and spit), but these bits and pieces are transmuted into non-human objects with which they blend and congeal:

> Now listen while he next produces
> The various combs for various uses,
> Fill'd up with dirt so closely fixt,
> No Brush could force a way betwixt.
> A Paste of Composition rare,
> Sweat, dandruff, Powder, Lead and Hair
> . . . .
> Nor be the handkerchiefs forgot
> All cover'd o'er with snuff and snot.
>   (20–24, 49–50)

At the end of the poem, Celia is then aptly recollected by the poet as order from confusion sprung: Celia's decomposing leavings have literally fused into a stiff paste of dandruff, puppy water, ear wax, pomatum, and sweat, "a nasty compound of all hues," literally sticking in the consciousness of Strephon and the reader.[14]

Swift could and did write non-satirically of memory. "Stella's Birthday, 1727" looks back at his friendship with Stella to find "[s]ome lasting Pleasure in the Mind:

> Which by Remembrance will assuage,
> Grief, Sickness, Poverty, and Age;
> And strongly shoot a radiant Dart,
> To shine through Life's declining Part.
> (30-34)

Yet even here the process of "reflecting on a Life well spent" leads Swift to images of homely physicality. Rather than relegate the past to "empty Shadows," "Forms reflected in a Glass," or "mere Chimaera's in the Mind,/ That fly and leave no Marks behind" (ll. 51-54), he proposes an intellectual and emotional digestive system, whereby the "Food of twenty Years ago" still lingers in "the Body." Just as "[e]ffects of Food remain," he urges Stells, so "each good Action past" becomes "the Nutriment that feeds the Mind" (ll. 60-62).

While Swift's striking images re-member and solidify, Pope's memory-images also change shape, but in doing so grow pliant and insubstantial. Things dissolve rather than dismember: "Memory's soft figures melt away" (*Essay on Criticism*, l. 59). Pope raises somewhat different issues of control — intellectual, emotional, artistic — over the act of remembering. For Pope, the changes worked by memory suggest literary precedents in Ovid, Homer, and Shakespeare. They too play a role in creating and, to use Pope's term, "uncreating." While he takes us further from Renaissance techniques for the control or manipulation of memory, he continues the Augustan belief that memory, not imagination, is the means to ideal truth.[15] Addison observes of Ovid that "[h]is Art consists chiefly in well-timing his Description, before the first shape is quite worn off, and the new one perfectly finish'd" (*Spectator*, 417).[16] For Pope, memory keeps these moments of overlap or transition perpetually alive; lingering traces of the past alter the present and the future; they produce motley mixtures, half-form'd creatures, and hybrid monsters. Ulysses' crew remembered that they had been men after Circe changed them to swine, an episode Pope had translated in his *Odyssey* and then parodied in the *Dunciad*. In Pope's work generally, the past exerts a constant pressure, urging the reader to glimpse an ever more remote but truer identity.

Swift associates memory with absence and desire by working through the bodily grotesque. Strephon, for example, remakes Celia in a way that satisfies his own mad needs. As a representative of the male desire to possess woman, he, like Petrarch before him, contemplates pieces of an absent mistress. Celia, as a whole presence, is less important than Strephon's frustrated desire.[17] In Pope, memory and the body are linked differently, more erotically, as memory's "soft figures" undergo change. Ovid focuses on the moments "before the first shape is quite worn off" because such moments hold the most intense sexual urgency. The pursuing god or satyr has just those last few seconds in which to achieve sexual union and gratify desire, and the fleeing nymph, to avoid rape and yield to another kind of physical change. As early as "Windsor Forest" (1713) Pope reworks such moments. The episode of Lodona and Pan introduces imagery that will later characterize Pope's metaphors for remembering and forgetting. Pan, "burning with desire," almost overtakes Lodona who feels his warm breath and the premonition of rape: "And now his Shadow reach'd her as she run,/ . . . And now his shorter breath with sultry Air/ Pants on her Neck and fans her parting Hair" (ll. 193, 195–96). The felt warmth of his breath is followed by transformation: "melting . . ./ In a soft, silver Stream [Lodona] dissolv'd away" (ll. 203–4).

In *An Essay on Criticism*, Pope writes of memory and imagination in similar imagery:

> Thus in the Soul while Memory
> prevails,
> The solid Pow'r of Understanding fails;
> Where Beams of warm Imagination
> play,
> The Memory's soft Figures melt away
> (56–59)

Memory is soft, changeable, feminine, stirring an almost erotic desire. To adapt T. S. Eliot's phrase in *The Wasteland*, the poet mixes memory and desire with a little imagination.[18] A kind of mating dance between mental faculties must go on if the mind is to be creative. Thus the sterile authors of *The Dunciad*, frustrated sexually and impotent artistically, are not equipped to be creative: "O Muse! relate (for you can tell alone,/ Wits have short Memories, and Dunces none" (ll. 619–20).

A relationship between memory, desire, and sexual difference similarly influences the portrait of Sporus in the *Epistle to Dr. Arbuthnot*. Lord Harvey's effeminacy is conveyed through images of softness: white curd, dimpling streams, froth. He is changeable, pliant, a mixture of male and female, beauty and ugliness, ineffectuality and danger. The metamorphoses to which he is subjected by the poet end in the "amphibious [and androgynous] Thing" breathing its hot satanic breath in seductive whispers at the ear of Eve. A similar configuration of images attends the softened resistance of Milton's Eve as the transformed serpent makes her memory of the divine commandment melt away. Miltonic echoes of *Paradise Lost*, Books 2 and 4, also suggest another mingled state. The fallen angels are tormented by memories of their former glory and thus they must enforce moral amnesia. Their burden (and humanity's) is that the lost state of innocence cannot be forgotten.

Memory, though not without its pains and frustrations, is associated with fertility and the impulse to create, the failure of memory with dangerous seduction and loss. Both are erotic, expressing both desire and fear of cycles of mutability. The Goddess Dulness is an anti-Mnemosyne, a wicked stepmother to the muse, a Circe to the poet. Her fecundity is a fecundity of the ephemeral, of the constant production of forgettable "momentary monsters [who] rise and fall" (*Dunciad*, line 83). Her "phantom" poet, in the heat of competition, "melted . . . from sight" (2.112). Her "Empire" predates human memory: "In eldest time, e'er mortal's writ or read" she "ruled in native anarchy the Mind" (lines 9-16). The mind without remembrance of history is chaotic, malleable, vulnerably soft, without fixed shape or order. The king of duncery will "peaceably forgot, at once be blest/ In Shadwell's bosom with eternal rest!/ Soon to that mass of Nonsense to return,/ Where things destroy'd are swept to things unborn" (lines 239-42). Dulness's "Opium" causes her sons to "leave all Memory of Sense behind" (line 276). Breathing the vapours from the land of dreams, drinking from "Lethe's streams," Dulness and the Dunces repeatedly associate sexuality and oblivion.

The sweeping historical vision of the *Dunciad*, Book 3, recounts "Old scenes of glory" soon to be forgotten. True to the pattern, learning may be turned by "one bright blaze . . . into Air" or is "dissolved in Port . . ." (line 338). In Book 4, memory has become, not creative re-membering, but "plying" with mere rote learning that will hang a jangling padlock on the mind. Britain's youth (her future), without clear memory of the past, "to gentle shadow all are shrunk,/ All melted down, in Pension, or in Punk" (lines 509-10). With images that suggest both political and psychological danger, Pope draws parallels between national historical crises and personal identity crises. "With that, a Wizard old his cup extends;/ Which who so tastes, forgets his former friends,/ Sire, Ancestors, Himself" (lines 518-20). In the vast forgetting, the "cultural amnesia" (Sitter's phrase), that closes the *Dunciad*, everything valuable is blurred, faded, dissolved. With memory, creativity is possible; without it, only uncreation and darkness.

As things and images melt away in Pope's work, we often are left, as the only enduring residue, with a text. Frequently this "text" consists of a single word. One of the most ancient metaphors for memory is writing: a scroll, a graven tablet, or a wax impression. Pope seems to endorse this metaphor. What we have left at the end of the *Dunciad* is a word, albeit an uncreating word.[19] Somewhat more consoling are the endings to *The Rape of the Lock* and "An Elegy To the Memory of an Unfortunate

Young Lady." Belinda's name, fixed forever in the celestial spheres, becomes the enduring memorial to her life: "This lock, the Muse shall consecrate to Fame,/ And mid'st the Stars inscribe Belinda's Name!" (4. 149-50). A similar fate attends the unfortunate young lady: "So peaceful rests, without a stone, a name,/ What once had beauty, titles, wealth, and fame" (lines 69-70). Pope tends to disembody and reduce the women to this single sign. Even the more impassioned "Epilogue to the Satires" ultimately consigns Pope's memory to the printed page, although he gets a whole verse and not just a word: "Yet may this Verse, (if such a Verse remain)/ Show there was one who held [Vice] in disdain" (Dialogue 1, lines 171-72).

The contrast between Pope's memorial texts and Swiftian debris is stark. Yet both writers combine their interest in the concept of memory with a concern for the kind of memories they might themselves leave behind. Swift had warned, in a "Letter to a Young Clergyman," that it is difficult to "drive home" anything that will be remembered "till the next Morning, or rather till the next Meal."[20] In "On Poetry: A Rhapsody," writing, in a deftly reductive image, becomes the next meal:

> Tho' Chickens take a Month to fatten,
> The Guests in less than half an Hour
> Will more than half a Score devour.
> So, after toiling twenty Days,
> To earn a Stock of Pence and Praise,
> Thy labours, grown the Critick's prey,
> Are swallow'd o'er a Dish of Tea;
> Gone, to be never heard of more,
> Gone, where the Chickens went before.
> (61-70)

In contrast to Pope's "if this Verse remain," Swift literalizes (and concretizes) the idea of authorial "remains" in *Verses on the Death of Dr. Swift*:

> Now Curll his Shop from Rubbish
> drains;
> Three genuine Tomes of Swift's
> Remains.
> And then to make them pass the glibber,
> Revis'd by Tibbalds, Moore, and Cibber.
> He'll treat me as he does my Betters.
> Publish my Will, my Life, my Letters.
> Revive the Libels born to dye,
> (197-203)

Spurious editions and biographies will use words to misrepresent him doubly: not only are the "Tomes" falsely attributed, but they are further "revis'd" by his enemies. While Swift agrees with Pope that an author's "remains" are his words, these are subject to the clumsy and even malicious changes of public remembrance.

Memory involves the poet in a history of texts and culture; it informs the poet's new representation of the world by supplying him with constantly altering images from the past. Memory not only creates, but becomes the test of art. Swift and Pope both wrote ironically about being misunderstood by their readers. One thinks of the self-consciousness of *Verses on the Death of Dr. Swift*, or the *Epilogue to the Satires*, or the *Epistle to Dr. Arbuthnot*. Of course, it is better to be misunderstood than to be completely forgotten.

What do the contrasts mean for readers of Swift and Pope? They clarify a difference between attitudes toward language. Pope exhibits greater confidence that the sign corresponds to something stable, that if the sign can endure, then its meaning will endure. When everything has melted down and dissolved away, the remaining residue or trace will be a printed word. Despite the parenthetical qualification in the *Epilogue to the Satires*, "(*if* this verse remain)," Pope seems to believe that it probably will remain, and that it will "show one" particular truth from the past. Swift seems unwilling to endorse the text in this way. Despite Gulliver's extreme effort at the precise reporting of his memoirs, the printer gets it wrong. It wasn't Brobdingnag at all, but Brobding*rag*, he complains in the letter to his Cousin Sympson. Yet that memory from the past has been irrevocably altered by the unreliability of the printed page and by memory's fascinating but frustrating transformations.

More moving examples of the relationship of memory to language come from Swift's correspondence. In 1708, he begins to recall his childhood with images of "charming custards" and "delicious holidays." But the revery soon changes to "bloody noses and broken shins," and to a memory of school as a kind of child's prison-house of language: "confinement ten hours a day to nouns and verbs" (*Correspondence*, 1:109). Much later (in 1737), he muses nostalgically over news of improvements at Moor Park, the scene of his youthful ambitions. "I have heard it is very much changed for the better, as well as the gardens. The tree on which I carved those words, *factura nepotibus umbram*, is one of those elms that stand in the hollow ground . . . but I suppose the letters are widened and grown shapeless by time" (*Correspondence*, 4: 89). The letters from Virgil's *Georgics* are distorted beyond recognition, like so many other memories dependent on language. Yet the leftover tangible tracts of the letters grow ever bigger and harder, with the aging elm.[21] Pope does not share this Swiftian ambivalence, in which meaning may be lost while disfigured and sometimes disgusting physical reminders of that lost meaning refuse to go away. Images of dissolving and melting in Pope ultimately endure because they are enshrined in the monument of print. The verse will show (for all its difficult hints and town facts) without growing wide and shapeless by time.

To pursue the contrast one step further, we can take Pope's *Imitations of Horace* as a case in point. Pope made certain that the Horatian original was printed on the page opposite to his imitation. That is to say, the remembered text, however transformed by the Augustan poet, still maintains an integrity of its own. Traces of it are preserved intact. Memory is truly a kind of writing and enabled by language. The flesh of the past may moulder away, but words are its bones.

Swift's use of the art of memory is a contrasting case in point. Through it, one can indulge in a brief escape, however illusory, from "confinement . . . to nouns and verbs" into an alternate room full of things — physical, sensory, and organic — whose things are seen and, in the case of Swift, smelt. The past does not hold stable facts but ingredients to be blended, or perhaps confused by the writer into rare compositions.

NOTES

1 *The Correspondence of Alexander Pope*, ed. George Sherburn, 5 vols. (Oxford: Clarendon Press, 1956), 2: 504–5.

2 Jonathan Swift, *A Tale of a Tub*, ed. A. C. Guthkelch and D. Nichol Smith (Oxford: Clarendon Press, 1920, rev., 1956).

3 John Sitter, *Literary Loneliness in Mid-Eighteenth-Century England* (Ithaca and London: Cornell University Press, 1982), 83–103.

4 *The Spectator*, ed. Donald F. Bond, 5 vols. (Oxford: Oxford University Press, 1965).

5 *The English Works of Thomas Hobbes*, ed. Sir William Molesworth, 4 vols. (London: John Bohn, 1839), 3: 6, 1: 398.

6 John Locke, *An Essay Concerning Human Understanding*, ed. Peter H. Nidditch (Oxford: Clarendon Press, 1950), bk. 2, chap. 10.

7 *Gulliver's Travels*, ed. Herbert Davis (Oxford: Basil Blackwell, 1965).

8 *The Poetry of Jonathan Swift*, ed. Harold Williams, 2nd ed., 3 vols. (Oxford: Clarendon Press, 1958). All quotations from Swift's poetry refer to this edition.

9 Cicero, *De Oratore*, bk. 2, sec. 86: 352–55. Other classical sources for this idea include *Ad C. Herennium libri IV* and Quintillian's *Institutio oratoria*. Frances Yates gives a detailed account of them in *The Art of Memory* (Chicago: University of Chicago Press, 1966), 1–49.

10 Swift's knowledge of *Ad C. Herennium* and of the rhetorics of Cicero and Quintillian is discussed in Charles Allen Beaumont, *Swift's Classical Rhetoric*

(Athens: University of Georgia Press, 1961). Swift also would have known the art of memory from his reading of later "dark authors" like Paracelsus, Irenaeus, and Vaughan, who stirred his youthful irony in *A Tale of a Tub*. See Guthkelch and Smith, ed., *A Tale of a Tub*, li–lv.

11 In *Rabelais and His World*, trans. Helene Iswolsky (Bloomington: Indiana University Press, 1984), 303–40, Mikhail Bakhtin describes the power of the grotesque to "escape oblivion."

12 The uneasy relationship in Swift's work (specifically in the poetry) between abstract and concrete, change and permanence, is treated by A. B. England in *Energy and Order in the Poetry of Swift* (Lewisburg: Bucknell University Press; London and Toronto: Associated University Presses, 1980).

13 *Ad C. Herennium* bk. 3. sec. 22. See also Yates, *Art of Memory*, 9–10.

14 It is possible to hear two plays on words in the phrase "order (ordure) from confusion (fusion) sprung."

15 Sitter, *Literary Loneliness*, 167.

16 Bond, ed., *Spectator*, 3: 565.

17 For a full discussion of memory and this poem, see Melinda Alliker Rabb, "The Art of Remembering in Swift's 'The Lady's Dressing Room,'" *Texas Studies in Literature and Language* (forthcoming, 1989).

18 "Mixing/ Memory and desire, stirring/ Dull roots with spring rain," *The Burial of the Dead*, ll. 2–4.

19 The familiar close to the *Dunciad* is: "Light dies before they uncreating word;/ They hand, Great Anarch! lets the curtain fall;/ And Universal Darkness buries All" (lines 654–56).

20 *The Prose Works of Jonathan Swift*, ed. Herbert Davis, 13 vols. (Oxford: Clarendon, 1929–65), 9:69.

21 The significance of the Virgilian allusion, contemplated first by the young and then by the older Swift, may be further illuminated by Peter J. Schakel's general discussion of Swift's poetic use of classical texts. Swift's earliest classical allusions (in the odes, written at Moor Park during the same years in which he carved the tree) seem superficial compared to his late and more personal transformations of them. See *The Poetry of Jonathan Swift: Allusion and the Development of a Poetic Style* (Madison: University of Wisconsin Press, 1978).

Gender and Race in
Yarico's Epistles to Inkle:
Voicing the Feminine/Slave

MARTIN WECHSELBLATT

Over forty years ago, in what is still one of the finest overviews of noble savagery in seventeenth- and eighteenth-century literature, Wylie Sypher wrote: "Two legends sustain the tradition of the noble Negro—that of Oroonoko and that of Inkle and Yarico."[1] While the first of these two narratives has remained familiar through Aphra Behn's most famous work, the second has been all but forgotten, in spite of the fifty recorded poems, plays, operettas, ballets, and occasional pieces it generated in Europe and New England between 1711 and 1830.[2]

Recently, Peter Hulme has given Richard Steele's influential version of the tale its first sustained close reading in his *Colonial Encounters*,[3] though without connecting its use of the deserted heroine motif to his analysis of its colonialist apologetics. This connection seems worth investigating since the popularity of Yarico's story was maintained in England primarily through the verse form of *heroic epistles* from this Amerindian native woman to the English trader who betrays their love and sells her into slavery.

The following essay will show how certain aspects of the pathetic heroine's representation in the heroic epistle, a genre intimately involved with the emergence of humanitarian sensibility, links the sentimentalized slave to a much broader system of thought concerned with representing trade as a civilizing agent of progressive "refinement." In fact, as Yarico's epistles demonstrate, the two levels of domestic reorganization and geo-political expansion were aspects of the same process of change, and were accepted as such by contemporaries.[4] In terms of moral philosophy and social theory, "sensibility" and "primitivism" merged early on in the period, thus enabling the domestic values and economic aspirations of "the middling sort" to be situated within, and forge a link between, national and world history.

I

The story of Yarico and Inkle finds its way into the genre of the heroic epistle through an early historical account and a popular prose redaction of that account in *The Spectator*. An Amerindian woman named Yarico, who "for her love lost her liberty," first appears in the pages of John Ligon's *True and Exact Account of the Island of Barbadoes* (1657).[5] In *Spectator* 11 (13 March 1711), written by Richard Steele, Ligon's story is retold (and considerably embellished) by Arietta, a fashionable, but sensible, woman of the world, whom Mr. Spectator finds at home debating a town fop over the relative unfaithfulness of the sexes.[6]

The story, as Arietta tells it, concerns an English seaman shipwrecked in the Caribbean, but saved from the bloodthirsty natives by the princess Yarico, who shelters him in a cave. They conceive a child, whereupon Inkle promises to take Yarico back to England as his wife. When they eventually arrive together in Barbados, however, Inkle sells her into slavery in order to recoup the money his father has lent him for the expedition. Moreover, since she is carrying a child he is able to get twice Yarico's market value.

As in Ligon, Steele's lovers are fascinated with the visible signs of their racial and cultural differences. But even though Steele writes that "the European was highly charmed with the limbs of the naked American" and that "the American was no less charmed with the dress, complexion and shape of the European, covered from head to foot," it is nevertheless the "naked American" whom Steele makes the locus of dress and its cultural significations one sentence later: "She was, it seems, a person of distinction, for she everyday came to him in a different dress, of the most beautiful shells, bugles and bedes." Whereas for Steele's shipwrecked seaman Yarico's attractiveness lies in her native nakedness, for Steele the polemicist her significance also lies in her dress: the portable goods of the colonial world which, paradoxically, her nakedness wears. Although he has been shipwrecked, Steele's trader has nonetheless found his way to the *plenum* of portable goods which that world offers the European market, and to that figure of otherness, the naked native, who is here made the vehicle of its bounty: "She likewise brought him a great many spoils, which her other lovers had presented to her; so that his cave was richly adorned with all the spotted skins of beasts, and mostly party-coloured feathers of fowls, which that world afforded."

In a mode of projection characteristic of colonialist representation, the native herself is made to function as the appropriator of native goods for the European. Moreover, exploiting both the sexual and commercial desirability of the female native, Steele has the savage woman offer up to the English trader those "spoils" she has won from her native lovers. The language of Yarico's seduction takes the form of a promise that, should she return with Inkle, she will enjoy an even more marvelous variety of luxuries than she has been able to provide him within her primitive state:

> In this manner did the lovers pass away their time till they had learned a language of their own, in which the voyager communicated to his mistress, how happy he should be to have her in his country, where she should be cloathed in such silks as his waistcoat was made of, and carried in houses drawn by horses, without being exposed to wind or weather.

Although there is a considerable difference between a lavishly appointed cave and a coach and six, it is still a difference of degree alone, of more highly refined and innovative forms of luxury. Both Steele's civilized man and native woman are, from the very beginning, traffickers in "spoils"; and if fashion could make a lady out of a lady's maid (as Fielding complained), it could make a metropolitan Englishwoman out of a naked native, especially one who already comes to her lover "every-day in a different dress." Because she is simultaneously native and female, according to Steele, Yarico occupies representative positions at both ends of the market, as both the source and ultimate consumer of its goods.[7]

Steele's opinion of trade's civilizing potential was urban, Whig, and progressive; but, like the position of the "moderns" in their debate with the "ancients," such a view had to take account of those who saw in it a challenge to traditional English society's relatively stable status assignments and concentration of economic and political power in the landed aristocracy. Against the "ancients'" claims to an unbroken continuity with established cultural values, the "moderns" theorized qualities of "taste" and sensibility which, though originally confined to a cultivated minority, had already become attainable, in the years between the publication of Shaftesbury's *Characteristics* and the first *Spectator* paper, by any and all of those readers who frequented London's coffee houses.[8] As Lois Whitney points out: "The language of sensibility passed very early into the literature of primitivism."[9] One result of the merging of these two initially separate discourses was that together they provided a link between the theory underwriting the cultural and political aspirations of "the middling sort" and the economic expansionism they pursued in acquiring national influence. By placing "the primitive" on the same progressive, temporal axis as "the civilized" (a move central to primitivism), the pro-trade faction could situate what appeared as their break with traditional social organization within a "universal history" of the progressive "refinement" of all God's creation.[10] Since trade functioned as the preeminent means for distributing the scattered elements of that creation (one of Defoe's favorite notions), it could also function as a means for disseminating the more advanced expressions of English civilization, Christianity foremost among them.

Steele's polemic in *Spectator* 11 moves within this merging of sensibility and primitivism into an apology for mercantilism. In representing Yarico's primitive acquisitiveness and consumerism, the text naturalizes on the body of the female native what is a morally problematic effect of trade in contemporary England. For if the increasing access to commodities encouraged a morally problematic growth in "artificial appetites" threatening the stability of traditional society, then evidence of a "primitive" who is both the origin of trade's wealth (in her goods as well as her readiness to circulate them) a consumer in her own right transforms civilization's apparently "artificial appetites" into natural ones and trade itself into the link between primitive and civilized society.[11]

Once this naturalization of trade's disruptive social effects is accomplished and trade itself has been rendered a civilizing agent, the narrative can restrict its moral criticism to the figure of the greedy merchant whose total reduction of human value to market value gives trade a bad name. On his arrival within English territories, therefore, Steele's Inkle abuses the bond of trust his promise represents, using his "information" of Yarico's pregnancy "to rise in his demands upon the purchaser."[12]

Mr. Spectator (who stands in for the contemporary reader as the story's model audience) is moved to tears by Arietta's story, his spontaneous outpouring of pity and benevolence countering both Inkle's false "vow" and the fop's wit, learning, and "ornament."[13] An imaginative community of sympathizers is produced by Yarico's suffering as the reader's benevolent feelings of commiseration are called forward by Mr. Spectator's own sympathy with the heroine's betrayal.[14]

We are never given the fop's reaction to the story of Yarico, and the original point of dispute is dissolved in, rather than decided by, Mr. Spectator's tears. Insofar as it invokes general conventions for representing the pathetic heroine, Arietta's story cannot, in fact, effectively dispute the fop's charge of women's unfaithfulness, since the point of whether or not a pathetic heroine like Yarico is guilty of willful misconduct is never placed at issue within the moral economy of her pathos. Despite the fact that they have been tricked into illicit relations, the women of the heroic epistle (like Drayton's Rosamond or his Jane Grey) and of the pathetic tragedy (like Jane Shore or *The Orphan*'s Monimia) are as "guilty" as willful offenders in terms of the conventional necessity for their punishment. At the same time, however, in order to become the vehicle for benevolent pity, the pathetic heroine must be established in some sense as a victim of forces beyond her control. She is therefore portrayed as self-deceived, self-betrayed—represented in the final instance as a victim not of male perfidy or the public world her desire impinges upon, but of her own, private, desires themselves.[15]

This kind of affective representation, which, by eliciting the sympathy of an audience for the suffering of a heroine such as Jane Shore, actually mitigates the responsibility of the society around her, is reproduced in Steele's paper through the mediation of Mr. Spectator's outpouring of sentimental benevolence. He pities her, and in so doing validates the culture of which he represents a normative product, while the perfidious Inkle is cast out as an aberration. The entire movement teaches the reassuring lesson that commercial society is capable of regulating itself through its production of an ever more highly refined sensibility.[16]

II

The first work in English to revive Steele's story, and the first which sets it to verse, is the anonymous "Story of Yarico and Inkle, from the eleventh *Spectator*" (1734). It has been suggested that the invocation identifies its author as a woman:[17]

> Ye virgin train, an artless dame inspire,
> Unlearn't in schools, unblest with celestial fire,
> And the dire arts of faithless man relate.[18]

This is no very strong evidence of the author's gender. The invocation may suggest that a male author has taken up Steele's strategy of placing Yarico's story in the mouth of a woman. The speaker goes on in her invocation to compare her act of writing to the creation of *Pandora*, thereby tapping an ancient tradition for representing woman as both the cause and effect of her own victimization by men. As we shall see, this strategy of displacing moral responsibility for the suffering which ensues from woman's "creation" by men, suggested here only through allusion, is central to the formal organization of the heroic epistle.

The first version of the tale to adopt the form of the heroic epistle is the anonymous "Yarico to Inkle, An Epistle" of 1736. The dedication is to a Miss Arabella Saintloe, and it is from her that the poem's male author petitions for the authority with which to compose the native woman's lament:

> O *Saintloe*, brightest of the virgin train,
> Approve my numbers, or I write in vain!
> To you fair patroness these lines belong,
> Life of my hopes, and ruler of my song!
> . . . .
> Superior labour to a muse like mine.
> Yet still she keeps the dazzling height in view,
> And, faintly, copies what she learnt from you.[19]

The first line recalls the "artless" author/ess of the earlier poem, who invokes her own muses as "the virgin train." Our present author invokes the woman Saintloe's membership in a similar group, pleading the comparative inadequacy of his own muse to this specific poetic task. It is to Saintloe that "these lines belong"; his muse "only copies what she learnt from [her]." We might take this for the conventional blandishments of an admiring gentleman, if not for the implicit assumptions about women enforced both by the tale itself and by the generic form of the heroic epistle.

As it was developed by Ovid, and in its reemergence in England during the sixteenth and seventeenth centuries, the heroic epistle was the preeminent form before the novel for ventriloquizing the female voice and representing women's inner lives: the special poetic form through which its authors could create a public revelation of interiority, otherness, and the private, "feminized" qualities increasingly defining the social identity of women in early modern Europe.[20] In Samuel Daniel's *A Letter form Octavia to Marcus Antonius*, for instance, the heroine writes to her errant husband in Egypt:

> We in this prison of ourselves confined,
> Must here shut up with our own passions live,
> Turned in upon us and denied to find
> The vent of outward means that might relieve. . . .[21]

If, as the prefaces to Dryden's and Saltonstall's collections suggest, the heroic epistle's readership was intended to be female, it offered, as an epistolary form, the intimate revelation of one woman's private desires to another, within a self-enclosed circuit of supposedly feminine meaning. As a heroic form, it isolated the feminine subject in the aftermath of male action (betrayal); further, it granted women a speaking self, the verbalization of an interiority which we could call "individuality," but (as in pathetic tragedy and the novel of sensibility) without the freedom males possessed to alter their situations by confronting the agencies responsible. Women's power of verbal affect thus replaces the possibility of their social effectiveness. The heroic epistle displays the privacy of feminine inner life in the anguished aftermath of male betrayal, universalizing its pathos for society at large, while at the same time enclosing and separating off the heroine's suffering as ultimately self-inflicted— making enclosure and separation the conditions of its possibility. Thus the initial conflict between victim and betrayer shifts to an emphasis on a difference within the self-contained and socially isolated psyche of the guilty victim. We should recognize in this the general outlines of the "exemplar to her sex," of the unique yet representative woman, so prominent in the novel from *Clarissa* onward and so important to the development of the cult of domesticity.

Since the heroic epistle recounts the narrative of events from the point at which the heroine has assumed responsibility for them, the question of where blame lies has been decided from the outset by banishing the conflict between private, feminized desire and public, male corruption to the pre-history of the heroine's incorporation of it; and the poem need never bring the two actors and levels of explanation back into contact with each other. Consequently, these poems have a structure open at one end, in the sense that the heroine's plea for the return of her lover will never be answered, because it need never be to fulfill the poem's formal design. Such pleas, though the heroine's reason for speaking out, are themselves entirely excessive to the formal structure which from the start dissolves the act of male betrayal in the rhetoric of female self-betrayal. It is therefore not surprising that these poems should register a knowledge of their own excessiveness, reflected in what their heroines say about their acts of enunciation.[22] Consider, for instance, Daniel's *Octavia to Marcus Antonius*:

> But whither am I carried all this while
> Beyond my scope, and know not when to cease?
> Words still with my increasing sorrows grow:
> I know to have said too much, but now enow.[23]

As nearly any example of the genre would show, the price paid by the heroine for the privilege of speaking her mind is confinement within it, while the language with which she speaks it comes unmoored from the world to which linguistic signs customarily point; her "words grow" without ever attaching themselves to objects outside the "labyrinth"[24] of her interiority.[25]

The importance of physical and figural confinement for the representation of interiority in the bourgeois heroine (that is, for her representation primarily as an interiority) is famously clear in Richardson. When Clarissa, after being confined to the house, beings to criticize her family, she stops herself and writes: "Why roves my pen?" For the guilty victim of such betrayals by society, when the body is contained the pen roves, seemingly of its own accord. Similarly, in Pope's *Eloisa to Abelard*, the heroine begins her letter to Abelard but stops after only ten lines:

> Oh write it not, my hand—the name appears
> Already written—wash it out, my tears!
> In vain lost Eloisa weeps and prays,
> Her heart still dictates and her hand obeys.[26]

The external distance separating Eloisa's desire from its object is rewritten at the outset of her letter as a conflicted, internal distance inhabiting her own psyche.[27]

To return to the opening of the 1736 "Yarico to Inkle, an Epistle," we can now read more specifically the male author's claim for the comparative inadequacy of his voice and his consequent need to appropriate the woman Saintloe's. "These lines belong to" her, in short, by virtue of her gender and of his genre.

Yarico, however, is a voicing not only of the feminine, but of the West Indian native and the transported slave as well. In this version, Yarico herself articulates a desire to be allowed to pass from the master-slave relationship of colonialism to the domestic sphere of companionate love:

> O redeem me, while you've power to save,
> And make me yours, if I must be a slave!
> Your faithful slave, indeed I'll ever prove,
> And with continued care attend my love.[28]

The removal of the native woman to England as Inkle's wife or mistress would change the social context of their relationship, but the terms would clearly remain the same. Since the merging of sensibility with primitivism achieved a means of conceptualizing the progressive refinement of domestic society through market relations by situating them within a "universal history" of cultural progress, it is not surprising to find the poem placing both domestic and colonial domination on the same axis. Yarico as wife or mistress would indeed "continue" in the same relationship to her man as Yarico the slave to her master, so deeply nested within each other are the two on the ideological level.

It is the fact that the two forms of domination are mutually reinforcing components of the same system of thought against which Yarico is shown protesting by attempting to separate her role as childbearer from that of potential forced laborer:

> And think, O think on the dear load I bear!
> Must the poor babe a mother's suffering share?
> . . . .
> This is the portion destined to be thine,
> Thou heir to all the wrongs that now are mine![29]

Yarico's child, however, as well as her betrayal and her utterance, are all characterized by Yarico herself as the work of a single "author":

> To Inkle she complains, to him who taught
> Her hand in language to express her thought.[30]

> Forgive, thou still-loved author of my pain! —
> My griefs are heavy and I must complain.[31]

Yarico cannot appeal to their child as evidence for the supersession of the colonialist by the domestic relation because her child, like her tale, is the product of the same male writing:

> And if in distant years some hapless maid
> Shall be by faithless, barbarous man betrayed,
> . . . .
> Then shall the comparison be made,
> So trusted Yarico, and was betrayed.[32]

Identifying herself with both the child and with the tale Inkle has "fathered" through her, Yarico's argument acknowledges her as written into what social identity she has by Inkle's act of betrayal. Yarico stakes her identity on the link to its father which the child provides her, even as she stakes it on the interpolation of her "still living story"[33] within the exemplary narratives of the father's culture.

Through her ineffectual appeal to her status as the bearer of Inkle's child, Yarico reveals the mutual implication of domestic and colonial tyranny within the merging of sensibility with primitivism. Daniel's Octavia also, but in a more direct manner of protest, confronts the double standard, locating the cause of her self-estrangement in the relation of women's reproductive role to the preservation of male property rights:

For, should we too (as God forbid we should)
Carry no better hand on our desires
Than your strength doth, what interest could
Our wronged patience pay you for your hires?
What mixture of strange generations would
Succeed the fortunes of uncertain sires?
What foul confusion in your blood and race
To your immortal shame and our disgrace?[34]

A woman's "shame," in this formulation, functions like the legitimacy of the child she bears to insure the continued self-possession and self-identity of her society.[35] In her chastity, her ability to be "shamed," woman is the guardian of private property, while not herself able to claim ownership. The same coupling of female exemplarity with the necessity for stabilizing the continuity of male property rights can be seen to inform Yarico's epistles, in the narrative logic whereby Inkle's sale of Yarico, as well as her transformation into an exemplary heroine, result from his need to make good his financial obligation to his father.

Daniel's Octavia may be fully aware of the connection between women's domestic oppression and the maintenance of male freedom, whereas Yarico (new to the contradictions of European society) only gradually encounters it. But the shade of difference in the forthrightness with which the two heroines present critiques of the status quo is of much less significance than the fact that the heroic epistle, through its separation of ("feminized") language from the world of (male) action, can give these critiques such a central place in its heroines' representations: articulating the contradictions in women's lives, while circumscribing what one is to do about them.[36]

Both the anonymous "Yarico to Inkle, an Epistle," of 1736 and the Countess of ****'s 1738 "An Epistle from Yarico to Inkle, After he had left her in Slavery," make use of an identical figure to establish the moment and mode of Yarico's self-betrayal:

There I beheld you, trembling as you lay,
And, e'er I knew it, look'd my soul away.[37]

I well remember that unhappy day,
In which I gazed my liberty away.[38]

We saw how in Steele's *Spectator* version the native woman herself became the agent of her culture's appropriation by a male trader, bringing to him those "spoils" she has won from her native lovers. By "gazing" on her future enslaver, the native woman in these two poems is again rendered the agent of her own appropriation, while simultaneously erasing the narrative history of her enslavement, as though her "gaze" effected his internalization. Edward Jerningham's "Yarico to Inkle, an Epistle" (1766) performs this self-appropriation somewhat differently. Jerningham gives even greater thematic emphasis to the pivotal moment of the colonial "gaze" by carefully elaborating a narrative of "shame" around a moment of reversal in the visibility of colonizer and colonized to each other.

As usual, Yarico is smitten at once by the appearance of the Englishman: "Behold thy foes advance—My steps persue, / To where I'll screen thee from their fatal view."[39] They retire to a cave and engage in the usual dalliance, until its natural climax:

> How as we wantoned on the flowery ground,
> The loose robed pleasures danced unblamed around:
> Till to the sight the growing burden proved,
> How thou o'ercam'st, and how, alas! I Lov'd![40]

Once the evidence of their encounter becomes inscribed "to the sight" on the body of the native woman, the text reverses emphasis from Yarico as "screen" and protector of Inkle, to Inkle as conqueror of the native woman. Or rather, though her initial dominance is wrested from her and given to Inkle, she continues to function as a "screen," now attracting to herself the "fatal view[s]" no longer of her fellow natives but of Inkle's merchant countrymen:

> But pleasure on the wings of time was born,
> And I *exposed* a prey to grinning scorn
> Of low born traders—mark the hand of fate![41]

> Lo! every hope is poisoned in its bloom,
> And horrors *watch* around this guilty womb.[42]

> Must I the shafts of infamy sustain?
> To slavery's purposes my infant train?
> To catch the *glances* of his haughty lord?[43]

What Yarico now "screens" by absorbing it into herself is the actual history of her enslavement, accomplished in the moment of shared, equal partnership in pleasure with Inkle. What she enjoyed with him "unblamed" behind the "screen" of her protection (of him, from the male natives) becomes inscribed upon her visibility (to him and his male countrymen) as "shame":

> No longer vainly suppliant will I bow,
> And give to love what I to Hate owe;
> Forgetful of the race from whence I came,
> With woe acquainted, but unknown to shame.[44]

In the 1736 and 1738 versions Yarico is made to internalize the process of her enslavement, simultaneously occupying the positions of both victim and victimizer. In Jerningham, Yarico absorbs the process of her enslavement within the opaque "screen" of her "shame," her visibility to the white man.[45]

III

We may now more explicitly define the intersection of patriarchy and colonialism which the formal logic of female transgression in the heroic epistle makes possible. As so many examples of eighteenth-century humanitarianism demonstrate, it was as a similarly reflexive and self-enfolding subject of betrayal that both the slave's race and homeland were represented by contemporaries in this period. James Thomson's famous lines, in *The Seasons*, sound a common note:

> But come, my Muse, the desert barrier burst
>   . . . ardent climb
> The Nubian mountains, and the secret bounds
> Of jealous Abyssinia boldly pierce.
> Thou art no ruffian, who beneath the mask
> Of social commerce com'st to rob their wealth;
> No holy fury thou, blaspheming Heaven,
> With consecrated steel to stab their peace.
> . . . .
> Thou, like the harmless bee, mayest freely range,
> From mead to mead bright with exalted flowers,
> From jasmine grove to grove; . . .
>   −a world within itself
> Disdaining all assault. . . .[46]

"A world within itself," turned in upon itself, disdaining the "burst" and "pierce" of missionary zeal's "stab," but open to the flights of Thomson's Muse—this is pseudo-Africa, that "unformed" region of mercantile and poetic opportunity of which Swift wrote:

> So geographers, in Afric Maps
> With savage pictures fill their gaps,
> And o'er uninhabitable downs
> Place elephants for want of towns.[47]

Literally "a wide extended blank,"[48] the continent invited both the poet and the geographer to fill its "gaps," while the trade exploited its human resources. Edward Long describes Africa as "a wilderness," from which, he adds, "many are never reclaimed."[49]

In spite of his championing of "natural rights," and in order to account for slavery, John Locke, in his *Second Treatise of Government*, employs the classical theory that slavery is the consequence of being captured in a "just war,"[50] which enabled him to rather awkwardly by-pass the issue of the English slave trade. The "just war theory" did, however, bequeath a context for others to focus on the indigenous African slave trade. In 1705 William Bosman describes slavery as so frequent and common in Africa that "the most potent negro can't pretend to be insured" against it as a result of tribal warfare.[51] In *The Sugarcane*, James Grainger urges the slave owner to consider the origins of his property: "perhaps / Fortune, in battle for his country fought, / gave him a captive to his deadliest foe."[52] Later in the century, the king of Dahomey, Bossa Ahadee, became a handy exemplar of the native slaver, reportedly selling his own people into captivity when he ran out of prisoners; and Robert Norris, who wrote an account of Ahadee's reign, described "slavery and oppression" as uniform throughout Africa.[53]

If the "just war" theory seems to us today to have been stretched to its limits in describing the activities of the native Africans, the important thing was that it seemed to show slavery originating with, and endemic to, the natives themselves. William Snelgrave, in his *New Account of Guinea*, reported that even mothers sold their own children into slavery.[54] In Thomson's words again, "The parent sun himself / Seems over this world of slaves to tyrannize."[55] The frequent emphasis given to both monstrous motherhood and the monstrousness of native female anatomy in many of these accounts can also be read within the logic of feminine transgression formulated by Drayton's Jane Grey: "Well knew'st thou what a monster I would be, / When thou did'st build this labyrinth for me."[56]

We have seen how in *Spectator* 11 slavery functions for Steele as a thematic medium through which to separate the evil effects of market culture from the essentially healthy state of English trade. A similar movement of containment and revision recurs throughout the century in discussions of the slave trade itself. Once their own slave trade had been recast as the alternative to indigenous African barbarity, the English could then (as in their rivalry with the Spanish in the Americas) cast themselves as relative liberators. Archibald Dalzell writes that: "Whatever evils the slave trade may be attended with . . . it is mercy . . . to poor wretches, who, for a small degree of guilt, would otherwise suffer from the butcher's knife."[57] James Boswell similarly argued, quoting Thomas Gray, that "to abolish this trade would be to — 'shut the gates of mercy on mankind.' "[58] This type of apologetic appeared in numerous texts throughout the century, even before Bossa Ahadee was reported to have killed 4,000 prisoners of war whom he could not sell.

As Gordon Lewis has noted, the first outright refutation of this humanitarian pro-slavery appeal to what I have referred to as African "self-betrayal" was Wadstrom's account of his Guinea voyage in 1789, *Observations on the Slave Trade*, with its factual evidence of the way Europeans had enlarged what was a local trade into an international commercial system. In his own attempt to refute this same argument, Clarkson boarded fifty-seven slave ships before he was able to find one seaman willing to give evidence of the marauding expeditions upriver in the Calabar region.[59]

But the work of the leading abolitionists such as Clarkson and Wilberforce diverted from the assurances of political economy, and was premised on a significant distrust of the systematically civilizing and self-regulatory potential of commercial society which had informed so much of eighteenth-century thought on the slave trade. Whereas for "Hume, Smith, Millar, or Tucker, commerce was the motor force behind the growth of manners and the progress of society," Burke stood political economy on its head, reversing this relationship to locate in pre-commercial society that civilizing force which developed into commercial systems for the circulation of goods and the spread of culture.[60] Burke was influenced by his reading of Robertson's histories of Asia and America, as well as by the impact of the French Revolution; and his approach reflects a growing crisis in theorizing the relationship between commerce and culture, economic systems and social organization. The former could no longer be entirely trusted to determine the latter, as political economy argued and as had seemed to be possible from the beginning of the century.

The abolitionists, by contrast, derived much of their ideological agenda from the moral reform movements which had been gaining influence throughout the century, and which by 1800 were making serious demands for the reform of "Old Corruption" in government, as well as for stricter forms of social policing that would correct aspects of social behavior exacerbated by the progress of commerce. Speaking of one such group, whose ideological antecedents reach back to the age of Steele, Reginald Coupland writes:

> Its activities, in which Wilberforce took a vigorous part for many years, were mostly directed against blasphemous and indecent publications, but it busied itself also with attempts to enforce a stricter observance of Sunday among the poor, to suppress such indecorous rustic festivities as "wakes," and so forth. In 1802 its place was taken by the better known Society for the Suppression of Vice — better known if only as the butt of

Sydney Smith's mordant humour. "A corporation of informers," he called it, "supported by large contributions" and bent on suppressing not the vices of the rich but the pleasures of the poor, on reducing their life to "to its regular standard of decorous gloom," while "the gambling houses of St James remained untouched."[51]

As E. P. Thompson has shown, such movements for the regulation and rationalization of lower class life are directly connected to the rise of market culture and the transition from archaic, feudal forms of master-servant dependency, through paternalism, to the creation of a working class of "free laborers" from out of the nation's surplus reserve of "masterless men."[62] In the sphere of bourgeois domestic life we find a related rage for the inculcation of morality as "propriety" in the century's ever growing production of conduct books aimed at the daughters of "the middling sort," and in the novel's assimilation of their conventions.

According to Gordon Lewis, "the abolitionists sought, in Clarkson's phrase, to establish the principle that commerce itself should have its moral boundaries."[63] The clamoring for reform, from both above and below, had reached such a pitch in the first period of industrialization that commerce itself appeared to be inadequate to the task of its own regulation and to the refinement of English sensibility which it was supposed to bring about. Wilberforce scorned this "delicate sensibility" as "distinct from plain practical benevolence."[64] For the next half century the challenge faced by the ruling class to its own hegemony would be the extent to which it could reform its clientage system and the economy without undermining the basic "parliamentary balance" through which it governed. "In a deeply conservative political system," writes Robin Blackburn, "abolition of the slave trade became not so much the most urgent, as the least controversial, reform that could be undertaken."[65]

Abolition, then, was part of a wider movement of thought which, while still in the process of dismantling the last vestiges of mercantilism in response to "the vision of a pacified global system of commerce,"[66] was also rethinking relations between the family, the worker, the state, and economic policy.

Popular notions of both what was possible for English women and of what new policies imperial trusteeship entailed had thus undergone considerable change by the beginning of the nineteenth century. In the case of women, their dislocation from traditional forms of economic production, starting in the seventeenth century, led to their gradual social "empowerment" as symbolically central but economically ancillary figures within the household. Thus women in commercial society, economically marginalized, sexually pacified, and symbolically centralized, came to serve as a basis for moral authority insulated from the competitive spirit and relative values of the market. That is, women functioned increasingly as potential correctives for an economic system that could not entirely be trusted to correct itself. Still, the distance measured from the heroic epistle's "feminized" language, which constructed female interiority as the product of a separation between public and private, action and desire, to the cult of domesticity, is not particularly striking: "Irrespective of the author's biological gender, moreover, language itself was thought of [in the nineteenth century] as essentially feminine in nature when detached from the competitive ways of the marketplace and rooted in the emotions and values of the home."[67] Women like Mary Wollstoncraft, who thought this new form of empowerment unacceptable, nevertheless found the conventions for representing female experience which developed along with it as difficult, if not impossible, to step outside of, as Yarico had found them in her pleas to Inkle.[68]

In the case of the colonized, abolition and emancipation certainly ended the crude form of economic exploitation to which they were subject. But the sentimentalized native remains the essential ingredient in colonial rhetoric well into the nineteenth century, after England found its "mission" among nations in extending the fight against slavery into the African interior.[69] Abolition of the trade and emancipation may have flown in the face of England's manifest economic interest; but in regard to both the short term interests of the nation's internal stability, the imperative to reform government and unite the nation under a moral standard (not to mention a war with France), as well as in the long term development of England's imperial reach, the dismantling of slavery represented a clear ideological gain for the status quo. Abolition achieved these results without entailing a departure from the basic global trajectory of market culture and its promise to bring an ever greater organization of productive forces into being (at home, in the home, and abroad).

Both English women and the colonized were, then, caught up in the "progress" of English commercial society as it adapted itself, on the domestic and international levels, to the demands of developing industrial capitalism. Both women and the colonized were to emerge from the crises of the nineteenth century in new positions of relative "empowerment" which, on the whole, fulfilled the promise of producing "free" individuals and a wider scope for commercial hegemony recognized at the beginning of this period by projectors such as Defoe. My argument has been that by joining the African's "self-betrayal" to the pathetic heroine's "self-betrayal" the heroic epistle could cement the bond between sensibility and primitivism, England's domestic reorganization and its imperial aspirations, to provide a unilateral self-justification for

England's emerging oligarchy. This in itself was crucial during a century in which both social theories and lived experience altered rapidly and continually.

One troubling question still remains. Steele's early *Spectator* paper, though a model instance of the sentimentalized native topos, is aimed less (if at all) at the evils of the slave trade, or at trade *per se*, than at certain problematic moral and social effects of England's expanding market culture.[70] But what appears paradoxical is that, even though Yarico's story was to be repeated in many subsequent versions during the consolidation of a popular abolition movement, these later works rely on all the same representational conventions. As the studies of Bissell, Fairchild, Sypher, and others demonstrate, the basic conventions for representing the sentimentalized native undergo very little modification between the rise of sensibility and its gradual replacement by more "utilitarian" systems, in spite of the mobilization of the abolition movement.[71] What is even more paradoxical, both anti- and pro-slavery factions made use of what was essentially the same ensemble of conventions for representing the slave in order to argue entirely opposed courses of action. Therefore, how are we to identify a shift toward an anti-slavery position in any of the various texts of sensibility in the period? If both anti- and pro-slavery positions make use of the same basic "lexicon," to what could Coleman's comedic treatment of the Yarico and Inkle story, for instance, be said to clearly point?

What evidence we have suggests that there is, on the contrary, no direct connection between the economic and social forces motivating the maintenance or abolition of slavery in the eighteenth century, and the ideological content of the sentimentalized native as a rhetorical trope. We have seen how far back the conventions for representing female interiority in the epistles of Yarico to Inkle go in the history of the heroic epistle itself. At the same time that sensibility and primitivism produced a discourse which situated the bourgeoisie in national and world historical terms, the pro-slavery position seems to have become commonly associated with a retrograde social outlook. C. Duncan Rice observes that: "The sentimental revolution against slavery was complete by the 1760's, as indeed was the theoretical argument against it."[72] The evidence of Steele's *Spectator* paper and Behn's *Oroonoko* might even suggest an earlier date, at least for the "sentimental revolution." To judge from the available evidence, the dominant view by the first third of the century seems to have been that slavery was an evil, but one necessary to England's continued economic growth.

It was into this cleavage between social commonplace and economic practice that Yarico's epistles stepped, providing, through the heroic epistle's pathetic heroine, a means of representing the reality of their contradiction in terms of seemingly self-evident and long standing conventions about the nature of the other (female or native), within a general apology for commercialism. The pathos of the heroine in this tradition separated the subject's suffering from the social context from which it emerges. Extrapolating from this, the social function or ideological content of Yarico's epistles (and the reason for their immense popularity) can perhaps be best understood as their preservation of certain foundational attitudes, basic to commercialism, toward the colonial enterprise, during a period of relative instability in social theory and great upheavals in actual society. Both pro- and anti-slavery factions could make use of the sentimentalized native because this trope tapped basic elements in the "lexicon" of commercial society, part of what Barthes calls the rhetoric of the bourgeoisie: "a group of fixed, regulated, insistent figures in which the various forms of mythic meaning come to be arranged."[73]

By the early nineteenth century, sensibility, if not primitivism, had outlived its usefulness as a means for coming to terms with the socially dynamic character of commercial society. It endured well beyond its prime as a kind of "survival" until economic and social relations had been transformed sufficiently for alternative systems of thought to achieve wider currency, though the sentimentalized native, like "the deserving poor," has never quite disappeared.[74] Coleman's comedic *Inkle and Yarico* is essentially an eighteenth-century domestic comedy (with negroes), whose variation on the tragic motif signals little else than its exhaustion.[75] Though these social conventions of representation remained unchanged through the century, however, what people were expected to do in response to them did change quite a bit. The previously effective combination of primitivism and sentiment could no more cope with the increasing frequency and violence of slave revolts, than imaginative sympathy could comprehend the actions of the Luddites. Wilberforce understood this. In Coleman's case, his play would have had a different ending if his leading man had not refused to play the part unless Inkle was finally reformed. In the end, Inkle is taught by his moral (and social) superiors to choose a marriage for love over a marriage for gain.[76] The simple representation of Inkle's unremitting greed, as a kind of "limit instance" of human behavior in commercial society, could no longer function as the vehicle for generating the impression of society's self-regulatory power (as in Steele)—no more than the heroine's pleas could remain unaddressed, or her pathos stand in for social reform. In the case of Yarico's epistles another development occurs at about the same time, one equally remedial: Inkle begins to write back, begging pardon.

NOTES

1 Wylie Sypher, *Guinea's Captive Kings: British Anti-Slavery Literature of the XVIII Century* (Chapel Hill: University of North Carolina Press, 1942), 108.

2 The definitive survey of these works is Lawrence Price's *Yarico and Inkle Album* (Berkeley: University of California Press, 1937).

3 Peter Hulme, *Colonial Encounters* (London: Methuen, 1986).

4 Hulme asserts that, in order to place the tale within the discourse of colonialism, "the pathos of the deserted heroine motif" needs to be separated from "the fully political issue of slavery." The following essay is, as much as anything else, an attempt to coordinate that aspect of bourgeois apologetics attuned to the great changes made in women's socioeconomic position by the development of commercial society, with the contemporaneous expansion of English economic power through colonial slavery. See *Colonial Encounters*, 253.

5 John Ligon, *True and Exact Account of the Island of Barbadoes* (London, 1657), 55.

6 All quotations are from *The Spectator*, ed. Donald F. Bond (Oxford: Clarendon Press, 1965), 47–51.

7 On the contemporary figuration of women as the motor force behind mercantile expansion see Louis A. Landa, "Pope's Belinda, The General Emporie of the World, and the Wonderous Worm," *South Atlantic Quarterly* 70 (1971): 215–35.

8 See Joan Pittock, *The Ascendancy of Taste* (London: Routledge and Kegan Paul, 1973); Raymond Williams, *Keywords: A Vocabulary of Culture and Society*, rev. ed. (New York: Oxford University Press, 1983), 313–15; James H. Bunn, "The Aesthetics of Mercantilism," *New Literary History* 11 (1980):303–21; and Walter Jackson Bate, *From Classic to Romantic: Premises of Taste in Eighteenth-Century England* (Cambridge, MA: Harvard University Press, 1946).

9 Lois Whitney, *Primitivism and the Idea of Progress in English Popular Literature of the Eighteenth Century* (Baltimore: The Johns Hopkins University Press, 1934), 108.

10 On primitivism's single time line see Johannes Fabian, *Time and the Other: How Anthropology Makes its Object* (New York: Columbia University Press, 1983); and P. J. Marshall and Glyndwr Williams, *The Map of Mankind: Perceptions of New Worlds in the Age of Enlightenment* (Cambridge, MA: Harvard University Press, 1983). On the concept of a "universal history" see these works and Ernst Breisach, *Historiography: Ancient, Medieval, and Modern* (Chicago: University of Chicago Press, 1983).

11 For the moral problem of luxury and the debates surrounding its relation to economic growth see John Sekora, *Luxury: The Concept in Western Thought, Eden to Smollet* (Baltimore: The Johns Hopkins University Press, 1977). Provocative accounts of consumerism in the period are given by Neil McKendrick, John Brewer, and J. H. Plumb, *The Birth of a Consumer Soci-*

ety: The Commercialization of Eighteenth-Century England (Bloomington: Indiana University Press, 1985).

12 Recent scholarship has enabled us to see in the new concept of "information" the intersection of the period's concern with both market and social self-regulation. As John Brewer has noted, information privately acquired by merchants regarding the activities of their fellows was a crucial aspect of the credit system, transforming "character" into a commodity subject to market fluctuations (a notion which particularly bothered Fielding). Information of changing conditions in areas of production and along shipping routes, of secret trade agreements and other factors liable to influence the market, was a constant source both of wealth and of moral ambivalence about the effect of market relations on social behavior.

The emergence of privately held "information" as a commodity in itself is most dramatically visible in eighteenth-century England's increasing reliance on informers to bring evidence against suspected criminals. Such informers, drawn from the ranks of the so-called criminal class itself, would receive monetary rewards graduated according to the degree of the crime. This system of criminal detection was welcomed by property owners to the extent that it respected the liberty of free born Englishmen, who would not put up with the powers of arbitrary arrest and search exercised by the French. It was welcomed by the more entrepreneurial of criminals, such as Jonathan Wild (or as represented by Gay's Peachum), because it actually encouraged the development of a type of organized crime controlled by a central "kingpin" who exploited the thieves under his command until it became more profitable to turn them in than to keep them. As Gordon Lewis has pointed out, citing John Fielding, one of the particular areas of the authorities' interest was in the information concerning the "secret societies" reputedly formed by escaped and manumitted slaves among the criminal underclass "aimed at self-protection and at persuading other slaves to abscond."

Members of the societies for moral reform also functioned as informers, though without pay, turning in their fellow subjects to the authorities for breaches of the Sabbath, swearing, etc. Further information on the abolitionist reformers will follow.

The key advantage to regulating social behavior through informers, as Henry Fielding recognized, was that by their means society policed itself, the criminal class "betrayed itself," without external intervention. For the history of a "self-regulating" commercial and civil society see Albert O. Hirschman, *The Passions and the Interests: Political Arguments for Capitalism before Its Triumph* (Princeton: Princeton University Press, 1977); and John Brewer, "Commercialization and Politics," in McKendrick et al., *Consumer Society*, 197-264. See also Henry Fielding, *An Enquiry into the Causes of the Late Increases of Robbers* (1750), in *The Complete Works of Henry Fielding, Esq.*, ed. William Ernest Henley, 9 vols. (New York: Croscup and Sterling, 1902), *Legal Writings*, 5-127; E. P. Thompson, *Whigs and Hunters: The Origin of the Black Act* (New York: Pantheon Books, 1975), esp. 63-85, 216-21; and

Gordon K. Lewis, *Slavery, Imperialism, and Freedom: Studies in English Radical Thought* (New York: Monthly Review Press, 1978), 22. On the early moral reform societies see Thomas A. Horne, *The Social Thought of Bernard Mandeville: Virtue and Commerce in Early Eighteenth-Century England* (New York: Columbia University Press, 1978). On the emergence of information as an empirical category of experience in commercial society see Walter Benjamin, "The Storyteller: Reflections on the Works of Nicolai Leskov," in *Illuminations*, ed. Hannah Arendt, trans. Harry Zohn (New York: Schoken Books, 1969), 83–109. See also n.14 below.

13 One notes that Steele's version gives much greater emphasis to the breaking of promises than Ligon's original. Susan Staves has shown that in the wake of the Restoration Settlement English drama reflects a marked cynicism regarding the efficacy of vows, as the law begins to regard oaths as merely words to support testimony that might or might not correspond to facts. The expansion of market culture and especially the loosening of mercantile restrictions on trade correspond, on the other hand, to a renewed emphasis on theorizing the conditions which make promises binding, as well as to a renewed insistence on the fundamental place of the promise in both commercial and domestic relations. The non-verbal language of sensibility, as a medium for social self-regulation, no doubt partially compensated for this gap in accountability, or so the centrality of the promise in Hume's philosophy of sympathy would suggest. Susan Staves, *Players' Scepters: Fictions of Authority in the Restoration* (Lincoln: University of Nebraska Press, 1979), 222–23; P. S. Atiyah, *The Rise and Fall of Freedom of Contract* (New York: Oxford University Press, 1979); Thomas L. Haskell, "Capitalism and the Origins of Humanitarian Sensibility, Part II," *American Historical Review* 90 (1985):339–61; David Hume, *A Treatise of Human Nature*, ed. P. H. Nidditch (Oxford: Clarendon Press, 1978), 518–45; and Jerome Christensen, *Practicing Enlightenment: Hume and the Formation of a Literary Career* (Madison: The University of Wisconsin Press, 1987), chap. 5.

14 For the *Spectator*'s production of sympathy in the reader, on the model of a "theatrical" structure of emulation between actor and audience, see Michael Ketcham, *Transparent Designs: Reading, Performance and Form in the Spectator Papers* (Athens: University of Georgia Press, 1985). Christensen discusses similar theatrical strategies of sympathetic persuasion in Hume (*Practicing Enlightenment*, 76–79, 228–31, 259–61), as well as Hume's insistence on the centrality of female mediators for a society held together by sympathetic emulation (chap. 4). The latter of these issues is touched on by J. G. A. Pocock regarding eighteenth-century commerce and sociology in *Virtue, Commerce, and History: Essays on Political Thought and History, Chiefly in the Eighteenth Century* (Cambridge: Cambridge University Press, 1985), 117ff. For Adam Smith see David Marshall, *Figure of Theater: Shaftesbury, Defoe, Adam Smith, and George Eliot* (New York: Columbia University Press, 1986), chap. 7. Jean-Christophe Agnew has argued convincingly that market culture tended to conceive of human relations along deeply theatrical

lines of sympathetic projection in *Worlds Apart: The Market and the Theater in Anglo-American Thought, 1550-1750* (Cambridge: Cambridge University Press, 1986).

Of the creation of a national debt, and the "reality conferred on the new government" oligarchy at mid-century, Agnew writes that "court and country parties were sharply divided on the repayment fiction, but few ever doubted for a moment that it was a fiction. What the debate over the national debt brought home to these men of power was . . . that security lay as much in the promise of a performance as in the performance of promises" (158). The significance of information and informers (discussed in n.12), and of the transitional replacement of the promise by sympathy's non-verbal, theatrical language of emulation (discussed in n.13) come together interestingly in Thomas Heywood's contention, mentioned by Agnew, that actors "were able to provoke spontaneous confessions from criminals concealed in the audience through the reenactment of their crimes on the stage—hence Hamlet's 'Murder of Gonzago' " (134). The heroic epistle's use of "self-betrayal" will follow, but it is important to note that the concept has wide epistemological and political implications for commercial society in association with the concept of self-regulating economic and social systems.

15 See Cynthia S. Matlack, " 'Spectatress of the Mischief Which She Made': Tragic Woman Perceived and Perceiver," *Studies in Eighteenth-Century Culture* 6 (1977):317–30; Susan Staves, "British Seduced Maidens," *Eighteenth-Century Studies* 14 (1980/81):109–34; Eugene M. Waith, "Tears of Magnanimity in Otway and Racine," *French and English Drama of the Seventeenth Century*, ed. Waith and Judd D. Hubert (Los Angeles: William Andrews Clark Memorial Library, U.C.L.A., 1972); Maximillian E. Novak, "Criticism, Adaption, Politics, and the Shakespearean Model of Dryden's *All for Love*," *Studies in Eighteenth-Century Culture* 7 (1978):375–87; and Laura Brown, *English Dramatic Form, 1660-1760; An Essay in Generic History* (New Haven: Yale University Press, 1981), chap. 3.

16 On the role of imaginative sympathy in social self-regulation see Ketcham, *Transparent Designs*, Christensen, *Practicing Enlightenment*, and Agnew, *Worlds Apart*.

17 Price, *The Yarico and Inkle Album*, 9.

18 "The Story of Yarico and Inkle, from the 11th *Spectator*," anon., (London, 1734), "Dedication," ll. 1–3.

19 "Yarico to Inkle, An Epistle," anon., (London, 1736), "Dedication," ll. 1–4, 13–14.

20 Though many of the conventions associated with the representation of female interiority in the novel were first developed within this poetic form, the heroic epistle has received little attention as a genre. Two exceptions are Gillian Beer, " 'Our Unnatural No-Voice': The Heroic Epistle, Pope, and Women's Gothic," recently collected in *Modern Essays on Eighteenth-Century Literature*, ed. Leopold Damrosch, Jr. (Oxford: Oxford University Press, 1988),

379–411; and Linda Kaufman, *Discourses of Desire: Gender, Genre, and Epistolary Fictions* (Ithaca: Cornell University Press, 1986), chap. 1.

21 Samuel Daniel, *A Letter from Octavia to Marcus Antonius*, in *The Complete Works in Verse and Prose of Samuel Daniel*, ed. Alexander Grossart, 5 vols. (London and Aylesbury: Hazel, Watson, and Viney, Ltd., 1885), 1:126–27.

22 The notion that women's language is somehow "excessive" or ungovernable is by no means unique to the heroic epistle, and is closely bound up with the notion of women's ungovernable lustfulness. As Patricia Parker has recently shown, the difference between male *copia* and female *copiousness* became something of a commonplace in medieval and Renaissance rhetorical theory. Both notions of women's excessive language and of their ungovernable lust, though relatively constant throughout the history of European civilization, tend to reemerge with particular emphasis during periods of disruptive political and economic transition (depending, to a large extent, on the effects such moments have on women's socioeconomic position). A case in point is the period in England stretching from the rise of the revolutionary sects in the 1640s, which gave women an unprecedented opportunity to speak out as "prophets" and social critics, to the consolidation of a governmental oligarchy and of rudimentary class alignments during the mid-eighteenth century. Between these fall the political and economic upheavals of the late seventeenth century, reflected in the pathetic tragedy, and the "rage of party" factionalism which give us, among other representations, Pope's Belinda and Addison's female personification of the credit system and the national debt (see *Spectator* 3). As it has been often noted, the relative stablization of England's governing elite and their economic policies during the mid-eighteenth century corresponds to a gradual shift, at least "among the middle classes," from emphasizing women's inordinate sexual desires, to "the notion, exemplarised by Richardson's *Pamela*, that women were sexually passive and utterly unlascivious." Keith Thomas, *Religion and the Decline of Magic* (New York: Charles Scribner's Sons, 1971), 569. Also see Thomas's account of female prophets in "Women and the Civil War Sects," *Past and Present* 13:42–62; Patricia Parker, *Literary Fat Ladies: Rhetoric, Gender, Property* (New York; Methuen, 1987); and Susan Bruce, "The Flying Island and Female Anatomy: Gynecology and Power in *Gulliver's Travels*," *Genders* 2 (Summer 1988):60–76. On the "feminization" of commercial activity see Pocock, "The Mobility of Property and the Rise of Eighteenth-Century Sociology," in *Virtue, Commerce, and History*, 103–23, esp. 113–14.

23 Daniel, *Octavia to Marcus Antonius*, *Works*, ed. Grossart, 1:138.

24 "Well knewest thou what a monster I would be / When thou didst build this labyrinth for me." "Jane Grey to Gilford Dudley," in Michael Drayton, *Collected Works*, ed. J. William Hebel (Oxford: Clarendon Press, 1961), 2:296.

25 The self-reflexive excess of Octavia's "feminized" language, signs isolated from the world they reach out to, should be compared to Daniel's hopes for the socially transformative power of English as it follows the progress of those

modern day Anthonys, like his mentor Fulke Greville, into the new world; for instance, as expressed in these lines from *Musophilus*:

> And who in time knows whither we may vent
> The treasure of our tongue, to what strange shores
> This gaine of our best glorie shall be sent,
> To inrich unknowing nations with our stores?
> What worlds in th' yet unformed Occident
> May come refin'd with th' accents that are ours?
>
> (957–62)

26 Alexander Pope, *Eloisa to Abelard*, ll. 13–16, in *The Poems of Alexander Pope*, A Reduced Version of the Twickenham Text, ed. John Butt (New Haven: Yale University Press, 1963), 252.

27 It should be noted, however, that Eloisa's power to act is also foreclosed by Abelard's dismemberment, a circumstance unique to this heroic epistle. The theme of castration as an avenue for transferring authority to the female (while also circumscribing her power of contestation) is by itself an interesting idea for further research; Christensen has identified a similar strategy as central to Hume's philosophy of sympathy and his approach to modern authorship. See *Practicing Enlightenment*, chap. 4.

28 "Yarico to Inkle, an Epistle," 2–3.

29 Ibid., 3.

30 Ibid., 1.

31 Ibid., 15.

32 Ibid., 8.

33 Ibid., 15.

34 Daniel, "Octavia to Marcus Antonius," *Works*, ed. Grossart, 1:127.

35 Daniel's Octavia laments the "wound" that Antonius has inflicted on her by his betrayal. Shortly thereafter, however, she draws a moral from her experience by rewriting that betrayal as self-betrayal: "For deepest wounds the hand of our own shame." The "wound" here, we might say, describes the gap between victim and betrayer which Octavia has, in the process of moralizing her experience, internalized as self-aggression. To the world, the visible sign of her psychic containment and self-division goes by the name of "shame." Daniel, *Works*, ed. Grossart, 1:134.

36 Gayatri Chakravorty Spivak has investigated the emergence in the nineteenth-century novel of what she calls "the female individualist," whose essential characteristic is to provide a space of contestation within dominant ideology, providing it with a way of acknowledging the presence of social contradiction, while foreclosing the possibility of a more radical critique. See "Three Women's Texts and a Critique of Imperialism," *Critical Inquiry* 12 (1985): 243–61. The generic origins of this type of strategic containment in the representation of women seem to lie in the heroic epistle. Gillian Beer's reading of the genre's influence on "women's gothic" supports my view, but see the opposing implications of Linda Kauffman's argument for female empowerment in *Discourses of Desire*, chap. 1.

37 "Yarico to Inkle, an Epistle," 4.

38 The Countess of ****, *"The Story of Yarico and Inkle" and "An Epistle from Yarico to Inkle, After he had left her in Slavery,"* (London, 1738), 14.

39 Edward Jerningham, "Yarico to Inkle, an Epistle," (London, 1766), 5.

40 Ibid., 11

41 Ibid., 10, emphasis added.

42 Ibid., 14, emphasis added.

43 Ibid., 14–15, emphasis added.

44 Ibid., 16.

45 Since "shame" in the heroic epistle functions as the condition of possibility for the heroine's representation, it can be lifted only at the cost of her being. Rosamond, in Drayton's "Rosamond to Henry II," writes:

> Since my shame so much belongs to thee,
> Rid me of that by only murdering me.

46 "Summer," ll. 747–73, in James Thomson, *The Seasons and The Castle of Indolence*, ed. James Sambrook (Oxford: Clarendon Press, 1972), 57–58.

47 "On Poetry: A Rhapsody," (1713), ll. 179–82, in *Jonathan Swift: The Complete Poems*, ed. Pat Rogers (New Haven: Yale University Press, 1983), 526.

48 *The plan for the Association for Promoting the Discovery of the Inland Parts of the Continent of Africa* (1778). Quoted in Sypher, *Guinea's Captive Kings*, 31.

49 Quoted in Sypher, *Guinea's Captive Kings*, 41.

50 *Second Treatise of Government*, ed. C. B. Macpherson (Indianapolis: Hackett Pub. Co., 1980), 17.

51 William Bosman, *New and Accurate Description of the Coast of Guinea* (London, 1705). Quoted in Sypher, *Guinea's Captive Kings*, 32.

52 James Grainger, *The Sugarcane* (London, 1764), bk. 4, ll. 218–20.

53 Robert Norris, *A Short Account of the African Slave Trade* (London, 1789). Quoted in Sypher, *Guinea's Captive Kings*, 36.

54 William Snelgrave, *A New Account of Guinea* (London, 1734), 160.

55 Thomson, "Summer," ll. 84–85, p.61.

56 Drayton, "Jane Grey to Gilford Dudley," *Works*, ed. Hebel, 2:296.

57 Archibald Dalzell, "Preface" to *The History of Dahomy* (London, 1793).

58 James Boswell, *The Life of Samuel Johnson*, ed. R. W. Chapman (Oxford: Oxford University Press, 1980), 878.

59 Lewis, *Slavery, Imperialism, and Freedom*, 42.

60 Pocock, *Virtue, Commerce, and History*, 188.

61 Reginald Coupland, *Wilberforce: A Narrative* (Oxford: Oxford University Press, 1923), 55, quoted in Robin Blackburn, *The Overthrow of Colonial Slavery, 1776–1848* (New York: Verso, 1988), 142.

62 E. P. Thompson, "Patrician Society, Plebian Culture," *Journal of Social History* 7 (1974): 382–405.

63 Lewis, *Slavery, Imperialism, and Freedom*, 71.

64 William Wilberforce, *A Practical View of the Prevailing Religious System of*

Professed Christians in the Higher and Middle Classes of Society, Contrasted with Real Christianity (1797; repr., New York, 1856), 272n.

65 Blackburn, *Colonial Slavery*, 295; see also 141–42.

66 Ibid., 310.

67 Nancy Armstrong, "The Rise of Feminine Authority in the Novel," *Novel* 15 (1982): 131.

68 As Mary Poovey has argued, Wollstonecraft's unfinished attempt to rewrite the representation of female experience in *Maria: Or the Wrongs of Woman* was constantly betrayed by the conventions bequeathed to her by the discourse of sensibility. Arietta's argument in *Spectator* 11 is similarly undermined by the formal conventions of the story she tells. *The Proper Lady and the Woman Writer: Ideology as Style in the Works of Mary Wollstonecraft, Mary Shelley, and Jane Austen* (Chicago: University of Chicago Press, 1984).

69 "The abolition of slavery in all British territories did not eliminate concern about slavery elsewhere, but the British began to see themselves less and less as perpetrators of the slave trade and more and more as the potential saviors of the African. The blame for slavery could now be displaced onto others — onto Americans, for example. Blame was increasingly displaced onto Africans themselves for maintaining the slave trade as a chief form of economic exchange." Patrick Brantlinger, "Victorians and Africans: The Genealogy of the Myth of the Dark Continent," *Critical Inquiry* 12 (1985): 173.

70 Steele is, in fact, writing two years before the treaty with Spain would give England rights to the *Asiento*, or commercial monopoly on the Atlantic slave trade.

71 See Benjamin Bissell, *The American Indian in English Literature in the Eighteenth Century* (New Haven: Yale University Press, 1925); Hoxie Neale Fairchild, *The Noble Savage; A Study in Romantic Naturalism* (New York: Columbia University Press, 1928); and Eva Beatrice Dyke, *The Negro in English Romantic Thought* (Washington, D.C.: The Associated Publishers, 1942).

72 C. Duncan Rice, "Literary Sources and the Revolution in British Attitudes to Slavery," in *Anti-Slavery, Religion, and Reform: Essays in Memory of Roger Anstay*, ed. Christine Bolt and Seymour Drescher (Folkstone, England: William Dawson, 1980), 326. Rice makes the point that there is no convincing way to tie in what appear to be "intellectual set pieces" and clearly anachronistic references to the pro-slavery position (when the theme appears at all in the literature of sensibility), with the popular trajectory of the abolition movement after 1760. Instead he concentrates on the, still not very conclusive, history of the theme's reception. Most of the changes he plots, however, occur after abolition.

73 Roland Barthes, *Mythologies*, trans. Annette Lavers (New York: Hill and Wang, 1972), 150.

74 The notion, for instance, that the primitive mentality is analogous to a "child's" belongs to this later period, but is clearly a variation on the basic primitivist view; however, it was one which allowed a greater emphasis to be

placed on "educating" the colonial subject by utilitarian theorists such as Bentham.

75 Adela Pinch has pointed out to me a particularly good, though late, example of the heroic epistle's exhaustion as a vehicle for the sentimentalized native in Wordsworth's "The Complaint of a Forsaken Indian Woman," whose climactic lines run:

> Too soon, my friends, ye went away;
> For I had many things to say.
>
> (49–50)

76 On the composition of Coleman's play see the editor's "Introduction" to *The Plays of George Coleman the Younger*, ed. Peter A. Tasch (New York: Garland Publishing, 1981), xvii-xx.

History as Monument:
Gibbon's Decline and Fall

FRANK PALMERI

Near the end of the penultimate chapter of the *History of the Decline and Fall of the Roman Empire*, Gibbon for the second time juxtaposes and laments the most famous pillagings of Rome: for six days by Alaric's soldiers in 410, and even more destructively for seven months in 1527 by soldiers serving Charles V (7:308).[1] In the seventy-first and final chapter, he revisits the remains of the architectural glories of the Antonines which he had celebrated in his second chapter and, echoing the beginning of his history, closes it with a meditation on the ruins that survived into the fifteenth century and his own day.[2]

Since the architectural monuments function as a synecdoche for the empire itself, this consideration of Roman ruins and of the causes for their deterioration provides a fitting conclusion for the entire *Decline and Fall*. Gibbon thus concludes and sums up his *History* as a project of coming to terms with the loss of ancient Rome. He alludes to works of verbal and visual art in this chapter in order to make imaginatively present a series of possible strategies for accommodating such massive cultural loss: from triumph over the previous culture or devaluation of it, to idealizing elevation of this lost culture, accompanied by contempt for what survives in the present. Although these reactions could succeed each other in the history of an individual or a culture, Gibbon implies less a sequence than a layering of possible alternatives. Gibbon's own project takes account of these earlier stages but itself exemplifies a further stage of the process of mourning, the melancholy process of working through in detail the memory of the lost object as a precondition to finally accepting the death of the preceding, generative culture as an unalterable fact.[3]

Gibbon devotes most of the first paragraph of this final chapter to a passage he quotes from Poggio Bracciolini's *Historiae de varietate fortunae*, on the vicissitudes of fortune. In this passage, Poggio has climbed the Capitoline hill with a friend to view the remains of ancient Rome, just as Gibbon in his last chapter invites his reader to join him in his survey of and meditation on the same ruins. A fifteenth-century historian and discoverer of classical texts, Poggio was one of the first to realize the differences between historical eras, especially classical and medieval cultures. He wrote dialogues satirizing religious enthusiasm and ecclesiastical corruption as well as indecent *facetiae*. Sharing Gibbon's historical awareness and many of his interests and attitudes, Poggio serves as Gibbon's double within the narrative, allowing him to bridge the three centuries between the end of the narrative of the *Decline and Fall* and his own time. Gibbon does not simply adopt and reiterate the passage he quotes from Poggio; he also makes it his own by translating it into his distinctive English, so that at the beginning of the seventy-first and culminating chapter of his history of Rome and its empire, he utters his own words in his own voice, as he synchronizes his voice and words with Poggio's across three centuries.

Poggio first remembers Aeneas's visit to Evander in *Aeneid*, Book 8, where Virgil contrasts the thick underbrush of the Capitoline in Evander's days of rustic simplicity, poverty, and virtue with the polished columns and golden roofs of the Forum in the imperial times of Augustus. Now, Poggio laments, history has come full circle, and the hill has returned to a semi-civilized, pastoral state (in Gibbon's translation):

> The forum of the Roman people, where they assembled to enact their laws and elect their magistrates, is now enclosed for the cultivation of pot-herbs, or thrown open for the reception of swine and buffaloes. The public and private edifices, that were founded for eternity, lie prostrate, naked, and broken, like the limbs of a mighty giant. (7:314)

The juxtaposition in the Forum of his own day of grazing cattle with the ruins that resemble a giant's scattered limbs demonstrates to Poggio the incommensurability between shrunken moderns and colossal ancients. Although Poggio invokes the wheel of fortune in this passage, his own time does not return to an exact duplication of Evander's, because the departure of greatness produces a sense of desolation and loss unknown to the original pastoral world. The third age of Rome, in which he lives, has reverted to semi-pastoral humility, but it lacks the virtue of the first age as well as the civilization of the second.

Gibbon's translation of Poggio's meditation in this final chapter on the decline of Rome from glorious past into a domesticated present translates into words a kind of painting extremely numerous and popular throughout the late seventeenth and eighteenth centuries — *capricci*, caprices, or imaginary architectural views painted and drawn by Canaletto, Panini, Guardi, and Piranesi, among many others. *Capricci* often juxtapose massive classical ruins — untopped columns, half-submerged arches overgrown with shrubs — with a diminutive humanity oblivious among its everyday activities to the colossal fragmentary remains of ancient times. A related, more inclusive, genre, the *vedute*, or views, depicts an architectural subject in accurate topographical detail. *Vedute* often also contain alterations from the topographical relations among buildings on a site. Conversely, most *capricci* include accurate depictions of recognizable buildings and monuments. The considerable overlap between the two genres results because both can express an artist's vision of the relation between different eras, between works of man and works of nature, between imperial and pastoral worlds.[4]

In translating *vedute* and *capricci* into prose in his concluding chapter, Gibbon allusively includes a wide range of possible views of the relation between pagan antiquity and the Christian era. Paintings of ruins from the fifteenth through the eighteenth century sometimes depict that relation as complementary; more often, they emphasize a fundamental opposition between the two eras. Paintings from the later seventeenth and eighteenth centuries, which invert the relative proportions they assign to ruins and to Christian or contemporary elements, reverse the judgment of paganism and Christianity that characterizes works of the fifteenth and sixteenth centuries.

Gibbon might be transcribing an eighteenth-century *capriccio* when he reflects that because of the medieval Romans' obliviousness to the accomplishments of their past, "the fairest columns of the Ionic and Corinthian orders, the richest marbles of Paros and Numidia, were degraded, perhaps, to the support of a convent or a stable" (7:325). The implicit equivalence between the last two structures only partially relieves the melancholy nature of the observation. But in fifteenth- and sixteenth-century *Adorations* (where ruins appear most frequently), pastoral elements such as stables and cattle signal a triumph, not a degradation or decline. For example, in Rogier van der Weyden's *Adoration of the Kings* in the central panel of the St. Columba altarpiece (mid-fifteenth century, Figure 1), a stable with its thatched roof emerges from the ruined walls of

Figure 1. Rogier van der Weyden, *Adoration of the Kings*, St. Columba altarpiece (mid-fifteenth century). Munich, Alte Pinakothek. Marburg/Art Resource, NY (110768).

two rooms. From the inside room, a cow and donkey observe the infant, while from the right the three kings, and from the left the donor pay their homage to him. The generalized ruin confirms what the anachronistic crucifix implies—that with this birth, a new order emerges from the preceding one. The thatched roof, stable, or shed in such a painting signifies the New Testament, and the ruins signify the old law by alluding to the palace of David or of Solomon.[5] In the middle and late fifteenth century, many Flemish painters, including van der Weyden and Jan van Eyck, also developed an opposition between Romanesque and Gothic elements in their *Adorations* as a means of designating the opposition between the old law and the new.[6]

Soon after the middle of the fifteenth century, however, many paintings of the adoration, especially in Florence, begin to include classicizing ruins that allude to the Roman Temple of Peace, which, according to legend, fell into ruin on the night of Christ's birth. Ruins that are identi-

Figure 2. Sandro Botticelli, *Adoration of the Magi* (1483–85). Florence, Uffizi. Alinari/Art Resource, NY (603).

fiably classical and sometimes specifically Roman thus signify the crumbling of the imperial pagan order upon the birth of Christ.[7] Botticelli's *Adoration of the Magi* (1483–85, Figure 2), which depicts three generations of Medici and their friends as the adoring kings and their retainers, reiterates from earlier nativities the ruined wall that supports a stable roof — perhaps signifying the stone rejected by the builder, that is, Christ, which yet became the cornerstone of the Church. But in the left background, Botticelli includes an incomplete and broken series of classical arches, which probably allude to the Temple of Peace and imply that the newborn child will replace not only the law of Moses but also the law and culture of Rome and of classical antiquity.[8] The ancient pagan world has begun to figure as significantly as Jewish law as a source of cultural authority in the past. Ghirlandaio's *Adoration of the Magi* (1487), painted soon after a visit to Rome, similarly places the adoration in front of a sequence of classical arches that have not yet crumbled, but whose one break in their top anticipates their disintegration as a sign of the coming reign of the newborn child. The adoration of the infant by the kings of the earth anticipates that all nations will be ruled by this child, even the Roman empire after a resistance of centuries.[9]

In the background of Raphael's *Virgin with the Veil*, three figures stand in the ruins of an arch, while two figures descend from there to a city with classical architecture in the distance behind the Virgin's back. In the foreground, the infant Christ, his mother, and the young John occupy a space not in a stable but in a quiet spot, a *hortus conclusus* in the midst of large blocks of stone, perhaps parts of an edifice that once included the arch and wall behind them. These three large, colorful, and lifelike figures signify the new age that will replace the old one signified by the diminutive monochromatic figures and buildings in the background. Such fifteenth and sixteenth-century *Nativities* and *Adorations* indicate the birth of a pastoral Christian order that supersedes the culture of pagan antiquity. If in their exultant triumph over classical culture, the Middle Ages repressed their cultural ancestor, these Renaissance paintings imply a returning recognition, a more moderate devaluation, of the classical in relation to the dominant Christian culture of their time. Gibbon's perspective, especially in the first half of the *Decline and Fall*, inverts that expressed in these fifteenth- and sixteenth-century *Adorations*, since it celebrates the defeated pagans and arraigns the victorious Christians. But, like these paintings, Gibbon's history also views Christianity as the determined cultural rival of paganism, and sees the spread of Christianity as a principal cause of the downfall of the Roman empire.

The significance of classical ruins in paintings changes by the middle of the seventeenth century, reflecting in part a growing interest in portraying forms of contemporary life, and also an increased awareness of the distance separating cultures and epochs. J. B. Weenix's *Coast Scene with Classic Ruins* (1649, Figure 3), mixes monuments of different periods and cultures with a courting couple, a rearing horse, masts and sails, which all point to energetic activity in the present. Weenix here juxtaposes the momentary transience of a slice of contemporary life with monuments which testify to the effects of time. Depicting temporal as spatial distance, he marks the movement from background to foreground as a movement from distant past by stages into the present: from the eroding Egyptian pyramid, to the fragmentary classical columns, to the modern porphyry tomb. Like Raphael's, this painting contrasts exuberant life in the foreground with the stillness and silence of the past, but life here is secular and passing, not Christian and timeless.

Weenix correlates contemporary figures with Egyptian as well as classical culture, but Claude Lorrain, in his landscapes and in his *veduta* of

Figure 3. J. B. Weenix, *Coast Scene with Classic Ruins* (1649). Reproduced by permission of the Trustees of the Wallace Collection, London.

the Campo Vaccino (1636, Figure 4), juxtaposes contemporary seventeenth-century Romans and their buildings specifically with the remains of the ancient Roman Forum, producing neither a simple nostalgic melancholy nor a simple satiric indignation, but a composite vision which combines melancholy, along with acceptance and accuracy of depiction. To unify his composition, Claude eliminates the cattle market that cluttered an earlier view of the campo from the same vantage point (by Swanevelt, 1631). Claude focuses interest not on the resulting large open area but on the combination of styles around the campo and on the various groups in the foreground, of whom the more well-to-do face the campo and gesture toward it, while their poorer countrymen, lounging on the platform of an ancient temple, listen attentively to their companions. In Claude's soft afternoon shadow, contemporary buildings remain distinct from yet not in conflict with classical structures.

In Claude's *capricci* as well, people in contemporary pastoral scenes merit as much sympathetic interest as does a majestic ruin, and both are usually overshadowed by the natural landscape. In the *Pastoral Capriccio with the Arch of Constantine* (1651), for example, a figure putting off in a boat from the bank of a river in the foreground links the group there (a lounging man with a rifle, perhaps a relaxed hunter, two women, and a child) with a pair of figures on the other side of the river (a woman who appears to be finishing a wash and perhaps putting on a stocking, and a male companion, who moves off in the direction of the cattle). These two in turn are linked to the arch by shambling cattle who proceed in a wide curve out of the river and into the background, attended by a figure who points toward the ruins. As in Weenix's *Coast Scene*, the distance from background to foreground designates a progression from past to present. But whereas that progression in Weenix remains paratactic and lacking in transitions, Claude links the monuments of the classical past with the contemporary conversing figures through the backwards "S" composed of the cattle and the river. The animals and the river connote the continuous gradual passage of time, not as a process that separates but as one that links different ages. Claude depicts the Arch and the Colosseum in meticulous detail but also in the soft yellow light of a sunset on the right, and he includes with them figures whose everyday activities and conversations merit our interested observation. This *Pastoral Capriccio* and the *veduta* of the Campo Vaccino exemplify Claude's conception of ancient and modern as complements, not as irreconcilable opposites. For Claude, human activity in both past and present coincides with and expresses the encompassing work of natural forces.

Gibbon's characteristic method of perceiving historical significance in the second half of the *Decline and Fall*—through juxtapositions of

Figure 4. Claude Lorrain 1600–1682, *The Roman Forum*, also called: *The Campo Vaccino*, 1636. Reproduced by permission of the National Gallery of Art, Washington, DC, Rosenwald Collection (B-23149).

widely separated events that occurred on the same geographical site — closely approximates Claude's practice of juxtaposing declining classical majesty with contemporary pastoral drama in its shadow. Like Claude, Gibbon assimilates historical revolutions to natural processes, conceiving of the opposition between cultural epochs not as the result of violent upheavals, but as the result of gradual incremental changes that produce ironic, often melancholy transformations in the course of centuries and millenia. His history of human works assumes an almost geological dimension.

Most eighteenth-century *capricci* and *vedute* alter Claude's balance between ruins and human figures. The imaginary tombs for English noblemen from the first decades of the century provide an indication of this change. The *Capriccio: Tomb of Lord Somers with Ruins and Landscape* (1726), with architecture probably by Canaletto, figures by Piazetta, and foliage by Cimaroli, again aligns background with antiquity and foreground with the present, though it also identifies the sarcophagus as that of an illustrious British noble of the preceding generation. The contiguity of a huge and complex tomb with a towering Ionic column just behind it produces a visual unity that links Somers, the recent lord chancellor, with the achievements of the ancient past. But both the tomb and the ruins dwarf the figures of the survivors who pay homage and mourn in the present. With monuments that now loom over the living, such a *capriccio* reveals a desire to devalue and subordinate the present in relation to a magnified past.

Also from the first half of the eighteenth century, Leonardo Coccorante's *capriccio*, *Port of Ostia in Calm Weather* (Figure 5), like Weenix's *Coast Scene*, juxtaposes ruins with bustling activity near water. But it too dramatically reduces the scale of the humans in relation to the ruins, and thus more sharply evokes the loss and diminution that time effects. The large number of such works by both minor and major figures illustrates that the magnification of ruins and reduction of human figures constituted a widespread and accepted convention in *capricci* of the first half of the eighteenth century. In these paintings, the humans remain unmindful of the silent ruins that tower over them and their affairs. Thus, in Francesco Guardi's *Cappriccio with Ruins on the Seashore* (1760s, Figure 6), all the humans look down; none observes the ruined arch that shares with the earth its clayey color and its ability to sustain vegetation. Having virtually reverted from a cultural product to a part of nature, this wild and noble arch combines elements of both. By the middle of the eighteenth century, it is the ruins, not the human figures, that testify to a triumph, even if it is an achievement that is past and faded.

Figure 5. Leonardo Coccorante, *Port of Ostia in Calm Weather* (first half of eighteenth century). Reproduced by permission of the Lowe Art Museum, University of Miami, Coral Gables, Florida, Samuel H. Kress Collection.

Figure 6. Francesco Guardi, *Capriccio with Ruins on the Seashore* (1760s). Reproduced by courtesy of the Trustees, The National Gallery, London.

Piranesi, finally, locates such a return of ruins to nature and to oblivion in the city of Rome itself and its environs. He includes in his *veduta* of the Campo Vaccino (c. 1750, Figure 7) massive columns two-thirds buried in earth, and his campo is cluttered with buildings, overgrown with trees, and marked by carriage ruts, an incoherent and unlovely urban pastoral. In striking constrast with Claude's contemporary human figures, who possess features, expressions, and narrative interest, Piranesi's diminutive humans resemble insects in their relation to the monuments of the ancient Forum (it takes an effort to notice the pair of observers in the lower right hand corner, for example), and their activities produce the same sense of frenetic inconsequentiality as do those of ants from our perspective. According to the scale of Piranesi's engraving, modern humanity lacks any terms of comparison or relation with the men of antiquity and their ancient structures, whose gigantic ruins here decline not into serene Christian pastoral, but into a scene of urban disorder. Piranesi's monuments seem to struggle like half-buried gods or monsters against being swallowed by the unending accumulation of specks of earth and time.

In the *vedute* of Hadrian's Villa, Piranesi carries these tendencies even further. His caption to the *veduta* of the Heliocaminus (c. 1756, Figure 8) recalls that in this room Hadrian displayed his most beautiful and valuable statues, having arranged that the sun would illuminate them through the windows from above and would also provide the heat for the space. In Piranesi's time, vines have overgrown the structure and trail down through vacant window openings. The space into which they hang, entirely lacking warmth and beauty, diametrically contradicts its former function, being filled now only by sunken fragmentary columns, prowling dogs, and human figures whose gestures indicate such extreme emotional states as depression, exasperation, and self-address. In this, as in other Piranesi prints, if the human figures are not swallowed by shadows or the powerful encroachments of nature, they exist apart from conversation with others in melodramatic isolation resembling that of madmen.

The fifteenth- and sixteenth-century *Adorations* implied that Christianity overcame and displaced a Rome already figuratively in ruins. The figures in these paintings dominate both the ruins and the diminutive cities in the background. Reversing these proportions, the gigantic ancient monuments in eighteenth-century *capricci* and *vedute* loom over diminutive moderns and their works, implying that the ancient Romans were giants. Piranesi goes furthest to imply that the transformation of a classical temple or monument to a stable or a structure of nature constitutes not a triumph but a degradation that leads to mad rebellion against

Figure 7. Giovanni Battista Piranesi, "Campo Vaccino," plate 15, *Vedute di Roma* (1750). From *The Mind and Art of Giovanni Battista Piranesi* by John Wilton-Ely. Copyright © 1978 Thames and Hudson Ltd. Reprinted by permission of the publisher.

Figure 8. Giovanni Battista Piranesi, "Hadrian's Villa, Tivoli, The Heliocaminus," plate 133, *Vedute di Roma* (1756). From *The Mind and Art of Giovanni Battista Piranesi* by John Wilton-Ely. Copyright © 1978 Thames and Hudson Ltd. Reprinted by permission of the publisher.

contemporary survivals. Claude's light assimilates ancient ruins and contemporary life, and, more importantly, binds both as examples of natural form. Perhaps only he and Guardi hold classical and contemporary in balance and suspension, as complementaries that participate equally in an encompassing natural order. Both these artists can conceive of works of man returning without protest to works of nature.

Gibbon allusively combines all these perspectives in his meditative last chapter. Like Piranesi, Gibbon regards the ruins of Rome as the limbs of a giant, and regrets that civilization embodied in the Forum has regressed to nature, or to an urban pasture.[10] Yet he avoids Piranesi's bitter rage and his diminishment of contemporary culture. Gibbon, for example, explicitly exonerates Christians from the responsibility for the greater part of the losses, assigning much of the blame instead to the destructive inattention of medieval and modern Romans themselves. To this historical and human cause, he adds, in a way that recalls Claude or Guardi, the workings of natural forces including water, fire, and time (7: 317-20).

Gibbon's translation of Poggio reveals a comparably allusive layering of alternate reactions to the fall of empire. Having to remind himself that this "hill of the Capitol, on which we sit, was formerly the head of the Roman empire, the citadel of the earth," Poggio exclaims, "This spectacle of the world, how is it fallen! how changed! how defaced!" With this series of exclamations, Gibbon through Poggio juxtaposes widely separated times and perspectives to produce a chorus of responses — including grief, celebration, and melancholy — to the fall and fragmentation of the Roman empire.[11] Poggio's words allude first of all to the night of the fall of Troy and Aeneas' dream of Hector's disfigured shade. Aeneas laments the contrast between this spectacle and the sight of Hector in his glory:

> Ah god, the look of him! How changed
> From that proud Hector who returned to Troy
> Wearing Achilles' armor. (*Aeneid*, Book 2, ll. 368-70)[12]

Hector, covered with gore and dirt, enjoins Aeneas to flee the burning city and save the Trojan gods for their translation to Rome.

Poggio's exclamations also echo a passage that expresses exactly the opposite judgment on a fallen empire and its gods' defeat: "How art thou fallen from heaven, O Lucifer, son of the morning! how art thou cut down to the ground, which didst weaken the nations!" (Isaiah 14:12). Prophesying the destruction of Babylon and its being "thrust down into the pit," Isaiah exults in the fall of the Assyrian empire and the triumph of its enemy, the god of Israel.

Milton would also allude to the same two passages in his own narrative of a contest between competing claimants to divinity and the disfiguring fall of one of them. Awaking after his fall into the lake of fire, Satan utters these first words to Beelzebub:

> If thou beest hee; But O how fall'n! how chang'd
> From him, who in the happy Realms of Light
> Cloth'd with transcendent brightness didst outshine
> Myriads though bright. (*Paradise Lost*, Book I, ll. 84–86)

Both Isaiah's exclamation and this reiteration of it are addressed to devils; Milton's Lucifer describes his henchman in terms that apply equally to himself. Although he does not intend to, Satan here gives the same evidence as Isaiah of the power of the god that lays his adversaries low and sends them to the pit. Milton's additional allusion to Virgil draws a parallel between Aeneas's reaction to fallen Hector and Satan's reaction to fallen Beelzebub. Milton links Satan with earlier epic heroes because his judgment of the fall of empire coincides with Isaiah's; both insist that all empires of this world descend from Satan and are doomed like him to fall.

Gibbon thus allusively introduces and juxtaposes possible responses to the destruction of empire. Isaiah and Milton celebrate the fall of Babylon and Rome, along with the complementary triumphant elevation of their god. Virgil mourns the horrific fall of Troy, the Trojans' deaths and disfigurements. Poggio's melancholy indignation, with its recognition of the differences between historical times, places him with Petrarch and Rienzi, whose recognition of such loss Gibbon has quoted earlier: "Where are now these Romans? their virtue, their justice, their power? why was I not born in those happy times?" (7: 270). Juxtaposing the epic poets of pagan Rome and Christian Britain with the Jewish prophet and the Renaissance Italians, Gibbon makes these alternatives available to the reader's imaginative intelligence. He does not scornfully condemn or dismiss Milton's celebration and Isaiah's exultation; nor does he simply embrace Virgil's grief and Petrarch's regret. He holds in suspension both responses to the empire's fall. His conclusion implies a tolerance of opposed points of view, an inclusive rather than an exclusive vision, an ironic openness and elegiac melancholy. The layers of allusions in Gibbon's adapted and translated quotation from Poggio resemble the layers of ruins on the same site, and the layers of attitudes toward ruins in the *Adorations*, *capricci*, and *vedute* painted from the fifteenth through the eighteenth centuries.

Such accretions of meaning through ironic layering in Gibbon's concluding chapter provide a culmination consistent with his method of historical interpretation in the second half of the *Decline and Fall*, where he repeatedly juxtaposes the histories of different people, alternate beliefs, and multiple frames of reference in order to construct a complex, many-sided, and ironic view of his subject. Instead of satirizing one religion and celebrating another, for example, he juxtaposes his descriptions and analyses of Islam, paganism, and Christianity. Throughout his last three volumes, he depicts historical figures as extremely ambiguous, stressing the inadequacy of relying on a single or even a double angle of vision in evaluating character. He increasingly concentrates on parallels between ancient and later times to bring into focus the contrasts between periods, and to register revolutions in human affairs as losses that occasion melancholy and ironic reflections. Gibbon transforms the exclusive, parodic satire that marks the first half of the *Decline and Fall* into the inclusive, ironic vision he achieves in the second half.[13]

Almost alone among ancient Roman monuments, Trajan's one hundred foot column still remains entire and upright, although since the time of Pope Sixtus V it has been capped, ironically, with a statue of St. Peter. The "scattered fragments" of the empire, the dismembered limbs of the Roman architectural giant, cannot be rejoined and restored; but they can be recollected, that is, vividly and thoroughly remembered. Gibbon's response to the ruins of the Roman Forum, therefore, consists not only of melancholy, but also of the creative work of remembering and retelling. From this perspective, Gibbon's entire history contributes to a project of reconstituting the authority and values of the felicitous time of Trajan and the Antonines. In the absence of architectural monuments in their original integrity, it is the historian's mind, ranging over the vast materials of history to organize a massive epic narrative, which provides a modern equivalent to the heroic accomplishments of the ancient world. The concluding chapter reveals that Gibbon intends his work as a monumental history—not in the sense of such exhaustive nineteenth-century collections of documents of national history as the *Monumenta Germaniae Historica*—but in a more literal, architectural sense appropriate for the subject of his history. Gibbon presents *The History of the Decline and Fall of the Roman Empire* itself as a fitting replacement for the Roman architectural monuments that survive only in ruins. He intends his history to commemorate what has gone before by serving as a grave marker for the Roman empire.[14]

In his *Autobiographies*, Gibbon shows his awareness of the paradoxical possibilities for the survival of linguistic monuments when he anticipates that the *Decline and Fall* "may perhaps, a hundred years hence, still continue to be abused." Observing that an eighteenth-century work that is received well in London "is speedily read on the banks of the Delaware and the Ganges,"[15] he imagines his future readership extending outward in space as well as time. The first volume of the *Decline and Fall* appeared in the year of the Declaration of Independence; the last three volumes were published in the year the U.S. Constitution was adopted. By citing America as an important source of his future readership, Gibbon implies his recognition that the British empire, like the Roman, will decline and pass away. But the sway of the English language will survive British imperial power, just as the preeminence of Latin long outlived Roman rule. Virgil and Horace are still read fifteen centuries after the fall of the Latin empire. Framing his history as a meditation on the ruins of that empire and as a lasting memorial to its acts, Gibbon demonstrates an equivalent awareness that his work will survive the decline and fall of the British empire.[16]

N O T E S

1 References are to volume and page numbers from the *History of the Decline and Fall of the Roman Empire*, ed. J. B. Bury (London, 1909; New York: AMS Press, 1974). Gibbon's earlier remarks on the sacks of Rome occur in relation to Alaric in chapter 31, 3: 339–48. Leo Braudy stresses the increasing importance Gibbon attaches to the persistence of geographical sites through different historical eras, in *Narrative Form in Fiction and History: Hume, Fielding, and Gibbon* (Princeton: Princeton University Press, 1970), 242–45.

2 According to the final sentence of the *History*, the work was conceived as Gibbon sat meditating among the ruins of the Capitol twenty years earlier. For the well-known account of the conception of the *Decline and Fall*, see *The Autobiographies of Edward Gibbon*, ed. John Murray (London: John Murray, 1896), 302. Patricia B. Craddock underscores the metaphoricity of "ruins" when she points out that, despite Gibbon's seeming particularity in this last chapter and in his account of the conception of the *Decline and Fall* in the *Memoirs*, there were no ruins on the Capitoline hill in his day. "Edward Gibbon and the 'Ruins of the Capitol,' " in *Roman Images: Selected Papers from the English Institute* (Baltimore: The Johns Hopkins University Press, 1982), 63–82. "Ruins" function primarily as rhetorical figures in Gibbon and elsewhere.

3 Freud analyzes the process of mourning as a painful recollection and working through of strong emotional attachments preparatory to accepting the loss of the person or object that had been their focus, in "Mourning and Melancholia," *Collected Papers*, trans. Joan Riviere (New York: Basic Books, 1959), 4: 152–70. In this essay, Freud also explores the divergence of energies from the process of mourning into states of melancholic depression and manic elation. With Freud's analysis in mind, a drawing such as Fuseli's, of the artist in

despair at the works of antiquity, would indicate a regression in the process of mourning the loss of antiquity; it fetishizes ancient culture by hallucinating in exaggerated form the foot of an ancient statue that dwarfs the body of the despairing modern artist.

4 Canaletto described his *capricci* as "vedute ideale" and the more topographically accurate *vedute* as "prese da i luoghi" on the title page to a collection of his engraved *vedute*. See J. G. Links, *Canaletto* (Ithaca: Cornell University Press, 1982), 138–41. Like Canaletto, Piranesi also included *capricci* and *vedute* in collections of their engravings; *capricci* could be considered a subset of the genre, *vedute*.

5 For these possibilities, see Lotte Brand Philip, "The Prado Epiphany by Jerome Bosch," *Art Bulletin* 35 (1953): 269, 281.

6 On this signifying practice, see Erwin Panofsky, *Early Netherlandish Painting: Its Origins and Character* (Cambridge, MA: Harvard University Press, 1964), 134–37.

7 On the frequent inclusion of ruins of the Temple of Peace in Florentine nativities of the quattrocento, see André Chastel, *Art et humanisme à Florence* (Paris: Presses universitaire de France, 1959), 239. On the legend of the Temple of Peace, see Henrik Cornell, *The Iconography of the Nativity of Christ* (Uppsala: A.-B. Lundequistska Bokhandeln, 1924), 48–50.

8 Rab Hatfield observes that the arches on the left of this painting carry a classical meaning and probably refer to the Temple of Peace, whereas the jagged corner seems to carry a Biblical meaning and refers either to the Tabernacle of David or to the stone the builders rejected. *Botticelli's Uffizi "Adoration": A Study in Pictorial Content* (Princeton: Princeton University Press, 1976), 64.

9 Ghirlandaio's earlier *Adoration* (1485) over the altar in the Sassetti Chapel in Sta. Trinità uses imagined classical inscriptions to displace anxieties about the power of earlier cultures and to assert a non-problematic progression from Judaism and paganism to Christianity. See Friedrich Saxl, "The Classical Inscription in Renaissance Art," *Journal of the Warburg and Courtauld Institutes* 4 (1941): 19–46.

10 Gibbon possessed a copy of Piranesi's *Vedute di Roma*, purchased probably during his visit to Rome in 1764; see Geoffrey Keynes, *The Library of Edward Gibbon* (London: Jonathan Cape, 1940), 222.

11 W. B. Carnochan first noted the conflation of texts in Gibbon's quotation from Poggio, in "Gibbon's Silences," *Johnson and His Age*, ed. James Engell (Cambridge, MA: Harvard University Press, 1984), 384. He sees these texts all contributing to the silence produced by contemplation of the fall of Rome; he does not observe or elaborate on the contradictory attitudes embraced by the different texts to which Gibbon alludes. Carnochan's analysis also appears, with minor revision, in his *Gibbon's Solitude: The Inward World of the Historian* (Stanford: Stanford University Press, 1987), 71–73. In this book Carnochan analyzes perspective in the *Decline and Fall* on an analogy with

landscape paintings as an alternation between long-distance and close-up point of view (68–70, 73–78).

12 Translated by Robert Fitzgerald (New York: Vintage, 1984).

13 As Leo Braudy argues, Gibbon makes use in the second half of the *Decline and Fall* of a "rhetoric of relative judgment," *Narrative Form in Fiction and History*, 247.

14 Gibbon thus joins many poets who have asserted that linguistic monuments may outlive both political empires and the monuments they erect in stone and metal: Virgil establishes his own epic as an appropriate memorial for Nisus and Euryalus in *Aeneid*, Book 9, ll. 446–49; Horace calls his poetry his "monument, destined to outlast bronze and to tower above pyramids" in *Odes*, Book 3, no. 30; in *Metamorphoses*, Book 15, Ovid asserts that his poem will outlast the anger of Jupiter and the star of Augustus Caesar. In Sonnet 55, Shakespeare also asserts the power of poetry to outlast the language of public praise engraved in stone: "Not marble nor the gilded monuments of princes shall outlive this pow'rful rime."

15 *Autobiographies*, ed. Murray, 338–39.

16 When he was working on the middle volumes of his history, near the end of the war between Britain and her American colonies, Gibbon wrote to his friend Georges Deyverdun that "the Decline of the Two Empires, the Roman and the British, advances with equal steps. I have contributed, however, much more effectively to the former," quoted in J. W. Johnson, "Gibbon's Architectural Metaphor," *Journal of British Studies* 13 (1973): 60.

For very helpful suggestions that pointed the way when this paper was at an early stage of its conception, I am grateful to Patricia B. Craddock. A later version of this paper was read by an NEH Institute on Image and Text in the Eighteenth Century, directed by Michael Fried and Ronald Paulson; I am indebted for valuable comments and suggestions to the participants in the institute, especially Ellen Handler Spitz and Heather McPherson.

A Prince's Sojourn in
Eighteenth-Century Canada

FREDERICK A. HALL

On 18 August 1791 the *Quebec Gazette* with great fanfare announced
the arrival of a royal personage:

> Last Thursday evening arrived here His Majesty's ships, Ulysses and
> Resistance in seven weeks from Gibraltar, having on board the 7th or
> Royal Regiment of Fusiliers under the command of the Colonel HIS
> ROYAL HIGHNESS PRINCE EDWARD.
> On Saturday at the Castle of Saint Lewis HIS ROYAL HIGHNESS
> received the respectful compliment of the officers of the garrison Civil
> and Military, the Clergy, Merchants, Citizens etc.
> In the afternoon the Ladies of Quebec were likewise introduced to HIS
> ROYAL HIGHNESS. . . .[1]

This young prince of twenty-five, already colonel of a regiment, was
Prince Edward Augustus (1767–1820), the fourth son of King George III
and Queen Charlotte. The prince had just finished a tour of duty in
Gibraltar following the completion of his education. As he waited in the
line of succession to the British crown, Edward, like all his brothers, was
instructed to make himself a respectable Christian, good man, and useful
member of society.[2] For this purpose, King George had laid out a specific
plan of education for his young sons which included time spent in Germany and in studying Latin, English composition, French, German,

247

English history, and of course military training, this last to include engineering, artillery, and military tactics.[3]

In the specific case of Prince Edward, he was sent to Luneburg and Hanover at the age of nineteen, six years before his arrival at Quebec. In a letter to his father in 1785 the dutiful son claimed: "I study every morning, Sundays excepted, from 6 till 10, and in the evening, when I am not invited anywhere, I amuse myself with a little musick. . . ."[4] This reference to entertaining himself with music is the first mention of what was to become a lifelong passion for the arts, especially music and theater. Although it is not clear if Edward ever received any formal musical training, he did enjoy singing.[5] It is very likely that regimental musicians taught him the basics of music and to play some instruments.

The rigorous schedule of study ensured that the prince shunned "low company, idleness and dissipation."[6] Lieutenant-Colonel George Wangenheim, an overbearing taskmaster, was put in charge of Edward's military training and he proceeded with great diligence to mold this weak young man into a good German officer. Despite Wangenheim's watchful eye, Edward succeeded in acquiring a substantial debt only two years after his arrival. His allowance could not cover the expenditures for furnishings and entertainment expected of a prince. King George was furious and chastized him for his debts and particularly for squandering the equivalent of a colonel's salary on the "futile addition to the Band of Musick and Drummers of the Regiment."[7] Edward acceded to his father's demands to rectify this state of affairs, informing the king in an apologetic reply that he had followed his orders and discharged all "supernumerary musicians, drummers and fifers. . . ."[8]

Edward's troubles with his father were only beginning. After a two-year stay in Geneva to escape the bitter cold and generally inhospitable climate of Hanover, Edward could no longer stand the separation from his family and the pleasures of England. Without permission he went home in the fall of 1789; after some futile attempts to see his father and to be accepted at public events, he was finally sent off in disgrace to Gibraltar—a fate worse than being stationed in Geneva. This summary dismissal to a lonely outpost left Edward in a state of depression. In his haste to reach Gibraltar many things had been left behind in Geneva, including his precious collection of music which he planned to take to Canada in prospects of receiving this new posting.[9] To boost his spirits Edward also arranged for a woman to join him at Gibraltar, and in the companionship of Thérèse-Bernardine Mongenet (1760–1830), known as Madame de St Laurent, he found great comfort—the fact that she was a trained singer was an added bonus. He wrote to his brother Clarence that now Gibraltar did not seem so bleak:

I feel this want of resources perhaps less than any man, for I manage with the assistance of a little music, a few books, & a little small talk with four or five officers, who constantly live in my family, to fill up as chearfully as I can those moments when professional business does not occupy me. Besides I have at present a young woman living with me who I wrote over to, to come from France to me. . . .[10]

Edward knew that another posting was imminent and he hoped that it would be Europe. However, on 14 February 1791 the Gibraltar Garrison Orders announced that the Seventh Regiment of Foot or Royal Fusiliers were to be sent to Canada in the spring. Edward was honored by many events prior to his departure, including a magnificent ball with dancing and singing to the accompaniment of the band until midnight. He finally sailed on 24 June with a retinue that the *Times* sarcastically called "rather domestic than Princely; a French Lady, his own man, and a Swiss valet, composing his whole suite."[11]

Upon Edward's arrival in Quebec two months later, the *Quebec Gazette* reflected the excitement that was felt by curious English and French residents as they waited to catch a glimpse of the king's son and his mysterious French companion.

[August 1791] On Tuesday the 7th Regiment disembarked on the beach or landing place in the Lower town, where, after having formed HIS HIGHNESS in compliment to the garrison made them perform the usual evolutions of a salute the drums beating and music playing, God Save the King. They then marched up to the parade before the Castle, where being drawn up in the presence of a great concourse of spectators they were viewed by His Excellency Lord Dorchester and His Honor General Clarke, his Royal Highness commanded in person, in a manner that shewed the Prince not less than the soldier.[12]

At the close of the ceremonies, the regiment marched up Port Louis Street and deposited the regimental colors in front of Edward's new residence. After the obligatory welcomes made over several days by various levels of Quebec society and military personnel, Edward settled into the daily routine of Quebec. Because he was the son of a king, Edward's attendance was sought and expected at many public functions. The presence of royalty created a crowded social calendar as each social matriarch of Quebec hoped that Edward would accept an invitation to her special event. As a result the paper records many balls, assemblies, and mixed entertainments during the first year of Edward's stay.

Quebec was already a well-established garrison town when Edward arrived. Since the Treaty of Paris in 1763, the British had made Quebec one of its major defence points. After the American War of Independence, the fortifications became even more important when the British established Quebec as the military headquarters for what remained of their possessions in North America. The arrival of thousands of American loyalists after the Revolution gave Canada a large population of English-speaking citizens loyal to the crown; but Quebec still retained its French character beneath the veneer of British bureaucracy and commerce. French residents detested the British but had learned to tolerate their presence. Although the Catholic Church had retarded the development of public secular activities, the British presence had encouraged the older residents and newly-arrived loyalists to produce some concerts and plays. The first notice of a public theatrical presentation was published in 1765; subscription concerts appeared in press notices as early as 1770, and public concerts at inns and taverns were advertised periodically. As the *Quebec Gazette* noted: "It is a prevailing custom in this Garrison, of inviting one another to Balls, Dances, House-Warmings, &c. . . ."[13] Undoubtedly, the loyalist emigrants from the American colonies and the militia stationed at the garrison combined forces in the 1780s to present various theatrical/musical presentations, including tragedies or mainpieces, interludes of songs and dances, and so-called afterpieces which were often mixed entertainments, farces, or even occasionally comic operas.

Elizabeth Simcoe (1762–1850), wife of John Graves Simcoe, lieutenant governor of Upper Canada, arrived at Quebec only three months after Edward, and the following entries in her diary for November 1791 illustrate the impact Edward had on the community:

> I went to a Subscription Concert. Prince Edward's Band of the 7th Fusiliers played and some of the officers of the Fusileers. The music was thought excellent. The Band costs the Prince 8 hundred a year.[14]

> I went to Church. The Service is performed in a Room occasionally used as a Council Chamber. Prince Edward always goes to Church and his band plays during the Service. . . .[15]

> I went to a Concert & afterwards to a dance at the Fusileers' Barracks.[16]

In a letter and in diary entries for February and March of 1792, Mrs. Simcoe recounted more activities of the band and mentioned some of the social entertainments enjoyed by residents:

> The Officers act Plays. I think of you as I know it is your favourite amusement indeed I think there are more amusements & gaiety here than a winter at Bath affords & that you would not expect in so remote a Country. The Prince's Band cost him near five hundred a year being a selection of fine performers so you may suppose the Concerts are not to be despised. . . .[17]

The Fusileers are the best dancers, well dressed & the best looking figures in a Ball Room I ever saw. They are all musical & like dancing & bestow as much money, as other Regts. usually spend in wine, in giving Balls & Concerts which make them very popular in this place where dancing is so favourite an amusement . . .[18]

Mrs. Simcoe's comments reveal the active social lives enjoyed by the privileged classes in Quebec. She points out that many of Edward's officers were musical, indicating that Edward's choice of men to serve with him was influenced by his artistic tastes. For example, Captain Smyth, one of the prince's trusted officers, was a talented keyboard player who accompanied Edward and Madame de St Laurent in impromptu private concerts at Edward's official residence.[19] Another officer stationed in Quebec advertised in the Quebec paper that he had to return to England and was selling "a parcel of Genteel Household Furniture, a Harpsichord, etc. etc."[20]

It was not only Edward's bandsmen who participated in Quebec's musical life. Two immigrants, one a German-born musician and the other a Boston loyalist, illustrate the contributions of talented residents. Johann Friedrich Conrad Glackemeyer (1759–1836),[21] born at Hanover twenty-six years before Edward's stay in the electorate, arrived at Quebec in 1777 and later probably served as band conductor for a regiment under the command of Baron von Riedesel.[22] He taught viol, bass-viol, violin, and piano and was an early importer of music and musical instruments. Glackemeyer sold goods to the townspeople and to members of Edward's band. An advertisement that appeared in November 1792 listed overtures by Johann Stamitz (1717–1757), Johann Baptist Vanhal (1739–1813), Franz Joseph Haydn (1732–1809), and Johann Sterkel (1750–1817) — "all for a compleat orchestra," quartets by Ignace Pleyel (1757–1831), a few Vauxhall songs, country dances, and the "best Italian Fiddle, Violoncello, and Tenor strings. . . ."[23] Glackemeyer participated in subscription concerts during the 1790–1791 season, and presumably Edward took advantage of the talents of this able musician. It has even been claimed by an early chronicler that Glackemeyer became the bandmaster of Edward's regiment.[24] Jonathan Sewell Jr. (1766–1839) arrived from New Brunswick after his father, the former attorney-general of Massachusetts, and his family had fled from Boston to the Canadian maritimes. An actor and skilled violinist,[25] Jonathan Jr. made Quebec his home, having been called to the bar in Lower Canada in 1789. Edward asked him to lead a small orchestra in which Glackemeyer also must have participated. These musicians, in combination with other residents and the Royal Fusiliers band, produced a series of public and private entertainments during Edward's sojourn at Quebec.

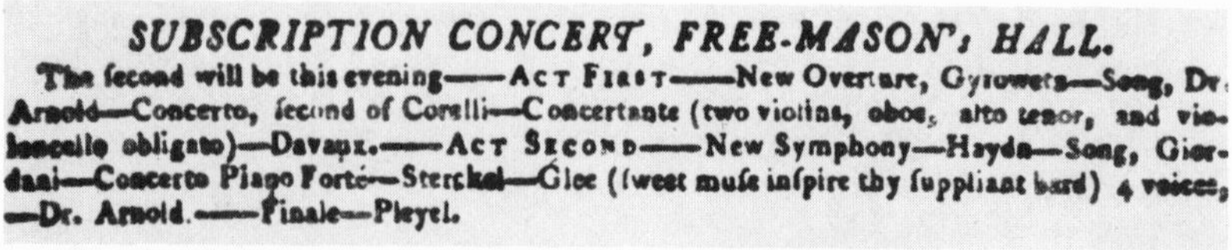

SUBSCRIPTION CONCERT, FREE-MASON'; HALL.

The second will be this evening——Act First——New Overture, Gyrowetz—Song, Dr. Arnold—Concerto, second of Corelli—Concertante (two violins, oboe, alto tenor, and violoncello obligato)—Davaux.——Act Second——New Symphony—Haydn—Song, Giordani—Concerto Piano Forte—Sterckel—Glee (sweet muse infpire thy suppliant bard) 4 voices, —Dr. Arnold.——Finale—Pleyel.

Figure 1. Advertisement for Second Subscription Concert. Quebec Gazette, 22 November 1792.

Edward's band became the central attraction at many festivities and an important musical resource. The officers and band members participated in the second season of subscription concerts which began in November 1792 and concluded the following February. During this winter season eleven concerts were presented to the public — approximately one each week. In addition to these weekly concerts, balls, suppers, assemblies, and theatrical presentations involved band members and officers of the Fusiliers. And, of course, the band was on the parade ground regularly, under the review of Edward and visiting dignitaries.

The composers represented on the subscription concerts ranged from the London favorites Samuel Arnold (1740-1802), Charles Avison (1709-1770), George Frideric Handel (1685-1759), Johann Christian Bach (1735-1782), and Thomas Augustine Arne (1710-1778) to the continental composers Pleyel, Adalbert Gyrowetz (1763-1850), Wolfgang Amadeus Mozart (1756-1791), and Haydn. The compositions included orchestral overtures, symphonies, pianoforte concertos, songs, and glees. Patrons of the theater could enjoy *She Stoops to Conquer* [Oliver Goldsmith], *Who's the Dupe?* [Hannah Cowley], *Miss in Her Teens* [David Garrick], and the comic operas *Choleric Fathers* [Thomas Holcroft; William Shield], and *The Padlock* [Isaac Bickerstaff; Charles Dibdin].

Edward was probably involved directly in the planning of these musical and theatrical seasons because he preferred to participate fully in all aspects of the regiment's activities. His fastidious nature and penchant for exacting detail are noted in letters and at times probably drove his officers and men to distraction.[26] By 1793 Edward was already restless. He wanted desperately to see military action and considered that Quebec was unlikely to be attacked by the Americans. To give him some solace, he had Madame de St Laurent, his band, and the rounds of social engagements, but his request for "Novellists Magazines, a small collection of the best French novels," plays and the works of Rousseau indicate that his days were not as exciting as he might have wished. On 2 October 1793 he was given the rank of major general in the army and on Christmas Eve was told that he was to be sent to the West Indies. Edward was elated; one of his captains wrote to a friend that "there was packing up of all the Brass Drums, Instruments &c. not to be opened until he comes back to the Regt."[27] Edward departed from Quebec on 22 January 1794.

After an exciting but brief campaign in which he actually saw some military action and received recognition for bravery, Edward travelled to Halifax in the hope that he might now be allowed to go directly home from this Atlantic port. He arrived in May 1794. By the end of the month a ship had arrived in the Halifax harbor with his possessions and his regimental band which he had left in Quebec. Edward soon learned that he was to be stationed at the garrison until further notice.

Halifax had been established by the British in 1749, less than fifty years prior to Edward's arrival. In that brief time the militia and towns-people had created an attractive and commercially viable settlement. William Dyott, whose regiment had been stationed in Boston before arriving in Halifax in 1787, described Edward's new posting:

> The town of Halifax is prettily enough situated on a hillside, at the top of which there is a citadel and block-house. The houses are all built of wood, and in general painted white or yellow, which has a very pleasing effect, particularly in summer. The streets extend from north to south along the side of the hill, and are intersected by cross streets, extending from the shore up the hill towards the block-house. . . . There are three barracks, which would contain from 600 to 1000 men. There are also two churches, both very neat buildings of wood, and one or two meeting-houses. There is a square in town called the Grand Parade, where the troops in garrison parade every evening during the summer; and where all the belles and beaux of the place promenade, and the bands remain to play as long as they walk.[28]

In 1789 theatrical productions were moved from the Great Pontac Inn to a building which the officers of the garrison and gentlemen of the town had constructed. Dyott in a diary entry for February 1789 noted that "it was as complete a thing for the size as I ever saw, boxes and a first and second pit."[29] All theatrical and musical performances patronized by Edward took place in this Halifax theater.

Edward took command of a garrison in desperate need of repair. In his military correspondence to England he complained about rotting floors and roofs and inadequate accommodation. Thus Edward attempted to put aside his desire to return to England and involved himself totally with the affairs of his new position. Once more he turned to his beloved woman and his band to distract him from the boring daily military routine. At this stage, however, Edward encountered great difficulties in maintaining his band. Desertions by musicians to other regiments or across the border to the United States reduced the number of performers available for parades and entertainments. In a letter written in October 1795 Edward outlined his problems and needs to his aide in London:

I little thought when I mentioned that to you, that my Band would be so completely wrecked by the present time as it now is, the Master Scavoye, having given us warning, agreeable to his engagement, to be free at Michaelmas next; the Trumpet (Muck) whose time lapses at the end of April, having refused to enter into a new engagement; my two Bassoons, 1st Clarinet and one Trumpet (all four soldiers) having deserted about a fortnight since to the States, being enticed away under promise of uncommon wages by one of their comrades (a showman). Our Tambour de basque, who deserted from furlow about two months before; thus, the labour of six years is entirely lost, and from having the very best Band (without exception) in the King's Service, I have now, worse than none, a very incomplete and bad one. In this dilemma, I have written to a Man at Brunswick of the name of Bies who served under me before in the Band of the Guards at Hanover, when I was their Colonel, to engage for me for a term of not less than six, and if possible of eight years, a complete Band of tricolor, the first and principal condition being that none of them have ever served in France, or have the least appearance of harbouring French principles. . . . The whole that I have stipulated to pay them previous to their reaching London is six pounds sterling per man, two of which is to be paid them at Hanover by Mr. Falcke, one of the first Magistrates of that city, and the other four at Hamburgh [sic] by Mr. Hamburg the British Consul, whose respective draughts I request you will therefore honor the former to the amount of twenty four, the other to the amount of forty eight pounds. I beg at the same time to observe that I never yet have received the Trumpets which I requested you to send out, and that I now request you will be good enough to forward them by the December Packet, if not hy the January, together with a bass Sackbut, agreeable to the following directions. The Trumpets to be of brass not of copper, perfectly plain without embossment or engraving, of the largest size possible, and with crooks for every tone; the bass Sackbut to be in like manner perfectly plain and of the largest size. Captain Smyth of my regiment, my major of brigade, who will be the bearer of this letter to you, and who is a most excellent musician, will be able to give you still fuller directions respecting them. I will trouble you immediately on the receipt of this, to write to Mr. Hamburg, the British Consul at Hamburgh that he may have directions to pay the sum of four pounds to any musician who shall produce an engagement signed with my name, and coming from Hanover, not exceeding the number of thirteen. . . .[30]

Judging from the evidence contained in this letter, published concert notices, and average sizes of military bands of this period, one can estimate the size and cost of the band which Edward maintained in Halifax at his own expense. British regimental bands had a minimum of eight musicians. For example, the band of the Royal Artillery contained pairs of horns, trumpets, and bassoons with four oboes or clarinets; some players were also expected to be able to play flute, violin, cello, or bass when necessary.[31] By 1794 the Grenadier Guards maintained a band consisting of one flute, six clarinets, three bassoons, three horns, one trumpet, two serpents, and one percussionist.[32] The duke of York, Edward's brother, had even introduced to England a band of twenty-four men following his return from Germany. Edward could not have possibly afforded this large number of players but probably maintained a band of thirteen to sixteen musicians. As he stated in his October letter, the British consul was to pay up to thirteen musicians from Hanover to join the Royal Fusiliers. Edward did not consider recruiting English performers but relied on the musical traditions that he had known when he stayed at Hanover. Because Britain had treaties with the principalities of Hesse, Brunswick, and Waldeck and since George III retained his title of elector-prince of Brunswick-Luneburg, it was relatively easy to recruit German players.

Still not satisfied, Edward turned to other regiments stationed in Canada in his efforts to find musicians. In a letter to Robert Prescott (c. 1726-1815), commander of the British forces in North America,[33] he noted he had heard that the Fourth Regiment and First Battalion of the Sixtieth Regiment were to be drafted; he requested that Prescott allow him to recruit some musicians from these regiments. In particular he wanted one man, a Hanoverian named Peterson, who had previously been in the duke of York's Coldstream Guards. He also wrote to major general Beckwith in Bermuda requesting the transfer of a musician from the Forty-seventh to the Royal Fusiliers. The costs of maintaining this band are difficult to determine. In one of his letters Edward states that drummers in the Royal Artillery were paid sixty-nine pounds eleven shillings and six pence salary; presumably some musicians received more than this wage because of their skills. Mrs. Simcoe had claimed that the band cost Edward five or eight hundred pounds, but it seems likely that Edward actually spent at least one thousand pounds annually on salaries, plus additional money for uniforms and instruments. Edward's pay as major general was 3,650 pounds annually, suggesting that he spent approximately one third of his salary on his band.

Edward not only occupied himself with rebuilding his band but also with transforming the country house loaned to him and Madame de St Laurent by Sir John Wentworth (1737-1820), lieutenant governor of Nova Scotia. This house, located near the Bedford Basin six miles from town, became the prince's private retreat. Across the road he built a rotunda, surmounted by a golden ball, which was the location for musical entertainment and from where the band serenaded Edward when he entertained at his lodge. "Latticed summer-houses, rocky grottoes and tiny Chinese temples"[34] were added to the rustic landscape behind the lodge.

Edward and Madame attended most social functions and entertainments, and the prince's official patronage of theater and music encouraged the garrison and town performers to produce more entertainments. Halifax attempted in many ways to imitate the social life of London; and as a result numerous balls, assemblies, drawing room functions, official receptions, and anniversary dinners were held. At least two major performances of plays and music were presented each month at the theater. Inns and taverns also advertised various mixed entertainments and regular private chamber concerts occurred at the garrison and at the prince's lodge. The regimental band assumed the same role as it had in Quebec — performing at these public and private entertainments, at church services, and on the grand parade in front of St. Paul's Church. A formal dress parade was held weekly, and the band played appropriate music at other occasions for couples to process along the grand parade and on the adjoining streets.

Between 7 August 1794 and 18 June 1800 Halifax newspapers list eighty-six different plays, operas, and mixed entertainments, most of which Edward officially patronized (see Appendix). The number of concerts and theatrical presentations in Halifax could not equal London, but under Edward's direction actors and musicians emulated on a modest scale the current trends of English theaters. Thirty-two works presented in Halifax had also been produced in London for at least five seasons between 1790 and 1800; thirteen plays and operas were produced in these same ten seasons, and another seven works were performed during nine seasons in London. In fact, all but fourteen works enjoyed by Halifax audiences had been produced at least once in London theaters during the decade 1790 to 1800. Most plays were comedies and farces such as *The Dramatist* (Frederick Reynolds) and *Miss in her Teens* (David Garrick). A few ballad operas were presented — *The Poor Soldier* (John O'Keeffe; music compiled by O'Keeffe and William Shield), *The Devil to Pay* (John Mottley & Charles Coffey), and *The Ladies' Frolick* (James Love; music compiled by William Bates and Thomas Arne). Most musical productions were comic operas from the second half of the eighteenth century, including: *The Castle of Andalusia* (John O'Keeffe; music compiled by Samuel Arnold), *Duenna* (Richard Sheridan; Thomas Linley Sr., Thomas Linley Jr.), and *No Song, No Supper* (Prince Hoare; Stephen Storace) which was produced at Halifax in 1798, just eight years after its Drury Lane premiere. Comic operas were the current popular entertainment with London audiences. Drury Lane, Covent Garden, and the Little Theatre in the Haymarket featured the genre as part of an evening's entertainment, often combining comic opera with a play. These operas, with their simple airs, difficult arias, and spoken dialogue, rivalled London theater in popularity.

"A Grand Medley of Entertainments" presented at Mr. Noonan's tavern typified the less formal extravaganzas attempted by entertainers. The first three acts contained a "set of curious artificial wax-work figures," a magic figure who danced a jig and at the same time changed her face into several different forms, an Italian scaramouche dance, and surprising philosophical experiments and deceptions. The final act presented "a grand view of Earl Howe's engagement" and victory over the French on the first of June; the newspaper advertisement claimed "part of the vessels will be seen sinking, some dismasted, and others blowing up — Also a view of Britannia's triumph — with the fishes sporting in the waves."[35]

Instrumental concerts held at inns and taverns were arranged by Edward's musicians. The British Coffee House, for instance, featured the prince's band with local musicians in a series of programs. In December 1797, for example, a benefit concert for Mr. Scavoye, Edward's director of music and clarinetist, featured a symphony by Leopold Kozeluch (1747-1818), concertos for solo violin, flute, and clarinet, and a *concertante* work for bassoons and clarinet.[36] The *concertante* pieces programmed for these and other concerts were ideal for regimental bandsmen in that several different instruments were featured and individual solo roles not particularly demanding. In January 1798 a benefit for the musician Mr. Duplessy, who had served in Quebec with Edward, included some of the same concertos, but supplemented a horn concerto and a "symphony concertante" for two violins.[37] Typical instrumental programs during these years consisted mainly of works written by eighteenth-century composers who were already popular in England and continental Europe. Compositions by Christian Bach, Gyrowetz, and Franz Kotzwara (ca. 1750-1791) had long been featured in London performances, especially the Hanover Square Series and the Ancient Concerts. Edward's musicians also performed works by composers active in Vienna and Mannheim who were known to Parisian and London audiences: Joseph Schmittbaur (1718-1809), Carl Toeschi (1731-1788), and Vanhal typified these orchestral musicians who also composed various instrumental pieces; not surprisingly, the composers' works likewise appeared on concert programs in Philadelphia, New York, and Boston. Orchestral overtures, symphonies, and *concertante* works typical of Edward's programs were scored for a minimum standard orchestra of the period, consisting of eight instrumental lines, four of which were strings

HALIFAX THEATRE.

BY THE DESIRE OF
HIS ROYAL HIGHNESS PRINCE EDWARD.

TO-MORROW EVENING, the 18th Inftant.
Will be prefented,

AN OPERA CALLED
ROSINA;
In Two Acts.

To which will added, the ENTERTAINMENT of
LETHE.

Between the Play and Farce, will be an Interlude.

Tickets for the Boxes 5s.———Pit 3s.
To prevent the avenues from being too much crowded,
both doors of the Pit will be kept open as ufual.

The Doors to be opened at Six, and the Performance to
begin precifely at Seven o'Clock.

The MANAGERS inform thofe Ladies and Gentlemen who
takes places in the Boxes, that Mr. *Minns* will deliver Tickets at the fame time, for any number of Seats taken.

Tickets to be had, and Places taken in the Boxes, of Mr.
Minns.

No Money to be taken at the Door, nor any Perfons admitted behind the Scenes.

VIVANT REX ET REGINA!

☞ Complaints having been made that the high head
dreffes of fome of the Ladies who occupy the front feats of the
Boxes, obftruct the fight of thofe who fit behind them :———
The Managers do therefore take the liberty of mentioning it,
with a firm affurance that the inconvenience will be remedied.

⁎ The MANAGERS once more requeft that thofe Perfons who have Bills againft the Theatre, will be fo good as
to bring them in immediately ; otherwife they will not be an-
fwerable for the Payment of them.

Figure 2. Royal Gazette and Nova Scotia Advertiser, 17 March 1795.

with optional harpsichord; the remaining four performed by oboes or flutes and French horns. Clarinets were occasionally substituted for oboes, and additional lines could have been inserted for trumpet or bassoon.

Despite this varied menu of entertainment, Edward's longing for England was not assuaged. He wrote to his brother, the prince of Wales, in the fall of 1799 that "the contrast between the comforts and the beauty of England, with the want of every resource and the drearyness of Nova Scotia, is certainly very glaring. . . ."[38] His numerous letters to England urging friends to convince the king to allow him to come home finally produced results. Word arrived he was to sail to England, and on 3 August 1800, after many farewell parties and entertainments, Edward, now the duke of Kent, bade farewell to his friends at Halifax.

Edward had spent six years and eight months in Canada, the longest that any son of a reigning monarch has remained in the country. During this period, Edward's military contributions to these two colonial garrison towns were significant: the Quebec and Halifax garrisons were refurbished, defences improved, and new buildings constructed. His cultural influence, though equally important, is less tangible and consequently more difficult to assess.

From published evidence we know that Edward attended or patronized productions of approximately one hundred major musical and theatrical works and an equal number of public concerts and mixed entertainments at which he heard several hundred instrumental and vocal works. One can only speculate about how many private chamber concerts took place at the garrisons and in Edward's Quebec and Halifax residences. This young prince, who became the duke of Kent and commander-in-chief of North America while serving in the colony and who was to become the father of Queen Victoria, set a standard of cultural patronage that few in Canada would be able to emulate.

NOTES

1 *Quebec Gazette*, 18 August 1791. The author gratefully acknowledges the assistance of Rebecca Green who searched Quebec newspapers for references to Prince Edward Augustus.

2 Arthur Aspinall, ed., *The Later Correspondence of George III*, 5 vols. (Cambridge: Cambridge University Press, 1962), 1:xvi.

3 Ibid., xviii.

4 Ibid., no. 216.

5 *Adventures and Recollections of Colonel Landmann*, 2 vols. (London: Colburn, 1852), 1:193.

6 Aspinall, *George III*, 1:xvii.

7 Ibid., no. 393; written to Edward at Hanover.

8 Ibid.

9 Ibid., 2:no. 561; letter from Lieutenant Colonel R. Symes to Major General R. Grenville. "Prince Edward desires me to request you will mention it to the King how earnestly his Royal Highness wishes to have with him his books, papers and musick from Geneva; should his Majesty be pleased to allow his Royal Highness to go to Canada the want of them will there be a very great misfortune."

10 Cited in Mollie Gillen, *The Prince and His Lady* (London: Sidgwick and Jackson, 1970), 21, from Royal Archives MS 46669.

11 Ibid., 25.

12 *Quebec Gazette*, 18 August 1791.

13 Ibid., 19 January 1767.

14 Mary Quayle Innis, ed., *Mrs. Simcoe's Diary* (Toronto: Macmillan, 1965), 39.

15 Ibid.

16 Ibid., 50.

17 Ibid.; letter to Mrs. Hunt, 13 February 1792.

18 Ibid., 52

19 *Adventures and Recollections of Colonel Landmann* 1:193. "I had the honour to receive a card stating, that 'Major Vesey had been commanded by his Royal Highness to invite me to dine at his country residence,' on Bedford Basin. . . . Coffee and tea being over, the Prince, condescendingly sang a duet with Madame St. Laurent, accompanied by Captain Smith, a first-rate pianist."

20 *Quebec Gazette*, 5 January 1792.

21 Dr. Helmut Kallmann has kindly provided this biographical information. Glackemeyer's given names, birthdate, and arrival in Canada have been established by Kallmann's recent research. See "Frédéric Glackemeyer: des données nouvelles sur sa vie et son style musical," *Les Cahiers de l'ARMuQ* 8 (May 1987): 86–92.

22 Helmut Kallmann, Gilles Potvin, and Kenneth Winters, eds., *Encyclopedia of Music in Canada* (Toronto: University of Toronto Press, 1981), 379.

23 *Quebec Gazette*, 1 November 1792.

24 Kallmann, *Encyclopedia of Music in Canada*, 379.

25 William Notman, *Portraits of British Americans* (Montreal, 1867), vol. 2, and Kallmann, *Encyclopedia of Music in Canada*, 863.

26 One example is Edward's reaction to the news that his brother the duke of York had altered the dress of his drum major and band when he returned from Germany. Edward immediately asked for "a pattern of half of each coat, in coarse cloth, with white cotton to represent the silver lace, yellow the gold, to be sent secretly." He sent the helmets of all his officers, sergeants, musi-

cians, and drummers back to London to be altered. Cited in Gillen, *The Prince and His Lady*, 57.

27 Cited in Gillen, *The Prince and His Lady*, 81.

28 Reginald W. Jeffery, ed., *Dyott's Diary* (London: Constable, 1907), 1:30.

29 Ibid., 61

30 The letterbooks of Prince Edward, duke of Kent from September 1794 to May 1800, Royal Archives ADD. 7/57-698, no. 202, 27 October 1795. Quoted with the gracious permission of Her Majesty the Queen.

31 Stanley Sadie, ed., *The New Grove Dictionary of Musical Instruments* (London and New York: Macmillan, 1984), 1:123.

32 Ibid., 125.

33 Letterbooks, 19 June 1797.

34 Gillen, *The Prince and His Lady*, 96.

35 *Royal Gazette and Nova Scotia Advertiser*, 13 and 26 January 1795.

36 Ibid., 5 December 1797.

37 Ibid., 30 January 1798.

38 Aspinall, *George III*, 4: no.1487.

Appendix

Halifax Performances

The following is a listing of the known musical and theatrical performances which took place during the time Prince Edward Augustus was in Halifax. All performances were officially patronized by Edward except those marked with an asterisk (*). The main venue was the Halifax Theater; some concerts took place at other locations, such as the British Coffee House and Noonan's Tavern. For each play the author is given in square brackets; for opera the author's name is followed by the name of the composer(s). Entries for concerts provide the titles of works and names of composers as published in the newspapers.

This Appendix is based on the author's research and on the listings of theatrical and musical presentations in: Sidney M. Oland, "Materials for a History of the Theatre in Early Halifax" (M.A. thesis, Dalhousie University, 1966).

Scheduled Date	*Summary of Performances*
*7 Aug. 1794	A Grand Medley of Entertainments, "Philosophical Experiments and Deceptions . . . A Grand View of the Siege of Gibraltar . . . the play of the Children in the Wood," etc. [Different versions of above presented by Mr. Maginnis on:

	9, 14, 16, 21, 23, 28, 30 Aug.; 2, 4, 6, Sept. 1794]
*16 Sept. 1794	Entertainment by Mr. Hackley, "Balance Master . . . A number of astonishing Feats of Activity in three acts." [Different versions of above presented on: 23, 25, 27 Sept. 1794]
30 Dec. 1794	The Mock Doctor [Henry Fielding] The Poor Soldier [John O'Keeffe; John O'Keeffe & William Shield]
*31 Dec. 1794	Whittington and His Cat "by a curious set of Artificial Wax Work Comedians with a variety of other curious Entertainments . . ." [Repeat performances on: 1, 2, 3, 6, 7, 8, 9, 10 Jan. 1795]
*13 Jan. 1795	A Grand Medley of Entertainments . . . "by a set of curious artificial wax-work figures . . ." [Repeat performances on 15, 21, 23, 27, 29 Jan.; 3 Feb. 1795]
14 Jan. 1795	Love-A La-Mode [Charles Macklin] The Agreeable Surprise [John O'Keeffe; Samuel Arnold]
4 Feb. 1795	Catherine and Petruchio [David Garrick] Appearance Is Against Them [Elizabeth Inchbald]
25 Feb. 1795	Midas [Kane O'Hara; various comps.] The Lying Valet [David Garrick]
4 Mar. 1795	Catherine and Petruchio [David Garrick] Midas [Kane O'Hara; various comps.]
18 Mar. 1795	Rosina [Frances Brooke; William Shield] Lethe [David Garrick]
15 Apr. 1795	Ways and Means [George Colman, Younger] The Poor Soldier [John O'Keeffe; John O'Keeffe & William Shield]
*15 July 1795	Ways and Means [George Colman, Younger] The Agreeable Surprise [John O'Keeffe; Samuel Arnold]
*7 Aug. 1795	Ways and Means [George Colman, Younger] Midas [Kane O'Hara; various comps.]

6 Nov. 1795	Mixed Entertainment given by Signor Tronche "Dancing a Hornpipe on the Tight Rope . . ."
22 Dec. 1795	The Beaux Stratagem [George Farquhar] Half an Hour After Supper [?]
3 Feb. 1796	Turkish Gratitude [?] Crotchet Lodge [Thomas Hurlstone]
24 Feb. 1796	The Castle of Andalusia [John O'Keeffe; compiled by Samuel Arnold] The Family Party [George Colman, Younger]
19 Mar. 1796	The Humours of a Village ["comic opera . . . written by a performer"] The Widow's Vow [Elizabeth Inchbald]
30 Mar. 1796	The Castle of Andalusia [John O'Keeffe; compiled by Samuel Arnold] Miss In Her Teens [David Garrick]
*1 Apr. 1796	Concert. For the Benefit of A. Scavoye. 1st Act. 1st Simphony a Grand Orchestre, Pleyel; 2d-Song; 3d. Concerte for the Clarinette; 4th. Simphony Concertante, Pleyel; 5th. New Simphony, Pichl; 2d Act. 6th. Simphony concertante for two Violins; 7th. Song, the Soldier tired of War's Alarms; 8th. Quartette, Pleyel; 9th. Trio, for Horns; 10th. Chorus; 11th. New Simphony, Schmit Bauer.
6 Apr. 1796	The Box-Lobby Challenge [Richard Cumberland] High Life Below Stairs [James Townley]
20 Apr. 1796	The Rage! [Frederick Reynolds] The Devil To Pay [John Mottley & Charles Coffey]
*29 Apr. 1796	The Padlock [Isaac Bickerstaff; Charles Dibdin] Bon Ton [David Garrick]
26 Oct. 1796	The Miser [Henry Fielding]
11 Jan. 1797	Douglas [John Home] The Mayor of Garratt [Samuel Foote]
28 Jan. 1797	The Dramatist [Frederick Reynolds]
30 Jan. 1797	[Repeat of 28 Jan. program]
1 Feb. 1797	[Repeat of 28 Jan. program]

*27 Feb. 1797	The Rivals [Richard Sheridan] The Ghost [H. James]
5 May 1797	The Dramatist [Frederick Reynolds] Matelot's Provinceaux [ballet]
14 July 1797	Crotchet Lodge [Thomas Hurlstone] The Poor Soldier [John O'Keeffe; John O'Keeffe & William Shield]
15 Sept. 1797	Collins's Evening Brush. "Modern Spouters; Stage Candidates . . . Bunglers and Bogglers . . . Interspersed with a Variety of Comic Songs . . ."-
8 Nov. 1797	Olio or Attic Evening's Entertainment. "Composed of the Sublime, the Pathetic, the Humerous and the Musical . . ."
13 Dec. 1797	Concert by Subscription. For the Benefit of Mr. Scavoye Act 1st. Simphonie of Kozeluc; Concerto de Violin; The Song of — Hark the dreadful sound of war; Concertante for Bassoons and Clarinett of Vogel; Act 2d. Concertante for Violin, Hautboy, Violoncello — Pleyel; Concerto for flute — Stamitz; The Song of Robinhoods Hill; Concerto for Clarinetts of Vogel; Henry the Fourth Overture.
3 Jan. 1798	A Cure for the Heart Ache [Thomas Morton]
17 Jan. 1798	The West Indian [Richard Cumberland]
31 Jan. 1798	Notoriety [Frederick Reynolds]
7 Feb. 1798	Concert by Subscription . . . for the Benefit of Mr. Duplessey. [sic] Act 1st. The Siege of Gibraltar arrang'd by Mr. Duplessy. Concerto for the Flute. — By Vienne. Song. — By Dr. Arnold. Horn Concerto. — By Fonto. Simphonie. — By Kozeluc. Act 2d. Simphonie Concertante for two Violins. — By Davaux.

	Concerto for the Clarinett. —By Vogal. A Song in Rosina. A Concerto for the Flute. —Stamitz. Simphonie. —By Kozeluc.
14 Feb. 1798	Richard Coeur de Lion [John Burgoyne; André Grétry adapted by Thomas Linley Sr.]
7 Mar. 1798	Abroad and at Home [Joseph Holman; William Shield] No Song, No Supper [Prince Hoare; Stephen Storace]
14 Mar. 1798	The Midnight Hour [Elizabeth Inchbald] No Song, No Supper [Prince Hoare; Stephen Storace]
21 Mar. 1798	The Brothers [Richard Cumberland] No Song, No Supper [Prince Hoare; Stephen Storace]
30 Mar. 1798	Duenna [Richard Sheridan; Thomas Linley Sr., Thomas Linley Jr.] The Deuce is In Him [George Colman, elder]
18 Apr. 1798	How To Grow Rich [Frederick Reynolds] The Return [Richard Sheridan?]
25 Apr. 1798	George Barnwell [George Lillo] [or The London Merchant] The Wrangling Lovers [William Lyon]
2 May 1798	The Jew [Richard Cumberland] The Miller of Mansfield [Robert Dodsley]
9 May 1798	The Jew [Richard Cumberland] The Miller of Mansfield [Robert Dodsley]
30 May 1798	The Will [Frederick Reynolds] Barnaby Brittle [?]
6 June 1798	The Will [Frederick Reynolds] Rosina [Frances Brooke; William Shield]
20 June 1798	Barnaby Brittle [?] Rosina [Frances Brooke; William Shield]
11 July 1798	The City Romp [T. Lloyd?] Chrononhotonthologos [Henry Carey]
8 Aug. 1798	Who's The Dupe? [Hannah Cowley]

	Robinson Crusoe [Richard Sheridan; Thomas Linley Sr.]
15 Aug. 1798	[Repeat of 8 Aug. program]
21 Sept. 1798	The Deaf Lover [Frederick Pilon] My Grandmother And Other Fairies [Prince Hoare; Stephen Storace]
12 Oct. 1798	The Tempest [William Shakespeare] The Waterman [Charles Dibdin; Charles Dibdin]

[Because of an injury, Edward left for England in October 1798 and returned to Halifax 6 Sept. 1799]

8 Jan. 1800	The Liar [Samuel Foote] Miss In Her Teens [David Garrick]
29 Jan. 1800	Inkle and Yarico [George Colman Jr.; Samuel Arnold] [subsequently cancelled—music lost]
31 Jan. 1800	The Old Maid [Arthur Murphy] Robinson Crusoe [Richard Sheridan; Thomas Linley Sr.]
5 Feb. 1800	[repeat of 31 Jan. program]
12 Mar. 1800	Matilda [Thomas Francklin] The Village Lawyer [George Colman, elder]
*27 Mar. 1800	The Battle of the Nile The Ladies' Frolic [James Love] The London Beau [?]
16 Apr. 1800	The Provoked Husband [Colley Cibber] The Village Lawyer [George Colman, elder]
28 May 1800	King Richard The Third [William Shakespeare] Seeing is Believing [Richard Jodrell]
18 June 1800	Cheap Living! [Frederick Reynolds] Seeing is Believing [Richard Jodrell]

Time in Rasselas:
Johnson's Use of Locke's Concept

REGINA HEWITT

From specific calculations of months and years through general observations about age to indefinite beginnings on "one day," references to
time appear insistently in *Rasselas*.[1] Despite more than four hundred
allusions to moments, hours, days, weeks, months, years, seasons,
cycles, intervals, and frequency of occurrences, the narrative offers little
quantifiable information about its events. One can ascertain that approximately four years elapse between the prince's awakening to his discon-
tent and escaping from the Happy Valley: he realizes that he is unhappy
one day when he is twenty-six years old, spends the next twenty months
considering the prospect of escape, four more months resolving to use
future time more productively, ten months searching for a way out, and
one year waiting for the artist to be ready for flight. But he conspires
with Imlac during an unspecifiedly long rainy season, which interferes
with further calculations.[2] Similarly, indefinite references prevent the
calculation of how much time the characters spend in the world between
escaping and deciding to return to Abissinia.

Johnson's references seem pointedly unconcerned with fixed and measured time, except as it affects his characters whose awareness of time the
references convey.[3] In effect, Johnson displays in his narrative what
Locke describes as the perception of time. Fundamental to Locke's idea
of time is the idea of duration, which consists of "the distance between

. . . the appearance of any two Ideas in our Minds" (2.14.3).[4] Actual duration, "go[es] on in one constant, equal, uniform Course," and time provides hypothetically constant, equal, uniform measures for manageable portions of duration (2.14.21). But no one perceives duration in itself. One perceives only one's own "train of thought," the succession of one's ideas (2.14.4). The nature and variety of one's ideas, together with emotional and other factors, affect the seeming rapidity of the passage. Johnson's narrative privileging of perceived time over measured time suggests that his use of Locke goes beyond assimilation or dissemination of Locke's view on this subject. Johnson seems to use Locke's account of time metonymically to represent the proper place of philosophy in the intellectual universe. Johnson posits the concept as a function, not a value: philosophy serves as a discipline to describe phenomena that obtain, not a system to be idealized in its own right. The functional view of philosophy contrasts with and eventually overrides the episodic intrusions of autonomous philosophies that issue in the Happy Valley and that trouble the characters' "choice of life." In this paper, I wish to call attention to Johnson's use of time in *Rasselas* to establish the ascendency of philosophy over philosophizing.

Repeatedly, Johnson illustrates the trains of thought passing through his characters' minds. First, Rasselas entertains the idea of escaping; next, he confronts the idea of an obstacle to escape; then, he becomes obsessed with the idea of specifically how much time has elapsed between his resolve to escape and his consequent failure (4). While Rasselas entertains his first idea, he rests content with it. Consumed in the "visionary bustle" of his single idea, he does not notice the passing of twenty months, a period of time first made known to the reader by the narrator. Rasselas does not entertain the second idea until he enacts a visionary chase and bumps into a mountain. Then the idea of an obstacle succeeds the idea of escape, creating a distance between his two thoughts and allowing him to become aware of duration. Rasselas then makes elaborate calculations backwards to arrive at the figure of twenty months and reevaluate as lost or wasted that period which was to him otherwise happy. Rasselas has not even an indefinite expression of time for this period prior to his calculations. The omission and the elapsing of twenty months, a remarkably long time to pass without the intrusion of a second idea, mark the sequence as Johnson's most exaggerated example of such mental processes.

Sometimes Johnson narrates this pattern of apprehension, as when he states that an additional ten months "passed chearfully away" for Rasselas, though he was engaged in "fruitless searches" for a passage out of the Happy Valley. They "passed chearfully" because Rasselas was absorbed in studying the anatomy of plants and insects (5). Only subsequent awareness of the disjuncture between botanical knowledge gained and exit unfound produces the idea of ten months fruitlessly elapsing. More often, Johnson uses a vague or indefinite expression to show his characters' engagement in an idea or activity and to indicate their attention to the thought itself and not the time. In contrast, he uses a specific measure of time to show the succession of one thought after another and the concomitant sense of time arising from it. For example, while Rasselas is searching for the passage under Imlac's direction, he does not become absorbed in the search itself but keeps in mind the object of escape. Because he remains aware of his frustration, he notes the passing of each of four days spent unsuccessfully. Once he finds the passage, he becomes engrossed in digging out and cares only that he engages in it "day after day" and accomplishes it "in a short time" (13). Johnson does not tell his readers precisely how long it took, leaving them to wonder if anything needing to be worked at "day after day" could really be effected "in a short time." Only Rasselas's perception matters here. To him, four unproductive days seem as ponderously long as the previously mentioned ten and twenty months, while any number of productive days reduces the passing of time itself to something vaguely unimportant.

Johnson does not confine this pattern of thinking to Rasselas's mind alone. Imlac's narrative shows his own consciousness operating in a parallel way. During his long first voyage, he invents thoughts and activities to relieve his consciousness of "barren uniformity." "Sometimes," he reports, he imagined himself in other places, and "sometimes" he learned navigation (9). His failure to state how long the voyage lasted or what proportion of time he allotted to each activity implies his perceptual engagement in the thought itself and not reflection upon its passage. Similarly, he says he spent "a few months" learning to converse with the natives of Agra, the exact time of study consumed by the study itself (9). With his impatience to return home comes his awareness of time, and he recalls that precisely ten months intervened between his desires and their fulfillment (12).

The pattern obtains for Pekuah as well. After the first stages of her captivity, which she describes only as "some days" in which she was "diverted from impatience [and reflection on time passing] by the novelty of the place," she grows aware of the "tediousness of time" (39). Here Johnson substitutes narrative statement (as he did when he explained the "chearful passing" of ten months for Rasselas) for the contrast of general and specific awareness of time in the character's consciousness, but he returns to the latter technique when dealing with the hermit's and astronomer's trains of thought. The hermit expresses his first happiness at his retreat as lasting "for some time," the happiness superseding the time in importance, but his succeeding frustration makes him recollect that he has been a hermit for precisely fifteen years (21). The astronomer's real engagement in contemplation occupies "days and nights," and "one day," he believes he accomplishes the regulation of the weather. Only upon perceiving his occupation as a burden does he recall that he began his contemplations ten years before and that he has regulated the weather for five years (41, 42).

Johnson even enacts in writing the pattern of apprehension he imputes to his character's consciousnesses. In an incident following the escape, Johnson has Imlac end his pupils' language study after "two years" in order to replace linguistic learning with social learning (16). The two-year figure appears less than three full pages after the escape. Johnson's narrative handling of time makes it seem that his characters cannot have been in the world for as long as two years, and he creates that impression by his use of indefinite expressions. From the report of the escape to the mention of two years of language study, no precise times are documented. The interval is paced entirely in general terms: "in the morning," "in a few days," "several weeks," "for a time," "some months," "when the time came," "soon," "for some days," "next day," "immediately," "gradually," "for a long time." The lack of exactitude blurs the succession of events in readers' minds as they become absorbed in the travellers' wonder, and the sudden reminder of two years passing intrudes arrestingly.

By repeatedly showing that a Lockian mode of apprehending time simply obtains, the narrative affords Locke's account the status of an explanation rather than a theory. As the account defines the proper importance of time, that is, as nothing more and nothing less than an act of reflection upon a train of thought, so Johnson's strategy defines the proper importance of philosophy, that is, as nothing more and nothing less than a generalization about a mental process. It follows, then, that any attempt to invest time or philosophy with an independent significance, any attempt to turn the calendar — or the theory — into a controlling principle of action, will be revealed as aberrant in light of Johnson's reiterated pattern.

While Johnson shows Rasselas's ability to apprehend time as consistent with the Lockian pattern, he also shows Rasselas's conclusions about the significance of time as deviant from the appropriate valuation. In introducing Rasselas's misapprehension, Johnson turns again to Locke. Rasselas discovers time as a relation by setting up a comparison like that with which Locke explains the notion. Rasselas, however, changes some significant terms, making his comparison a parody of Locke's and discovering a wrong relation with respect to time.

According to Locke, "Words of time, . . . such as Young, Old, etc." describe "relative" and not "positive" ideas; therefore, they can be applied only "to those Things, which we can observe in the ordinary course of Things, by a natural decay to come to an end, in a certain period of time; and so have in our Minds . . . a Standard, to which we can compare the several parts of their Duration" (2.26.4). One decides if any person is young or old by comparing the number of years that individual has lived with the number of years in the general standard, which Locke puts at seventy years. An individual is young if "his Age is yet but a small part of that which usually Men attain to," old if his age nears the total number of years, "which Men do not usually exceed" (2.26.4).

Rasselas sets up his pseudo-comparison after the encounter with the mountain makes him cognizant of time having elapsed. He follows Locke insofar as he posits a general standard to which he compares an individual, himself, for the purpose of gaining relative information about that individual. His standard likewise pertains to human life, which he counts as forty years by excluding "the ignorance of infancy" and the "imbecility of age" (4). Rasselas does not care about the "ordinary" duration of life but about the "true" duration of life. He substitutes a value term, "true," for Locke's term "ordinary" (4). He tries to judge data that Locke only observes. The transformation renders the comparison useless, but Rasselas draws a conclusion from it nonetheless. Comparing the twenty months he is newly aware of to his forty year standard, he deduces that he has "mused away the four and twentieth part" of his life. Rasselas dismisses that fraction as time "lost," "squandered" (4). He states, of course, a literal impossibility. Since time is not anything in its own right, indeed is nothing more than a hypothetical measure of distance between thoughts, it cannot be "lost" or "squandered." It also cannot be "filled up," the mistaken prospect with which Rasselas consoles himself when he "rejoices in his youth because in many years much might be done" (4).

This false idea of time as a reality with which something must be done informs much of the unhappiness and failure afflicting the characters throughout, beginning with the idea of the Happy Valley. The Happy Valley is predicated on the belief that the succession of thoughts can be controlled and that time can thereby be filled for all people perpetually by one idea.

In order to represent its stasis, Johnson presents the Happy Valley with an emphasis on the continuity of its unmeasured duration: it is a "perpetual" retreat established by "the wisdom or policy of antiquity"; its palace, of a design "fully known to none but some ancient officers," has "stood from century to century" and houses the wealth of "a long race of monarchs" (1). The Happy Valley attempts to sustain the condition represented in the verbal still life of Johnson's opening description by controlling the succession of its inhabitants' ideas rather than, as one might first expect, by preventing the succession entirely. Indeed, preventing the succession would be impossible, as Johnson shows metaphorically by allowing a rainy season to intrude even in the Happy Valley (7). Since this external phenomenon cannot be excluded, it is "co-opted," made into a productive part of the system. Likewise, the internal phenomenon of succeeding ideas is put to work for the system, and this use accounts for the rigid structuring of time in the Happy Valley.

The hours of any given day are divided into specific times for meals, for walks and sleep, for propagandistic songs and lectures (2, 4). Any individual's deviation from the routine is noted and investigated, as evidenced by the Sage's observation and pursuit of Rasselas (3). The years are distinguished one from another by the emperor's annual visit, which lasts exactly eight days (1). While "revelry and merriment [are] the business of every hour from the dawn of morning to the close of even," that single object is not, indeed cannot, be accomplished by a single or generalized direct pursuit, for, left unguided, that thought would quickly pass to another. Rather, through "frequent enumerations of different enjoyments," a succession of thoughts with the same object is posited (2). One might say that the method of the Happy Valley involves a "short circuiting" rather than a "derailing" of the train of thought.

Like the scheme of the Happy Valley, the purpose of the journey takes its shape from the idea that time can be filled. The travellers are to "see all the conditions of humanity," then "make [their] choice of life" (16). The plan implies that there is a "right" or a "best" way to dispose of time; that the travellers will discover the way; and that they will thereupon fill all the time remaining in their projected lives according to the dictates of the "right" way. The ideal choices that they posit after their many adventures confirm the plan completely: Rasselas wants total control of "a little kingdom"; Nekayah wants to head a women's college, so as to "divide her time between the acquisition and communication of wisdom, and raise up for the next age models of prudence, and patterns of piety"; Pekuah wants to be "fixed in [the] unvariable state" of prioress at the Convent of Saint Anthony; Imlac and the astronomer want to surrender their wills and "be driven along the stream of life without directing their course to any particular port" (49).

These ideal schemes exclude all vicissitude: there is no variety, no potential for growth and change. Pekuah explicitly voices her desire for fixity, but the wish underpins the others' fantasies as well. Rasselas has only to set the boundaries of his kingdom and limit the number of his subjects to effect his wish for total control (control, of course, implying the desire to impose fixity); Nekayah conceives of "wisdom" as a set body of knowledge to be reduced to "models" and "patterns" that will eliminate the need for future generations to make a choice of life even one time; Imlac and the astronomer want to become non-reflective beings, like Locke's dreamless sleepers or his theoretical man with only one idea, persisting in a single state of mind despite all inducements to active consciousness (2.16.4).

The characters have constructed their own versions of the Happy Valley, tempting the reader to conclude that they learned nothing from all their experiences. Johnson, however, does not end *Rasselas* with the articulation of his characters' schemes. He ends with a narrative comment that his characters know their wishes cannot be obtained and that they resolve "to return to Abissinia." This comment suggests that the characters have grown and changed considerably. They must have given up the false notions of time as a quantity to be filled with which they started the journey and replaced them with the proper understanding of time and the succession of ideas reflected in Johnson's Lockian pattern. This much is implied in the knowledge imputed to the characters. The resolution imputed to them suggests returning home as a metaphor for embracing the mundane and commonsensical. Thus, it implies that the characters can now accept the mere actuality of time and that this acceptance will enable them to turn their attention to thought and activity according to the merits of the thoughts or activities and not according to their ability to fill up time. In other words, the final comment suggests that the characters have outgrown making a "choice of life" and are now ready to live.

As Johnson prepares his characters to use rather than idealize time, he prepares his readers to use rather than idealize philosophy. Johnson takes Locke's account as accurate and normative but avoids separating the theory from the phenomena it explains. The narrative incorporation of Locke's philosophy differs from the narrative depiction of other philosophies that characters have elevated into controlling ideals. Predictably, perhaps, given Johnson's documented antagonism toward Stoicism,[5] the contrast appears most striking with respect to the Stoic's unsustainable program (18), but it clearly highlights the deflation of Nature Philosophy (22), quietism (21), and other totalizing systems (23–30, 40–44). The rejected philosophies would exclude from the human condition what their principles cannot rein in; Johnson would have philosophy help humanity come to terms with the condition in which it finds itself.[6]

By using rather than idealizing Locke in *Rasselas*, Johnson does more than avoid the self-contradiction of replacing the idolatry of philosophy he criticizes with a "Lockolatry" of his own. He illustrates the view he endorses and he focuses the enormous mid-century interest in Locke on the practical dimension of Locke's achievement.[7] Locke set himself the limit of defining what people can know with certainty and how they can know it.[8] He anatomized human understanding within that limit and offered his conclusions to others with the expectation that they would find them helpful and reassuring. As he wrote in the Introduction to the *Essay*:

> We shall not have much Reason to complain of the narrowness of our Minds, if we will but employ them about what may be of use to us; for of that they are very capable: and it will be an unpardonable, as well as Childish Peevishness, if we undervalue the Advantages of our Knowledge, and neglect to improve it to the ends for which it was given us, because there are some Things that are set out of the reach of it. (1.1.5)

Locke's concentration on the advantages of the available scope aligns his priorities with those of Johnson, who values theory only when, as he writes in *Rambler* 81, it can be brought to bear on the "happiness of mankind."[9] By advancing his narrative with Locke's concept, Johnson follows and celebrates Locke not as an idealized theoretician but as a useful philosopher, and he helps his readers to do the same.

NOTES

1 For interpretations of the theological, structural, and ethical significance of references to time in *Rasselas*, see Geoffrey Tillotson, "Time in *Rasselas*," *Bicentenary Essays on Rasselas*, ed. Magdi Wahba (Cairo: S. O. P. Press, 1959), 97–103; Harold E. Pagliaro, "Structural Patterns of Control in *Rasselas*," *English Writers of the Eighteenth Century*, ed. John H. Middendorf (New York and London: Columbia University Press, 1971), 208–29; and Phyllis Gaba, " 'A Succession of Amusements': The Moralization in *Rasselas* of Locke's Account of Time," *Eighteenth-Century Studies* 10 (1977):451–63.

2 The scenes addressed occupy chapters 2–7. Future references to *Rasselas* appear parenthetically in the text by chapter number and are to the Oxford Edition of *The Works of Samuel Johnson*, vol. 1 of 11 (1825; repr., New York: AMS Press, 1970).

The precision of the calculation is dubious even before the intrusion of the rainy season. In chapter 4, the narrator refers to the period between Rasselas's resolve to escape and his encounter with the mountain in two different ways—

once as "twenty months," and again as a time during which "the sun had passed twice over him in his annual course." Thus, he raises the possibility that more than twenty months may have elapsed.

3 Johnson's practice seems deliberate especially in light of his knowledge of and interest in ways of measuring time as pointed out by Paul Alkon, "Johnson and Chronology," *Greene Centennial Studies*, ed. Paul J. Korshin and Robert R. Allen (Charlottesville: University Press of Virginia, 1984), 143-71.

4 John Locke, *An Essay Concerning Human Understanding*, ed. with an intro. by Peter Nidditch (Oxford: Clarendon Press, 1975), 181-82. All references to Locke are to this edition and appear parenthetically within the text by book, chapter, and section number as shown in the text for this reference. The prominence Sterne gives to Locke's account of time in *Tristram Shandy* might fruitfully be compared with Johnson's treatment of the account in *Rasselas*. Earl R. Wasserman, "Johnson's *Rasselas*: Implicit Contexts," *Journal of English and Germanic Philology* 74 (1975): 4, 22, and Emrys Jones, "The Artistic Form of *Rasselas*," *Review of English Studies* n.s. 18 (1967): 392-94, draw analogies between *Rasselas* and *Tristram Shandy*, but neither develops a full comparison.

5 See Donald Greene, "Johnson, Stoicism, and the Good Life," *The Unknown Samuel Johnson*, ed. John J. Burke and Donald Kay (Madison and London: University of Wisconsin Press, 1983), 17-38.

6 As Richard B. Schwartz points out in *Samuel Johnson and the Problem of Evil* (Madison and London: University of Wisconsin Press, 1975), 6, Johnson is antagonistic toward philosophers who do not show a "compassion for human suffering and a demand for its alleviation" as essential as is his own concern in the matter.

7 Kenneth MacLean, *John Locke and English Literature of the Eighteenth Century* (1936; New York: Russell and Russell, 1962) places Locke's vogue between 1725 and 1765 (2). See also Donald Greene, "Augustinianism and Empiricism: A Note on Eighteenth-Century English Intellectual History," *Eighteenth-Century Studies* 1 (1967):33-68 on the eighteenth century as an era "when Locke reigned virtually unchallenged" (52).

8 James Gibson, *Locke's Theory of Knowledge and its Historical Relations* (1917; Cambridge: Cambridge University Press, 1960), 2-10, emphasizes the nature and significance of Locke's specified scope.

9 Recall Schwartz, n. 6 above, who cites *Rambler* 81 among many Johnsonian texts in support of his argument. The consonance between Johnson and Locke's views on morality has been demonstrated by Paul Alkon, *Samuel Johnson and Moral Discipline* (Chicago: Northwestern University Press, 1967), who argues furthermore that Johnson often used "the naturalistic theories of Locke in the service of an endeavor to teach the moral discipline of the mind" (87). Hence, Johnson's use of Locke in *Rasselas* seems consistent not only with his general intellectual orientation but with his habitual practice as well, a practice perhaps most widely believed to obtain in the *Dictionary*. Johnson's use of Locke by assimilation and demonstration in the *Dictionary* has most

recently been addressed by Robert DeMaria, Jr., "The Theory of Language in Johnson's *Dictionary*," *Johnson after Two Hundred Years*, ed. Paul Korshin (Philadelphia: University of Pennsylvania Press, 1986), 159–74.

Aphra Behn in Search of the Novel

ROSE A. ZIMBARDO

In his brilliant book, *The Discourse of Modernism*, Timothy J. Reiss traces the development in Western discourse from what he calls "the discourse of patterning" to "analytico-referential discourse," the discourse of modernism that was born in the seventeenth century: "a passage from what we might call a discursive *exchange within* the world to the expressions of knowledge as reasoning *practice upon* the world."[1] A work of art rendered in the older "discourse of patterning" is what Paul de Man calls a "calligraphy" of emblems "rather than a mimesis."[2] That is to say, within the older system of discourse a work of art is the organization of a pattern of emblematic figures or abstract concepts "whose function is 'to guarantee ideal convertibility between the celestial and the terrestrial . . . the universal and the individual . . . nature and history.' "[3] This is the process that I described elsewhere as the "Imitation of Idea" which obtained in English dramatic art in the decades of the 1660s and early 1670s.[4]

The newer "analytico-referential discourse" creates distance between the eye of the perceiver and the objectified "reality" perceived. Reiss uses Galileo's invention of the telescope as a nexus of the change with which he is concerned. This newer discourse of modernism required the invention of the novel as its best artistic medium. Under the governance of the older discourse of patterning the function of a work of dramatic art was

277

to show a closed system of ideational relationships to the spectator which would reveal to him or her the harmonious systematic interaction among ideas, a model of the whole cosmological reality. It is true that the larger aim of such dramatic discourse was to disclose a method by which human participation within the metaphysical order occurs; that participation was of a kind by which we, as a species, are placed within the celestial-terrestrial system which the abstract discourse of patterning shows. For example, a character in one of Aphra Behn's early plays, *The Young King*, says:

> *Orisames*: I to my self could an *Idea* frame
> Of Man in much more excellence.
> Had I been *Nature*, I had varied still,
> And made such different *Characters* of Men
> They should have bow'd and made a God of me
> Ador'd and thank'd me for their great Creation. (act 2. sc. 1)[5]

Here "nature," or "reality," is a configuration of ideas; dramatic characters are concepts, and the function of dramatic discourse is to pattern a rhetorical design, a closed system analogous, as the human mind itself is analogous, to a metaphysical system of reality.

The new analytico-referential discourse created distance between subject and object, the human being and the world at which he looks; it also established a more intimate relationship between the human eye and the scaled down "reality" which the human eye could perceive and the human tongue describe. The older discourse erased the importance of the individual human being. Indeed, in English drama of the 1660s and early 1670s it is relatively unimportant which speaker declaims a set rhetorical speech; what is crucially important is the position of that set piece within the whole rhetorical design of the play. The newer discourse brought a manageable "outside" reality into the range of human perception, possession, and control. As Reiss puts it, "Its exemplary formal statement is *cogito-ergo-sum* (reason-semiotic mediating system-world). . . . Its principal metaphors will be those of the telescope (eye-instrument-world) and of the voyage of discovery (self-possessed point of departure — sea journey — country claimed as legitimate possession of the discoverer)."[6] It is interesting that Aphra Behn's late, best work, *Oroonoko*, not only employs the new analytico-referential discourse whose operation Reiss describes here, but also enacts what he considers one of its principal metaphors — the narrator "I" 's journey to Surinam, the reader's discovery of that colonial possession, and even the politico-economic consequences that such "possession" entails.

Aphra Behn is an important figure in seventeenth-century English literature because, had we no other remaining evidence than the works of Dryden and Behn upon which to judge, we could yet trace the course of one of the most important revolutions in aesthetics and consciousness that has occurred in the history of English thought. This is not to suggest that Behn was a great dramatist — she was not among the best of her time — nor to suggest that she was a theorist, as Dryden was. In part, her importance lies in the fact that she was an almost faultless barometer of popular taste and consciousness; she described herself as one "who is forced to write for Bread and not ashamed to owne it, and consequently ought to write to please (if she can) an Age which has given severall proofs it was by this way of writing to be oblig'd."[7] What makes Behn a crucially important figure, however, is that she was a pioneer in the invention of the novel; her *Oroonoko* is not only the first, but also one of the best, early English novels. This study therefore is entitled "Aphra Behn in Search of the Novel" because what I shall attempt to establish is the movement in Behn's practice that led her from using language in the service of an abstract design of discourse that patterns an ideational metaphysical "reality" to using an analytico-referential discourse that led her inevitably to the novel as her best medium of expression.

In Behn's first play, *The Forc'd Marriage*, or *The Jealous Bridegroom* (1670), the object of dramatic imitation is an ideal of heroic love and honor. Characters, as well as the speeches they declaim, are figures, or, to be more precise, placements within what Eric Rothstein called "a fixed grid of love and honor."[8] Discourse is declamation, set rhetorical pieces that are positioned within a dialectical progression that mounts toward a complex metaphysical concept, which it does not, indeed cannot, describe. Words are ideational counters; for example:

> *Erminia*: *Philander* never spoke but from a Soul
> That all dishonest Passions can controul;
> With flames as chaste as Vestals that did burn,
> From whence I borrow'd mine to make return . . .
> Upon my life no other thing he spoke
> But those from dictates of his Honour took. (act 1. sc. 4)

Words here are abstract counters for abstract concepts. They form a set rhetorical pattern, which, positioned in relation to a variety of other such set pieces, in turn, pattern the rhetorical design of the whole. So much is it the case that discourse figures a pattern here that at a climactic moment in the play language can be dispensed with altogether and the pattern achieved by mute, still figures positioned in significant gestural relation to one another. For example, act 2 of this first play begins with a *tableau vivant* called "The Representation of the Wedding." Quoted here is only a small exemplary fragment of a quite lengthy, detailed direction. Notice how the figures, arranged in relation to one another, form a complex, wordless configuration of theatrical signs:

> The *Curtain* must be let down and soft Musick must play: the *Curtain* being drawn up, discovers a scene of a Temple: the *King* on a throne bowing down to join hands of *Alcippus* and *Ermine* . . . without on the Stage *Philander* with his sword half-drawn held by *Galatea*, who looks ever on *Alcippus: Erminia* still fixing her eyes on *Philander; Pisano* passionately gazing on *Galatea; Aminta* on *Falatio*, and he on her; *Alcander, Issilia, Cleonatis*, in other severall postures, with the rest, all remaining without motion, whilst Musick softly plays; this continues 'till the Curtain falls. . . . [9]

What is significant in this example is that mute, motionless figures serve precisely the function that words or declaimed set-pieces serve within the whole design of the play. The king, bowing down from his throne, equals majesty condescending to heroic glory and beauty; the rightful lover with his sword half-drawn equals heroic love urging toward heroic beauty. His gesture is restrained by a figure, Galatea, that represents heroic honor's curb upon heroic love. The point is that in Behn's earliest play (wherein her practice is indistinguishable from that of her contemporaries of the sixties and early seventies) both characters and the discourse they declaim are figures, positions within a rhetorical design wrought by the discourse of patterning.

We begin, however, to see signs of Behn's desire to break the pattern quite early on in her career, both in her practice and in the comments she addresses to her audience in prefaces and remarks "To the Reader." Throughout her career Behn argued that she was better equipped to write plays than her male contemporaries because she was a woman, her argument being that "We [women] have nobler Souls than you [as] we prove/ By how much more we're sensible of Love" (Epilogue, *Sir Patient Fancy*, 1678) and that "plays have no great room for that which is men's great advantage over women, that is Learning," because plays are "intended for the exercising of man's passions not their understanding" (Preface, *The Dutch Lover*, 1673). Indeed, the male sensibility, hampered as it is by learning and affectation, she argues, is hamstrung by its own discourse: "for affectation hath always a greater share both in the action and discourse of men than truth or judgment have" (Preface, *The Dutch Lover*).

There is nothing remarkable in the notion that drama imitates "the Passions" and in her earliest practice Behn, like her male contemporaries, envisioned imitation of the passions as imitation of ideas, or abstract conceptions, of the passions, as we have seen in the passage from her first play quoted above. Earlier than most and in accordance with the epistemological changes governing her time, however, Behn became aware of the passions as being located not "out there" in the realm of abstract conceptualization but rather within the human psyche; more precisely, she began to see the passions as forces having their origins within the human psyche that are the vehicles by means of which the human connects with the metaphysical realm. Earlier than most, she became impatient with the restrictions that "imitation of idea" and the discourse of patterning required by it imposed upon the playwright. Addressing her male contemporaries, she said:

> Your Way of Writings out of Fashion grown.
> Method, and Rule — you only understand.
> Pursue that way of Fooling and be damn'd.
> Your learned Cant of Action, Time and Place,
> Must all give way to the unlabour'd Farce.
> (Epilogue, *Sir Patient Fancy*)

As early as her second play, *The Amorous Prince* (1671), and throughout her subsequent career as a playwright Behn began to choose as her sources the Spanish tale, the Italian novella, the history, and, finally, the documentary pamphlet. Of her twenty or so plays well over half were taken from romances or novellas, and the source of her last play, *The Widow Ranter*, or *The History of Bacon in Virginia* (produced after her death in 1690) was taken from a news pamphlet, "Strange News from Virginia being a free and true account of the life and Death of Nathaniel Bacon, Esq." (1677).

What is significant for our purposes is that almost from the beginning of her career Aphra Behn was straining against the strictures of dramatic convention and was beginning her search for the novel. Her best known plays — and possibly her worst — *The Rover I* and *II* exhibit what Michael McKeon, in his important book, *The Origins of the English Novel*,[10] calls "generic instability," that dislocation in generic form which, in Bahktinian terms, was the fertile soil in which the novel was born. Both *The Rover I* and *II* were taken from Thomas Killigrew's *Tomaso*, or *The Wanderer*, a strange closet drama written during the Interregnum and never intended for the stage. *Tomaso* is constructed in ten closely consecutive, but structurally loose acts. The action is the serial action of picaresque fiction, and, as Summers said, the work "may better be described as a dramatic romance than a comedy intended for the boards."[11] Behn does two interesting things in these plays. The first, and most important, is that she begins to free discourse from patterning. It would be totally wrong to say that she created character as we understand it today, that is, as the fictional simulation of people having psychology and interiority. It would be equally wrong to suggest that she had yet mastered analytico-referential discourse. Rather, she changes character from figural place-ment, or position, within a rhetorical design to free-floating type. The consequence is that discourse, while it is still very far from dialogue, becomes disembodied voice. Curiously, in some ways *The Rover* may be understood as a two-hundred-and-some year foreshadowing of Virginia Woolf's *The Waves*. Rather than placing set rhetorical pieces in relation to other set pieces within a dominant rhetorical design, the discourse of *The Rover I* and *II* consists in typologically determined "voices" that exist in interesting contrapuntal relation to one another.

The second important development in these two plays is Behn's crea-tion of gratuitous character/figures that are designed deliberately to break rhetorical consistency. The courtesans, Angelica Bianca and La Nuche, both of whom are heroines of Herculean "irregular greatness," are designed not only to break accepted moral and social conventions, but, by their extravagance of language (which, in an old-fashioned sixties heroic drama would be perfectly acceptable if placed properly within the confines of a mounting rhetorical design), are extrinsic to the design. Their function, rather, is to dislocate typology from the medley of "voices" upon which the plays depend.

Behn's best play of the seventies, the decade which I have called the great moment in English dramatic satire,[12] is *The Feign'd Courtesans* (1679). In it Behn was striving for the same disjunctive unity in concep-tualization toward which the giants of dramatic satire — Dryden, Wycherley, and Etherege — aimed, in which a heightened ideal plays in continuous juxtaposition against a downwardly exaggerated actual. Dry-den delineated the opposition most obviously in *Marriage a la Mode*, Wycherley and Etherege more subtly in *The Country Wife* and *The Man of Mode*. What is interesting here is that while her contemporaries render the necessary disjunctive unity of satire structurally, Behn does so dialog-ically. For example, in playing high (ancient model) against low (immedi-ate actual) where her contemporaries, especially Dryden, interplay planes of action, Behn achieves the effect in a differentiation between the voices:

> *Marcella*: The Evening's soft and calm as happy Lovers thoughts
> And here are Groves where meeting Trees
> Will hide us from the Amorous gazing Crowd
> *Cornelia*: What should we do here, sigh 'till our wandering Breath
> Has rais'd a gentle Gale among the boughs,
> To whose dull melancholy Musick, we

Laid on a bed of Moss, and new fall'n leaves
Will read the dismal tale of Eccho's love!
—No, I can make better use of famous Ovid. (act 2. sc. 1)

In the eighties Behn began to transform her dramatic discourse itself, to displace "discursive exchange *within* the [fictional] world" to analytico-referential "practice upon the world"—to use Reiss's terms again. Whereas in *The Feign'd Courtesans* satiric dialectic is contained within the discursive dimensions of the play's rhetorical design, in a play like *The City Heiress* (1682) Behn trains the disjunctive unity, which earlier was contained within a closed literary context, upon the actual circumstances of contemporary life. The satiric disjunction remains the same—that is, the ideal versus the satirically, downwardly exaggerated actual—but the dimensions of disjunctive interplay are secularized and made present. The charming "heroic" vices of "real" Tories (drinking, gambling, and whoring) are contrasted with the mean and despicable vices of "real" Whigs (hypocrisy, greed, and sedition). Character is still concept, but typologically rendered though it is, it is realized in terms of a contemporary situation, in much the way that a modern newspaper cartoonist might exaggerate and typologize the figures and discourse of current political events.

It is in *The Lucky Chance* (1687) that we see clearly for the first time an authorial "I" looking at its world and novelistically describing the problematic condition of it. From her first play, *The Forc'd Marriage*, Behn had been concerned with the evils of forced marriage; but whereas in her first play the idea is elevated to the distant, heroic realm, in 1687 we are made to see the situation not as the occasion for a rhetorical "turn" or two within a dialectical progression but as a contemporary social problem. Character is no longer the delineation of concept or type. Action is no longer subservient to the demands of rhetorical patterning. Rather, a subject which had been fair game for light comic ridicule since Chaucer is presented for serious consideration and, discursively, for sober discussion:

Lady Fullbank: Oh how fatal are forc'd Marriages.
How many Ruins one such Match pulls on!
Had I but kept my Sacred Vows to *Gayman*
How happy had I been—how prosperous he!
Whilst now I languish in a loath'd embrace
Pine out my Life with Age—Consumptive Coughs. (act 2. sc. 1)

Here is the world of experience—consumptive coughs and all. Here is the present "I"—both writer and reader—looking through the instrument of analytico-referential discourse upon an immediate, familiar "reality."

Here is discourse that "practices upon" the world rather than shaping an abstract image of it. The actual circumstances leading to forced marriages are explored; Lucretia is driven to marry Sir Feeble Fainwood by economic necessity. Vows are not broken, as in a play of the early seventies, to set a particular dialectic antithesis between concepts of love and honor. Rather, as in life, persons are forced to break promises by social pressure and economic need.

The Lucky Chance was Behn's "new-modelling" of an old play, Shirley's *The Lady of Pleasure.* In her renovation Behn not only forces us to consider the stock literary situations of an earlier period from a contemporary vantage, and not only transforms discourse from declamation to dialogue, but she uses the specific descriptive techniques of a novelist to bring ideas into what Bahktin calls the "present of still evolving contemporary reality."[13] Over and over again in this play Behn forces us to look behind very old stock comic situations to explore the real circumstances that may underlie them. One such stock situation, prevalent since Jacobean "City Comedy," is that of an aristocratic lover, down on his luck, who is driven to solicit the help of his city landlady. Behn uses the new analytico-referential discourse to make us envision the situation as a novel would do. Lady Fullbank's steward, Bredwell, who has just launched the trick that will finally bring Gayman his reward for having given all for love, reports to Lady Fullbank the conditions under which Gayman lives. So detailed, so novelistic, is the description that it badly strains the limits of dramatic representation:

> *Bred.* . . . at the door [I] encountered the beastly thing he calls a Landlady; who look't as if she had been of her own Husband's making, compos'd of moulded Smith's dust. I ask'd for Mr. Wasteall [Gayman's assumed name] and she began to open—and did so rail at him, that what with her *Billingsgate*, and her Husband's hammers I was both deaf and dumb—at last the hammers ceased and she grew weary, and call'd down Mr. Wasteall, but he not answering—I was sent up a ladder rather than a pair of Stairs. . . .
> 'Tis a pretty convenient Tub, Madam, [Gayman's room]. He may lie a long in't, there's just room for an old join'd Stool besides the Bed, which one cannot call a Cabin, about the largeness of a pantry Bin, or a Usurer's Trunk: there had been Dornex Curtains to't in days of Yore; but they were now annihilated, and nothing left to save his Eyes from the Light, but my Landlady's Blue Apron, ty'd by strings before the Window, in which stood a six-penny Looking Glass, that shew'd as many faces as the Scene in *Henry* the Eighth, which cou'd but just stand upright, and then a Combcase fill'd it. (act 1. sc. 3)

The scene is not the ambiguous "A Room in Mrs——House" that we have found in earlier drama; rather, it describes a specific, and visualizable location, such as we are given by a novel. We are made by the description to notice particular details — the sizes, shapes, and colors of objects. We see the ragged apron at the window; we hear the smith's din. Consequently, as in a novel, we are made to enter into and experience the condition of poverty as it actually existed in London in 1687. Here is a discourse that "practices upon" the world, a telescopic instrument by means of which the reader/listener's eye focuses upon a known reality, which, by seeing, he may encompass and possess in consciousness.

At roughly the same time that she wrote *The Lucky Chance* Aphra Behn wrote a prose work, *The Adventure of the Black Lady* (ca. 1685, published 1696), of which George Woodcock says, "The incidents all take place in familiar London surroundings, and the lack of artificiality and elaboration gives the whole piece the air of a little vignette from real life. It is written in an easy, conversational style; which adds to the impression of its authenticity."[14] Of another prose work, written at the same time, *The Wandering Beauty*, Angeline Goreau writes: "This [the narrator's] 'I' was something new not only in literature but in history. It was a very early example of the growing self-consciousness of the individual, which would in the next century and a half develop into a 'given' in the way people thought about themselves. Aphra's focus on individual experience and self-expression was historically avant garde."[15]

This essay has focused on Behn's, the dramatist's, search for the novel. We find the same movement from the discourse of patterning to analytico-referential discourse in the progressive development of Behn's prose fiction. Her first prose work, *Love Letters between a Nobleman and His Sister*, while it is innovative in introducing the epistolary mode, employs the older discourse throughout. In Part 1, composed entirely of letters, it is virtually impossible, without reference to the title heads — "To Philander" or "To Syvia" — to distinguish among the voices of the letter writers. On the other hand, in her late novel, *Oroonoko*, so perfectly has Behn mastered the use of analytico-referential discourse, and so thoroughly aware is she of the operational difference upon a reader between the older and newer discourses, that she skillfully uses interaction between the two styles to create the first tragic novel in English. For example, she uses the older discourse when her aim is to delineate the spiritual essence of her hero: "the Greatness of Soul, those refined Notions of True Honour, that absolute Generosity, and Softness that was capable of the highest Passions of Love and Gallantery" (135). That is to say, she uses the "sacrosanct and traditional" language[16] of heroic romance when her aim is to shape a "Character of Mind" or to figure the Idea of Majesty[17] that Oroonoko the Prince represents. On the other hand, before Behn begins to tell Oroonoko's story, she uses the analytico-referential mode of discourse to create the setting in which his sufferings as Caesar the Slave will take place. The new mode of narrative discourse, full of accurately observed detail and almost scientific description, is used to make the exotic landscape and culture of Surinam familiar, and, more importantly, to make the reader, by virtue of the detailed landscape he has visualized, an inhabitant of the fictional world. The narrative of Coramantien, in which Oroonoko figures Majesty and ideal heroic love, is written wholly in the older discourse. Such is the glistening height from which the tragic hero falls. The narrative of Surinam is written largely in the newer discourse. It realistically pictures the crushing world of experience into which he falls.

Aphra Behn was by no means a great dramatist, but she may be considered the first English novelist, the first literary artist to master the telescope of analytico-referential discourse and to teach us, her readers, how to use that instrument.

NOTES

1 Timothy J. Reiss, *The Discourse of Modernism* (Ithaca: Cornell University Press, 1982), 30.
2 Paul de Man, "Pascal's Allegory of Persuasion," *Allegory and Representation*, ed. Stephen J. Greenblatt (Baltimore: The Johns Hopkins University Press, 1981), 1.
3 Reiss, *Modernism*, quoting Gerard Simon, 30.
4 Rose A. Zimbardo, *A Mirror to Nature: Transformations in Drama and Aesthetics, 1660–1732* (Lexington: University Press of Kentucky, 1986).
5 *The Works of Aphra Behn*, ed. Montague Summers, 6 vols. (London, 1915; repr., New York: Benjamin Bloom, 1967). All references to Behn's work are to this edition.
6 Reiss, *Modernism*, 31.
7 "To the Reader," Preface, *Sir Patient Fancy*, Summers, ed., *Works*, 4:115–16.
8 Eric Rothstein, *Restoration Tragedy* (Madison: University of Wisconsin Press, 1966), 31.
9 Summers, ed., *Works*, 3:305.
10 Michael McKeon, *The Origins of the English Novel* (Baltimore: The Johns Hopkins University Press, 1986), 20.
11 Summers, ed., *Works*, 1:4.
12 Zimbardo, *Mirror to Nature*, 9.
13 M. M. Bahktin, "Epic and Novel," *The Dialogue of Imagination*, trans. C. Emerson and M. Holquist (Austin: University of Texas Press, 1983), 19.
14 George Woodcock, *The Incomparable Aphra* (London and New York: T. V. Boardman, 1948), 167.

15 Angeline Goreau, *Reconstructing Aphra: A Social Biography of Aphra Behn* (New York: Dial Press, 1980), 281.
16 Bahktin, "Epic and Novel," 16.
17 Zimbardo, *Mirror to Nature*, chap. 2, "Imitation of Nature as Idea."

Discourses of Sexual Difference: Beau Wilson and the Mythologies of Homosexual Love

G. S. ROUSSEAU

"Homosexuality has always given rise to myths."
(John McRae, *Oscar Wilde and Others. Teleny*, London, 1986, 7)

" . . . one melting Extasy, thou alone can'st give, will recompense a thousand such Uneasinesses." (nobleman to Mr. Wilson, *Love-Letters*, 1723, 26-27)

I

In the late twentieth century we tend to believe, as the epigraph suggests, that the collective fantasy about homosexuals has remained constant throughout the ages. The notion is buttressed by an historical sense (however intuitive and primitive it may be) that homosexuals have existed — perhaps in similar proportions to their percentage of the population today — throughout the ages. Empirical history and social anthropology give the lie to such an idea, prompting us to reassess the sources of this belief about homosexual fantasy, if indeed it represents a concrete belief rather than amorphous dream.[1]

The story told here may be regarded as one empirical case history among several that adumbrates the point that homosexuality has given rise to myths. The specific episode, now obscure and largely forgotten, should not be given undue importance in its own right; nevertheless it serves to demonstrate in what drastically different ways subsequent generations have explained the complex arrangements and often ambiguous relations between the genders. In the case at hand, the explanations alternate between heterosexual and homosexual interpretations.

When Edward Wilson, the younger son of an old but clearly impoverished Norfolk family, was killed by John Law in a duel in 1694, there was no suggestion whatever of a homosexual motive for the murder or the merest hint that in real life Wilson had been a sodomite. Yet one generation later, by the 1720s, passionate male love was proffered as the explanation for his sudden death.[2] The patent disparity between these views, and the subtle ways in which the collective sexual fantasy altered in England during the generation between the 1690s and the 1720s, forms the heart of this story. And we are surely fortunate, insofar as the printed document that affords the best distinct source of evidence, the *Love-Letters*, has barely been discussed in the scholarly literature. Moreover, no English prose narrative of the English Restoration or early eighteenth century demonstrates the transformations of these mythologies of homosexual love better than the bizarre account of this now obscure figure, Edward Wilson, who rose from rags to riches in just a few months.

The task of narrating the story is complicated by varied strands that need to be disentangled. On the one hand, there are the so-called known facts, which, though few, need to be properly evaluated and documented. On the other hand, the much more elusive fantasy — even the collective fantasy of an entire society — remains to be grappled with. The latter is obviously less capable of documentation or any type of empirical authentification than the former. And if conjecture and unwarranted speculation seem apparent, I must respond, as did Foucault or Deleuze under these circumstances when in a similar impasse, that the collective fantasies of a culture cannot be reduced to series of empirical facts, like so many atomistic components or footnotes.[3] Nevertheless, in reconstructing the story an attempt is made to differentiate between these types of explanation and provide clues as to whether there is evidence or mere speculation about the hypothesis that in the generation from 1690 to 1720 a major transformation was occurring in the sodomitical subculture of London town.[4]

II

Here with the basic facts is John Evelyn, the noted if cautious diarist, commenting in the *Kalendarium* on or about 22 April 1694:

> A very young Gentleman named Wilson, the [younger] son of one who had not above 200 pounds per Annum: lived in the Garb & Equipage of the richest Noble man in the nation for House, Furniture, Coaches & 6

horses, & other saddle horses; Table & all things accordingly: Redeemed his Fathers Estate, gave portion to his sister; being challenged by one Laws a Scots-man, was now killed in a Duel, not fairly, the quarrel being because he tooke away his owne [i.e. Wilson's own] sister from lodging in a house, where this Laws had a Wench: which the Mistris of the lodging thinking a disparagement to her House, & loosing by it this Gentlewoman (namely Wilson's sister) who was a profitable Guest, Instigated the Scotchman to revenge it: Laws is taken & condemned for Murder: But the Mysterie is, how this so young gentleman, a sober young person, & very inoffensive, & of good fortune, did so live in so extraordinary Equipage; it not being discovered by any possible industry, by any his most intimate Friends, no, tho' they had endeavoured to make him reveale it being in drink: But they could never find it out: It did not appeare he either was kept by Women or Play, or Coyning, Padding; or that he had any dealing in Chymistry, but that he would sometimes say, that if he should live [to] never so great an age, he had wherewith to maintain it in the same affluence. He was very young, Civil, well natured, or no greate force in Understanding, but very Indifferent parts: All which was subject of much discourse and admiration.[5]

Two weeks earlier, on 9 April, Wilson was instantly killed in a duel by John Law (1671–1729), the ambitiously brilliant if also corrupt financier who was later to gain international notoriety as the French sponsor of the Mississippi Bubble in France and the New World.[6] Law was tried at the Old Bailey and found guilty of murder on 19 April, then sentenced to death on 20 April, two days before Evelyn wrote in his diary.[7] An appeal was made during the next three months and Law's sentence was commuted to a fine.[8] H. Montgomery Hyde, the biographer of Oscar Wilde, whose fascination with outlaws of different types extended to John Law, especially for his murder of Beau Wilson, has laid out the chronology of these events.[9] He explains how Law connived and lied to escape imprisonment; how he frantically appealed to his friends for assistance; and how, with their last-ditch attempts to rescue him, he fled to the Continent. Shortly after New Year's Day 1695, Law escaped across the North Sea, not to return to England for twenty-six years. Hyde also concludes, based on his own research, that the truth surrounding Law's role in Wilson's death would never be known: "It is unlikely after such a long lapse of time that the truth or falsity of this alleged episode and Law's part in it will ever be established."[10] Frustrating as this prediction is, it may well represent the limits of knowledge in this matter. Yet it is not Law's role in Wilson's murder that primarily concerns us here, but the mystery of Wilson's splendorous existence and the explanations given to account for it in two successive generations: his own of the 1690s and, later, in the aftermath of the South Sea Bubble, the generation of the

1720s — especially the explanations given then to the *menage* of Wilson, Elizabeth Villiers, and the mysterious "nobleman."[11]

Yet Evelyn's account, however limited, cannot be dismissed so rapidly. "Beau" having been a term long since used by the fashionable town (Beau Ranby, Jones, and others), its omission by the rigid, even stuffy, Evelyn is not remarkable. Yet it is curious that Evelyn nowhere uses the word, for it was under the name "Beau Wilson," rather than Edward Wilson, that our protagonist became legendary at the end of his very brief life. Even in the legal literature pertaining to his murder, he is often called Beau rather than Edward. Furthermore, Thomas Seccombe's life in the *Dictionary of National Biography* states that "in *1695* there appeared the *Love-Letters* between 'a certain late Nobelman' and the celebrated beau Wilson" (italics mine), and identifies the nobleman as the earl of Sunderland.[12] So far, there is no basis for either assertion: no edition of 1695 has ever been seen or known to have existed, and there is no reason to believe that Sunderland and Wilson were intimately connected, let alone that Sunderland was the secret of Wilson's wealth. Moreover, Seccombe held that a 1695 edition of Beau Wilson's *Love-Letters* formed the basis for the later one of 1723 (see n. 24 below). The surmise is unwarranted and deflects those who want to understand Wilson's sudden rise to riches and the explanations given for it: more specifically, the way Wilson's splendor reveals (in modern and admittedly anachronistic language) a bisexual model of the sodomite commonly assumed during the seventeenth-century *fin-de-siecle*.[13] By the 1720s — approximately a generation after Wilson's death — the new typology of the sodomite had begun to crystallize into one or the other: from the old-style bisexual sodomite who held a male on one arm and female on the other while kissing both, to the new-style sodomite who was exclusively homocentric and male oriented. Stated in terms approximating our own nomenclature, the later generation differentiated between an exclusively homosexual or heterosexual type, so that it was possible during the early 1720s, as we shall see, to write fiction that served as political propaganda to endorse or, more commonly, derogate the new typology. Such fierce exploitation of the newly formed homosexual type was less likely in the 1690s (here using the term homosexual again anachronistically but designating the sodomite who was exclusively interested in other men). By the 1720s, the new-style sodomite had become very much in evidence about the town: a source of easy ridicule for those seeking out targets and claiming that practically every young boy was a Ganymede who had been corrupted. Such facile identification would have been more difficult in the 1680s or 1690s, when the bisexual sodomite (one who kept a catamite who got buggered yet who was also seen with females) rather than the exclusively homosexual male prevailed.

Yet it is not Seccombe's brief sketch in the *Dictionary of National Biography* but a work of 1707–8 that proves genuinely useful in the reconstruction of our mysterious figure. This is a scandalous if perhaps authentic biographical account appended to Madame D'Aulnoy's *Memoirs of the Court of England in the Reign of Charles II* under the title "The Unknown Lady's Pacquet of Letters," the first part of which is titled "An Account of Beau Wilson's secret support of his public manner of living and the occasion of his death."[14] In the Huntington Library copy it occupies almost one hundred pages (521–616), pages so detailed in regard to Wilson's good looks and sexual appeal that one can hardly resist it for its own sexual, quasi-pornographic appeal. Seccombe was right to conjecture that it came from the pen of Mrs. Manley; this is beyond doubt. But what must intrigue us more than the authorship of "The Unknown Lady's Pacquet" is the way its contents get structurally encoded into a series of subplots that thrive on the early eighteenth-century reader's expectation about prose genre, especially genres exploiting the double account: two entirely separate versions of the same story.

Manley's account reveals Elizabeth Villiers (1657–1733), King William III's notorious mistress who was later to become the countess of Orkney, as Wilson's secret financier.[15] According to Manley's memoirs, the "lady" took every precaution to ensure that her identity should remain secret. But nothing could stop her from keeping her Norfolk stud in style. (Wilson was studlike as a consequence—according to Mrs. Manley—of the hypnotic effect his physique had on the lady the first time she saw him.)[16] To keep him, she bought him "Coaches, Saddles, Hunting, Race Horses, Equipage, Dress and Table"[17]—spoiling him to such a degree that he became the admiration not only of the town "but of the Whole World."[18]

The account relates, furthermore, that other than this woman of quality, there was "scarce any lady rich enough to keep him." But when Wilson became too inquisitive during their nocturnal assignations and ripped off her veil to learn her identity, Villiers arranged for Law to murder him and then supplied Law with the money to escape to France.[19] It is perhaps an improbable ending, overlooking the possibility of Wilson's having been kept by a male patron, but it is the sole explanation Manley chose to give and we must presume she had ample evidence for her account.[20] Her version contradicts John Evelyn's and Narcissus Luttrell's account that Law and Wilson quarreled over Wilson's removal of his sister from a brothel where Law kept his wenches.[21] But, as explained below (see n. 43), the contradiction may not be irreconcilable with the existing evidence. In short, "The Lady's Pacquet" remains a reliable source, revealing as well the developed readership that existed in 1708–9 for this kind of scandal *cum* fantasy. And it does not merely ramble on about all romance, but projects an economically based heterosexual fantasy that reverses the gender roles and their traditional power structures. Here, in Mrs. Manley's version, the aggressive, sophisticated, powerful, politically wise, and obviously affluent female courtier elevates the passive, naive, weak, apolitical, and patently impoverished young male from the countryside. Later on, in the 1720s, the possibility of female power as the source of this wealth and sexual bonding becomes liminal: by then it is a "nobleman" who must have been the keeper. One can appreciate, then, the significance of Manley's insights: that a woman was the source of Wilson's affluence. It was a fantasy very much in advance of the economic reality of its time. Finally, it was a female fantasy about the seductive power of male anatomy; especially about the woman succumbing to these male charms as she casts herself in the role of the nurturing mother-lover. It may not be extending oneself too far to imagine how Mrs. Manley's world was exhilarated by the detail of the female veil: the insistence on the mother-lover's anonymity during all their nocturnal assignations.[22] Here was the legendary Cupid and Psyche in reverse, as if myth and history had exchanged roles in recent times.

III

A limited search has produced no discussion of Beau Wilson during the fifteen years that elapsed between 1708 and the mid 1720s. During these decades a new generation grew up with new ideological values and a new sense of gender.[23] Many of those who had been alive in 1694, when Wilson was murdered, were now old and could have forgotten (and they probably did forget) the specific details. The new generation had to learn them anew. In so doing, the mythologies about gender and sex that arose in the aftermath of the economically topsy-turvy South Sea Bubble world were imposed; these developed from the continued urban sprawl in London and combined with the tumultuous socio-economic rearrangements throughout the kingdom after the summer of 1720 when the bubble burst. Furthermore, by 1723 the "town" had become much larger and more diversified than it had been in the 1690s, when it amounted to little more than the court. Still, the individual could discover the reasons for Wilson's personal rise to splendor and sudden death in a remarkable little work written in the mid-1720s: the notorious "love-letters" between two men.[24]

In documenting 1723 as the unassailable date of publication, I continue to believe that the work was issued, not as a fictional romance or genuine set of letters that was actually sent in 1694 or discovered sometime thereafter, but rather as a blend of political satire and narrative realism resulting from the widespread urban interest in the growth of sodomy within the town. This development of a sodomitical subculture, whose historiography is provided above in the opening endnotes, is crucial for understanding the genesis of the work. Those who consider the *Love-Letters* as either of the former (romance or actual letters), will naturally see no reason to account for its generation and publication within a particular year or find any external conditions that explain its genesis and publication. But they will nevertheless have a difficult time explaining why the *Love-Letters* appeared almost thirty years after the event; difficulty explaining why the letters, if authentic, should have remained undiscovered for such a long time, and—most importantly— how and by whom they suddenly appeared on the scene in 1723. It is true that letters are never fictional to the person reading them, but in this case they were letters involving a figure (Beau Wilson) who had become somewhat legendary between the time of his death in 1694 and the appearance of this work in 1723. The degree of his fame is difficult to estimate from the extant evidence. Today the work clamors to be understood by anyone interested in solving the mystery of its authorship and protagonist, and by anyone who asks why more copies have not survived. Only a handful of copies (in the Bodleian, the Huntington, and the Royal Library in the Hague) have been found, as well as two or three in private hands. The work is now so scarce that it fetches hundreds of pounds (the last amount seen was 1,200 pounds).[25] The Huntington Library had catalogued the work ca. 1920 as "published in 1712 by Daniel Defoe" until I protested in 1986 that it probably was not by him nor could it have been published in that year.[26]

Unlike some of Mrs. Manley's letters in "The Lady's Pacquet," the anonymous *Love-Letters* is not authentic; nor does the work constitute in any conventional sense a novel or novelette. Yet it provides an extraordinarily good read. The titlepage reads "London: printed by the bookseller A. Moore," whose shop was near St. Paul's and whose name (perhaps a pseudonym) first appeared in 1722, but this identification may be a fabrication, and Moore is not known to have specialized in pornography no matter how this genre is defined for the early eighteenth century.[27] Besides, "A. Moore" sounds like "a-mour" and "and more," and the calculating writer may have been exploiting the printer's homonymic and semiotic potential, though no evidence whatever exists to support this conjecture.

The letters are not dirty or pornographic in any sense that David Foxon and — more recently — Peter Wagner have suggested.[28] But they have the feel, as it were, especially the physical feel, of a cushy, if also a borderline dirty, and high-class work — this as the result of the book's continuous strips of ornament, ornate head and tail pieces, and facto-tums associated with this type of literature.[29] In this sense, and in the author's (surely fictional) proclamation that he "found these letters in a cabinet," the outrageous *Love-Letters* resemble the equally racy, if much less overtly homosexual, papers of 1706 "*Found in the Cabinet of the Great Almanzor.*"[30] I say "he," recognizing that the author could have been female, in which case much of my argument and interpretation will have to be altered; yet until there is some evidence of female authorship (of which there is none I know of now), I continue to speculate about a male writer of the *Love-Letters*. The "one shilling" price, common at the time for books of this size, may be a ruse: the work may have sold for less, just as hardcore homosexual pornography today often carries a high pricetag but sells for less. The significance of the town-house imaged on the headpiece on page one is unclear (unless it is Wilson's lodgings, known from "The Unknown Lady's Pacquet of Letters" to have been next to Hippolito's in Covent Garden).[31] Nor is it clear why the curved headpieces suddenly change to square ones at the point where the letters end and the observations start.[32] These old-type ornaments had been used as fillers for decades and may not signify anything important in identifying the author or targets of the *Love-Letters*, but is crucial to notice that the *Love-Letters* contain a bipartite structure within their double narrative recounting two completely separate versions of the same story: part 1 (pages 1–28) comprising twenty letters, including one which the author claims cannot be printed because its "subject" is still living — an Irish bull if ever there were one; and part 2 (pages 29–49), containing analytic observations on the twenty letters. Readers of the mid-1720s, who did not know the facts of thirty years before (1694), could not have pieced the story together from these letters: it is the observations that are crucial if the reader is to grasp the plot. Nor would readers then have asked whether the work was fact or fiction: they wanted rather to be persuaded, as when reading Defoe's realistic fictions, that this was not romance. But beyond a modicum of realism, they probably craved no proof of fact, or evidence, as we might today.

This 1723 version recounting Wilson's demise, unlike Manley's 1707-8 account, is a homosexual, or sodomitical, bourgeois fantasy primarily intended for the newly-broadened heterosexual *and* homosexual reading public: bourgeois because it embeds the by now familiar theme of rags to riches; sodomitical because here the secret nocturnal assignations are between man and man—sodomite and catamite—although a good deal of cross-dressing, transvestism, and deceptive hermaphroditism is also interwoven into both accounts of the events. As such, the *Love-Letters* surely constitute the most explicitly homosexual prose fiction in English literature printed before the publication of Oscar Wilde's *Teleny*,[33] and — what is more—can have been rivaled only by Thomas Cannon's *Ancient and Modern Pederasty investigated and exemplified* (1749).[34] Without Cannon's book, one hasn't a clue of what it contained. Moreover, this is the work that Cleland referred to when he was indicted in 1749 for the publication of the *Memoirs of a Woman of Pleasure* and when he later was publicly ridiculed as a sodomite.[35] Yet the *Love-Letters* cannot be a "real" nobleman's correspondence, and it would be risky for modern scholars to approach this text as if it represented authentic historical fact rather than a crafted piece of literature.

Along these lines of history versus literature, in the 1720s there would indeed have been readers who had heard how the earl of Castlehaven was hanged from a rope in 1631 after his acts of sodomy on his valet were discovered.[36] If these letters were authentic, the nobleman (whoever he was in 1723) would have taken action, and there would have been gossip and scandal at court. Nor can they be authentic letters of 1694 which someone has found in a cabinet: if authentic letters, why publish them now—thirty years later—unless there is good reason? Yet in actuality, there was very little printed comment about Wilson in the 1720s, and the ephemera of the time are virtually silent on his life.[37] Therefore, the modern scholar who approaches this text as if it were representative of "authentic history" is adopting perhaps the wrong approach. My thesis is rather that the *Love-Letters* represent fiction of a particular type: partly composed for a new heterosexual readership intrigued by the spread of sodomy throughout the town and eager to learn what the newly self-styled sodomites were really like; partly intended for the new homosexual subculture that was also reading by the 1720s and whose readers mythologized "Beau Wilson" as a new type of rags-to-riches hero.

The work's structure (double narrative) is calculated to dupe the reader at every point. It begins with a three and a half-page preface assuring readers that the letters are authentic, having been "found in the Cabinet of the Deceas'd" [i.e., the nobleman], and that the "Vice" here described—sodomy—has been realistically portrayed, without any attempt to disguise its true nature. The story depicts an anonymous London nobleman who has seen the handsome "Willie Wilson" at a play, where he becomes enamored of his looks. (Whether Wilson is handsome as epicene and effeminate or brawny and butch, we are never told.) He writes to Wilson ("My dear Willie") asking for a rendezvous "in

Greenwich Park at nine p.m. tomorrow," and promises splendid presents. Wilson declines, claiming there must be a mistake: he is not the nobleman's rival in love. The nobleman, recognizing what Wilson really is, interprets the protest otherwise and replies: "Then come away . . . my Willy . . . the Bath is ready, that I may wrestle with it, and pit it, and pat it, and — [suck or fuck][38] it; and then for cooler Sport, devour it with greedy Kisses; for Venus and all the *Poet's* Wenches are but dirty Dowdies to thee."

Wilson eventually succumbs and the two men become sexually intimate. But they must conceal the nature of their liaison to protect their social standing, and — equally important — hide the nature of their business. Both have heterosexual conquests despite their passionate homosexual attachment with each other and other men. But the nobleman keeps Wilson in such splendor that he becomes the "Wonder of the whole Town." As Evelyn had intimated in the passage already cited above, he "lived in the Garb & Equipage of the richest Noble man in the nation."

Wilson and the nobleman then enter into a mutual conspiracy to delude the town. First they separate, Wilson retiring to Tunbridge on grounds of ruined health. Then they feign to have fallen out with each other, in order that their friends may overlook their secret attachment. But a mishap changes all. "Lady V—l—s," herself kept by a mysteriously unnamed man in the narrative, has apparently been "the Person who had thus rais'd him" (32). Concerned that the rumors about Wilson consorting with a man may be true, she hires spies to follow him, only to discover his daily rendezvous. Spending his afternoons "at Court, Park, or Play" (33), he "dismiss'd his Equipage, and took a Chair, which carry's him to a private House near *Hyde Park* Corner, into which he enter'd by a Key he had with him." This is the nobleman's house, from which Wilson emerged in the early hours of the morning each day.

"Lady V—l—s" also sends other spies who attempt to procure lodgings in this "house," only to be rebuffed — so it cannot be a public house. Now the lady, veritably distracted, sets her spies on Wilson and his romantic patron. They discover that the same person who enters at ten exits at a back door "in the Habit of a Lady." Assisted by Villiers's "chief Engine *Johnasco*," they arrange for Wilson to be intercepted and arrested. (Johnasco's "Engine" name may now suggest a New-World Indian — *injun* — as it was widely known that Law had been in Mississippi, but Johnasco itself would have been read as nothing more than a standard way of distorting his real name, John.[39]) Wilson denies he is the wanted person, but to no avail. Johnasco and his men carry him off (crossdressed as a woman) to a "Spunging-House" (35) where they threaten he will remain until she/he can post bail. A few hours later, Johnasco continues with the stratagem devised by his mistress (i. e., Villiers). He arrives and professes love for the imprisoned Wilson, lamenting when he discovers that Wilson is already enamored of another: i. e., the nobleman whose house he has been frequenting. Johnasco now makes lewd advances to his male prisoner, who rebuffs them, claiming to belong to another. Johnasco continues his conquest, naturally discovering that Wilson is a male dressed as a woman—which Johnasco has known all along.

Now the sodomitical plot thickens. Introduced are a banished Frenchman, his daughter, and a beautiful young woman just arrived from the country—Cloris—this being a second inserted subplot within the double narrative. This heterosexual group composed of one male and two females—in gender, the antidote to the protagonists surrounding the nobleman (the beau and Lady V, as well as the second menage in the other subplot)—camouflage what is occurring between the nobleman and the beau.[40] Johnasco, hoping to dupe Lady V further, claims that the nobleman has left London, and that he (Johnasco) has observed the mysterious "woman" (Wilson) enter the apartment of the lord's steward. Johnasco reports he "found it was the Steward's Apartment," and that the occupant "was a *French* Gentleman" (37–38) claiming to be a Hugenot escaping from religious persecution. Johansco urges Lady V to acquaint the lord with this intelligence, as the intrigues are taking place in his house. Lady V follows his suggestion, and the nobleman plans his own (fraudulent) attack: he and Johnasco will entrap Wilson as he visits the steward's apartment. But no sooner have they captured their prey than the French steward disappears, and when Wilson is discovered he is betrothed to the Frenchman's daughter. The nobleman, claiming to Johnasco that the ruckus has been conducted over "*A Plot on a* French *Petticoat*" (39), insists that the two of them have accomplished what their "Counter-Plot" (39) was intended to resolve: to throw Lady V off the track.

It is now made clear that all persons within the nobleman's house have been bribed, just as Johnasco has. But Lady V is not the only one duped; Wilson also is. While Wilson is away from London, the aristocrat seduces Cloris, who—as we noted—was brought to London by her parents to be educated. The misogynistic nobleman seduces her, "*not so much to amuse the dull Time in his* [Wilson's] tedious Absence, as to stop the World's good natur'd Reflections on his Indifference that Way" (40–41). "That Way" is the crux of the matter, but why the lord needs to dupe the already persuaded town about his sodomitical nature is never made clear. Still, he takes up with Cloris and is humiliated. In public she "runs Pins in his false Calves" to "shew them that Age had depriv'd him of his natural ones" (42). The aging nobleman secretly swears revenge on her, and accomplishes this by duping her through flattery and ingratiation. He maintains her, as he had kept Wilson, in such fine clothes that even she succumbs, only to learn eventually the price she has had to pay. By this time Wilson returns to London and discovers his female rival. Cloris and Wilson meet, recognizing their common interest in the nobleman, but Wilson, assured by the lord that Cloris is no rival after all, calms himself. When Cloris least suspects conflict, and after having been impregnated by the lord, he drops her, charging that she has been unfaithful. Now the tables are turned from the false-calves episode, and Cloris vows eternal revenge.

The luxuriant sub-plot thickens even further as the story ends with yet another scene involving cross-dressing. Imitating Wilson, Cloris disguises herself in male clothing, decking herself out as a handsome youth capable of ensnaring "my lord." At dusk she intercepts his carriage and asks to speak with my lord privately. Attracted by the seemingly handsome young male, the lord listens, only to discover that Cloris (whom he has not recognized) has a pistol pointed at him. He tosses this instrument from her hands, beats her, and leaves her to die in the road. A soldier passing by takes pity — thinking the youth is male — and removes Cloris to the apartment where she had cross-dressed. Here, in shock, Cloris entreats him to bring Wilson, whom Cloris still believes (erroneously of course) is a woman, "not being able to die in Peace without seeing her" (48). Wilson arrives and discovers the distracted Cloris pregnant and bleeding. Three days later, she prematurely delivers a stillborn baby and dies. "Thus fell the unfortunate *Cloris*, a Sacrifice to one [the nobleman] who had not even the Excuse of once liking her; but work'd her Ruin, to gratify his own Pride, and mortify hers" (49). With this poignant sentence the fictional *Love-Letters* conclude, Wilson and the nobleman presumably living conjugally blissful in their sodomitical state.

IV

So much for the plot of the *Love-Letters* — what about the mystery of the nobleman? Who did finance the real Wilson and why the appearance of the *Love-Letters* in 1723 rather than a decade earlier or later?

There are three possibilities whose strengths and weaknesses I evaluate. In so doing, I demonstrate the defects of some of the possibilities in order to argue with concrete reasons for my rankings rather than to tear down straw men. I begin with the historical Wilson in 1694, and then proceed to the circumstances of 1723 that prompted the *Love-Letters*. But in examining these possibilities, I must make my position explicitly clear: namely, that the original historical Wilson of 1694 may have been no more than a shadow—a memory—for the writer of 1723. There remains no valid reason to conclude that the author of the 1723 *Love-Letters* ever knew the historical reality of what had happened in 1694: namely, those mysterious persons and events described by Evelyn and Manley. It is possible that the 1723 author had heard about the case and fabricated his fantasy based on just a few details, without knowing anything about the historical Beau Wilson or having the slightest clue who the real "nobleman" was, or even if there had been a real nobleman.

(1). *The Villiers Thesis.* First among these alternatives for 1694, and the one with the greatest plausibility in my view, is the Villiers-Wilson connection and the virtual certainty from the extant material, especially that of Mrs. Manley, that Villiers wanted Wilson for herself.[41] This situation may be an unassailable fact, but even so, Villiers—the king's whore—would not have expended all this money and energy to keep a country boy. If the original "nobleman" of 1694 is not Villiers herself—disguising her gender in an epoch when cross-dressing was so common—then we must search for larger fish. This possibility of Villiers in drag may be remote, but should not be entirely discarded. If she is indeed the source of the mystery, and if jealousy has prompted her to unravel the secret of Wilson's nocturnal meetings, then we can understand why she would expend a fortune (which she is known to have enjoyed as the king's mistress) to hire "Johnasco"—John Law—as her detective spy, and later insist that Law not be penalized.[42] Yet underlying all her actions after the unveiling is the wish to have Wilson murdered for penetrating to her real identity.

(2). *The Earl of Portland Thesis.* The second possibility (perhaps as likely as the first for a number of reasons but equally difficult to support) is that Wilson was kept by the very affluent Dutchman Hans William Bentinck, later earl of Portland and the king's "first favorite" before he was replaced by Justus van Keppel.[43] This is the Dutch Bentinck, of course, about whom dozens of catamitical aspersions are cast in the *Poems on Affairs of State* and almost as many in the Dutch ephemera of the time.[44] Even before Bentinck had arrived in England with William, he was known from rumor and reports to have been interested in other males in a homoerotic way, and—as we shall soon see—he quarreled bitterly with James Stanhope, the soldier and first earl, late in the 1690s over the ways in which the king's attention, and perhaps even favors, could be granted to these young men eager to be enlisted in his (the king's) service. Looking back from the perspective of the late 1690s, the Dutch or English in 1689 should not have been surprised that Bentinck would join William in England as a sort of catamitical favorite.

Once there, William showered him with titles, property, and vast amounts of money, as is now common knowledge among British historians of the reign of William and Mary.[45] In addition, Bentinck was widowed from 1688 until he remarried in 1700; he was a widower when Law killed Wilson in 1694.

In this scenario, Villiers and Bentinck are in competition for William's attention: she as Wilson's mistress (as Montgomery Hyde had argued and, again according to Hyde, as Villiers's maid had presumably corroborated), and Bentinck as Wilson's catamite. This type of bisexual menage accords with everything known about Bentinck and fits, moreover, into the Restoration model of the bisexual male heroically conceptualized with a woman on one arm and a man on the other.[46] But Bentinck is also the king's favorite. That is, William and Bentinck share a special relationship. Indeed, in this scenario Bentinck is the secret of Wilson's wealth. This hypothesis involves groups of favorites: the king consorting with his favorite Bentinck; Bentinck keeping Wilson.[47]

Such male favoritism was bound to disturb Villiers, not merely out of jealousy and for calculated economic reasons but because of her heightened curiosity to learn how Bentinck was frittering away the king's presents in his mysterious nocturnal life. Villiers, having bribed "Johnasco" Law to unravel the mystery, would naturally assist him to escape when he was under the gun of a death sentence.[48] She had her own identity to hide as Wilson's former keeper-lover, and even after his death wished to keep the matter secret. What would the king think if she had been squandering his considerable presents on this young Norfolkshire man, no matter how attractive he was? Moreover, Villiers had despised Bentinck from the time he arrived in England and was forever jealous of her sister Anne, who had married him in 1678 and died in 1688, leaving him a widower with six children.[49] Indeed, the catamitical Bentinck was her only serious rival with the king until Keppel replaced him.[50] In this scenario, Villiers would not have objected if John Law while fighting the duel had also killed Bentinck (perhaps instead of killing Wilson), although she was obviously disturbed that Wilson had pulled off her veil and discovered her identity. The last action belongs to the fictional version, so common in the romance tradition, and is practically impossible in real life. What Villiers had not banked on was the brawl—as we have noticed—at Hippolito's or elsewhere near Covent Garden, over the lodging of women. And the evidence that this hypothesis has more substance than its predecessor is that Villiers, more so than anyone else at the time, encouraged William to replace Bentinck with Keppel.[51] Did Villiers know that Bentinck was the mysterious nobleman? It would seem impossible for her not to have known in this scenario. Alternatively, did Bentinck know about Villiers? The answer must be affirmative. If this version has any plausibility, all three knew the identity of each other, Wilson only having learned who the woman was upon lifting her veil.

(3) *The King William III Thesis.* There is one more serious alternative explanation to consider before moving to the 1720s. This is the possibility (implausible, although not impossible in my view) that the king himself is the nobleman. Although he favored Portland, William had had other catamites, as the satire and drama of the period make patent.[52] Wilson—the handsome country boy newly come to town—possesses something the King wants, something Bentinck lacks, perhaps something to complement the other catamites. In this scenario, William himself keeps Wilson in the magnificent splendor that has baffled Evelyn and the town. In this hypothesis, Manley's letters in "The Lady's Pacquet" amount to no more than uninformed gossip derived from the knowledgeable if malicious duchess of Cleveland. Here, in this version, Villiers and Bentinck are allies in their joint jealously of and rivalry with Wilson. It is not Wilson they want but the king; both would oust Wilson if they could. It is bad enough—seeing this scenario from their point of view—to divide the king's pleasure and wealth as whore and catamite; to give up favoritism to this rustic and catamitical parvenu from the provinces entails more than they can tolerate. Therefore, Villiers enlisted Law, and possibly Bentinck as well (who may have contributed to Law's fee and, later on, toward the cost of his escape). In this hypothesis the king rather than Villiers or Bentinck loses Wilson through the machinations of his favorites who eliminate their rival in a duel.

The weaknesses of the hypothesis are manifold. The interpretation fails to explain why there was not more gossip about William, if he indeed had been the source of Wilson's wealth. It contradicts Mrs. Manley. It reveals a more vulnerable king—no matter how homosocial—than the facts permit. In my view, it is the least likely of all explanations.

But what if the anonymous author of 1723 knew none of this information: neither Evelyn's nor Manley's account or any detailed oral reports—only a memory, a shadow, of the original story, which he was now (in 1723) invoking for entirely other purposes? We assume that the hack was in possession of sources, but that may not have been the case. After all, Evelyn had said nothing whatever about the gender of Wilson's sponsor, merely writing that the mystery could never be solved and expressing his wonder how "this so young gentleman . . . did so live in so extraordinary Equipage."[53] Furthermore, Manley never alluded to any "nobleman:" she assured the world in her packets of letters (1707–8, 1718) that the mysterious keeper was a woman. In this scenario—the likeliest of all in my view as I have reconstructed this now largely forgotten episode within the history of sexuality—there was no nobleman in 1694, only a more recent one to be unearthed in 1723. That is, what we have are two entirely different versions of the same story. By reading backwards and imposing the second on the first (that is, interpreting the first of 1694 in the light of the second of 1723), we search for the wrong identity. There was indeed an historical Wilson whom Law killed and who was sumptuously kept by someone. But we need consult no figure other than Villiers to ascertain the source of the wealth because in 1694 there is no mention of any "nobleman." He enters in 1723 only, and it now remains to explain why.

V

Broke and somewhat bitter about his fate abroad, John Law returned to England on 20 October 1721, a little more than a year after the South Sea Bubble burst, the first time he had set foot on English soil for almost twenty-seven years.[54] The *Historical Register* for 1721 documents that within weeks he "was daily visited of persons of the first quality and distinction."[55] Soon Law discovered that he had more enemies than friends, this state of affairs developing despite his official pardon by George I for Wilson's murder.[56] What better way for one or a group of these enemies to embarrass Law now than by hiring a Grub Street hack to reify "Johnasco's" murder of 1694? True, but why invent a mythical "nobleman" who keeps Wilson if one's purpose is to embarrass Law by retelling the story of his murder of Wilson?

There are many possible responses. One embraces the suggestion supplied earlier: that the hack simply did not know the facts of 1694. Another is that the hack has a dual purpose: he wants to expose Law for the criminal he thinks he is (that is what he has been paid for),[57] but also imagines (or has been instructed to imagine) that a nobleman rather than female "V — — —" was the source of Wilson's riches. This constitutes the source of the story's complex double layer.

Yet let us not turn away from the matter of homosexual scandal so quickly. Glancing backward at the previous generation—the 1690s—it is true that scandal, rumor, and innuendo about William and his catamites plagued the king throughout his reign in England, abetted by fierce anti-Dutch propaganda in England that cast all Hollanders in the role of outsiders.[58] But after William died in 1702, the gossip disappeared almost immediately. By 1710, or 1715, there was no longer any buzzing of the variety that had flourished earlier, as new political woes and Jacobite worries plagued the nation. Of what political or social use then was a fiction like the *Love-Letters*—part satire, part realism—if it merely undertook to embarrass Law? And of what specific value in 1723, over a year and half after Law returned to England?[59] In asking this question I do not diminish the importance of Law but maintain that the invention of a mythical nobleman cannot be overlooked, especially inasmuch as it nowhere figures in any version previous to 1723.

Law does not remain the crux of the argument. Hyde has shown the depths of Law's despair during the winter of 1722–23, as he wrote his memoirs in unheated lodgings on Conduit Street London, and has demonstrated to what ends Law went to enlist the patronage of Robert Walpole, who was sympathetic but ultimately unreceptive.[60] By March 1723 the duke of Orleans, the French regent Law had served so diligently, had sent Law money in England, announcing that a legacy was also forthcoming.[61] Different camps of enemies, especially those prevailing on Walpole not to give Law any preferment, would have been all too quick to attack Law for expecting favors. But none of this entangled political labyrinth will explain the invention of the "nobleman" who figures so prominently in the *Love-Letters*. For that we must return to the developing administration of Robert Walpole at the turn of the decade, and look beyond Law to James Stanhope (1673–1721), the first earl of Stanhope, and his male protégés. We must do so if we believe that the hack has specific targets in mind (such as Law and Stanhope) when he writes. If, on the other hand, we are satisfied to construe the *Love-Letters* as fiction pure and apolitical, then we need only account for the narrative organization of the work and comment—as we already have done—on its form of the double narrative. My preference for specific targets in this case will become increasingly clear.

James Stanhope had served his country valiantly and distinguished himself as one of England's bravest soldiers by the time of his death in 1721.[62] Born into wealth and station, he indicated an interest in military life from early age, leaving his college at Oxford before graduating to join the army and serving King William in various campaigns in Italy and Flanders. During the years 1693–94 when our protagonist (Beau Wilson) was being kept so sumptuously, if also mysteriously in the town, Stanhope, now twenty-two, briefly returned to London; according to his biographer Aubrey Newman, in debt and petitioning his father for money.[63] It is unlikely, if not implausible then, that Stanhope had been the mysterious "nobleman" keeping Wilson. Like Law, Stanhope had also killed a man in a duel in 1694, in Brussels, perhaps inclining some to think that he was a possible, but in my view altogether unlikely, source of Wilson's wealth.[64]

Stanhope only remained in London for a few months in 1693–94, shipping out soon again for Flanders. His resourcefulness as a general was widely commended, culminating in national headlines by capturing Minorca in 1708. But by 1709 or 1710, his career as a soldier slowly collapsed, no matter how brilliant it had been; the War of the Spanish Succession, in which he had played such an important military role, coming to an end, and there being no more campaigns for him to head up. Instead, he continued in public service, in which he had already had some intermittent experience from 1702 onwards, the conventional route for one of his high station and public visibility. It is impossible to determine when the public knowledge of his homosexuality became widespread, but if a blazingly explicit passage in "The Golden Age Revers'd" — a political satire of 1703 in imitation of the fourth eclogue of Virgil — is any indication, it was already known by 1703:[65]

> Stanhope, that Offspring of unlawful Lust,
> Begot with more than Matrimonial Gust,
> Who thinks no Pleasure like *Italian* Joy,
> And to a *Venus* Arms prefers a Pathick Boy,[66]
> Shall thunder in the Senate and the Field,
> And reap what Fame, or Arts or Arms can yield.

More specifically for our purposes and for the political underpinnings of the *Love-Letters*, Stanhope was branded "a sodomite"[67] while campaigning in the general election of 1710 in Westminster London, not a surprising charge in view of his public image by then as well as his predictable reputation as a promoter of handsome young men both abroad and at home.[68] W. Speck, one of our most erudite contemporary commentators on politics during the reign of Queen Anne, comments on Stanhope's sodomy as a matter of known fact. "Although his homosexuality roused public comment," Speck writes, "it did not impede his political advancement."[69] Speck also calls attention to one of the many sources ridiculing Stanhope's sodomy: *An Excellent New Ballad being the Second Part of the Glorious Warrior*, a broadside that appeared in October 1710.[70] There must have been an abundance of other ephemera and caricature now lost to time, and Speck notes that "when at ease," Stanhope "could be a most agreeable companion, but under attack he tended to react violently — hence perhaps his nickname 'Hackum.' "[71] Speck's commentary, however, requires larger contexts of explanation than these local political ones; he must be understood in the terms of sexuality and gender that make him a more human figure than he has generally been considered by students of the age of Anne. For one thing, by the time that peace negotiations seemed imminent in 1710, there had been in London two large waves of arrests of sodomites: one in 1707, another in 1709.[72] In each instance, dozens of sodomites (the exact numbers remain contested) had been brought to trial, found guilty and punished. Fear and suspicion of a thriving and ever-growing subculture of sodomites permeated the metropolis on the eve of the general election of 1710 for which Stanhope stood. The mob's cry of sodomy might therefore indicate nothing more than its disapproval of the candidate on any number of grounds, not even indicating sexual preferment among them. In Stanhope's case, it was a cry based on widespread rumor and substance: the knowledge, at least among a segment of the court and aristocracy, of the soldier's blatant homosexuality and the way he had continued to indulge his sodomitical tastes through preferment and patronage of younger men.

For another thing, Stanhope's habits in preferment had extended back almost to the beginning of his career. For example, he had quarreled seriously with the earl of Portland, the Dutch Bentinck already discussed at length in connection with "The Earl of Portland Thesis." Aubrey Newman discusses this quarrel, considering it to have had serious repercussions and consequences for the court politics of the 1690s. "Although nothing further is known of this episode," he writes, "there was undoubtedly a certain amount of constraint thereafter between Portland and James Stanhope, and the latter believed it to have been responsible for blocking a projected appointment to a place in the King's Bedchamber."[73] In view of the links between Villiers and Portland discussed earlier in this account, the episode is not irrelevant, even if it does not suggest that Stanhope played any role whatever in financing Beau Wilson's career in London.[74] Nevertheless, it confirms beyond a doubt that at least some members of the mob knew what they were charging when they yelled sodomite. The popular literature of the day—ephemera, ballads, caricatures—also substantiates the sodomitical charge, as in the ballad of 1710 mentioned by Speck.[75] Moreover, Stanhope's friendships with other aristocrats he could trust were soaked in the dye of similar homoerotic tastes and habits, as was his very intimate tie to the eighth Earl of Huntingdon, George (1677-1705), an exact contemporary. Fellow officers who had served together on the Continent, their bond verged on what we today might called "deep and committed homosexual friendship," and their dozens of passionate letters, still in the archives at Chevening, indicate in no unclear terms the memories they shared of other young men they had perhaps preferred or even slept with. Huntingdon, for example, wrote to Stanhope on 11 July 1703: "The joy I had to hear you were well you may believe was not lessened by that naked and sincere friendship that appeared to me in every line of your letter, but I am sorry it is out of my power to make you such returns as I ought. I can only assure you if I had a new heart you should be master of that as well as you are of the old one. What would I not give to tell you this my wicked Stanhope over a glass of champagne in Paris with two or three pretty smiling unthinking fellows that know nothing and do everything."[76]

Can there be any doubt about these "pretty smiling unthinking fellows" or the naughty familiarity assumed in "my wicked Stanhope?" Who other than young men seeking fame and fortune — perhaps through conventional military routes but perhaps also through other forms of patronage — could have "known nothing yet done everything?" The words speak for themselves: precisely those who "know nothing and do everything" were the traffic in which Stanhope and his trusted homoerotic friends like Huntingdon were dealing.[77] Huntingdon's sentence in this letter calms any lingering doubts: "I don't despair but this may be brought yet before gray hairs and wrinkles make us virtuous." Actually, neither Huntingdon or Stanhope reformed, and it was unrealistic for either to believe that the octopus-like court, whose tentacles had always possessed means of gathering information, would not have uncovered these ingrained habits. Yet, if this type of written evidence is insufficient proof of the real tie between the two officers, in 1702 Huntington began to pay for Stanhope's premises (according to Newman at the rate of 400 per annum) and provided him with this amount until his death.[78]

Stanhope continued in public life after the turn of the century, more continuously from the time when his career as a soldier ended, but the real test of his mettle came in 1719 when he, together with Sunderland and James Craggs, Jr., supported the Peerage Bill. This legislation was intended, as J. F. Naylor has now definitively shown,[79] to delimit the number of lords who could be created, and one of its more dire effects was the exclusion of Walpole from the House of Lords: an action Walpole was never to forget and for which he never forgave the Whig triumvirate who were its architects. Stanhope himself was entrusted with effecting the specific exclusion of Walpole, a task that brought the two men into further conflict.[80] The bill polarized the Whigs — among whose members all the protagonists mentioned here can be counted — and caused deep division within their rank and file. From the start, Richard Steele, a Walpole supporter and fierce spokesman for the dissident Whigs, came out against it, as did the majority of the House of Commons; and Steele advocated his views in The Plebian, a paper "To be Continued Weekly," whose main purpose was to attack the bill's proponents.[81] When lashing out against Stanhope, Steele was cautious — as the mobs who cried sodomite against Stanhope in 1710 had not been — to tread lightly. But the Stanhope coalition nevertheless criticized Steele for his views. Reacting to the response, Steele brilliantly and allusively created a new contemporary Georgian scenario comparing England's military might of 1719 to that of the Lacedemonians and basing his analogies of power and authority on Ubbo Emmius' *Historia nostri temporis*. His genuine purpose was to show that Stanhope had taken a morbidly lascivious interest in young English soldiers, not unlike those Spartan ministers of state who inspected the ephebes (youths), to the point of undressing them and cohabiting with them as male concubines. It was an extraordinary charge in view of the political stakes in 1719. Yet having made this bold insinuation and created this Anglo-Greek analogy, Steele then claimed he had taken every care "to avoid the least Appearance of personal Reflection" against Stanhope:[82]

> AS to the Digression upon the *Ephori*, the PLEBIAN was very careful to avoid giving Offence. Amongst the many extraordinary Powers exercis'd by those Magistrates, there was one of a very uncommon nature; which was, That as they took upon themselves the sole Inspection of the Youth, they were particularly curious of the Persons of the *Boys*. They employ'd every tenth Day in examining the *Youths of about Fifteen, stark naked, Oportebat Ephebos decimo quoque die Ephoris se sistere sine veste*, Ubbo Emmius, des Re. La. p. 235, with whom *Crags* [i. e. James Craggs] agrees almost in the same words, in the Treatise mention'd in the former PLEBIAN, p. 78. What an ill Use was made of this Power, we may see in Emmius, p. 236, where speaking of the manner how the *Ephori* liv'd with *those young Men they lik'd best*, he says, *Iis* (Ephebis) *assiduo fere adhaerebant*. Which Words, for fear of offending the PLEBIAN Ladies, I am not at liberty to translate. However, it is very plain all this was omitted to avoid the least Appearance of personal Reflection.

This was a mild but nonetheless pungent warning to Stanhope and his Ganymedes in 1719 that the opposition could strike harder—and perhaps would attack—if provoked. The dissident Whigs had ready ammunition in Stanhope's homosexuality and would use it if need be, especially if Walpole continued to feel threatened through exclusion after 1721 and gave orders to retaliate. There was no reason for Walpole's supporters to make bolder claims about Stanhope at this time (1719): the way the famous soldier had thrown his weight at court, for example, to pretty boys who could serve as pages. Steele's *Plebian's* point was merely that those who stood in opposition to the Peerage Bill were well aware of Stanhope's Achilles-heel and would attack it if necessary. Walpole's defenders were also cognizant that throughout his career Stanhope had caused young men to become dependent on him for their professional advancement, and that he particularly encouraged those in whom he bore a special, and possibly homosexual, interest.[83] Even Steele, who had as we have just seen, struck at Stanhope's sore spot—the same Steele who elsewhere described the trope of sodomy as encoding forms of excessive political dependence on an older and more established political states- man.[84] What reason then is there to believe that the anonymous author of the *Love-Letters* would not play upon these well-known facts of Stan- hope's life? — the most suitable candidate for the "nobleman" in the early 1720s. That is, identifying Stanhope as the nobleman, while hoping that few readers would remember that he was only twenty-two in 1694 and almost certainly *not* the source of Wilson's wealth? The response that Stanhope had died in February 1721 and that the author of the *Love- Letters* waited over two years to publish is neither here nor there: the hack — if he was a hack — also took almost two years from the time Law had returned to England to write it, and it would be difficult to docu- ment a case that it was Law's particular relation to Walpole in April or May 1723 that was the sole *raison d'etre* for the *Love-Letters*.

The fact is that Walpole's animus against Stanhope cut much deeper. It is as plausible that the hack, writing for a pro-Walpole faction, or for Walpole himself, waited until Stanhope's death had taken a public toll before issuing the warning to similar young protégés serving at court and in the administration. On the basis of lapse of time one does not get very far. Along the line of the trope of sodomy rather than on the matter of dating, we are inclined today to surmise in our often anachronistic mode of thinking that sodomy was always a charge of illicit sexuality — especially buggery; and we are sometimes less receptive to its protean transformations in the Restoration and early eighteenth century than the historical and literary circumstances warrant. If we can bear Steele's Anglo-Greek analogy and trope of sodomy in mind, we may begin to comprehend how the *Love-Letters* were — in addition to being an embar- rassment to Law — a warning to all types of neophytes in the Walpole administration who were then patronized by older, more established, figures like the dark and swarthy Stanhope.[85]

VI

If this line of reasoning has any validity, the *Love-Letters* of 1723 served, among other things, as an admonition to political parvenus rather than as a commentary on the historical circumstances surrounding Wilson's murder in 1694. Indeed, it is preposterous while proceeding in this historical mode to inquire where Stanhope was in 1692–94 when Wilson was being kept so lavishly in London and to ask whether Stan- hope had been the mysterious nobleman supporting him.[86] The point is rather that the 1723 version builds on the legend that grew up in the aftermath of 1694; beyond that, all is geared for the present: the years

1721, 1722, 1723. Our author wants to embarrass Law—the main target—as well as issue a warning to young political protégés such as those (often handsome young men) Stanhope had preferred.

Furthermore, if this approach appears to read politics into literature more tenaciously, if perhaps also more deviously, than we are accustomed to today, there is nonetheless a valid historical reason to do so. But even more so than reading politics into literature, I have been attempting to show that social arrangements between the genders determine (not merely color) the explanations for historical events. In 1694 Evelyn did not leap to suspect a male as Wilson's keeper-lover. In 1707 Mrs. Manley was sure the person was female. By 1723 both a man and a woman were held accountable, and an unnamed nobleman was invented as the source holding the key to the entire mystery.

Nor did Wilson's bizarre legend die out after 1723. Even Horace Walpole, who continued to disguise his sexuality in old age although there was little reason for so doing given the reclusive manner in which he had lived at Strawberry Hill, blurrily remembered the events of 1694 almost a hundred years later. He wrote a long passage about Law in 1782 to one of his correspondents, speculating whether Law had killed all those in England he was reputed to have murdered, including Beau Wilson.[87] It is interesting that Walpole should have thought there were multiple murders ca. 1694, as there was no hint of numbers of murdered persons at the end of the seventeenth century or the beginning of the eighteenth. But by the 1780s, Walpole no longer knew how many victims were Law's and whether they had been male or female, heterosexual or homosexual. There had been so much gossip subsequent to the liaisons of Villiers, William, and Portland, and then again (in the 1720s) subsequent to the rumors about Law and possibly even Stanhope, as well as gossip about the sodomitical scandals that occurred during Horace Walpole's own adult life,[88] that Walpole could no longer remember whom exactly John Law had killed in his duels.

The anthropological matter begging to be understood is sexual commensurability, not exclusivity, as well as—in more literary domains—the new genre implications for realism. In reconstructing the mysterious Wilson we have continued to ask whether these figures—even William III—were either heterosexual or homosexual: the one or the other. Also, as expressed at the outset, we have continued to assume that for whatever reason homosexuality remains constant throughout time. In my view this entails a flawed approach. It is not a matter of either or, as in an exclusion principle, or as in old-style sodomite or new, but both at the same time: whore and catamite. If we can conceptualize William III (for example) with both Villiers and Bentinck, or Bentinck with Beau Wilson; or, by the same principle, Stanhope, and even Addison and Steele, as concommitantly whorish and sodomitical,[89] then it grows easier to conceptualize the reader's response to the anonymous *Love-Letters* after 1723.

NOTES

1 For male and female fantasies about homosexuals see: William J. Slattery, *The Erotic Imagination: Sexual Fantasies of the Adult Male* (Chicago: University of Chicago Press, 1975); David J. Spak, *An Exploratory Study of Gay Male Sexual Fantasies* (London: Macmillan, 1987); Klaus Theweleit, *Male Fantasies: Volume I: Women, Floods, History*, trans. Stephen Conway (Minneapolis: University of Minnesota Press, 1987), especially 53–57, 432–35; Françoise D'Eaubonne, *Eros Minoritaire* (Paris: André Balland, 1970), who describes the persistence of recurrent images in these collective fantasies; June Singer, *Androgyny: Toward a New Theory of Sexuality* (New York: Doubleday, 1977), who, unlike these others, demonstrates the radical fluidity of these fantasies about homosexuals; Margaret Walters, *The Nude Male: A New Perspective* (London: Paddington Press, 1978) and James M. Saslow, *Ganymede in the Renaissance: Homosexuality in Art and Society* (New Haven: Yale University Press, 1986), who show how the homosexual nude, among other visual types of the homosexual, has been visually imagined and idealized throughout the centuries; Jeffrey Meyers, *Homosexuality and Literature 1890–1930* (London: Athlone, 1977), who explains what this idealization has meant for the modern European imagination as expressed in some of its greatest literature. Theweleit comments that "in patriarchy, where the work of domination has consisted in subjugating, damming in, and transforming the 'national energy' in society, that desiring-production of the unconscious has been encoded as the subjugated gender, or femaleness; and it has been affirmed and confirmed, over and over again, in the successive forms of female oppression" (*Male Fantasies*, 432). The versions of Beau Wilson's story described below were indeed generated in what Theweleit classifies as a patriarchal society, and one could make a strong case along lines that in the Wilson-Villiers-mysterious nobleman triangle, Villiers emerges as the subjugated and oppressed female. My account not only raises the possibility, but also attempts to establish the known facts in order to permit such conjecture and speculation to go forward on firmer footing.

2 I discuss the lives of these figures below. In reconstructing Wilson's story and the cultural transformations and collective fantasies surrounding it, I have profited from discussions with Robert Adams Day, Milton Malkin, and Randolph Trumbach, as well as from hearing Professor William Roosen's 1988 talk at the American Society for Eighteenth-Century Studies (Knoxville, TN) on the same subject. Day's *Told in Letters: Epistolary Fiction before Richardson* (Ann Arbor: University of Michigan Press, 1966) is especially useful,

particularly his discussion of works by Mrs. Manley and Marie Catherine Aulnoy, also called the Countess d'Aulnoy, which are discussed below. My greatest debt, however, is to Trumbach, whose vast knowledge of sodomitical subcultures in seventeenth-and eighteenth-century England is unparalleled. In his writings he has substantiated my own sense, based in part on the material presented below and elsewhere, of the transformations in sodomitical stereotypes during this period; Trumbach's research on this matter will appear in 1990 in a forthcoming book entitled *The Sexual Life of Eighteenth-Century London.*

The modern historiography of the sodomite begins with a pioneering article by Mary McIntosh, "The Homosexual Role," *Social Problems* 16 (1968): 182-92, which has been reprinted in Kenneth Plummer, ed., *The Making of the Modern Homosexual* (London: Hutchinson, 1981), 30-44, with a "Postscript: 'The Homosexual Role,' " 44-49. Trumbach modified and expanded the historical dimension of McIntosh's position in "London's Sodomites: Homosexual Behavior and Western Culture in the Eighteenth Century," *Journal of Social History* 11 (1977): 1-33. The thesis of both works was that sodomitical subcultures at the end of the seventeenth and beginning of the eighteenth century flourished to a hitherto unprecedented degree and, perhaps owing to urban sprawl and the new pressures created by large cities (London, Paris, Rome, etc.), developed in specific ways and according to predictable arrangements. The findings of McIntosh and Trumbach were questioned by Alan Bray in *Homosexuality in Renaissance England* (London: Gay Men's Press, 1982), but were not sufficiently well-challenged to cause historians to veer from their basic agreement with them. Various continental historians substantiated the McIntosh-Trumbach position by demonstrating that the birth of this sodomitical subculture was not limited to England, but was occurring at approximately the same time throughout Western Europe. For France, see Philippe Ariès, "Réflexions sur l'historie de l'homosexualité," in Philippe Ariès and André Bejin, eds., *Sexualités occidentales* (Paris: Editions du Seuil, 1982), 81-97, and Michel Rey, "Parisian Homosexuals Create a Lifestyle, 1700-1750: The Police Archives," in Robert Maccubbin, ed., *'Tis Nature's Fault: Unauthorized Sexuality during the Enlightenment* (Cambridge: Cambridge University Press, 1988), 179-91. For Holland see: Dirk Jaap Noordham, "Homosocial Relations in Leiden (1533-1811)," in *Among Men, Among Women: Sociological and Historical Recognition of Homosocial Arrangements: Proceedings of the Amsterdam Conference 1983* (Amsterdam: University of Amsterdam, [1985]), 218-23, 603, and Arend H. Huusen, Jr., "Sodomy in the Dutch Republic during the Eighteenth Century," in Maccubbin, ed., *Nature's Fault*, 169-78.

More recently, Trumbach has substantiated his original claim made in the 1977 article in "Sodomitical Subcultures, Sodomitical Roles and the Gender Revolution of the Eighteenth Century," in Maccubbin, ed., *Nature's Fault*, 109-21; idem, "The Birth of the Queen: Sodomy and the Emergence of Gender Equality in Modern Culture, 1660-1750," in Martin Duberman, Martha

Vicinus, and George Chauncey, eds., *The New Social History of Homosexuality* (New York: New American Library, 1988); idem, "Sodomitical Assaults, Gender Roles, and Sexual Deviance in Eighteenth-Century London," in Kent Gerard and Gert Hekma, eds., *Sodomy in Early Modern Europe* (New York: Haworth Press, 1988), 221–47; idem, "Gender and the Homosexual Role: the Eighteenth and Nineteenth Century Compared," in Theo van de Meer and Anja van Kooten Nickerke, eds., *Homosexuality: Which Homosexuality? Proceedings of the 1987 Amsterdam Conference* (Amsterdam: University of Amsterdam, 1990). Further discussion of the historical formation of bisexual and homosexual roles among men is found in David Greenberg, *The Construction of Homosexuality* (Chicago: University of Chicago Press, 1988). For other works dealing with bisexual and homosexual subcultures during the Restoration and eighteenth century in England and the rest of Western Europe, see Wayne Dynes, *Homolexis: A Historical and Cultural Lexicon of Homosexuality* (New York: Gay Academic Union, 1985) and idem, *Homosexuality: A Bibliography* (New York: Garland, 1987).

Finally, my story, as readers will see, begs several questions about the agency of change among these social types: namely, what forces actually caused the old-style sodomite to be converted to the new one? This is not the place to discuss that very difficult transformation, and Trumbach has already begun to discuss it in the works cited in nn. 1–3, but I suggest in passing that the agent falls in the province of urban sprawl: the new large city, with a center and suburbs, and especially with the proliferation of prostitution under the stress of new economic necessity. That story, however, must be told elsewhere.

3 I have been influenced in my thinking about the history of sexuality, especially of sodomy and the more recently constituted homosexuality, by Foucault's multi-volumed *History of Sexuality* and by Gilles Deleüze and Félix Guattari's *Anti-Oedipus: Capitalism and Schizophrenia* (Minneapolis: University of Minnesota Press, 1983), with a preface by Michel Foucault.

4 My evidence in based to a large degree on the historical and historiographical materials listed in n. 2.

5 See E. S. de Beer, *The Diary of John Evelyn*, 6 vols. (Oxford: Clarendon Press, 1955), 5: 175–76.

6 For Law's life and career, see Adolphe Thiere, *The Mississippi Bubble: A Memoir of John Law*, trans. F. S. Fiske (New York: Townsend & Co., 1859); John Carswell, *The South Sea Bubble* (London: Cresset, 1960); H. Montgomery Hyde, *John Law: The History of an Honest Adventurer* (London: W. H. Allen, 1969), the most persuasive if least documented of the biographies; and Edgar Faure, *La Banqueroute de Law: 17 juillet 1720* (Paris: Gallimard, 1977), 21–24 for Law and Wilson.

7 For the gory details of Wilson's death and Law's apprehension, see the memorandum in the Public Record Office, London [PRO] SP 35 xviii 118, which, though unsigned, is attributed to James Johnston of Warristoun, then Secretary of State in Scotland. Hyde, *John Law*, 30, discusses the intervention of

William III in Law's apprehension and imprisonment: "It seems that it was the King's wish that [Beau] Wilson's family should have recourse to a civil action [i. e. against Law]. The following is an extract from the Secretary of State's Domestic Entry Book: "April 22 1694 Whitehall. Caveat that nothing pass relating to a pardon for John Laws [sic] sentenced to death for the murder of Mr. Edward Wilson till notice first be given to Mr. Robert Wilson brother of the deceased at his house in Stratton St. Berkeley Square." *Calendar of State Papers (Domestic) 1694–95*, 18.

8 See J. P. Wood, *Memoirs of the Life of John Law of Lauriston* (Edinburgh, 1824), 5–11. An advertisement appeared in the *London Gazette* on Monday, 7 January 1695, eight months after Wilson's murder, offering a £50 reward for Law's apprehension.

9 See Hyde, *John Law*, 30–32.

10 Ibid., 27.

11 Hyde claims (26), on the basis of the testimony of her maid, that "the lady [Villiers] was greatly struck by his [Wilson's] appearance." What John Evelyn omits (i. e., Wilson's stunning looks), the maid, recounting the source of her mistress's initial interest, therefore includes. Wilson's remarkable good looks thereby contribute to the mysterious story of his sudden rise to wealth from the very start. Yet Hyde does not indicate where the testimony of this maid is to be found. From it, Hyde also claims that "nothing was found among Wilson's belongings after his death [in 1694] which threw any light on the mystery of his wealth. As Beau lay dying on the ground in Bloomsbury Square, he handed his keys to a friend nearby and requested him to burn all his papers. The friend immediately went to the Wilson mansion, but the ensuing search revealed absolutely nothing of the slightest consequence. The most material document, we are informed, was a recipe bequeathed to the dead man by his grandmother 'to cure old women of the tooth-ache, so that no persons troubled with that distemper need doubt of a remedy' " (*John Law*, 27–28). It is impossible to evaluate the validity of these conclusions drawn by Hyde without some knowledge of his sources. My researches have so far produced no testimony of any maid (other than the fictional one, discussed below, in the *Love-Letters*), and I am puzzled about Hyde's source for the person who searched Wilson's premises after his death.

12 Leslie Stephen et al., eds., *Dictionary of National Biography*, 32 vols. (Oxford: Oxford University Press, 1882–), 21: 561–62. For Sunderland, see J. P. Kenyon, *Robert Spencer Earl of Sunderland 1641–1702* (New York: Longmans, 1958), 262, who does not identify him as the mysterious aristocrat supporting Wilson. If my argument about James Stanhope, provided below, is valid, it is easy to see why Sunderland, who was so often associated with Stanhope ca. 1720, could be identified as the source.

13 My evidence for these generalizations about types of sodomites and their transformations continues to be the historical, anthropological, and sociological studies listed in nn. 1–3. By anachronistic I mean, of course, that such designations as bisexual, homosexual, or heterosexual are here being imposed

on the civilization of Beau Wilson by a process of reading-in backwardly, their own terms being sodomitical or catamitical, especially when used with various adjectives prefixing them (i. e., woman-loving sodomite or boy-crazed catamite). For discussion of the justifications of this anachronistic language and the conditions under which it can be usefully invoked, see G. S. Rousseau, "The Pursuit of Homosexuality in the Eighteenth Century: 'Utterly Confused Category' and/or Rich Repository?" in Maccubbin, ed., *Nature's Fault*, 162–63. Trumbach in particular has explained why the bisexual model of the sodomite was functional in the 1690s and why it gradually disappeared as the eighteenth century progressed; see his works listed above in n. 2. My discussion, here and below, of old-style and new-style sodomites and their particular sexual arrangements in this period builds on Trumbach's bisexual and homosexual models in his works listed in n. 2.

14 Marie Catherine D'Aulnoy's (also called Aulnoy) *Memoirs of the Court of England in the Reign of Charles II* appeared in two versions in 1707 and 1708; in the 1707 edition were included, as 521–616, Mrs. Manley's "Lady's Pacquet of Letters, taken from her by a French Privateer in her Passage to Holland," describing in considerable detail the affair of Beau Wilson. The bibliographical knots of the composite work called the *Memoirs*, especially the sections that are authentic versus those that are fictional, are difficult to disentangle. For discussion which establishes that Mrs. Manley remains one of the three most important sources for Wilson's legend (Evelyn and the anonymous *Love-Letters* being the other two), see: Paul Bunyan Anderson, "Mistress de la Riviere Manley's Biography," *Modern Philology* 33 (1936): 272–73; William H. McBurney, *A Check List of English Prose Fiction, 1700–1739* (Cambridge, MA: Harvard University Press, 1960), 12–13, items 26, 28, 29, where McBurney lists Manley as the author of "The Lady's Pacquet of Letters"; Day, *Told in Letters*, 65–66; Rae Blanchard, ed., *The Letters of Richard Steele* (Oxford: Clarendon University Press, 1950), 425–39. Anderson, Mrs. Manley's biographer, printed a letter from Steele to Mrs. Manley, acknowledging her account of the amours and death of Wilson; see P. B. Anderson, "Mary de la Riviere Manley: A Cavalier's Daughter in Grub Street," (Ph. D. dissertation, Harvard University, 1931), 157. I have marshalled the materials of this letter in the account below and have used the edition of 1707 of the *Memoirs* in the Huntington Library, where the "Lady's Pacquet of Letters" is found on 521–616. The second edition of 1708, a copy of which is in the William Andrews Clark Memorial Library, differs slightly from its predecessor, but not in the details presented about Wilson's looks and charm, or his style of living and the way he was kept.

15 There is no authoritative biography of Elizabeth Villiers, but see nn. 41–42 below for information about her during this period.

16 It may be this account of Manley that Hyde was thinking of when he wrote (*John Law*, 26), perhaps excessively and without any documentation: "According to this source, Edward Wilson was discovered one hot summer evening lying on the grass in Kensington Gardens by a lady [i. e., Villiers] who

was taking the air there with her maid. In spite of his dejected expression the lady was greatly struck by his appearance. Being at the moment ripe for an adventure she instructed the maid to strike up an acquaintance with the young man. The result of this chance meeting was an assignation for the following night at midnight in St. James's Park."

17 Manley, "The Unknown Lady's Pacquet," 523.

18 Ibid.

19 In the 1718 edition of *The Lady's Pacquet broke open*, largely a reprint of the 1707–8 version, there is an engraving of the lady facing p. 18 with these words printed beneath it: "Beau Wilson's mistress," but there is no particular reason to think it is the portrait of Elizabeth Villiers. There is some likeness with existing portraits of Villiers but not enough to make a case. A copy of the 1718 edition is in the Houghton Library, Harvard University.

20 During the 1690s Manley was a confidante of her distant cousin Barbara, the Duchess of Cleveland, one of the best sources for court gossip anywhere in England. Day notes (*Told in Letters*, 65–66), with good reasons, that *The Lady's Pacquet* contains authentic letters by Mrs. Manley.

21 See Narcissus Luttrell, *A Brief Historical Relation of State Affairs from September, 1678 to April, 1714*, 6 vols. (Oxford: Oxford University Press, 1857), 3: 123.

22 Freudians would have a field day accounting for this detail in the heterosexual version of the story: i. e., the powerful rich woman as anonymous lover-provider in a phallocratically-centered mercantile society.

23 Here, again, based on the works listed in nn. 1–3.

24 The full title of this anonymous work containing forty-nine quarto pages is *Love-Letters Between a certain late Nobleman And the famous Mr. Wilson: Discovering The true History of the Rise and surprising Grandeur of that celebrated Beau* (London: Printed for A. Moore, near St. Paul's). It was probably issued in an edition running to ca. 500 copies (normal for the time), with no date given on the titlepage or in the prefatory material. All page references below are taken from the Huntington copy. Day is the first modern scholar to refer to this work (*Told in Letters*, 142–43, 225, 251) and deserves full credit for so doing; he has correctly perpetuated the date given by William McBurney in *A Checklist of English Prose Fiction, 1700–1739* (Cambridge, MA: Harvard University Press), 52 (no. 138), who, in turn, derived the date 1723 from the *Monthly Catalogue*, 4 vols. (London: Printed for John Wilford, 1723–30), 1, no. 4 (June 1723): 6, where it is listed under "New Miscellaneous Pamphlets," and from the copy he consulted in the Bodleian Library (shelfmark phi. e. 19), whose cataloguers correctly assigned it to the year 1723. The year 1723 is correct beyond all doubt for all these combined reasons, and is, furthermore, corroborated by the political implications (as we shall see below) to Stanhope, Walpole, and the return of John Law. There is, incidentally, no mention of the *Love-Letters* anywhere in the works of Pisanus Fraxi (Herbert Spencer Ashbee), certainly not in his *Catena Librorum prohibitorum* (London, 1885).

25 Sale Catalogue of Bernard Quaritch, "Rare Manuscripts and Pamphlets," Spring 1985.

26 The Huntington cataloguer may have conflated Defoe and Aphra Behn, who wrote *Love-Letters between a Nobleman and his Sister* (London: D. Brown, 1712), and this may have been the source of the date 1712.

27 For "A. Moore" see H. R. Plomer, *A Dictionary of the Printers and Booksellers Who Were at Work in England, Scotland, and Ireland from 1726 to 1775* (Oxford: Oxford University Press, 1932), 174–75, who lists Moore's first printed work as 1722, and David Foxon, "Index of Imprints" in *English Verse 1700–1750*, 2 vols. (Cambridge: Cambridge University Press, 1975), 2: 172. It is probably fanciful to conjecture that Moore's name was a pseudonym, but the possibility is there; he printed a few licentious works, including an edition of Petronius Arbiter. Burney lists six items for him in his *Checklist of English Prose Fiction*. My information about his works derives from Plomer, Foxon, McBurney, and a thorough search made through the *Eighteenth-Century Short Title Catalog*.

28 See David Foxon, *Libertine Literature in England, 1660–1745* (New York: New Hyde Park, 1966), and Peter Wagner's excellent study, *Eros Revived: Erotica of the Enlightenment in England and America* (London: Secker and Warburg, 1988).

29 As described by Foxon, *Libertine Literature*; I am also grateful to Nicholas Barker of the British Library who showed me just how conventional they were in upper-class scandalous literature.

30 "The Maxims of the Great Almanzor," in *A Collection of State Tracts*, 3 vols. (London, 1705–7), 2, (1706).

31 Manley, "The Unknown Lady's Pacquet of Letters," 530; nestled between brothels and bagnios, Hippolito's establishment was, according to Tom Brown, a lodging house much frequented by beaus.

32 The change was probably a conventional device intended as a clue to readers that the so-called genuine letters have ended and the commentary will begin; but whether this shift in headpieces always accompanied the double narrative I do not know. Day (*Told in Letters*, 142–43) says nothing about the matter.

33 Oscar Wilde et al, *Teleny* (1893–95), reprinted by John McRae in *Oscar Wilde and Others. Teleny* (London: Gay Men's Press, 1986).

34 On 13 November 1749 Cleland, upon being indicted, wrote to Lord Stanhope: "It is not eight months since the Son [Thomas Cannon] of a Dean and Grandson of a *Bishop* was mad and wicked enough to Publish a Pamphlet evidently in defence of *Sodomy*, advertised in all the papers" (quoted and discussed in Foxon, *Libertine Literature*, 54–55).

35 See Henry Merritt, "A Biographical Note on John Cleland," *Notes and Queries* 226 (1981): 305–6, for a discussion of Cleland's alleged sodomy and the sources for it. See also Peter Sabor, ed., *Memoirs of a Woman of Pleasure* (Oxford: Oxford Classics, 1985), 8.

36 Castlehaven's death for sodomy continued to be discussed during the Restoration and the account of his trial retold: see, for example, during the 1690s (the

period when Wilson was killed), *The Trial and Condemnation . . . of Lord Castlehaven* (London, 1699), and the discussion of it in Caroline Bingham, "Seventeenth-Century Attitudes toward Deviant Sex," *Journal of Interdisciplinary History* 1 (1971): 447–72.

37 The evidence for this assertion lies in a systematic search made of printed material from 1721 to 1723, which has turned up only the material presented in this paper. No doubt I have overlooked some items, but not enough can have eluded my search to alter the point about printed evidence related to Wilson's life.

38 While the repeated use of "it" heightens the author's rhetoric here, the ellipsis leaves no doubt about what the action is or what is being fondled.

39 In reconstructing the anonymous author's reasons for calling him "Johnasco," I show below that readers in 1723 were all too aware of Law's recent return to England from France.

40 Our anonymous author has anticipated the heterosexual triangles discussed by Eve K. Sedgwick in *Between Men: English Literature and Male Homosexual Desire* (New York: Columbia University Press, 1985), triangles in which two males, pursuing the same woman, or both being pursued by her, demonstrate their desire for each other.

41 For Elizabeth Villiers as she was perceived as a woman of the time, see William J. Cameron, *Poems on Affairs of State: Volume 5: 1688–1697* (New Haven: Yale University Press, 1971), passim, all volumes of which are now referred to as *POAS*.

42 Without belaboring the obvious I must continue to emphasize that based on printed evidence Villiers's relation to Law remains mysterious, as Hyde (see n. 6) has indicated. The mystery may be diminished if one is willing to believe that Villiers was, as I have been suggesting, first the ally-lover of Wilson, and then — after he insisted on ascertaining who she was — his enemy, so much so, that after turning on Wilson, Villiers hired Law to kill him. The crux in this explanation is the account provided by Evelyn (n. 5 above) about the boarding house in St. Giles in-the-Fields where Law lodged and the degree of its respectability. The story, perpetuated by Hyde and others, is that Law kept a mistress named Mrs. Lawrence, and that Beau Wilson's sister objected to her. When Wilson removed his sister from these apartments, the landlady imagined that her house had now got a bad reputation. She complained to Law, who then picked a fight with Wilson and killed him. It may well be that the story was apocryphal, that is, merely invented to explain Law's reason for the duel, and that Law's truer motive was his having been hired by Villiers to kill Wilson. I am suggesting, therefore, that the two stories are not incompatible: it should not be thought that just because Villiers hired Law to do her work, she was not also Wilson's lover earlier on.

43 For the often intimate homosocial liaisons among all these figures, see Marion E. Grew, *William Bentinck and William III: The Life of Bentinck Earl of Portland from The Welbeck Correspondence* (London: John Murray, 1924) and *POAS*, 5, especially the many references listed in the index and docu-

menting the close erotic bonds between the king and Bentinck. W. J. Cameron, the editor of *POAS*, 5, comments about Portland (42): "The monotony of the repeated charges of [Portland's] homosexuality [that is, throughout the *POAS*] is broken only by nauseous calumny." I do not cite the relevant Dutch literature here, printed or in manuscript, partly in the interests of space, but I am grateful to Dr. Guus Vendendaal of the Royal Library in the Hague, general editor of the *Rijks Geschiedkundige Pub.*, for providing me with an abundance of materials documenting Portland's fabulous wealth and interest in men while still in Holland.

44 See *POAS*, 5, passim, especially p. 38, and the Bentinck archives in the Royal Library at the Hague.

45 See, for example, Stephen Baxter, *William III* (London: Longmans, 1966) and Nesca Robb, *William of Orange*, 2 vols. (London: Heinemann, 1962-66), especially 2: 398-406, 448-50, where Robb discusses public perception of William's intimacy with Portland and the pervasive smears on their homosexuality.

46 See above nn. 1-3.

47 There is, of course, no printed evidence whatever for this conjecture; it remains speculation to the end. Nevertheless, one can be sure that Portland and Wilson would have taken every precaution to destroy any printed evidence documenting the possibility (that is, bank accounts, letters, diaries, etc.). Hyde comments (*John Law*, 28 and my n. 11 above) that those who went to Wilson's lodgings on the day Law killed him found nothing there revealing the identity of the mysterious nobleman.

48 For Law's "powerful friends" (that is, within the circle of Villiers), see John Carswell, *The South Sea Bubble* (London: Cresset Press, 1960), 8.

49 For their marriage see Grew, *William Bentinck and William III*, 268-89.

50 For the way William replaced one favorite with another and for Bentinck's eventual resignation in William's administration, see Grew, *William Bentinck and William III*, 268-89.

51 Ibid., 279-85.

52 See *POAS*, 5, passim and Terence Johnson, "Homosexuality on the Stage of Restoration and Early Eighteenth-Century England," (Ph. D. diss. University of California, Los Angeles, in progress), chaps. 2-3.

53 See E. S. DeBeer, *The Diary of John Evelyn*, 5: 175.

54 Hyde, *John Law*, 180.

55 Ibid., 183, where the pages from the *Historical Register* are quoted.

56 Among the reasons given for the pardon was the fact, documented in the courts of law, that Wilson's family withdrew the charges for murder it had made in 1694-95.

57 Everything in the writing of the *Love-Letters* suggests that the author is a hack who wrote because he was paid; surely his instructions were primarily to expose Law, hence the invention of Johnasco as a main character.

58 On the anti-Dutch campaign see G. S. Rousseau, "Holland: The Englishman's Lure," *Eighteenth-Century Life* (1990), forthcoming, and idem, " 'In the

House of Madame Van der Tasse, on the Long Bridge:' A Homosocial University Club in Early Modern Europe," in Kent Gerard and Gert Hekma, eds., *The Pursuit of Sodomy: Male Homosexuality in Renaissance and Enlightenment Europe* (New York: Haworth Press, 1989), 311–47.

59 Calculating from October 1721 to June 1723 when the *Love-Letters* were printed.

60 Hyde, *John Law*, 188–89. See also Faure, *La Banqueroute de Law*, 598–609.

61 Hyde, *John Law*, 189.

62 Among the best biographical sources Basil Williams's study, *Stanhope: A Study in Eighteenth-Century War and Diplomacy* (Oxford: Clarendon Press, 1932) is perhaps the most authoritative, but Aubrey Newman's *The Stanhopes of Chevening: A Family Biography* (London: Macmillan, 1969) is more understanding of Stanhope's character and the shape of his career. Both Williams and Newman are silent on Stanhope's homosocial proclivities.

63 See Newman, *The Stanhopes of Chevening*, 20–21.

64 For the duel of 1694, see *POAS*, 6: 525.

65 *POAS*, 6: 525.

66 An early usage of the vernacular term, from the Latin *pathicus*, denoting exclusively passive young catamites. It is more commonly found in the literature of the 1730s and 1740s; see Rousseau, "The Pursuit of Homosexuality in the Eighteenth Century," n. 13, 150, for a discussion of pathics.

67 See Harold Williams, ed., *Jonathan Swift Journal to Stella*, 2 vols. (Oxford: Clarendon Press: 1948), 1: 42. Using other contemporary documents than works by Swift, William T. Morgan, "An Eighteenth-Century Election in England," *Political Science Quarterly* 37 (1922): 595, points out that the Tory mob had branded Stanhope a sodomite throughout this general election.

68 I mention in passing that to his later discredit, Stanhope elevated William Cosby (1693–1736) in the American colonies. Cosby had served in the army and risen by the age of twenty-five to colonel and governor of Minorca. After that he was made governor of New Jersey, where he became involved in political difficulties that caused the authorities to inquire into the means by which he was elevated so quickly. On 31 March 1735 Lewis Morris wrote to James Alexander: "You shall know all I can discover of the great and worthy character of your great man [Cosby] who was once a handsome person of a man & the means of his rise known to every body acquainted with Lord Stanhope and almost to every body else;" a. s. l., New York Historical Society, Rutherford College. I am grateful to Eugene R. Sheridan, the editor of the Papers of Thomas Jefferson at Princeton University, for making a typescript of this letter, which will appear in his collected letters of Jefferson, available to me. There are no doubt many more references to Stanhope's sodomy than those I have found.

69 See W. A. Speck, *Stability and Strife: England 1714–1760* (Cambridge, MA: Harvard University Press, 1977), 186.

70 In *Swift's Verse: An Essay* (London: John Murray, 1929), 108–11, F. Elrington Ball attributed the ballad to Swift, but Harold Williams rejected the

attribution; see Williams, ed., *Poems of Jonathan Swift*, 3 vols. (Oxford, Clarendon Press, 1958), 3: 1087. Williams recounts the discovery of the ballads and its manuscripts (1087), a complex provenance, and notes that the election "drew forth a number of broadsides" in addition to these two ballads. I have seen the copy of the second ballad ridiculing Stanhope, especially his homosexuality, in the British Library.

71 Speck, *Stability and Strife*, 186.

72 The arrests of 1707 are referred to in an anonymous work of 1707, *Women-Hater's Lamentation* (London, 1707), those of 1709 briefly in John Dunton's "The He-Strumpet's, a Satyr on the Sodomite Club," in his *Athenianism*, 2 vols. (London, 1710), 2:93–99. Some discussion of these mass arrests is found in Alan Bray, *Homosexuality in Renaissance England* (London: Gay Men's Press, 1982), 93–96.

73 See Newman, *The Stanhopes of Chevening*, 25.

74 Matthew Prior, the English poet who was also the secretary of Portland's British embassy in Paris, remains a seminal figure in this quarrel. Prior, like Portland, despised Stanhope for reasons that remain murky and did what he could to blacken his name. Prior also sided with Portland in the quarrel against Stanhope and reported that Stanhope was leading a debauched life in Paris. But Prior's own sexuality remains so very much in doubt that one can hardly consider him a neutral observer in the matter. My sense is that all those implicated in the Paris intrigue—Portland, Stanhope, Prior—were perfectly well aware of the homosexual stakes involved; after all, William's actions had spoken plainly for themselves, and he had undeniably conferred privilege on those men who could court his deepest trust and devotion. See Newman, *The Stanhopes of Chevening*, 24–25, for further discussion of the matter. Prior's complex sexuality, however, is another matter that must be addressed on another occasion.

75 Speck, *Stability and Strife*, 186.

76 Quoted in Newman, *The Stanhopes of Chevening*, 27.

77 The phrase is borrowed from Eve K. Sedgwick, *Between Men: English Literature and Male Homosexual Desire* (New York: Columbia University Press, 1985), and is one that sheds light on many historical arrangements in the English culture of the Restoration and eighteenth century; not merely on its historical culture but its literature also (plays, poems, novels).

78 See Newman, *The Stanhopes of Chevening*, 90.

79 J. F. Naylor, *The British Aristocracy and the Peerage Bill of 1719* (Cambridge, MA: Harvard University Press, 1968).

80 J. H. Plumb, *Robert Walpole: A Biography*, 2 vols. (London: Cresset Press, 1956–60), 1: 126.

81 See Rae Blanchard, *Tracts and Pamphlets by Richard Steele* (Baltimore: The Johns Hopkins University Press, 1944), 457ff., who also provides background on the political circumstances and notes how Steele was criticized. Each number of the paper assumed knowledge of the previous one. Steele's

extended analogy is found on p. 465 (*Plebian*, no. 1), and specifically deals with Stanhope's homosexuality on p. 471 (*Plebian*, no. 2).

82 See Blanchard, *Tracts and Pamphlets of Richard Steele*, 471.

83 See Newman, *The Stanhopes of Chevening*, 87, who produces examples of Stanhope's correspondence over the appointment of pages who were apparently required to be "pretty brisk boys."

84 See Blanchard, *Tracts and Pamphlets of Richard Steele*, 468–82.

85 Commenting on his sodomitical lust, John Macky called him "a handsom [sic] black Man;" see A. R., ed., *Memoirs of the Secret Services of John Macky* (London, 1733), 54.

86 I have tried to explain why Stanhope was incapable of doing so financially, and I hope no one will think that at any point I have been suggesting Stanhope as the mysterious patron of 1694; I continue to believe it was Villiers.

87 See W. S. Lewis, ed., *The Yale Edition of Horace Walpole's Correspondence*, 48 vols. (New Haven: Yale University Press, 1937–83), 15:180.

88 For some of these, see G. S. Rousseau, "The Sorrows of Priapus: Anticlericalism, Homosocial Desire, and Richard Payne Knight," in G. S. Rousseau and Roy Porter, eds., *Sexual Underworlds of the Enlightenment* (Chapel Hill: University of North Carolina Press, 1987), 125–31.

89 Stanhope had married but in itself this proves nothing about his relation to younger men. I mention Addison and Steele because of the repeated charge in the 1720s, by the poet Pope among others, that they were "a couple of h — — — — [hermaphrodites, not homosexuals]"; see James Osborn, ed., *Observations, Anecdotes and Characters*, 2 vols. (Oxford: Clarendon Press, 1966), 1:80. Hermaphrodites, perfect and imperfect, normal and abnormal, ancient and modern, male and female, local and foreign, not homosexuals, were the concepts on the tongues of early eighteenth-century folk; much more work remains to be done on them than has been accomplished so far. The only use of the word "homosexual" in an eighteenth-century English text appears in Henry Fielding's *Adventures of Tom Jones* (1748), bk. 7, chap. 12, in the passage in which the vulgar militaristic Notherton claims that one of the soldiers in his regiment "always carries a *Homo* in his pocket," but the meaning here is different from our modern one and must be carefully differentiated. The *Oxford English Dictionary* is not to be trusted for its entries on either "homosexual" or "hermaphroditic."

Zealous in the Cause of Liberty: Self-Creation and Redemption in the Narrative of Ethan Allen

DANIEL E. WILLIAMS

Early on the morning of 10 May 1775, Colonel Ethan Allen led a small force of eighty-three Green Mountain Boys before the walls of Fort Ticonderoga. Realizing that reinforcements would take too long to arrive, he decided to attack the fortress before the British Regulars awoke and discovered his presence. At best, such a venture was a bold undertaking; at worst, it was a reckless attempt by a raw, undisciplined band of Yankee farmers to capture one of Great Britain's mightiest forts. Viewing the situation as "hazardous," Allen paused to offer encouragement to his men:

> Friends and fellow soldiers, you have, for a number of years past, been the scourge and terror of arbitrary power. Your valour has been famed abroad, and acknowledged, as appears by the advice and orders to me (from the general assembly of Connecticut) to surprise and take the garrison before us. I now propose to advance before you, and in person conduct you through the wicket-gate; for we must this morning either quit our pretensions to valour, or possess ourselves of this fortress in a few minutes; and, in as much as it is a desperate attempt, (which none but the bravest of men dare undertake) I do not urge it on any contrary to his will. You that will undertake voluntarily, poise your firelocks. (6-7)[1]

After finishing his speech, Allen led his men through the fort's outer gate and confronted the lone sentry. The guard raised his musket, but the gun snapped without firing, and the man then turned and ran into the fort's parade ground. Allen and his band pursued the guard into the fort and, once inside, he ordered his men to face the barracks, where most of the Regulars were still asleep.

At that moment, one of the guards inside the fort charged with his bayonet. Turning to meet the attack, Allen, with the flat edge of his sword, cracked the guard on the head, knocking him to the ground. Bleeding from the wound, and having dropped his gun, the defenseless man begged for quarter, which Allen granted on the condition that he lead him to the fort's commanding officer. After being taken to the door of the officers' quarters, Allen recounted the scene as follows:

> [I] ordered the commander (capt. Delaplace) to come forth instantly, or I would sacrifice the whole garrison; at which the capt. came immediately to the door with his breeches in his hand, when I ordered him to deliver to me the fort instantly, who asked me by what authority I demanded it; I answered, "In the name of the great Jehova, and the Continental Congress." (The authority of the Congress being very little known at that time) he began to speak again; but I interrupted him, and with my drawn sword over his head, again demanded an immediate surrender of the garrison; to which he then complied . . . . (8–9)

And so the strategic fortress of Ticonderoga fell, conquered by a strange, defiant group of Yankee farmers, whose only identifiable piece of uniform was a sprig of evergreen stuck into their caps. This dramatic scene of conquest, emotionally symbolic as well as militarily significant, almost instantly became part of the mythology which sprang up around the American Revolution.

Like most myths, this one was only partially true. But unlike most myths, this one did not slowly evolve through the mists of popular legend. One man, rather than many, was responsible for popularizing the vivid confrontation between British Regulars and Yankee farmers, between a startled, half-dressed British commander and his wild, sword-wielding adversary, and that man was Ethan Allen himself. In the narrative of his Revolutionary experiences, written four years later, Allen described the taking of Fort Ticonderoga in colorful detail and heroic terms, and it was from his description alone that the popular image emerged. Satisfied with Allen's splendid account, few have bothered to look beyond his version.[2]

Between Allen's experiences and his descriptions, however, there are a number of discrepancies. To begin, mighty Fort Ticonderoga was not so mighty. After receiving the fort from the French at the close of the Seven Years' War, the British had neglected to maintain the structure. With one outer wall broken through, and other walls and roofs crumbling, the fort's commander, less than a year before Allen's attack, complained to the home government that "the Fort and Barracks are in a most ruinous situation."[3] In addition to the general disrepair, Allen also neglected to mention that Ticonderoga was guarded only by a skeletal force of fifty soldiers, of whom only a handful were fit for duty and who had not even heard that war had erupted between the mother country and the colonies. Moreover, throughout the spring Captain Delaplace had shown more interest in maintaining his garden than he had in preparing his defenses. As for the rousing pre-attack speech, none of the other Ticonderoga accounts mentioned anything like it, and, in fact, Allen would have been foolish to pause within hearing distance of the gates and speak loud enough to be heard by eighty-three men, thereby jeopardizing the crucial element of surprise.

The famous confrontation between Delaplace, holding his pants in his hands, and Allen, waving his huge sword around his head and proclaiming the new order of God and Congress, as well proved to be more Allen than actuality. Allen did not mention that he was accompanied by another colonel, Benedict Arnold, who carried a commission and orders more official than any he had.[4] Nor did he mention that, in response to his shouts at the door of the officers' quarters, it was a British lieutenant, Jocelyn Feltham, and not Delaplace, who appeared pants in hand. Mistaking Feltham for the commander, Allen indeed demanded the surrender of the fort, but the lieutenant stalled, hoping that the Regulars would counterattack. When Allen realized his mistake, he shouted for the commander, threatening him with physical abuse if he did not appear, shocking both Arnold and Feltham.[5] After several minutes, Delaplace finally appeared, dressed in full uniform. Seeing that his troops were well guarded, he then surrendered his sword.

What Allen actually said during the final confrontation has also been amended by the later recollections of those who accompanied him to the officers' quarters. As opposed to initially shouting for the fort's surrender in the thunderous names of Jehova and Congress, one account stated that Allen shouted: "Come out of there, you damned old Rat," while another claimed that he called: "Come out of there you sons of British whores, or I'll smoke you out."[6] According to Feltham's own account, only later, as he stalled for time, did he ask Allen and Arnold by what authority they attacked Ticonderoga. Arnold immediately produced his fancy commission, while Allen, having no such document, declared that he was acting under the orders of the Connecticut government. Charles A. Jellison, Allen's most reliable biographer, states that at this point, Allen, having realized the historic significance of the moment, and having composed himself, searched for something more appropriate, more dramatic, to say.[7] To answer Feltham's question, and as well to compensate for his lack of official commission, Allen then invoked the powers of God and Congress.

So Ethan Allen lied, at least on one level. In order to make himself greater and grander than he really was, the braggart reduced the contributions of others and enlarged his own. For the sake of his own bloated vanity, he distorted historical fact. But this view is equally as superficial as it is undeniable. To conclude that Allen is a liar, simply another overrated Revolutionary hero, overlooks a much deeper and more significant level of historical — and literary — experience. In changing and rearranging the materials of his past, in shaping factual chaos into a narrative framework, Allen did not so much distort reality as he dramatized it.[8] He was, after all, author as well as character. The freedoms taken to enhance and embellish, not only in the Ticonderoga passages but throughout the narrative, were the same freedoms he claimed in his own life. Revolutionary long before there was a Revolution, Allen overran the established borders of his life at an early age and claimed the right to become whatever he wanted to be. Born in western Connecticut, he grew up in Cornwall, "at this time the crudest of frontier communities."[9] Without any formal education, and despite the limitations and the hardships of his isolated wilderness life, he soon proclaimed that he was a philosopher, that he was a gentleman, and that he was a leader of men. By giving utterance to his pretensions, by giving voice to his ambition, Allen became all of these things. For this man, whose wild presumptions recognized few boundaries, to articulate was to affirm.

The same self-creative powers that turned a backwoods frontiersman, notorious for his blasphemy and brawling, into a gentleman philosopher were employed in writing the narrative. Although sometimes syntactically crude and grammatically incorrect, Allen was an accomplished writer.[10] The narrative was by no means his only effort at writing. According to Jellison, he had a "compulsion" to write and would often lock himself away to turn scattered thoughts into written words.[11] Allen himself stated that "this method of scribbling I practiced for many years. From it I experienced great advantages in the progression of learning and knowledge."[12] Not only did he learn to shape and organize his thoughts this way, but he also discovered that he could create, or at least manipulate, perception and that, ultimately, reality was made up of perception.[13]

Most of Allen's actual publications were concerned with the controversy between the colony of New York and the settlers of the New Hampshire Grants, which first became the Republic of Vermont and later the state of Vermont. As the most prominent and colorful leader of the Grants, Allen led the Green Mountain Boys, the Grants militia, to oppose numerous New York sheriffs, surveyors, and settlers. But the skirmishes between Yorkers and Yankees took place in print as well as in the wilderness. In response to the proclamations issued by a succession of New York governors, Allen published a number of pamphlets, letters, and newspaper articles.[14] All acted as propaganda, promoting the cause of the Grants settlers, and in all of them he reduced the complexities of the conflict. The Yorkers were greedy, corrupt, land–hungry aristocrats who only pressed their claims for speculation and profit, while the Yankees were hard-working, independent, honest farmers who had both bought and earned their land. Such a reduction was too simplified to be true, but Allen gained sympathy for his cause. Although he signed his efforts as "A Lover of Reason and Truth," he at times took great liberty in relating the truth, using hyperbole and melodrama to depict the Yorkers as evil, brutal people.[15] Clearly, Allen understood that what is perceived assumes the place of what is and that writing controls perception. Conscious of the ideological implications of public discourse, he not only published in order to affirm and verify his cause, but also to create and shape his cause.

In his Revolutionary narrative, Allen's causes were both patriotic and personal, but in describing his experiences he merged the two, so that self came to reflect society. Using deliberate rhetorical strategies, he constructed a social reality that sharply displayed the conflict (as he perceived it) between two orders, the traditional British system, which emphasized class hierarchy, and the upstart American system, which promoted individual opportunism. In order to give life to the latter, he consciously manipulated his materials so that his example personified the greater contest between the mother country and the colonies. But Allen's narrative was not a tale of conquest; rather, it was a tale of captivity. Although he began with the capture of Ticonderoga, he quickly introduced his defeat and capture at Montreal, and in the rest of the narrative he dramatized his struggles to survive in British prisons.[16] Continually abused and nearly destroyed, he experienced great suffering and was witness to even greater horrors. Yet Allen, as he presented himself, was never defeated. Regardless of the brutality or the degradation, the cruelty or the humiliation, the character Allen was ever defiant, never passive.

Allen used the trajectory of his struggles to promote both himself and his society, but in doing so he as well conveyed a new set of standards and values. Just as he refused to concede that backwoods meant primitive, so too he refused to concede that captivity meant defeat. Using his self-creative powers, and despite substantial evidence to the contrary, he rejected any notion of his inferiority. As long as he perceived himself to be unconquerable (or at least as long as he presented himself to be), he was. Originally published in 1779 as *A Narrative of Colonel Ethan Allen's Captivity*, Allen's written account gave calculated credence to his defiance. Employing narrative techniques intended to evoke sympathetic reader response, he rearranged the traditional configurations of power. British generals and jailers were all described as powerless to overcome the will of one individual, and the more they conspired to defeat and destroy, the more they defeated themselves. Using imagination as a creative force, Allen attacked the British by altering traditional perceptions of authority and autonomy. By denying the influence of British governance, he seized the right to govern himself.

Allen's narrative, then, became a microcosm of the Revolution. By dramatizing his struggles against captivity, by celebrating his defiance against authority, the narrative illustrated the greater colonial struggle to secure political and social self-determination. Yet Allen's defiance was not a single act, but a process, and it was the process of rebellion that he so carefully narrated. By illustrating his steps from victory to defeat, and then from captivity to liberty, he provided and promoted a clearly marked path of resistance. By dramatizing his experiences through narrative, character, and context, by presenting himself as an example of resolute defiance, he demonstrated the self-creative power which the Americans required not only to defeat the British, but also to invent themselves and their nation.

Not long after "his" conquest of Ticonderoga, Allen joined the ill-fated invasion of Canada. Although his narrative was intentionally unclear on this issue, he held no official rank or commission in the invasion, serving only as a civilian scout. But Allen, as he characterized himself, was never a man to accept limitations. When given the task of journeying into the Canadian wilderness to inform the populace that the invading Americans meant them no harm, he heartily embraced his role. Instead of merely informing the inhabitants, he sought to convert them. In his narrative he stated: "I passed through all the parishes on the river Sorrel . . . preaching politics . . . and so far met with [as] good success as an itinerant" (14). Indeed, by his own account and those of his biographers, Allen became a successful preacher, converting hundreds to the American cause.[17] With his boundless enthusiasm and towering confidence, he used his powers of persuasion to proselytize for liberty.

In his narrative, Allen continued to proselytize. When describing the horrors of his captivity, he was as well "preaching politics," seeking to convert lukewarm and even indifferent readers.[18] As any good New Light itinerant, he attempted to move his audience by first scaring them with visions of hell, in this case British prisons, and then offering them salvation in the form of liberty. But liberty had to be earned, and by dramatizing his own example, Allen illustrated the requisite steps to political paradise. First, the unconverted had to be excited so that they would repent of their sinful indifference. Next, once they had been given a glimpse of the coming glory, they had to pass through a series of tests and hardships so that they could prove their commitment. Finally, they had to resist a number of temptations in which they were either tempted with visions of corrupt wealth and power or with political atheism. Judging by its popularity, Allen's narrative was as compelling as it was dramatic. First published serially in the tri-weekly *Pennsylvania Packet* in the late spring of 1779, the narrative "immediately became a best seller" and was republished eight more times within two years.[19] Certainly Allen succeeded in promoting the cause of liberty, and in so doing he as well succeeded in promoting his own self-created self.

In his "Introduction," Allen clearly articulated his intention to convert readers. Many, including "some men . . . appointed into office, in these States," were content to view the war "with the same careless indifferency, as they do the pages of the Roman history" (1). To attack political indifference, then, he published the "extraordinary scenes" of his captivity, especially "the cruel and relentless disposition of the enemy, towards the prisoners . . . " (1). Such statements point to an obvious rhetorical strategy; by depicting a cruel, oppressive enemy, Allen could make American readers feel that they were oppressed. The more ruthless the enemy, the more aroused the reader. But Allen was equally careful to introduce the dangers of "the tory influence" (1). He stated "that the instances [of such influence] are (I hope) but rare; and it stands all freemen in hand, to prevent their further influence, which . . . would be the most baneful to the liberties and happiness of this country . . . " (1-2). Here another strategy was announced; the Tories were enemies, and by separating them from the rest of colonial society, by depicting their invidious cruelty, Allen further reduced the complexities of conflicting loyalties.

At several points, both structurally and thematically, Allen's captivity narrative reflected the conventions of earlier Indian captivity narratives. Red coats and prison ships were easily moved into the place of red men and wilderness. Following the established pattern, Allen's entry into captivity was characterized by a sudden, violent movement away from the comfortable and the familiar. Having recklessly agreed to attack Montreal, he was captured after his supporting forces had failed to appear and after half of his own force had deserted. As a foreshadowing of what was to follow, Allen was nearly executed by both an Indian, whose "hellish visage" betokened "the wrath of devils and damned spirits," and the British commander, General Prescott, who thundered: "I will not execute you now, but you shall grace a halter at Tyburn, God damn ye" (24, 25). After being vexed by these devils, he then was given a taste of hell. Treated as a common criminal instead of as a prisoner of war, he was chained hand and foot and taken on board a British vessel in the St. Lawrence. Allen stated that "the irons were so close upon my ancles, that I could not lie down in any other manner than on my back. I was put into the lowest and most wretched part of the vessel, where I got the favour of a chest to sit on, the same answered for my bed at night" (26). Despite his entreaties, Allen declared that he remained on the chest for six weeks, enduring the severest of physical torments as well as the taunts of Tories.

This vision of hell, however, was only the beginning of Allen's narrative descent into human barbarity. He and the men who were captured with him were soon imprisoned on board a merchant ship bound for London. The ship's captain, Brook Watson, was "a man of malicious and cruel disposition," but even his cruelty could not match the malevolence of a group of Tories who sailed along as passengers. Allen declared that the prisoners were treated "with that spirit of bitterness, which is the peculiar characteristic of tories, when they have the friends of American in their power, measuring their loyalty to the English king, by the barbarity, fraud, and deceit which they exercise towards the whigs" (32). Packed into a small hold with no other furniture except "two excrement tubs," Allen and thirty-three others remained in their "filthy enclosure" for the entire voyage, suffering the abuses of "every blackguard sailor and tory on board" (33). According to Allen, their treatment was "derogatory to every sentiment of honour and humanity" (33). Their "den" indeed came to resemble hell. Allen stated:

> we were denied fresh water, except a small allowance, which was very inadequate to our wants; and in consequence of the stench of the place, each of us was soon followed with a diarrhoea and fever, which occasioned an intolerable thirst. When we asked for water, we were most commonly . . . insulted and derided; and to add to all the horrors of the place, it was so dark that we could not see each other, and were covered with body lice. (35)

Yet Allen, as he described himself, not only survived the miseries of this voyage, but he thrived in his adversity.

In his refusal to cower, Allen's responses to hardship and cruelty resembled earlier Puritan responses. In the doctrine of adversity, captive Puritans, such as Mary Rowlandson or John Williams, interpreted their afflictions as signs of God's concern, even as signs of God's favor.[20] The devilish Indians were allowed to commit their barbarities by divine will; through them, God was chastening and correcting his chosen. Hardship and cruelty were not only used to test the captive's faith, but to redirect his or her attention away from the vanities of self and world and back to God. As a freethinker, Allen did not resign his fate to Providence or surrender the self to God.[21] However, he did present the severities of his captivity as a test of his will, as an affirmation of his cause, and as a lesson in liberty. Fully aware of the narrative requirements in a tale of captivity, perhaps the most popular of all colonial genres, he shaped his experiences to reflect an easily identifiable pattern of affliction. When describing the hopelessness of his situation at Montreal, he remarked: "I perceived it would be a day of trouble, if not of rebuke . . . " (17).

Allen's "rebukes" came in many forms. In addition to the brutal conditions of his captivity, he described numerous instances in which he was derided; but derision merely inflamed his passion for liberty. When insulted, he insulted back. When abused, he attacked. At one point, when he was first thrust into the hell of the ship's hold, he clearly exhibited his refusal to accept inferiority. He wrote: "About the same time a lieutenant among the tories, insulted me in a grievous manner, saying that I ought to have been executed for my rebellion against New York, and spit in my face; upon which, though I was handcuffed, I sprang at him with both hands, and knocked him partly down" (33–34). This same defiant spirit was dramatized throughout the narrative. When the merchant ship unloaded its human cargo at Falmouth, the prisoners were marched through the city to Pendennis Castle, where they were to be held. Despite his filthy appearance, Allen proudly paraded before the "multitudes" who lined the streets and rooftops to glimpse the rebels. Once imprisoned at Pendennis, he continued to perform. Although expecting to be executed, he described his determination to conceal his fears from the guards and spectators, who "were perpetually shaking the halter" at him: "I nevertheless treated them with scorn and contempt, and . . . could conceive of nothing more in my power but to keep up my spirits and behave in a daring, soldier-like manner, that I might exhibit a good sample of American fortitude" (40).

As he described himself, Allen actually enjoyed performing for the hostile audiences that surrounded him when he was allowed to exercise in the castle green.[22] He declared that he "often entertained such audiences, with harangues on the impracticability of Great Britain's conquering the (then) colonies of America" (43). Whenever questioned concerning his motives for rebellion, he stated that he "expatiated on American freedom," and whenever he was given the opportunity to dramatize his political beliefs, he did (42). He described one encounter in which he entertained his spectators with an illustration of the new order he represented: "At one of these times I asked a gentleman for a bowl of punch, and he ordered his servant to bring it, which he did, and offered it [to] me, but I refused to take it from the hand of his servant; he then gave it to me with his own hand" (43).

In refusing to be served by the servant, Allen demanded to be recognized as a gentleman. Early in his life he had claimed for himself gentleman-status, and now, during his captivity, his greatest struggle was to maintain this status in the most abject circumstances.[23] When first captured, General Prescott had threatened to strike him with a cane, but the self-styled gentleman had responded with a defiant declaration that he was not to be beaten: "I told him [Prescott] he would do well not to cane me, for I was not accustomed to it, and shook my fist at him, telling him that that was the beetle of mortality for him . . . " (23). Not long after, when he was kept chained in the ship's hold, he wrote to Prescott requesting better treatment: "I reminded him of the kind and generous manner of my treatment to the prisoners I took at Ticonderoga; the injustice and ungentleman like usage, which I had met with from him, and demanded gentleman like usage . . . " (28). Although the treatment he received was brutal and degrading, he never stopped demanding to be "treated as other gentleman of my merit" (42). The refusal to drink from a servant's hand was but one example of a long series. Allen was determined to be recognized for his "merit." Like the Puritan captives who refused to surrender their faith, he refused to surrender his self-elevated conception of self.

Perhaps the severest tests of Allen's gentleman-status came during the next phase of his captivity. After King George III had decided that Allen and his fellow prisoners would not be hanged as traitors, they were sent back to America on a British man-of-war. But once on board he discovered that he was in a worse situation than before. He stated that "a Captain of a man of war was more arbitrary than a king, as he could view his territory with a look of his eye, and a movement of his finger commanded obedience. . . . I felt myself more desponding than I had done ay any time before . . . " (46). Allen soon received his first taste of the captain's tyranny.

> When we were first brought on board, Captain Symonds ordered all the prisoners, and most of the hands on board, to go on the deck, and caused to be read in their hearing, a certain code of laws, or rules for regulation and ordering of their behavior; and then in a sovereign manner, ordered the prisoners, me in particular, off the deck, and never to come on it again; for said he, this is a place for gentlemen to walk. (45)

Allen was then taken down into the ship to the "cable tire," where, he was told, "this is your place," but, true to his self-created character, he refused to remain in his "place" (45). He wrote that "two days after [the captain's hierarchy had been imposed] I shaved and cleansed myself as well as I could, and went on deck. The Captain spoke to me in great rage, and said, 'Did I not order you not to come on deck?' I answered him, that at the same time he said, 'That it was a place for gentlemen to walk;' That I was Col. Allen, but had not been properly introduced to him" (46).[24]

Throughout the return voyage, Allen repeatedly confronted the captain, seeking better food and better treatment, but all relief was denied. As conditions deteriorated, he accused Symonds of intentional abuse and neglect. In reply to one of his entreaties, Symonds responded: "that it was no matter how soon I was dead, and that he was no way anxious to preserve the lives of rebels, but wished them all dead" (54). Yet despite the harshness of his captivity, the character Allen bantered the captain whenever he had occasion. In reply to still another one of his requests, the captain stated that "he needed no directions of mine [as] to how to treat a rebel; that the British would conquer the American rebels, hang the Congress, and such as promoted the rebellion (me in particular). . . . I gave him for answer, that if they stayed till they conquered America, before they hanged me, I should die of old age" (55).

Allen, however, nearly died. Similar to earlier Puritan captives, his captivity, as he narrated it, was marked by a steady deterioration of body and mind. Before redemption was possible, the captive had to be figuratively destroyed, so that a newly converted self could emerge. But unlike the Puritan captives, Allen's reduction strengthened, rather than destroyed, his pride. After being transferred to another ship bound for Halifax, Allen and his fellow prisoners experienced even worse conditions than they had under Symonds. He stated that "I now found myself under a worse capt. . . . for Montague was loaded with prejudice against every body; and every thing that was not stamped with royalty; and being by nature underwitted, his wrath was heavier than the others" (58). Yet what made this part of his captivity all the more unbearable was the outbreak of smallpox and scurvy. Both sailors and captives began to succumb to the one or to the other or to both. Several of the crew died on the passage, and even Allen's health, once so sturdy, began to ebb: "I was weak and feeble in consequence of so long and cruel a captivity . . . " (59). When he applied for relief, he was refused: "I tried to reason the matter with him [Montague], but found him proof against reason; I also help up honor to view . . . but found his honor impenetrable, I then endeavored to touch his humanity, but found he had none" (59). Not only did the captain refuse any relief to the captives, but he also forbade the ship's surgeon from attending to any of the sick prisoners. But despite disease and death, Allen — as he portrayed himself — endured.

In Halifax the captives were placed on a small prison ship anchored in the harbor. With little food and no medicine, they soon reached their lowest point. But Allen, true to his idealized self, instead of expressing a selfish concern for self-preservation during this period of crisis, declared his loyalty to his fellow prisoners and to his cause:

> here [on the ship] we were cruelly pinched with hunger; it seemed to me that we had not more than one third of the common allowance; we were all seized with violent hunger and faintness; we divided our scanty allowance as exact as possible. I shared the same fate with the rest, and though they offered me more than an even share, I refused to accept it, as it was a time of substantial distress, which in my opinion I ought to partake equally with the test, and set an example of virtue and fortitude to our little commonwealth. (62)[25]

To save his men, many of whom were "dangerously ill of the scurvy," Allen wrote a stream of letters to Montague and to nearby doctors, but the only response was an order from the captain to the guards not to deliver any more letters (62).

Eventually, Allen's "little commonwealth" was removed to shore. The seriously ill prisoners were taken to a hospital, while Allen and the others were placed in the Halifax jail. This resulted in only slight improvement, for the jail was commanded by General Massey, a man — according to Allen — "as inflexible as the Devil himself" (66).[26] Placed in "one common large room, without regard to rank, education, or any other accomplishment" and with only "excrement tubs" as furniture, the problem of survival continued (65). Yet, despite their degrading circumstances, they refused to surrender their pride of self. "Our first attention," Allen declared, "was the preservation of ourselves and [our] injured little republic, the rest of our time we devoted interchangeably to politics and philosophy" (67). Within the narrative, then, the struggle for status, for affirmation of a new social order based on "merit," occurred simultaneously with the struggle for survival. No matter how severe "the malignant hand of Britain" fell upon them, the prisoners, especially Allen, refused to be humbled (68).

Allen's determination "to obtain gentleman-like usage" finally succeeded (68). After being shipped to New York, he was officially recognized as a gentleman when he was placed on parole along with other Revolutionary officers. As long as he stayed within the limits of his parole, as long as he kept his word of honor, he was free to roam the city from dawn to dusk. Honor, however, as Allen defined and described it, was a scarce commodity in New York, particularly among the British and

Loyalists who guarded the private soldiers. As Allen and his fellow officers walked about the streets of New York, the several thousand private soldiers and citizens taken captive during the various battles for New York were crowded into any available building, often into churches. Once imprisoned, they were left to starve.[27]

During his parole, Allen testified that he witnessed even crueler forms of captivity than he had experienced. Indeed, in the last part of the narrative he described shocking scenes of horror and suffering, far exceeding any of the torments he had survived. By his own estimate he stated that "about 2000 [prisoners] perished with hunger, cold, and sickness occasioned by the filth of their prisons" (93). Surrounded by scenes of atrocity and barbarity, Allen was taught a different sort of lesson. After struggling to secure his honor, he was shown all that was dishonorable, including the hypocrisies of the most elevated British gentlemen. Moreover, his role as a witness served as a test of his devotion. Having been reborn out of his own hell, having had his determination strengthened by the ordeals of imprisonment, his commitment to the cause of liberty was now tested. Spurning all temptations, Allen responded with outrage and indignation.

To create the context in which to interpret the scenes of horror, he wrote that, once "the private soldiers . . . were crowded into churches," they were abused and insulted by "slavish Hessian guards . . . by merciless Britons . . . but above all [by] the hellish delight and triumph of the tories over them, as they were dying by hundreds" (79). To justify the tone of his outrage, he added:

> This was too much for me to bear as a spectator; for I saw the tories exulting over the dead bodies of their murdered countrymen. I have gone into the churches, and seen sundry of the prisoners in the agonies of death, in consequence of very hunger, and others speechless and near death. . . . The filth of these churches (in consequence of the fluxes) was almost beyond description. The floors were covered with excrements. . . . I have seen in one of these churches seven dead at the same time, lying among the excrements of their bodies. . . . I have seen whole gangs of tories making derision, and exulting over the dead, saying there goes another load of damned rebels. (79–80)

Allen's language of indignation conveyed a significant political message. The bitter paradoxes were all too apparent. The churches, instead of offering comfort and refuge, had been turned into a secularized hell.[28] Yet his depiction of the "tories" clearly suggested that this hell on earth had been created by men corrupted by a false political faith. As devils, the "tories" had perverted all values and modes of behavior in their attempt to oppress those who believed in liberty. But in describing this man-made hell, Allen as well implied that those who could maintain their faith in liberty, those who refused to give in to despair, still could achieve salvation.

As he described his experiences, Allen offered proof both of his loyalty and that of other prisoners. He mentioned the sufferings, for example, of two brothers who preferred death over dishonor. Starving and sick, the brothers "had been urged to enlist in the British service, but had both resolved to die first" (83). Yet "the resolution of the two brothers" was by no means exceptional (84). "Many hundreds . . . " he stated, "submitted to death rather than enlist in the British service" (83). Similarly, Allen exhibited the same resolution when he was tempted. He stated that one day he was contacted by "a British officer of rank and importance," who offered to make him "a colonel of a regiment of new levies (alias tories) in the British service" (94). The officer further proposed that Allen accompany him to England, where he would be introduced to high British officials and "probably to the king" (94). The officer added that "I should be cloathed equal to such an introduction, and instead of paper rags, be paid in hard guineas" (94). Once this grand tour was competed, he was then to "embark with General Burgoyne, and assist in the reduction of the country" (94). In return for his services, he was to receive "a large tract of land, whether on the New Hampshire grants, or in Connecticut . . . " (95). According to the narrative, Allen wasted little time in rejecting the offer, and indescribing the scene of rejection he carefully fashioned an appropriate typological context: "I viewed the offer of land to be similar to that which the devil offered Jesus Christ. 'To give him all the kingdoms of the world, if he would fall down and worship him.' [sic] when at the same time the damned soul had not one foot of land upon earth" (95). Allen rejected the devil's offer, and in doing so he displayed his strength of resolution. In this resisting of temptation he reinforced his rhetorical dichotomy of good and evil. In order to earn redemption (liberty), he had to maintain his faith by enduring affliction and by resisting evil, regardless of the vicissitudes of war.

One of the more obvious differences between Allen's captivity and earlier Puritan narratives was that, for the most part, he was not isolated. Throughout his captivity he was imprisoned with a number of other American prisoners, who equally shared his ordeals and his commitments. His struggle to achieve liberty, then, reflected a national as well as individual movement. The hell created by the British was shared by many who, like Allen, longed for liberty. Despite the "insatiable thirst for cruelty" of their guards, they denied and disdained the power which curtailed their freedom (96). In the concluding pages of his narrative, Allen carefully documented the examples of other captives who suffered, endured, and defied. Arrested on what he called "artful, mean and pitiful pretences" he had his parole revoked and was placed in the "provost-gaol" of New York (97).[29] There he observed numerous attempts by the guards to reduce the prisoners either to submission or to death. One patriot officer, Allen testified, was kept four months in the dungeon "with murderers, thieves, and every species of criminal, and all for the sole crime of unshaken fidelity to his country; but his spirits were above dejection, and his mind unconquerable" (98). Similarly, several other officers were variously abused and imprisoned because of "their fidelity and zealous attachment to their country's cause" (101). According to Allen, the British used the Provost dungeons in order to destroy the new patriot faith. He wrote that "It [the use of the Provost dungeons] may be with propriety called the British Inquisition, and calculated to support their oppressive measures and designs, by suppressing the spirit of liberty" (104).

Yet no matter the torments of the British Inquisition, Allen and his fellow prisoners remained faithful to liberty, refusing to re-embrace the old orthodoxy of King and Parliament. Instead of submitting, they rebelled, once again creating their own social order despite dungeon walls and abusive guards. As a final act of self-creative power, Allen reaffirmed the new order by damning those who damned him. In order to exercise this power of self, he leveled his rage against Sir William Howe, then commander of the British forces, and Joshua Loring, a Tory who had been responsible for the prisoners' commissary. Far from exhibiting the honor expected of a gentleman of his rank, Howe — according to Allen — had "prescribed and directed the murders and cruelties" against the captives, while Loring, in response, had carried out Howe's directives. To place their inhuman hypocrisies in an appropriately hellish context, Allen stated:

> This Loring is a monster! . . . There is not his like in human shape: He exhibits a smiling countenance, seems to wear a phiz of humanity, but has been instrumentally capable of the most consummate acts of wickedness . . . murdering premeditately (in cold blood) near or quite 2000 helpless prisoners, and that in the most clandestine, mean and shameful manner (at N. York.) He is the most mean spirited, cowardly, deceitful, and destructive animal in God's creation below, and legions of infernal devils, with all their tremendous horrors, are impatiently ready to receive Howe and him . . . into the most exquisite agonies of the hottest regions of hell fire. (107)

By transporting Howe, one of the highest British officials, and Loring, one of the highest Tories, to the lowest regions of hell, Allen symbolically corrected the system of values which had been corrupted by unnatural abuses of power. More than simply illustrating his insolence and his indignation, such transporting gave added emphasis to the self-creative power of liberty. By turning the highest into the lowest, by denying the traditional distinctions of rank, and by redefining the qualities of "merit," he demonstrated the strength of his beliefs to refashion the world. Indeed, he dramatized his revolutionary zeal.

Ultimately, Allen's faith was rewarded. In May of 1778, after nearly three years of captivity, he was exchanged for a British officer of equal rank. His redemption, having been arranged by Washington, resulted in his salvation. In commenting upon his release, Allen and Elias Boudinot, his American escort, agreed that "sweet liberty was the foundation of our gladness" (122). When crossing the Hudson to Elizabethtown, New Jersey, he stated that he "sailed . . . in a transport of joy, [and] landed on liberty ground" (122–23). In the new social order, which Allen so enthusiastically embraced, liberty was salvation.[30] After returning to Vermont, Allen's friends appropriately greeted him "as one rose from the dead" (124). There, while celebrating his resurrection, he declared: "we moved the flowing bowl, and rural felicity, sweetened with friendship, glowed in each countenance" (124).

Certainly, Allen's narrative journey had taken him, literally and figuratively, through hell. His return "from the dead" signified a successful pilgrimage which had brought him through the gradual stages of conversion. His early enthusiasm had been tested, strengthened, and shaped by the ordeals of captivity, finally resulting in a passionate commitment to liberty. His faith in the joys of liberty had enabled him to endure all the damning he had been subjected to by British officers and Tory jailers. His narrative, written within a year of his return, carefully displayed his journey, and, like the testimonies of earlier captives, it demonstrated his devotion and confirmed his redemption.

Moreover, the narrative was intended to promote, as well as demonstrate, political salvation. For the sake of readers Allen retraced his steps from victory to defeat, from captivity to liberty, and from reckless eagerness to firm resolve. The lessons learned along the way were well illustrated, and readers, by following his narrative journey, could experience for themselves his insights and his perceptions. Through the trials and torments of his captivity he taught that submission to tyranny resulted in a death of one sort or another, that happiness depended on liberty, and that liberty demanded total commitment. In this way the narrative itself served as a converting influence. In his introduction he had proclaimed his intention to attack indifference, and throughout his narrative he had carried on this attack, reducing the complexities of issues, describing the war as a conflict between good and evil, and filling his pages with scenes of cruelty intended to arouse indignation. His most compelling lesson, however, was his self-created self.

Throughout his life, Allen was recognized for his originality. Despite misgivings about his military leadership, Washington was favorably impressed with Allen. In a letter written shortly after their meeting, Washington wrote that "there is an original something in him that commands admiration; and his long captivity and sufferings have only served to increase if possible, his enthusiastic zeal."[31] Similarly, Jeremy Belknap, the New Hampshire historian, commented to a friend that Allen was "an original in his way, but as rough and boisterous as the scenes he has passed through."[32] His friend, Ebenezer Hazard, agreed, yet added a note of caution: "Allen is an original; at least I never met with a genius like him. Had his natural talents been cultivated by a liberal education, he would have made no bad figure among the sons of science; but perhaps his want of such an education is not to be lamented, as, unless he had more grace it would make him a dangerous member of society."[33] What Washington and Belknap praised, and what Hazard feared, was Allen's self-creative power. Alexander Graydon, who was imprisoned in New York with Allen, declared: "I have seldom met with a man, possessing . . . a stronger mind, or whose mode of expression was more vehement and oratorical. Notwithstanding that Allen might have had something of the insubordinate, lawless frontier spirit in his composition. . . . he appeared to me to be a man of generosity and honor."[34] In reality, at least in some respects, Allen was indeed "lawless." Because of his defiance of New York sheriffs and settlers, he was a wanted criminal with a price on his head. Yet, just as he refused to limit his ambitions and proclaimed himself to be a gentleman philosopher, so too he refused to acquiesce to either New York's or Great Britain's view of him as a criminal. Allen recognized that, for those who believed in liberty, lawless often meant limitless.

Shortly before he was to be released, Allen was removed form the Provost jail and taken to Staten Island, where he recuperated and rested for two days. As he was drinking wine with several British officers one evening, he remarked: "I made an observation on my transition from provost criminal to the company of gentlemen, adding that I was the same man still . . . " (121). Social distinctions, he implied, depended on perceptions, not on intrinsic values. The differences between a criminal and a gentleman were adjudged by society, and such judgments were at best subjective. Self-perception, rather than social perception, was more important in determining essential distinctions. To create his self, Allen freely selected from a variety of possible self-definitions, and through this artistic process of self-creation he proclaimed himself to be a hero of the Revolution, a gentleman of honor, and a saint of liberty. His narrative fully reflected the freedoms he took in self-creation. That he lied, enhanced, or reshaped was immaterial. *A Narrative of Colonel Ethan Allen's Captivity* at once affirmed his proclamations of self and demonstrated his power of self-creation.

NOTES

1 The standard edition is Ethan Allen, *A Narrative of Colonel Ethan Allen's Captivity*, ed. Brooks Hindle (New York: Corinth Books, 1961). All further citations will be taken from this volume.
2 Scholarship on Ethan Allen has been limited primarily to biographical works. For the most reliable biography, see Charles A. Jellison, *Ethan Allen Frontier Hero* (Syracuse: Syracuse University Press, 1985). For an older yet still valuable work, see John Pell, *Ethan Allen* (Boston: Houghton Mifflin, 1925). For other biographical works, see Stephen H. Holbrook, *Ethan Allen* (New York: Macmillan, 1944) and Edwin P. Hoyt, *The Damndest Yankee: Ethan Allen and His Clan* (Brattleboro, VT: The Stephen Greene Press, 1976). Because of the controversial nature of *Reason the Only Oracle of Man* and the controversy over its authorship, Allen's religious beliefs have been discussed by Clarence Gohdes, "Ethan Allen and His Magnum Opus," *Open Court* 43 (1929): 129-51; B. T. Schantz, "Ethan Allen's Religious Ideas," *Journal of Religion* 18 (1938): 183-217; and Arnold Smithline, "Ethan Allen," in *Natural Religion in American Literature* (New Haven: College and University Press, 1966). Although a popular and influential work, little attention has been given to Allen's *Narrative*; still the fullest discussion can be found in Moses Coit Tyler, *The Literary History of the American Revolution* (1897; repr., New York: Frederick Ungar, 1966). Brief but helpful is Hindle's "Introduction," in the Corinth edition (4-6). For comments on Allen's character as it was presented in the *Narrative*, see John Ditsky, "The Yankee Insolence of Ethan Allen," *Canadian Review of American Studies* 1 (1970): 32-38; and Dana Doten, "Ethan Allen's Original Something," *The New England Quarterly* 11 (1938): 361-66. For the most perceptive analysis of Allen's character and his place in the historical imagination, see John McWilliams, "The Faces of Ethan Allen: 1760-1860," *The New England Quarterly* 49 (1976): 257-82.
3 Allen French, *The Taking of Ticonderoga in 1775: The British Story* (Cambridge, MA: Harvard University Press, 1928), 14.
4 Although Allen attacked Ticonderoga at the request of several members of Hartford's Committee of Correspondence, the request was unofficial, as was his military rank. Arnold officially had received both his orders and rank from the Massachusetts Committee of Safety. The only thing that Arnold lacked and which Allen had, however, was a military force. Allen's Green

Mountain Boys refused to follow Arnold when he suddenly appeared with his commission to lead the attack. As a compromise, Allen and Arnold entered the fort together.

5 Feltham's written account is quoted in full in French, *Taking of Ticonderoga*, 43–54. According to Feltham, Allen threatened "neither man woman or child should be left alive in the fort[.] Mr. Arnold begg'd it in a genteel manner but without success, it was owing to him they were prevented getting in Capt. Delaplaces room, after they found I did not command" (44).

6 Jellison, *Ethan Allen*, 118..

7 Ibid.

8 Although certain incidents and figures are sometimes rearranged and others entirely omitted, Allen's *Narrative* is thought to be generally reliable. Jellison states: "Clearly this account is not entirely above suspicion for braggadocio, even to the extent of inserting a whopping big lie now and then. On the whole, however, it is probably an essentially accurate record of what actually happened. At least, on nearly all those points (admittedly few) for which collateral evidence has been found, Ethan's account bears up very well. As a historical document it is perhaps as reliable as most—and it is infinitely more interesting" (161). In view of recent metahistorical approaches to history, Allen's *Narrative* is no different from any other historical text in its selective presentation of the past as a story. Certainly Allen anticipated his readers and shaped his materials (both character and context) in an attempt to appeal to them. For a valuable discussion of metahistorical views on the uses of the past, see Hayden White, "The Historical Text as a Literary Artifact," in *The Writing of History*, eds., Robert H. Canary and Henry Kozicki (Madison: University of Wisconsin Press, 1978), 41–62; and "The Value of Narrativity in the Representation of Reality," *Critical Inquiry* 7 (1980): 5–27.

9 Jellison, *Ethan Allen*, 2.

10 Allen is commonly considered to be a careless writer. According to George F. Scheer and Hugh F. Rankin, *Rebels and Redcoats: The American Revolution Through the Eyes of Those Who Fought and Lived It* (New York: Da Capo Press, 1986), Allen wrote "with a careless regard for detail" (51). I would argue, however, that he wrote indeed with a careful regard for detail, especially for those details which he reshaped to better fit his narrative requirements. In order to merge self with society, in order to present his experiences as a microcosm of the Revolution . . . he carefully selected and arranged his materials. As McWilliams, "Faces of Allen," has noted, he attentively polished his prose for publication (267), and as Jellison, *Ethan Allen*, has noted, he took great pride in his publications (45, 65, 206).

11 Jellison, *Ethan Allen*, 13.

12 Ibid.

13 With his great size and swagger, Allen had enormous presence, and it was for his popular presence that he was chosen to lead the Grants settlers. In his various publications, he naturally attempted to establish the same image. For other examples of Revolutionary leaders who manufactured literary reflec-

tions of themselves, see Albert Furtwangler, *American Silhouettes: Rhetorical Identities of the Founders* (New Haven: Yale University Press, 1987) and Mitchell Robert Breitwieser, *Cotton Mather and Benjamin Franklin: The Price of Representative Personality* (Cambridge: Cambridge University Press, 1984). For a comprehensive analysis of literary reflections of the Revolution, see Michael Kammen, *A Season of Youth: The American Revolution and the Historical Imagination* (New York: Oxford University Press, 1978).

14 For a complete list of Allen's publications, see Hindle's "Bibliography" in the Corinth edition of the *Narrative*, 127–31.

15 Jellison, *Ethan Allen*, 45. Allen, while posing as a simple farmer, was himself deeply involved in land speculation.

16 Allen was a prisoner in various British ships and prisons for thirty-two months, from September 1775 to May 1778. Only the first part of the *Narrative* describes his actions before he was captured at Montreal, while the rest (nearly 100 pages of a 130-page text) describes his captivity experiences.

17 According to Jellison, Allen was ideally suited to the task of converting Canadians and Indians to the American cause. In response to his successes, one of the American officers commented: "Colonel Allen has been very serviceable in bringing in the Canadians and Indians. The Indians of all tribes and the Canadians who join us, have all learned English enough to say Liberty and Bostonian, and all call themselves Yankees. The Indians boast much of it and will smite themselves in their breasts, saying 'me Yankee' " (Jellison, *Ethan Allen*, 151). In his response to Allen's political proselytizing, Ditsky stated that there was "seldom one who brought not religious fanaticism but religious zeal in matters political forward in arguing the case for his fellows" (35).

18 My argument here and throughout the essay is that Allen, in shaping his experiences into a "captivity narrative," consciously exploited a commonly recognized rhetorical framework of redemption, perhaps the most popular of all rhetorical forms in early New England. By adapting the language and structure of religious experience, he made use of a shared system of values and references which, when altered to fit his narrative requirements, imbued his account with significance on both social and individual levels. In his secularized scheme, liberty (both his and America's) becomes merged with salvation. For a valuable analysis of the use of religious experience in personal narratives, see Daniel B. Shea, *Spiritual Autobiography in Early America* (Princeton: Princeton University Press, 1968). For a recent work discussing the individual process of redemption in Puritan New England, see Charles Lloyd Cohen, *God's Caress: The Psychology of Puritan Religious Experience* (New York: Oxford University Press, 1986). For a discussion of how popular writers made use of the conversion process as a narrative structure, see Daniel E. Williams, "Behold a Tragic Scene Strangely Changed into a Theater of Mercy: The Structure and Significance of Criminal Conversion Narratives in Early New England," *American Quarterly* 38 (1986): 827–47.

19 Jellison, *Ethan Allen*, 219. Allen's *Narrative* remained popular throughout the nineteenth century, reaching nineteen editions by 1854. Allen's character,

however, reached even higher levels of popularity. In his novel, *The Green Mountain Boys* (1839), Daniel Thompson refined—and romanticized—the basic rhetorical persona which Allen had developed out of himself in the *Narrative*. Thompson's novel was hugely successful, reaching fifty editions by 1860. Less popular but equally interesting was Melville's *Israel Potter: His Fifty Years in Exile* (1854), which depicted Allen during his captivity in England. As these examples indicate, Allen achieved a remarkable level of popularity by the mid-nineteenth century. For a valuable discussion of Allen's characterization in Thompson and Melville, see McWilliams, "Faces of Allen."

20 In her narrative, Rowlandson referred to her Indian captors as "a scourge to His People" (Alden T. Vaughan and Edward W. Clark, eds., *Puritans among the Indians* [Cambridge, MA: Harvard Unviersity Press, 1981], 69). After quoting Hebrew 12: 6 ("For whom the Lord loveth he chasteneth and scourgeth . . . ") in her conclusion, she stated: "But now I see the Lord had His time to scourge and chasten me. . . . Affliction I wanted and affliction I had, full measure (I thought) pressed down and running over. Yet I see when God calls a person to anything and through never so many difficulties, yet He is fully able to carry them through and make them see and say they have been gainers thereby. And I hope I can say in some measure, as David did, 'It is good fore me that I have been afflicted' " (75). Similarly, John Williams maintained that "an afflicting god was to be glorified. . . . " He referred to the ordeals of his captivity as "divine rebukes" sent to correct him (176, 169).

21 Allen's religious beliefs tended to stress the autonomy of the individual. As a Deist, he rejected all organized religion based on revelation. Since all individuals were unique, every person was entitled to his or her own particular revelation, and such revelations came, not from previously inherited sacred texts, but from the observation of nature. As a reflection of God's perfection, nature manifested order and harmony. Equally reflecting God's goodness, individuals could thus comprehend moral and religious laws for themselves by observing nature. All that an individual found to be repugnant to reason in organized religion could be discarded, especially all that belonged to "superstition." In celebrating both nature and human nature, Allen rejected his family's Calvinism, which he believed was a perversion of God's nature and an insult to human reason. Instead of demanding blind obedience, God had allowed individuals to rationally determine for themselves their own codes of behavior. According to Smithline, Allen's deistical rejection of organized religion "can be viewed as a manifestation of revolutionary democratic thought" (32).

22 Allen apparently loved to be the focus of attention. Whenever surrounded by an audience, no matter how hostile, he attempted to entertain through self-dramatization. According to Jellison, he was an "inveterate showman, taking obvious delight in being the center of much public curiosity and attention" (218). In view of its vivid descriptions and humor, his narrative can be seen as another attempt to captivate an audience.

23 Although he rigorously claimed gentleman-status, Allen did not always behave as a gentleman according to eighteenth century standards of polite behavior. As indicated with the incident with the Tory lieutenant who spit in his face, Allen often resorted to physical and verbal violence when provoked. His persistent claims to gentleman-status, then, offer even greater evidence of his self-creative power. In contrast to traditional conventions, which relied on exterior social identifications, Allen's self-definition was an individual process. I am indebted to A. Owen Aldridge for his insights into Allen's departures from eighteenth-century standards of social etiquette.

24 As a self-promoted mythic figure, Allen had many stories told about him. Holbrook related a different version of Allen's confrontation with Symonds over walking rights to the quarterdeck. Instead of Symonds, Allen confronted an even more austere figure of authority, Lord Cornwallis. According to Holbrook, Cornwallis became angered when he saw Allen trespassing in an area reserved for gentlemen: " 'Mr. Allen,' he said, 'do you know that the quarterdeck is the place fore gentlemen?'

'Yes, by God, I do,' the Colonel responded, 'and that's the reason I'm here' " (121). For a sample of Ethan Allen tall tales, see Holbrook, *Ethan Allen*, 257–73.

25 Allen's emphasis here, as well as in similar references, demonstrates another redemption requirement. According to Cohen, *God's Caress*, "conversion accomplishes more than knitting the soul to Christ; it also establishes bonds of affection within the holy community" (221). In his narrative framework, the experience of captivity not only brought individuals to a true awareness of liberty and tyranny, but it also bonded them together into a new society of mutual concern.

26 Allen often equated British soldiers and American Tories with devils, and in doing so he again made use of a pre-existing and readily recognizable rhetorical structure. Traditionally, Satan and his followers had to be overcome in order to achieve redemption. The Devil, according to Cohen (*God's Caress*), was a "conversion frustrator" who sought to destroy the individual's search for salvation (216). Compromise was out of the question.

27 For a discussion of the deplorable conditions under which prisoners were kept by both sides during the war, see Charles H. Metzger, S. J., *The Prisoner in the American Revolution* (Chicago: Loyola University Press, 1971).

28 In view of Allen's defiant Deism, it is not hard to imagine the satisfaction he took in describing the British use of churches as prisons. Like Paine, he believed that organized religions enslaved individuals. According to Doten, "Allen's Original Something," Allen "loved the role of the Glorious Rebel, Champion of Liberty, Defender of Oppresed . . . (365). After opposing political tyranny, he turned his attention to religious tyranny, resulting in the publication of *Reason the Only Oracle*. In this controversial text, Allen continued to assume the role of liberty's champion, attacking sectarian oppression and superstition.

29 Allen actually had been caught in minor parole violations. Jellison, *Ethan*

Allen, has stated that Allen simply became bored with the limitations of his parole and violated its conditions as a challenge to British authority (174–75).

30 Equally appropriate for the narrative's conclusion, Allen's last scenes depicted him in the company of the highest ranking colonial officials and generals, including George Washington, proving that redemption resulted in salvation.

31 Jellison, *Ethan Allen,* 178.

32 Pell, *Ethan Allen,* 169.

33 Ibid., 170.

34 Jellison, *Ethan Allen,* 171.

Pygmalion's Dream in
Herder's Aesthetics, or Male Narcissism
as the Model for Bildung

DOROTHEA E. VON MÜCKE

In the first issue of the *Rheinische Thalia* (1785), Friedrich Schiller provides an account of a visit to the Mannheim sculpture gallery as seen through the eyes of a hypothetical Danish traveler. Schiller begins his "Brief eines reisenden Dänen" by depicting the traveler's reaction to the misery and poverty which assault him in their stark contrast to the pomp and luxury of the ducal gardens and palace:

> Eine hohläugige Hungerfigur, die mich in den blumigten Promenaden eines fürstlichen Lustgartens anbettelt—eine sturzdrohende Schindelhütte, die einem prahlerischen Palast gegenübersteht—wie schnell schlägt sie meinen auffliegenden Stolz zu Boden! Meine Einbildung vollendet das Gemälde. Ich sehe jetzt die Flüche von Tausenden gleich einer gefräßigen Würmerwelt in dieser großsprechenden Verwesung wimmeln—Das Große und Reizende wird mir abscheulich.—Ich entdecke nichts mehr als einen siechen, hinschwindenden Menschenkörper, dessen Augen und Wangen von fiebrischer Röte brennen und blühendes Leben heucheln, während daß Brand und Fäulung in den röchelnden Lungen wüten.[1]
> (A hollow-eyed starving figure, which begs from me among the blooming promenades of a ducal amusement garden—a collapsing shingle hovel opposed to a pompous palace—how fast do they strike down my soaring pride! My imagination completes the painting. And now I can see the curses of thousands like a ravenous world of worms swarming among this boasting decomposition—The great and delightful is abominable to me.—I don't discover anything but a sickly,

349

languishing human body, whose eyes and cheeks burn with a feverish
redness and simulate blooming life, while gangrene and putrefaction are
raging in the rattling lungs.)

The tourist can no longer enjoy the beauty of the princely architecture
and gardens, since the misery of the underprivileged — starvation, disease, homelessness — pervades even those delightful and luxurious places.
The two extremes are joined in the image of the human body, where the
sites of beauty become a mere simulation of health and life, a facade over
the truth of disease and death. What could have been an occasion for a
political critique is perceived as a physical and personal threat: the
"curses of the thousands" are turned into the "swarming worms of
putrefaction."

However, the Danish traveler does not remain with this "painting" of
his imagination, this *vanitas* still life, reminding him of his own mortality
and raising doubts about the immortality of the human soul. In fact, the
entire scenario up to this point is merely the prelude to the visit to the
Mannheim sculpture gallery, where the contemplation of Greek art
restores to our tourist the belief in man's perfectibility:

> Warum zielen alle redende und zeichnende Künste des Altertums so sehr
> nach Veredlung? Der Mensch brachte hier etwas zustande, das mehr ist,
> als er selbst war, das an etwas GröBeres erinnert als seine
> Gattung — beweist das vielleicht, daß er weniger ist, als er sein
> wird? — so könnte uns ja dieser allgemeine Hang nach Verschönerung
> jede Spekulation über die Fortdauer der Seele ersparen.[2]
> (Why do all the speaking and painting arts of antiquity aim so much at
> refinement? Man was able to accomplish something greater than he
> was, which reminds us of something greater than his species — could this
> perhaps prove that he is less than he will be? — then this common
> tendency towards beautification could save us any further speculation
> about the permanence of the soul.)

The sculptures of the Mannheim gallery represent the height of Greek art
and serve as a document and reminder that it is in and through art that
man can overcome his present situation of imperfection and suffering.

Though Schiller published this brief article ten years before the *Letters
on the Aesthetic Education* we already note the shift from a potential for
political critique and intervention towards what he then came to call "the
detour *via* the realm of beauty."[3] With this shift the aesthetic, particularly
the art of classical antiquity, and above all Greek sculpture, becomes the
locus of transforming man's misery. According to Schiller, art becomes
the condition of the possibility of man's perfectibility by providing him
with a very specific model of refinement, sublimation, and idealization.
This move towards what German literary and intellectual history has

called Classicism and Neo-Humanism clearly announces itself in this fetishization of Greek sculpture; it not only entails a rupture with the Enlightenment semiotics of representation and the *epistemé* of rationalism but also produces a new kind of subjectivity, which emerges under the name of "Bildung."

The reason for beginning this essay on the neo-humanist obsession with Greek sculpture with this passage from a lesser known essay by Schiller lies with a fairly topical issue. Currently in 1988–89, one would be tempted to "historicize" Schiller's "apolitical" turn to neo-classicist aesthetics as a response to the French Revolution or, more precisely, to the Reign of Terror. This earlier piece from 1785, which displays the neo-humanist admiration for Greek sculpture, could be brushed aside and labeled in moralist terms as an "escape" from "alienation," beginning industrialization, social injustice, poverty, etc. But this narrow, yet fairly abstract, historical reading fails to come to a fuller understanding of this period's obsession with the medium of sculpture. It is in view of this question that in my preliminary attempt to characterize this fascination I have used the term fetishization. For I want to emphasize that Greek sculpture functions, as can be seen in the above quoted Schiller passage, as a vehicle of a specific form of denial. The unpleasant facts (the mortality of the body, poverty, disease and suffering) are not repressed, but their acknowledgement is strangely suspended, held at bay by a more pleasant perception (the beauty and immortality of man's ideal and soul). What the fetish accomplishes is a particular type of illusion, not one that entirely absorbs its beholder and cancels out any other perception, but an illusion which (though the beholder is conscious of its illusionary status) exercises an apotropaic power over an otherwise unbearable threat to the beholder's sense of physical and psychic integrity. And yet, the model of fetishism alone does not suffice to refine our understanding of the transformative power which is attributed to the contemplation of Greek sculpture. In other words, what is at stake is a more detailed understanding of how sculpture above all artistic media is supposed to modify the beholder's relation to the body and to shape his soul.

It is well known that the name for the neo-humanist sublimation script, *Bildung*, cannot easily be translated into English. Among the many possibilities one might recall: formation, growth, foundation, constitution, organization, form, shape, physiognomy, structure, forming, development, training, culture, higher education, accomplishments, polish, and good breeding. The term *Bildung* gains weight in the last decades of the eighteenth century at the time when both language and the subject are invested with an organic depth and an individual history in terms of an entelechial development. At that time *Bildung* comes to replace —

increasingly with a polemical edge—the term *Erziehung* (education, in the more external and technical sense). *Bildung* is used in the description of artifacts, mainly sculptures, as well as in the description of humans; in the case of humans, *Bildung* refers to the human body and face as well as the human mind—quite frequently as the outer appearance acquires a diaphanous quality with regard to the mind. The term is furthermore applied to the arts, to the creative activity of the sculptor and poet and denotes the poesis of a self-sufficient beautiful construct. In brief, the term *Bildung* entails a certain ideal of signification, aesthetic production, and reception, as well as a certain ideal of education as it emerges towards the end of the eighteenth century. This particular coalescence of pedagogical, aesthetic, and semiotic concerns will be examined in Herder's notes on sculpture, particularly in a close reading of his formulations about the soul-shaping impact of an aesthetic object, and about the ideal relation between the subject and an aesthetic object. It will be demonstrated how in Herder's writings on sculpture we can situate the emergence of this aesthetic medium as a model object for that type of aesthetic signification that will culminate in the classical/romantic symbol and for that relation to the aesthetic object, which will be occupied by the subject of *Bildung*.

Before turning to Herder's writing on sculpture, let me briefly summarize an aspect of the epistemic shift in which is situated the new subjectivity of *Bildung* and which can be localized in Herder's theory of language from 1771, the *Abhandlung über den Ursprung der Sprache*. What distinguishes Herder's origin-of-language essay from all of his predecessors and contemporaries is its fundamentally humanist anthropology: language is not a divine gift (as it is for Süßmilch), nor a gradually developed vehicle of knowledge (as it is for Condillac), but it is the crucial condition of man's humanity. It is through language that the weak and disoriented human creature gains control over his environment, because language allows him to focus his sensory perceptions and to organize his otherwise diffuse and erratic drives and impulses. In his narrative about the first word Herder distinguishes man through his capacity of reflexion ("Besonnenheit"), the ability to behold and contemplate peacefully an object. In fact, Herder sees in language a "sphere of mirrors," the medium of reflexion and contemplation that constitutes the objects of the world as well as the subjectivity of their beholder. In contrast to the partial objects that respond to a specific animal instinct like hunger or heat, human language, the word, consisting of sound and a hallucinated sight, can produce a total object and with it the autonomous human subject. In language man finds his "sphere of mirroring" ("Sphäre der Bespiegelung") which defines the boundaries of his interiority and his exteriority. Thus, what separates man from the animal realm is his primarily narcissistic constitution which coexists with his language-forming ability.[4]

But further details about Herder's essay are not necessary here. The intention is merely to indicate how in the neo-humanist conceptualization of language, language no longer functions primarily as a vehicle of knowledge or as a mere system of representations but, rather, becomes the locus of human subjectivity, the condition of the possibility of man's freedom and history—and, more specifically how this subjectivity is structured in a self-reflexive, narcissistic manner.[5] From here we turn to some aspects of Herder's aesthetics and pursue how he charts the relation between a beholder and an aesthetic object.

While Herder was working on his treatise on the origin of language he also started to elaborate an aesthetic theory of sculpture, of which he published a final version in 1778 under the title: "Einige Wahrnehmungen über Form und Gestalt aus Pygmalions bildendem Traume." In the context of the classical *epistemé*, Diderot's aesthetics, as well as Lessing's *Laokoon*, evolve around the *image sensible*, the hallucinated sight modelled on the pictorial *tableau* which is supposed to mirror the *tableau mouvant* of the soul. With Herder these aesthetic ideals of illusion have come to an end. In a way, one could read his writings about sculpture as the rewriting of Diderot's *Lettre sur les aveugles* and *Lettre sur les sourds et muets*. The place and function of the *tableau* is to be taken up by sculpture as the new model object, where the prevalence of the sense of sight is to be replaced by the sense of touch. Furthermore, Herder wants to revise Lessing's theory of the arts, which rests on the opposition of figures and colors in a spatial order versus articulated sounds in a temporal order. Sculpture, according to Herder, is an artistic medium in its own right. It would be wrong to subordinate it under the flat surface of painting which is only accessible to the sense of sight. Instead of the sight versus sound opposition, Herder proposes a tripartite system for the various arts:

painting	music	sculpture
surface	sound	body
sight	hearing	touch/feeling
coexistence	succession	coexistence and succession
space	time	force

In light of Herder's treatise on the origin of language, one would not necessarily expect this valorization of the sense of touch, since in the *Ursprung* essay he allowed the ear to occupy the place of the privileged organ, while the sense of touch could only convey very confused sensations. However, the sense of touch in the *Ursprung* essay and in the writings about sculpture is not one and the same. It is not even quite correct to speak of tactile sensations with regard to the later writings. The feeling which Herder discusses in his writing on sculpture is not localized in the process of the fingertips feeling the texture of a surface, but refers to the total comprehension of the spatial form, of the body's organization in space, the *Körpergefühl* (body feeling) that provides the beholder with a comprehensive notion of an organized totality.

In one of the studies for his essay on sculpture, entitled "Philosphie des Wahren, Guten und Schönen aus dem Sinne des Gefühls," Herder writes:

1. Gehfühl ist der erste, profondste und fast einzige Sinn der Menschen: die Quelle der meisten unsrer Begriffe und Empfindungen: das wahre, und erste Organum der Seele Vorstellungen von außen zu sammeln: der Sinn, der die Seele gleichsam ganz umgibt, und die andren Sinnen als Arten, Theile oder Verkürzungen in sich enthält: die Maße unsrer Sinnlichkeit: der wahre Ursprung des Wahren, Guten, Schönen!
2. Die Seele fühlet sich in die Welt hinein. Da sie in ihren Kräften durch Raum und Zeit eingeschränkt ist: so kann sie nicht alles unmittelbar erkennen: einiges aber, und dies wird ein Spiegel des Andern: das ist der Leib. Er ist also von ihr durch eine Art von fühlbarer Anziehung gebildet; diese Attraktion ist aber noch völlig zu berechnen, so wie das Fühlbare in ihr aus der Bildung des Fötus noch zu experimentiren. Alsdenn wirds offenbar werden, daß die Seele sich einen Körper durchs Gefühl und zum Gefühl von außen bilde, oder sich fühlend in die Welt hineinbilde!
3. Entwicklung des Gefühls in den ersten Augenblicken der Kindlheit. Wie ein Kind die ersten Begriffe fühlend bekommt. In welcher Ordnung? Daß oft die abstraktesten Begriffe die ersten Fühlideen sind. Die erste Ontologie de Gefühls: von Seyn, Außer uns seyn, Raum, Zeit, Kraft, Körper, u.s.w.[6]
(1. Feeling is the first, most profound and almost the only sense of men: the source of the majority of our notions and sensations: the true and first organ of the soul to gather ideas from the exterior world: the sense which surrounds the soul in its entirety and which contains in itself the other senses as species, parts or abbreviations: the measure of our sensuality: the true origin of the true, the good and the beautiful.
2. The soul makes its way into the world through feeling. Since its forces are restricted by space and time: it cannot know everything in an immediate manner, only some things, which then become the mirror of the other: that is the body. Thus the body is formed by the soul through an attraction accessible to feeling; this attraction remains to be figured out in its entirety, as well as that which can be felt needs to be explained through the formation of the fetus. Then it will become obvious that the soul forms itself a body through feeling and for the feeling of the exterior, or that it forms itself in the world in a feeling manner!

3. Development of feeling in the first moments of childhood. How a child attains its first notions in a feeling manner. In which order? That frequently the most abstract notions are the first ideas of feeling. The first ontology of feeling: of being, being exterior to ourselves, space, time, force, body, etc.)

In these rather fragmentary and cryptic notes, Herder attributes to "feeling" and the body the "mirror" function, which in his treatise on the origin of language he attributed to the sense of hearing and the first word. The surface or skin of Herder's fetus, endowed with tactile sensibility, surrounds the little creature, gives it unity by separating an inside from an outside, while it also establishes the possibility of contact between this inside and its exterior. Thus, feeling constructs the body as the model for the soul's perception of the world.[7] On the basis of this observation, Herder postulates that though feeling might be the most primitive sensation, it, nevertheless, is also at the foundation of the most abstract comprehension. To the extent that feeling, according to Herder, is always related to the totality of the body, it never remains on the surface: feeling is exactly that arresting of an object which goes beyond its mere surface to its structure and depth where it denotes the immediate grasp of the idea or notion. In that sense, feeling means a special access to truth, and, indeed, Herder writes: "Im Gesicht ist Traum, im Gefühl Wahrheit." (In the sense of sight there is dream, in feeling truth.)[8]

As the synthesized comprehension of a *Gestalt*, feeling is far removed from actual sensory perception: rather, it can be described as a certain spatial hallucination of an ideal object. Furthermore, we must not forget that while the *Ursprung* essay deals with sensory perceptions *per se*, the aesthetic writings on sculpture primarily discuss perceptions vis-à-vis representations. While the primary issue of the subject's constitution in the *Ursprung* essay involved the defense against overstimulation, the artistic media in the sculpture essays have already mastered this obstacle. In Herder's terms, one could say that once faced with aesthetic objects, once in the realm of representations, man has already found his sphere of mirrors, his reflexion.

Herder's choice of Greek sculpture as the privileged kind of aesthetic representation has to be understood within the context of a broader project of a cultural critique. Herder is not concerned with these art objects in terms of an historical inquiry of art. Rather, the sculpture provides him with a heuristic device for describing an ideal type of signification. Thus, we can trace Herder's interest in artistic products in terms of their ability to shape subjectivity. If Greek sculpture becomes the paradigm for the aesthetic object, according to Herder, what are its qualities? They can be summarized in these lapidary terms: Greek sculpture is the spatially isolated representation of a beautiful and vigorous nude human body, preferably in polished marble, and certainly without the use of colors.

This eighteenth-century view of sculpture deserves further elaboration. As a spatial representation, sculpture provides an image of the body in its totality and accessibility to the senses of sight and feeling. As an isolated entity the sculpture asserts a certain independence from its environment. A sculpture has to have its own center of gravity without becoming frozen; it can thereby combine calmness and movement, displaying its autonomy and force. The Greeks chose to represent only those human bodies that were free of any imperfections. It is here, in particular, that the polished white marble of the Greeks proves its superiority, for the Greeks had the good taste to avoid color and bodily details:

> Viel feinere Sachen, als Tünche und Kuhhaut müssen von der Statue wegbleiben, weil sie dem Gefühl widerstehen, weil sie dem *tastenden Sinne* keine *ununterbrochne schöne* Form sind. Diese Adern an Händen, diese Knorpel an Fingern, diese Knöchel an Knien müßen so geschont und in die Fülle des Ganzen verkleidet werden; oder die Adern sind kriechende Würme, die Knorpel aufliegende Gewächse dem stillen dunkeltastenden Gefühl. Nicht ganze Fülle *Eines* Köpers mehr, sondern Abtrennungen, losgelöste Stücke des Körpers, die seine Zerstörung weißagen, und sich eben daher schon selbst entfernten (27).
> Wer hat nicht gesehen, wie bei abgenommenen ersten Gipsabdrücken eines Gesichts jedes *einzelne* Haar so widrig und unsanft thut, als jede Pockengrube oder jede fatale Unebenheit und Lostrennung vom Antlitz. Die einzelnen Härchen schauern uns durch, es ist wie eine Scharte im Messer, nur etwas was die Form hindert und nicht zu ihr gehöret. Der Griechische Künstler *deutet* also nur *an* . . . (29).
> (Many finer things than color and cowhide have to be kept away from statues, for they resist the feeling, for they are not a continuous beautiful form for the feeling of touch. These veins at the hands, these gristles on the fingers, these knuckles on the knees have to be treated with caution and clothed by the fullness of the whole; else the veins are crawling worms, the gristles protruding growths for the silent sense of touch in the dark. No longer fullness of *One* body, but separations, isolated pieces of the body, which predict its destruction, and should be already removed for this very reason. Who has not seen how in the first plaster masque of a face *each individual* hair sticks out in such an obstinate and ungentle manner, like any pockmark or fatal unevenness and separation from the human face. The individual hairs make us shudder like a dent in a knife, they merely oppose the form and do not belong to it. Therefore the Greek artist only *suggests*. . . .)

Note how the perfect smoothness of the Greek marble is opposed to the plaster of a death mask, how, according to Herder, only Greek sculpture can provide us with that ideal dermal surface, which constitutes the oneness of the body. Like Lacan's infant of the mirror stage, the beholder of the Greek statue appreciates in this representation, *via* a certain imaginary identification, the wholeness and health of his own body, a protection from fragmentation and disintegration.[9] This imaginary identification presupposes a specific degree of stylization and idealization.[10] The representation is not to be judged in terms of a proximity to nature; details in particular have to be ruled out.[11] Instead of referring the beholder to a concrete human body of hair, fat, cartilage, veins, etc., the sculpture is supposed to represent an ideal — the human body will come to stand in for the human soul, or for the ego, which cannot be represented and which props itself on an idealized body image.[12]

But how does the Greek artist allow the beholder to identify himself with an ideal body, how does he suggest this immortal body? The sculpture manages to signify this ideal body in a manner that painting cannot. Herder analyzes the particularity of the medium by looking at how the Greeks draped clothes on their statues:

> Zu *bekleiden*, daß doch nicht *verhüllt* würde? Gewand anzubringen, und der Körper doch seinem Wuchs, seine schöne runde Fülle behielte? Wie seinen wenn er *durchschiene*? In der Bildnerei, bei einem Solido kann nichts durchscheinen: sie arbeitet für die Hand und nicht fürs Auge. Und siehe, eben *für die Hand* erfanden die feinen Griechen Auskunft. Ist nur der tastende Finger betrogen, daß er Gewand und zugleich Körper taste; der *fremde* Richter, das Auge muß *folgen*. Kurz, es sind der Griechen *nasse Gewänder* (22).
>
> (To dress the body without covering it up? To dress the body so as to retain its growth and beautiful, rounded fullness? What if it were to *shine through*? In the sculpture of somebody like Solido nothing can shine through: this kind of sculpture works for the hand and not for the eye. And look, it was exactly *for the hand* that the Greeks solved the problem. If the touching finger is deceived that it feels clothes and the body simultaneously; the *alien* judge, the eye must *follow*. In brief, it is the Greeks' *wet clothing*.)

Only the surface of Greek sculpture can function like a specific screen that, on the one hand, veils the material details of the concrete body from the eye, while on the other hand, it appeals to the hallucinatory feeling of the body by which the beholder identifies with the sculpture. Thus, the sculpture acquires a certain diaphanous quality, a transparency with regard to this ideal body.

We might ask here, how Herder sees this identification with an ideal body?[13] In his essay on sculpture Herder elaborates a long and detailed semiotics of the human body. However, his interest is not in physiognomy, not in deciphering individual marks and characteristics, but in a demonstration of how the human body is the only natural sign and embodiment of an internal perfection:

> Die Wohlgestalt des Menschen ist also kein Abstraktum aus den Wolken, keine Komposition gelehrter Regeln oder willkürlicher Einständnisse, sie kann von jedem *erfaßt* und *gefühlt* werden, der, was Form des Lebens, Ausdruck der Kraft im Gefäße der Menschheit ist, *in sich* oder *im andern* fühlet. Nur die *Bedeutung innerer Volkommenheit ist* Schönheit (56).
>
> (The well shaped human form is not something abstract out of the clouds, not a composition according to learned rules or arbitrary agreements, it can be *grasped* and *felt* by everybody, who feels *in himself* or *in an other* the form of life, the expression of force in the vessel of humanity. Only the *signification* of an *internal perfection* is beauty.)

Herder vehemently rejects a notion of signification and beauty that would require the activity of the symbolic understanding, rather than being universally accessible to the intuitive understanding:

> Man darf hier abermals weder in Buchstaben noch in Wolken studiren, sondern nur *seyn* und fühlen: Mensch seyn, blind empfinden, wie die Seele in jedem Charakter, in jeder Stellung und Leidenschaft *in uns* würke, und denn tasten. Es ist die laute Natursprache, allen Völkern, ja selbst Blinden und Tauben hörbar (58).
>
> (Again one must not study in letters or in clouds, one must merely *be* and *feel*: be human, and sense blindly how the soul operates in each character, in each position and passion *in us*, and then touch. It is the loud language of nature, audible to all peoples, even to the blind and deaf.)

In the contemplation of Greek sculpture man gains an immediate access to the ideal of beauty and hears the language of nature which is beyond material signifiers, as well as beyond mere sensory data, since it speaks through his soul—that is, in the contemplation of Greek sculpture the soul defines its own shape.

The sculpture is not so much a sign for something else; rather, its semiotic status shifts towards the classical-romantic symbol, which has a necessary internal relation to what it signifies.[14] The process of signification achieves a quasi-organic character. Instead of a model of reading, we find the model of an osmosis, or assimilation. Beholding a sculpture will effect a mutual metamorphosis of object and subject:

> Jedes Beugen und Heben der Brust und des Knies, und wie der Körper ruht und wie in ihm die Seele sich darstellt, geht stumm und unbegreiflich in uns hinüber: wir werden mit der Statue gleichsam verkörpert oder diese mit uns beseelet (60).

(Each bending and raising of the chest and the knee, and how the body rests and how the soul represents itself in it, transfuses us in a silent and incomprehensible manner: such that we are embodied, as it were, through the statue and it is endowed with a soul through us.)

In the sculpture we do not perceive an other but the soul receives through the sculpture an image of itself. It is only in this sense that the initially mysterious title of Herder's essay, "Some Observations on Form and *Gestalt* from Pygmalion's Shaping Dream," begins to make sense: what endows the product of Pygmalion's hands with life is the passionately narcissistic love for this ideal representation of himself.

From here we can link the narcissistic aspect of Pygmalion's dream with the subject's constitution in language. In the origin-of-language essay, the white, soft, and wooly sheep, the total object of a "disinterested interest," was given its mark by the soul through its sound, allowing the soul to constitute and stabilize itself. In the white, full, and smooth, but well defined and hard body of the sculpture, the soul then can find a representation of itself in terms of a secondary narcissism; its ego-ideal will be reflected in the mirror of a humanist idealism:

Wir treten an eine Bildsäule, wie in ein heiliges Dunkel, als ob wir jetzt erst den simpelsten Begriff und Bedeutung der Form und zwar der edelsten, schönsten, reichsten Form, eines Menschlichen Körpers, uns er tasten müßten. Je einfacher wir dabei zu Werke gehen, und wie dort Hamlet sagt, alle Alltags-kopien und das Gemahl — und Gekritsel von Buchstaben und Zügen aus unserm Gehirn wegwischen: desto mehr wird das stumme Bild zu uns sprechen und die heilige Kraftvolle Form, die aus den Händen des grösten Bildners kam und von seinem Hauch durchwehet dastand, sich unter der Hand, unter dem Finger unsres innern Geistes beleben. Du Hauch dessen, der schuf, wehe mich an, daß ich bei seinem Werke bleibe, treu fühle und treu schreibe! (41).
(We approach a sculpture as if we were entering into a sacred darkness, as if we had to feel for ourselves for the first time the simplest notion and meaning of form, the most noble, beautiful and rich form, the one of a human body. The simpler the manner we go about it, and if, as Hamlet says, all trivial fond records, all saws of books are erased from our brain: the more the silent image will speak to us, and the sacred, forceful form, coming from the hands of the greatest sculptor and standing there animated by his breath, will enliven itself under the hand, under the fingers of our inner spirit. Breath of the one who created, blow towards me, that I remain truthful to his work, that I may feel and write authentically.)

While Ovid's Pygmalion, disappointed with the love of flesh and blood women, made for himself a beautiful ivory girl who through his passionate love is endowed with life and finally becomes his wife, Herder's Pygmalion relates to the sculpture in terms of a complex narcissistic structure. The erotic attraction towards an Other is replaced by a desire for an ideal self; the statue is to endow Pygmalion with the form of his own soul. Not only does the beholder of the statue find in it a representation of his ideal body and soul, but he also encounters the creative genius of an Other who commands him to remain truthful to his work. "To feel and write authentically, true to the breath of the one who created" — what does this mean other than to read and write according to the hermeneutic ideal of grasping the "essence" of an author's individuality, that totalizing spirit that prohibits the attention to the materiality of the letter, which would disrupt the beautiful autonomy and continuity of the self of *Bildung*. Thus the sculpture finally becomes that ideal aesthetic object or "interface" that provides the seam or suture (for it has to stitch up the wounds of absence and mortality) through which man inserts himself into the order of creation, the order of sense and the senses.

When I say that sculpture becomes the model object for man's relation to the aesthetic and to himself, that it provides him with a representation of an ideal self, I am also stressing the gendered aspect of the notion of *Bildung*. Of course, Enlightenment pedagogy possessed two different models for the education of boys and girls, if we think, for instance, of the difference between the education of Emile and that of Sophie. However, not until the last decades of the eighteenth century does the discourse of a fundamental gender polarity pervade the entire discourse on language and the arts.[15] In Rousseau's case, there is no *a priori* difference between women's or men's access to language, and it must be the work of culture to institute a gendered access to the realm of representations. However, in the *Urprung* essay, Herder attributes the fundamentally human, the language-forming ability only to the male biped.[16] It is exactly at the point when language is no longer conceived of as a mere representation of things in the world, or a vehicle of knowledge, when it becomes the humanizing factor due to its reflexivity, that the discourse on language produces a gender polarization. And this state carries over into the discourse on the arts. If man forms himself through language he learns to love his ideal self through aesthetic objects.

We have seen how Herder transforms the Pygmalion story, how he celebrates the enthusiastic love for the aesthetic object as a mirror of the self.[17] We have also seen how this enthusiastic love becomes the paradigm for a hermeneutic model of reading in the spirit, which needs to screen out both the materiality of the letter and the materiality of the body as disruptive signs of absence and mortality. We return now to the introductory statement of this essay, that is, with Herder's aesthetics we can localize an epistemic break. This rewriting of the Pygmalion story is highly significant with regard to Herder's position *vis à vis* the Enlightenment. Herder not only rehabilitates enthusiasm, by contrasting the "cold" rationality of a distanced beholder with the passionate love of the art lover who identifies with his object, but this enthusiasm is very specifically inscribed into a model of male narcissism. If I call this model of love naricissistic, I want to emphasize that it is not the libidinal investment of an Other, but the love of an Other as that which one is, was, or would like to be, an auto-sufficient, independent, and immortal being.[17] Any libidinal object investment, the passionate love of an Other, is perceived as a threat to the stable boundaries of the self. And it is here that Herder depicts the other kind of enthusiasm, the dangerous and condemnable fanaticism, described as female sexuality. In his brief notes on Hemsterhuis, entitled "Über Selbstheit und Liebe," he writes about that other kind of enthusiasm:

Es ist die allgemeine Erfahrung, daß in alle Schwärmereien Weiber verwickelt gewesen; oft wurden die Männer nur angesteckt durch Weiber, die sie, wie es hieß neu gebahren. Den Männern waren sie also gleichsam Mittlerinnen der Gottheit; und wie sie sich die Gottheit, insonderheit den menschlichen Gott dachten, und ihn empfanden, davon liegen ja so viele Schriften und Briefe der Welt vor Augen. Die Ohnmacht, die die heilige Theresia vor dem Altar fühlte, als der himmlische Amor ihr Herz berührte, konnte, wenn sie in diesem Augenblick nur körperlich betrachtet würde, schwerlich von einer andern Art seyn, als den jede Ohnmacht der Liebe hat: denn in den Säften des Körpers ist Liebe und Liebe an Wirkungen gleich, wer auch der Gegenstand seyn möge. Bei allen Gefühlen dieser Gattung ist also auch dem unschuldigsten Herzen die größeste Behutsamkeit nöthig; selbst im Strom der Göttlichen Liebe bleibts immer nur ein menschliches Herz. Alle Mittlerinnen, und wenn es die Mutter Gotttes selbst wäre, sind gefährlich: so wie dem weiblichen Herzen alle irrdische und (zu sinnlich empfunden) selbst der himmlische Mittler es seyn kann. Von ganzer Seele, von allen ihren Kräften will Gott geliebet seyn, nicht aber vom gährenden Nervensaft in einem kranken epileptischen Körper.[18]

(It is confirmed by general experience that in all kinds of fanaticism there have been women involved; often men were only infected by women, who then, as it used to be phrased, made them reborn. They were, so to speak, mediators of the divinity for men; and how they imagined the divinity, particularly the human god, how they felt him, about this there are so many writings and letters for the eyes of the world. The fainting which Saint Theresa experienced before the altar when the divine amor touched her heart, this fainting fit, if considered from a physical angle, could hardly be of a different kind than any other fainting of love: for in the juices of the body there is no difference between love and love with regard to its effects, regardless of its objects. In all feelings of this kind, even the most innocent heart needs to be very cautious; even in the stream of divine love it remains merely a human heart. All female mediators, and even if it were the mother of

God, are dangerous: as for any female heart all earthly and even [if too sensuously experienced] the divine mediator may be dangerous. God wants to be loved by the entirety of the soul, by all its forces, not by the fermenting nerve juices of a sick, epileptic body.)

In contrast to the discourse of Enlightenment, where the dangers of enthusiasm are conceived of as the disruption of rational discourse (for the fanatic disregards the established discursive regulations), in the discourse of neo-humanism, enthusiasm can supersede the narrow limits of rationality, either furthering the aims of *Bildung* or becoming utterly noxious, depending on whether it serves to stabilize or destabilize the boundaries of the male ego.

NOTES

1 Friedrich Schiller, "Brief eines reisenden Dänen," (*Rheinische Thalia I*, 1785) in *Sämtliche Werke* (Munich: Hanser, 1984), 5: 879, translation mine.

2 Ibid., 883.

3 See Friedrich Schiller, "Über die ästhetische Erziehung des Menschen in einer Reihe von Briefen," *Sämtliche Werke*, 5: 571.

4 See especially pp. 26–35 in Johann Gottfried Herder, *Abhandlung über den Ursprung der Sprache*, ed. Hans Dietrich Irmscher (Stuttgart: Reclam, 1966).

5 For a detailed analysis of Herder's origin-of-language essay in this context, see my "Language as the Mark of the Soul: Herder's Narcissistic Subject," forthcoming in Kurt Müller-Vollmer, ed., *Herder Today* (Berlin, New York: Walter de Gruyter).

6 *Herders sämtliche Werke*, ed. Bernhard Suphan (Berlin: Weidmannsche Buchhandlung, 1892), 8: 104.

7 Freud in chapter 2 of "Das ich und das Es" describes the importance of the sense of touch and body-feeling in the separation of ego and id: "Der eigenen Körper und vor allem die Ober fläche desselben ist ein Ort, von dem gleichzeitig äußere und innere Wahrnehmungen ausgehen können. Er wird wie ein anderes Objekt gesehen, er gibt aber dem Getast zweierlei Empfindungen, von denen die eine einer inneren Wahrnehmung gleichkommen kann." In the same context he also emphasizes the constructedness of this representation of the ego: "Das Ich ist vor allem ein körperliches, es ist nicht nur ein Oberflächenwesen, sondern selbst die Projektion einer Oberfläche." *Studienausgabe*, 3: 294. ("A person's own body, and above all its surface, is a place from which both external and internal perceptions may spring. It is seen like any other object, but to the touch it yields to kinds of sensations, one of which may be equivalent to an internal perception. . . . The Ego is first and foremost a bodily ego; it is not merely a surface entity, but is itself the projection of a surface." [i.e., the ego is ultimately derived from bodily sensations, chiefly

from those springing from the surface of the body. It may thus be regarded as a mental projection of the surface of the body, besides, as we have seen above, representing the superficies of the mental apparatus. This footnote first appeared in the English translation of 1927, in which it was described as having been authorized by Freud. It does not appear in the German editions.]) "The Ego and the Id," in *On Metapsychology: The Theory of Psychoanalysis*, trans. James Strachey, The Pelican Freud Library, (Harmondsworth, England: Pelican Books, 1987), 364.

8 Johann Gottfried Herder, "Einige Wahrnehmungen über Form und Gestalt aus Pygmalions bildendem Traume" (1778) in *Herders sämtliche Werke*, ed. Bernhard Suphan (Berlin: Weidmannsche Buchhandlung, 1892), 8: 9. Page references to this edition will be given in parentheses; translations will be mine. For the position of Herder's writings about sculpture in the development of his aesthetics, see also Hans Dietrich Irmscher's "Mitteilungen aus Herder's Nachlaß," *Euphorion* 54 (1960): 281-94.

9 Lacan describes the identificatory movement of the mirror stage in the following words: "We have only to understand the mirror stage as an identification, in the full sense that analysis gives to the term: namely the transformation that takes place in the subject when he assumes an image—whose predestination to this phase—effect is sufficiently indicated by the use, in analytic theory, of the ancient term imago. This jubilant assumption of his specular image by the child at the infans stage, still sunk in his motor incapacity and nursling dependence, would seem to exhibit in an exemplary situation the symbolic matrix in which the I is precipitated in a primordial form, before it is objectified in the dialectic of identification with the other, and before language restores to it, in the universal, its function as subject. This form would have to be called the ideal-I, if we wished to incorporate it into our usual register, in the sense that it will also be the source of secondary identifications, under which term I would place the functions of libidinal normalization. But the important point is that this form situates the agency of the ego, before its social determination, in a fictional direction, which will always remain irreducible for the individual alone, or rather, which will only rejoin the coming-into-being (*le devenir*) of the subject asymptotically, whatever the success of the dialectical syntheses by which he must resolve as I his discordance with his own reality." Jacques Lacan, "The mirror stage as formative of the function of the I," in *Écrits*, trans. from the French by Alan Sheridan (New York, London: Norton, 1977), 2. What is important in the Lacanian description of the mirror stage is the fact that this image is a construct and a fiction, that the identification does not produce a simple recognition but a fundamental "méconnaissance."

10 Hans Dietrich Irmscher's essay "Grundzüge der Hemeneutik Herders" in Johann Gottfried Maltusch, ed., *Bückeburger Gespräche über Johann Gottfried Herder 1971* (Rinteln: Bösendahl, 1973), 17, defends Herder against those interpretations which see him merely as the forerunner of historicism. He explains Herder's sophisticated notion of hermeneutic understanding which takes into account the limited horizon of understanding as productive

for the hermeneutic process. Irmscher points out the relevance of Herder's writings on sculpture and shows how the position of the understanding subject is grounded in his sense of his own body. With regard to the Greek sculpture he remarks that this isolated representation of the nude human body becomes for Herder an image of autonomous individuality (see pp. 31–33). In this attempt to know the individual, as it is developed through the image of the sculpture, Irmscher sees the beginning of morphology and the departure from the classical *epistemé* with its insistence on natural history and the *mathesis* of the classificatory table (see p. 34). Irmscher, however, though emphasizing the "Köpergefühl" as constituting Herder's hermeneutics, does not consider this feeling as constructed with the aid of an idealized fiction, as based on a *méconnaissance*. The essay by Dietrick Harth, "Ästhetik der 'Ganzen Seele'," in Johann Gottfried Maltusch, ed., *Bückeburger Gespräche über Johann Gottfried Herder 1975* (Rinteln: Bösendahl, 1976), 119, sees Herder's concept of "literarische Bildung" as the development of the hermeneutic notion of a divine "Verstehen." Though Harth does not consider the specific role of the ideal body, he acknowledges the idealizing and fictional component in Herder's concept of the soul, which he sees as a compensatory move in idealist aesthetics vis-à-vis modern alienation.

11 For an excellent study of how Hegel's aesthetics in part continue to participate in this neo-classicist rejection of the detail, see chapter 2 of Naomi Schor, *Reading in Detail: Aesthetics and the Feminine* (New York and London: Methuen, 1987), esp. 23–29.

12 See André Green, "L'Angoisse et le narcissisme," in *Narcissisme de vie-narcissisme de mort* (Paris: Éditions de Minuit, 1983), 133–73, esp. 139: "Le Moi travaille sur les représentations, il est travaillé par les représentations, il ne peut être représenté. Il peut, et même il ne peut faire que cela, avoir des représentations d'objet. C'est par l'affect que le Moi se donne une représentation irreprésentable de lui-même." (The Ego works on representations, it is worked on by representations, it cannot be represented. It can have representations of the object, and this is the only thing it can do. It is through the affect that the Ego gives itself an unrepresentable representation of itself.)

13 In "Übers Erkennen und Empfinden in der menschlichen Seele," Herder writes: "Der Körper ist in Absicht der Seele kein Körper: ist ihr Reich: ein Aggregat vieler dunkel vorstellenden Kräfte, aus denen sie ihr Bild, den deutlichen Gedanken sammlet. Sie sind also würklich voneinander abhängig und für einander zusammengeordnet. . . . Kurz, der Körper ist Symbol, Phänomen der Seele in Beziehung aufs Universum." (For the soul, the body is not a body: it is its realm: an aggregation of many obscure forces of the imagination out of which the soul forms its image, i.e., the clear thought. They are actually interdependent and made for one another. . . . In brief, the body is a symbol, a phenomenon of the soul in its relation to the universe.) Suphan, ed., *Herder's Werke*, 8: 250. See also Joe K. Fugate's *The Psychological Basis of Herder's Aesthetics* (The Hague, Paris: Mouton, 1966), a study which shows how all of Herder's writings on aesthetics are intimately bound up with

Herder's notion of the human soul as a unified totality of man's faculties, his perceptions, and creative potential. Fugate's study also points out how Herder's notion of feeling and the body are connected to the soul. Herder's aesthetics, thus, are shown as a critique of rationalism. In his conclusion Fugate attempts to highlight the difference between Herder's and Schiller's aesthetics; Schiller seems to remain a rationalist, an idealist, and a dualist, as opposed to Herder who emphasizes process, natural development, and the unity of the soul. Unfortunately, Fugate gives relatively little attention to Herder's concept of language and the soul's construction in language. More attention to Herder's "Besonnenheit" in relation to Schiller's "ästhetischer Zustand" would have brought those two writers into closer proximity.

14 Cf. Tzvetan Todorov, *Theories of the Symbol* (Ithaca: Cornell Unviersity Press, 1982), 153–64.

15 Cf. Karin Hausen, "Die Polarisierung der 'Geschlechtscharaktere' — eine Spiegelung der Dissoziation von Erwerbs-und Familienleben." In Werner Conze, ed., *Sozialgeschichte der Familie in der Neuzeit Europas* (Stuttgart: Klett, 1976), 363–93.

16 See: "Ists denn nicht Gesetz und Verewigung genug, diese Familienfortbildung der Sprache? Das Weib, in der Natur so sehr der schwächere Teil, muß es nicht von dem erfahrnen, versorgenden, sprachbildenden Manne Gesetz annehmen? Ja heißts Gesetz, was bloß milde Wohltat des Unterrichts ist?" (Isn't there enough law and eternity in this family tradition of language? Woman, in nature so much the weaker part, doesn't she have to accept the law from the experienced, providing, and language-forming man?) Herder, *Abhandlung über den Ursprung der Sprache*, 99.

17 For a survey how the earlier eighteenth century dealt with the Pygmalion story, mainly in either terms of a seduction scenario or in terms of artistic genius, see Hans Sckommodau, *Pygmalion bei Franzosen und Deutschen im 18. Jahrhundert*, Sitzungsberichte der wissenschaftlichen Gesellschaft an der Johann Wolfgang Goethe-Universität Frankfurt am Main, 8, no. 3 (1969).

18 See Sigmund Freud, "Zur Einführung des Narziβmus," *Studiennausgabe* (Frankfurt am Main: Fischer, 1982), 3: 56.

19 "Über Selbstheit und Liebe," Suphan, ed., *Herder's Werke,* 15: 319–20.

The Review in Desfontaines's
Nouvelliste du Parnasse:
The Development of Literary Criticism

PAUL BENHAMOU

There has been growing interest in the French periodical press over the last two decades,[1] but comparable attention has not been paid to the evolution, character, and reception of the literary review in eighteenth-century French journals.[2] While the scope of this paper does not permit full-scale examination, it does take an initial step by analyzing the objectives and rhetoric of reviews written by Abbé Desfontaines for *Le Nouvelliste du Parnasse*. The journal is an ideal case study because it was relatively short-lived, consisting of only fifty-four letters in three volumes appearing between January 1731 and March 1732, and because it was born of Desfontaines's efforts to rewrite the guidelines of literary journalism.

For all practical purposes, the French periodical press may be dated from the seventeenth century. By an established system of privileges and monopolies, the three major periodicals of that age divided the spectrum of information. Political news was handled by the *Gazette*, founded in 1631. Erudition was the domain of the *Journal des savants*, started in 1665. Literature and society were the focus of the *Mercure de France*, begun in 1672.

In the eighteenth century, the older journals faced increasing competition. According to the *Bibliographie de la presse classique* established by Jean Sgard, the number of periodicals grew rapidly, expanding to 42 by

1720, to 70 by 1740, to 114 by 1760.[3] As the number of titles increased, so did the number of copies printed and sold. The public responded favorably to this new medium, which cost less and could be read more quickly than complete works. Readership could rise to around 10,000 — not large by today's standards, but significant in eighteenth-century terms.

Announcements of new books, summaries of their contents, and even a limited amount of evaluation were early features of the periodicals. Most readers appreciated being able to "voir en racourci ce qu'il y a de plus beau dans tous les livres," but some reproached "la trop grande liberté qu'on s'y donn[e] de juger de toutes sortes de livres."[4] The *Journal des savants*, object of such a complaint, retreated to the straightforward summaries that were the hallmark of the seventeenth-century book review. As its editor put it, "il faut avouer c'était entreprendre sur la liberté publique, et exercer une espèce de tyrannie dans l'empire des Lettres, que de s'attribuer le droit de juger des ouvrages de tout le monde."[5]

At least one eighteenth-century editor was less docile. Influenced by the *Spectator* of Addison and Steele, as well as by the emerging spirit of freedom and curiosity, Pierre François Guyot Desfontaines intervened directly in the literary scene by judging books — and authors — and by forming a personal relationship with readers through the epistolary form.

Desfontaines's approach was not popular with writers, most of whom tolerated only reluctantly even the impersonal abridgements of their work typical of the established journals and who were, in any case, predisposed to dislike the whole concept of the periodical. Montesquieu wrote in his *Lettres persanes*, "il y a une espèce de livres que nous ne connaissons point en Perse et que me paraissent ici fort à la mode: ce sont les journaux. La paresse se sent flattée en les lisant."[6] Voltaire detested the "petites gazettes volantes," flyers in which "des hommes incapables de rien produire dénigrent les productions des autres."[7] Rousseau, who tried to start a journal with Diderot in 1749, later expressed contempt for the "barbouilleurs de papier," the scribblers among whom he could have ruined his career. "Un ouvrage périodique," he wrote to Vernes, "n'est qu'un ouvrage éphémère, sans mérite ni utilité, dont la lecture négligée et méprisée par les gens lettrés, ne sert qu'à donner aux femmes et aux sots de la vanité sans instruction, et dont le sort, après avoir brillé le matin sur la toilette, est de mourir le soir dans la garde-robe."[8]

Diderot himself was attracted by the financial possibilities of journalism, as is shown by a letter to Sophie Volland: "Savez-vous qu'il s'agit de me faire pensionnaire du *Mercure* pour quinze cents livres, à condition de fournir une feuille tous les mois? Il y a plus d'un mois que cette agréable perspective dure."[9] In a letter to Grimm, nonetheless, he called journalism a "triste et plat métier," and complained, "il est si difficile de produire une chose, même médiocre; il est si facile de sentir la médiocrité! Et puis toujours ramasser des ordures, comme Fréron ou ceux qui se promènent dans nos rues avec des tombereaux. . . . "[10]

Grimm, who became editor of the *Correspondance littéraire, philosophique et critique* in 1753, shared the dislike of his fellow *philosophes* for those who criticized them; and he condemned unwittingly what he himself was doing in his own literary journal when he wrote: "Je ne trouve rien de plus inutile dans le monde que les faiseurs d'extraits. Les bons ouvrages n'en ont pas besoin parce qu'il faut les lire et non s'en rapporter à un extrait sec et insipide qui, ou prétexte d'en donner la substance, n'en offre que le squelette."[11] Many writers had Desfontaines directly or indirectly in mind when they thus condemned journals and journalists.

Desfontaines is known today primarily through Voltaire's negative comments in *Le Préservatif* (1738) and throughout his correspondence; but as Thelma Morris has so ably demonstrated, he was an important figure on the Paris literary scene. His influence can be dated to the early 1720s when he reviewed a book on religion by Abbé Houtteville, a member of the Académie française, and a popular play by Houdar de La Motte.[13] Employing the biting irony that was to become his trademark, he criticized both works on stylistic grounds, and in addition excoriated de La Motte's play for its departure from the rules of good drama and good taste. The approach, which revolutionized literary criticism, was one he carried to the pages of his *Nouvelliste du Parnasse*.

It is not too much to say that in launching this periodical Desfontaines intended to redefine the nature of the journal and the journalist, both of which were still conceived in seventeenth-century terms. Since by classic definition the journal was largely a collection of excerpts and the journalist their selector, Desfontaines informed his readers that "nous ne faisons pas un journal, mais seulement des réflexions dont nous souhaitons que les gens d'esprit et de goût reconnaissent la justesse en lisant les livres."[14] His subtitle, *Réflexions sur les ouvrages nouveaux*, signalled his approach, as did the foreword to the first issue: "On ne parlera que des ouvrages absolument nouveaux. On s'étendra particulièrement sur les nouvelles pièces de théâtre, et sur les petits livres qui ont le plus de cours dans le monde. . . . "[15] The foreword also showed Desfontaines's intention to restrict his field of inquiry to *belles-lettres*, which he later called his "sphère,"[16] and to avoid religious and political matters. "Nous croyons devoir nous interdire certaines facultés, et particulièrement la théologie et toutes les hautes sciences qui ne sont point du ressort du Parnasse," he told his readers. "Vous voyez bien qu'étant privés de la liberté de parler de ces choses, nous avons un champ bien moins vaste que tous les auteurs des journaux littéraires."[17] Desfontaines also denied several times that he was a journalist. "On est résolu de s'abstenir [de faire des extraits] pour n'avoir aucunement l'air de journaliste,"[18] he said, later adding, "je me suis défendu l'extrait des ouvrages, ce qui est du ressort d'un journaliste."[19]

His goal for the periodical was clear: "Notre but . . . n'a jamais été de faire des extraits des livres nouveaux; nos lettres sont destinées à des réflexions sur les ouvrages d'esprit et sur d'autres, lorsqu'ils amènent l'occasion de dire des choses agréables ou curieuses."[20] From his statement that "un nouvelliste du Parnasse ne doit pas être un gazetier; il doit penser, juger et raisonner,"[21] it is clear that Desfontaines was carving out the role of literary critic. As such, he considered it his primary duty "de faire respecter la raison, le goût, la langue et l'usage,"[22] and "de rendre un compte fidèle des ouvrages nouveaux, et d'en juger selon notre portée après les avoir lus exactement."[23]

Like Pierre Bayle, Desfontaines believed that the Republic of Letters was a free state, and that literary criticism was necessary to its advancement. He let it be known that he would tell the truth about "mauvais auteurs";[24] he took it upon himself to defend classical standards, putting authors "sur leurs gardes, de les forcer d'écrire mieux, et de leur apprendre à respecter le public et à se respecter eux-mêmes."[25] To oversensitive writers like Voltaire, who reacted negatively to critical evaluation of their work and claimed Desfontaines wrote only satire, he took great pains to clarify his position: "Nous jugeons librement; mais nou tâchons toujours d'assaisonner nos jugements et nous nous interdisons absolument tout ce qui pourrait blesser personnellement qui que ce soit. Nous jugeons parce que les auteurs ne publient leurs ouvrages qu'afin qu'on en juge."[26] Desfontaines saw himself as the "guardian and keeper" of the Temple of Fame,[27] the preserver of good taste and classical standards. Quoting his Jesuit mentor Father Porée, he announced that " 'les critiques sont aussi nécessaires dans la République des Lettres qu'une cour de justice l'est dans un état policé' ";[28] and, convinced he was performing an indispensable task, he asked "quel progrès ferait-on dans les sciences et dans les arts sans l'oeil de la critique?"[29]

It is evident that Desfontaines believed the role of the literary critic was significant not only to authors and readers, but also to literary history. In this context, he described the *Nouvelliste* as "d'utiles mémoires qui pourront servir un jour à l'histoire du bel-esprit et des talents de ce siècle."[30] Although his approach antagonized many authors of his time, his journal had great appeal for such men and women of letters as Président Bouhier, Mathieu Marais, and Mme. de Graffigny, all of whom recognized the new role the reviewer was assuming in the Republic of Letters. Reader satisfaction is clear in the following exchange: after reading the *Nouvelliste*, Marais wrote Bouhier that "on se souvient avec plaisir des *Nouvelles de la République* de Bayle en les lisant; le sel y est à pleines mains. . . . Si vous ne l'avez pas lu vous aurez bien du plaisir, et si vous l'avez lu, vous avez dû en avoir." Bouhier's response to the work was that predicted by Marais: "Enfin j'ai eu le plaisir de rire comme vous pour mes cinq sols, et j'ai reçu tout à la fois les seize lettres du *Nouvelliste du Parnasse*. Je les ai dévorées comme vous pouvez bien penser, et j'y ai trouvé beaucoup de sel et de grâce."[31]

In addition to the content and style of the *Nouvelliste*, readers appreciated the epistolary form in which Desfontaines communicated his views on literary works, finding in it the "spectators" and fictitious correspondents popular in the early part of the eighteenth century.[32] Desfontaines's journalistic use of the letter—until the end of the seventeenth century the great channel of communication of the intellectual elite—was not new (the *Gazette*, the *Mercure*, and the *Journal des savants* all included letters from correspondents and readers), but his exploitation of the genre was especially effective.

Each letter pretended to address an anonymous male correspondent who had asked the reviewer to comment on new books and who on occasion reacted to these remarks. Typically, a letter began with such phrases as, "Vous me demandez, Monsieur, des nouvelles du Parnasse"; or, "Vous voulez, Monsieur, que je vous dise ce que je pense des journaux français qui s'impriment aujourd'hui"; or "Vous m'invitez depuis longtemps, Monsieur, à vous entretenir des *Commentaires* latins d'Ausonius publiés à Paris."[33] The epistolary dialogue gave a certain informality to the review, and it allowed the reader to become the interlocutor of the reviewer, someone who listened and responded.

This was certainly Desfontaines's intention. "Ce n'est pas sans raison que nous avons choisi le genre épistolaire, outre que le style en est libre et aisé, certains tours qui lui sont familiers donnent de l'éclat et de la vivacité aux réflections," he said in Letter 12 of the *Nouvelliste*, adding "qu'on se souvienne en même temps que nous écrivons des lettres, où non seulement il est permis de badiner mais qui, destituées de cet agrément seraient froides et insipides."[34]

Besides addressing himself to an imaginary reader at the beginning of each review, Desfontaines maintained the artifice of the letter form throughout the text with such questions and admonitions as: "Avez-vous vu des *Dialogues critiques et philosophiques* imprimés en Hollande chez

Bernard?"; or, "Relisez cette critique que je vous envoie"; or, "Que pensez-vous de cette métaphore martiale?"; or, "Souvenez-vous, je vous prie, du passage de Montaigne. . . . "[35] He concluded each review with the traditional formula, "Je suis, Monsieur, votre . . . "[36] (without, however, signing his name).

Desfontaines proved himself a master of the letter form, and even carried his fictitious correspondence to a new level of reality by pretending to react to comments from his imagined correspondents: "J'ai lu avec plaisir, Monsieur, ce que vous m'écrivez sur le roman intitulé *Les Amours d'Aristée et de Télésie*. . . . Ce jugement, qui en général, est assez vrai, ne m'empêchera pas de vous faire remarquer quelques petits défauts qui m'ont frappé."[37] He also announced that he would include letters from readers in the *Nouvelliste*, even if they were critical of his reviews: "Nous insérons volontiers dans nos Lettres, celles qu'on nous fera l'honneur de nous adresser sur les matières qui peuvent être de notre ressort; il n'y aura qu'à les faire remettre au sieur Chaubert, notre libraire; nous promettons même de faire honneur à celles où l'on combattrait nos sentiments, pourvu qu'elles soient judicieuses et polies."[38] That some readers appear to have accepted his challenge only demonstrates Desfontaines's mastery of the epistolary game. Most if not all of these supposed responses were in fact written by Desfontaines himself.[39]

Like a letter, the length of the reviews in the *Nouvelliste* was not prescribed. Desfontaines could devote twenty pages to Voltaire's *Brutus*, a single page to that same author's *Histoire de Charles XII*. Elsewhere, there were three consecutive letters reviewing a single novel, *Séthos*, by Abbé Terrasson. He even wrote a forty-four page letter on his favorite target, the poet-dramatist Houdar de La Motte, at the end of which he confessed, "Je crois, Monsieur, que c'est assez parler des *Discours* de M. de La Motte: si ma lettre est plus longue qu'à l'ordinaire, c'est que je vous écris sur un auteur qui donne beaucoup à penser à ses lecteurs, et leur fournit d'utiles et longues réflexions."[40] Most reviews were not nearly so long, however, and Desfontaines often truncated them as though bored, using such phrases as "Sans m'engager à une ennuyeuse analyse, il me suffit de vous dire . . . "; or, "Mais c'est assez vous parler de cette glorieuse *Histoire romaine*: je n'ai plus rien à vous en dire."[41] Obviously, there were no editorial guidelines for the length of his reviews. Neither a letter nor the reflections it conveyed was meant to be constrained within a set number of lines.

An examination of the style of the critical discourse in the *Nouvelliste du Parnasse* reveals immediately how much Desfontaines enjoyed being center stage instead of withdrawing behind his text. He preferred the personal pronoun *je* to the more erudite *nous*: "Je n'ai point encore examiné ce livre . . . "; "je doute que . . . "; "j'ose dire que . . . "; "je suis sûr que. . . . "[42] Throughout the review, Desfontaines's voice was clear, even though there were three other editors: "c'est une société de quatre personnes qui ont entrepris cet ouvrage périodique," the publisher announced in the first issue.[43] This new style of direct intervention in the Republic of Letters, at a time when individualism was on the rise, undoubtedly pleased many French readers.

The main characteristic of Desfontaines's reviewing style was its variety, which he justified by saying, "Nos lettres sont nécessairement conformes aux matières que nous traitons. Il nous est aussi impossible d'être enjoués lorsqu'il s'agit de livres sérieux que d'être sérieux quand il est question d'ouvrages d'une autre nature."[44] As the exchange between Marais and Bouhier quoted earlier shows, however, what his readers appreciated most were the irony and wit constantly at play in his work.

There is no doubt that he was the master of the well-turned phrase and the extended metaphor. He described De La Grange's tragedy *Amasis* as "une maison où il y a quelque architecture singulière mais où toutes les pierres ne sont ni bien taillées, ni bien posées; c'est un édifice qui n'est passable que de très loin. Si vous le regardez de près, tout y est gothique et sans aucun goût."[45] At the end of a devastating review of an essay entitled *Dissertation sur le goût*, Desfontaines said, "Après toutes ces remarques, vous ne serez pas étonné que l'auteur accorde à ceux qui ne savent pas le grec la faculté de prononcer plus sainement que ceux qui le savent, sur le mérite essentiel des écrits d'Homère. Ce paradoxe part d'un homme de bon goût."[46]

That his liveliness was deliberate can be seen in his second review of the *Critique desintéressée des journaux*, a French periodical published in Holland in 1730: "J'oubliais presque de vous parler de la *Critique desintéressée des journaux*; ce que je vous en ai dit dans ma seconde lettre, ne vous a pas prévenu en faveur de cet ouvrage; j'ai pourtant eu la patience de le lire; en vérité ces critiques desintéressés qui s'annoncent comme les grands médecins de la République des Lettres, sont bien propres à faire mourir les lecteurs d'ennui."[47] And when his brief comments on Gaullier's *Grammaire* resulted in a long rebuttal by that author published in the *Mercure de France*, Desfontaines replied: "Dix lignes que nous avons écrites à l'occasion de la dernière brochure de M. G. ont produit une réponse de dix pages insérées dans le *Mercure* d'octobre. Quelle brillante fécondité!"[48]

When Desfontaines reviewed well established authors such as Voltaire or Rollin, he altered his technique somewhat to "déguiser notre légère censure sous un air de louange."[49] In writing of Voltaire's *Brutus*, for example, he said, "Malgré ses défauts, qui sont considérables, il faut bien avouer qu'à plusieurs égards, c'est un ouvrage digne d'estime et digne de son auteur. . . . Presque tous les vers de cette tragédie sont des vers de génie et à l'exception d'un petit nombre qui semblent négligés, plus on les lit, plus ils plaisent."[50] Charles Rollin's *Histoire ancienne* suffered similar praise: "Rien de plus noble et de plus épuré que les réflexions de M. R. Mais elles sont d'ordinaire trop longues, ce qui est une dissonance dans une histoire où les faits sont pressés et abrégés. . . . "[51]

Earlier, another of Rollin's works, the *Traité des études*, had been subjected to the same treatment. After inquiring with false diffidence, "Me sera-t-il permis de hasarder mon jugement sur le *Traité des études* de M. Rollin?," Desfontaines went on to credit the author with having "peint agréablement ses pensées; son style est vif, et élégant; mais . . . ses fréquentes contradictions font de la peine à des lecteurs attentifs; elles se dérobent à la plupart des lecteurs entrainés par les agréments du style."[52] Desfontaines was not yet done with Rollin and his *Traité*, however, for he used this review to remind his readers that Rollin's views on rhetoric had been roundly attacked by Balthazar Gibert in *Règles de l'éloquence*. That Gibert had stopped short of identifying by name the author of the erroneous views was an oversight Desfontaines was prepared to explain and redress: "M. Gibert attaque quelquefois M. Rollin dans son nouvel ouvrage, mais il ne le nomme pas; ainsi ce n'est plus une guerre ouverte."[53] After revealing what Gibert had wished to conceal, Desfontaines praised him (and thus indirectly criticized Rollin) by noting "qu'il entend la matière qu'il traite; que les principes de[s] grands maîtres sont bien expliqués, et qu'il y a de la dialectique dans ce qu'il écrit sur l'art oratoire où l'imagination a tant de part."[54] The review ended in another of Desfontaines's effective techniques, that of comparing two works, their authors (and even their antecedents): "En égard à l'ordre et la méthode, la rhétorique de M. Gibert tient beaucoup de celle d'Aristote; et M. Rollin semble s'être formé sur Quintilien qui donne rarement des préceptes sans ornement."[55]

This technique could be used benignly, however, as it was in Letter 16 when, after praising the *Panégyrique de la Régence de Madame Royale, Marie-Jeanne-Baptiste de Savoie* by the Abbé de Saint Réal, Desfontaines introduced another work by saying, "Le plaisir que m'a donné la lecture de ce *Panégyrique*, n'est rien en comparaison de celui que j'ai eu en lisant les *Réflexions nouvelles* de M. de la R****."[56] He even refrained from exposing the author, as he had exposed Gibert's formerly anonymous target, perhaps because he felt it unnecessary: "Quoiqu'on désigne le nom de l'auteur d'une manière un peu énigmatique, il y a tant de finesse dans ses sentiments, tant de délicatesse dans l'expression, qu'on reconnaît aisément cet écrivain célèbre. . . . "[57]

Positive reviews such as those making up Letter 16 were not Desfontaines's norm, and in the end his aggressive approach caused the downfall of the *Nouvelliste du Parnasse*. Its privilege of publication was revoked in March 1732 by a decree of the Council of State. This was an event predicted by at least two of his readers[58] and, it seems, anticipated by Desfontaines: "la vérité, que nous ne craignons point de dire, doit nécessairement indisposer contre nous plusieurs mauvais auteurs, et qui pis est, leurs amis et leurs patrons," he said in Letter 32; "nous avons beau séparer leur personne de leurs ouvrages, et nous abstenir de toute invective et de toute impolitesse: ils ne s'accommodent point de cette distinction si raisonnable; leur orgueil veut des louanges, et leur délicatesse s'offense du moindre trait de critique."[59] In the interest of self-justification, he ignored the fact that his separation of author and work was sometimes so fine as to be invisible. Many writers complained loudly about him to the officials of the Librairie; but their complaints were more contributory than causative factors in the revocation of his privilege. More important was the publication, in early 1732, of *Les Mémoires de Madame de Barneveldt*, a *roman à clé* that created a scandal in Paris through its easily identifiable characters, and which was erroneously (and perhaps slyly) attributed to Desfontaines.[60]

Whatever injured authors thought of his comments, and despite his disclaimer that "nous ne donnons . . . nos jugements que comme de simples avis, ou comme des témoignages, et non comme des décisions,"[61] both Desfontaines and his contemporaries knew that he had redefined the journal and had developed the new genre of literary criticism. As the editor of the *Mercure de France* wrote in 1735 when Desfontaines launched his second journal, *Observations sur les écrits modernes*, "il est le premier qui ait ajouté de la grâce et de la chaleur à l'intérêt de l'analyse, il est le premier qui ait su résumer un livre de façon à en montrer toutes les beautés, tous les défauts comme si vous l'aviez lu vous-même d'un bout à l'autre."[62] Desfontaines himself stated, with what may have been false modesty, that he was performing "un petit travail . . . agréable et utile."[63] Others besides the editor of the *Mercure* were to recognize his true contribution. Among the many posthumous accolades offered him, that of C. M. Giraud is representative: "Né avec un goût sûr et délicat, et cultivé par la lecture des Anciens, il sut allier dans ses écrits la force et le naturel des Grecs et des Latins à la politesse de sa nation. (. . .) On peut dire qu'il fut le créateur de ce genre de critique inconnu jusqu'à lui. . . . Il fallait un homme tel que lui pour venger l'honneur des lettres et s'opposer aux progrès du mauvais goût."[64] Through his reviews, Desfontaines both created and legitimized the role of the professional critic in the Republic of Letters.

NOTES

1 See, for example, Raymond Birn, "The French-Language Press and the *Ency-clopédie*, 1750-1759," *Studies on Voltaire and the Eighteenth Century* 55 (1967):263-86; Jean Sgard, ed., *Dictionnaire des journalistes (1600-1789)* (Grenoble: Presses universitaires de Grenoble, 1976) and its five supplements; Pierre Rétat, ed., *Le Journalisme d'ancien régime, questions et propositions* (Lyon: Presses universitaires de Lyon); Paul Benhamou, "The Periodical Press in the *Encyclopédie*," *French Review* 59 (1986):410-17.

2 Two notable exceptions are Pierre Rétat, "Rhétorique de l'article de journal: *Les Mémoires de Trévoux*," in *Etudes sur la presse au XVIIIe siècle* (Lyon: Presses universitaires de Lyon, 1978), 81-99; and Rémy Saisselin, *The Literary Enterprise in 18th-Century France* (Detroit: Wayne State University Press, 1979), esp. 93-98.

3 Jean Sgard, *Bibliographie de la presse classique (1600-1789)* (Geneva: Slatkine, 1984). The phenomenon did not go unnoticed. At the beginning of the century, Dutch scholar Gisbert Cuper wrote Abbé Bignon, then editor of the *Journal des savants*, "le nombre [des journaux] devient trop grand et l'on pourrait appeler ce siècle le siècle des journaux" ["the number of journals has gotten so out of hand we could call this the century of journals"] (quoted by H. J. Reesink, *L'Angleterre et la littérature anglaise dans les trois plus anciens périodiques français de Hollande, de 1684 à 1709* [Paris: Champion, 1931], 86).

4 "To see in abbreviated form the best part of every book" . . . "the excessive liberty of judging all kinds of books." *Journal des Savants*, 4 January 1666 (repr. [Amsterdam: Pierre le Grand, 1679]), 1:187.

5 "It must be acknowledged that assuming the right to judge the works of all writers infringed on the public liberty, and exerted a kind of tyranny over the Republic of Letters." Ibid.

6 "A kind of book we don't have in Persia seems very popular here: I mean, periodicals. Reading them makes a virtue of sloth." Montesquieu, *Lettres persanes*, ed. Paul Vernière (Paris: Garnier, 1960), 225.

7 "Men incapable of producing anything disparage what others produce." Voltaire, *Oeuvres complètes*, ed. Louis Moland (Paris: Garnier, 1877-1885), 21:278.

8 "A periodical is an ephemeral work, lacking in both merit and utility. It is scorned by men of letters, and serves only to give women and fools a gloss of instruction. Its fate is to shine on the toilet table in the morning and die in the toilet chamber at night." Rousseau, *Corespondance complète*, ed. R. A. Leigh (Geneva: Institut et Musée Voltaire, 1966), 153:116. See also, J. P. Le Bouler, "Jean-Jacques Rousseau journaliste: 'Le Periffleur,' " *Revue des sciences humaines* (January-March 1974), 145-53.

9 "Do you know I may get 1500 *livres* from the *Mercure*, provided I write a column every month? I've had this pleasant prospect in front of me for over a

month." Diderot, *Correspondance*, ed. G. Roth (Paris; Editions de Minuit, 1958), 4:76.

10 "Journalism is a sad and servile trade. It is so difficult to produce something, however mediocre; it is so easy to sniff out mediocrity! And then always having to pick up garbage, like Fréron or those who walk our streets with dumpcarts." Ibid., 259. It should not be forgotten that Diderot's "garbage collector" Fréron was trained by Desfontaines.

11 "I don't find anything more useless than those who write extracts. If a work is good, we have to read it. We can't rely on a dry and insipid extract that pretends to give the heart of the matter but instead gives only its skeleton." *Correspondance littéraire*, 15 July 1755, 1:397.

12 Thelma Morris, "L'Abbé Desfontaines et son rôle dans la littérature de son temps," *Studies on Voltaire and the Eighteenth Century* 19 (1961).

13 Ibid., 34; Saisselin, *Literary Enterprise*, 99–101.

14 "We are not writing a journal but reflections, the soundness of which we hope will be recognized by men of intelligence and taste when they read the books themselves." *Le Nouvelliste du Parnasse, ou Réflexions sur les ouvrages nouveaux*, 3 vols. (Paris: Chaubert, 1731–1732), 1:3.

15 "We shall speak only of absolutely new works. We will deal particularly with new plays, and with the minor books most popular with readers." Ibid.

16 Ibid., 3:170.

17 "We believe we should avoid some areas, particularly theology and all the noble sciences that do not belong to Parnassus. . . . You can see that because we do not allow ourselves to speak of these matters, our arena is much smaller than that of all the authors of literary journals." Ibid., 2:2–3.

18 "We are determined not to write extracts, so that we will in no way resemble a journalist." Ibid., 1:3.

19 "I have refused to write extracts; that is the province of the journalist." Ibid., 1:117.

20 "Our goal . . . has never been to write extracts of new books. Our letters are intended as reflections on the works of the mind, and on other matters when they provide an opportunity to make a few pleasant and interesting comments." Ibid., 1:178.

21 "The writer from Parnassus should not be a gazetteer; he must think, weigh, and reason." Ibid., 2:3.

22 "To force respect for reason, taste, language and its use." Ibid., 2:365.

23 "To read new books carefully, render a faithful account, and evaluate them as honestly as we can." Ibid., 3:67–68.

24 "Bad authors." Ibid., 2:363.

25 "Put authors on their guard, force them to write better, and teach them to respect both the public and themselves." Ibid., 2:194.

26 "We judge freely; but we always try to season our judgments, and we absolutely refuse to say anything that could hurt someone personally. We judge because authors publish their work so that we can judge it." Ibid., 2:4.

27 Saisselin, *Literary Enterprise*, 97.

28 "Critics are as necessary in a Republic of Letters as a court of law in a civilized state." *Nouvelliste*, 2:194.

29 "What progress could be made in the arts and sciences without criticism?" Ibid., 2:16.

30 "Useful diaries that may someday contribute to the history of the wit and talent of this century." Ibid., 2:2.

31 "In reading [the *Nouvelliste du Parnasse*], one is pleasantly reminded of Bayle's *Nouvelles de la République*. It is laced with wit. . . . If you haven't read it, you can look forward to enjoying yourself, and if you have, you've enjoyed yourself already"; "I have finally had the pleasure of laughing like you for my five *sols*. I received the sixteen letters of the *Nouvelliste du Parnasse* all at once. I devoured them, as you can well imagine, and found them full of wit and style." H. Duranton, ed., *Correspondance littéraire du Président Bouhier* (Saint-Etienne: Publications de l'université de Saint-Etienne, 1974), vol. 2, letters 436 and 441.

32 Michel Gilot and Jean Sgard, "Le Journaliste masqué, personnages et formes personnelles," in Rétat, *Le Journalisme*, 286–313.

33 "You ask me, Sir, for news from Parnassus"; "You want, Sir, that I tell you what I think of the French journals printed today"; "You have long urged me, Sir, to speak to you of the Latin *Commentaires* of Ausonius published in Paris." *Nouvelliste*, 1:5, 1:253, 2:337.

34 "It is not without reason that we have chosen the epistolary form, for not only is its style free and natural, but certain of its conventions lend brightness and vivacity to our thoughts. . . . Remember that we are writing letters, where playfulness is not only permitted but required, for without it our reflections would be cold and insipid." Ibid., 1:278–80.

35 "Have you seen the *Dialogues critiques et philosophiques* printed in Holland by Bernard?"; "Reread this piece of criticism I am sending you"; "What do you think of this martial metaphor?"; "Think, please, of the passage in Montaigne. . . . " Ibid., 1:25, 1:33, 2:170, 2:170.

36 "I am, Sir, your. . . . "

37 "I have read with pleasure, Sir, what you wrote me about the novel entitled *Les Amours d'Aristée et de Télésie*. . . . That your evaluation is generally correct will not prevent me from pointing out a few shortcomings that attracted my attention." *Nouvelliste*, 1:161.

38 "Letters sent to us by readers will be included in the *Nouvelliste* if they address matters within our scope. Just send them to M. Chaubert, our publisher. We will even publish those that attack our opinions, provided they are written with thought and civility." Ibid., 1:340, note.

39 See, for example, 1:340 and 3:122. In the edition of the *Nouvelliste du Parnasse* kept in the Bibliothèque Nationale (Rés. Z.2979–81), which is supposed to have belonged to Desfontaines's collaborator François Granet, the source of these anonymous letters is revealed each time by a manuscript note in the margin: "écrit par le Nouvelliste" ["written by Desfontaines"].

40 "I believe, Sir, I have said enough on the *Discours* of M. De La Motte. If my

letter is longer than usual, it's because I am writing you about an author who makes his readers think, and who provides them with lengthy and profitable reflection." *Nouvelliste*, 1:167.

41 "Rather than get involved in a tedious analysis, I will say only that"; "I have said enough about this illustrious *Histoire romaine*: I have nothing more to tell you about it." Ibid., 1:167, 2:204.

42 "I haven't yet looked at this book"; "I doubt that"; "I dare say that"; "I am sure that." Ibid., 1:18, 1:35, 1:101. To critics who reproached him for his lack of erudition, he replied, tongue-in-cheek, "Ignorez-vous que pour certaines gens c'est avoir une vaste et profonde érudition, que de joindre beaucoup de hardiesse à une grande ignorance" ["Don't you know that for some people, a vast and profound erudition means joining audacity to great ignorance?"]. Ibid., 3:186.

43 "Four persons are collaborating on this periodical." Ibid., 1:4. Desfontaines's collaborators were Granet, Castre d'Auvigny, and La Clède.

44 "Our letters necessarily conform to the subjects we treat. It is as impossible for us to be playful when we deal with serious books as it is to be serious when the works are not." Ibid., 3:67.

45 "A house of peculiar architecture, in which the stones are neither well cut nor well laid. As an edifice, it is acceptable only from afar; if you look at it closely, everything is primitive and pedestrian." Ibid., 1:141.

46 "After these remarks, you will not be astonished to learn that the author feels those who don't know Greek have a greater ability to judge the works of Homer than those who do. This paradox comes from a man of taste." Ibid., 3:180.

47 "I almost forgot to mention the *Critique desintéressée des journaux*. What I told you about it in my second letter did not predispose you in its favor. I have had the patience to read it, however. In truth, these disinterested critics who proclaim themselves the great doctors of the Republic of Letters are likely to make their readers die of boredom." Ibid., 1:288–89.

48 "The ten lines I wrote about M. G[aullier's] last pamphlet resulted in the ten-page response published in the *Mercure*. What brilliant fecundity!" Ibid., 2:333.

49 "To mask our mild criticism behind a cover of praise." Ibid., 2:364.

50 "Despite its faults, which are considerable, we must admit that it is in many respects worthy of esteem and worthy of its author. . . . Nearly all the lines of this tragedy are lines of genius and, except for a few that seem unpolished, the more one reads them, the more pleasing they become." Ibid., 1:70,.

51 There is nothing more noble or refined than the reflections of M. R[ollin]. Most are too long, however, and this creates a discordant note in a history where the facts are compressed and abridged. . . . " Ibid., 3:268–69.

52 "May I be permitted to offer my judgment of the *Traité des études* by M. Rollin?. . . . painted his thoughts with grace; his style is lively and elegant; his frequent contradictions pain attentive readers, they are missed by readers carried away by his style." Ibid., 1:40.

53 "M. Gibert sometimes attacks M. Rollin in his new work, but he doesn't name him; this way, it is no longer open warfare." Ibid., 1:39.

54 "He understands the subject he is dealing with; the principles of the great masters are well explained, and there is logic in what he says about the art of oratory in which the imagination plays so important a role." Ibid.

55 "In order and method, M. Gibert's rhetoric is very close to that of Aristotle; M. Rollin seems to have been trained by Quintilian, who rarely offers his precepts unadorned." Ibid., 1:41.

56 "The pleasure I received in reading this *Panégyrique* is nothing compared to that which I had in reading the *Réflexions nouvelles* by M. de la R****." Ibid., 1:380.

57 "Although the author's name is given in a somewhat enigmatic manner, his views are so refined, and their expression so graceful, that we can easily recognize this celebrated writer." Ibid., 1:380. The author referred to was Marquis Henri-François de La Rivière. Desfontaines sometimes cloaked himself in a spurious anonymity. In the multi-layered Letter 32, for example, he pretended that his true identity was not yet known, and that "le nom même assez connu de ceux à qui on nous fait l'honneur d'attribuer ces Lettres, est une espèce de rideau. . . . Nous nous applaudissons de l'*incognito*. . . . " ["the well-known persons to whom these letters have the honor of being attributed are a kind of curtain. We congratulate ourselves on our *incognito* . . . "]. Ibid., 2:367.

58 Mathieu Marais wrote Président Bouhier on 27 April 1731 that "cet ouvrage est si vrai qu'il ne peut durer" ["This work is so true it cannot last"]. Bouhier agreed: "Je crois néanmoins qu'on peut en faire le même horoscope qu'un Italien faisait d'un enfant qui avait l'esprit trop au-dessus de son âge. Ce qui veut dire: *non durata*" ["I believe all the same that it will have the same fate as an Italian predicted for an overly intelligent child. In other words, it won't last"]. Duranton, *Correspondance*, vol. 2, letters 436 and 441.

59 "We are not afraid to tell the truth, and this necessarily sets many bad writers against us; what is worse, their friends and patrons must also oppose us. . . . Try as we might to separate their person from their work, and to abstain from all invective and incivility, they are unable to accept this reasonable distinction. Their pride demands praise, and their sensitivity is offended by the slightest criticism." *Nouvelliste*, 2:363.

60 See Françoise Weil, *L'Interdiction du roman et la Librairie, 1728–1750* (Paris: Aux amateurs du livre, 1986), 161–75; and Morris, "L'Abbé Desfontaines," 48.

61 "We offer . . . our judgments as mere opinion, or testimony, and not as decrees." *Nouvelliste*, 2:364.

62 "He is the first to temper analysis with grace and warmth, the first who knew how to sum up a book in a way that so revealed its beauties and flaws that it was as if you had read it yourself from beginning to end." *Mercure de France*, May 1735, quoted by Morris, "L'Abbé Desfontaines," 145.

63 "A pleasant and useful little work." *Nouvelliste*, 2:367.

64 "Born with a sure and delicate taste he cultivated by his reading of the Ancients, he knew how to combine in his writings the strength and simplicity of the Greeks and Romans with the polished civility of his nation. . . . One can say that he was the creator of a kind of criticism heretofore unknown. . . . A man such as he was necessary to vindicate the honor of literature and to check the advance of tastelessness." C. M. Giraud, "Préface," in Abbé de La Porte, *L'Esprit de l'abbé Desfontaines, ou Réflexions sur différents genres de science et de littérature. . . .* 4 vols. (London: Clément, 1757), 1:7. See Morris, "L'Abbé Desfontaines," 125–26, for similar statements by Meusnier de Querlon and Abbé Irailh. In reading Giraud's eulogy, we should remember that as a teacher of rhetoric at Bourges, Desfontaines had taught the *dispositio*, and could draw from the classical rules of exordium, narration, proof, and peroration in defining the form, tone, and focus of his commentary.

Just *When* Did
*"British bards begin t'Immortalize"?**

TREVOR ROSS

I begin with an image, the now familiar image of a young author working in the humbling presence of his canonical fathers. The author is Christopher Smart, as he is depicted in the frontispiece to his periodical *The Universal Visiter.*[1] Smart is seated at a writing desk, at work on the next issue of his paper. He is gazing up at a row of five busts, raised on a mantel and surrounded by an oversized laurel wreath. The busts bear representations of Chaucer, Spenser, Shakespeare, Waller, and Dryden. Each bust has a verse legend inscribed on its base. These verses are reprinted below the frontispiece:

> To CHAUCER! who the English Tongue design'd:
> To SPENCER! who improv'd it, and refin'd:
> To Muse—fir'd SHAKESPEAR! who increas'd its Praise,
> Rich in bold Compounds, & strong-painted Phrase,
> To WALLER! Sweet'ner of its manly Sound:
> To DRYDEN! who its full Perfection found.

Behind the busts are bookshelves containing a number of folios, including the works of Gower, "Hubert," Sidney and eighteen other English authors. Above these bookshelves is a Latin inscription which tells us this is Apollo's Temple of the English. In addition to this engraving, a miniature of "A. Cowley" is reproduced on the title page, which also bears the following epigraph:

> Sounding with Moral Virtue was his Speech,
> And gladly would he learn, and gladly teach.
> CHAUCER

We may choose to read this image of the young ephebe writing under the influence of his great English masters as somehow typical of the eighteenth century. It is, after all, during this century when collected editions and handsomely-printed folios of the works of esteemed national poets begin to appear in large quantities in England. During the middle decades of the century, as well, there develops a minor vogue for busts and portraits of well-known English authors.[2] In many of these portraits, the subject is shown wearing a laurel wreath; Kneller and Richardson both drew a proudly laureated Pope. Above all, it is during the eighteenth century that the English people first seem to think highly of their own literature, so highly that young poets like Smart begin to experience "anxiety" under the burden of a newly-discovered English literary tradition.

Yet the reality is a little more complicated than this reading of the frontispiece suggests. Folio editions and frontispiece engravings of English poets had been produced since the sixteenth century. Portraits of eminent national authors had been commissioned for private collections since at least the Caroline age. And English poets had been shown wearing laurels in frontispieces ever since a laureated Skelton appeared in a woodcut before a collection of his works printed in the early 1540s.[3] As for the anxiety of influence, Smart's burden is somewhat more immediate than the pressure of tradition on the individual talent: Johnson reports that Smart's contract for *The Universal Visiter* "was for ninety-nine years," during which period Smart was bound to write nothing else.[4]

I wish to contest the claim that the English began to make and celebrate a canon of their literature only sometime in the eighteenth century. This claim was put forward a few years ago by Howard Weinbrot, in an essay on Thomas Gray. Weinbrot in fact devoted nearly half of his essay to providing evidence for what he called the eighteenth century's "increased affection for national letters." After presenting his evidence, Weinbrot declared that "the information in the first part of this essay of course is intended to be suggestive rather than exhaustive; it is prolegomena to a longer study of the rise of British and the decline of classical literature and values during the Restoration and the eighteenth century. This should appear sometime before the second coming."[5] Second coming or no, I have been working on such a study, in the possibly vain hope of meeting Pope's challenge to "Fix the year precise / When British bards begin t'Immortalize" (*Epistle to Augustus*, ll. 53–54). I have concluded that it is misleading to suggest that English literature began to be "affectionately" received only during the eighteenth century. Certainly neoclassical standards gave way to more indigenous Romantic values during this period. But this should not be taken to mean that the canon of national letters was "formed" only in the generations following the deaths of Pope and Swift. That canon-formation is a late occurrence seems to be a common assumption among literary historians. In *The Ordering of the Arts in Eighteenth-Century England*, Lawrence Lipking contends that, prior to Johnson's *Lives of the English Poets*, "there was . . . no canon of what was best." Marilyn Butler argues for an even later date in a recent lecture entitled "Revising the Canon," where she states categorically that "a single, official English literary history emerges only in the 1820s."[6]

One crucial distinction must be emphasized here: canon-formation is not literary history. They are related activities, but it is more useful to see them as contrasting functions. When we practice literary history we are relating literary works to a wider context, to other works, to aspects of the author's personal history or of a broader socio-political history, to the history of ideas, genres, conventions, printing, and so on. Yet when we select or "elect" a canon of great works of art, we are removing those works from their historical context, and inserting them in an imaginary pantheon that we assume will last forever. Though canon-formation is never an apolitical gesture, we often find it reassuring to believe that canonical texts themselves are empowered with an authority that is beyond politics. A canonical text, we say, possesses an aura, a sacredness, a value and a meaning that survive the text's contextual origins and the "test of time."

If we accept this definition of canon-formation, then it is possible to argue that the idea of a national canon of letters has been the hope and purpose of English authors from very early on. In fact, canon-making may be considered an inevitable consequence of self-consciousness in writing, a phenomenon that "begins" when authorship itself begins. What is probably the oldest extant poem in the language, *Widsith*, is in part a mythic "canonization" of the medieval minstrels, idealized in the legendary title character who travels far and wide to sing of and immortalize countless Saxon kings. Canon-making, in this way, originates in the self-defining gestures of authors eager to legitimize their profession and to lend aura and authority to their tradition and its writings. Chaucer, it seems clear, was nominating himself to a European canon in the *envoi* to *Troilus and Criseyde*, just as his followers, in calling him the first "refiner" of the vernacular, were installing him at the head of a new indigenous canon. Consciously-fashioned canonical texts such as *The Shepheardes Calender* and Jonson's 1616 folio *Workes* are equally gestures at self-definition though, in these works, the spotlight is on the individual poet rather than the tradition as a whole.

Canon-making of an institutional nature is inaugurated during the Elizabethan period. Poets' Corner in Westminster Abbey, the closest thing in England to an actual pantheon of dead authors, comes into being at this time, the bodies of Spenser, Drayton and others being interred in the vicinity of a monument to Chaucer first erected in 1555. Most of the major works of Elizabethan criticism and national historiography contain roll calls of authors, usually beginning with Chaucer and then moving quickly to Sidney, Spenser, and "other most pregnant wits of these our times, whom succeeding ages may justly admire."[7] Already, in 1595, there appears a proposal calling on English universities "to canonize your own writers"; the proposal includes a list of potential nominees, including Spenser and Shakespeare, and a lengthy discussion of how an official canon might both raise England's reputation abroad and help quell dissent at home.[8] Even nobles are exposed to this secular canonizing, in the masques and entertainments held in their honor. In one of Ben Jonson's masques, *The Golden Age Restor'd*, the eminent bards Chaucer, Gower, Lydgate, and Spenser are called before Astraea "to wait upon the age that shall your names new nourish."[9] My personal favorite of these episodes occurs in William Drummond's "Entertainment" for King Charles I's visit to Edinburgh in 1633. According to Drummond's instructions, "a Mountaine dressed up for *Parnassus*" was to be built in the middle of an Edinburgh roadway. On top of this Highland Parnassus, there would stand the Scottish canon, represented by impersonations of Duns Scotus, Gavin Douglas, and, interestingly enough, George Buchanan. Buchanan was the author of a controversial history of Scotland that was later used by Republican apologists to defend the execution of King Charles.[10]

Prior to the eighteenth century, there is at least affection for the idea of a national canon. That said, a change does occur between 1660 and 1780, a change that is related to the rise of criticism and literary history. The nature of this change is suggested in something Richard McKeon has written in relation to the history of Christian dogma. "In the course of the development of canon law," McKeon argues, "the art of rhetoric, which takes into account the character and authority of speakers, the circumstances and sensibilities of audiences, and the modes and styles of communications, was transformed into an art of interpretation by which apparent contradictions of conflicting canons might be removed or justified by consideration of differences of audiences, circumstances, and intentions as they determine differences of meaning in what is said."[11] By analogy, when early English authors or critics wish to praise a work, they merely assert its value. They make claims for it, usually with reference to standards derived from classical rhetoric, such as "eloquence." They assume, not entirely incorrectly, that the tastes and sensibilities of their readers are much like their own. Yet when more and more critics make identical claims about increasingly diverse works, there is bound to be disagreement. And it is no use trying to impose new standards because these will inevitably conflict with established standards. A solution is to relax the absoluteness of standards, using historicist arguments such as "times change," "tastes change," or "the aims and styles of writing change." In this way, interpretations of changing values gradually replace or supplement declarations of value. In other words, it is the practical necessity of overcoming contradictions in the definition of the English canon that leads to the rise of literary history and interpretive criticism in the eighteenth century.

Among the evidence Weinbrot cites for increased affection for the canon is a statement by Charles Gildon from 1694, near the time when the controversy of the Ancients and Moderns was reaching its peak. Says Gildon, "We have the Honor to have more and better Poets than ever Greece or Rome saw."[12] English writers have been making claims like this for a long time. John Denham, eulogizing Cowley's death in 1667, declares proudly:

> By *Shakespear*'s, *Jonson*'s, *Fletcher*'s lines,
> Our Stages' lustre *Rome*'s outshines.
> ("On Mr. Abraham Cowley," lines 11–12)

We can go back further. Almost twenty years before the appearance of the first "Golden" English work, *The Shepheardes Calender*, the poet Barnaby Googe tells his readers that "English verse . . . is little inferior to the pleasaunt verses of the auncient Romaines. . . . There hath flourished in England so fine and filed phrases, and so good pleasant Poets as may countervayle the doings of *Virgill, Ovid, Horace, Juvenal*, &c." Or how about the antiquarian John Bale, writing in the 1550s on how it was that the erudition of ancient British bards and druids had outclassed even Greek learning?[13]

Statements such as those just quoted are rhetorical assertions, of the kind that permeated practical criticism in England until the end of the seventeenth century. Asking whether these statements are true or whether they indicate broad cultural aspirations is like asking the same thing of modern advertising. Like advertisements, these statements contain distortions of the truth and yet they do reflect certain cultural expectations.

And it is with this type of statement that early English poets, critics, and publishers chose to promote the value of the English literary canon.

By "practical criticism," I do not mean only the early rolls of authors. Included here are such items as printers' addresses to the reader, commendatory verses, prologues and epilogues, and elegies to dead poets. By modern standards, these items contain very little if any descriptive or interpretive criticism, but they are filled with claims and declarations calculated to influence the reception of literary works. It is in these items that we can find the early English canon being made. Indeed, because one of the dominant conventions of testimonial verses is to set the author's name alongside those of celebrated precursors, enduring public awareness of the canon owes something to the art of puffery.[14] Puffery is a marketing strategy, as are many of the other rhetorical statements of early criticism. In printers' prefaces, for example, there frequently appears a peculiar figure usually called the "learned reader." "I esteeme more the prayse of one learned Reader," says the poet George Gascoigne, "than I regard the curious carping of ten thousande unlettered Tattlers."[15] Gascoigne is trying to sell his poetry by pandering to his audience's sense of its own learned superiority. The learned reader is a figure of elitist canon-making; and "he" — it is always "he" — is one of a number of devices designed to persuade actual readers to buy and praise the book.

The learned reader is an extraordinarily long-lived character. "He" has never entirely left us, and yet he originates in a very old theory of the classic. For early critics, the canonical text is the one that has retained some timeless truth despite the vulgarity and changefulness of common humanity. The learned reader does not express this theory, though. He remains a device for manipulating audience responses. Contrast the learned reader to the common reader who, though equally a rhetorical figure, is not a marketing tool. The common reader personifies an interpretation rather than an assertion of value. "He" (or "she") is an abbreviated form of the theory that says the meaning of the canonical text survives for common humanity, in all its diversity. The common reader appears most famously in Johnson's "Life of Gray," where Johnson uses the figure to defend the high reputation of Gray's *Elegy Written in a Country Church-Yard.*[16] Johnson has little respect for Gray; the poet who wants nothing more than to keep to his private chamber represents, for Johnson, elitist posturing at its worst. But Johnson likes Gray's *Elegy.* Johnson uses the common reader to get around the difficult question of why it is that an apparently negligible poet like Gray has managed to produce one great canonical poem. "I rejoice," Johnson writes, "to concur with the common reader. . . . The *Churchyard* abounds with images which find a mirror in every mind, and with sentiments to which every bosom returns an echo."[17] By considering only the poem's reception among a diverse audience, Johnson brushes aside the perceived contradiction between Gray the bad poet and his *Elegy* the great poem. Instead of fashioning an audience for the canon through rhetorical suasion, Johnson simply accepts the public's judgment in whatever choices it makes.

The idea of a common reader dates from the early decades of the seventeenth century, a period of strain if not crisis for the English literary system. Divisions of one kind or another have been recognized in the English tradition almost from the start: medieval authors of "learned" or religious works routinely set their literature above popular forms, while classical rhetoric dictated that all works had to be judged in accordance with a strict hierarchy of genres. It is only in the early seventeenth century that conflicts emerge within the definition of the official "learned" canon. Initially, these conflicts are restricted to the formation of rival schools of poetry: the "sons of Ben," the "Donne circle," Drayton and the "Spenserians." Gradually, however, the literary system in England, which had been rigidly stratified during the Elizabethan period, begins to lose some of its definition and "structural integrity."[18] Professional authors, already laboring under censorship, now had to compete against a growing mob of gentlemanly amateurs who were trying their hands at playwriting, formerly the exclusive trade of anonymous writers-for-hire. In addition, the market for popular drama was disintegrating, to the accompaniment of a good deal of imperious opinion-making on the part of the courtiers. Reacting to this assault, professionals like Massinger uphold a notion of the "publique test" for literary works, as if this were a valid alternative to the elitism of the courtiers.[19] Frustrated "laureate" poets like Drayton likewise oppose the idea of "publique censure" to the excessive sense of privacy and privilege among the coterie poets.[20] The "public test" is a forerunner of the "common reader," though it is equally an oblique expression of nostalgia for the glory days of Elizabethan consensus, when all readers of learning seemed to have the same sensibilities.

The courtiers keep to their private chambers; there they meet as a definable community for whom there still exists a sense of the aura and controlled intimacy of literary performances. By preserving an atmosphere of consensus, it is easy for the courtiers to believe in the rightfulness of their judgment. Gildon, in the work quoted above, recounts how one such gathering brought together several prominent members of the Caroline court to debate the relative merits of Shakespeare and the ancients: "on that appointed day, my Lord *Falkland*, Sir *John Suckling*, and all the Persons of Quality that had Wit and Learning, . . . met there, and upon a thorough Disquisition of the point, the Judges chose by agreement out of this Learned and Ingenious Assembly, unanimously gave the Preference to SHAKESPEAR."[21] The unanimity masks anxiety. It is no coincidence that at this time there occurs a marked increase in elegies and testimonials as Royalist poets desperately seek to hold on to a sense of community. A record number of them (over fifty!) contribute commendatory verses to the 1651 edition of the works of fellow royalist William Cartwright. "He shall be read as Canon," says one of the commenders.[22] On the other side, Parliament closes the theaters. Censorship, in a sense, emanates from a fear of conflicting canons. As McKeon notes, the "Greek word 'heresy' is derived from election or selection: everyone elects what seems to him best."[23]

With the Restoration, the conflicts become formalized in the familiar competing standards of Ancient versus Modern, French versus English, the rules versus native genius. Scholars have recently begun to look at other, less "literary" conflicts. The emerging political parties of the Restoration, for example, were eager to claim canonical texts for their cause, and to base value judgments on their own paradigms of Tory stability and Whig liberty. Whig publishers of the 1680s and 1690s strategically republish works by Marvell, Milton, and other republican writers to coincide with political events like the Exclusion Crisis and the Glorious Revolution.[24] Milton's nephew, Edward Phillips, compiles a catalogue of authors, the *Theatrum Poetarum* (1675), that gives short shrift to Cleveland and other royalist poets. A dozen years later, Phillips's catalogue is rewritten by the Tory William Winstanley in an effort to restore the reputations of authors like Cleveland who devoted their careers to "Vindicating the Royal Interest, and undeceiving the People." In 1713, Samuel Croxall produces Whig revisions of Spenser, "Design'd as Part of his Fairy Queen but never printed," which provokes an angry response from *The Examiner*: "to have Treason and Sedition utter'd in the Name and Language of Spenser, is an Iniquity that has few Precedents."[25] Naturally this Tory critic goes on to quote some notably absolutist passages from Spenser's original. All these examples may indicate a "desperate quest for authentication" among rival parties, though with Cleveland, and perhaps Spenser, it is as much a case of a party seeking cultural legitimation as it is of a minor scholar trying to rehabilitate a forgotten author with the help of partisan rhetoric.[26]

The conflict that interests me is the one the English canon has with itself, or rather, with its older self. By the mid-seventeenth century, the language of the earliest poets seemed very remote and could not conceivably be praised under the prevailing standards of eloquence. One solution was to revise the canon, a solution put forward by the poet George

Daniel in "An Essay; Endeavouring to ennoble our English Poesie by evidence of latter Quills; and rejecting the former." Daniel proposes that Chaucer be dropped from the list:

> in-authentike Chaucer's furnishment,
> Adds nothing to our Poesie, in his Store;
> Nor let vs call him Father anie more.[27]

Chaucer was still being read at the time by Pepys and other readers of learning. It is just that his greatness could not be described under the terms of classical rhetoric. Revision of the canon on this scale would, however, expose a particularly troubling contradiction. Chaucer had been at the head of the canon for some 250 years. As Robert Greene asked in 1590, "who hath bin more *canonized* for his works than Sir Geoffrey Chaucer?"[28] Chaucer was no passing fashion. Removing him from the canon was tantamount to admitting that all works of the canon could not be expected to last. Waller says as much in his poem "Of English Verse," where he claims that English poets should hope for no more than a lifetime of love. But immortality has been the prime operative trope behind canon-formation and, indeed, poetry since the dawn of the West. Without the prospect of immortality, the making of canons is absurd. To reject the old poets is, in essence, to accept the contradiction that the making and revising of canons cannot but affirm the death of poetry.

Authors would continue to revise the canon and to look for new poetic fathers. Dryden, for one, selects Waller to be "the father of our English numbers," but Chaucer remains for Dryden the "father of English poetry."[29] Earl Miner has argued that Dryden "was the first to conceive of Chaucer as a classic"; this, despite the fact that the famous defense of the poet in the "Preface to the *Fables*" seems to do no more than rehearse "the major Elizabethan conceptions of Chaucer."[30] The importance of the preface lies not in its declaration of Chaucer's permanent value, but rather in the way in which Dryden uses a historical argument to diminish the authority of prevailing and conflicting standards. For all his talk of a language coming to "perfection," Dryden's case rests on an idea of change, of languages and standards growing obsolete. "Customs are changed," he says, "and even statutes are silently repealed, when the reason ceases for which they are enacted." Or, more starkly, "mankind is ever the same, and nothing lost out of Nature, though everything is altered." Dryden admits that Chaucer is "not harmonious to us," yet rather than apply a rigid principle of eloquence, Dryden says that "they who lived with [Chaucer], and some time after him, thought [his verse] musical."[31] There are, in other words, different audiences, circumstances, and intentions to be considered. This is not the first time a historicist interpretation has been taken up in the defense of an old text. But it is the first time such an interpretation has been used to help retain an undeniably great yet very distinctive and "irregular" poet in the English canon. Dryden's historicism allows for a plural canon, something totally unheard of in earlier English criticism. The contradictions of permanence and change, obsolescence and perfection, plurality and harmony, all still exist but Dryden has removed them from the discourse of canon-making; they are, for him, among the inevitable contradictions of history and civilization.

Within a decade of Dryden's preface, critics are referring to English works as "classics." Elijah Fenton, in a testimonial to Thomas Southerne, tells him his plays "shall stand / Among the chosen classics of our land."[32] Canon-formation may not be a late occurrence but the normative usage of "classic" is. It appears late in antiquity. Originally the Latin term designated the top tax bracket. Only in the second century A.D. is it used to refer to the top rank of authors. It appears relatively late in English, too, in the late 1620s.[33] The reason for these late debuts is that the term "classic" itself expresses an awareness of "belatedness."[34] The Elizabethans tended to think of antiquity as a rival empire that had declined and dispersed. For the Jacobean pessimists, antiquity seemed more like a remote Golden Age, whose towering works of art had nonetheless survived the Fall. A similar attitude is present when critics start to call English works "classics." Thus Fenton, at the same time as he praises Southerne, looks back with nostalgia at a former time:

> There was an age (its memory will last!)
> Before Italian airs debauch'd our tastes.[35]

This sense of belatedness inevitably translates into disaffection over the conditions and literary production of the present: "it must be confessed that we have *classic-authors* in our own language also, a proper study of whose elegant works would make us look with contempt on the prettiness so profusely lavished on the compositions of some modern writers."[36] Because of their agedness, however, classics retain an element of strangeness and need to be made ready for the modern reader. As George Sewell says in his preface to "Volume Seven" of Pope's *Shakespeare*, "what then has been done by the really Learned to the dead Languages, by treading backwards into the Paths of Antiquity and reviving and correcting good old Authors, we in Justice owe to our own great Writers, both in Prose and Poetry. They are in some degree our *Classics*."[37] Here, then, is the paradox of canon-making: English writings begin to be called "classics" at the very moment when they begin to seem remote, obscure, in need of revival, correction, "modernization."

Pope had nothing to do with the seventh volume of his edition of Shakespeare—it was merely Sewell's reprint of an earlier spurious "volume seven" from Rowe's edition. He may therefore have been targetting Sewell when he mocked the indiscriminate usage of "classic" in the *Epistle to Augustus*. Mimicking the voice of critical fashion, Pope says,

> "Who lasts a Century can have no flaw,
> I hold that Wit a Classick, good in law."
> (55–56)

Pope ridicules the mindlessness of such prescriptions, in much the same way as he criticizes elsewhere the provincialism of observing an exclusively national canon.[38] Yet, surely, Pope felt "affection" for national letters. He wrote several imitations of earlier English poets. His edition of Shakespeare was intended to make the plays more intelligible for the readers of his time. He even helped raise funds for Shakespeare's monument in Poets' Corner.

Johnson refers to Horace's one-hundred-year rule in his "Preface to *Shakespeare*." Shakespeare, he says, "has long outlived his century, the term commonly fixed as the test of literary merit." The hundred-year rule is but one of many interpretations of canonical value found in Johnson's criticism:

-the common reader; or,

-"length of duration and continuance of esteem;" or,

-"it has had the best evidence of its merit. . . . Few books, I believe, have had a more extensive sale;" or,

-"To judge rightly of an author, we must transport ourselves to his time, and examine what were the wants of his contemporaries, and what were his means of supplying them."[39]

Strictly speaking, these methods of determining value are contradictory: canon-making by appeal to the "generality," to the "test of time," to sales figures, or to literary history. No doubt modern scholars will continue to try to reconcile Johnson's contradictions and to close what Johnson never wished concluded. But it is with these and other interpretations that Johnson, and those who follow him, justify an English canon composed of authors as diverse as, respectively, Gray, Shakespeare, Bunyan, and Dryden.

There is no real increase in affection for national letters in the eighteenth century. There are more readers and many of them remain unfamiliar with classical literature—for the majority of the British people, English became a literary language at the moment the Bible was translated into the vernacular. There are more editions of the works of early English authors, though this partly results from a relaxation of copyright laws on old books. There is more formal recognition given to English poetry in the universities, though this stems from the rise of the "new rhetoric," which made it possible to think of the "belles lettres" as a separate category of writing and hence a distinct discipline.[40] There is expansion of the canon to include works before Chaucer and popular forms like ballads and novels. There is also contraction, or at least rankings of selections—Shakespeare rises as Waller falls. What does happen in the eighteenth century is not an increase in approval for the canon, but a gradual removal of conflict in how it is defined. With the publication of Johnson's *Lives*, canon-making in England seems to become ordered and systematic though, in one important way, it also becomes more flexible and open to change.

NOTES

*I would like to thank Brian Corman and Laura Hopkins for their invaluable assistance in the preparation of this article.

1 The frontispiece appears before the reprint volume, *The Universal Visiter and Memorialist. For the Year 1756* (London, 1756).

2 In a letter dated 25 June 1761, Robert Dodsley asks William Shenstone to choose a pair of statues from among a list that includes the pairings "Locke and Newton," "Chaucer and Spencer," "Shakespeare and Milton." Adds Dodsley, "When you have fixed upon which Pair you will have, you will let me know whether you will have them white or bronzed." Quoted in *Five Hundred Years of Chaucer Criticism and Allusion (1357–1900)*, ed. Caroline F. E. Spurgeon, 3 vols. (Cambridge: Cambridge University Press, 1925), 3:93.

3 Woodcut from John Skelton, *Certayn Bokes coppied by Mayster Skelton Poet Laureat* (London, c. 1545), reproduced in David Piper, *The Image of the Poet: British Poets and their Portraits* (Oxford: Clarendon Press, 1982), 9.

4 James Boswell, *The Life of Samuel Johnson, LL.D.*, ed. George Birkbeck Hill, rev. L. F. Powell, 6 vols. (Oxford: Clarendon Press, 1934–1950; with corr., 1964), 2:345.

5 Howard D. Weinbrot, "Gray's 'Progress of Poesy' and 'The Bard': An Essay in Literary Transmission," in *The Age of Johnson*, ed. James Engell (Cambridge, MA: Harvard University Press, 1984), 315, 322 n.24. Ratios like Weinbrot's that set the "rise of British" against the "decline of Classical litera-

ture" seem typical of the unverifiable, rhetorical claims that characterize canon-making in its early phase. Authors have been placing the English above the classical canon since at least the sixteenth century, while there are many who maintain that the classics "decline" only in this century: "I rather think we are now passing through a period when the greatest classical authors are changing guard, and that Homer and Virgil have had their day." Robert Birley, *Sunk Without Trace* (London: Hart-Davis, 1962), 12. It would seem rather that the nature of this "guard" is gradually altered to include both the ancients and the moderns.

6 Lawrence Lipking, *The Ordering of the Arts in Eighteenth-Century England* (Princeton: Princeton University Press, 1970), 3; Marilyn Butler, "Revising the Canon," *Times Literary Supplement* (4–10 December 1987), 1349.

7 William Camden, *Remains Concerning Britain*, ed. R. D. Dunn (Toronto: University of Toronto Press, 1984), 294.

8 William Covell, *Polimanteia* (London, 1595), sig. Q2^v.

9 Ben Jonson, *Works*, ed. C. H. Herford, Percy Simpson, and Evelyn Simpson, 11 vols. (Oxford: Clarendon Press, 1925–1952), 7:425.

10 William Drummond of Hawthornden, *Poetical Works*, ed. L. E. Kastner, 2 vols. (Manchester: Manchester University Press, 1913), 2:123. On the politics of Buchanan's *History*, see David Norbrook, "*Macbeth* and the Politics of Historiography," in *Politics of Discourse: The Literature and History of Seventeenth-Century England*, ed. Kevin Sharpe and Stephen N. Zwicker (Berkeley: University of California Press, 1987), 78–116.

11 Richard McKeon, "Canonic Books and Prohibited Books: Orthodoxy and Heresy in Religion and Culture," *Critical Inquiry* 2 (1975): 794.

12 Charles Gildon, *Miscellaneous Letters and Essays* (London, 1694), sig. A8^r.

13 Barnaby Googe, pref. to his translation of Marcellus Palingenius, *The Zodiake of Life* (London, 1565) sig. ($\neq$)3^v; John Bale, *Scriptorum Illustrium maioris Brytanniae . . . Catalogus*, 2 vols. (Basel, 1557–1559), 1:4.

14 This convention has a long history in England. Among the editorial apparatus appended to the "authorized" manuscripts of Gower's works are two sets of commendatory verses that go so far as to compare the English poet's output to Virgil's. Gower is in fact said to have the upper hand over Virgil because of his ease at writing in three languages. C. G. Macaulay has included these verses in his edition of Gower's *English Works*, 2 vols. (London: Early English Text Society, 1901), 2:479.

15 George Gascoigne, *The Posies*, 2nd ed. (London, 1575), sig. ¶iiij^v–¶¶^{r}.

16 This is not the figure's first appearance in English criticism. In the "Dedication of the *Æneis*" (1697), Dryden offers the point that whether or not Virgil broke a poetic rule in extending the action of his poem beyond a year "is of no more concernment to the common reader, than it is to a ploughman, whether February this year had 28 or 29 days in it." *Essays*, ed. W. P. Ker, 2 vols. (Oxford: Clarendon Press, 1900), 2:204. See Clarence Tracy, "Johnson and The Common Reader," *Dalhousie Review* 57 (1977): 405–23.

17 Samuel Johnson, *The Lives of the English Poets*, ed. George Birkbeck Hill, 3 vols. (Oxford: Clarendon Press, 1905), 3:441.

18 As Richard Helgerson has explained, the Elizabethan literary system recognized three classes of authors: the courtly amateur like Sidney, the semi-anonymous professional like Greene, and, in between, the ambitious "laureate" poet like Spenser (who shared with the amateur a schooling in civic humanism yet differed from the amateur in relying, like the professional, on an expanding print culture). This hierarchy, Helgerson argues, provided authors with a set of enabling definitions and a "clarity of outline from a structure of sharply opposed forces. Humanist expectations played against amateur prodigality; amateur prodigality, against laureate seriousness; laureate seriousness, against professional anonymity. But by the time the Caroline poets began to make themselves known, the tension had gone out of this system of oppositions and had not yet redistributed itself to create a new pattern of authorial roles. The old building still stood, but nothing was holding it up." *Self-Crowned Laureates: Spenser, Jonson, Milton and the Literary System* (Berkeley: University of California Press, 1983), 186.

19 Philip Massinger, "A Charme for a Libeller," in Peter Beal, "Massinger at Bay: Unpublished Verses in a War of the Theatres," *Yearbook of English Studies* 10 (1979): 199. Courtiers have never refrained from maligning popular forms, but this elitist posturing is by the 1630s something a lot more aggressive, with the courtiers apparently making a conscious effort to direct the tastes of the town. Massinger, in this poem, is responding to a particularly strident set of commendatory verses written by Thomas Carew for William Davenant's play *The Just Italian* (1630). Carew, in these verses, compares the "Rabble" of Massinger's theater to an "untun'd Kennell" that treats drama like a piece of "meat" (cited in Beal, 190).

20 Michael Drayton, *Works*, ed. J. William Hebel, rev. Kathleen Tillotson and Bernard Newdigate, 5 vols. (Oxford: Shakespeare Head Press, 1931-1961), 3:231.

21 Gildon, *Miscellaneous Letters*, sig. G3^v

22 Ralph Bathurst, pref. to William Cartwright, *Comedies, Tragi-Comedies, with other Poems* (London, 1651), sig. **2^v. Bathurst is punning on Cartwright's clerical calling. P. W. Thomas has discussed the relation between Cavalier "morale-boosting" gestures like the Cartwright volume and the crystallization of a classicism that "images the centralizing and institutionalizing tendencies of the aristocratic élite, tendencies only fortified by the upheaval of 1646." *Sir John Berkenhead 1617-1679: A Royalist Career in Politics and Polemics* (Oxford: Clarendon Press, 1969), 133-40, 176-79.

23 McKeon, "Canonic Books," 792. Annabel Patterson has discussed how seventeenth-century authors learned to avoid censorship by shrouding their politically-sensitive material behind a "functional ambiguity." In this way, Patterson suggests, political censorship helped generate the modern view of "literature" as a peculiarly refined discourse. *Censorship and Interpretation: The Conditions of Writing and Reading in Early Modern England* (Madison:

University of Wisconsin Press, 1984), 4–18. It is also worth speculating on how the notion of a secular canon of literature was based not only on the Biblical model but equally on its opposite, the idea of a profane "apocrypha" or index of proscribed books. After all, "blacklists" of controversial or offensive titles are a common feature of early anti-romance and anti-theatrical tracts. Moreover, the authors of those tracts implicitly endorse the idea of select canon whenever they call upon images of social anarchy caused by unrestrained eclecticism and cultural pluralism. Thus these self-styled guardians of public well-being routinely insist on the profusion of bad literature compared to the scarcity of good works, inveigh against what they perceive to be the vastly disproportionate attention lavished on "improper" books over others considered more suitable readings, and put forward the alarming possibility that civilization may lose its few valuable tomes amid an endless torrent of worthless printed trash. *Pace* Benjamin, there is no dream of literary pantheons that is not at the same time a vision of hellish Dunciads.

24 On the publishing activities of the republican "Calves-Head Club," see A. B. Worden, ed., *Edmund Ludlow's A Voyce From the Watch Tower*, Camden Society Publications, 4th ser., 21 (London: Royal Historical Society, 1978): 17–21.

25 William Winstanley, *The Lives of the Most Famous English Poets* (London, 1687), 220; Samuel Croxall, *An Original Canto of Spenser* (London, 1713) and *Another Original Canto of Spenser* (London, 1714); *The Examiner*, vol. 5, no. 6 (14–18 December 1713): 2.

26 Sharpe and Zwicker, "Politics of Discourse: Introduction," *Politics of Discourse*, 13.

27 George Daniel of Beswick, *Poems*, ed. Alexander B. Grosart, 4 vols. (Boston, Lincolnshire, 1878), 1:81.

28 Robert Greene, *Greenes Vision* (London, written 1590; pub. 1592), sig. C3^r.

29 John Dryden, pref. to William Walsh, *A Dialogue Concerning Women* (London, 1691), quoted in *The Critical Opinions of John Dryden: A Dictionary*, ed. John M. Aden (Nashville: Vanderbilt University Press, 1963), 275; and "Preface to *Fables, Ancient and Modern*," in *Essays*, ed. Ker, 2:257.

30 Earl Miner, "Chaucer in Dryden's *Fables*," in *Studies in Criticism and Aesthetics, 1660–1800*, ed. Howard Anderson and John S. Shea (Minneapolis: University of Minnesota Press, 1967), 59, 71.

31 Dryden, "Preface to *Fables*," 2:267, 263, 258.

32 Elijah Fenton, "An Epistle to Mr. Southerne, from Kent, January 28, 1710/11," in *Works of the English Poets*, ed. Alexander Chalmers, 21 vols. (London, 1810), 10:399.

33 The *OED*'s earliest entry for "classic," as an adjective denoting the literature of ancient Greece and Rome, dates from 1628. Massinger, in the poem quoted above, contrasts the excessive privacy of the coterie poets to the wide and unrestricted popularity of the "Classique Poets" (199). On the normative usage of "classic" in antiquity, see Ernst Robert Curtius, *European Literature*

and the Latin Middle Ages, trans. William R. Trask (New York: Harper & Row, 1963), 249.

34 That classics are the absent presences against which latecomers define themselves is evident from a revealing statement by Charles-Augustin Sainte-Beuve near the end of his essay "What is a Classic?" (1850): "Let us be satisfied with feeling them [the classics], with interpreting them, with admiring them, and for ourselves, latecomers that we are, let us try at least to be ourselves." Trans. A. J. Butler, repr. in *Critical Theory Since Plato*, ed. Hazard Adams (New York: Harcourt Brace Jovanovich, 1971), 562.

35 Fenton, "An Epistle to Mr. Southerne," 10:399.

36 W. Z., "Parallel between the French and English Writers, Part II," *The Universal Museum and Complete Magazine* (October 1765), 527.

37 George Sewell, pref. to "Volume Seven" of Pope's edition of Shakespeare's *Works*, repr. in *Shakespeare: The Critical Heritage 1623–1801*, ed. Brian W. Vickers, 6 vols. (London: Routledge and Kegan Paul, 1974–1981), 2:419.

38 Pope may also be responding ironically to John Dennis's sharp comment on his earlier prescription of "Threescore" for canonical status in the *Essay on Criticism*: "Now what does young Mr. *Bays* mean by *our second life*, and by *bare Threescore*? If he speaks of himself, and means threescore days, he means too much in Reason: But if he speaks of *Chaucer, Spenser*, and *Shakespear*, and means threescore Years, he means too little in Conscience. 'Tis now a hundred Years since *Shakespear* began to write, more since *Spencer* flourished, and above 300 Years since *Chaucer* died. And yet, the Fame of none of these is extinguish'd." John Dennis, *Critical Works*, ed. Edward Niles Hooker, 2 vols. (Baltimore: The Johns Hopkins University Press, 1939–1943), 1:410.

39 Samuel Johnson, *Works*, ed. A. T. Hazen et al. (New Haven: Yale University Press, 1958–in progress), 7:60–61; Boswell, *Life*, 2:238; Johnson, *Lives*, 1:411.

40 See Wilbur Samuel Howell, *Eighteenth-Century British Logic and Rhetoric* (Princeton: Princeton University Press, 1971).

Restoration and Repression: The Language Projects of the Royal Society

JOEL REED

Historians studying the eighteenth century need not look to V. N. Voloshinov to realize that "the word is the most sensitive index of social changes"; writings of the early 1700s show an awareness of language's social context two hundred years before Voloshinov made his observation, even if those doing the work would find themselves opposed to Voloshinov's motivations.[1] At the close of the seventeenth century members of the Royal Society were doing the most important work on the English language, Thomas Sprat and Bishop John Wilkins in particular. We might in retrospect call their work socio-linguistics and, in Sprat's case, a kind of discourse analysis, for they were especially concerned with the social context of language usage, with the two-way relationship between language and the society which speaks it. Of course, an important distinction between Voloshinov and his predecessors in sociolinguistics is that while Voloshinov's project was linked with one of the most important revolutions of our century, we can link the Royal Society's linguistics to the most significant counter-revolutionary movement of theirs: the Restoration.[2]

Paralleling the restoration of the monarchy were Sprat and Wilkins's efforts to restore language to an earlier, mythic purity, a double return of the repressed that is by no means coincidental. The politics of Royal Society linguistics is at least as significant as the Society's scientific contributions to the study of language for what it reveals about the political and ideological shifts at the turn of the century. In their work we see an important conjunction of the beginnings of scientific discourse, the episteme of rational experimentalism that Timothy Reiss investigates, and a much older theological discourse which in the context of the Restoration could only be called a politico-theology.[3] Royal Society discourse analysis was particularly concerned with the relation between a fallen language and a fallen state, and with the proposition that a language saved from the fall, a language redeemed, could play a part in saving from corruption the state which speaks that language.

This linguistic politico-theology was developed in two closely linked texts. Sprat's *History of the Royal Society* (1667) and Wilkins's *Essay Towards A Real Character and a Philosophical Language* (1668) were printed for the Royal Society only a year apart, though the chronology of the texts must be complicated by the fact that Wilkins had completed his *Essay* in 1665, and it was nearly completely in print in 1666 when it was destroyed by the London fire.[4] Thus, deciding which came first, Sprat or Wilkins, and which text is the primary or original one in the politico-theological linguistics, is more complex than it might seem from publication dates; the matter is complicated still further when we realize that Wilkins acted as a supervisor and ghost writer of Sprat's *History*.[5] Of course, this conjunction does not suggest that we regard these texts as identical; Wilkins's invention of a universal language is precisely an example of the kind of research that Sprat refers to as the Royal Society's principal work, while Sprat's text, rather than being a particular scientific study, has other functions. His history was written only five years after the Society received its charter from Charles II, but Sprat takes advantage of his project to work in a statement of intentions—a manifesto of sorts—as well as a "Defence and Recommendation of Experimental Knowledge."[6] But an investigation of the development of a new discourse that relies heavily on the older theological forms allows us to see their work, at least on language and language history, in a close and even complementary relation.

The Restoration plays an important role in their linguistic projects, both as a political and ideological ground, for what motivates Royal Society linguistics is precisely the restoration of an Adamic language and a return to an earlier time and social order that can be used to push forward new national projects. In a passage often quoted from the *History of the Royal Society*, Sprat writes that the goal of the Royal Society's "manner of discourse" is: " . . . to return back to the primitive purity, and shortness, when men deliver'd so many things, almost in an equal number of words. They have exacted from their members, a close, naked, natural way of speaking . . . bringing all things as near the Mathematical plainness, as they can" (*History*, 113). This passage is significant because of its interweaving of two important, complex themes. Sprat leads his readers back to Adamic language theory and forward to a discourse of science and rationality. The combination of these two themes exemplifies the heterogeneous structure of cultural formation that Raymond Williams posits in his discussion of dominant, residual, and emerging cultures. Williams's concept of historiographic periodization allows room for exceptional cultural elements at any given time; to speak of a dominant cultural practice does not mean that this practice can only be characterized through a single, totalizing view. In any dominant or hegemonic culture can be found traces of that culture's history, as well as newly incorporated social values and meanings.[7] The double theme of Royal Society discourse—its reliance on the residual Judeo-Christian utopia of Eden and its evocation of the emerging discourse of scientific rationalism—plays important roles in legitimating the social order of the Restoration.[8]

The importance of a residual theology is clear in the nostalgia of Sprat's emphasis on the return back to the pure origins of language, or on the restoration of language to its pure state, and is similar to that of Wilkins in his *Essay*. Purity lies in the prehistory of English, in a language that we do not know, but only know of, as told to us through the Judeo-Christian tradition. Wilkins retells the story of this language: "the first language was con-created with our first Parents, they immediately understanding the voice of God speaking to them in the Garden" (*Essay*, 2). Fluency in the first language was immediately accessible to Adam and Eve through God's voice, through the divine act of speech itself. The Jewish scholar Gershom Scholem emphasizes the centrality of this divine speech act in his theoretical work on sacred languages. His reference to "le 'dit' de la langue, son contenu"[9] defies the profane conception of the signifier/signified opposition. Wilkins also finds that the unity of content with form is an indication of the sacred language, and in Wilkins we see that the origin of this language goes back to the beginnings of the world, to a pure origin before the Fall. In Eden the name for something not only referred to an object, but also communicated its essence; the chasm between signifier and signified was closed as the name presented an immediate understanding of the referent.

The Edenic language was lost with the expulsion of Adam and Eve, though linguistic multiplicity did not develop until the collapse of the Tower of Babel. This is a familiar history, though particular attention should be drawn to the importance of the double fall in this version of linguistic history. Because of Adam and Eve's fallen state, time itself will inevitably corrupt language. It is because of this inevitable corruption that the Royal Society's manner of discourse must be a "return back to the primitive purity" (*History*, 113), where Sprat's use of purity carries both a sense of an unmixed language, one free from other influences, and a theological sense of a language undefiled or uncorrupted.

Despite this implicit acknowledgment of a corrupt language, Wilkins posits a counter-reading which suggests that the very notion of language, and of the letters that compose it, has sacred associations: " . . . something should also be premised concerning letters, the Invention of which was a thing of so great Art and exquisiteness, that Tully doth from hence inferr the divinity and spirituality of the humane soul, and that it must needs be of a farr more excellent and abstracted Essence then mere Matter or Body, in that it was able to reduce all articulate sounds to 24 Letters" (*Essay*, 10). While highlighting the secular nature of language in this passage by admitting its "Invention," a creation by man rather than God, Wilkins also suggests the possibility that a relationship between a divine spirituality and the human can be found through the materiality of letters. This play between the secular and the sacred allows the possibility that a sacred language can be humanly created, an important justification for the other mixtures found in these texts, those of science and religion, theology and politics. It appears from the passage that the major manifestation of this divinity is in the artfulness of language paradoxically made all the more artful through its simplicity. For it is with the reduction of all possible sounds to only two dozen letters that Wilkins closes his paragraph, and reduction (as the necessary course to take towards a return to or restoration of the Adamic tongue) is an important aspect of both his and Sprat's linguistic ideal.

Citing the Bible, Wilkins points out that not all languages are equally sacred. Hebrew is the most sacred language, if not the sacred language of Eden, for it is both the oldest and the simplest: "the ancient Hebrew Character hath the priority before any other now known . . . And 'tis amongst rational arguments none of the least, for the truth and Divine Authority of the Scripture, to consider the general concurrence of all manner of evidence for the Antiquity of the Hebrew, and the derivation of all other Letters from it" (*Essay*, 11). Emphasizing Hebrew's position as the earliest language since the fall, Wilkins also reminds his readers that in the past he had "proposed the Hebrew Tongue as consisting of fewest Radicals."[10] Simplicity, or in Sprat's terms "primitive purity," that stresses the importance of a reduced number of signs necessary for communication is important in defining the divine nature of language.

Wilkins was not the only universal language projector of his time, nor was he unique in finding a connection between linguistic simplicity and signs of divinity. Leibniz also makes this connection. In a letter written to Princess Elizabeth in 1678, Leibniz debates Descartes's views on the proof of God's existence and finds that it is in the simple, in itself—what he will later call the monad, "a *simple* substance," "the elements of things"—that evidence of God's existence can be found.[11] As does the Royal Society, Leibniz connects this relation of simplicity and divinity to linguistic investigations:

> . . . cette caractéristique représenterait nos pensées véritablement et distinctment et quand une pensée est composée de quelques autres plus simples, son caractère le serait aussi de même . . . ce qui est le fondement de ma caractéristique l'est aussi de la démonstration de l'existence de Dieu; car les pensées simples sont les éléments de la caractéristique, et les formes simples sont la source des choses. . . . si elle est accordée il s'ensuit que la nature de Dieu qui enferme toutes les formes simples absolument prises, est possible.[12]

In many ways Leibniz's description of this characteristic sounds like Sprat's presentation of Royal Society discourse. His emphasis on the true and clear representation of thought is similar to Sprat's concern with a "short" manner, while the importance of simplicity as a sign, and even proof, of God's existence can also be found in Wilkins. If anything Leibniz is clearer on the interrelations of the sacred with a simple or "pure" language than the British, though their relations are evident. Leibniz, in fact, knew of Wilkins's work on universal languages, and, though Wilkins had died by the time of Leibniz's first visit to London, the German philosopher was able to meet with Robert Boyle and other members of the Royal Society.[13] The connections of the Leibnizian language project and those of the German *Sprachgesellschaften* to the projects of the Royal Society are evident both on this personal level, and in the less subjective historical move towards a politico-theological view of language. It is their connection that also separates them, for both the German *Sprachgesellschaften* and the British Royal Society were working towards particularly nationalistic projects; they used the same theoretical models to assert their own linguistic superiority and primacy.[14]

The "shortness" that Sprat highlights in Royal Society discourse is another approach to the simplicity that Wilkins valued both in Hebrew and in the establishment of his "real character," of which he writes that "the reducing of all things and notions, to such kind of Tables, as are here proposed . . . would prove the shortest and plainest way for the attainment of real Knowledge, that hath been yet offered to the World."[15] Sprat attempts this valorization of reduction through the importance he places on the delivery of "so many things, almost in an equal number of words" (*History*, 113), a delivery, incidentally, which he personally found impossible to accomplish. With this equation of things with words he introduces elements of the emerging discourse of experimentalism. Simplicity is valued in the Royal Society's discourse, but we can also see in this simplicity the importance of proportion, that things should be represented in an equal number of words, or that the words should be in proportion to things, a measure of symmetry which would also be a way to close the gap between the signifier and the referent. This proportion is measured with the skills learned from mathematics, the logic of quantification that is here an integral part of the sacred, primitive, naked language. The importance of these linguistic views lies in this integration of the sacred with the scientific logic of measuring and quantification, and in the political importance that this combination had for Restoration England.

It was the Royal Society's intention to create a language, a creation that would turn back to what existed before language. Though their most radical language projects — such as Wilkins's — never caught on, the Royal Society was able to develop a discourse that would sanctify their already secular and corrupt language, and this was done with an explicitly utilitarian goal in mind. As with Wilkins's aims for his universal language, efficiency of communication was the goal of Royal Society discourse. With both Wilkins's creation of a new universal language and Sprat's redemption of English, efficiency of communication would be in the national interest.

In the section entitled "Experiments advantageous to the Interest of our Nation," Sprat makes explicit the relationship between the Royal Society's works, including their linguistic reforms, and national interest. He begins: "It now follows in the last place, that I examin the Universal Interest of the English Nation" (*History*, 419). While this effectively calls our attention to the nationalistic theme of the section to follow, we may find this passage suggestive in its odd use of "Universal." In conflating the universal with the national, Sprat introduces the interests universal to all of the English, while he also suggests that what is good for the English is good for the world, an important leap made possible though another element of the theological. If the English were divine, if they were a sacred or a chosen people, they might be able to help others; their personal interests would best serve the world. On the next page Sprat asserts, "There are very many things in the Natural Genius of the English, which qualify them above any other for a Governing Nation" (*History*, 420). There is a divine power implicit in the word "natural" as Sprat uses it, suggested earlier in its relation to the purity of the Royal Society's "naked, natural way of speaking." A tracing of this divinity is further supported by what Sprat calls "a good sign, that Nature will reveal more of its secrets to the English, than to others; because it has already furnished them with a Genius so well proportioned, for the receiving, and retaining its mysteries" (*History*, 114-15). There are really two "good signs" here; the first is a sign of the logic of the sacred, marked in the logic of proportion which governs the natural and mystical revelation, and the second is a sign of nationalism, of national advantage and the power that knowledge brings to its first discoverers.

The Royal Society is the mediator of this national advantage. Sprat outlines a number of ways that England could improve, and discusses in each how the Society's work will lead to that improvement. Sprat writes that "The first thing that ought to be improv'd in the English Nation, is their Industry"; after positing various ways of accomplishing this, he writes that "the tru Method of increasing Industry, is by that cours which the Royal Society has begun" (*History*, 421-22). Sprat finds the second need for improvement in the "English . . . inclination to every Novelty, and vanity of foreign countries, and a contempt of the good things of our own, . . . This wandring, and affected humor Experiments will lessen, above all other studies. They will employ our thoughts about our native conveniences: they will make us intend our minds, on what is contain'd within our own Seas" (*History*, 424). Experimental practice, the emerging cultural form that the *History* defends, will strengthen the national culture and national market by closing off the British borders to international "wandring." Sprat discusses other national interests which the Royal Society will serve as well. He is more thorough than Wilkins, who generalizes the utility of his universal language project as "that most obvious advantage which would ensue, of facilitating mutual Commerce, amongst the several Nations of the world, and the improving of all Natural knowledge; It would likewise very much conduce to the spreading of the knowledge of Religion."[16]

While Wilkins presents his advantages within the rhetoric of universality and mutual benefits, Sprat believes commerce or industry and natural knowledge should be used to a particularly English advantage. The importance of "religious knowledge" in Wilkins's utilitarianism, however, presents a more complex problem; it is connected through divine or sacred qualities to the natural knowledge which we earlier saw as a uniquely English advantage. The importance for the British nation in particular of this religious knowledge is increased through the by now familiar connections of colonial exploration to missionary settlement throughout the world. But religious knowledge also brings the Society back to a consideration of language itself, through the sanctity of the Royal Society's languages that were either created from nothing in Wilkins's case, or saved from corruption. If we consider that these sacred languages may be used best, as Wilkins says, to communicate the knowledge of religion, a theory of language emerges that is completely self-reflexive: a theory of a sacred language that can only talk about conditions of sanctity and ways to achieve those conditions. This theory calls for material conditions that must in fact already exist to demonstrate its sanctity. That is, the very thing that it says it will make possible must already be present for this sacred language to be sacred. With the development of their languages Wilkins and Sprat are able to move from a rotten language, one that decomposes with every change, and hence at every moment, to a language of closure, that refers only to itself and its own (pre)conditions. This language communciates other things as well — an instrumentalization of this sacred language, and its sanctification through instrumentalization.

Sprat suggests the ultimate instrumentalization of the sacred language when he brings together the topics of nationalism, utility, sanctity, and the institution. The last benefit Sprat finds in the work of the Royal Society and its discourse of rational experimentalism is "Obedience to the Civil Government": " . . . we ought to be very watchful that they [the works of the Society] prove not offensive to the Supreme Power: For being that the King has honor'd them with His Royal Patronage, it is but just that the Praerogatives of His Crown should be no losers by their increase" (*History*, 427). Sprat writes of the danger from the supreme power, the power by whose grace the Society's work and language is allowed to continue. But there is an important slippage of power here: Sprat's supreme power is secular, as is his sacred language — secular and utilitarian, yet divine — allowed to exist through supreme grace. In the face of the potential jealousy that the supreme power may feel if it should be the loser by the Society's "increase," Sprat assures his readers that "[t]he Work [of the Society] is so vast, that it cannot be perform'd without the assistance of the Prince: It will not therefore undermine his Authority whose aid it implores" (*History*, 429). Sprat's solicitation of the prince is no accident. Among its functions, the *History* both thanks Charles II for his support and asks for continued assistance. This is displayed most graphically in Sprat's reproduction of the charter the society was granted in the section following "The incouragements the R. S. has receiv'd at home" entitled "From the Royal Family" (*History*, 129, 133). Thus Sprat makes it clear that, rather than undermining royal authority, the Society and its work will support monarchy by enlightening the Supreme Power's subjects:

> Experiments . . . will take away all pretence of idleness, by a constant cours of pleasant indeavors; they will employ men about profitable

Works, as well as delightful; by the pleasure of their Discoveries they will wear off the roughness, and sweeten the humorous peevishness of the mind, whereby many are sowr'd into Rebellion. (*History*, 428)

From this passage it seems that the Royal Society's activities are simply so much busy work, distractions that will keep men's minds in their laboratories and away from the social causes of political dissent.

It should not come as a surprise to find that when the Society proposed institutionalizing their sacred utilitarian language the themes we have been looking at remained in the foreground. The English Academy would be the most pertinent of the Society's innovations to our discussion, and there too we find the importance of reduction in language and the connection of this redemption to the state. Here, however, in the specific proposal of a new state institution, nationalistic themes take on a more militant character. The section of Sprat's *History* entitled "A proposal for erecting an English Academy" contains an abridged history of language that is explicitly concerned with the nationalistic implications of the politico-theological. Sprat connects a strong language to a strong state, historically supporting this connection:

> . . . the purity of Speech, and greatness of Empire have in all Countries, still met together. The Greeks spoke best, when they were in their glory of conquest: The Romans make those times the Standard of their Wit when they subdu'd, and gave Laws to the World: And from thence, by degrees, they declin'd to corruption; as their valour, their prudence, and the honor of their Arms did decay. (*History*, 41)

With this passage Sprat makes explicit a connection that has only been implicit thus far; in so doing he exposes a violence that is latent in the control of discourse and its channeling into one particular mode. The salvation of the language and the nation does not come through prayer and good deeds, but rather through a crusade against threatening territories. The state and the language become so closely and aggressively bound together in this imperialist history because in this section Sprat is concerned with the creation not only of a new—though sacred—discourse, but also with the promotion of this discourse as the official language, the state's language, which is enmeshed with the fate of the state itself. The opposite of purity—corruption or decay—is also present in this passage; there are historical connections between linguistic corruption and the decline of an empire or state.

The first, though not the most important, task of the Academy would be the improvement and regulation of English. It is in this improvement that Sprat rediscovers the importance of reduction to the restoration of purity: " . . . if some sober and judicious Men, would take the whole

Mass of our Language into their hands, as they find it, and would set a mark on the ill Words; correct those, which are to be retain'd; admit, and establish the good . . . " (*History*, 42). His proposal is for a careful judging and disciplining of the language; words that are beyond rehabilitation will be disciplined with "a mark" that implicitly will lead to their censorship out of the lexicon, while those with a chance of correction might be saved. This linguistic judgment occurs within the framework of a moral judgment of "the good" versus "the ill" or bad, and this will be an established judgment, as if it were set down in a book of Roman laws.[17] A subtext here that suggests a leap from this linguistic-moral judgment to a process of political judgment is evident through the passage's framing in Sprat's text by a history which proves his thesis of the connection of pure speech to great empires. The logic which finds a homologous relationship between pure speech and great empire might by extension view that which corrupts speech, the "ill" words Sprat refers to, in the same way it sees those who threaten the greatness of the empire. In the wake of the Restoration, the republicans, the Diggers, and Levellers at their most radical fringes would take on the "mark" of the "ill."

The extension of Sprat's logic away from the socio-linguistic and in the direction of the socio-political is more than implicit, as is clear in the importance he gives to the Academy's second function. Rather than expanding on the Academy's function as linguistic jurists, a function that might be expected to be its most important, Sprat quickly moves on to describe what "greater Works" may be "found out for it" (*History*, 42). With the production of an official history of the civil war the Society would add one more layer to the development of its politico-theology, moving from the creation of a sacred-utilitarian language, through the institutionalization of this language, and ultimately to the inscription of this language in a sacred text. Sprat is very clear about this text's function: "The effects of such a Work would be wonderfully advantageous, to the safety of our Country, and to His Majesties Interest: for there can be no better means to preserve his Subjects in obedience for the future, than to give them a full view of the miseries, that attended rebellion" (*History*, 44).

Conflating the safety of the state with that of the king, Sprat blends those whose safety and interests might lie elsewhere with those whose interests are with the monarch. This conflation is suggested in the earlier reference to "*some* sober and judicious Men" who would make up the Academy, though Sprat avoids specifically suggesting who this would be. If, however, we take the Society itself as a model for the Academy, we would find that just such a conflation occurred. Sir Henry Lyons, in his history of the Royal Society, asserts that "at no time was there any attempt on the part of the Society . . . to limit admission to the Fellowship to any social class, or to hinder the entry of skilled craftsmen or any candidate of middle-class parentage. . . . [18] Lyons may have been temporarily blinded by his desire to dedicate his text to the Royal Society, a dedication graciously acknowledged by the Society's president in a prefatory note. Lyons also points out that though there was only one peer in the list of original Society members, "on December 12 [1660] barons and all of higher rank were declared to be eligible for election as a special privilege on the same day that they were proposed."[19] Indeed, a list of the Fellows from 1663 to 1687 reveals far more earls, dukes, and politicians than merchants or artisans.[20] This early privilege must have increased in the Society's first hundred years, for by the late eighteenth century most of the Fellows "belonged to the aristocracy either by birth or by virtue of their positions and affiliations. . . . The Royal Society had indeed become a gentlemen's club . . . seemingly unaffected by the winds of reform and equality that were blowing more and more strongly around it."[21]

Though the Society may have been oblivious to the revolutionary movements of the late eighteenth century, those of the seventeenth century had a profound effect on how it conceived its projects. This effect becomes clear in the connection between the reference to obedience and subjection in the description of the proposed Academy's history of the wars, to those references of the socio-linguistic political history Sprat previously presented, the history of subjection of an Empire to Laws. Sprat writes that the Romans "gave Laws to the World," no doubt consciously using language which we might expect — as Sprat was himself a clergyman — to be reserved for Moses. But while the Romans are the lawgivers, the sacred text is to be the enforcer of the laws. This enforcement is to take place through a deterrent sentence meted out not in the hopes of rehabilitation of the criminal, but to preempt any future transgressions of the law. The Academy's history would be the inscription of a public execution, presenting in "full view" the wrath and revenge of a supreme king.[22] This justice is not only that of an angry god, but is also related to the benevolence of a god who would execute justice in the interests of "safety," a merciful justice which by preventing the possibility of rebellion would preserve the peace of a strong state.

Within a humanistic and rational investigation of linguistics and the history of language lies a violence that is not confined to the field of discourse. The violence of institutional efforts to control language is also a form of controlling political dissent, and in the seventeenth century this double violence occurred through the same gesture. This gesture was in some ways a retrograde one in its dependence on the older religious discourse, yet this was a necessary return as the Royal Society pushed forward the new discourse of rationality and analysis by attaching it to the older form. The sanctification of a secular-utilitarian discourse was one way to ensure the existence of this new discourse in a time of transition. But the violence of this discursive transformation, like the violence that latches itself onto understandings of the sacred, or the violence of a rationality as reductive as the Royal Society's, is always just below the surface of that very discourse. For Restoration language reformers, the violence of repression was preferable to that of rebellion.

NOTES

1 V. N. Voloshinov, *Marxism and the Philosophy of Language* (Cambridge, MA: Harvard University Press, 1986), 19.

2 Jacques Derrida suggested the direction of this investigation in the seminars he conducted at the University of California, Irvine, in the spring of 1987. I would like to thank Jane Newman and especially Robert Folkenflik for their comments and suggestions as I worked through various drafts of this essay.

3 Timothy Reiss traces the development of "analytico-referential" discourse in seventeenth-and eighteenth-century texts in *The Discourse of Modernism* (Ithaca: Cornell Unviersity Press, 1982).

4 Thomas Sprat, *History of the Royal Society* (London, 1667; repr., St. Louis: Washington University Studies, 1958); and John Wilkins, *Essay Towards A Real Character and a Philosophical Language* (London, 1668; repr., Menston: The Scolar Press, 1968). The history of Wilkins's text is from the editor's preface. Unless otherwise noted, subsequent references to Sprat's *History* and Wilkins's *Essay* will be included parenthetically in the text. I have maintained the old spelling in the quotations from Sprat and Wilkins.

5 See Hans Aarsleff's discussion of the relationship of Wilkins to Sprat's work in *From Locke to Saussure: Essays on the Study of Language and Intellectual History* (Minneapolis: University of Minnesota Press, 1982), 231–32, 259; P. B. Wood lends further support to their connection in "Methodology and Apologetics: Thomas Sprat's *History of the Royal Society*," *The British Journal for the History of Science*, no. 43 (1980): 3–4. Also see Francis Christensen, "John Wilkins and the Royal Society's Reform of Prose Style. Part One," *Modern Language Quarterly* 7 (1946): 179–87; and Christensen, "John Wilkins and the Royal Society's Reform of Prose Style. Part Two," *Modern Language Quarterly* 7 (1946): 279–90.

6 Sprat, *History*, "Advertisement to the Reader."

7 Raymond Williams, "Base and Superstructure in Marxist Cultural Theory," *New Left Review*, no. 82 (1973): 3–16. Fredric Jameson's comments on Wil-

liams's hypothesis, though brief, are helpful. See *The Ideologies of Theory, Essays 1971–86, Volume 2: Syntax of History* (Minneapolis: University of Minnesota Press, 1988), 178–79.

8 Brian Vickers discusses the political importance of the Royal Society's alliance with the Church of England as a self-legitimating move: "I would like to suggest that we see this union of the two bodies, one old, one very new, rather as a self-legitimating move by the Royal Society to attach itself to the established center. . . . I would see [this union] as a political grouping, power politics from the center against the radicals and ec-centrics"; "The Royal Society and English Prose Style: A Reassessment," in *Rhetoric and the Pursuit of Truth: Language Change in the Seventeenth and Eighteenth Centuries* (Los Angeles: William Andrews Clark Memorial Library, 1985), 51–52. While Vickers's work on the Society is important, it is necessary to see that this self-legitimation also served the Restoration state itself. In aligning the Royal Society to the monarchy Sprat does much more than just promote the Society; he also ensures the protection of the state.

9 Gershom Scholem, "Une Lettre inedite de Gerschom [*sic*] Scholem a Franz Rosenzweig. A propos de notre langue. Une confession." *Archives de sciences sociales des religion* 60 (1985): 83–84.

10 See the prefatory "Epistle to the Reader" in Wilkins.

11 The definitions of the monad are from Leibniz's *Monadology*, trans. Robert Latta, *The Monadology and Other Philosophical Writings* (London, 1898; repr., New York: Garland, 1985), 217, 218.

12 "This characteristic would represent our thoughts truly and clearly and when thought is composed of other, more simple thoughts, its character will also be simple . . . that which is the foundation of my characteristic is also the demonstration of the existence of God; because simple thoughts are the elements of the characteristic, and simple forms are the source of things. . . . if this is granted, it follows that the nature of God who encloses all simple forms absolutely, is possible." Gottfried Wilhelm Leibniz, "Lettre a la Princesse Elisabeth" (1678), in *G. W. Leibniz: Oeuvres choisies*, ed. L. Prenant (Paris: Librarie Garnier Freres), 60. My attention was drawn to this passage by a reference in Jacques Derrida's *Of Grammatology*, trans. Gayatri Spivak (Baltimore: The Johns Hopkins University Press, 1976), 331.

13 For background on Leibniz and the Royal Society see Aarsleff, *From Locke to Saussure*, 72; Latta, *Monadology*, 7; and John M. Mackie, *Life Of Godfrey William Von Leibniz on the Basis of the German Work of Dr. G. E. Guhrauer* (Boston: Gould, Kendall, and Lincoln, 1845), 70–73.

14 For a discussion of the importance of a politico-theology to the German language societies, see Jane Newman, "Redemption in the Vernacular: The Language of Language Theory in Seventeenth-Century *Sprachgesellschaften*," *Monatshefte* 79 (1987): 10–29.

15 Wilkins, *Essay Towards a Real Character*, Dedicatory Epistle to William Lord Viscount Brouncker.

16 Ibid.

17 The relationship of language to the law in eighteenth-century thought is a rich topic in and of itself. See John Barrell's discussion in *English Literature in History, 1730–1780: An Equal, Wide Survey* (London: Hutchinson, 1983), 110–19, 174–75.

18 Sir Henry Lyons, F. R. S., *The Royal Society, 1660–1940: A History of Its Administration under Its Charters* (Cambridge: Cambridge Unviersity Press, 1944), 29.

19 Ibid., 22.

20 Thomas Birch, *The History of the Royal Society of London For Improving Of Natural Knowledge From Its First Rise* (London, 1756–57; repr., New York: Johnson Reprint Corporation, 1968), 1: xxxiv–xlv.

21 Dorothy Stimson, *Scientists and Amateurs, A History of the Royal Society* (New York: Henry Schuman, 1948), 161–62.

22 The work of Michel Foucault and many of the New Historicists is behind my perspective on this enscribed execution. Much of this work examines the violence of representions of physical punishment in various historical and literary contexts. See Foucault's *Discipline and Punish: The Birth of the Prison,* trans. Alan Sheridan (New York: Vintage, 1979); Leonard Tennenhouse, *Power on Display: The Politics of Shakespeare's Genres* (New York: Metheun, 1986); Jonathan Goldberg, "The Poet's Authority: Spenser, Johnson, and James VI and I," *Genre* 15, nos. 1–2 (1982): 81–99; Stephen Greenblatt, "Murdering Peasants: Status, Genre, and The Representation of Rebellion," *Representations*, no. 1 (1983): 1–29; and Stephen Orgel, *The Illusion of Power: Political Theater in the English Renaissance* (Berkeley: University of California Press, 1975).

Approaches to Narrative and History: The Case of the Donation of September 7, 1789 and its Images*

VIVIAN P. CAMERON

When several wives and daughters of artists, dressed in white gowns, their hair beribboned with the tricolor, presented a patriotic donation of their jewels to the National Assembly of France on 7 September 1789, the event received extensive coverage in the newspapers and even attracted the attention of printmakers.[1] For a twentieth-century audience, the fascination with a story which today would probably be relegated to the women's pages appears perplexing, but the event had profound meanings for eighteenth-century audiences reading those written and visual accounts. An investigation of selected images in relation to established theories about the portrayal of historical events, various issues of pictorial narrative, and the ideology conveyed by the images may help us to understand the attention this particular donation received.

In reviewing the evidence, we find conflicting interpretations about the narration of history in the eighteenth century. History, we are informed by the *Encyclopédie*, is "le récit des faits données pour vrai; au contraire de la fable, qui est le récit des faits donnés pour faux." Voltaire continued:

> Les premiers fondemens de toute *Histoire* sont les récits des pères aux enfans, transmis ensuite d'une génération à une autre; ils ne sont que probables dans leur origine, & perdent un degré de probabilité à chaque génération. Avec le tems, la fable se grossit, & la vérité se perd. . . .[2]

The effects of time on memory, we are informed, alter truth and transform it into something else, a story or a fable rather than history. After a lengthy discussion of what is known about history from antiquity to the eighteenth century, Voltaire testified that "toute certitude qui n'est pas démonstration mathématique, n'est qu'une extrême probabilité. Il n'y a pas d'autre certitude historique." He added that ". . . les tems historiques auroient dû être distingués eux-mêmes en vérités & en fables."[3] Thus, history is, at best, an imprecise science, where facts can be — if this is not a contradiction in terms — only probable.

Art theorists of the eighteenth century, however, had no such uncertainty about history. Writing in 1757, Abbé Batteux affirmed that:

> L'Histoire peint ce qui a été fait. La Poësie, ce qui a pu être fait. L'une est liée au vrai, elle ne crée ni actions, ni acteurs. L'autre n'est tenue qu'au vraisemblable: elle invente: elle imagine à son gré: elle peint de tête. L'Historien donne des exemples tels qu'ils sont, souvent imparfaits. Le Poëte les donne tels qu'ils doivent être. Et c'est pour cela que . . . la Poësie est une leçon bien plus instructive que l'Histoire.[4]

Believing his arguments equally valid for painting as for poetry, Batteux advocated painting an historical event appropriately revised to convey its moral message with great effect. The circumstances, the disposition of the figures, their attitudes, their expressions, the contrasts, and the like, could all be invented. In agreement with Batteux's ideas about history, the amateur, Charles H. Watelet, later theorized:

> Le devoir du peintre d'*histoire* est d'élever l'âme par la noblesse du sujet. . . . Ainsi point de tableaux d'*histoire* sans poësie. . . . Ainsi bien loin d'astreindre le peintre d'*histoire* à la fidélité d'un biographe ou d'un historien, on doit exiger qu'il traite les sujets à la manière d'Homère, ou d'Euripide.[5]

The opposition between painter and historian was repeatedly emphasized by Watelet: "Les faits que cet art représente, ne sont pas sous nos yeux, ils ne sont transmis à notre pensée que par le récit des historiens; c'est notre imagination seule qui s'en forme des tableaux, et c'est aussi l'imagination que l'art doit satisfaire."[6] Thus, for such art theorists, historians dealt with certainty and facts, which, through the invention and imagination of the artist, could and should be transformed into history paintings. The reality of history is translated through visual means into another language, that of art with its own conventions and rules and, more importantly, with its emphasis on invention.[7] The historical event

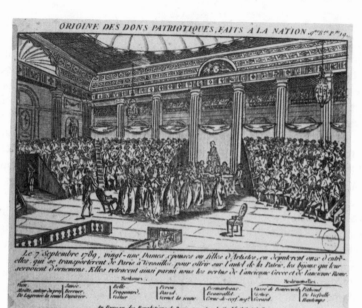

Figure 1. *Origine des dons patriotiques, faites à la nation,* from *Révolutions de Paris,* no. 9, 5–12 September 1789. Paris, Musée Carnavalet (Photo: Author).

was not merely represented, fact by fact, but altered and transformed, sometimes to a startling degree to include even allegorical figures.[8]

The issue of invention in narration was as germane for printmakers as it was for painters, as the Abbé Du Bos, the early eighteenth-century theorist, pointed out, referring to prints as pictures without coloring.[9] Invention included the composition, the lighting effects, the attitude of all of the figures, the position of all of the objects within the work, etc. As Watelet explained, "*L'invention* du peintre ne consiste pas dans la faculté d'imaginer le sujet, mais dans celle de disposer dans son esprit le sujet de la manière qui convient le mieux à son art, quoi qu'il l'ait emprunté des poëtes, des historiens, ou d'une simple tradition. . . ."[10]

The printermakers who depicted the donation of September 7, 1789 all used invention, but in different ways. The anonymous printmaker who created one of the first illustrations of the event (Figure 1) was employed by the new radical left-wing newspaper, the *Révolutions de Paris.* The work appeared in the weekly issue covering the events of 5 through 12 September.[11] The scene is executed in a crude shorthand, a kind of pictographic style that might be a sign of the haste with which the work was executed or, more likely, a sign of the lack of the skill of the unidentified printmaker, who was absorbed in representing the basic elements of the story to accompany the newspaper report, written by the eighteen-year old journalist, Elysée Loustallot. Loustallot began his story by calling attention to those idle French noblemen who played at everything and made no sacrifices for their country. Contrasted to such lethargy was the exemplary activity of simple citizenesses who gave their most precious possessions to the National Assembly. In exchange for those gifts, that institution offered them chairs, a privilege, Loustallot explained, given only to "cours souverains," that is, royalty or perhaps more specifically, the king.[12] The chairs signified not only the approbation of the deputies but also the temporary prestige of sovereignty and authority, as the women were honored and became, so to speak, queens for the day.

Working with the writer or the text, the printmaker translated the ideas presented by Loustallot, not the happiest of situations according to Watelet, who stated that the task was easier if the artist could invent his own subject.[13] In the top half of the print, rising above the figures, is the very recognizable meeting room of the National Assembly in the Hôtel des Menus Plaisirs at Versailles (compare Figure 2), its Doric colonnade an appropriate setting for this patriotic donation. Below this, the printmaker split the focus between the women, centralized in the midst of the deputies, and an isolated chair in the right foreground which faces left, away from the action. For the viewer, who is placed on the right, above the women, as though among the deputies on the top tier of an invisible set of bleachers, that empty chair, isolated against the flagstones of the floor, appears to be closer and even more prominent than the women.

The idea of dramatizing an apparently insignificant element in the scene was not new. Dandré-Bardon, discussing "Invention" in his *Traité de peinture*, mentioned that one means of introducing novel ideas into a work was to make the essential part of an historical event episodic, while focusing on something less important within that event.[14] While the illustrator for the *Révolutions de Paris* may not have been familiar with this text nor even the Venetian paintings which Dandré-Bardon analyzed, that was the strategy which he adopted. Hence, the chair in the right foreground is not mere furniture but an actor within the drama. In illustrating Loustallot's text, the printmaker produced a work which is more than merely a reportage of an event. Rather it is a poetic gesture, which offers the very kind of invention advocated by the theorists, "une leçon bien plus instructive que l'histoire."[15]

One of the constraints on invention in the eighteenth century was the concept of unity of time, action, and place, which was upheld by many theorists.[16] As Batteux stated, "L'action doit être singulière, une, simple, variée," and he was simply repeating what others, such as Du Bos, had

OFFRANDES FAITES A L'ASSEMBLÉE NATIONALE PAR DES DAMES ARTISTES

Figure 2. Pierre Gabriel Berthault after Jean-Louis Prieur, *Offrandres faites à l'Assemblée nationale par des dames artistes le 7 septembre 1789*. Paris, Bibliothèque Nationale (Photo: Author).

written earlier: "Un tableau ne représente même qu'un instant d'une scène."[17] Other theorists, however, felt that a more extended sense of time could be conveyed in visual works. In his essay, "Composition," for the *Encyclopédie*, Diderot claimed:

> Il y a pourtant des occasions où la présence d'un instant n'est pas incompatible avec des traces d'un instant passé: des larmes de douleur couvrent quelquefois un visage dont la joie commence à s'emparer. Un peintre habile faisit un visage dans l'instant du passage de l'âme d'une passion à une autre, & fait un chef-d'oeuvre.[18]

This transcendence of the single moment was paraphrased by Pernety in his *Dictionnaire portatif*, and later expanded by Watelet:

> C'est que l'esprit humain qui, dans un continuel mouvement, passe sans cesse du passé au présent, du présent à l'avenir, ne peut fixer la représentation bien faite d'une action instantanée, sans mêler à l'idée qu'il en prend, des idées antérieures & surtout des idées postérieures.[19]

Watelet was theorizing a more complex rendering of an event which could now be stretched into several moments.[20] While it is true that a painting (or print) has a temporal unity — unlike a written work — what is proposed here is that a visual work can have an extended temporality, which activates the imagination of the beholder into reflecting on actions both preceding and following the moment depicted, as well as envisaging them. One of the best demonstrations of this method of reading a visual work is Diderot's analysis of Fragonard's *Coresus Sacrificing Himself in Place of Callirhoe*. Diderot constructed a five-part drama around the event, although only the denouement was represented in the painting.[21]

The reader of the *Révolutions de Paris* was likewise intended to consider the moments preceding the donation as well as those following them. One was to imagine some relation between the women and the chair although by depicting the donation and this honor, the printmaker seems, in fact, to have violated the concept of the unity of time by presenting two moments in a story. These were enumerated in great detail in Loustallot's article: the entrance of the women dressed in white and adorned with the national cocard; the box of jewels carried by one of them; the address of the speechlessly shy women delivered by a deputy; the reference in that speech to the example of the Roman women living during the time of Camillus who gave their jewels to fulfill a vow made to Apollo after a victory over the Veii; the request for the establishment of a national bureau of gifts to help erase the national debt; the presentation of the casket of jewels to the secretary of the National Assembly; the response from the president; and the petition of the donors to remain for the duration of this session of the National Assembly.[22]

Within this sequence of events, the obviously significant moment, the donation, is chosen for emphasis in accordance with the aesthetic theories of the time.[23] But since Loustallot stressed the sovereign honor offered to the women, the printmaker placed that donation not in the forefront but in the middle ground. It is the empty chair which occupies the foreground. Indeed, it was honor which the women themselves sought, according to a phrase in their oration: "dans les arts, on cherche plus la gloire que la fortune; notre hommage est proportionné à nos moyens, & non au sentiment qui nous l'inspire."[24] Influenced by the models of virtue painted by artists whom they knew, these artists' wives and relatives, including Mesdames Vien and David and Mademoiselle Gérard, sought to distinguish themselves through their sacrifice.[25]

The printmaker, however, was not capable of emulating his artistic superiors in representing a narrative, although he did indicate some awareness of general academic cliches by centralizing the women in the print and by introducing a railing in the bottom left as a compositional

sequence or juxtaposition and paintings or prints appears to have attracted little critical and theoretical attention in the eighteenth century although it must have been a concern of any artist who depicted a cycle, particularly one concerning history. Du Bos, in analyzing the problem of allegory in history painting, mentioned that a spectator might notice the order and arrangement of canvases in Rubens's cycle of the life of Marie de Medici, but he did not elaborate on how these might be read as interrelated.[38] Dandré-Bardon also made no mention of such associations in his extensive discussion of the colors of the individual paintings that composed this cycle.[39] There are hints that adjacency produced meaning. Batteux, who argued for a singular action within one scene, discussed narrative as a sequence:

> La première partie ne suppose rien avant elle; mais elle exige quelque chose après; c'est ce qu'Aristote appelle le commencement. La second suppose quelque chose avant elle, & exige quelque chose après: c'est le milieu. La troisième suppose quelque chose auparavant & ne demande rien après: c'est la fin.[40]

Thus, a sequence of works, whether literary or visual, presented a beginning, middle, and end, and hence was interconnected. But his analysis went no further.

Prieur and Berthault's sequence begins with the Oath of the Tennis Court on 20 June 1789 and ends with the August 1792 days when statues of the kings of France were overthrown and destroyed. The *Offrandes faites à l'Assemblée nationale par des dames artistes le 7 septembre 1789* is part of a cycle of works, a pictorial chronicle, a tale of disjunctive events, bracketed with scenes of resistance to authority, which appears to comply with a statement from the original prospectus for the project by Claude Fauchet: "La nature social . . . est sublime dans ses bouleversements et ses orages, qui préparent l'équilibre des éléments et la sérénité. . . ."[41] This schema of sublime storms, however, was balanced by "des événements heureux et des prodiges de vertus," which would lead to liberty. The donation of 7 September 1789 would be clearly placed within the latter series of events. The entire group is a narrative (the prospectus uses the word "narration") of chronologically arranged, distinct events, which prepare for "la sérénité des beaux jours," that is, the utopian dream of liberty which interrelates and interconnects the events depicted.

But it is not only the chronological sequence that determines the story, but adjacency that creates meaning. The print of the donation, for instance, was preceded and thereby introduced by a scene depicting the departure for prison of M. Besenval, the commander-in-chief of the armed forces in Paris on 14 July. By the time the print was conceived, he had been publicly accused of creating disorder and fear, and of abrogating his responsibilities. The print which succeeded the donation represented the benediction of the flags of the national guard at Notre-Dame on 27 September. Prieur and Berthault framed an act of generosity with one scene depicting punishment for the abuse of authority and another showing symbols of the new authority honored. Within this extensive narrative series dealing with liberty, the triad of prints relates to the new authority, acknowledged both symbolically and financially by the donation of the French women.

If, as Barbara Herrnstein Smith has suggested, we should investigate narratives not only as structures but as acts which "are functions of the variable sets of conditions in response to which they are performed,"[42] then we must consider that Prieur and Berthault, both revolutionaries (Prieur so radical that he would be guillotined in 1795), were, in fact, working on the print of the donation in 1792 when France was at war and threatened by foreign invasion.[43] France was then a nation that needed "de nouveaux sacrifices consommés avec un nouvel enthousiasme."[44] Like the print which accompanied Loustallot's account, the subject of Prieur and Berthault's print was selected with a specific agenda in mind: to remind the French of previous sacrifices made for their country. Indeed, a text which appeared on separate sheets accompanying the print stated that the new authority needed further monetary sacrifices, that the abolition of feudal rights and privileges made France particularly vulnerable to its enemies at a time when its financial underpinnings were shaky.[45] Despite the fact that this donation disrupted a crucial discussion of the royal veto, debated and finally authorized on 11 September, Prieur and Berthault chose the less significant episode because the donation appeared to unite the nation whereas the vote revealed a nation divided (673 deputies voted for the motion, 325 against, and 14 abstained). In addition, Prieur used all the artistic devices at his disposal: the panoramic view, the incredible detail of architecture, gesture and expression, the precise but dramatic lighting, devices of invention which ignore the inaccuracy and imprecision of memory to serve the implicitly persuasive purpose of encouraging the sacrifices needed to achieve unity.

Prieur's traditional approach evokes the standards of history painting which would have been clearly understood by his intended audience, who were expected to collect the prints as they were issued, in contrast to the readers of the *Révolutions de Paris*, who were presumably expected to throw away the newspapers once they read the news. Larger than the usual vignettes, the prints, each of which measures approximately eight by ten inches, were not only intended for private collectors but also proposed as works to be placed in public schools, in public depositories, and in libraries in order to reach and accordingly persuade a more extended readership.[46]

Just as Prieur and Berthault asserted that they were presenting the truth ("la verité"), so François Janinet claimed that his serialized pictorial chronicle was a "histoire fidèle." Janinet's *Gravures historiques des principaux evénements de la Révolution de France et code des loix décrétées par l'Assemblée nationale*, advertised in the *Gazette de France* on 26 January 1790, consisted of fifty-two plates, one issued weekly, along with eight pages of text, conceived, written, and illustrated by this artist alone.[47]

One of the most celebrated printmakers of the time, Janinet had previously executed works after the paintings of historical subjects by Jean-Jacques LeBarbier, paintings of gallant subjects by Fragonard, Lawrence, and others. So he brought that knowledge of the academic tradition and its ideas about history and invention to his illustrations. Like most of the works in his series, the print of 7 September 1789, entitled *Plusieurs citoyennes de Paris, portant à l'Assemblée nationale leurs bijoux et leurs diamants pour servir à l'acquit de la dette publique* (Figure 3), presents a close-up view of the event. Unlike Prieur and Berthault, who portrayed an entire panorama yet lovingly attended to every detail in the scene to convince the viewer of its veracity, Janinet, like artists at the Salon, focused on the most important parts of the drama.[48] This, in fact, was the advice of a number of art theorists, Watelet among them: "Ainsi les grandes compositions qui représentent un peuple assemblé, une bataille, une cérémonie, causeront toujours un plaisir moins vif & moins d'*intérêt*, qu'un excellent ouvrage qui représente une seule figure ou un fort petit nombre de figures."[49]

Therefore, Janinet represented only a part of the National Assembly and a selected number of the deputies, donors, and visitors in the gallery. But it is not just that crowds are less interesting. They are an obstacle. "Quoique la nature semble autoriser l'excès des détails, ces excès est un obstacle à l'*effet* théâtral, & à l'effet pittoresque."[50] It was that very theatrical effect that Janinet was able to capture so well by means of the play of chiaroscuro. A brilliant light unites the women (here reduced to only three) and their spokesman (in the lower right-hand corner) with a seated deputy in the center and with the officials of the National Assembly who rise above them on the left. In the penumbra of the lower left corner, grouped in a circle, are some deputies, one of whom points to the women. As a counterweight to that group, Janinet placed a fourth group of figures on the right seated at a long table just above the donors. To

Figure 3. François Janinet, *Evénement du 7 sept. 1789*. 1789. Paris, Bibliothèque Nationale (Photo: Bibliothèque Nationale).

emphasize the drama, above the figures is the hall of the National Assembly in dramatically receding perspective.

While the text of the print illustrating the *Révolutions de Paris* made reference to examples of antique donors, Janinet's print is very different. By reducing the donors to three, Janinet alludes to the Three Graces, with their spokesman, M. Bouché, acting as the hero Paris. Nor is this reference quixotic. As the accompanying text affirms, Janinet clearly had this myth in mind: "L'une d'elles, jeune & jolie, portoit dans une cassette l'offrande destinée à la patrie, on croyoit voir Venus entourée par les Graces." The gesture of M. Bouché appears to be presenting the women, as much as offering the box of jewels. Gesture and text agree: women belong "à ce sexe enchanteur . . . qui, par un charme, inexprimable, fait à son gré le bonheur ou le tourment de nos jours. . . ."[51] This is the language of the boudoir rather than that appropriate to a patriotic donation.

If the reference to the past is entirely different in this print, what about the concept of adjacency or sequentiality? Placed in its proper chronological position, the print would be situated between two confrontational scenes: *M. Walche apaise des furieux qui veulent ravager son chateau . . .* (16–17 August) and *Les Femmes voulant pendre l'abbé Lefevre et les hommes voulant incendier les papiers* (5 October 1789). In this case, the donation is used for the purpose of antithesis. In contrast to the scenes of disorder, destruction, and even murder which frame it, the donation print served, according to the accompanying text, as a sign of peaceful beneficence, of goodness, "de ce généraux dévouement à la chose publique."

Perhaps it was this general public devotion that motivated Janinet to commence this chronicle, which began with a scene of the opening of the Estates general on 5 May 1789 and ended abruptly with the fire at the chateau of Buzet and the murder of M. de Buzet, colonel of the royal grenadiers of Guyenne on 8 January 1790. Why he never completed an intended second volume is unknown, and this makes it difficult to interpret the ideology of the entire enterprise although Janinet claimed that it was to be an impartial account. Available in several formats and at different prices, the work was advertised in the conservative *Gazette de France*. Numerous prints in the series dealt favorably with the king and other authorities. On the other hand, the text appended to the print of the donation claimed that ". . . la France venoit à peine d'enfanter la liberté sur la couche ensanglantée du despotisme. . . ."[52] And there are the subsequent prints of allegorical figures, such as Liberty and Fraternity, etched after the works of others, which could be cited as evidence of patriotism. Nevertheless, there are certain contradictions between his opposition to despotism and his support of royalty, combined with the comments about women, "ce sexe enchanteur," words which are the language of the *ancien régime*, that of *bon ton*.

When Laurent Guyot included the donation (Figure 4) in his series of eight prints, recording episodes from the fall of the Bastille to the return of the royal family on 6 October 1789, being a monarchist, he completely transformed the event. Framed by an oval, reminiscent of paintings of the mid-eighteenth century such as overdoors, the scene is pictured in an

Figure 4. Laurent Guyot, *Les Dames artistes.* . . . Paris, Bibliothèque Nationale (Photo: Author).

outdoor setting with an open circular temple crowned with a seated statue and an antique tripod serving as an altar. The artist was clearly familiar with academic rules of composition since he used a repoussoir figure (presumably an allegorical figure of France with a rudder) in the right foreground and centralized his principals around the tripod. Vapors of incense issuing from the latter mingle with the clouds in the air and with the mist within the temple, joining the female donors in the center with the crowd of followers on the left and with the orator within the temple on the right. Discourse and action are thereby related. The sacrifice itself, virtuous and paradigmatic, recalls antique prototypes pictured by Joseph-Marie Vien.[53] Its message is intensified by the use of a well-established symbol, the pelican nursing her young at the altar (the pelican, symbol of sacrifice and salvation or mother love). The sacrifice of the donors is acknowledged by the background figures: clergymen, soldiers, and other patriotic contributors, who emulate the central benefactors.

That the historical event has been almost totally imagined is evident by the numerous departures from the reported facts. Not only has Guyot transformed the setting, but he has added allegorical characters to the eighteenth-century cast. This is an example of what Dandré-Bardon called a mixed composition, combining the marvelous with the historic, which would lend the subject "plus de force, plus d'agrément, & quelque fois plus de clarté," all for the purpose of intriguing the spectator.[54] Like Janinet, Guyot reduced the number of donors to three, suggesting the Three Graces. Since the inscription refers to the contributors as "dames artistes" (an appelation likewise used by Prieur and Berthault), Guyot might have been alluding to the three prominent female academicians: Elizabeth Vigée-Lebrun, Anne Vallayer-Coster, and Adelaide Labille-Guiard (who did not participate in the donation although the fourth female academician, Madame Vien, did). The relationship with the arts, at which this allusion hints, is made clear by the inscription. ". . . tous les Français et nombre d'étrangers animés du même sentiment, ont manifesté leurs voeux en imitant ces nobles artistes. . . ." Guyot wanted to stress the nobility and originality of the artists and, by implication, the arts in general. His sentiments were shared by the editor of the right-wing *Journal de Paris*, the academician D. Garat, who wrote: "Les beaux Arts, par ce sacrifice, se sont associés à la Liberté naissante. . . . La liberté va leur créer un nouveau monde & de nouveaux modèles."[55]

How new was this world and these models in Guyot's print? Some of his transformations may be indebted to newspaper accounts. A Temple of Immortality, where the names of the women would be inscribed, was mentioned in the moderate *Le Courier français*.[56] Gorsas, that pre-revolutionary radical writing in *Le Courier de Versailles à Paris*, referred to the Graces.[57] Such citations, however, may well have recalled pictorial counterparts of ceremonial rituals by Vien and others that are more probable sources for this printmaker, who was so familiar with the academic world.

Ideologically, these antecedents, as well as the elegance of Guyot's style, the attenuation of the figures, and the use of the words "dames" and "noble" in the accompanying text, are all parts of a narrative that appears to confirm "noble" behavior during a period when such behavior was in question. The temple, the altar, the union of various classes in the background of the print are all signs of a golden age, a utopia, more explicitly heralded in the songs of the period.[58] In constructing his new world, Guyot was certainly familiar with the advice of eighteenth-century theorists such as Batteux (whose ideas in *Les Beaux Arts réduits à un même principe* had been published more than forty years before), and he poeticized or dehistoricized the donation of 7 September 1789. Unlike the radical artist, Jacques-Louis David, however, Guyot used a retrograde style. The new world is actually the old, that of the *ancien régime*, and that is confirmed by the past tense of the text. Since the other scenes in the series, depicting the fall of the Bastille and the October days of 1789, are situated in accurately rendered settings, the fantasy of the donation print may also express Guyot's nostalgia for a world, however mythical, now lost.

The donation of 7 September 1789 was not the first patriotic sacrifice made for the new revolutionary France, despite the attestations by Guyot, by the anonymous artist working for the *Révolutions de Paris*, and by others.[59] This historical event was chosen, however, by artists and journalists alike to establish a mythology about gift-giving, which would grant it either middle-class or noble legitimacy. The episode was invested with even greater significance by all of the printmakers through various narrational strategies: emphasis on the episodic; adjacency; antithesis; sequentiality; inscriptions; and, most important, artistic invention. Accordingly, the donation acquired additional meanings: a sign of national unity; the utopian dream of liberty; the acknowledgement of the authority of the new National Assembly; peaceful beneficence; and a signifier for the nobility of art. Ultimately, the donation of 7 September 1789 became a mythic symbol that far surpassed the hopes of the original donors.

NOTES

* I would like to thank the Social Sciences and Humanities Research Council of Canada, whose generous support made the research for this article possible.
1 The donors included Mesdames Moitte, Vien, Lagrenée, Suvée, Beruer, Duvivier, Fragonard, Peyron, David, Vernet, Belle, Vestier, Desmarteaux, Beauvarlet, Cornedecerf, et Mlles. Vassé, Vestier, de Bonrecueil, Gérard, Pithoud, Hautemps, Viefville. Madame Vien and Mademoiselle Gérard were known artists.
2 "The first foundation of all *history* are the narrations of fathers to their children, transmitted subsequently from one generation to another. They are only probable in their origin and lose a degree of probability each generation. With time, the fable increases, and the truth is lost." "Histoire," *Encyclopédie ou dictionnaire raissoné des sciences, des arts et des métiers*, 35 vols. (Paris, 1751–80), 8: 220, 221.
3 Ibid., 223, 224.

4 "History paints that which was done. Poetry that which could have been done. One is related to the truth. It creates neither actions nor actors. The other relies entirely on the conceivable; it invents, it imagines to its liking, it paints in one's head. The historian gives examples such as they are, often imperfect. The poet gives them as they ought to be. And it is for this reason that . . . poetry is a much more instructive lesson than history." Charles Batteux, *Les Beaux Arts réduits à un même principe* (Paris, 1747), 24, 29.

5 "The duty of the history painter is to elevate the soul by the nobility of the subject. . . . Thus no paintings of history without poetry. . . . Thus, far from restricting the painter of history to the fidelity of a biographer or a historian, one ought to require that he treat subjects in the manner of Homer or Euripides." Charles Watelet, *Dictionnaire des arts de peinture, sculpture et gravure*, 5 vols. (Paris, 1792; repr., Geneva: Minkoff, 1972), 3: 37.

6 "The facts that this art [history painting] represents are not before our eyes. They are only transmitted to our thought through the narration of historians; it is our imagination alone which develops paintings from them, and it is also the imagination which art ought to satisfy." Ibid., 41.

7 Ibid., 183–84. See also Michel Dandré-Bardon, *Traité de peinture, suivi d'un essai sur la sculpture* (Paris, 1765), 80–90.

8 See Jean-Baptist Du Bos, *Réflexions critiques sur la poësie et sur la peinture*, 6th ed., 3 vols. (Paris, 1755), 1: 176–85; Dandré-Bardon, *Traité de peinture*, 97–98; and Watelet, *Dictionnaire des arts*, 1: 54–56.

9 See Du Bos, *Réflexions critiques*, chap. 48.

10 "The invention of the painter does not consist of the power of imagining the subject, but of that of arranging the subject in his mind in the manner which best agrees with his art although he may have borrowed it from poets, historians, or a simple tradition. . . ." Watelet, *Dictionnaire des arts*, 3: 183.

11 *Révolutions de Paris*, no. 9, 5–12 September 1789, 19–22. The version illustrated is a separate print now in the collection of the Musée Carnavalet in Paris. It differs from the examples in the bound editions of the journal in the Bibliothèque Nationale and at Yale University, owing perhaps to the fact that there were ten editions of each issue of the journal then being printed. The most important difference is the eleven female delegates in the Carnavalet version, which agrees with the text below all of the prints, as opposed to the ten women in the Bibliothèque Nationale and Yale editions. However, in all other important details, the prints are identical, including the caption and the placement indication ($9^{me}.R^{er}.P^{ge}.19$) in the upper right corner. Presence of the latter confirms that the Carnavalet version was once incorporated within the journal.

12 *Révolutions de Paris*, no. 9, 5–12 September 1789, 19.

13 Watelet, *Dictionnaire des arts*, 3: 183.

14 Dandré-Bardon, *Traité de peinture*, 84–85.

15 Batteux, *Les Beaux Arts*, 24.

16 See Rensselaer W. Lee, *Ut Pictura Poesis: The Humanistic Theory of Painting*

(New York: W. W. Norton and Company, 1967), 61–66, for a discussion of this.

17 Batteux, *Les Beaux Arts*, 65; and Du Bos, *Réflexions critiques*, 1: 387.

18 "There are, however, some occasions when the present instant is not incompatible with the traces of an elapsed instant: tears of sorrow sometimes cover a face when joy begins to appear. A skillful artist knows how to capture the face in the instant when the soul passes from one passion to another and creates a masterpiece." "Composition," *Encyclopédie*, 3: 773.

19 "It is because the human spirit, which, in a continual movement, passes ceaselessly from the past to the present and from the present to the future, is not able to fix the fully developed representation of an instantaneous action without mixing into the idea which he has of it, some ideas prior to it and especially some ideas following it." Dom Antoine-Joseph Pernety, *Dictionnaire portatif de peinture, sculpture et gravure; avec un traité pratique des différentes manières de peindre* (Paris, 1757), 77; and Watelet, *Dictionnaire des arts*, 2: 223.

20 For a further discussion of the temporal in painting, see Lee, *Ut Pictura Poesis*, 63–66.

21 Denis Diderot, "Salon de 1765," in *Salons*, ed. Jean Seznec and Jean Adhémar, 4 vols. (Paris, 1957–67), 2: 188–98; and *Diderot et l'art de Boucher à David* (Paris: Hôtel de la Monnaie, 1984–85), 204–12. I am grateful to Mary Sheriff for her discussion of this with me.

22 *Révolutions de Paris*, no. 9, 5–12 September 1789, 20–22.

23 "Composition," *Encyclopédie*, 3: 772. See also Gotthold Ephraim Lessing, "Laocoon, On the Limitations of Painting and Poetry," trans. Ellen Frothingham, in *Neoclassicism and Romanticism 1750–1850*, ed. Lorenz Eitner, 2 vols. (Englewood Cliffs, NJ: Prentice-Hall, 1970), 1: 23–24.

24 *Révolutions de Paris*, no. 9, 5–12 September 1789, 20.

25 The example of the Roman women donating their jewels was pictured by Nicolas-Guy Brenet in a work entitled *Piété & générosité des dames romaines*, exhibited at the Salon of 1785 (no. 7). The Salon livret states that the women offered their jewelry because gold was rare and scarce. Plutarch (*Lives*, "Camillus," VII-VIII) mentioned that after the victory over the Veii, all the booty was enjoyed by the soliders, who did not bring the required tenth to the public treasury. Hence, the women, in fact, bailed out the men for their excesses.

26 See Watelet, *Dictionnaire des arts*, 3: 177; Du Bos, *Réflexions critiques*, 1: 245–47; and Batteux, *Les Beaux Arts*, 172–73.

27 The practice of giving a caption to a print was common. For painting, it was more unusual, although Dandré-Bardon had advised artists to render an ambiguous work intelligible by adding an inscription, which, he pointed out, Annibale Caracci had done in the Farnese Gallery and Raphael in his *Parnassus*. See his *Traité de peinture*, 94.

28 *Révolutions de Paris*, no. 9, 5–12 September 1789, 27.

29 For an illustration, see Robert Rosenblum, *Transformations in Late Eigh-*

teenth Century Art (Princeton: Princeton University Press, 1967), pl. 86 and his discussion on 86–87.

30 *Révolutions de Paris*, no. 9, 5–12 September 1789, 24.

31 On the Berthault-Prieur works and the entire prospectus for the *Tableaux de la Révolution française*, see Maurice Tourneux, ed., *Bibliographie de l'historie de Paris pendant la Révolution française*, 5 vols. (Paris, 1968, reimpression of 1890), 1: 35–56. The work was revised in 1798 and retitled *Collection complète des tableaux historiques de la Révolution française*. The series appeared in 1802 in a three-volume set, the first volume illustrated with sixty-eight prints by Berthault after Prieur's drawings. With each revision, the accompanying text was changed to reflect the changing political beliefs of the editor and/or period.

A print that resembles the Prieur-Berthault donation was engraved and etched by N. Ponce after a drawing by Antoine Borel. It can be found in the Collection de Vinck, Bibliothèque Nationale, Paris. For more information, see François Louis Bruel et al., *Un Siècle d'histoire de France par l'estampe, 1700–1871. Collection de Vinck. Bibliothèque Nationale. Département des Estampes*, 8 vols. (Paris, 1909–79), 2: 395–396 n. 2847.

32 The Ponce print, cited in n. 31, shows a barrel roof. See, however, Pierre-Adrien Pâris, *Hôtel des Menus-Plaisirs, Versailles, 1787*, in Rosenblum, *Transformations in Late Eighteenth Century Art*, pl. 143, where the veiled oculus is quite evident. Another scene of the donation, which indicates the correct ceiling for the room, is also illustrated in Rosemblum, pl. 87.

33 Watelet, *Dictionnaire des arts,* 3: 183–84; and Dandré-Bardon, *Traité de peinture*, 106, on "Composition," where he talks about placing the central group in the center and also attracting the attention of the spectator by "quelque accident de lumière."

34 See Bruel, *Un Siècle d'histoire de France*, 1:190.

35 Tourneux, *Bibliographie de l'histoire de Paris*, 1: 35. The Ponce print seems to have had the same intent.

36 Dandré-Bardon, *Traité de peinture*, 92.

37 In addition to Bruel, for information about Prieur, see *La Révolution française. Le Premier Empire. Dessins du Musée Carnavalet* (Paris: Musée Carnavalet, 22 February–22 May 1982), 127; and Tourneux, *Bibliographie de l'histoire de Paris*, 1: 33–34.

38 Du Bos, *Réflexions critiques*, 1: 196.

39 Dandré-Bardon, *Traité de peinture*, 235–306.

40 "The first part does not assume anything before it; but it requires something after. It is what Aristotle calls the beginning. The second supposes something before it and requires something after it: it is the middle. The third supposes something preceding it and demands nothing after: it is the end." Batteux, *Les Beaux Arts*, 164.

41 Tourneux, *Bibliographie de l'historie de Paris*, 1: 35.

42 Barbara Herrnstein Smith, "Narrative Versions, Narrative Theories," in *On*

Narrative, ed. W. J. T. Mitchell (Chicago and London: University of Chicago Press, 1981), 226.

43 Tourneux, *Bibliographie de l'historie de Paris*, 1: 33–35 and 42.

44 Ibid.

45 See the prospectus, probably by M. de Chamfort, who succeeded Claude Fauchet, in *Tableaux de la Révolution française ou collection de quarante-huit gravures* (Paris, n.d.), 3. The Bibliothèque Nationale call number for this is La^{32}18.

46 See Bruel, *Un Siècle d'histoire de France*, 2: 8; Tourneux, *Bibliographie de l'histoire de Paris*, 1: 58–59; and *L'Art de l'estampe et la Révolution française* (Paris: Musée Carnavalet, 27 June–20 November 1977), 33, no.164.

47 We can see a relationship between this work and paintings such as Joseph-Benoît Suvée's *Admiral Coligny confronts his assassins*, exhibited at the Salon of 1787.

48 Watelet, *Dictionnaire des arts*, 3:178.

49 "Thus, the large compositions which represent an assembled people, a battle, a ceremony, always cause a pleasure less intense and of less interest than an excellent work which represents a single figure or a very small number of figures." Ibid., 2:115.

50 Both quotations are taken from the cahier for the print, 2.

51 Ibid., 1. For a list of the other subjects in the series, see Tourneux, *Bibliographie de l'histoire de Paris*, 1:58–59.

52 See Diderot, *Salons*, 1: pls. 73 (Vien, *Proserpine ornant le buste de Cérès*) and 74 (Vien, *Offrande à Vénus*).

53 Dandré-Bardon, *Traité de peinture*, 102.

54 *Journal de Paris*, no. 252, 9 September 1789, 1144.

55 *Le Courier français*, no. 65, 8 September 1789, 313.

56 *Le Courier de Versailles à Paris*, 66, 11 September 1789, 179.

57 See Cornwell B. Rogers, *The Spirit of Revolution in 1789* (Princeton: Princeton University Press, 1949), 52–70.

58 A few other prints of the event exist (see Bruel, *Un Siècle d'histoire de France*, 2: 397–98, particularly nos. 2854, 2857, and 2858); however, the use of invention is similar.

59 In addition, Olympe de Gouges wrote a political brochure in 1788 entitled *Lettre au peuple, ou Projet d'une caisse patriotique par une citoyenne*, asking for a national coffer for patriotic donations. On 27 August 1789, an anonymous woman published an essay entitled "Proposition d'une Femme citoyenne pour établir les moyens de remédier à toutes les calamités qui environnent la France . . .," in *Journal d'etat et du citoyen*, supplement to no. 3, 27 August 1789, 62–64. For earlier donations, see *Extrait des procés-verbaux de l'Assemblée nationale, contentant des dons patriotiques antérieurs au 7 septembre 1789* (Versailles, 1789).

Contributors to Volume 19

PAUL BENHAMOU, Associate Professor of Foreign Languages and Literature at Purdue University, initially presented this essay at the 1988 South Central SECS meeting in Fayetteville, AK. He has contributed to the *Dictionnaire des journalistes* and has published indexes to two eighteenth-century journals, as well as articles on journals and journalists in the Age of Enlightenment.

THOMAS F. BONNELL is Associate Professor of English at Saint Mary's College, Notre Dame and is currently preparing a book about booksellers and the English poetical canon from 1770 to 1810. His essay was read at the 1988 ASECS conference in Knoxville, TN.

BRUCE ALAN BROWN is Assistant Professor of Music at the University of Southern California, Los Angeles. He has written extensively on Gluck, Mozart, and eighteenth-century theater and has prepared an edition of Gluck's opéra-comique *Le Diable à quatre*. He is currently working on a study of *Gluck and the French Theatre in Vienna* for Oxford University Press. His essay was first presented at the 1987 ASECS conference in Cincinnati, OH.

VIVIAN P. CAMERON, Assistant Professor of Art History at Acadia University, first presented her essay at the 1987 ASECS conference. Her most recent scholarly endeavors are two books: *Women, Culture, and Society in Paris during the French Revolution: Images of Women in High Art and Popular Culture* and *Reflections of the Tarnished I: Images of Louis XVI*.

FREDERICK A. HALL, whose essay was first presented at the 1987 Northeast ASECS conference in Kingston, Ontario, is Associate Professor of Music and Associate Dean of Humanities at McMaster University. He has published a number of articles on music and musicians in Canada in the eighteenth century and has co-edited a recent volume, *Musical Canada*.

REGINA HEWITT, Assistant Professor of English at the University of South Florida, is presently completing a study of Wordworth's thought and work in the context of problems inherited from the empirical tradition. Her paper was read initially at the 1988 ASECS conference.

GRANT I. HOLLY, Professor of English and Comparative Literature at Hobart and William Smith College, has published on Swift, the novel, and literary theory. He is currently at work on a manuscript entitled *Theory as the Sublime: Essays on the Interrelationships between Eighteenth-Century Culture and Contemporary Theory*. His essay was originally presented at the 1988 ASECS conference.

THOMAS JEMIELITY, Associate Professor of English at the University of Notre Dame, is currently working in two research areas, the satire of the Hebrew prophets and Edward Gibbon's analysis of religion in *The Decline and Fall*. His article was first read at the ASECS conference in 1988.

DOROTHEA E. VON MÜCKE is Assistant Professor of German at Columbia University. She has published on Herder, Schiller, and Kleist and is generally working on a study about the emergence of new literary genres in the eighteenth century in the context of contemporary language theory. Her article stems from a paper first presented at the 1988 ASECS meeting.

FRANK PALMERI, Assistant Professor of English at the University of Miami, first presented a version of his essay at the 1988 ASECS conference. He has published on Swift and Pynchon and has recently completed a book, *Satire in Narrative*.

MELINDA ALLIKER RABB is Associate Professor of English at Brown University. She is the author of articles on Swift, Pope, Richardson, Fielding, Sterne, and Godwin and is completing a book on satire and memory. Her essay was first presented at the 1988 ASECS conference.

JOEL REED, who is completing his graduate studies in English and critical theory at the University of California, Irvine, first presented his essay at the 1988 Western SECS meeting in Long Beach, CA. His study derives from a broader work in the politics of language reform and its relationships to the eighteenth-century novel.

CEDRIC D. REVERAND II, Professor of English at the University of Wyoming, has written various articles on Dryden and Pope and is the author of a forthcoming book from the University of Pennsylvania Press, *Dryden's Final Poetic Mode: The Fables*. His essay was presented at the 1988 ASECS meeting.

TREVOR ROSS, whose essay was read at the 1988 ASECS conference, recently defended his doctoral thesis, "Albion's Parnassus: The Making of the English Literary Canon," at the University of Toronto.

G. S. ROUSSEAU, Professor of Eighteenth-Century Studies at the University of California, Los Angeles, initially presented his essay at the 1988 ASECS conference. He and Roy Porter have just completed the third volume of a trilogy of books dealing with sexuality during the Enlightenment, *Exoticism in the Enlightenment*, published by Manchester University Press.

MARY ANNE SCHOFIELD, Professor of English at Saint Bonaventure University, presented this essay at the 1987 East Central ASECS meeting in Collegeville, PA. She is currently the president of NEASECS. She is the author of several books on Eliza Haywood, as well as the co-editor of *Fetter'd or Free? British Women Writers, 1670–1815* and the forthcoming *Curtain Calls: British and American Women and their Relation to the Eighteenth-Century Theatre*. Her book, *Disguising Romances in Feminine Fiction, 1713–1799*, is also forthcoming.

SUSAN STAVES, Professor of English at Brandeis University, presented her essay at the 1988 ASECS conference. She is the author of *Player's Scepters: Fictions of*

SUSAN STAVES, Professor of English at Brandeis University, presented her essay at the 1988 ASECS conference. She is the author of *Player's Scepters: Fictions of Authority in the Restoration* and a forthcoming book on critical legal history of married women's separate property, 1660–1833.

JAMES GRANTHAM TURNER'S essay was first read at the 1987 Midwestern ASECS conference in Evanston, IL. Currently Professor of English Language and Literature at the University of Michigan, he is the author of *The Politics of Landscape: Rural Scenery and Society in English Poetry, 1630–1660, One Flesh: Paradisal Marriage and Sexual Relations in the Age of Milton*, and numerous articles on seventeenth- and eighteenth-century topics. His most recent project is a book entitled *Libertinism and Erotic Representation in England, 1650–1750*.

JACK UNDANK, Professor of French at Rutgers University, first read his essay in Knoxville at the 1988 ASECS meeting. Although widely published on various eighteenth-century topics, he is best known for his work on Diderot, including critical editions of the author, a commemorative collection entitled *Diderot: Digression and Dispersion*, and a critical study, *Diderot Inside, Outside, & In-Between*.

ARAM VARTANIAN, William R. Kenan Professor of French Literature at the University of Virginia, is the author of *Diderot and Descartes: A Study of Scientific Naturalism in Enlightenment, Le Mettrie's "L'Homme machine": A Study in the Origins of an Idea*, and a critical edition of *Bijoux indiscrets* for the Diderot *Oeuvres complètes*. His article was read at the 1988 ASECS conference.

MARTIN WECHSELBLATT is currently completing his doctoral dissertation, entitled "The Rhetoric of Colonialism in Eighteenth-Century England: The Case of Samuel Johnson," at Cornell University. The present essay, which was read at the 1988 ASECS meeting, is part of a larger project dealing with nationalism and the construction of social identity in England between 1640 and the French Revolution.

DANIEL E. WILLIAMS, Assistant Professor of English at the University of Mississippi, first presented his essay at the 1987 ECASECS meeting. He is in the process of completing an anthology of early-American criminal narratives and is also working on a study of narrative self-creation in eighteenth-century American literature.

ROSE A. ZIMBARDO, Professor of English Literature at the State University of New York, Stony Brook, has written extensively on the Restoration, eighteenth-century topics, and Shakespeare. Her most recent book, *A Mirror to Nature: Transformations in Drama and Aesthetics, 1660–1732*, appeared in 1986. Her article was first presented at the 1987 NEASECS conference.

Executive Board, 1988-1989

President: ISAAC KRAMNICK, Associate Dean, College of Arts and Sciences and Richard J. Schwartz Professor of Government, Cornell University

Past President: GLORIA FLAHERTY, Professor of German and Fellow of the Institute for the Humanities, The University of Illinois at Chicago

First Vice-President: PAUL ALKON, Professor of English, University of Southern California

Second Vice-President: ARAM VARTANIAN, William R. Kenan Professor of French, University of Virginia

Executive Secretary: R. G. PETERSON, Professor of English and Classics, St. Olaf College

Treasurer: RENÉE WALDINGER, Professor of French, City College and Graduate School, City University of New York

Members-at-Large: DEWEY F. MOSBY, Director of the Picker Art Gallery, Charles A. Dana Creative Arts Center, Colgate University (1989)
VIRGINIA HARTT RINGER, Professor of Philosophy, California State University, Long Beach (1989)
MICHAEL FRIED, Professor of Humanities and the History of Art, The Johns Hopkins University (1990)
SUSAN STAVES, Professor of English, Brandeis University (1990)
DANIEL HEARTZ, Professor of Music, University of California, Berkeley (1991)
DAVID CARRITHERS, Adolph Ochs Professor of Government, University of Tennessee, Chatanooga (1991)

Business Manager: THOMAS R. LACY, St. Olaf College.

Institutional Members

*of the American Society
for Eighteenth-Century Studies*

American Antiquarian Society
Arizona State University
National Library of Australia
University of Calgary
University of California, Davis
University of California, Irvine
University of California,
    Los Angeles/William Andrews
    Clark Memorial Library
University of California, San Diego
California State University,
    Long Beach
Carleton University
Case Western Reserve
    University
University of Cincinnati
City College, CUNY
Claremont Graduate School
Cleveland State University
Colonial Williamsburg
    Foundation
University of Colorado at Denver
University of Connecticut
Dalhousie University
Emory University
University of Evansville
Folger Institute of Renaissance and
    Eighteenth-Century Studies
Fordham University
Georgia Institute of Technology
Georgia State University
University of Georgia
Gettysburg College
Hamilton College
Haverford College
Herzog August Bibliothek,
    Wolfenbuttel

University of Illinois at Chicago
Institute of Early American History
    and Culture
John Carter Brown Library,
    Brown University
The Johns Hopkins University
University of Kansas
University of Kentucky
Kimbell Art Museum, Fort Worth
Lehigh University
Lehman College, CUNY
Los Angeles County Museum of Art
McMaster University/Association
    for 18th-Century Studies
University of Michigan, Ann Arbor
University of Minnesota
Mount Saint Vincent University
State University of New York,
    Binghamton
State University of New York,
    Fredonia
Northern Illinois University
Northwestern University
The Ohio State University
University of Pennsylvania
Purdue University
University of Rochester
Rosenberg & Stiebel, Inc., New
    York
Rutgers University
Smith College
Smithsonian Institution
University of Southern
    California
University of Southern
    Mississippi
Swarthmore College

Sweet Briar College
Syracuse University
University of Tennessee,
    Knoxville
University of Texas at Austin
Texas A&M University
Texas Tech University
Towson State University
Trinity College, Connecticut
Tulane University
University of Tulsa
University of Utrecht, Institute for
    Comparative and
    General Literature

University of Victoria
University of Virgina
The Voltaire Foundation
Washington University, St. Louis
Westfalische Wilhelms-Universitat,
    Munster
The Henry Francis du Pont
    Winterthur Museum
University of Wisconsin, Milwaukee
Yale Center for British Art
Yale University
Zentralbibliothek der Deutschen
    Klassik, Weimar

Sponsoring Members

of the American Society
for Eighteenth-Century Studies

Herman Asarnow
Mark S. Auburn
Jeffrey Barnouw
Jerry C. Beasley
J.M. Beattie
Pamela J. Bennett
Charles L. Beyer
L.J. Bianchi
Carol Blum
Thomas F. Bonnell
Martha F. Bowden
George C. Branam
Leo Braudy
Elizabeth Brophy
Morris R. Brownell
Stephen N. Brown
Martha L. Brunson
John L. Bullion
James H. Bunn
Max Byrd
Joseph A. Byrnes
W.B. Carnochan
Vincent Carretta
David W. Carrithers
Richard G. Carrott
Ellmore A. Champie
Thomas M. Columbus
Henry S. Commager
Brian Corman
Gustavo Costa
Howard J. Coughlin
James Cruise
David W. Dangremond
Charles G. Davis
William P. Davisson
Virginia P. Dawson
Robert Adams Day
Martha Dietz
John Dowling
Lee Andrew Elioseff
Antoinette Emch-Deriaz
Roger Emerson

Jan Fergus
Beartrice Fink
Carol Houlihan Flynn
Roderick S. French
Joy Frieman
Jack Fruchtman Jr.
Frank J. Garosi
James Garrett
Morris Golden
Peter B. Goldman
Josephine Grieder
Dustin H. Griffin
Walter Grossmann
Leon M. Guilhamet
Diana Guiragossian-Carr
Phyllis J. Guskin
Madelyn Gutwirth
H. George Hahn
Roger Hahn
Elizabeth Harries
Karsten Harries
Edward Harris
Marilyn Harris
Phillip Harth
Donald M. Hassler
Philip H. Highfill, Jr.
Kinzo Higuchi
Emita B. Hill
Robert H. Hopkins
Adrienne D. Hytier
Margaret C. Jacob
Thomas Jemielity
Wilbert Davis Jerome
Denis Jonnes
Frank A. Kafker
Martin Kallich
Charles A. Knight
Gwin J. Kolb
Yvonne Korshak
Carl R. Kropf
Colby H. Kullman
Thomas R. Lacy

441

Patrons
of the American Society
for Eighteenth-Century Studies

Lawrence G. Blackmon
T.E.D. Braun
Patricia Brückmann
Chester Chapin
Louis Cornell
Frank H. Ellis
Charles N. Fifer
Basil Guy
Diether H. Haenicke
Alfred W. Hesse
Stephen Holliday
J. Paul Hunter
Kathryn Montgomery Hunter
Annibel Jenkins
Judith Keig
J. Patrick Lee
Maynard Mack
H.W. Matalene
Helen L. McGuffie
Donald C. Mell, Jr.

John H. Middendorf
Virginia J. Peacock
R.G. Peterson
James Pollak
John Valdimir Price
Jack Richtman
Edgar V. Roberts
Ronald C. Rosbottom
Helen E. Searing
English Showalter
Elizabeth Stewart
Keith Stewart
J.E. Stockwell, Jr.
Rebecca Stockwell
Connie C. Thorson
James L. Thorson
Teri Noel Towe
Robert W. Uphaus
Howard D. Weinbrot
Calhoun Winton

Index of Names

Italicized page numbers indicate names treated extensively.